Southern Literary Studies

Southern Literary Studies

LOUIS D. RUBIN, JR., EDITOR

SOUTHERN WRITERS
A Biographical Dictionary

SOUTHERN WRITERS

A Biographical Dictionary

Edited by **ROBERT BAIN**

JOSEPH M. FLORA
and
LOUIS D. RUBIN, JR.

Louisiana State University Press
Baton Rouge and London

Copyright © 1979 by Louisiana State University Press
Manufactured in the United States of America

Designer: Albert Crochet
Typeface: VIP Caledonia
Typesetter: G & S Typesetters, Inc.
Printing and binding: Thomson-Shore, Inc.

LIBRARY OF CONGRESS CATALOGING IN PUBLICATION DATA

Main entry under title:

Southern writers.

(Southern literary studies)
   1.   American literature—Southern States—Bio-bibliography.   2.   Authors, American
—Southern States—Biography.   I.   Bain, Robert.   II.   Flora, Joseph M.   III.   Rubin,
Louis Decimus, 1923–   IV.   Series.
PS261.S59   810′.9′975[B]   78–25899
ISBN 0–8071–0354–3
ISBN 0–8071–0390–X pbk.

Dedicated to

LEWIS LEARY (1906–). Lewis Gaston Leary was born in Blauvelt, N.Y., April 18, 1906, the son of Lewis Gaston Leary, a Presbyterian minister, and Beatrice Emily Knight Leary. He was educated in public schools and at the University of Vermont, where he received his B.S. in 1928. After teaching for three years at the American University in Beirut, Lebanon, in 1931 he began graduate study at Columbia University, and in 1932 was awarded the M.A. In 1932 he was married to Mary Warren Hudson, of Miami, Fla. After study at Columbia, he joined the faculty of the University of Miami in 1935, and was appointed associate professor in 1938. He completed his doctoral dissertation and was awarded the Ph.D. in 1941, the same year that he published the biography *That Rascal Freneau*.

That fall he went to Duke University, where, except for a three-year tour of duty with the Office of Strategic Services in the Middle East during World War II, he remained through 1951. It was at Duke, as a colleague of Jay B. Hubbell, that he began his work in southern literature of the colonial and early national periods. In 1951 he published *The Literary Life of Nathaniel Tucker*. He returned to Columbia University as visiting professor in the fall of 1951 and joined that faculty permanently the following year, becoming chairman of the Department of English and Comparative Literature in 1962. In 1968 he was appointed William Rand Kenan, Jr., Professor of English at the University of North Carolina at Chapel Hill, serving until his retirement in 1976.

As scholar in American literature Lewis Leary has by no means confined his interests and activities to any single period or genre; nor has he hesitated to move with ease and authority among the various kinds of scholarship. He has shown himself equally at home in literary criticism, historical scholarship, textual criticism, and bibliography. He has written extensively on writers as various as Irving, Whittier, Pound, Clemens, Norman Douglas, and Faulkner. He has edited volumes in the Mark Twain and Washington Irving editions of the Center for the Editions of American Authors. He has published facsimile editions of the complete works of Philip Freneau. His several compilations of *Articles in American Literature* have proved indispensable reference sources for his profession. It was appropriate that in 1976 the American Literature Section of the Modern Language Association awarded him the Jay B. Hubbell Medal for Distinguished Achievement in American literary study.

His work on southern authors has touched almost every period of literature in the South. He began with Joseph Brown Ladd and Nathaniel Tucker and he has continued by writing on William Byrd II, George Washington Harris, Poe, Clemens, Lanier, Kate Chopin, Lafcadio Hearn, Cable, Thomas Wolfe, Faulkner, and Richard Wright.

His time at Chapel Hill may have been the final position of his career as an active teacher, but in no way was it a finale. On the contrary, he managed to astound an entire English department with his energy, buoyancy, good fellowship, and cantankerousness. His zest for teaching and zeal for scholarship have invigorated his students and inspired his colleagues, three of whom, as editors of this volume, dedicate it to him in affection and admiration.

WORKS: *Idiomatic Mistakes in English* (1932). *That Rascal Freneau: A Study in Literary Failure* (1941). Ed., *The Last Poems of Philip Freneau* (1945). Ed., *Doctoral Dissertations in American Literature, 1933–1945* (1946). Comp., *Articles on American Literature, 1920–1945* (1947). *The Literary Life of Nathaniel Tucker* (1951). Ed., *Method and Motive in the Cantos of Ezra Pound* (1954). Comp., *Articles on American Literature, 1900–1950* (1954). Ed., *The Unity of Knowledge* (1955). Ed., *Israel Potter: His Fifty Years of Exile*, by Herman Melville (1957). Ed., *Contemporary Literature Scholarship: A Critical Review* (1958). Ed., *Selected Writings of Henry David Thoreau* (1958). Ed., *Miss McCrea: A Novel of the American Revolution*, by Michael René Hilliard d'Auberteuill, with Eric LaGuardia (1958). *Mark Twain* (1960). Ed., *American Literary Essays* (1960). Ed., *Mark Twain's Letters to Mary* (1961). Ed.,

Home as Found, by James Fenimore Cooper (1961). *John Greenleaf Whittier* (1962). Ed., *Mark Twain's Wound* (1962). Ed., *The Essential Longfellow* (1962). Ed., *The Autobiography of Benjamin Franklin* (1962). *Washington Irving* (1963). Ed., *The Teacher and American Literature* (1965). Ed., *Modern Chivalry*, by Hugh Henry Brackenridge (1965). *Norman Douglas* (1968). Ed., *Mark Twain's Correspondence with Henry Huttleston Rogers* (1969). Comp., *Articles on American Literature, 1950– 1968* (1970). Ed., *The Writings of Joseph Brown Ladd* (1970). Ed., *The Awakening and Other Stories*, by Kate Chopin (1970). *Southern Excursions: Essays on Mark Twain and Others* (1971). *William Faulkner of Yoknapatawpha County* (1973). Ed., *The Complete Published Writings of Nathaniel Tucker* (1973). Ed., *Criticism: Some Major American Writers* (1973). *Soundings: Some Early American Writers* (1975). Ed., *The Writings in Prose and Verse of Hezekiah Salem* (1975). Ed., *The Poems (1786) and Miscellaneous Works (1788) of Philip Freneau* (1975). *American Literature: A Study and Research Guide* (1976). Ed., *Poems (1795) of Philip Freneau* (1976). Ed., *Poems (1809) of Philip Freneau* (1976). Ed., *Poems (1815) of Philip Freneau* (1976). Comp., *Articles on American Literature, 1968–1975* (1977). Numerous poems, articles, and reviews.

ROBERT BAIN
JOSEPH M. FLORA
LOUIS D. RUBIN, JR.
University of North Carolina
Chapel Hill

CONTENTS

PREFACE

Southern Writers: A Biographical Dictionary is designed to be a work in which brief and informative sketches of the lives of authors associated with the American South are made available within a single volume.

As editors, we drew up names of writers who might be included and sent them to a group of scholars of southern literature for comment and elaboration. With the help of such comments, we compiled a master list. We then set about grouping those writers to be included into categories based upon our judgment of their importance. Some few authors would require sketches of 1,000 words or so in length. A second group would be treated in sketches of about 750 words. Still others would receive 500-word treatment. But by far the largest number of writers were set for 300 words. These writers—the so-called "minor" figures—would be perhaps the most important group in the book, since it is the lesser known authors for whom reliable biographical material is often least available. The student can find material on the life of Poe or Clemens or Thomas Wolfe from a number of reference sources and a choice of available biographies. Similar information on William Crafts or Olive Tilford Dargan is much less accessible.

The problem, of course, was where to draw the line, and admittedly, such judgments had to be somewhat subjective. In any event, if the reader wishes to know why writer X is included, when writer Y is not, we can only declare that it is because we believed the X belonged and Y did not.

With contemporary writers, the problem was perhaps most acute. There was no possible way to include all or even most of the currently active southern writers in a reference book and still have room for writers no longer living. So we tried to adopt some rules of procedure. Except for a few obvious instances, all sketches of contemporary writers were to be of uniform 300-word length. In most instances a writer had to have published at least four books of poetry, fiction, or whatever. He or she had to be identified with the region not merely geographically but imaginatively. Beyond that, the question of inclusion and exclusion came down again to editorial judgment.

Toward gathering these sketches, we drew up lists of possible contributors, seeking to find for each author to be included a scholar familiar with his life and work. When that was impossible, we sought someone who had done work on the particular time during which the author flourished, or, failing that, someone authoritative in the work of authors whose writings were similar to those of the subject. We also announced the details of the project in the newsletter of the Society for the Study of Southern Literature and invited persons willing to prepare sketches to offer their services. As might have been expected, the more obscure the author, the more difficult it was to find someone to write about him. Ultimately, however, we found scholars to prepare every one of the sketches we desired for this book.

Southern Writers: A Biographical Dictionary is a project of the Society for the Study of Southern Literature, a group formed in 1968 for the purpose of stimulating and enhancing sound scholarly study in the literature of the South. It is the latest of a number of bibliographical projects of the society, among which are the annual checklist of scholarship in southern literature, which appears in each spring issue of the *Mississippi Quarterly*; a book, *A Bibliographical Guide to the Study of Southern Literature*, published by the Louisiana State University Press in 1969; and a forthcoming volume, *Southern Literary Culture*, to be published by the University of Alabama Press, which constitutes a listing of doctoral and master's theses on southern literature, and is an updating, considerably enlarged, of an earlier volume bearing that title. Our book is designed to be used along with such work; it does not therefore include checklists of scholarship.

Yet another project, for which the National Endowment of the Humanities awarded the society a grant some seven years ago, was to have been a bibliographical checklist of first printings of works by southern authors. But those who undertook this project have never completed it. We, therefore, asked the contributors of each biographical sketch to append a list of the subject's first printings, with dates. Although the more exhaustive and bibliographically fastidious checklist would obviously be more desirable, *Southern Writers: A Biographical Dictionary* provides titles and dates, and thus represents, to a degree, a fulfillment of a scholarly obligation incurred through acceptance of the National Endowment for the Humanities grant.

Here, then, is a volume offering biographical sketches of 379 southern authors. It represents the work of 172 scholars, and we, as the editors, willingly accept responsibility for all questions of inclusiveness.

For their assistance in the preparation of this book we wish to acknowledge the good offices of the Department of English at the University of North Carolina at Chapel Hill and also the chairmen of that department during the time of publication, William Harmon and James R. Gaskin.

Five clerical assistants deserve special thanks: Joyce Bradshaw, Karen Niklason, Mary Dawson, Karen Nelson, and Ramona Cook. We wish to acknowledge also a grant from the Smith Fund of the University of North Carolina which aided in the preparation of the manuscript. Most of all, we thank the many scholars whose contributions made this volume possible.

ROBERT BAIN
JOSEPH M. FLORA
LOUIS D. RUBIN, JR.

JAMES RUFUS AGEE (1909–1955). James Rufus Agee was born on November 27, 1909, the son of Hugh James Agee and Laura Whitman Tyler. His early years were spent in Knoxville, Tenn., where his mother's family resided; ties also were maintained with the Agees of rural LaFollette, Tenn. Three years after his father's death in 1916, Agee entered St. Andrew's School near Sewanee, Tenn., where he was a student through 1924. He attended Knoxville High School in 1924–25, toured France and England in the summer, and entered Phillips Exeter Academy in fall of 1925. At Exeter he contributed regularly to the *Phillips Exeter Monthly*. Enrolled at Harvard College in 1928, he produced poetry and fiction for the *Harvard Advocate*, of which he was editor in 1931–1932. Upon graduation, he became a staff writer for *Fortune* for which he wrote continuously until 1936 when he lived for six months in Anna Marie, Fla., to pursue his own writing.

In 1933 he married Olivia Saunders, but they were divorced in 1939. His second marriage, to Alma Mailman in 1939, ended in divorce in 1944, and that same year he married Mia Fritsch. One son was born of the second marriage; two daughters and a son were born of the final one.

Agee's first book, *Permit Me Voyage* (1934), manifests his uneasiness with conventional modes of writing, and much subsequent production in the 1930s was experimental, serving as preparation for *Let Us Now Praise Famous Men* (1941), his documentary text, which grew from his assignment to write a *Fortune* article about tenant farmers. Agee traveled throughout the South during the summer of 1936, but his second book was five years in the making. A respect for the "dignity of actuality" informs that text, his criticism, and all his significant prose.

In 1939 he became a book reviewer for *Time* magazine, a post he

1

held through 1941; in 1942 he began writing film criticism for
Time as well as a biweekly film column for the *Nation*. He wrote
movie criticism for both publications through 1947 and also other
essays for *Time*. His success as film critic made it possible in the
late 1940s for him to write film scripts; by 1948, the year he completed the commentary for Helen Levitt's *The Quiet One*, and
scripts based on Stephen Crane stories, he was regularly producing
scenarios; his later important screenplays include *The African
Queen* and *The Night of the Hunter*, and the Omnibus television
series on Lincoln.

During his final several years Agee wrote scripts and autobiographical fiction. *The Morning Watch* (1951) uses St. Andrew's
School as its setting. *A Death in the Family* (1957), published posthumously, is a detailed reconstruction of childhood.

Agee's reputation is largely a posthumous one, furthered greatly
by the publication of his autobiographical *A Death in the Family*,
which received the Pulitzer Prize in 1957, two years after he died
from a heart attack on May 15, 1955, in New York City. Father
James Harold Flye, a lifelong friend from St. Andrew's, edited a
collection of Agee's letters (1962), and collections of criticism,
screenplays, poetry, and prose have been published.

WORKS: *Permit Me Voyage* (1934). *Let Us Now Praise Famous Men* (1941).
The Morning Watch (1951). *A Death in the Family* (1957). *Agee on Film:
Reviews and Comments* (1958). *Agee on Film: Five Film Scripts* (1960).
Let Us Now Praise Famous Men, 2nd ed. (1960). *The Letters of James
Agee to Father Flye* (1962; 1971). *Four Early Stories by James Agee*
(1964). *The Collected Short Prose of James Agee* (1968). *The Collected
Poems of James Agee* (1968).

VICTOR A. KRAMER
Georgia State University
Atlanta, Ga.

EDWIN ANDERSON ALDERMAN (1861–1931). A university
president and crusader for popular education, Edwin A. Alderman
was born May 15, 1861, to James and Susan Jane Corbett Alderman of Wilmington, N.C. Alderman attended Wilmington private

schools and Bethel Military Academy near Warrenton, Va., then enrolled at the University of North Carolina in 1878. After his graduation in 1882, he taught school in Goldsboro for three years before becoming the town's superintendent of schools. In 1889 he resigned to organize teachers' institutes for the state board of education.

Abandoning secondary for higher education, Alderman taught at the new Normal and Industrial School for Women at Greensboro in 1892 and at the University of North Carolina the following three years. In 1896 he was elected president of the latter institution, but resigned in 1900 to accept the presidency of Tulane University. After four years there, he left to become president of the University of Virginia, a post he held until his death on April 29, 1931.

An able fund raiser and politician, Alderman worked to strengthen the academic standing and commitment to public education of all three universities. Throughout his career, Alderman championed popular education as a necessity in a democracy. In 1901 he participated in the formation of the Southern Education Board and until 1907 actively campaigned in its behalf.

His administrative duties and educational crusades left Alderman little time for scholarly work of his own. He published a series of grade school readers and collaborated on a biography of J. L. M. Curry, an earlier educational reformer. Alderman contributed his name and a few sketches to *The Library of Southern Literature* but did little editorial work. Although not a prolific author, Alderman was a powerful and popular orator; in 1924 he delivered the eulogy to Woodrow Wilson before the United States Congress.

WORKS: *Classics Old and New: A Series of School Readers* (1906–1907). *J. L. M. Curry: A Biography*, with Armistead C. Gordon (1911).

> GAINES M. FOSTER
> University of North Carolina
> Chapel Hill

JAMES LANE ALLEN (1849–1925). James Lane Allen, a romancer who wrote in an age of realism, was born in the bluegrass region of Kentucky on December 21, 1849. He learned a love of nature from his parents and from farm life. After he became a writer, his word landscapes were likened to the paintings of Corot. He felt that nature in his books was transcendent of a mere local-color backdrop for his characters.

Allen's family was impoverished after the Civil War, but he earned his way through Kentucky (Transylvania) University, graduating with honors in 1872. Although he was a lifelong bachelor, he supported his family for many years. He taught, primarily Latin, at various lower schools, at Richmond College, Richmond, Mo., and at Bethany College (W.Va.) through 1884. He had received an M.A. in 1877.

Upon publishing a number of articles and stories in the 1880s, Allen decided to leave teaching for a writing career. By 1893 his legal residence was New York City, where he lived until he died. His first book, *Flute and Violin* (1891), was a collection of his magazine stories, from *Harper's* and *Century*. The tales were sentimental and moralistic. His next major publication, the novelette *A Kentucky Cardinal* (1894), became a best seller for about a decade. The story poetically described the bluegrass landscape, and told of its Thoreauvian hero's frustrating love for an unpoetic, self-centered woman. His most popular novel, *The Choir Invisible*, appeared in 1897. It was another love story, but one involving the philosophic dilemma of determinism versus freedom of the will.

In his next two novels, *The Reign of Law* (1900) and *The Mettle of the Pasture* (1903), he swerved toward realism. He asked whether religious faith could be maintained in an age of evolutionary thought, and he became almost Jamesian in probing the psyches of his characters. After a silence of about six years, Allen published *The Bride of the Mistletoe*, a novelette whose mythic dimension, in 1909, seemed obscure to readers and critics. Other books, and a posthumously printed collection of stories, *The Landmark*, failed to regain for him his reputation.

Allen had attacked the Howells school of realism, had corresponded with many leading literary figures, and had often been called the Hawthorne of his time. But his own fiction made of him only a minor master. In 1916 he was honored when his portrait was placed in the Lexington Public Library. Various illnesses marred his later life. He died on February 18, 1925, and was buried three days later back in his native Kentucky.

WORKS: *Flute and Violin and Other Kentucky Tales and Romances* (1891). *The Blue-Grass Region of Kentucky and Other Kentucky Articles* (1892). *John Gray: A Kentucky Tale of the Olden Time* (1893). *A Kentucky Cardinal: A Story* (1894). *Aftermath* (1895). *Summer in Arcady: A Tale of Nature* (1896). *The Choir Invisible* (1897). *The Reign of Law: A Tale of the Kentucky Hemp Fields* (1900). *The Mettle of the Pasture* (1903). *The Bride of the Mistletoe* (1909). *The Doctor's Christmas Eve* (1910). *The Heroine in Bronze: or A Portrait of a Girl* (1912). *The Last Christmas Tree: An Idyl of Immortality* (1914). *The Sword of Youth* (1915). *A Cathedral Singer* (1916). *The Kentucky Warbler* (1918). *The Emblems of Fidelity: A Comedy in Letters* (1919). *The Alabaster Box* (1923). *The Landmark* (1925).

WILLIAM K. BOTTORFF
University of Toledo
Toledo, Ohio

WASHINGTON ALLSTON (1779–1843). Washington Allston was born on November 5, 1779, on a rice plantation on Waccamaw Neck, Georgetown District, S.C. He was the son of Captain William Allston, a Revolutionary officer, and Rachel Moore, of a prominent Dutch and Huguenot family. After Captain Allston's death in 1781 she married Dr. Henry Collins Flagg, a Revolutionary physician.

Allston was educated at private schools in Charleston, S.C., in Newport, R.I., and at Harvard College, where he graduated in 1800. From 1801 to 1807 he was in London, Paris, and Rome painting and studying art. He returned to Cambridge, Mass., for three years and married Ann Channing. He returned to England, where he remained until 1818, and where he achieved acclaim as a painter.

He spent the remainder of his life in Cambridge and Cambridgeport. In 1830 (his first wife having died in 1815) he married

Martha Remington Dana. These years were generally sad ones, chiefly because he was unable to finish the large canvas "Belshazzar's Feast," and because his patronage declined. He died on July 9, 1843.

Allston wrote a volume of poems, *The Sylphs of the Seasons, and Other Poems* (1813), a Gothic romance, *Monaldi: A Tale* (1841), and a series of lectures on art, *Lectures on Art and Poems* (1850). But he was more eminent as a painter than as a writer. In both creative fields he was predominantly romantic. Brooding landscapes and solitary portraits, without accessories, are his hallmarks in painting. Biblical subjects predominate among his historical paintings. His poems are fanciful and often Gothic; several are sonnets addressed to works of art and artists. His lectures on art give him stature as an idealistic aesthetician; they depend to a degree on Coleridge, whom he knew.

WORKS: *The Sylphs of the Seasons and Other Poems* (1813). *Monaldi, a Tale* (1841). *Lectures on Art and Poems* (1850).

NATHALIA WRIGHT
University of Tennessee
Knoxville

GEORGE ALSOP (1636?–1673?). Outlines of George Alsop's life are at best uncertain. The frontispiece engraving of Alsop in his only book, *A Character of the Province of Mary-Land* (London, 1666), lists his age as 28 in that year, making his birthdate 1638. But he was probably born on June 19, 1636, in Westminster, London, the son of Rose and Peter Alsop. A younger brother was named Peter.

Alsop's father was a tailor, and young George served a two-year handicraft apprenticeship in London before migrating to Maryland because of his Royalist sympathies. There he indentured himself for four years to Thomas Stockett, a frontier planter living near the Susquehanna Indians. Because Alsop was literate, Stockett evidently employed him as a secretary-accountant and perhaps as an agent in the Indian trade. When his indenture ended in December, 1662, Alsop remained in Maryland at occupations unknown;

he suffered ill health before returning to England late in 1663 or early in 1664. At the suggestion of Lord Baltimore or one of Baltimore's agents, Alsop gathered his letters from Maryland to his parents and friends, and wrote the four numbered chapters of his book, plus an essay on the Susquehanna Indians. The book's purpose was to promote migration to the colony. What happened to Alsop thereafter is even more uncertain. He may have taken clerical orders; he probably lived beyond 1673, for his name appears in his father's will of 1672.

The only book written by an indentured servant in America, *A Character* abounds in extravagant wit and bawdy humor. An ardent Royalist and Anglican, Alsop satirizes in prose and verse the Puritans of the Old and New Worlds, and pokes fun at Englishmen who would rather live at home in poverty than adventure to Maryland, which he calls *"The Miracle of this Age."*

WORKS: *A Character of the Province of Mary-Land* (1666).

ROBERT BAIN
University of North Carolina
Chapel Hill

A. R. AMMONS (1926–). Archie Randolph Ammons, born in Columbus County, N.C., February 18, 1926, did not receive very much attention or recognition until he was about 45 years old. His first book, *Ommateum* (1955), was published in a small limited edition, and nine years went by before his first generally available collection, *Expressions of Sea Level* (1964), was published. After that time, however, he produced a book almost every year, and his *Collected Poems 1951–1971* (which won the 1973 National Book Award) is almost 400 pages long. Three other volumes ought to be added to *Collected Poems 1951–1971* to comprise the whole Ammons canon: *Tape for the Turn of the Year* (a long poem published in 1965 but not included in *Collected Poems*), *Sphere: The Form of a Motion* (1974), and *Diversifications* (1975). On February 18, 1976, Ammons' 50th birthday, he could look back over a productive career crowned, at long last, by recognition and acclaim, including two honorary degrees and the rich Bollingen Award.

Ammons received a B.S. from Wake Forest College in 1949 and worked thereafter at various jobs in North Carolina and New Jersey. For a time he was principal of an elementary school in the remote coastal community of Hatteras, N.C., and for several years he was an executive of a company that manufactured biological glassware. In 1964 he joined the faculty of Cornell University as an instructor, and after ten years had risen rank by rank until he was named Goldwyn Smith Professor of the Humanities.

As sympathetic critics (particularly Harold Bloom) have observed, Ammons belongs in the practical-visionary succession of American poets whose chief ancestor is Emerson, with Wallace Stevens and William Carlos Williams as the main twentieth-century exemplars. Ammons' specialties are the epigram, the middle-sized nature lyric, and the lengthy and rather casual verse-essay or verse-diary.

WORKS: *Ommateum* (1955). *Expressions of Sea Level* (1964). *Tape for the Turn of the Year* (1965). *Corsons Inlet* (1965). *Northfield Poems* (1966). *Selected Poems* (1968). *Uplands* (1970). *Briefings* (1971). *Collected Poems 1951–1971* (1972). *Sphere: The Form of Motion* (1974). *Diversifications* (1975). *The Selected Poems, 1951–1977* (1977). *The Snow Poems* (1977).

WILLIAM HARMON
University of North Carolina
Chapel Hill

HARRIETTE ARNOW (1908–). Harriette Simpson was born on July 7, 1908, in Wayne County, Ky., where her parents had previously taught in rural schools. After attending Berea College for two years, she taught in a remote, one-room school in Pulaski County, an experience that later served as background material for her first novel, *Mountain Path*. She also taught school after her graduation from the University of Louisville in 1930, but in 1934 she moved to Cincinnati where she supported herself by taking odd jobs, frequently as a waitress, and worked on her writing. Two of the short stories she wrote during this period were anthologized in *O. Henry Memorial Award Prize Stories*. In 1939 she married Harold Arnow. They have two children and now live in Ann Arbor, Mich.

In 1944 she moved to Detroit, where her husband was a reporter for the Detroit *Times*. Her experiences in that severely over-crowded city during World War II are reflected in her best-known novel, *The Dollmaker*, for which she received many awards. Gertie Nevels, the strong central character of the book, is be-wildered by the ethnically heterogeneous environment she finds when she moves with her husband and five children from a tenant farm in the Kentucky hills to a cramped unit of a wartime housing development in Detroit.

Arnow has written three other novels, two historical studies, and several short stories and articles. The setting for all of her fiction is Kentucky or Michigan. Her characters are presented realistically, but they sometimes are involved in sensational events. Her work conveys a sense of appreciation for the stoic hardiness of the Ken-tucky mountain people, as well as an insistence upon the necessity of aesthetic elements in their lives.

WORKS: *Mountain Path* (1936). *Hunter's Horn* (1949). *The Dollmaker* (1954). *Seedtime on the Cumberland* (1960). *Flowering of the Cumber-land* (1963). *The Weedkiller's Daughter* (1970). *The Kentucky Trace: A Novel of the American Revolution* (1974). *Old Burnside* (1977).

NANCY C. JOYNER
Western Carolina University
Cullowhee, N.C.

THOMAS BACON (1700?–1768). Probably a native of Cumber-land County, England, little is known about Bacon before he ap-pears as a customs collector in Dublin in the 1730s. He published a study of the Irish tax system in 1737 and edited two Dublin news-papers, 1742–1743. Bacon entered the Anglican priesthood in 1745 and sailed for Maryland where he was rector of St. Peter's Parish, Talbot County, for thirteen years. From 1758 until his death he served All Saints, Frederick County, the richest parish in the province.

Along with James Sterling and Thomas Cradock, Bacon repre-sented the best the Anglican ministry contributed to colonial Mary-land culture. He became an honorary member of the Tuesday

Club in 1745 and frequently attended the Annapolis organization's meetings where his poetry, violin playing, and musical compositions enlivened the proceedings. He was the most widely published author in colonial Maryland, and his sermons on charity schools and the education of slaves were printed and reprinted in America and Britain, with the last edition appearing 75 years after his death. As a political writer Bacon remained an articulate champion of the proprietary party and the interests of the established church. As a humanitarian he advocated educational opportunities for poor whites, slaves, and German immigrants in the province.

Bacon is best known for his compilation of the *Laws of Maryland* which Lawrence C. Wroth acclaimed as "the most important of the legal publications of the Province of Maryland . . . and a specimen of typography which was not exceeded in dignity and beauty by any production of an American colonial press." Surveying the totality of his contributions, J. A. Leo Lemay concluded: "In an age when clergymen dominated literature and society, Bacon led the Maryland clergy."

WORKS: *A Compleat System of the Revenue of Ireland.* . . . (1737). Ed., Dublin *Mercury* (January 23–September 25, 1742), Dublin *Gazette* (September 28, 1742–July 12, 1743). *Two Sermons, Preached to a Congregation of Black Slaves* . . . (1749). *Four Sermons, Upon the Great and Indispensible Duty of All Christian Masters and Mistresses to Bring Up Their Negro Slaves in the Knowledge and Fear of God.* . . . (1750). *A Sermon Preached . . . Before a Society of Free and Accepted Masons* . . . (1753). *An Answer to the Queries on the Proprietary Government of Maryland* . . . with Cecilius Calvert (1764). *Laws of Maryland.* . . . (1765). *Four Sermons . . . Viz. Two Sermons to Black Slaves and Two Sermons for the Benefit of a Charity Working School.* . . . (1753, 1783 reprint only copy now extant). *Writings.* . . . (1843). "Proceedings of the Parochial Clergy," *Maryland Historical Magazine*, III (1908), 257–73, 364–84.

DAVID CURTIS SKAGGS
Bowling Green State University
Bowling Green, Ohio

GEORGE WILLIAM BAGBY (1828–1883). Journalist, essayist, and humorist, George William Bagby was born on August 13,

1828, in Buckingham County, Va. His mother suffered years of poor health and died when Bagby was eight. Thus he grew up mainly on the plantations of his aunt and of his grandfather and was educated in field schools in Buckingham and Prince Edward counties. The ambiance of the "spring and gourd" Virginia of his youth would furnish in later years the material for his best writing.

When Bagby was ten, his father, a Lynchburg merchant, sent him north for his education, first at Edgehill School, in Princeton, N.J., and later to M. L. Hurlbut's school in Philadelphia. In 1849 he graduated from the University of Pennsylvania with a degree in medicine and returned to Lynchburg to practice. By 1853, however, he had turned to journalism, joining with George W. Latham to publish the Lynchburg *Express*.

After the failure of the *Express* in 1856, Bagby continued to contribute sketches and essays to local newspapers. From 1857 to 1859 he served as Washington correspondent for several newspapers. From February to December of 1858 he contributed eight "Mozis Addums" letters to the *Southern Literary Messenger*. These dialect letters of a semiliterate rural Virginian were popular and were no doubt in part responsible for Bagby's being named editor of the *Messenger* in May, 1860. Poor health forced Bagby to leave the Confederate Army after short service in 1861. He returned to Richmond, continued as editor of the *Messenger* until 1864, and became Richmond correspondent for newspapers throughout Virginia and the South.

After an unsuccessful postwar attempt to establish a newspaper in rural Virginia, Bagby accepted a post as custodian of the state library, which he held from 1870 to 1878. During this difficult financial period he supplemented his income by writing some of his best sketches of antebellum Virginia life. His gently irreverent and lightly satirical portraits, such as "The Old Virginia Gentleman" and "The Southern Fool," moved him beyond the idealized plantation romances of the period and made him popular on the lecture circuit. He died in Richmond on November 29, 1883.

WORKS: *Mozis Addums' New Letters: Lettur Wun* (1860). *The Letters of Mozis Addums to Billy Ivvins* (1862). *John M. Daniel's Latch Key: A Memoir of the Late Editor of the Richmond Examiner* (1868). *What I*

Did with My Fifty Millions (1874). *Meekins's Twinses: A Perduckshun uv
Mozis Addums* (1877). *Canal Reminiscences: Recollections of Travel in
the Old Days on the James River and Kanawha Canal* (1879). *A Week
in Hespidam: Being the First and Only True Account of the Mountains,
Men, Manners and Morals Thereof* (1879). *John Brown and William
Mahone: An Historical Parallel Foreshadowing Civil Trouble, 1860–
1880* (1880). *Selections from the Writings of Dr. George W. Bagby* (1884).
The Old Virginia Gentleman and Other Sketches, ed. Thomas Nelson
Page (1910). *The Old Virginia Gentleman and Other Sketches*, ed. Ellen
M. Bagby (1938).

RITCHIE D. WATSON, JR.
Randolph-Macon College
Ashland, Va.

JOSEPH GLOVER BALDWIN (1815–1864). Well-known in his
day as a jurist, but more interesting to posterity as a writer of satirical and realistic sketches and tales about flush times on the Mississippi and Alabama frontier, Joseph Glover Baldwin was born on
January 21, 1815, at Friendly Grove Factory, Va. He devoured
Shakespeare, Scott, and Irving as a boy, and went to work at fourteen to help with the family finances. He was one of seven children
born to Eliza Cook and Joseph Clarke Baldwin, a businessman.
Joseph read law in the office of an uncle and a cousin; in 1835 he
assisted his older brother Cornelius in putting out the Lexington
(Va.) *Gazette* (later the *Union*), and for six months in 1835–1836
copublished the Buchanan (Va.) *Advocate and Commercial Gazette*. In 1836 he left for the turbulent Mississippi frontier. He
practiced law in DeKalb, Miss. (1836–1837), in Gainesville, Ala.
(1837–1850), and Livingston, Ala. (1850–1854). He married Sidney Gaylord White in 1840; of their six children, only Alexander,
Joseph, and John lived to maturity.

Between 1851 and 1853 he wrote the 26 sketches and satires
that appear in his most notable volume, *The Flush Times of Alabama and Mississippi* (1853). Drawing heavily on his experiences
as an attorney, Baldwin sketched vivid and authentic portraits of
shifty lawyers, unlettered judges, inept prosecutors, slippery cli-
ents, and other frontier types, as well as doing pungent but basi-

cally serious profiles of colorful but respected colleagues such as Sergeant S. Prentiss. Like Augustus Baldwin Longstreet, Thomas Bangs Thorpe, and other humorists of the Old Southwest, Baldwin's aim in part was realistic depiction of a lawless, colorful era that was passing, or had passed, away. In 1853 he also published, in the *Southern Literary Messenger*, a satirical and wholly imaginary account of "California Flush Times." Subsequently he wrote serious essays on Jefferson, Hamilton, Jackson, Clay, and Randolph, collected and published as *Party Leaders* (1855).

Partly because of defeat in politics and partly in response to the lure of a new country, Baldwin emigrated to California in 1854, where he soon achieved success at the bar despite the lawlessness and confusion rampant in the legal profession at the time of his arrival. In 1858 he was elected associate justice of the California Supreme Court but was defeated in his campaign for U.S. senator (1860). During the Civil War, Baldwin, a southern sympathizer, made a business trip to the East (1863) and sought permission to visit members of his family in Virginia, behind the Confederate lines. Although his request was denied, he obtained an interview with President Lincoln, who told him that *Flush Times* was one of his favorite books.

After returning to California in 1864, he began a realistic account "The Flush Times of California." At this time, financial difficulties arising from unprofitable mining investments harassed him. Operated on for a minor ailment, he developed tetanus and died, either from the infection or from opiates administered as antidotes, on September 30, 1864.

Baldwin's contribution to the humorous realism of the Old Southwest is weakened by his too-frequent striving for literary gentility and by the scantiness of his output. Nonetheless, his one significant volume holds a unique place in southern literary history by virtue of the vivid and, at times, even grotesque depictions of scenes and character types of the frontier bench and bar and through the author's deft use of his own extensive legal knowledge and experience to authenticate these scenes and types.

WORKS: *The Flush Times of Alabama and Mississippi* (1853). *Party Leaders: Sketches of Thomas Jefferson, Alex'r Hamilton, Andrew Jackson,*

*Henry Clay, John Randolph, of Roanoke, Including Notices of Many
Other Distinguished American Statesmen* (1855). *The Flush Times of
California* (1966).

NORRIS YATES
Iowa State University
Ames

JOHN BARTH (1930–). John Barth was born on May 27, 1930, in
Cambridge, Md., the son of John J. (a candy store owner) and
Georgia Simmons Barth. He has a twin sister, Jill, and an older
brother, William. After graduating from Cambridge High School,
Barth, who wanted to be a jazz musician, attended the Julliard
School of Music in New York City briefly, moving on to Johns
Hopkins University to major in journalism. While working in the
library at Hopkins, he discovered many of his literary "love af-
fairs"—most notably Scheherazade. He received his B.A. from
Johns Hopkins in 1951 and an M.A. in creative writing in 1952.
From 1953 to 1965 he taught English at Pennsylvania State Uni-
versity. Between 1965 and 1974 he held a similar position at the
State University of New York at Buffalo, resigning to return to
Johns Hopkins, where he now teaches in the creative writing program. In 1950 Barth married Harriette Anne Strickland; they are
the parents of three children: Christine, John, and Daniel.

His first novel, *The Floating Opera* (1956), was written in the
first three months of 1955 and was inspired by his memories of an
old showboat that had played the tidewater Maryland area during
his childhood. Although it received a mixed critical reception, *The
Floating Opera* was the runner-up for the 1957 National Book
Award for fiction. In 1967 Barth published a revised edition of the
novel, restoring to its text passages that his publishers had insisted
he remove eleven years earlier.

The End of the Road (1958) was written during the last three
months of 1955 and is what Barth calls a "companion-piece" to his
first novel. But it was Barth's third novel, *The Sot Weed Factor*
(1965), which placed him among the most important American
novelists since World War II. The novel is based on the life of poet
Ebenezer Cooke, whose satirical poem about colonial Maryland

gave Barth his title and his subject. Cooke, self-proclaimed "Poet and Virgin," sets out to claim his inheritance in the New World and to write an epic Marylandiad. As he struggles to preserve his innocence through a series of increasingly bizarre experiences, the Marylandiad gives way to a bitter but comic satire on the new continent and on the darker sides of human nature to which Cooke is exposed. In 1967 Barth published a slightly revised edition of this novel.

In 1966 Barth continued his experimentation with the picaresque novel in *Giles Goat-Boy*, the first-person chronicle of the life and teachings of George Giles, who left the goat farm to become a tutor in the human university. Reminiscent of Swift, this *"Bildungsroman ad absurdum"* is, as one critic puts it, "part sacred book, animal fable, science-fiction fantasy, political allegory, educational satire, epic, and what not else." *Giles* was also widely acclaimed. Also in 1966 the National Institute of Arts awarded Barth a grant ($2,500), and the Creative Arts Commission of Brandeis University recognized his achievement in fiction.

Lost in the Funhouse (1968) is a collection of shorter pieces, which explore, in Barth's words, "ways in which the phenomenon of the disembodied authorial voice can be used metaphorically." Of the fourteen pieces, most are designed either for live voice or for tape or for various combinations of the two, rather than for print. Barth has been an effective recorder and reader of his own work. In his most recent work, *Chimera* (1972), Barth is again reworking and playing with traditional fictional forms and points of view.

Barth once remarked, "God wasn't too bad a novelist, except he was a Realist." John Barth has made it his task to continue to dream up "unreal" views of the world that will be more satisfactory than the "real thing."

WORKS: *The Floating Opera* (1956). *The End of the Road* (1958). *The Sot-Weed Factor* (1960). *Giles Goat-Boy: or The Revised New Syllabus* (1966). *Lost in the Funhouse* (1968). *Chimera* (1972).

JACKSON R. BRYER
University of Maryland
College Park

WILLIAM MALONE BASKERVILL (1850–1899). William Malone Baskervill was born on April 1, 1850, in Fayette County,
Tenn., the son of John and Elizabeth Malone Baskervill, his father
a physician, Methodist preacher, and planter. He attended local
schools until 1865, when he was sent to Indiana Asbury University
(now DePauw) for a year. Upon his return home he studied privately with a tutor until in 1872 he went to Randolph-Macon College in Virginia, where he followed an elective course and never
received a degree. In 1874 he went to Leipzig to study at the university there, remaining until the fall of 1876; in December of that
year he went to Wofford College in South Carolina to teach Latin.
In the summer of 1877 Baskervill married Florence Adams, and
in the summer of 1878 he went again to Leipzig to complete his
doctoral work. After the sudden death of his wife following childbirth, he returned to the United States in February, 1879, and in
June of that same year returned to Wofford College to teach Latin
and Greek. He completed the requirements for a Ph.D. in 1880,
his dissertation studying the Anglo-Saxon text of Alexander's Epistle to Aristotle. In 1881 he was called to the chair of English at
Vanderbilt University. He later married Jane McTyeire, the
youngest daughter of Bishop H. N. McTyeire, one of the founders
of Vanderbilt, and they were the parents of William Malone
Baskervill, Jr. (1888–1953), who became managing editor of the
Baltimore *News*. Baskervill died September 6, 1899, at the height
of his activities as teacher and critic.

Although Baskervill completed several linguistic and language
studies, he is better remembered today for his critical writings on
the literature of the South. He formulated plans for "a pioneer
attempt to survey the entire field of . . . post-bellum [southern]
literature, to indicate its inherent unity, and to work out some of
the details characteristic of its production and of the product itself." His plans originally involved twelve short papers dealing
with various post–Civil War southern writers, largely of the
local-color movement, but by the time of his death the study had
grown to include papers on many writers. Volume I of *Southern
Writers: Biographical and Critical Studies* was published in 1897.

Volume II of the same title was completed by Baskervill's students and published in 1903.

WORKS: Ed., *Andreas: A Legend of St. Andrew*, in *Library of Anglo-Saxon Poetry* (1885). Ed., *Students' Anglo-Saxon Dictionary*, with James A. Harrison (1885). Ed., *An Outline of Anglo-Saxon Grammar*, with James A. Harrison (1887). *Shall the Negro Be Educated or Suppressed? A Symposium*, with W. M. Beckner, C. F. Smith, and G. W. Cable (1889). Ed., *English Grammar for High School and College Use*, with James W. Sewell (1895). *Southern Writers: Biographical and Critical Studies*, 2 vols. (I, 1897; II, 1903). Ed., *School Grammar of the English Language* (1903).

RANDALL G. PATTERSON
Belhaven College
Jackson, Miss.

JOHN SPENCER BASSETT (1867–1928). Born on September 10, 1867, at Tarboro, N.C., to Mary Wilson and Richard Baxter Bassett, John Spencer Bassett was educated in public and private schools of eastern North Carolina, at Trinity College (Duke University) from which he graduated in 1888, and at Johns Hopkins University where he received his doctorate in 1894. With his wife of two years, Jessie Lewellin, he then returned to Trinity as professor of history.

In addition to teaching, Bassett wrote articles and books, increased library holdings of southern materials, initiated publication of the *Historical Papers of the Trinity College Historical Society*, and founded and edited the *South Atlantic Quarterly* (1902–1905). A liberal stand on the race question, reflected in his editorials, nearly caused his dismissal from Trinity in 1903. Nevertheless, sustained by the college, he withstood attacks from without, winning a significant victory for academic freedom.

Bassett's interest in the history of North Carolina yielded monographs on its colonial government, the Regulator movement, and slavery. His work on the "peculiar institution," though pathbreaking, emphasized merely its legal aspects.

In 1906 *The Federalist System*, Bassett's contribution to the prestigious *American Nation* series, brought him wider recognition. That same year he accepted an appointment at Smith College in Massachusetts, mainly because, as he wrote later, he desired "a peaceful atmosphere."

Although Bassett broadened his scholarly interests at Smith, he continued to work in regional history, publishing a two-volume *Life of Andrew Jackson* (1911), his finest book. Bassett believed sectionalism to have been the formative force in the Jacksonian era. He viewed Jackson himself as a product of, and spokesman for, the frontier, portraying him sympathetically, yet fairly. Some years later, Bassett supplied a needed source by editing *The Southern Plantation Overseer as Revealed in His Letters* (1925), long the standard work on that subject. On January 27, 1928, accidental death cut short his work as editor of the *Correspondence of Andrew Jackson*.

Bassett was a pioneer in the critical study of southern history. His courage, competence, and commitment to seek the truth give him a high place among historians of the South.

WORKS: *The Constitutional Beginnings of North Carolina, 1663–1729* (1894). *Regulators of North Carolina* (1895). *Slavery and Servitude in the Colony of North Carolina* (1896). *Anti-Slavery Leaders of North Carolina* (1898). *Slavery in the State of North Carolina* (1899). Ed., *The Writings of "Colonel William Byrd of Westover in Virginia, Esqr."* (1901). *The Federalist System, 1789–1801* (1906). *Life of Andrew Jackson,* 2 vols. (1911). *A Short History of the United States* (1913). *The Plain Story of American History* (1916). Ed., *Correspondence of George Bancroft and Jared Sparks, 1823–1832* (1917). *The Middle Group of American Historians* (1917). *The Lost Fruits of Waterloo* (1918). *Our War with Germany: A History* (1919). Ed., *Selections from the Federalist* (1921). Ed., *The Westover Journal of John A. Selden, Esqr., 1858–1862* (1921). Ed., *Major Howell Tatum's Journal While Acting Topographical Engineer (1814) to General Jackson, Commanding the Seventh Military District* (1922). Ed., *Letters of Francis Parkman to Pierre Margry* (1923). Ed., *The Southern Plantation Overseer as Revealed in His Letters* (1925). Ed., *Correspondence of Andrew Jackson,* 7 vols. (1926–35; 3 vols. completed at Bassett's death). *Expansion and Reform, 1889–1926* (1926). Ed., with others, *The Writing of History* (1926). *The League of Nations: A Chapter in World Politics* (1928). *Makers of a New Nation* (1928).

Martin Van Buren, Secretary of State, in Samuel Flagg Bemis, *The American Secretaries of State and Their Diplomacy*, IV (1928).

WAYNE MIXON
Mercer University
Macon, Ga.

HAMILTON BASSO (1904–1964). Joseph Hamilton Basso was born on September 5, 1904, in New Orleans; he attended Tulane University from 1922 to 1926 but did not complete his law degree. After a short residence in New York City he returned in 1927 to New Orleans and became a reporter for the *Tribune*, the *Item*, and the *Times-Picayune*. He knew Sherwood Anderson and William Faulkner and other contributors to the *Double Dealer*, where he first published. His first novel, *Relics and Angels*, appeared in 1929. After marriage in 1930 to Etolia Simmons, he moved to western North Carolina, where he lived periodically until the early forties. From 1935 to 1937 he served as an associate editor of the *New Republic*, to which he contributed over 30 book reviews and articles. From 1937 to 1939 he traveled and lived in Europe, particularly southern France, England, and Italy. He received the Southern Authors Award in 1939. Basso was a contributing editor of *Time* magazine in 1942 and 1943 and then became an associate editor of the *New Yorker*, to which he contributed profiles, stories, essays, and reviews until the 1960s. In 1955 he was elected to the National Institute of Arts and Letters. He died on May 13, 1964, in Weston, Conn.

Basso's work as a journalist influenced his novels, which, like those of his friend Thomas Wolfe, reveal a dual vision of love and contempt for the South. His most notorious work, *Sun in Capricorn* (1942), deals with Huey Long's political chicanery; and his most famous novel, a best seller, *The View from Pompey's Head* (1954), typifies his technique of the young, politically liberal southerner who returns home and comes into conflict with the remains of an old conservative social order.

WORKS: *Relics and Angels* (1929). *Beauregard: The Great Creole* (1933). *Cinnamon Seed* (1934). *In Their Own Image* (1935). *Courthouse Square*

(1936). *Days Before Lent* (1939). *Wine of the Country* (1941). *Sun in Capricorn* (1942). *Mainstream* (1943). Ed., with Etolia S. Basso, *The World from Jackson Square* (1948). *The Greenroom* (1949). *The View from Pompey's Head* (1954). *The Light Infantry Ball* (1959). *A Quota of Seaweed* (1960). *A Touch of the Dragon* (1964).

JAMES E. ROCKS
Loyola University
Chicago, Ill.

FRANCES COURTENAY BAYLOR (1848–1920). Frances Baylor was born on January 20, 1848, at Fort Smith, Ark., where her father James L. Dawson was stationed. Later she moved to other military posts in San Antonio and New Orleans. Her mother, Sophie Baylor Dawson, was a member of a famous Virginia family, and near the end of the Civil War she resumed her maiden name for herself and Frances and returned to Virginia to reside with relatives. At war's end, the whole family went to England for an extended stay, returning to Winchester, Va., in the late 1860s.

During the 1870s Frances Baylor wrote a number of newspaper sketches and considerable poetry, but her first success was an Anglo-American novel of manners in 1886. For *Lippincott's Magazine* she had written "The Perfect Treasure," a lively humorous sketch of the social adventures of an American family in England. She had followed with another sketch, "On this Side," of the parallel misadventures of an English family visiting America. It was these two sketches that were combined for the novel *On Both Sides* (1886), which was widely praised and went through eleven editions. Her second novel, *Behind the Blue Ridge* (1887), concerns the mountain people of her region of Virginia, and beyond the sentimentality and inept plotting there is considerable realistic grasp of local speech, manners, and customs. She wrote a number of juvenile stories; one of them, *Juan and Juanita* (1887), a small classic of its sort, has gone through many editions and is still found in most libraries. Her short stories and sketches, including a number from *Atlantic Monthly*, were collected and published as *A Shocking Example, and Other Sketches* (1889).

In 1896 she married George S. Barnum of Savannah, Ga., where she lived briefly, and they later moved to Lexington, Va. After her husband's death about 1900, she returned to Winchester, where she died on October 19, 1920.

WORKS: *On Both Sides* (1886). *Behind the Blue Ridge* (1887). *Juan and Juanita* (1887). *A Shocking Example and Other Sketches* (1889). *Claudia Hyde* (1894). *Miss Nina Barrow* (1897). *The Ladder of Fortune* (1899). *A Georgian Bungalow* (1900). *Remaking a Man: One Successful Method of Mental Refitting* (1919).

C. CARROLL HOLLIS
University of North Carolina
Chapel Hill

RICHMOND CROOM BEATTY (1905–1961). Richmond Croom Beatty was born in Shawnee, Okla., on January 6, 1905, the son of William Henry and Caroline Barbour Beatty. He grew up in Birmingham, Ala., where on May 7, 1927, he married Floy Ward. They had no children.

He attended Birmingham-Southern College, from which he received his A.B. (1926), and Vanderbilt University, from which he received his M.A. (1928) and his Ph.D. (1930). From 1930 to 1935 he taught at West Tennessee State Teachers College (Memphis State University) and from 1935 to 1937 at the University of Alabama. In 1937 he returned to Vanderbilt where he remained until illness forced his retirement in 1956. From 1956 until his death, on October 9, 1961, he was literary editor of the Nashville *Tennessean*.

A prolific writer and editor, Beatty edited or coedited more than a dozen books, including two widely used textbooks: *The Literature of the South* (with Floyd C. Watkins and Thomas Daniel Young) and *The American Tradition in Literature* (with Sculley Bradley and E. Hudson Long). He published more than 100 essays in *PMLA*, *American Literature*, *Sewanee Review*, *Yale Review*, and elsewhere. He was the author of four biographies, the best known of which is the first, *William Byrd of Westover* (1932).

WORKS: *William Byrd of Westover* (1932). *Bayard Taylor* (1936). *Lord Macaulay* (1938). *James Russell Lowell* (1942).

THOMAS DANIEL YOUNG
Vanderbilt University
Nashville, Tenn.

KATHERINE BELLAMANN (1877–1956). In 1945 after the death of her husband, musician-novelist Henry Bellamann, Katherine McKee Jones Bellamann returned to her native Mississippi to resume a writing career that had lapsed since the publication of her first novel, *My Husband's Friends* (1931). At the time of her death in 1956 she had completed a novel that her husband had left unfinished, *Parris Mitchell of Kings Row*, composed a modest amount of poetry, and written a novel based on the life she had known as a child growing up in rural Mississippi near the small town of Carthage where she was born on October 7, 1877.

She met Henry Bellamann at Methodist Girls' College in Tuscaloosa, Ala. They were married on September 3, 1907, at Carthage and moved to Columbia, S.C., where Henry was dean of the School of Fine Arts at Chicora College from 1907 to 1924. Having studied voice in Europe and New York, Katherine was preparing to make her debut at *l'Opera Comique de Paris* when she developed asthma and was forced to abandon her career as a professional singer. As a voice teacher in New York, where she and Henry moved in 1924, she achieved distinction. Desi Arnaz and Eddie Arnold were among her pupils.

Bellamann's writing career was strongly influenced by that of her husband. Although Henry Bellamann, who grew up in Fulton, Mo., was primarily interested in music, serving as chairman of the examining board of the Julliard School, as a director of the Curtis School of Music, and briefly as head of the Department of Music at Vassar, he completed seven novels and one book of poems. *Kings Row* (1940) was his most successful novel.

Katherine Bellaman died in Jackson, Miss., on November 8, 1956. The Bellamann papers were given to Mississippi College at Clinton.

WORKS: *My Husband's Friends* (1931). *Parris Mitchell of Kings Row*, with Henry Bellamann (1948). *The Hayvens of Demaret* (1951). *Two Sides of a Poem* (1955). *A Poet Passed This Way* (1958).

ROBERT L. PHILLIPS, JR.
Mississippi State University
Starkville

LERONE BENNETT, JR. (1928–). Historian, journalist, editor, and social critic, Lerone Bennett, Jr., was born on October 17, 1928, in Clarksville, Miss., the son of Lerone and Alma Reed Bennett. After attending public schools in Jackson and working on the local Negro weekly *Mississippi Enterprise*, Bennett matriculated to Morehouse College, Atlanta, in 1945; there he edited the college newspaper and completed his B.A. in 1949. He pursued graduate study briefly at Atlanta University before joining the staff of the Atlanta *Daily World*, first as a reporter (1949–1951) and then as city editor (1952–1953). Bennett moved to Chicago to become associate editor of *Ebony Magazine* (1953–1958); in 1958 he was elevated to senior editor of *Ebony*, one of the most influential magazines concerned with black America. He married Gloria Sylvester on July 21, 1956; they have four children. The Bennetts reside in Chicago.

In addition to his writing and editorial duties, Bennett was visiting professor of history at Northwestern University (1969–1971) and became chairman of African-American Studies there in 1972. He received the Capital Press Club Award for Book of the Year (1963); the Patron Saints Award from the Society of Midland Authors in 1965 for his biography of Martin Luther King, Jr., *What Manner of Man*; and a D. Litt. from Morehouse College in 1966. A senior fellow of the Institute of the Black World (1969), Bennett is also a member of the board of directors of the Martin Luther King Memorial Center and a member of the Black Academy of Arts and Sciences.

Bennett's books have focused on black American history and on the analysis of Negro Americans' struggle for civil rights. *Before the Mayflower: A History of the Negro in America, 1619–1966* and

Black Power U.S.A.: The Human Side of Reconstruction, 1867–1877 are historical studies recounting the conditions of black Americans and of their contributions to U.S. culture. *What Manner of Man* traces the life of Dr. King, showing his impact on the nation and the world, and *Pioneers in Protest* presents biographical essays on black leaders from Crispus Attucks to modern times. Bennett has contributed articles, poems, and stories to popular magazines, and he played a major role in the publication of *Ebony*'s three-volume *Pictorial History of Black America* (1971).

WORKS: *Before the Mayflower: A History of the Negro in America, 1619–1964* (1962; rev., 1966). *The Negro Mood, and Other Essays* (1964). *What Manner of Man: A Biography of Martin Luther King, Jr.* (1964; rev., 1965, 1968, 1976). *A Confrontation: Black and White* (1965). *Black Power U.S.A.: The Human Side of Reconstruction, 1867–1877* (1967). *Pioneers in Protest* (1968). *The Challenge of Blackness* (1972). *The Shaping of Black America* (1975).

ROBERT BAIN
University of North Carolina
Chapel Hill

WENDELL BERRY (1934–). Wendell Berry lives in Henry County, Ky., where he was born on August 5, 1934. He took his B.A. and M.A. from the University of Kentucky in 1956 and 1957, has taught briefly at Georgetown College (Ky.), Stanford University, and New York University, and since 1964 has taught creative writing at the University of Kentucky. He is the recipient of two prizes from *Poetry Magazine*, both a Guggenheim and Rockefeller Foundation Fellowship, and a 1971 award from the National Institute of Arts and Letters. In 1957 he married Tanya Amyx; they have two children. It is important that he is a farmer as well as a writer, for the one vocation informs the other.

Berry divides his creative energies almost equally among poetry, novels, and essays, but in each genre his principal subject matter is the land. In such volumes of poetry as *Farming: A Handbook* and *The Country of Marriage* his chief metaphor is tilling the soil. His three novels, *Nathan Coulter, A Place on Earth*, and *The Memory of Old Jack*, investigate the lives of middle-class farming families. Many of his essays reflect his stance as a pacifist and conservationist; some are strongly ecological, such as *The Unforeseen Wilderness*. All of his works are infused with a single vision: the moral and intellectual responsibility of the individual to his fellows and to the land that nurtures him.

Berry's style is characterized by high wit as well as the broad humor of the southern frontier tradition. He uses both free verse and traditional verse forms in his poetry, which is predominantly quiet, direct, and unpretentious. His principal fictional technique is realistic, emphasizing the development of and the relationships among the characters who inhabit his re-creation of northern Kentucky.

WORKS: *Nathan Coulter* (1960). *November Twenty-Six, Nineteen Hundred Sixty-Three* (1964). *The Broken Ground: Poems* (1964). *A Place on Earth* (1967). *Openings* (1968). *Findings* (1969). *The Long-Legged House* (1969). *The Hidden Wound* (1970). *Farming: A Hand Book* (1970). *The Unforeseen Wilderness: An Essay on Kentucky's Red River Gorge* (1971). *A Continuous Harmony: Essays Cultural and Agricultural* (1972). *The Country of Marriage* (1973). *The Memory of Old Jack* (1974). *Sayings and Doings* (1975). *Three Memorial Poems* (1977). *Clearing* (1977). *The Unsettling of America: Culture and Agriculture* (1977).

NANCY C. JOYNER
Western Carolina University
Cullowhee, N.C.

DORIS BETTS (1932–). Doris June Waugh Betts was born at Statesville, N.C., on June 4, 1932, the daughter of William Elmore and Mary Ellen Freeze Waugh. She received her education in the Statesville public schools, at the University of North Carolina at Greensboro (1950–1953), and later at Chapel Hill (1954). On July 5, 1952, she married Lowry M. Betts, an attorney; they have three children—Doris Lewellyn (b. 1953), David Lowry (b. 1954), and Erskine Moore (b. 1960). Since 1957 Betts and her family have resided in Sanford, N.C.

Betts began her career writing for North Carolina newspapers, among them the Statesville *Daily Record* (1946–1950), the Chapel Hill *Weekly* (1953–1954), and the Sanford *Daily Herald* (1957–

1958). She received a Guggenheim Fellowship in creative writing (1958–1959) and edited the Sanford *News Leader* (1960). In 1966 Betts joined the English faculty of the University of North Carolina at Chapel Hill, where she teaches creative writing, and where she was director of freshman-sophomore English from 1972 to 1977. She received a Tanner Award for excellence in undergraduate teaching in 1973. The state of North Carolina honored her in 1975 with its Medal for Literature.

Jonathan Yardley says, "Doris Betts has been writing remarkable stories for two decades, and the lamentable truth is that attention, by and large, has not been paid." Yet Betts's reputation as a first-rate fiction writer grows. She won the Mademoiselle College Fiction Contest (1953) and the U.N.C. Putnam Prize for her first collection of stories, *The Gentle Insurrection* (1954). *The Astronomer and Other Stories* (1966) and *The River to Pickle Beach* (1972) received critical praise, and she has three times won the Sir Walter Raleigh Award for best fiction by a North Carolinian—for *Tall Houses in Winter* (1958) in 1959; for *The Scarlet Thread* (1965) in 1966; and for *Beasts of the Southern Wild* (1973) in 1974. *Beasts of the Southern Wild* was also one of twelve finalists for the National Book Award in 1973. Betts is completing a novel tentatively titled "Stepping Westward" and a collection of stories, yet untitled. She has not collected her essays and poems.

WORKS: *The Gentle Insurrection* (1954). *Tall Houses in Winter* (1958). *The Scarlet Thread* (1965). *The Astronomer and Other Stories* (1966). Ed., *Young Writer at Chapel Hill* (1968). *The River to Pickle Beach* (1972). *Beasts of the Southern Wild and Other Stories* (1973).

ROBERT BAIN
University of North Carolina
Chapel Hill

ROBERT BEVERLEY (*ca.* 1673–1722). The first native Virginian to write a history of the colony, Robert Beverley was born on his father's plantation in Middlesex County, in about 1673. About his childhood we know only that he was educated in England, at Beverley Grammar School in Yorkshire, perhaps. In 1697 he married Ursula Byrd, daughter of the first William Byrd. She died at the birth of their son, William, less than one year after the marriage, and Beverley never remarried.

Beverley early began a promising political career: he held several clerkships with the colonial government by 1696, and in 1699 he was elected to the House of Burgesses from Jamestown. While in London (1703–1705) to defend a lawsuit over some property, Beverley wrote indiscreet letters home alleging self-serving political maneuvering on the parts of Governor Francis Nicholson and the surveyor general of customs. Repercussions from the governor and the crown effectively ended Beverley's public career. He spent the rest of his life as a private citizen, amassing before his death on April 21, 1722, one of the largest estates in Virginia.

The business trip to London brought about Beverley's one book of note, *The History and Present State of Virginia, in Four Parts* (1705). Annoyed at the amount of error about Virginia and Virginians in the manuscript of Oldmixon's *British Empire in America* (1708), Beverley wrote a more "tolerable account." With lively curiosity, a ready eye for detail, a sometimes bawdy humor, and unabashed candor, Beverley covers, in succession, the history, the natural products, the Indians, and the current state of Virginia.

In 1722 he revised the *History*, deleting many of his idiosyncratic judgments. In the same year he also published *An Abridgement of the Publick Laws of Virginia*, a working manual for magistrates and planters. His only other known work is the note on a map drawn by the Creek Indian, Lambatty, a note sometimes called "The Account of Lambatty," still unpublished.

WORKS: *The History and Present State of Virginia, in Four Parts* (1705; rev., 1722). *An Abridgement of the Publick Laws of Virginia* (1722).

FREDA F. STOHRER
Old Dominion University
Norfolk, Va.

JOHN PEALE BISHOP (1892–1944). John Peale Bishop was born on May 21, 1892, in Charles Town, W.Va. His mother was of old Virginia stock and his father of New England heritage—a prefigurement of the ambiguities of his later life. Instinctively a southerner and one of the first modern writers to articulate a defense of the Old South, he lived most of his adult life away from the South and was never identifiably a member of any literary or ideological group. In 1939, when asked about his loyalties, he declared, "I have always believed that literature should oppose to any system, no matter how perfectly conceived, the 'minute particulars' of mankind."

His schooling set back by a protracted illness, Bishop entered Princeton in 1913, a year after he had published his first poem in *Harper's Weekly*. Soon a mainstay of the *Nassau Lit*, he embarked upon lifelong friendships with Edmund Wilson and Scott Fitzgerald. By the time of his 1917 graduation he had assembled poems enough for a slim volume ironically titled *Green Fruit*. After more than a year's service in France with the AEF, Bishop plunged into the literary life of New York. From 1920 to 1922 he was an editor at *Vanity Fair*, and for a while one of Edna Millay's suitors. In 1922 he married Margaret Hutchins, who had an independent income. The Bishops spent most of the next decade in Europe, where three sons were born and where Bishop worked sporadically at fiction and poetry. While abroad, the Bishops kept mostly to themselves; Allen Tate, who did visit them, believed Bishop had not been altogether happy in "that charming isolation," that he would have profited from a "sympathetic literary society," and his increased productivity after the family's return to America in 1933 bears out Tate's judgment. In 1935, when the Bishops took up permanent residence on Cape Cod, he published the fine novel *Act of Darkness* and an accomplished volume of poetry, *Minute Particulars*; in the next half-dozen years, in spite of ill health, he wrote frequently for significant periodicals, served as chief poetry reviewer for the *Nation*, and was involved with several editing ventures. His health continued to worsen, and in 1943, after working for a short while as Archibald MacLeish's assistant at the Library of Congress, a severe heart attack forced his return to Massachusetts. Now bedridden most of the time, he continued to work at poems he himself would never see published; on April 4, 1944, he died in Hyannis Hospital.

WORKS: *Green Fruit* (1917). *The Undertaker's Garland* (1922). *Many Thousands Gone* (1931). *Now With His Love* (1933). *Minute Particulars* (1935). *Act of Darkness* (1935). *Selected Poems* (1941). *Collected Essays* (1948). *Collected Poems* (1948).

ROBERT WHITE
York University
Toronto, Ont.

ARTHUR BLACKAMORE (*ca.* **1679–post-1723).** Arthur Blackamore is another of those ghostly figures from early southern literary history. He was evidently born in London about 1679, for he entered Christ Church College, Oxford, on May 17, 1695, at the age of sixteen. In September, 1707, Blackamore was sent to Virginia as a schoolmaster or as a tutor for a planter's children. Shortly after arriving in Virginia, he became master of the grammar school of the College of William and Mary, and perhaps also a professor of humanity in the college.

At Williamsburg, Blackamore befriended William Byrd II and Commissary James Blair. From his arrival in Virginia until his departure for London in 1717, Blackamore fought the battle of the books and of the bottle, periodically turned out of his teaching position or "put on trial" for "being so great a sot." After a decade of fluctuating between bouts of drunkenness and periods of remorse and reform, he returned to England late in 1717, apparently to take orders in the Anglican Church and to cure his alcoholism. Whether he achieved either is uncertain. He may have kept a school after returning to England, but after 1723, he seems to have dropped out of sight.

In 1716, following Governor Alexander Spotswood's successful expedition beyond the mountains, Blackamore wrote a Latin poem celebrating the event, "Expeditio Ultramontana." The Latin poem has been lost, but a translation into English by the Reverend George Seagood was published in the *Maryland Gazette* of June 24, 1729.

After returning to London, Blackamore published two novels. The first, *The Religious Triumverate, Display'd in Three Ecclesiastical Novels* (1720), was dedicated to Governor Spotswood and includes thinly veiled satirical portraits of several Virginians, including Commissary Blair, with whom Blackamore had quarreled. The second, *Luck at Last; or, The Happy Unfortunate* (1723), was dedicated to "Mr. David Bray Merchant, of Virginia," and is a precursor of such sentimental novels as Samuel Richardson's *Pamela*.

WORKS: *The Religious Triumverate, Display'd in Three Ecclesiastical Novels. I. Heathen Priestcraft; Or, The Female Bigot. II. Presbyterian Piety; or the Way to get a Fortune. III. The Cloven-Hoof; Or the Anabaptist Teacher Detected* (1720). *Luck at Last; or, The Happy Unfortunate* (1723; repr. as *The Distress'd Fair, or Happy Unfortunate*, 1737; also in *Four Before Richardson*, ed. William H. McBurney, 1963). *Arthur Blackamore's Expeditio Ultramontana* [1716], ed. Earl G. Swem (1960).

ROBERT BAIN
University of North Carolina
Chapel Hill

JAMES BLAIR (1655?/56?–1743). James Blair, the son of a Church of Scotland minister, was born in May, 1655 or 1656, in Banffshire, Scotland. He was educated at Marischal College (Aberdeen) and in 1669 entered the University of Edinburgh, where he received an M.A. (1673). Ordained in 1679, Blair was minister of Cranston Parish, near Edinburgh, until 1682, when he refused to sign the Test Oath required of Scotch clergy under Catholic James II. After three years in London as a clerk of the Master of Rolls, he accepted appointment as missionary to Henrico Parish, Va., and arrived there in 1685. In 1687 he married seventeen-year-old Sarah Harrison, daughter of Benjamin Harrison, a councilor and wealthy planter. They had no children.

From his arrival in Virginia until his death on April 18, 1743, Blair influenced greatly affairs of the Old Dominion through three powerful offices. Appointed in 1690 as commissary (deputy) to the bishop of London, Blair was the Anglican spiritual leader of the colony. His appointment to the Virginia Council in 1694 increased his power. He was a principal founder of the College of William and Mary (chartered 1693), its first president, and was instrumental in 1699–1700 in moving the capital from Jamestown to Williamsburg. In 1710 he became rector of Bruton Parish. Blair held the offices of commissary, councilor, and college president until his death. A combative man, he was chiefly responsible for the recall of three colonial governors, and though sometimes vitriolic and excessive, he showed a whiggish concern for colonial rights, which gave rise to increasingly independent thought among Virginia's leaders.

Blair was evidently a prolific writer of letters, reports, and essays, but most of these papers have been lost. He was well known through the Anglican community for his five-volume sermon series, *Our Saviour's Divine Sermon on the Mount* . . . (London, 1722), a work republished in England (1740) and translated into Danish (1761) and a fixture of clerical libraries for a century. Blair was also a principal author of *The Present State of Virginia, and the College*, a book written in 1697 but not published until 1727 in London.

WORKS: *Our Saviour's Divine Sermon on the Mount, Contain'd in the Vth, VIth, and VIIth Chapters of St. Matthew's Gospel explained, And the Practice of it recommended in divers Sermons and Discourses* . . . , 5 vols. (1722, 1740). *The Present State of Virginia, and the College*, with Henry Hartwell and Edward Chilton (1727). *A Paraphrase of Our Saviour's Sermon on the Mount, Contained in V, VI, VII Chap. of St. Matthew's Gospel* (1729).

PARKE ROUSE, JR.
Williamsburg, Va.

RICHARD BLAND (1710–1776). Scion of a leading family of the Tidewater planter-aristocracy, Richard Bland was born in Williamsburg, Va., on May 6, 1710; he was educated at William and Mary College and assertedly (though not provably) the University of Edinburgh. He taught himself enough law to qualify for the Virginia bar in 1746. In 1742 he was elected to the House of Burgesses from Prince George County and reelected continuously to that seat until 1775, serving thereafter in the first House of Delegates until his death. In the sporadic and intensifying crises that culminated in the Revolutionary War, Bland was a leading Virginia spokesman for libertarian causes. In 1773 he was appointed to the Virginia committee of correspondence, and he served as a delegate in the first two Continental Congresses, declining a third election (in August, 1775) because of poor health. Bland was thrice married. By his first wife, Anne Poythress, he had twelve children, most of whom survived him. He died in Williamsburg, October 26, 1776.

He was known among his contemporaries as a man of profound learning. Celebrated in his day for his prodigious knowledge of Virginia history, he was an avid collector of books and manuscripts. After his death, Jefferson bought the collection; it was among the 6,500 volumes Jefferson sold the Library of Congress in 1815 and was lost when fire gutted the library in 1851.

Although Bland lent his pen exclusively to ecclesiastical and political controversy, his four extant pamphlets constitute some of the most polished prose in eighteenth-century America and a literary output unsurpassed in quantity in southern colonial political history. His surviving essays concern incidents and issues surrounding the Pistole Fee controversy, the Two-Penny acts and the Stamp Act. There are no known copies of treatises he is said to have written on land tenure in Virginia, on water baptism (refuting the Quakers), and on establishing an American episcopate. Additionally, he contributed several letters to the *Virginia Gazette* (in the 1760s) of which copies are missing.

In his pamphlets Bland delineated arguments that were later expounded by such better-known figures today as Patrick Henry, George Mason, and Thomas Jefferson. He laid the bases for the political beliefs of the dominant party of Virginia in the Revolution. His most accomplished belletristic effort is a pamphlet entitled *The Colonel Dismounted*, published in 1764 in Williamsburg over the signature "Common Sense." In sustaining this fictional persona and a mock inversion of roles, Bland displays great satiric skill and literary sophistication.

WORKS: *A Modest and True State of the Case* (1753; surviving only in part as *A Fragment on the Pistole Fee*, ed. W. C. Ford, 1891). *A Letter to the Clergy of Virginia* (1760). *The Colonel Dismounted: or The Rector Vindicated* (1764). *An Inquiry into the Rights of the British Colonies* (1766).

CARL DOLMETSCH
The College of William and Mary
Williamsburg, Va.

ALBERT TAYLOR BLEDSOE (1809–1877). Albert Bledsoe was born on November 9, 1809, the eldest son of Moses Bledsoe, editor of the Frankfort (Ky.) *Commonwealth*. At West Point he was a classmate of Robert E. Lee and Jefferson Davis, but after his graduation in 1830 he left the army to study philosophy and theology at Kenyon College in Ohio. The mathematics he had learned at West Point was of practical value at Kenyon where he taught it to support himself. Similarly, he was an instructor in mathematics at Miami University while studying law. In 1836 he married, and in 1838 moved to Springfield, Ill., where he practiced law for ten years. He knew Abraham Lincoln and Stephen Douglas, who practiced in the same courts, but his real interests were still in theology. He completed his brilliant and surprising study, *Examination of President Edwards' Inquiry into the Freedom of the Will*, while living in Springfield. A development of these ideas resulted in *Theodicy* in 1853, the most widely used southern theological work of the century, which with his reputation in religious circles as a polemicist led to his nickname, "The Arminian Sledge Hammer."

From 1848 to 1854 he taught mathematics at the University of Mississippi and at the University of Virginia from 1854 to 1861. He became assistant secretary of war under Jefferson Davis, who sent him, as the region's best controversialist, to London to explain the southern side. He returned in February, 1865, and published his most impassioned work the following year, *Is Davis a Traitor; or Was Secession a Constitutional Right Previous to the War of 1861?* In 1867 he went to Baltimore to edit the *Southern Review*, with initial help from William Hand Browne and later assistance from his talented daughter, Sophia Bledsoe Herrick. Widely known as the most trenchant defender of the Lost Cause, Bledsoe consumed his great mental and physical energy in endless controversies in a journal the impoverished region could not support. Yet the magazine, brilliantly combative as it is, is his monument, for his daugher could continue it only a few months after his death on December 8, 1877.

WORKS: *An Examination of President Edwards' Inquiry into the Freedom of the Will* (1845). *A Theodicy: or Vindication of the Divine Glory, as Manifested in the Constitution and Government of the Moral World* (1853). *Three Lectures on Rational Mechanics: or The Theory of Motion* (1854). *An Essay on Liberty and Slavery* (1856). *Is Davis a Traitor: or, Was Secession a Constitutional Right Previous to the War of 1861?* (1886). *The Philosophy of Mathematics, with Special Reference to the Elements of Geometry and the Infinitesimal Method* (1867).

C. CARROLL HOLLIS
University of North Carolina
Chapel Hill

MAXWELL BODENHEIM (1892–1954). Born in Hermanville, Miss., on May 26, 1892, Bodenheim moved with his family to Chicago about eight years later. Dismissed from high school, he joined the army, and after trying to obtain a discharge, deserted, attempted suicide, and ended his army career in Fort Leavenworth. In 1911–1912 he bummed around the Southwest, before returning to Chicago where he and Ben Hecht (Bodenheim's ambivalent but lasting friend) played minor roles in the Chicago literary revival.

In 1915 he went to New York where he worked with the *Others* group, including William Carlos Williams and Alfred Kreymborg. In 1918 he married Minna Schein and published his first book of poetry, *Minna and Myself*. Two years later they traveled to England where their son, Solbert, was born. In 1923 he published his first novel, *Blackguard*, and began work for Hecht's *Chicago Literary Times*. His third novel, *Replenishing Jessica*, temporarily suppressed, became a best seller. Bodenheim again traveled to Europe in 1931, but by 1934 he was down on his luck, trying unsuccessfully to break into the California movie industry. He returned to New York and to comparative poverty as a Greenwich Village character.

In 1938 Minna divorced him, and the following year he married Grace Finan, an invalid. Fired from the Federal Writer's Project in 1940 for his alleged communism, he worked on as a poet, publishing *Lights in the Valley* (1942). His wife died in 1950, and he possibly married Ruth Fagan the next year. After a stormy relationship, Bodenheim and his lady were murdered by Harold Weinberg during a drunken debauch on February 7, 1954.

Bodenheim's poetry is thematically various, but in general depends on its imagery which is often ludicrously inappropriate. As a novelist, he ranges from fictional autobiography to semipornography, from personal attack to proletarian protest. The poetry and the novels are minor.

WORKS: *Minna and Myself* (1918). *Introducing Irony* (1922). *The Sardonic Arm* (1923). *Against This Age* (1923). *Blackguard* (1923). *Crazy Man* (1924). *Replenishing Jessica* (1925). *Ninth Avenue* (1926). *Returning to Emotion* (1927). *The King of Spain* (1928). *Georgie May* (1928). *Sixty Seconds* (1929). *Bringing Jazz!* (1930). *Naked on Roller Skates: A Novel* (1930). *A Virtuous Girl* (1930). *Duke Herring* (1931). *Run, Sheep, Run* (1932). *6 A.M.* (1932). *New York Madness* (1933). *Slow Vision* (1934). *Lights in the Valley* (1942). *Selected Poems of Maxwell Bodenheim, 1914–1944* (1946).

> WILLIAM L. GODSHALK
> University of Cincinnati
> Cincinnati, Ohio

ROBERT BOLLING (1738–1775). Robert Bolling of Chellowe, Buckingham County, Va., was born on August 17, 1738, the son of John and Elizabeth Blair Bolling of Varina, Henrico County, and through his great-grandmother Jane Rolfe Bolling a direct descendant of Pocahontas. He was educated under John Clarke at Wakefield, Yorkshire, and read law in the office of Benjamin Waller, Williamsburg, although there is no evidence that he maintained a practice. He was a Burgess for (successively) Chesterfield and Buckingham counties, sheriff of the latter, and appears to have commanded the county militia, since he is frequently styled "Colonel." By his first wife, Mary Burton, he had a daughter; his second wife, Susannah Watson, bore him four children. He was a delegate to the July Convention of 1775, and died shortly thereafter on July 21, 1775.

Bolling contributed essays on vineculture to the *Virginia Gazette* in 1773. His manuscripts contain several original songs (others are in the Hubard Papers of the Southern Historical Collection at the University of North Carolina) and drawings that indicate an aptitude for domestic architecture. But he apparently thought of himself primarily as a writer. By 1766 he had contributed 35 poems to English periodicals. Most of his published works were derivative love poems, or satires in the Horatian mode, but his manuscripts, still uncollected, contain a number of bawdy narratives. A commonplace book, *Hl: arodiana*, is in the possession of Bolling descendants. Other manuscripts, in the Brock collection of the Henry E. Huntington Library, are: *A Collection of Diverting Anecdotes, Bon Mots and Other Trifling Pieces by Bolling, junr.*, 1764; *Pieces Concerning Vineyards & Their Establishment in Virginia* (which includes a collection of poems "intended to attract a stronger public attention to vine planting in Virginia, writ in 1772"); and *La Gazzetta de Parnaso or Poems, Imitations, Translations &c by Bolling junr.* Bolling's only published work to date is a brief genealogical memoir, written in French; it was translated as a childhood exercise by a Bolling descendant, and published in 1868.

WORKS: *A Memoir of a Portion of the Bolling Family of Virginia*, No. IV, Wynne's Historical Documents from the Old Dominion (1868).

> CHARLES BOLTON
> Xavier University
> Cincinnati, Ohio

JOHN HENRY BONER (1845–1903).

JOHN HENRY BONER (1845–1903). John Henry Boner was born on January 31, 1845, the younger son of a hatter, in the Moravian village of Salem, N.C., in a house now restored. He attended the Salem Boys' School and, when thirteen, was apprenticed to Blum Brothers, printers. After the Civil War he founded the short-lived Salem *Observer*, then briefly was editor of the Asheville *Pioneer*. An ardent Republican, he became reading clerk of the Constitutional Convention of 1868 in Raleigh and held a similar position with the state house of representatives 1869–1870. After marriage to a young Raleigh woman, he found work with the Government Printing Office in Washington, D.C., first as a compositor and then as a proofreader. With the inauguration of Grover Cleveland in 1884, he lost his job, but was invited by Edmund Clarence Stedman, who had been impressed by the poems in *Whispering Pines*, to come to New York, where he was on the staff of the *Century Dictionary* then being prepared, and was Stedman's assistant in compiling *A Library of American Literature* (11 vols., 1888–1890).

Under Stedman's aegis, Boner became literary editor of the New York *World*, made lexicographical contributions to the *Standard Dictionary*, and was chosen as editor of the *Literary Digest*, with whose publishers he had a disagreement in 1897. His hasty resignation as editor brought on inevitable financial problems. His health broke, and he returned in 1901 to his old post in Washington, where he died two years later on March 6, 1903. Boner's rhythmical love poems and nostalgic lyrics about his boyhood in Old Salem evince his admiration for Edgar Allan Poe, whom he consciously emulated. Shortly after Boner's death, his friends sponsored the publication of a collection of his poems.

WORKS: *Whispering Pines* (1883, 1954). *Some New Poems* (1901). *Poems* (1903).

RICHARD WALSER
North Carolina State University
Raleigh

SHERWOOD BONNER (1849–1883). Katharine Sherwood Bonner McDowell, one of four children of Dr. Charles Bonner and Mary Wilson Bonner, was born in Holly Springs, Miss., on Feb-

ruary 26, 1849, and died of cancer in that same town on July 22,
1883. She married Edward McDowell, son of a prominent Holly
Springs family, on February 14, 1871, and bore him one child,
Lillian, on December 10, 1871.

When the Civil War destroyed much of her town and the family's personal property, Bonner's formal education in the local
schools terminated; she was sixteen, but she continued to study
under her father's tutelage. Her 1869 diary notes that she contributed stories to Boston and to Mobile, Ala., newspapers. In early
1873 the McDowells moved to Texas, but she and her daughter
returned to Mississippi in August. Later the same year, Bonner left
the child with relatives and went to Boston. There she became the
amanuensis of Henry Wadsworth Longfellow. In 1876 she went to
Europe and sent articles about her experiences to Memphis and
Boston newspapers. She returned to Boston in late summer of
1876.

Family problems and responsibilities forced her to spend portions of the next two years in Mississippi and Texas, but she continued to contribute short stories to several magazines. Harper and
Brothers published her only novel, *Like Unto Like*, in 1878. *Dialect Tales* and *Suwanee River Tales*, short story collections, appeared in 1883 and 1884 respectively. When her father and brother
fell victims of the yellow fever epidemic in 1878, she returned to
Mississippi to live, but the growing rift with her husband caused
her to return to Boston in the spring of 1879. In 1880 she went
to Illinois to establish residency for the divorce that she received
in May, 1881.

Her health began to deteriorate that year, but with the help of
her friend Sophia Kirk she continued to write and publish. Her
"Gran'mammy" stories were probably the first in Negro dialect to
appear in a monthly journal. Her Tennessee and Illinois dialect
stories were the first of their type to be published. Her literary
merit lies in the realistic manner in which she was able to fit the
turbulent years from 1860 to 1875 and the embryonic modern
America into a remarkable literary form that is more fact than
fiction.

WORKS: *Like Unto Like: A Novel* (1878). *Dialect Tales* (1883). *Last Will and Testament* (1883). *Suwanee River Tales* (1884).

DORRIE BUSBY NORWOOD
Tennessee Technological
University
Cookeville

ARNA WENDELL BONTEMPS (1902–1973). Arna (shortened from Arnaud) Bontemps' name betokens the French Creole element in his ancestry—as very considerably did his personal appearance. He was born on October 13, 1902, in Alexandria, La. His family, however, fled the South in 1905 when he was only three, and he grew up in Los Angeles, where he graduated from Pacific Union College in 1923. When he came east in 1924, already interested in writing, although he had once planned to be a doctor, he landed in the vortex of the Harlem Renaissance.

Bontemps was one of the more substantial contributors to the Renaissance. That he was, however, failed to be a subject of due notice until long after the Renaissance was over.

Langston Hughes and he bore toward each other a striking physical resemblance. They were born in the same year. Once they met, they became lifelong close friends. Temperamentally alike, they were both also much the same in their versatility as writers.

Bontemps married, and enjoyed the possession of a fine, large family. He taught in the 1920s in New York City, in the 1930s in Alabama and Chicago. He studied at Columbia, acquired an advanced degree from the University of Chicago and, from 1943 until 1965, served as university librarian at Fisk University, where, from 1965 until 1968, he was director of University Relations. By the 1960s he was in great demand as a speaker. He had never stopped writing. Poet, novelist, short-story writer, essayist and writer of juveniles, he was also an editor and anthologist. In 1968 he resumed the role of teacher, first at the Chicago Circle campus of the University of Illinois and then at Yale, where he was also curator of Yale's James Weldon Johnson Collection. Returning to

Nashville, where he had built a home on a hill, and to Fisk as writer-in-residence, he died on June 4, 1973.

WORKS: *God Sends Sunday* (1931), dramatized as *St. Louis Woman* (1966). *Popo and Fifina: Children of Haiti*, with Langston Hughes (1932). *You Can't Pet a Possum* (1934). *Black Thunder* (1936). *Sad-Faced Boy* (1937). *Drums at Dusk* (1939). Ed., *Golden Slippers: An Anthology of Negro Poetry for Young People* (1941). *Father of the Blues, the Autobiography of W. C. Handy*, with W. C. Handy (1941). *The Fast Sooner Hound*, with Jack Conroy (1942). *We Have Tomorrow* (1945). *They Seek a City* (1945), with Jack Conroy, rev. as *Anyplace But Here* (1966). *Slappy Hooper: The Wonderful Sign Painter*, with Jack Conroy (1946). *The Story of the Negro* (1948). *The Poetry of the Negro: 1746–1949*, with Langston Hughes (1949). *George Washington Carver* (1950). *Chariot in the Sky* (1951). *Sam Patch, the High, Wide and Handsome Jumper*, with Jack Conroy (1951). *Lonesome Boy* (1955). *Frederick Douglass: Slave Fighter* (1958). *The Book of American Negro Folklore*, with Langston Hughes (1958). *100 Years of Negro Freedom* (1961). Ed., *American Negro Poetry* (1963). *Personals* (1964). *Famous Negro Athletes* (1964). Ed., *Hold Fast to Dreams* (1969). Ed., *Great Slave Narratives* (1969). Ed., *The Harlem Renaissance Remembered* (1972). *The Old South: "A Summer Tragedy" and Other Stories of the Thirties* (1973).

BLYDEN JACKSON
University of North Carolina
Chapel Hill

KATE LANGLEY BOSHER (1865–1932). Kate Lee Langley was born in Norfolk, Va., on February 1, 1865, to Charles Henry and Portia Deming Langley. Both parents were from families long prominent in the state. She grew up in Norfolk and graduated in 1882 from the Norfolk College for Young Ladies. On October 12, 1887, she married Charles Gideon Bosher and moved to Richmond, where she lived for the rest of her life.

Bosher's first novel, *"Bobbie,"* was published in 1899 under the pseudonym Kate Cairns. A second novel, *When Love is Love*, followed five years later, but it was her third novel, *Mary Cary, "Frequently Martha,"* which sold well and made her a popular writer of the day. Bosher published six more novels, the last in

1919. Most of her stories were sunny and cheery. They were readable, amusing, and often sentimental.

Kate Langley Bosher was active in Richmond social affairs as well as in civic, historical, political, and educational endeavors. She was an ardent force in the struggle for woman's suffrage in Virginia, and after that battle was won, she was an organizer of the League of Women Voters, serving on both state and local boards of that organization. She was president of the Woman's Club of Richmond and held membership in the Daughters of the American Revolution, United Daughters of the Confederacy, and Daughters of the American Colonists. She also belonged to the Richmond Writers' Club, the Artists' Club, and the Cosmopolitan Club of New York.

A gracious, charming, and much-loved woman, Kate Bosher died in Norfolk on July 27, 1932. Funeral services were conducted at her home, 2030 Monument Avenue, Richmond, and she was buried in Hollywood Cemetery.

WORKS: *"Bobbie"* (1899). *When Love is Love* (1904). *Mary Cary, "Frequently Martha"* (1910). *Miss Gibbie Gault* (1911). *The Man in Lonely Land* (1912). *The House of Happiness* (1913). *How It Happened* (1914). *People Like That* (1916). *Kitty Canary* (1918). *His Friend Miss McFarlane* (1919).

DOROTHY McINNIS SCURA
University of Richmond
Richmond, Va.

JONATHAN BOUCHER (1738–1804). An outspoken Loyalist and Anglican minister, Jonathan Boucher was born on March 12, 1738, at Blencogo, Cumberland County, England, the son of James Boucher, a shiftless schoolmaster and alehouse keeper, and Ann Barnes Boucher. He studied at the free school at Bromfield and then at Wigton, where he continued his studies and began teaching at the age of sixteen. At eighteen, he was usher in a school at St. Bee's kept by the Reverend John James, who helped him secure a position as tutor to a planter's children at Port Royal, Va. Boucher sailed for Virginia in April, 1759.

In 1762 Boucher went to England to take orders in the Anglican
Church, returning in the summer of 1763 to Virginia, where he
moved to the rectory of St. Mary's in Caroline County, bought a
small plantation, and opened a boys' school. There he taught
"Jacky" Custis, step-son of George Washington. Appointed rector
of Saint Anne's at Annapolis in 1770, Boucher was active in social
and literary life, attending the theater, writing verses as prologues
to plays, and becoming the first president of the Homony Club,
a literary society. Later he took Queen Anne's Parish, Prince
George County, Md., and married Eleanor Addison, whose dowry
enabled him to purchase a plantation on the Potomac River.

Boucher preached actively against the revolutionaries in the
1770s, often with a pair of pistols lying on the pulpit. He was
burned in effigy for his Tory sympathies and left Maryland for
England on September 10, 1775, never to return to America.
Boucher spent the last nineteen years of his life as a vicar near
Epsom. His Maryland property was confiscated by the revolutionaries, but he received compensation from the British government. He died on April 27, 1804.

A poet and linguist, Boucher is best remembered for works dealing with the Revolutionary period. *A View of the Causes and Consequences of the American Revolution* (1797), thirteen sermons
preached in America between 1763 and 1775, recounts the coming
of the Revolution from a Tory perspective. Boucher's autobiography, *Reminiscences of an American Loyalist, 1738–1789,* also
treats the turmoil of his American years and was not published
until 1925.

WORKS: *A View of the Causes and Consequences of the American Revolution* (1797). *Reminiscences of an American Loyalist, 1738–1789,* ed.
Jonathan Bouchier (1925).

ROBERT BAIN
University of North Carolina
Chapel Hill

JAMES BOYD (1888–1944). James Boyd was born on July 2, 1888, in Harrisburg, Pa., to Eleanor Gilmore Herr and John Yeomans Boyd. He attended the Hill School (1901–1906), Princeton University (1906–1910), and Trinity College, Cambridge. Commissioned a second lieutenant in the United States Army Ambulance Service, he served from August, 1917, to July, 1919.

In 1919 Boyd established a permanent home in Southern Pines, N.C., and began his career as a writer. Within a year, his stories and articles began appearing in *Scribner's Magazine, Century Magazine, American Mercury*, and elsewhere. Many were set in the sandhills region of North Carolina. By 1922, Boyd had turned primarily to the writing of the historical novels upon which his literary reputation chiefly rests. Boyd's historical novels represented major steps in the development of the genre, carrying it beyond the older historical romance through greater historical accuracy, psychological and sociological awareness, moral and aesthetic sensitivity, and formal control. The novels were the major basis for Boyd's election to the National Institute of Arts and Letters (1937) and the Society of American Historians (1939).

Widely involved in the cultural life of North Carolina, Boyd served as president of the North Carolina Literary and Historical Association (1927–1928), and was on the original board of the North Carolina Society for the Preservation of Antiquities. In 1941 he bought and became editor of the nearly defunct Southern Pines *Pilot* and transformed it into a progressive regional newspaper. In 1940–1941 Boyd organized and directed the national Free Company of Players, which presented a series of original radio dramas on democratic themes.

In 1917 Boyd married Katharine Lamont of Millbrook, N.Y. They had three children: James, Jr. (b. 1922), Daniel (b. 1924), and Nancy (b. 1927). He died on February 25, 1944. His papers and manuscripts are in the Firestone Library at Princeton University and the Southern Historical Collection at the University of North Carolina.

WORKS: *Drums* (1925). *Marching On* (1927). *Long Hunt* (1930). *Roll River* (1935). *Bitter Creek* (1939). Ed., *The Free Company Presents*

(1944). *Eighteen Poems* (1944). *Old Pines and Other Stories*, ed. Richard
Walser (1952).

DAVID E. WHISNANT
University of Maryland,
Baltimore County
Baltimore

ROARK WHITNEY WICKLIFFE BRADFORD (1896–1948).
Roark Bradford was born on August 21, 1896, on his family's cotton plantation located near the Mississippi River in Lauderdale
County, Tenn. His father, Richard Clarence Bradford, and his
mother, Patricia Adelaide Tillman Bradford, were both descended
from families prominent in colonial and southern history. Bradford's literary career may be traced back to his childhood attraction
to the bizarre versions of biblical stories he heard from a plantation
Negro minister. After a moderate amount of formal schooling in
Halls, Tenn., Bradford joined the armed services of the United
States in 1917 and was commissioned a second lieutenant in the
artillery reserve. Discharged in 1920, he married Lydia Sehorn
of Columbia, Miss. Following her death some years later he married Mary Rose Sciarra Himler of Indianapolis, Ind. Serving as
a reporter on various southern newspapers, Bradford eventually
became night city editor of the New Orleans *Picayune*. He left
the *Picayune* in 1926 to free lance and never returned to regular
civilian employment. From 1942 until 1946 he was on duty as a
lieutenant in the naval reserve. He died in New Orleans on November 13, 1948, of an amoebic infection contracted while on a
mission with the Navy off the African coast.

His childhood fascination with Negro storytelling reawakened by
his experiences with native storytellers both in the Cajun country
of Louisiana and in the city of New Orleans, Bradford centered
his literary efforts on tales about Negro life. In 1927 his short story
entitled "Child of God" won the O'Henry Memorial competition.
Fame came to Bradford when a book of stories, *Ol' Man Adam an'
His Chillun*, was adapted by Marc Connelly for the theater as
The Green Pastures. Bradford and Connelly were jointly awarded
a Pulitzer Prize. Although Bradford wrote one novel, *The Three-*

Headed Angel, about white settlers in the Cumberland Mountains, and in two novels, *This Side of Jordan* and *Kingdom Coming*, tried to deal seriously with Negro life, he based most of his fiction on sentimental and comic stereotypes of the Negro character. His stories (many uncollected ones may be found in the files of *Collier's Magazine*) are clearly now significant only in the historical sociology of American literature.

WORKS: *Ol' Man Adam an' His Chillun* (1928). *This Side of Jordan* (1929). *How Come Christmas* (1930). *John Henry* (1930). *Ol' King David and the Philistine Boys* (1930). *Kingdom Coming* (1933). *Let the Band Play Dixie* (1934). *The Three-Headed Angel* (1937).

LEWIS P. SIMPSON
Louisiana State University
Baton Rouge

BENJAMIN GRIFFITH BRAWLEY (1882–1939). Born in Columbia, S.C., on April 22, 1882, Benjamin Brawley was a precocious child nurtured on Greek and Roman classics. As a youth, he excelled in his studies, graduating with honors from Atlanta Baptist College (now Morehouse College) in 1901. After teaching one term in Georgetown, Fla., he began his career as an English instructor at Morehouse, where he remained from 1902 to 1910. During this period, he continued advanced study, earning a second A.B. at the University of Chicago (1906) and an M.A. at Harvard University (1908). From 1910 to 1912, Brawley taught at Howard University but returned to Morehouse for a second eight-year period (1912–1920). Then, embarking upon two new ventures, he conducted a socioeducational survey of the Liberian Republic and, on his return to America, became an ordained minister. He served as pastor of Messiah Baptist Church in Brockton, Mass., during 1921–1922, before returning to teaching, an occupation which was for him as sacred a calling as the ministry. In his professorships at Shaw University (1923–1931) and at Howard University (1931–1939), as at Morehouse earlier, he distinguished himself as a scholarly teacher.

Brawley was also a minor poet, a frequent contributor to periodicals, and a prolific writer of books in social and literary history.

Among his books, two emphases spread over three stages of his career may be noted: race-centered books, 1913–1921; general interest books, 1921–1932; race-inspired books, 1933–1938. Although Brawley explored racial themes, he never accepted the atavistic, sensational character of black people popularly reflected in literature of the 1920s. On this point, he differed with many Harlem Renaissance writers. In literature, however, as in other areas, Brawley observed standards of traditional morality, correctness, and good taste which (long before he died on February 1, 1939) developed into the "Brawley Tradition" of excellence in personal and scholarly conduct.

WORKS: *A Toast to Love and Death* (1902). *The Problem and Other Poems* (1905). *A Short History of the American Negro* (1913). *History of Morehouse College* (1917). *The Seven Sleepers of Ephesus; A Lyrical Legend* (1917). *Africa and the War* (1918). *The Negro in Literature and Art in the United States* (1918). Ed., *New Era Declamations* (1918). *Your Negro Neighbor* (1918). *Women of Achievement* (1919). *A Short History of the English Drama* (1921). *A Social History of the American Negro* (1921). *A New Survey of English Literature* (1925). *Freshman Year English* (1929). *Dr. Dillard of the Jeanes Fund* (1930). *A History of the English Hymn* (1932). Ed., *Early Negro American Writers* (1935). *Paul Laurence Dunbar: Poet of His People* (1936). *Negro Builders and Heroes* (1937). *The Negro Genius* (1937). Ed., *The Best Stories of Paul Laurence Dunbar* (1938). *Sojourner Truth*, with Arthur Huff Fauset (1938).

PATSY B. PERRY
North Carolina Central University
Durham

CLEANTH BROOKS (1906–). The son of Cleanth and Bessie Lee Witherspoon Brooks, Cleanth Brooks was born on October 16, 1906, in Murray, Ky., and spent his youth in several small towns in that state and in west Tennessee where his father served as a Methodist minister. From 1920 to 1924 he attended the McTyeire School in McKenzie, Tenn. He was graduated Phi Beta Kappa from Vanderbilt University in 1928. After earning his M.A. from Tulane University the following year, he studied as a Rhodes

Scholar at Exeter College, Oxford University, from which he received the B.A. (Honors) in 1931 and the B. Litt. in 1932.

From Oxford he went directly to Louisiana State University where he remained until 1947. On September 12, 1934, he married Edith Amy Blanchard. In 1935 Brooks, Robert Penn Warren, and others founded the *Southern Review*, which before its demise in 1942 had become one of the most significant literary quarterlies ever published in the United States.

Since leaving Louisiana State University, Brooks has held a number of other distinguished positions. He was a Fellow of the Library of Congress (1951–1962), cultural attaché, American Embassy, London (1964–1966), and twice a Guggenheim Fellow (1953, 1960). From 1947 until his retirement in 1975, as Gray Professor of Rhetoric, Brooks was a member of the English department of Yale University. Since his retirement, he has been visiting professor at several universities and continues his scholarly work on William Faulkner.

Brooks's reputation as "The best living 'reader' or interpreter of difficult verse," to use John Crowe Ransom's phrase, is based on his first two books: *Modern Poetry and the Tradition* (1939) and *The Well Wrought Urn* (1947). His reputation as one of the most illuminating and provocative commentators on the works of William Faulkner is the result of his *William Faulkner: The Yoknapatawpha Country* (1963). His greatest impact upon the way literature is read today, however, has probably come from three textbooks of which he is coeditor: *Understanding Poetry*, with Robert Penn Warren (1938); *Understanding Fiction*, with Robert Penn Warren (1943); and *Understanding Drama*, with Robert B. Heilman (1945).

WORKS: Ed., *An Approach to Literature*, with Robert Penn Warren and John Thibaut Purser (1936, 1939, 1952, 1964, 1975). Ed., *Understanding Poetry*, with Robert Penn Warren (1938, 1950, 1956, 1960). *Modern Poetry and the Tradition* (1939). Ed., *Understanding Fiction*, with Robert Penn Warren (1943, 1959). Ed., *Understanding Drama*, with Robert B. Heilman (1945). *The Well Wrought Urn: Studies in the Structure of Poetry* (1947). Ed., *Modern Rhetoric*, with Robert Penn Warren (1949,

1958, 1972). Ed., *Fundamentals of Good Writing: A Handbook of Modern Rhetoric*, with Robert Penn Warren (1950). Ed., *An Anthology of Stories from the Southern Review*, with Robert Penn Warren (1953). Ed., *Tragic Themes in Western Literature*, with others (1955). *Literary Criticism: A Short History*, with W. K. Wimsatt (1957). Ed., *The Scope of Fiction*, with Robert Penn Warren (1960). *The Hidden God: Studies in Hemingway, Faulkner, Yeats, Eliot, and Warren* (1963). *William Faulkner: The Yoknapatawpha Country* (1963). *American Literature: A Mirror, Lens, or Prism?* (1967). *A Shaping Joy: Studies in the Writer's Craft* (1971). Ed., *American Literature: The Makers and the Making*, with Robert Penn Warren and R. W. B. Lewis, 2 vols. (1973). *William Faulkner: Toward Yoknapatawpha and Beyond* (1978).

THOMAS DANIEL YOUNG
Vanderbilt University
Nashville, Tenn.

WILLIAM GARROTT BROWN (1868–1913). William Garrott Brown was born in Marion, Ala., on April 24, 1868, and remained there until 1889. After preparatory schooling in his native town, he graduated from Howard College in 1886. He devoted a year to independent study and writing for the Montgomery *Advertiser*, after which he taught English for two years at the Marion Military Institute. He then entered Harvard, where he spent thirteen years: three as a student, nine as an assistant in the university library, and one as a lecturer in American history. Increasing deafness prevented either an academic or a political career; and he turned to writing, soon winning an enviable reputation as a literary historian and essayist. Albert B. Hart asserted that Brown was "one of the few men in the country who has got something to say and can say it."

A textbook *History of Alabama* appeared in 1900. He contributed volumes on Andrew Jackson and Stephen A. Douglas to Houghton Mifflin and Company's Riverside Biographical Series. His reputation as a southern historian rests largely upon *The Lower South in American History* (1902), a collection of lectures and essays dealing in part with the civilization of the cotton states from 1820 to 1860. Brown's antebellum novel, *A Gentleman of the*

South: A Memory of the Black Belt (1903), revealed that fiction was not his forte. A life of Oliver Ellsworth was his last book except for a posthumous collection on political topics, *The New Politics and Other Papers* (1914).

In 1906 Brown found that he had tuberculosis and abandoned projected historical studies; however, he kept up a lively interest in politics and was a regular contributor to newspapers and periodicals until his death on October 19, 1913.

WORKS: *A History of Alabama* (1900). *Andrew Jackson* (1900). *Stephen Arnold Douglas* (1902). *The Lower South in American History* (1902). *A Gentleman of the South: A Memory of the Black Belt, from the Manuscript Memoirs of the Late Colonel Stanton Elmore* (1903). *The Foe of Compromise and Other Essays* (1903). *The Life of Oliver Ellsworth* (1905). *The New Politics and Other Papers* (1914).

Norman D. Brown
University of Texas
Austin

WILLIAM WELLS BROWN (*ca.* 1815–1884). The son of a white father and mulatto mother, William Wells Brown was born a slave in Lexington, Ky., *ca.* 1815. At the age of ten he was taken from Lexington to St. Louis, Mo., to work on a river steamboat that traveled the Ohio and Mississippi rivers. Although still a slave he was hired out to the newspaper office of Elijah Lovejoy, abolitionist editor of the St. Louis *Times*. In his first attempt to escape slavery Brown, along with his mother, reached Illinois, where the two were captured and returned to their master. As punishment the mother was sold into the South. Brown's second attempt was successful when, at the age of nineteen, he walked away from his master in Cincinnati. It was Wells Brown, a Quaker who befriended him after the escape, from whom he took his name.

William Wells Brown became a spokesman for the antislavery movement. His job as a steward on a Lake Erie steamboat enabled him to assist escaping slaves. He improved his language skills to the extent that he became a vocal participant and prolific writer in abolitionist and temperance movements. He became so well known that Victor Hugo invited him to address the Paris Peace Congress. Brown remained in England until 1854, when he was granted his freedom. In England he published his first novel, *Clotel; or, The President's Daughter*. Not only did the story treat the controversial topic of miscegenation, but dared to imply that Clotel was the mulatto daughter of Thomas Jefferson.

After his return to the United States, Brown resided in Buffalo, N.Y. He was the first black American man of letters, the first black American dramatist, and the first black American writer of a travel book. He died in Chelsea, Mass., on November 6, 1884.

WORKS: *Narrative of William Wells Brown, a Fugitive Slave* (1847). *Three Years in Europe: or, Places I Have Seen and People I Have Met* (1852). *Clotel; or The President's Daughter: A Narrative of Slave Life in the United States* (1853). *The Escape; or A Leap for Freedom: A Drama in Five Acts* (1858).

ELAINE MITCHELL NEWSOME
Fayetteville State University
Fayetteville, N.C.

WILLIAM HAND BROWNE (1828–1912). William Hand Browne was born in Baltimore on December 31, 1828, of a famous Maryland family and dedicated much of his life to Maryland history. Educated for medicine, he refused to enter that profession, preferring to help his brother in a profitable commission business while pursuing literary and antiquarian investigations as a hobby. In 1863 he married and moved out of the city, and throughout the war he traveled widely in the South without taking any active part in military affairs.

After the war he devoted himself to helping restore the South to its former cultural place in the nation, and in so doing he had much to do with making Baltimore a focal point for southern writers. As an initial step in this enterprise, he coedited the *Southern Review* with Albert Taylor Bledsoe in 1867. Bledsoe's fierce controversies in defense of the Lost Cause were not suited to Browne's milder temperament, and Browne left to coedit the *New Eclectic Magazine*, later known as the *Southern Magazine*. He quickly made it the principal literary journal in the South. He even tried editing a weekly, the *Statesman*, to cover literature, art, and music, as well as politics, but the pace was too hectic, and he dropped the venture in 1871. His friend Richard Malcolm Johnston helped him write the *Life of Alexander H. Stephens* in 1878, and other literary friends assisted him in the many texts he published on literature and local history. In 1876 he was an advisor in the founding of Johns Hopkins University and became its librarian in 1879, as well as lecturer in literature. His literary interests continued, and he published a concise English dictionary as well as scholarly works in his favorite specialty, early Scotch poetry.

But Browne's major contribution, completed with remarkable regularity considering the enormous amount of scholarly research and editorial exactness required, was the *Archives of Maryland*, the 30-volume presentation of the colonial and provincial records. To these he added his books on the Calverts, his editing of the Calvert Papers for the Maryland Historical Society, and his own contributions and reviews to the *Maryland Historical Magazine*, of which he was the first editor. He was much loved and admired in Baltimore, was witty and gracious all his life, and remained active until his death on December 13, 1912, in his 84th year.

WORKS: *Speech in the House of Delegates of Virginia, on the Removal from the Commonwealth of the Free Colored Population* (1853). *Wheat, Its Worth and Waste*, with Thomas J. Hand (1862). Trans., *Hammer and Anvil*, by Friedrich Spielhagen (1870). *English Literature*, with Richard Malcolm Johnston (1873). Trans., *A Lear of the Steppe*, by Ivan Turgenieff (1874). *History of Maryland*, with J. Thomas Scharf (1877). *The Clarendon Dictionary* (1882). Trans., *Greece and Rome, Their Life and Art*, by Jakob von Falke (1882). *Archives of Maryland*, I (1883)–XXX (1910). *Life of Alexander H. Stephens*, with Richard Malcolm Johnston (1884). *Maryland, the History of a Palatinate* (1884). *Selections from the Early Scottish Poets* (1887). *The Tail of Rauf Coilyear: A Scottish Metrical Romance of the Fifteenth Century* (1903).

C. CARROLL HOLLIS
University of North Carolina
Chapel Hill

THOMAS BURKE (1747?–1783). Thomas Burke, born in Ireland of a prominent Catholic family, received a good education, but a disagreement with kinsmen when he was about sixteen prompted him to immigrate to America. In Accomack County, Va., he studied medicine and wrote, often in shorthand, pastoral poems and youthful love lyrics. His "Triumph, America!" on the repeal of the Stamp Act in 1766 expressed his detestation of the English and, according to a letter he wrote, brought him fame. He participated poetically in the political quarrels of the late 1760s, but only two of his unsigned contributions in Purdie's *Virginia Gazette* have been identified. In 1770 he was married and living in Norfolk, having changed his profession to law. Two years later he settled in Hillsborough, N.C., and in 1775–1776 served in the North Carolina Provincial Congresses, then spent four years as a member of the Continental Congress in Philadelphia, where he sharpened his poetic pen with patriotic paeans and addresses to the ladies.

In June, 1781, he was elected governor of North Carolina, but was captured by the Tories in September and imprisoned in Wilmington and Charleston. In January, arguing violation of its terms, he broke his parole, returned to Hillsborough and resumed the governorship. When he was criticized by valued friends for what they considered an unjustified breach of the parole, his tense Irish sense of honor was deeply wounded, and though urged to stand for reelection, he refused. A saddened man, he died a year and a half later on December 2, 1783. Only three of Burke's 24 extant poems were printed in his lifetime, though many of them—often derivative, replete with classical names and typical eighteenth-century allusions—were circulated in manuscript. His last poem, after Cornwallis' defeat, was a hymn to peace.

WORKS: *The Poems of Governor Thomas Burke of North Carolina* (1961).

RICHARD WALSER
North Carolina State University
Raleigh

FRANCES HODGSON BURNETT (1849–1924). Although Frances Hodgson wrote her first story in her rural home near Knoxville,

Tenn., this ambiance figures only negligibly in her voluminous literary production. The daughter of an ironmonger, she was born in Manchester, England, on November 24, 1849. In 1865, just a few days after Lincoln's assassination, Frances' mother, now widowed, sailed with her children for America to join her brother in Knoxville.

Instead of new opportunities, the Hodgsons found the rigors of Reconstruction awaiting them. It was necessary for Frances to pick grapes in order to buy the paper, ink, and stamps for writing and submitting her first story. "Hearts and Diamonds," her first published effort, appeared in *Godey's Lady's Book* in June, 1868, when Frances was only nineteen. Encouraged by Richard Watson Gilder, Frances continued to write, and for the remaining 56 years of her life made her livelihood from her pen.

Most of her fiction was cast in the romantic mold of contemporary popular magazines, but her use of the native Lancashire dialect is quite authentic; and her portrayal of contemporary life is usually considered realistic. It is perhaps for two children's books that she is best remembered: *Little Lord Fauntleroy* (1886) and *The Secret Garden* (1911). The success of the former was phenomenal: its seven-year-old protagonist with his long locks, velvet suits with lace collars, and refined manners became an international model for the dress, grooming, and demeanor of a generation of reluctant little boys.

She produced more than 50 book-length titles (many were collections of short magazine fiction) and more than a dozen plays. She enjoyed vast popularity and financial success both in England and America and crossed the Atlantic 33 times. Despite the rewards of fame and wealth, she experienced two unhappy marriages —first to Dr. Swan Burnett of Knoxville, then to Dr. Stephen Townsend of London. The death of one of her two sons is reflected in her fiction in various ways. She died on October 29, 1924.

WORKS: *That Lass o' Lowrie's* (1877). *Surly Tim* (1877). *Theo* (1877). *Dolly* (1877). *Pretty Polly Pemberton* (1877). *Earlier Stories*, 1st Ser. (1878). *Kathleen* (1878). *Earlier Stories*, 2nd Ser. (1878). *Miss Crespigny* (1878). *A Quiet Life* and *The Tide on the Moaning Bar* (1878). *Our*

Neighbor Opposite (1878). *The Lass of Lowrie's* (1878). *Jarl's Daughter*
(1879). *Natalie* (1879). *Haworth's* (1879). *Louisiana* (1880). *A Fair Bar-*
barian (1881). *Esmerelda* (1881). *Young Folks' Ways* (1883). *Through*
One Administration (1883). *Little Lord Fauntleroy* (1886). *A Woman's*
Will or Miss Defarge (1887). *Sara Crewe* (1887). *Editha's Burglar* (1888).
The Fortunes of Philippa Fairfax (1888). *The Real Lord Fauntleroy*
(1888). *The Pretty Sister of José* (1889). *Phyllis* (1889). *Little Saint Eliza-*
beth (1890). *Nixie* (1890). *Giovanni and the Other; [Children I Have*
Known] (1892). *The Drury Lane Boys' Club* (1892). *The Showman's*
Daughter (1892). *The One I Knew Best of All* (1893). *Piccino and Other*
Child Stories [The Captain's Youngest] (1894). *The Two Little Pilgrims'*
Progress (1895). *A Lady of Quality* (1896). *His Grace Osmonde* (1897).
The First Gentlemen of Europe (1897). *In Connection with the De Wil-*
loughby Claim (1899). *The Making of A Marchioness* (1901). *The Methods*
of Lady Walderhust (1901). *A Little Princess* (1902). *The Pretty Sister*
of San José (1903). *In the Closed Room* (1904). *That Man and I* (1904).
The Dawn of A Tomorrow (1906). *The Troubles of Queen Silver-Bell*
(1906). *Racketty Packetty House* (1906). *The Cozy Lion* (1907). *The*
Shuttle (1907). *The Spring Cleaning* (1908). *The Good Wolf* (1908). *Barty*
Crusoe and His Man Saturday (1909). *The Land of the Blue Flower*
(1909). *The Secret Garden* (1911). *My Robin* (1912). *T. Tembaron* (1913).
The Lost Prince (1915). *Little Hunchback Zia* (1916). *The White People*
(1917). *The Head of the House of Coombe* (1922). *Robin* (1922). *In the*
Garden (1925).

WELFORD DUNAWAY TAYLOR
University of Richmond
Richmond, Va.

WILLIAM BYRD OF WESTOVER (1674–1744). The most important southern writer before Thomas Jefferson, William Byrd
busied his 70 years as a farmer, businessman, lawyer, politician,
amateur physician and naturalist, and womanizer. The son of Mary
(1653–1699) and William Byrd I (1652–1704), he was born on
March 28, 1674, at his father's frontier plantation near the falls
of the James River. His father had migrated from London before
1670 to inherit the plantation and Indian trade of his kinsman,
Thomas Stegge. In 1673, William Byrd I married Mary Horsemanden Filmer, an eighteen-year-old widow and daughter of War-

ham Horsemanden. Besides William II, the Byrds had three daughters—Susan, Mary, and Ursula—and a son, Warham, who died in infancy.

At the age of seven (1681), Byrd sailed for England, where he lived until 1696. He received his early education in the classics at Felsted Grammar School in Essex and throughout his life read Latin and Greek, as well as the modern languages. After studying business in Holland in 1690, he returned to London to work in the mercantile house of Perry and Lane. He entered Middle Temple to study law in 1692 and was licensed to practice in 1695. In London, Byrd befriended such prominent scientific and literary figures as Charles Boyle, William Congreve, and William Wycherley. On April 29, 1696, he was elected to the Royal Society.

When Byrd returned to Virginia in 1696–1697, he was elected to the House of Burgesses from Henrico County. Late in 1697, he was in London representing his father and Governor Edmund Andros in a dispute with the Reverend James Blair over the building of the College of William and Mary. His second residence in England ended in 1705 when he was called home after his father's death.

From 1705 to 1715, Byrd settled at Westover on his father's Virginia estate. He married Lucy Parke, daughter of Colonel Daniel Parke, on May 4, 1706; they had four children, two of whom survived infancy—Evelyn (1707–1737) and Wilhelmina (b. 1715). Byrd added to his land holdings, continued to build his library, which numbered more than 3,600 volumes at his death, and won appointment to the Governor's Council in 1709. A dispute with Alexander Spotswood and business debts of his dead father-in-law's estate carried Byrd to England in 1715.

Except for a brief sojourn in Virginia in 1720–1721, Byrd spent the years between 1715–1726 in England. Lucy, who had arrived in London in the summer of 1716, died of smallpox on November 21, 1716, and Byrd spent the next years searching for a second wife and intriguing with ladies, high and low. He courted several young heiresses unsuccessfully before marrying Maria Taylor (1698–1771), a wealthy woman of 25 in May, 1724. They had four children—Anne (1725–1757), Maria (1727–1745), William III (1728–

1777), and Jane (b. 1729). Still in debt and with a growing family, Byrd returned to Virginia in the spring of 1726.

He resumed his seat on the Governor's Council on April 28, 1726, and in 1727 was appointed one of three Virginia commissioners to settle the boundary dispute with North Carolina. In the spring and fall of 1728, the Virginia and North Carolina commissioners surveyed the line. Byrd recorded the events of this survey in his two most important works—*The Secret History of the Line* and *The History of the Dividing Line*. In 1732 he traveled to Colonel Spotswood's home at Germanna to learn about iron mining; this account became *A Progress to the Mines*. He recorded his exploration of his frontier lands in 1733 in *A Journey to the Land of Eden*. None of these works was published during Byrd's life, but they circulated among friends in manuscript.

During these years, Byrd built the house which still stands at Westover (*ca.* 1730–1731), secured vast acreage, founded Richmond (1737), planned to settle his western lands with Swiss colonists, reduced his debts, and sought political preferment. He was president of the Governor's Council in 1743, and when he died on August 26, 1744, had paid his debts and owned 179,440 acres. He was buried at Westover.

A central figure in shaping the political and cultural life of Virginia, Byrd built one of the best private libraries in America and was a lifelong patron of the College of William and Mary. Although he published little during his life, he was a compulsive writer. His letters, diaries (kept in shorthand), journals, and literary exercises provide an excellent window for viewing life and letters in Virginia in the first half of the eighteenth century.

WORKS: "An Account of a Negro Boy That Is Dappled in Several Places on His Body with White Spots," *Philosophical Transactions*, XIX (London, 1698), 781–82. Verses by "Mr. Burrard" in *Tunbrigalia: or, Tunbridge Miscellanies, for the Year 1719* (1719). *A Discourse Concerning the Plague, with Some Preservatives Against It*, by a "Lover of Mankind" (1721). *Neu-gefundes Eden* by "Wilhelm Vogel" (Berne, Switzerland, 1737), ed. and trans. R. C. Beatty and W. J. Mulloy as *William Byrd's Natural History of Virginia* (1940), Byrd's notes, but mainly a reprint of John Lawson's *A New Voyage to Carolina* (1708). *The Westover Manu-*

scripts, ed. Edmund Ruffin (1841) includes *The History of the Dividing Line, A Progress to the Mines*, and *A Journey to the Land of Eden*; other editions of this work are by Thomas H. Wynne (1866) and John S. Bassett (1901). *William Byrd's Histories of the Dividing Line Betwixt Virginia and North Carolina*, ed. W. K. Boyd (1929) prints for the first time *The Secret History*; this work was reissued by Percy G. Adams (1967). *Accounts as Solicitor General of the Colonies* (1913). *Description of the Dismal Swamp and a Proposal to Drain the Swamp* (1922). *The Secret Diary of William Byrd of Westover, 1709–1712*, ed. Louis B. Wright and Marion Tinling (1941). *Another Secret Diary of William Byrd of Westover*, ed. Maude H. Woodfin and Marion Tinling (1942). *The London Diary (1717–1721) and Other Writings of William Byrd of Virginia*, ed. Louis B. Wright and Marion Tinling (1958). *The Prose Works of William Byrd of Westover*, ed. Louis B. Wright (1966). Wright is editing Byrd's letters, and the Virginia Historical Society owns an unpublished commonplace book for 1722–1732.

ROBERT BAIN
University of North Carolina
Chapel Hill

JAMES BRANCH CABELL (1879–1958). James Branch Cabell, America's greatest purveyor and creator of myth for comic purposes through the mid-twentieth century, was born on April 14, 1879, in Richmond, Va. On both sides Cabell descended from aristocratic Virginia families; many of his fictions probe the vanities of the Virginia aristocracy. By nature intellectual and meditative, Cabell pondered the inconsistencies in the stories he heard his elders relate about the fallen Confederacy. To the contemporary myths connected with the Confederacy, he supplemented a keen appreciation of classical myth. He became a lifelong student of the mythic and the occult.

Cabell was a brilliant student at the College of William and Mary, and he later published poems written for the college literary magazine, as well as a college paper on William Congreve. As an upperclassman Cabell taught French and Greek; both literatures were to color his major fictions. In 1898 Cabell graduated with highest honors, an event briefly threatened when Cabell withdrew his name, angry at being a victim of campus gossip because he was a good friend of a college librarian accused of being homosexual. Ultimately Cabell's name was cleared and his graduation proceeded. In this time of uncertainty he met Ellen Glasgow, who was visiting the campus. Later the association would become major for both writers.

After graduation Cabell worked briefly as a copyreader for the Richmond *Times*, but the next year (1899) he was working for the New York *Herald*. By 1901 he was back with the *Times*; strangely he was soon the subject of Richmond gossip again—this time as the probable murderer of one of his mother's cousins. Angered and hurt by the accusations, Cabell fancied himself something of the devil's own dear son as he labored during the next ten years as a genealogist, a profession that would be reflected in his future books, especially in his magnus opus, *The Biography of the Life of Manuel*. During these years, he began publishing stories in national magazines, and in 1904 he published his first novel, *The Eagle's Shadow*. Surprisingly, Cabell worked in coal mine operations in West Virginia during 1911–1913. By his own testimony he was gathering material for his writing by living the life of a Restoration rake, but this pattern ended decisively when he met Priscilla Bradley Shepherd at the Rockbridge Alum, a popular summer resort in Virginia. Mrs. Shepherd, some four and a half years Cabell's senior, was a widow with five children. He and Mrs. Shepherd were married on November 8, 1913. Their only child, a son—Ballard Hartwell—was born on August 25, 1915.

In 1919 Cabell became editor of the Virginia War History Commission, a post he held through 1926. In 1919 he also became genealogist for the Virginia chapter of the Sons of the American Revolution. The real event of 1919, however, was the publication of *Jurgen*, the book that made the quiet, shy Cabell one of the most controversial writers in America. He became an international figure when on January 14, 1920, his publisher was summoned to appear in court for violating New York's pornography law. The Cabell boom was on, and it would last through the 1920s. *Jurgen* was exonerated on October 19, 1922. The event was an important milestone in the struggle for a freer treatment of human sexuality. *Jurgen* and its author were taken as symbols of the ultra-sophistication of the 1920s. Cabell was aligned closely with the "smart set," and H. L. Mencken was one of his staunchest defenders.

Following publication of *Jurgen*, Cabell revised his earlier work to make it conform to his scheme for Manuel's biography. The definitive edition of the biography appeared in eighteen volumes from 1927–1930 as the Storisende Edition of *The Works of James Branch Cabell*. Cabell marked the completion of this labor by publishing for a time thereafter under the shortened name Branch Cabell. Much of his later writing was autobiographical and philosophical, with Cabell meditating on the ironies, pleasures, and pains of the creative life. He did write three fictional trilogies in succeeding years, but never regained the public he had enjoyed in the 1920s, sometimes known as the James Branch Cabell era.

From 1932 to 1935 Cabell served—with George Jean Nathan, Ernest Boyd, Theodore Dreiser, Eugene O'Neill, and Sherwood Anderson—as an editor of *The American Spectator*. After 1935 he was plagued by attacks of pneumonia and began making frequent removals to St. Augustine, Fla. Florida's legendary past and history came to absorb him much as Virginia's had, and this interest found expression in his last fictional works. In St. Augustine, Priscilla Bradley Cabell died on March 25, 1949. On June 15, 1949, Cabell married Margaret Waller Freeman, a younger woman with whom Cabell had been associated in 1921, when he had edited three issues of *The Reviewer*, Richmond's literary magazine. Cabell died on May 5, 1958, in Richmond.

WORKS: *The Eagle's Shadow* (1904). *The Line of Love* (1905). *Branchiana* (1907). *Gallantry* (1907). *Chivalry* (1909). *The Cords of Vanity* (1909). *Branch of Abingdon* (1911). *The Soul of Melicent* (1913). *The Majors and Their Marriages* (1915). *The Rivet in Grandfather's Neck* (1915). *The Certain Hour* (1916). *From the Hidden Way* (1916). *The Cream of the Jest* (1917). *Beyond Life* (1919). *Jurgen* (1919). *Domnei* (1920). *The Judging of Jurgen* (1920). *Figures of Earth* (1921). *The Jewel Merchants* (1921). *Joseph Hergesheimer* (1921). *The Lineage of Lichfield* (1922). *The High Place* (1923). *Straws and Prayer-Books* (1924). *Retractions* (1926). *The Silver Stallion* (1926). *The Music from Behind the Moon* (1926). *Something About Eve* (1927). *Ballades from the Hidden Way* (1928). *The White Robe* (1928). *Sonnets from Antan* (1929). *The Way of*

Ecben (1929). *Some of Us* (1930). *Townsend of Lichfield* (1930). *Between Dawn and Sunrise* (1930). Storisende Edition of *The Works of James Branch Cabell* (1927–30). *These Restless Heads* (1932). *Special Delivery* (1933). *Ladies and Gentlemen* (1934). *Smirt* (1934). *Smith* (1935). *Preface to the Past* (1936). *The Nightmare Has Triplets* (1937). *Smire* (1937). *The King Was in His Counting House* (1938). *Of Ellen Glasgow* (1938). *Hamlet Had an Uncle* (1940). *The First Gentleman of America* (1942). *The St. Johns* (1942). *There Were Two Pirates* (1946). *Let Me Lie* (1947). *The Witch-Woman* (1948). *The Devil's Own Dear Son* (1949). *Quiet, Please* (1952). *As I Remember It* (1955). *Between Friends: Letters of James Branch Cabell and Others*, ed. Padraic Colum and Margaret Freeman Cabell (1962). *The Letters of James Branch Cabell*, ed. Edward Wagenknecht (1975).

JOSEPH M. FLORA
University of North Carolina
Chapel Hill

GEORGE WASHINGTON CABLE (1844–1925). George Washington Cable, one of the first progressive writers of the New South, was born in New Orleans on October 12, 1844, the son of Rebecca Boardman and G. W. Cable. His father's German background and his mother's New England protestantism contributed to his own sense of isolation in a community whose leaders were primarily French and Catholic. Cable's position as an outsider may have stimulated his interest in sociological problems and made him more sensitive to the needs of minorities, especially southern blacks.

At his father's death, Cable, only fifteen, terminated his formal education and took a job at the local customhouse until his enlistment as a Confederate soldier at nineteen. After the Civil War he continued his old job and married Louise Bartlett on December 7, 1869; they had four daughters and a son. In February, 1870, Cable accepted a position on the New Orleans *Picayune*, where his "Drop Shot" column, though occasionally controversial, was well received. At this time Cable began writing a series of short stories and was discovered by Scribner's Edward King, who was touring Louisiana in search of materials for his "Great South" series. Although Scribner's rejected "Bibi," Cable's story of a tormented slave-prince, on the grounds of its unpleasant subject matter, they published his character sketch of an old Creole, "'Sieur George," in 1873. Richard Watson Gilder, editor of *Scribner's Monthly* and the *Century*, considered Cable one of his leading local colorists, who would contribute to Gilder's plan for reconciling the North and South through literature. H. H. Boyesen also took an interest in Cable's writing and initiated a correspondence helpful to the latter's career.

In 1879 Cable's *Old Creole Days*, a collection of short stories, was published, and the first installments of *The Grandissimes*, which incorporated the "Bibi" materials, appeared in *Scribner's Monthly*. In 1880 *The Grandissimes* was published in book form, as was *Madame Delphine*, a novella. These two books represent Cable's highest achievement, anticipating the complex drama of Faulkner's works. Each deals with racial injustice, the continuing problems caused by exploitation of the black community, and the Creoles' resistance to social change.

By 1882 Cable began a full-time career as a writer, completing *Dr. Sevier*, a serious novel dealing with prison reform, which was followed by a *Century Magazine* exposé, "The Convict Lease System in the Southern States," and a history, *The Creoles of Louisiana*. These three works, openly polemical, offended Gilder and caused tremendous resentment throughout the South. A reading tour with Mark Twain brought Cable some additional income and popularity, but his increasingly fervent publications on the Negro's dilemma, especially "A Freedman's Case in Equity" and the first edition of *The Silent South*, made him notorious in New Orleans. He felt pressured to move his family to Northampton, Mass., in 1885.

There, in 1886, Cable organized the Home Culture clubs, racially integrated reading groups designed to raise the educational level of average citizens. The success of the movement was due in part to the national atmosphere of self-improvement and upward mobility in the last quarter of the nineteenth century. The clubs published a journal in 1892, called first the *Letter* and later in 1896 the *Symposium*.

When Cable was 50 he published *John March, Southerner*, an

ambiguous portrait of a southern aristocrat during the Reconstruction era; this was his last attempt at social satire. He continued to be an outspoken essayist, but his fiction became unashamedly romantic. The public taste of the period and his editors reinforced his tendency toward sentimentalism. *The Cavalier*, written in 1901, was Cable's greatest popular success with Julia Marlowe starring in a dramatic version of the novel a year later.

Cable's first wife died in 1904. Afterwards he was married to Eva Stevenson, who died in 1923, and to Hannah Cowing, who survived him. Energetic till the end, he published three novels while in his seventies; he died on January 31, 1925, at age 81. He shaped an optimistic vision of technological progress in the New South and the eventual integration of the races. Perhaps because he remained too dependent on the family magazine audience and the taste of his editors, Cable did not live up to his early potential as a major southern writer. Nevertheless, in his best fiction he transcended the limitations of the local color genre and revealed a daring and prophetic intelligence.

WORKS: *Old Creole Days* (1879). *The Grandissimes* (1880). *Madame Delphine* (1881). *The Creoles of Louisiana* (1884). *Dr. Sevier* (1884). *The Silent South* (1885). *Bonaventure* (1888). *Strange True Stories of Louisiana* (1889). *The Negro Question* (1890). *The Busy Man's Bible* (1891). *A Memory of Roswell Smith* (1892). *John March, Southerner* (1894). *Strong Hearts* (1899). *The Cavalier* (1901). *Bylow Hill* (1902). *Kincaid's Battery* (1908). *"Posson Jone'" and Père Raphaël* (1909). *Gideon's Band* (1914). *The Amateur Garden* (1914). *The Flower of the Chapdelaines* (1918). *Lovers of Louisiana* (1918).

KIMBALL KING
University of North Carolina
Chapel Hill

ERSKINE CALDWELL (1902–). Erskine Caldwell's father, the Reverend Ira Sylvester Caldwell, was a preacher of the Associate Reformed Presbyterian Church, which Robert Cantwell describes as a small, highly literate, intellectual, strong-willed, socially progressive, and courageous sect that believes each autonomous congregation should choose its own minister. The Reverend Caldwell was serving in Newnan, Ga., Coweta County, 40 miles southeast of Atlanta when his son Erskine was born on December 17, 1902. (Caldwell later, inexplicably, has said 1903.) Caldwell's mother was Carrie Preston Bell Caldwell, of an old Staunton, Va., family. She actively assisted her husband in his ministry and ran a small school; Erskine was very close to her and received much of his primary and secondary education from her, at school or at home.

In 1906 the Reverend Caldwell and his family left the White Oak Church of Newnan, served several churches, including a rough assignment in Atoka, Tenn., and returned to Wrens, Ga., in 1919, where he remained until his death in 1944. Near Wrens one finds the locale of Caldwell's famous *Tobacco Road*.

Erskine was enrolled in his father's alma mater, Erskine College, in Due West, S.C., in September, 1920. Caldwell attended three semesters, dropped out, returned in the fall of 1922, then attended the University of Virginia for one year, 1923–1924, on a DAR scholarship, spent the summer and fall of 1924 studying at the University of Pennsylvania, and returned to Virginia for the spring semester of 1925. Although Caldwell never graduated, he can hardly be described as a self-educated rustic.

In 1925 Caldwell married Helen Lannegan of Charlottesville by whom he had three children: Erskine Preston, Dabney Withers, and Janet. They lived in Maine from 1925 through 1932, while Caldwell worked at odd jobs and wrote (and had rejected) over 100 stories and novelettes.

His first published work was an article, "The Georgia Cracker," 1926. His early writing, published in "little" magazines, caught the attention of Maxwell Perkins, who accepted some stories for *Scribner's Magazine*, gave Caldwell encouragement, and published *American Earth* and *Tobacco Road*. After a disagreement with Perkins, Caldwell went to Viking Press.

From 1925 to 1926 Caldwell worked on the Atlanta *Journal*; in 1933–1934, 1938, and 1942–1943 he wrote for Hollywood. During the late 1930s and early 1940s he worked as a foreign correspondent in Prague, Moscow, Mexico, and Madrid. He covered the Spanish Civil War. In 1938 Caldwell lectured at the New School for Social Research in New York City.

Caldwell divorced his first wife in 1938 and married the photographer Margaret Bourke-White in 1939. He traveled in China, Mongolia, and Turkestan in 1940 and was in Russia when Hitler attacked in 1941. He wrote powerfully of the Russian land and people. Because of his great popularity in Russia and his indictments of many aspects of American capitalism, some have labeled him a Communist, an accusation Caldwell denies.

Caldwell's professional collaboration with Bourke-White was a great success; the marriage, however, ended in divorce in 1942. That same year he married June Johnson. They had one son, Jay Erskine, divorced, and in 1957 Caldwell married his present wife, Virginia Moffett Fletcher. They live in Dunedin, Fla.

Caldwell is, in every sense, a professional writer. Although early in his career he supported himself with odd jobs and was the editor of a series of regional studies, *American Folkways* (1940–1955), he has not relied on teaching or other sources of income. He is a prolific writer, and if the quality of his work has fallen off in recent years, we must still not ignore either his enormous popularity or the power of his early work.

WORKS: *The Bastard* (1929). *Poor Fool* (1930). *American Earth* (1930). *Mama's Little Girl* (1932). *Tobacco Road* (1932). *God's Little Acre* (1933). *Message for Genevieva* (1933). *We are the Living* (1933). *Journeyman* (1935). *Kneel to the Rising Sun* (1935). *Tenant Farmers* (1935). *Some American People* (1935). *The Sacrilege of Alan Kent* (1936). *You Have Seen Their Faces*, with Margaret Bourke-White (1937). *Southways* (1938). *North of the Danube*, with Margaret Bourke-White (1939). *Trouble in July* (1940). *Jackpot* (1940). *Say! Is This the U.S.A.?*, with Margaret Bourke-White (1941). *All Night Long* (1942). *Moscow under Fire* (1942). *All-Out on the Road to Smolensk* (1942). *Russia at War*, with Margaret Bourke-White (1942). *Georgia Boy* (1944). *Tragic Ground* (1944). *A Day's Wooing and Other Stories* (1944). *Stories of Erskine Caldwell*, selected by Henry Soidel (1944). *A House in the Uplands* (1946). *The Caldwell Caravan* (1946). *The Sure Hand of God* (1947). *This Very Earth* (1948). *Place Called Esterville* (1949). *Episode in Palmetto* (1950).

Humorous Side of Erskine Caldwell, ed. Robert Cantwell (1951). *Call It Experience* (1951). *A Lamp for Nightfall* (1952). *The Courting of Susie Brown* (1952). *Love and Money* (1952). *Complete Stories* (1953). *Gretta* (1955). *Gulf Coast Stories* (1956). *Certain Women* (1957). *Molly Cottontail* (1958). *Claudelle Inglish* (1958). *When You Think of Me* (1959). *Jenny by Nature* (1961). *Men and Women*, selected by Carvel Collins (1961). *Close to Home* (1962). *The Last Night of Summer* (1963). *Around About America* (1964). *In Search of Bisco* (1965). *Where the Girls Were Different* (1965). *Woman in the House* (1965). *Deer at Our House* (1966). *In the Shadow of the Steeple* (1967). *Writing in America* (1967). *Miss Mamma Aimée* (1967). *Deep South* (1968). *Summertime Island* (1968). *The Weather Shelter* (1969). *Little House in the Uplands* (1970). *A Swell-Looking Girl* (1972). *The Earnshaw Neighborhood* (1972). *Close to Home* (1972). *Annette* (1974). *Afternoons in Mid-America* (1976).

DONALD R. NOBLE
University of Alabama
Tuscaloosa

FRANCES BOYD CALHOUN (1867–1909). *Miss Minerva and William Green Hill* (1909), Frances Boyd Calhoun's only book-length title, is much better known than its creator. She was born on Christmas day, 1867, in Mecklenburg County, Va. Before moving to Tennessee in 1880, she lived in Warrenton, N.C., for some two years. She attended the Tipton Female Seminary in Covington, Tenn., from which she graduated in 1885. Thereafter she helped her father edit a local newspaper. Some of her early poetic efforts were published here and in one of the Memphis dailies.

After teaching for seven years in the Covington city school, she married George Barret Calhoun, in 1903. He died a year later, and it was not until the spring of 1908 that she mailed to a Chicago publisher the manuscript of her novel, on which she had worked for two years. She broke the publisher's silence with a prodding letter in late summer, and the manuscript was quickly accepted and published (it appeared on February 6, 1909). Four months later, on June 8, 1909, Frances Calhoun died, without ever knowing the success her book was to achieve.

Miss Minerva and William Green Hill became a minor classic of popular southern fiction. It ultimately went through more than 50 printings, and in 1918 a sequel appeared, titled *Billy and the Major*. This continuation, written by Emma Speed Sampson (1868–1947), was but the first of eleven continuations, the last being *Miss Minerva's Vacation* (1939), all by Sampson.

The germs of Calhoun's fictional treatment were found among individuals and incidents she witnessed in Covington, but recent research has shown that she exercised considerable authorial license. Attention in the novel is focused upon three groups of characters: the spindly old maid, Miss Minerva, and the rotund Major, her long-time suitor and a Confederate veteran; Minerva's nephew "Billy" Hill and his three playmates; and various blacks. Calhoun was sharply attuned to the local ambiance, but her story concerns the universal problem of the distance that separates the child and adult worlds. Though the stiff Aunt Minerva at first listens to Billy "in frozen amazement and paralyzed silence," she ultimately comes to love him, in spite of his pranks and frequent scrapes with authority.

WORKS: *Miss Minerva and William Green Hill* (1909).

> WELFORD DUNAWAY TAYLOR
> University of Richmond
> Richmond, Va.

WILLIAM EDWARD CAMPBELL. See William March.

TRUMAN CAPOTE (1924–). At his birth on September 30, 1923, in New Orleans, Capote was named Truman Streckfus Persons. His mother, later divorced, married Joseph Garcia Capote, a Spanish Cuban textile manufacturer. After his parents' divorce when he was four, Capote spent the next six years chiefly with elderly unmarried cousins in Monroeville, Ala. Here the friends his own age were Edwin and Harper Lee; the latter's novel *To Kill a Mockingbird* reflects this period. Capote remembered small-town southern life in "A Christmas Memory," first published in 1956 and later adapted for radio and film. Memories of a childhood in which he felt isolated and insecure also figure in *Other Voices, Other Rooms* (1948), his celebrated first novel.

In 1935 Capote rejoined his mother and continued his education at Trinity School and St. John's Academy in New York. During a year at Greenwich High School, Millbrook, Conn., he was encouraged to write by an English teacher, Catherine Wood. When seventeen, Capote spent a year in New York, where he worked for the *New Yorker*, first as a mailroom clerk and later as a feature writer. He moved to New Orleans and began his career with "Miriam," published in *Mademoiselle* in 1945 and given the O. Henry Award in 1946.

Capote has devoted himself to writing and to living an artistic life. He often lives abroad but always keeps a New York apartment because he is "a city fellow." Evocative narration and description characterize his travel essays, reportage, interviews, and stage and film plays as well as his fiction. His most experimental work is the "nonfiction novel" *In Cold Blood*, based on five years of research into the 1959 murder of the Clutter family in Holcomb, Kan.

Honors include membership in the National Institute of Arts and Letters, the Institute's creative writing award in 1959, and O. Henry Awards in 1946, 1948, and 1951.

WORKS: *Other Voices, Other Rooms* (1948). *A Tree of Night and Other Stories* (1949). *Local Color* (1950). *The Grass Harp* (1951). *The Grass Harp*, drama (1952). *The Grass Harp, A Tree of Night, and Other Stories* (1956). *House of Flowers* (1954; 1968). *The Muses Are Heard* (1956). *Breakfast at Tiffany's* (1958). *Commentary for Richard Avedon's Observations* (1959). *Selected Writings* (1963). *In Cold Blood* (1965). Intro., *The Collected Works of Jean Bowles* (1966). *A Christmas Memory* (1966). *The Thanksgiving Visitor* (1968). *Trilogy: An Experiment in Multimedia*, three short stories adapted for film with Eleanor and Frank Perry (1969). *The Dogs Bark: Public People and Private Places* (1973).

LOUISE GOSSETT.
Salem College
Winston-Salem, N.C.

HODDING CARTER (1907–1972). Journalist Hodding Carter, Jr., gained national prominence in 1946 when he was awarded the Pulitzer Prize for editorials in his Greenville (Miss.) *Delta Democrat-Times* attacking religious and racial intolerance. Born February 3, 1907, in Hammond, La., the son of William Hodding and Irma Dutartre Carter, he received his B.A. from Bowdoin College in 1927. After completing a degree in journalism at Columbia in 1928, he became a Teaching Fellow in the English Department at Tulane. He began his career in journalism as a reporter for the New Orleans *Item* and worked briefly as night bureau chief for United Press in New Orleans and bureau chief for Associated Press in Jackson, Miss. In 1932 he and his wife, the former Betty Werlein of New Orleans, moved to Hammond where they began the *Daily Courier*. Carter gained a reputation as a relentless foe of the Huey Long regime. At the urging of David Cohn and William Alexander Percy, the Carters moved to Greenville in 1936 and began the *Delta Star* in competition with an established paper which Carter was able to purchase in 1938 to form the *Delta Democrat-Times*. In 1939 Carter was a Nieman Fellow at Harvard and in the spring of 1940 was on the staff of *PM* in New York. During World War II he was coauthor of a book on civil defense, served as editor for *Yank* and the Cairo edition of *Stars and Stripes*, and was an intelligence officer in the War Department. Returning to Greenville after the war, he devoted his time to scholarship, writing, and newspaper editing. From 1962 to 1970 he was writer-in-residence at Tulane. He died April 4, 1972.

Although he was primarily a journalist campaigning for human rights, he was also a historian, a novelist, and a poet, having published biographies, histories of the lower Mississippi Valley, two novels (*The Winds of Fear* and *Flood Crest*), and one collection of poems. In addition to his Pulitzer Prize and Nieman Fellowship, he won honorary degree from Harvard and Bowdoin, a Guggenheim Fellowship, the Southern Literary Award, the William Allen White Citation for Journalistic Merit, and many other awards. Always interested in southern literature, he was instrumental in founding the Levee Press, which during its brief existence published handsome editions of Welty, Faulkner, and William Alexander Percy.

WORKS: *Lower Mississippi* (1942). *Civilian Defense of the United States*, with R. Ernest Dupuy (1942). *The Winds of Fear* (1944). *Flood Crest* (1947). *Southern Legacy* (1950). *Gulf Coast Country*, with Anthony Ragusin (1951). *Where Main Street Meets the River* (1952). *John Law Wasn't So Wrong: The Story of Louisiana's Horn of Plenty* (1952). *Robert E. Lee and the Road of Honor* (1955). *So Great a Good: A History of the Episcopal Church in Louisiana and of Christ Church Cathedral, 1805–1955*, with Betty Carter (1955). *The Marquis de Lafayette: Bright Sword for Freedom* (1958). *The Angry Scar: The Story of Reconstruction* (1959). *First Person Rural* (1963). *Doomed Road of Empire: The Spanish Trail of Conquest*, with Betty Carter (1963). *The Ballad of Catfoot Grimes and Other Verses* (1964). *So the Heffners Left McComb* (1965). *The Commandos of World War II* (1966). Ed., *The Past as Prelude: New Orleans, 1718–1968* (1968). *Their Words Were Bullets: The Southern Press in War, Reconstruction, and Peace* (1969). *Man and the River: The Mississippi* (1970).

ROBERT L. PHILLIPS, JR.
Mississippi State University
Starkville

WILLIAM ALEXANDER CARUTHERS (1802–1846). The second son of eleven children of a prominent Rockbridge County, Va., merchant, William, and Phebe Alexander Caruthers, Caruthers was born in Lexington, Va., and attended Washington College there, now Washington and Lee University, without graduating. In 1823 he received his diploma from the medical school of the University of Pennsylvania and that July in Savannah married Louisa Catherine Gibson, daughter of the Whitemarsh Island planter Robert S. Gibson. The couple settled at Lexington and eventually produced five children.

During 1829–1835 Caruthers resided in New York City, where he practiced medicine (notably in the plague year, 1832, described in his first novel, *The Kentuckian in New-York*) and gained entree to Gotham's literary circles. The publication there in 1834–1835 of his epistolary novel *The Kentuckian* and his historical romance *The Cavaliers of Virginia* established him as the earliest Virginia novelist of importance and, with William Gilmore Simms and John Pendleton Kennedy, as one of the first southern novelists of significance. *The Kentuckian* is notable as an early example of the "intersectional" genre, but its passing derogation of slavery has caught the eye of critics to the exclusion of its preponderantly sentimental aspects. The widely popular *Cavaliers of Virginia* lent wings to the fixing of the "cavalier" stereotype and became the first book-length work in any field to treat the subject of Bacon's Rebellion (1676). At this period Caruthers grew friendly with James K. Paulding, and later advised Secretary of War John Bell that Paulding and he had "published books together," though the titles have not been identified.

Forsaking New York early in 1835, Caruthers took his family back to Lexington, where he lingered until some time in 1837. By spring that year he was settled permanently in Savannah. There he published his last known novel, and ablest work, "The Knights of the Golden Horse-Shoe," monthly in the local *Magnolia* in 1841, marking its author as one of the earlier Georgia novelists of record. Without the adjective, the romance appeared in book form at Wetumpka, Ala., in December, 1845. *The Knights* became not only the first extended treatment of Governor Alexander Spotswood's expedition across the Blue Ridge Mountains in 1716, but also the first book-length work of any sort to commemorate that statesman. Now, too, Caruthers' article "Climbing the Natural Bridge" (*Knickerbocker Magazine*, July, 1838), his eyewitness account of the first ascent, in 1818, by a Washington College schoolmate, James H. Piper, evolved into one of American journalism's more legend-provoking items.

At Savannah the novelist practiced medicine, dealt in real estate, served on the board of aldermen, and helped found the Georgia Historical Society. In politics he was a Whig, in religion a converted Episcopalian. He died of tuberculosis on August 26, 1846, at Marietta, Ga., and is buried in an unlocated grave in the cemetery of Saint James Episcopal Church there. No known likeness of Caruthers has been located.

WORKS: *The Kentuckian in New-York, or the Adventures of Three Southerns*, 2 vols. (1834). *The Cavaliers of Virginia, or the Recluse of Jamestown . . .* , 2 vols. (1834–35). *The Knights of the Horse-Shoe; a Traditionary Tale of the Cocked Hat Gentry in the Old Dominion* (1845). *The Drunkard; from the Cradle to the Grave. A Lecture, Delivered Before the Savannah Temperance Society . . .* (1840). *A Lecture, Delivered Before the Georgia Historical Society . . .* (1843).

CURTIS CARROLL DAVIS
Baltimore, Md.

WILBUR JOSEPH CASH (1900–1941). W. J. Cash was born on May 2, 1900, in Gaffney, S.C., a cotton-mill town in the Carolina Piedmont. His father, John William Cash, was manager of the company store of Limestone Mills; his mother was Nannie Hamrick Cash. The Cashes were of Scotch-Irish and German descent, and were devout Baptists. After an early education in Gaffney and across the state line in Boiling Springs, N.C., and after brief stays at two colleges, W. J. Cash in 1920 entered Wake Forest College, a Baptist institution in North Carolina. Wake Forest was in many ways a liberal and progressive institution, and it was here that Cash began to read in earnest such iconoclasts as H. L. Mencken and James Branch Cabell. He also reaffirmed his earlier vow to become a writer, especially an interpreter of the southern mind.

After graduating from Wake Forest and briefly holding jobs as a teacher and reporter, Cash joined the staff of the Charlotte *News* in 1926. In 1929 he began to contribute articles on the South to Mencken's *American Mercury*, and it is obvious that Mencken was the greatest early influence on Cash. In the late 1920s Cash also began to work on the book he was later to entitle *The Mind of the South*. He continued to work on the book during the 1930s, and in 1937 returned to the Charlotte *News* as associate editor and editorial writer. In February, 1941, *The Mind of the South* was published. That spring Cash left for Mexico where he was to spend a year working on a novel under a Guggenheim Fellowship. On July 1, 1941, he committed suicide in Mexico City.

Cash's single book, *The Mind of the South*, is regarded as one of the best attempts to define and explain the nature and the temper of the southerner. Writing basically from the viewpoint of a liberal southerner—but one with a distaste for undiscriminating "progress" and boosterism—Cash helped to demolish the myth of the aristocratic Old South. He contended that "the old ruling class had never been a fully realized aristocracy," that virtually no aristocrats had existed in most southern states, and that "the intellectual and aesthetic culture of the Old South was a superficial and jejune thing . . . not a true culture at all." In his book Cash treated most thoroughly the Carolina Piedmont he knew so well—the rise of the upland cotton planter in the early nineteenth century, the growth of the textile mill and mill village in the late nineteenth century. But he also concerned himself with the antebellum southern frontier of Alabama and Mississippi and with the more general topics of southern race relations, politics, and religion.

Cash was one of many southerners who have attempted to interpret and "explain" the South to outsiders and to themselves. He spent virtually his entire adult life in the writing of his single book, and it is in this book that the southern mind received perhaps its fullest treatment.

WORKS: Eight essays on the South in the *American Mercury* (1929–35). *The Mind of the South* (1941).

FRED HOBSON
University of Alabama
Tuscaloosa

MADISON JULIUS CAWEIN (1865–1914). Madison Julius Cawein was born and died in Louisville, Ky., and lived there all his life except for three years in his early teens spent across the river in New Albany, Ind. He was born on March 23, 1865. His father, "Dr." William Cawein, an herbalist and compounder of "vegetable" family medicines, may have had some influence on the poet's dedication to nature. His mother was a spiritualist who thought she had the capacities of a medium, possibly a generative factor in the supernatural fantasies of much of Cawein's poetry. For six years after graduation from Louisville Male High in 1886, he was cashier in the local Newmarket Pool Hall, a center for the then legal off-track betting industry. Thereafter Cawein depended on the uncertain income from his books and contributions to periodicals in one of the least lucrative of literary genres. His dependence on literary production for a livelihood could account for his virtual enslavement to romantic and Victorian lyric traditions, which held a firm appeal for traditional readers of poetry through Cawein's lifetime. He had a wide circle of literary acquaintances in Kentucky and in the nation, and often visited, for example, Edward Arlington Robinson in New York, Henry van Dyke in Princeton, and James Whitcomb Riley in Indianapolis. He died on December 8, 1914.

Cawein wrote some 2,700 lyrics, of which about 1,500 are originals, the remainder revisions. Although his genuine passion for nature, in the best romantic tradition, inspired many admirers, the consensus today is that most of his work is the product of a fatigued genius with a few purple patches that have found their way to anthologies. In his own day he was generally respected, with the solid endorsements of such figures as William Dean Howells and Edmund Gosse. Richard H. Stoddard condemned his work as "execrable," but later he mistook Cawein's "Noera," published anonymously in a newspaper, for a hitherto unknown Elizabethan lyric. From a regional standpoint, Cawein is the first Kentucky poet with national recognition before the 1930s.

WORKS: *Blossoms of the Berry* (1887). *The Triumph of Music, and Other Lyrics* (1888). *Ascolon of Gaul, with Other Poems* (1889). *Lyrics and Idyls* (1890). *Days and Dreams* (1891). *Moods and Memories, Poems* (1892). *Poems of Nature and Love* (1893). *Red Leaves and Roses* (1893). *Intimations of the Beautiful, and Poems* (1894). *The White Snake and Other Poems; Translated from the German into the Original Meters* (1895). *The Garden of Dreams* (1896). *Vndertones* [sic] (1896). *Idyllic Monologues* (1898). *Shapes and Shadows* (1898). *Myth and Romance, Being a Book of Verse* (1899). *One Day & Another, a Lyrical Eclogue* (1901). *Kentucky Poems* (1902). *A Voice on the Wind and Other Poems* (1902). *Weeds by the Wall* (1904). *The Vale of Tempe* (1905). *Nature-Notes and Impressions, in Prose and Verse* (1906). *An Ode August 15, 1907, at the Dedication of the Monument Erected at Gloucester, Massachusetts, in Commemoration of the Founding of Massachusetts Bay Colony in the*

Year Sixteen Hundred and Twenty-Three (1908). *The Poems of Madison Cawein,* 5 vols. (1908). *The Giant and the Star, Little Annals in Rhyme* (1909). *New Poems* (1909). *The Shadow Garden (a Phantasy) and Other Plays* (1910). *Poems* (1911). *So Many Ways* (1911). *The Poet, the Fool and the Faeries* (1912). *The Message of the Lilies* (1913). *Minions of the Moon; a Little Book of Song and Story* (1913). *The Republic, a Little Book of Homespun Verse* (1913). *The Poet and Nature and the Morning Road* (1914). *The Cup of Comus, Fact and Fancy* (1915).

LAWRENCE S. THOMPSON
University of Kentucky
Lexington

FRED CHAPPELL (1936–). Fred Chappell was born on May 28, 1936, in Canton, N.C. He grew up in Haywood County in the mountains of North Carolina and graduated from Canton High School in 1954. Both his parents were teachers. He left Duke University and worked for some time with his father in furniture and agriculture at Candler, N.C. He graduated from Duke in 1961. As a graduate student at Duke, Chappell was a National Defense Education Act Fellow. His thesis for his master's degree (1964) was a concordance to the English poems of Samuel Johnson. At Duke he studied writing with William Blackburn. On August 2, 1959, he married Susan Nicholls of Canton. They have a son, Heath. In 1967–1968 they spent a year in Florence on a Rockefeller grant. In 1968 he was awarded a $2,500 grant by the National Institute of Arts and Letters. Since 1964 he has taught writing and literature at the University of North Carolina at Greensboro.

By the time Chappell went to Duke he had published both fiction and verse. (His science fiction was published under a pseudonym.) He has published in major journals and in various anthologies. He seems to be at his best in his frequent explorations of his rural mountain roots. His first novel, *It Is Time, Lord* (1963), is in some ways autobiographical and has a central character who explores his past trying to gain meaning for his present and future. *The Inkling* (1965) portrays a growing boy's awareness of himself and his world as both that world and his perception of it change. (The town in the book echoes Canton.) *Dagon* (1968) takes its central character through surrealistic experiences in which myth and reality blend as both change. His first volume of poetry, *The World Between the Eyes* (1971), won for him the Roanoke-Chowan Poetry Award. His fourth novel, *The Gaudy Place* (1973), has a setting based on Asheville, is less somber than his previous novels and reveals through various points of view how the world of a teenage prostitute becomes entangled in that of a professor's son from the other side of town. *River: A Poem* (1975) uses free verse, couplets, blank verse, and terza rima, with water as a unifying image.

WORKS: *It Is Time, Lord* (1963). *The Inkling* (1965). *Dagon* (1968). *The World Between the Eyes* (1971). *The Gaudy Place* (1973). *River: A Poem* (1975). *Bloodfire* (1978).

JULIAN MASON
University of North Carolina
Charlotte

BRAINARD BARTWELL CHENEY (1900–). Born on June 3, 1900, in Fitzgerald, Ga., to Brainard Bartwell and Mattie Lucy Mood Cheney, Brainard Cheney grew up in Lumber City, Ga., on the Ocmulgee River. Cheney was educated at The Citadel (1917–1919), the University of Georgia (1924), and Vanderbilt University (1924–1925). On June 21, 1928, he married Frances Neel, who became a respected reference librarian and member of the faculty of the Peabody Library School, Nashville, Tenn. The Cheneys live outside Nashville, in Smyrna.

Cheney worked as a bank clerk, a lumber dealer, and a school principal before becoming a newspaperman. As a member of the staff of the Nashville *Banner* (1925–1942), Cheney was particularly interested in political reporting; and he was directly involved in Tennessee politics as executive secretary to U.S. Senator Tom Stewart (1942–1945) and on the public relations staff of Governor Frank Clement (1952–1958). Cheney's writing has also been varied: several uncollected short stories; two plays which have been produced, "Strangers in This World" and "I Choose to Die"; and five novels published between 1939 and 1975. For his writing

Cheney received a Guggenheim Fellowship (1941) and an award from the Georgia Writers Association for *This Is Adam* (1958).

This Is Adam and *Devil's Elbow*, set in Cheney's native south Georgia like his earlier novels, carry the Hightower family from the turn of the century to the 1930s. These are the first two volumes of a trilogy which Cheney completed with *In Pursuit of Happiness*. As interesting as Cheney's fiction is his correspondence, which was purchased by the Joint University Libraries, Vanderbilt University, in 1972. The letters, from 1932–1933 to 1970, constitute a significant body of literary criticism and biographical information written to and from correspondents such as fellow southern authors Caroline Gordon, Allen Tate, Flannery O'Connor, Robert Penn Warren, and Andrew Lytle.

WORKS: *Lightwood* (1939). *River Rogue* (1942). *This Is Adam: A Novel* (1958). *Devil's Elbow: A Novel* (1969). *In Pursuit of Happiness* (1975).

> MARTHA E. COOK
> Longwood College
> Farmville, Va.

MARY BOYKIN MILLER CHESNUT (1823–1886). The eldest daughter of Mary Boykin and Stephen Decatur Miller, a lawyer who served his state as congressman, senator, and governor, Mary Boykin Miller was born at Pleasant Hill, S.C., on March 31, 1823. She attended private schools in Camden and Charleston and proved an apt student of French, German, history, and literature. While studying in Charleston, she met, as a girl of thirteen, James Chesnut, Jr., whom she married four years later, on April 23, 1840. She and her husband, a Princeton graduate, settled in Camden, where Chesnut practiced law, and where they resided until her husband's election to the U.S. Senate took them to Washington.

Her husband's term as senator ended abruptly upon his resignation from the upper chamber to lead the secessionist movement in South Carolina. Mary Chesnut accompanied her husband to Montgomery and Richmond, where he served under Jefferson Davis, and to Columbia, where he commanded South Carolina's reserve forces. At intervals during the Civil War, she resided at her father-in-law's plantation, Mulberry. Once the war ended, the Chesnuts returned to Camden, where she died on November 22, 1886, and was buried at Knight's Hill, the family cemetery.

She began the work *A Diary From Dixie*, which was to become a primary source of information about Confederate leaders and southern society during the Civil War, on February 15, 1861, and closed her account on August 2, 1865. What began as a diary became something less and more than she intended it to be, for she sometimes entered nothing for days, weeks, or months and once filled a hiatus from August 2, 1862, to October 27, 1863, by writing memories of that interval. Following the war, she transcribed her diary, revising and polishing it as she did, and planned to publish it. She left it, unpublished at her death, in the hands of her friend Isabella Martin.

WORKS: *A Diary From Dixie*, ed. Isabella Martin and Myrta Lockett Avary, contains 150,000 of the original 400,000 words (1905). *A Diary From Dixie*, ed. Ben Ames Williams, contains approximately 300,000 words (1949).

JOHN L. IDOL, JR.
Clemson University
Clemson, S.C.

CHARLES WADDELL CHESNUTT (1858–1932). Charles W. Chesnutt was not only a pioneer in writing about problems of the very light-skinned Afro-American, but he also was an important writer of regional realism, primarily about the area around Fayetteville, N.C., where his ancestral roots were deep and where he lived during his formative years between ages eight and 25. He was born on June 20, 1858, in Cleveland, Ohio, because in 1856 his parents had left North Carolina to escape the oppressions of slavery. In 1866 the family returned to Fayetteville, where Chesnutt was to grow up and then marry and begin a family. Although Chesnutt could easily pass as white because of his light color, all his life he chose to remain a black man, a situation which in the South limited severely his possibilities for learning.

After teaching and serving as a principal in Fayetteville, in Charlotte and surrounding areas, and then in Fayetteville again, Chesnutt finally decided to seek better social and cultural circumstances. In 1883 he moved to New York, planning to put to use there his self-taught ability to take shorthand at 200 words per minute. Before long he moved to Cleveland, where his family joined him. He lived in Cleveland the rest of his life, enjoying a reputation as: court reporter; lawyer; interested citizen; member of many local civic and cultural organizations; member of Booker T. Washington's Committee of Twelve, the Open Letter Club, and the General Committee of the NAACP; member of the bibliophile Rowfant Club; and, of course, as author. He died on November 15, 1932.

Chesnutt published his first story when he was fourteen, in a small Negro weekly newspaper. In 1885 one of his stories was published by the new McClure newspaper syndicate. He was to publish a great many articles and pieces of short fiction in such magazines as *Atlantic Monthly*, *Overland Monthly*, *Outlook*, *Family Fiction*, *Puck*, and *Critic*. Both his fiction and nonfiction usually dealt with the South. One of his interests was folklore, which is reflected in his skillful dialect and especially in the plots of the stories of his first book, *The Conjure Woman*, in 1899. These are told by Uncle Julius, a well-drawn former slave who cleverly uses tales of conjuring to his own ends. A second volume of stories, *The Wife of His Youth, And Other Stories of the Color Line*, also was published in 1899. These stories are of a different type from those of *The Conjure Woman* and are of a sociological bent. Also, in 1899 Chesnutt's life of Frederick Douglass was published.

Chesnutt published three novels: *The House Behind the Cedars* (1900), dealing with the pathos of miscegenation and "passing"; *The Marrow of Tradition* (1901), based on the 1898 race riot in Wilmington, N.C.; and *The Colonel's Dream* (1905), with a plan for economic and social help for the Reconstruction South. Although Chesnutt published no more books, his social concerns continued to be invested in public involvement both locally and nationally and in further articles and short fiction. In 1928 he was awarded the Spingarn Medal by the NAACP.

WORKS: *The Conjure Woman* (1899). *Frederick Douglass* (1899). *The Wife of His Youth, And Other Stories of the Color Line* (1899). *The House Behind the Cedars* (1900). *The Marrow of Tradition* (1901). *The Colonel's Dream* (1905). *The Short Fiction of Charles W. Chesnutt* (1974).

JULIAN MASON
University of North Carolina
Charlotte

THOMAS HOLLEY CHIVERS (1809–1858). Born on October 18, 1809, on a plantation near Washington, Ga., Thomas Holley Chivers is an elusive figure, best known for his relationship with Edgar Allan Poe. Planning to be a doctor, Chivers received his M.D. from Transylvania College in 1830, but soon abandoned medicine for poetry, and published *The Path of Sorrow*, poems about his early unhappy marriage about which little is known.

In 1832 he began spending most of his time in New York and soon married Harriet Hunt of Massachusetts. Then came *Nacoochee*, with a preface stating his theory of the transcendental nature of poetry, and in 1840 he became acquainted with Poe, and their strong friendship and correspondence began. One of Poe's first statements about Chivers was that he was "one of the best and one of the worst poets in America," but when Chivers protested, Poe smoothed things over. Chivers often wrote harshly in his letters and demanded immediate reply, but Poe never took offense. To Chivers, both correspondence and conversation were arenas for debate—deadly serious, tolerating no levity.

Eonchs of Ruby, the book containing "Isadore," "To Allegra Florence in Heaven," "The Vigil of Aiden," and other poems labeled as plagiarism of Poe, came out in 1851, and long controversy began. William Gilmore Simms wrote advising Chivers to give Poe up as a model, and Chivers warned him against "the Jackasses of America . . . my sap-headed enemies who bray nonsense." Poe had read many of these poems before he died in 1849 but never mentioned plagiarism.

Chivers published during his lifetime eleven volumes of drama and poetry and wrote a biography of Poe, which was not published till 1952. *Virginalia*, containing "Apollo" and "Rosalie Lee," and *Search After Truth*, a study of mysticism and occultism, are significant volumes. In 1855 he returned from New York to his childhood home, and, writing to the last, soon moved to Decatur, Ga., where he died on December 18, 1858.

WORKS: *The Path of Sorrow* (1832). *Conrad and Eudora* (1834). *Nacoochee* (1837). *The Lost Pleiad* (1845). *Search After Truth* (1848). *Eonchs of Ruby* (1851). *Virginalia* (1853). *Memoralia* (1853). *Atlanta* (1853). *Heroes of Freedom* (1856). *The Sons of Usna* (1858). *Selected Poems of Thomas Holley Chivers*, ed. Earl Henry (1935). *Chivers' Life of Poe*, ed. Richard Beale Davis (1952). *The Correspondence of Thomas Holley Chivers*, ed. Emma Lester Chase and Lois Ferry Parks (1957), Vol. I of *Complete Works*, no other volumes yet published.

JOHN O. EIDSON
University System of Georgia
Atlanta

KATE CHOPIN (1851–1904). The daughter of an Irish commission merchant and a French-Creole mother, Kate Chopin was born Katherine O'Flaherty on February 8, 1851, in St. Louis. Educated in convents there, she was something of a rebel against the restraints of formal education and social conventions, reading books of her own choice and writing schoolgirl poems and imaginative short sketches. In 1870 she married Oscar Chopin, a banker and cotton broker of Louisiana. During an extended honeymoon tour through Europe, she met Victoria Chaflin, later Victoria Woodhull, already prominent as an outspoken advocate of women's rights, birth control, and free love, who warned the young bride against becoming trapped in the useless and degrading life of most married women.

Settling in New Orleans, the Chopins entertained elegantly but without ostentation. In 1879 they moved to a plantation in Natchitoches in northwestern Louisiana, spending summers at Grand Isle on the Gulf of Mexico. Gracious in performing necessary social duties, the young outsider from Missouri was nevertheless looked on with some disapproval by aristocratic neighbors: she dressed unconventionally, smoked cigarettes, and though a devoted wife and the mother of six children, she enjoyed escape from household duties by taking long exploratory walks through the streets of New Orleans and horseback rides through byways of back country Louisiana, meeting and talking with people of all kinds and classes.

When her husband died in 1883, Chopin attempted for more than a year to carry on the work of the plantation, but then returned to St. Louis. Partly in order to assuage her grief, she began to recreate memories of her life among the Creoles and Acadians of Louisiana in short stories, which from 1889 until 1902 appeared in such popular magazines as the *Atlantic Monthly*, *Vogue*, *Saturday Evening Post*, and *Youth's Companion*. Her first attempt at a novel, *At Fault*, is cluttered with complications of plot, but ends happily with the marriage of a man from the North to a Creole widow, owner of a large plantation. Her second novel, *The Awakening*, is not cluttered at all, but is a masterwork of compression— focusing on a woman's attempt to free herself from restraints imposed by tradition and society.

The quest for freedom is a theme that runs through much of Chopin's writing, and though the quest may end in failure, it is most often found to be praiseworthy. The theme is prefigured in a sketch she wrote in her late teens about an animal that escapes from its cage to discover a world filled with hardship and danger but in which he is free to battle for survival. In *The Awakening* Edna Pontellier throws aside restraints of marriage and motherhood to discover a life of her own. That she finally fails and that hers is ultimately a tragedy of self-deceit seem less important than that she had been awakened to possibilities of self-expression not realized. The only freedom finally available to her was the freedom of death by suicide.

Many of Chopin's short stories touch lightly on the Cajun's joyous freedom or on Creole codes of manners and morals. Among the more bold stories is "A Respectable Woman," which reveals a married woman attracted, briefly, to a man who is not her husband and to possibilities for escape from matrimonial bonds. "The

Storm," too outspoken to be accepted for publication during her lifetime, revealed emotion that may sweep people beyond convention. "Athénaise," a longer story, vies with *The Awakening* as Chopin's most successful revelation of a woman who will not accept the inevitable with patient resignation and breaks from the cage of marriage to explore, though timidly and in innocence, a short-lived independence. Her return, finally, to her husband is proof, not that she had been wrong to seek freedom, only that in the male-managed world into which she had been born, escape was impossible. After the publication of *The Awakening*, severely attacked as an immoral book, Chopin wrote little and published less. She died from a brain hemorrhage on August 30, 1904, after an active day at the St. Louis World's Fair, where her interest had been caught up again by possibilities for a more secure freedom for people of whatever class or sex. Her forthright portrayal of women in their search for emancipation shocked many of her generation, but has gained her a large following in ours, often for reasons beyond that of her artistry, which is often superb.

WORKS: *At Fault* (1890). *Bayou Folk* (1894). *A Night in Acadie* (1895). *The Awakening* (1899). *The Complete Works of Kate Chopin*, ed. Per Seyersted, 2 vols. (1969).

LEWIS LEARY
University of North Carolina
Chapel Hill

EMILY TAPSCOTT CLARK [BALCH] (1892–1953). Clever and witty from childhood, Emily Clark was redheaded and homely. She was the daughter of the rector of St. James Episcopal Church in Richmond, Va., and she attended Miss Jennie Ellett's School. Although she prepared for Bryn Mawr, she chose instead to remain in Richmond and write for newspapers.

In 1921 she was a founder of the *Reviewer*, a literary magazine. In her role as chief editor and regular contributor to the journal, Clark met many of the well-known literary figures of the day and collected written contributions from such writers as H. L. Mencken, Gertrude Stein, and Sinclair Lewis. She gave up the *Reviewer* in 1924 to marry Joseph Swift Balch, 68, an explorer, sportsman, and writer, who was a wealthy and socially prominent Philadelphian.

After her husband's death in 1927, she remained in Philadelphia, where she contributed articles and book reviews to various newspapers and where she was a patron of the arts. She left two-thirds of her estate to the University of Virginia upon her death on July 2, 1953, the income from the fund to be used for the purpose of "stimulating appreciation and creation of American literature."

Seven of her satirical portraits of thinly disguised Richmonders were collected in her first book, *Stuffed Peacocks*. In a second volume her gift at characterization was again demonstrated: *Innocence Abroad*, which tells of her experiences with the *Reviewer*, includes twelve chapters that present portraits of prominent writers who contributed to the journal.

Clark also published pieces in *Saturday Review*, *Smart Set*, *American Mercury*, and *Virginia Quarterly Review*. Gerald Langford has edited the lively letters of Clark to Joseph Hergesheimer during the *Reviewer* days in *Ingenue Among the Lions* (Austin: University of Texas Press, 1965).

WORKS: *Stuffed Peacocks* (1927). *Innocence Abroad* (1931).

DOROTHY McINNIS SCURA
University of Richmond
Richmond, Va.

JOHN HENRIK CLARKE (1915–). John Henrik Clarke was born in Union Springs, Ala., on January 1, 1915, descended, he says, "from a long line of sharecroppers." When he was four, he moved to Columbus, Ga., where he worked as a caddie at the Fort Benning Officers Club, but left the South for New York in 1933 to study creative writing, first at the League of American Writers School and Columbia University, later at New York University.

Since then Clarke has produced a number of short stories, some of which have been collected in anthologies of black writers, a book of verse (*Rebellion in Rhyme*, 1948), and a novel. Today, however, Clarke's reputation rests mainly on his work as associate editor of *Freedomways* and cofounder and fiction editor of the *Harlem Quarterly*, and his support of Harlem-based black cultural enterprises like the Harlem Writers Guild. In a 1965 conference of that organization Clarke vigorously criticized Ralph Ellison as being "in flight from his own people."

Clarke is a prolific journalist and has served notably as feature writer on African subjects for the Pittsburgh *Courier*, where his book *The Lives of Great African Chiefs* was first published serially between September, 1957, and March, 1958. Harold Cruse's *The Crisis of the Negro Intellectual*, which is almost unfailingly hostile to Clarke, credits him with being "an Africanist of long standing, one of the few devoted American Negro specialists in African history outside university cloisters."

Clarke has consolidated his influence as a leading black spokesman through serving as coordinator and special consultant for a CBS-TV and Columbia University series, "Black Heritage, a History of Afro-Americans," in addition to conducting a teacher training course, "Colloquium on Black History, Dimensions of the Black Experience," at Columbia (1969) and lecturing on African and Afro-American subjects at New York University, the New School for Social Research, Hunter College, and Cornell University.

Most recently, Clarke has edited *Malcolm X: The Man and His Times* and *William Styron's Nat Turner: Ten Black Writers Respond*, while continuing to publish heavily in black periodicals.

WORKS: Ed., *Harlem: A Community in Transition* (1964). Ed., *Harlem, U.S.A.* (1966). Ed., *American Negro Short Stories* (1966). Ed., *William Styron's Nat Turner: Ten Black Writers Respond* (1968). Ed., *Malcolm X: The Man and His Times* (1969).

> JOHN AGAR
> Valdosta State College
> Valdosta, Ga.

JOHN BELL CLAYTON (1906–1955). Born on October 28, 1906, into a Craigsville, Va., farm family which traced its ancestry back to the Pre-Revolutionary era, John Bell Clayton was the son of

John Bell and Mary McCausland Clayton. He was educated at local schools and the University of Virginia. After three years he left the university without a degree for a newspaper career, beginning with the Charlottesville (Va.) *Daily Progress* (1928–1932) and later graduating to the Washington (D.C.) *News* (1933–1936). He was editor of the Charlottesville *Daily Progress* (1938–1940). During World War II he served with Office of War Information in San Francisco, where he collaborated with Ernie Pyle. From 1944 to 1950 he was an associate editor of the San Francisco *Chronicle*. He was twice married: in 1930 to Millicent Pearsall (the marriage ended in divorce in 1945) and in 1945 to Martha Carmichael, the sister of composer Hoagie Carmichael. John Bell Clayton, Jr. was born to the first marriage.

Clayton began writing fiction after the war, and his second published story, "The White Circle," won the O. Henry Prize in 1947. His first novel, *Six Angels at My Back* (1952), met critical and commercial success, allowing the author to devote full time to his fiction. *Wait, Son, October Is Near* (1953), Clayton's second novel, demonstrates his real talent as a writer of the American South. He was at work on a fourth novel when he died suddenly on February 10, 1955. A posthumous collection, *Strangers Were There* (1957), brings together unpublished and published shorter pieces. Fine stories such as "The Silence of the Mountains," "A Warm Day in November," and "Sunday Ice Cream," along with the novel *Wait, Son, October Is Near* remain Clayton's best and most enduring works, especially impressive as the products of only one decade in the writer's life.

WORKS: *Six Angels At My Back* (1952). *Wait, Son, October Is Near* (1953). *Walk Toward The Rainbow* (1954). *Strangers Were There* (1957).

> JOSEPH R. MILLICHAP
> University of Tulsa
> Tulsa, Okla.

SAMUEL LANGHORNE CLEMENS [MARK TWAIN] (1835–1910).

Novelist, humorist, and satirist, Samuel Langhorne Clemens was born in Florida, Mo., on November 30, 1835, into a family that had joined the westward movement and shared the frontier expectations of the time. His father, John Marshall Clemens, traced his ancestry to early Virginia; his mother, Jane Lampton, was descended from settlers of Kentucky in Daniel Boone's time. The family moved in 1839 to the Mississippi River town of Hannibal, where young Sam Clemens observed and absorbed the life of the slave-holding river towns that would furnish the substance of his best works. At the age of fourteen, two years after the death of his father, he became a printer's apprentice, and during the next eight years worked as a printer in the main eastern and midwestern cities. According to his account, he was on his way to South America when he persuaded Horace Bixby to teach him steamboat piloting. (Such accounts must be read in an awareness of the creative recollection through which he produced such accounts, particularly in the autobiographical writings of his late years.)

Clemens was on the river from 1857 to 1861, accumulating the experience he later recreated in "Old Times on the Mississippi" (1877; later the first 20 chapters of *Life on the Mississippi*, 1883). After the Civil War closed commerce on the river, he joined a company training for service in the Confederate Army in a brief episode that he reported in the farcical narrative "The Private History of a Campaign that Failed" (1885). In the summer of 1861 he went to Nevada, accompanying his brother Orion, who had been appointed secretary to the territorial governor. The stagecoach journey is described in *Roughing It* (1872), and a year in mining ventures furnished characters and episodes that he later put to literary use. While a reporter for the Virginia City *Enterprise*, he first signed himself Mark Twain, a name derived from river steamboating. There and in San Francisco he learned from his associates the methods of journalistic satire and hoax and extravagance; and with the encouragement of Artemus Ward he sent east his story "Jim Smiley and His Jumping Frog." After visiting the Sandwich Islands in 1866 and lecturing afterward, he traveled to New York by way of the Isthmus of Panama and published *The Celebrated Jumping Frog of Calavares County, and Other Sketches* (1867).

In June, 1867, Clemens joined the excursion of the *Quaker City* to the Holy Land, an adventure he reported in newspaper letters and afterward shaped into *The Innocents Abroad* (1869). Married to Olivia Langdon in 1870, he served briefly as editor and part owner of the Buffalo *Express* and continued journalistic writing. In *Roughing It* he employed, with modifications, the method of fictionizing his own travels and observations that had proved successful in *The Innocents Abroad* and was to serve him well, with various adaptations, in later works. In *The Gilded Age* (1873), a novel written jointly with Charles Dudley Warner, he began drawing on the southern and autobiographical materials that would appear in *Tom Sawyer* (1876), *Life on the Mississippi* (1883), the second half of which was based on a tour of the river in 1882, *Huckleberry Finn* (1885), *Pudd'nhead Wilson* (1894), and some of his best sketches and stories.

Clemens settled at Hartford in 1872, and in that year made the first of his many excursions of varying length abroad to arrange for publication of his works, to lecture, to reduce the expenses of his household, and to gather materials for travel accounts. *A Tramp Abroad* (1880) resulted from a residence in Germany and Italy; *Following the Equator* (1897), from his lecture tour around the world. In the winter of 1884–1885 he and George W. Cable traveled four months giving joint readings from their works in cities of the United States and Canada. From his association with Cable, beginning in 1881, and from Cable's writings, he drew encouragement to deepen his questioning and his understanding of the race question, as revealed particularly in the development in this regard from *Tom Sawyer* to *Huckleberry Finn* and to *Pudd'nhead Wilson*.

Clemens had in his makeup much of the reliance on an unrealistically rosy future that his father possessed and that he gave Colonel Sellers in *The Gilded Age*. A fondness for gadgeteering such as he gave Sir Boss in *A Connecticut Yankee in King Arthur's Court* (1889) caused him to invest in a sequence of inventions; through investments in his publishing house, Charles L. Webster and Company, and the Paige typesetter he fell into bankruptcy at the age of 60. An inveterate reformer, Clemens in *The Gilded Age* attacked public and private corruption during the Grant administration; he carried on an extended affair of love and anger with the

South, with his awareness of shortcomings in the region the more
painful because the South was the nostalgic home of his boyhood;
in *A Connecticut Yankee* he satirized institutions and those responsible for them with a tone of disillusionment that remains after the
farcical action has closed. Such late works as "The Man That Corrupted Hadleyburg," "What Is Man," *The Mysterious Stranger*,
and various manuscript fragments that have been published since
his papers became open in 1936, evidence a deepening cynicism
and a darkened view of human nature and the meaning of existence.

Only one member of Clemens's family survived him, his daughter Clara. His son Langdon died in infancy; his daughter Susan in
1896; his wife in 1904; his daughter Jean in 1909. A main under-
taking of his last four years was the imaginative recollection of
his early years and the dictation of his autobiography.

WORKS: *The Celebrated Jumping Frog of Calaveras County, and Other
Sketches* (1867). *The Innocents Abroad* (1869). *Mark Twain's (Burlesque)
Autobiography* (1871). *Roughing It* (1872). *The Gilded Age* (1873–74).
Mark Twain's Sketches, New and Old (1875). *The Adventures of Tom
Sawyer* (1876). *A True Story and the Recent Carnival of Crime* (1877).
Punch, Brothers, Punch! (1878). *A Tramp Abroad* (1880). *The Prince and
the Pauper* (1882). *1601: or Conversation as It Was by the Social Fireside
in the Time of the Tudors* (1880, 1882). *The Stolen White Elephant* (1882).
Life on the Mississippi (1883). *Adventures of Huckleberry Finn* (1885).
A Connecticut Yankee in King Arthur's Court (1889). *The American
Claimant* (1892). *Merry Tales* (1892). *The £1,000,000 Bank-Note and
Other New Stories* (1893). *Tom Sawyer Abroad* (1894). *The Tragedy of
Pudd'nhead Wilson and the Comedy of Those Extraordinary Twins*
(1894). *Personal Recollections of Joan of Arc* (1896). *Tom Sawyer
Abroad, Tom Sawyer, Detective, and Other Stories* (1896). *Following the
Equator* (1897). *How to Tell a Story and Other Essays* (1897). *The Man
That Corrupted Hadleyburg and Other Stories and Essays* (1900). *A
Double Barrelled Detective Story* (1902). *My Debut as a Literary Person*
(1903). *A Dog's Tale* (1904). *Extracts From Adam's Diary* (1904). *King
Leopold's Soliloquy* (1905). *What Is Man?* (1906). *The $30,000 Bequest
and other Stories* (1906). *Eve's Diary* (1906). *Christian Science* (1907).
A Horse's Tale (1907). *Is Shakespeare Dead?* (1909). *Extract From Cap-
tain Stormfield's Visit to Heaven* (1909). *The Mysterious Stranger* (1916,

1969). *Mark Twain's Speeches*, ed. A. B. Paine (1910). *Letters, Arranged with Comments*, 2 vols.; ed. A. B. Paine (1917). *Autobiography*, 2 vols., ed. A. B. Paine (1924). *Notebook*, ed. A. B. Paine (1935). *The Autobiography of Mark Twain*, ed. Charles Neider (1959).

ARLIN TURNER
Duke University
Durham, N.C.

IRVIN SHREWSBURY COBB (1876–1944). Irvin Shrewsbury Cobb was born on June 23, 1876, in Paducah, Ky., the second of four children of Joshua and Manie Saunders Cobb. His father was a Confederate veteran. He was a keen observer of life and local characters in his native McCracken County and knew most of the local characters, prominent and otherwise. He left school to become a reporter for the Paducah *Daily News*, and after serving on the staffs of the Cincinnati *Post* and Louisville *Evening Post*, he returned to Paducah in 1901 as managing editor of the Paducah *Democrat*. In 1904 he went to New York where he got a job with the *Evening Sun*. His reportage of the Russo-Japanese Peace Conference at Portsmouth, N.H., was so spritely that he won a position on Joseph Pulitzer's *World* as staff humorist. Here he gained prominence by his column, "Through Funny Glasses," also his brilliant reporting of the trial of Harry K. Thaw in 1907. From 1911 to 1922 he was staff contributor to the *Saturday Evening Post*, thereafter for *Cosmopolitan* until 1932. After heavy losses in the crash of 1929, he moved to Hollywood and wrote scenarios and acted, with particular success as the captain in "Steamboat Round the Bend," with Will Rogers, who had previously appeared in a movie based on Judge Priest. Cobb died on March 10, 1944.

His reputation as a good-natured, original humorist whose style was replete with original witticisms, often based on traditional Kentucky character, was first established in his column "Sour Mash" for the Louisville *Evening Post*. In 1912 his *Back Home* introduced Judge Priest, already known to *Saturday Evening Post* readers, and subsequent books exploited the kindly old mint-julep-drinking Confederate veteran whose favorite avocation was helping innocents in trouble. In 1915 and 1917 the *Post* sent him to Europe, and he was among the first to expose the British propaganda about German "atrocities." His "*Speaking of Prussians—*" (1917) and *The Glory of the Coming* (1918) dealt with the war in tones of humorous exaggeration devoid of hate. His autobiography, *Exit Laughing* (1941), was received as a climactic finale in which he retained his genius as a humorist to the end.

WORKS: *Back Home: Being the Narrative of Judge Priest and His People* (1912). *Cobb's Anatomy* (1912). *Cobb's Bill-of-Fare* (1913). *The Escape of Mr. Trimm: His Plight and Other Plights* (1913). *Europe Revised* (1914). *Roughing It De Luxe* (1914). *Paths of Glory: Impressions of War Written at and near the Front* (1915). "*Speaking of Operations—*" (1915). *Fibble, D.D.* (1916). *Local Color* (1916). *Old Judge Priest* (1916). *The Lost Tribes of the Irish in the South: An Address by Irvin S. Cobb at the Annual Dinner of the American Irish Historical Society, Waldorf-Astoria Hotel, January 6, 1917* (1917). *Those Times and These* (1917). "*Speaking of Prussians—*" (1917). *The Glory of the Coming: What Mine Eyes Have Seen of the Americans in Action in This Year of Grace and Allied Endeavor* (1918). *The Thunders of Silence* (1918). *Eating in Two or Three Languages* (1919). *The Life of the Party* (1919). *From Place to Place* (1920). *One Third Off* (1921). *J. Poindexter, Colored* (1922). *Sundry Accounts* (1922). *A Laugh a Day Keeps the Doctor Away: His Favorite Stories as Told by Irvin S. Cobb* (1923). *Snake Doctor and Other Stories* (1923). *Stickfuls: Compositions of a Newspaper Minion* (1923). *Goin' on Fourteen, Being Cross-Sections out of a Year in the Life of an Average Boy* (1924). *Indiana* (1924). *Kansas* (1924). *Kentucky* (1924). *Maine* (1924). *New York* (1924). *North Carolina* (1924). *Alias Ben Alibi* (1925). "*Here Comes the Bride—*" *and So Forth* (1925). "*Oh, Well, You Know How Women Are!*" (1926). *On an Island That Cost $24,000* (1926). *Prose and Cons* (1926). *Some United States: A Series of Stops in Various Parts of the Nation with One Excursion Across the Line* (1926). *Chivalry Peak* (1927). *Ladies and Gentlemen* (1927). *All Aboard: Saga of the Romantic River* (1928). *The Abandoned Farmers: Humorous Account of a Retreat from the City to the Farm* (1929). *Irvin Cobb at His Best* (1929). *The Man's World* (1929). *Red Likker* (1929). *Both Sides of the Street* (1930). *To Be Taken Before Sailing* (1930). *Incredible Truth* (1931). *Down Yonder with Judge Priest* (1932). *Many Laughs for Many Days: Another Year's Supply (365) of His Favorite Stories as Told by Irvin S. Cobb* (1933). *Murder Day by Day* (1933). *One Way to Stop a Panic* (1933).

Faith, Hope and Charity (1934). *Irvin S. Cobb's Own Recipe Book, Written by Mr. Cobb for Frankfort Distilleries, Incorporated* (1934). *Azam: The Story of an Arabian Colt and His Friends* (1937). *Judge Priest Turns Detective* (1937). *Favorite Humorous Stories of Irvin Cobb* (1940). *Four Useful Pups* (1940). *Glory, Glory, Hallelujah!* (1941). *Exit Laughing* (1941).

LAWRENCE S. THOMPSON
University of Kentucky
Lexington

MONCURE DANIEL CONWAY (1832–1907). Spending his boyhood in Falmouth, Stafford County, Va., where he was born on March 17, 1832, Moncure Conway came from a family rooted in Jeffersonian liberalism and orthodox Methodism. After graduating from Dickinson College, Carlisle, Pa., in 1849, he served Methodist circuits in Rockville, Md. Meeting there Hicksite Quakers, he admired their serenity, their intuitive religious experience, and humanitarian concern for all human beings—especially slaves.

Early in life Conway had begun questioning the supernatural aspects of his faith, the emphasis on salvation, and the reality of damnation. Forsaking Methodism, he left the South in 1853 to enter Harvard Divinity School. He soon met Ralph Waldo Emerson, whom he had previously read. Emerson opened his library to Conway and urged him to read the oriental texts. In 1856 Conway's radical antislavery sermons cost him his pastorate of the Unitarian Church in Washington, D.C. Accepting a church in Cincinnati, Ohio, he later edited the *Dial*, twelve issues in 1860, the western organ of transcendentalism. Conway, however, was a latter-day transcendentalist—more a rationalist than a transcendentalist, more of the Theodore Parker than of the Emerson stamp.

In 1863 he lectured in England for the Union cause. The following year he assumed leadership of the ultraliberal South Place Chapel at Finsbury, London, remaining until 1884. During his years at Finsbury and later, he traveled and lectured in both America and Europe. He died in Paris on November 15, 1907.

His most important contribution to literatrure is the biography
of Thomas Paine and the editing of Paine's works. He published
biographies of Emerson, Hawthorne, and Carlyle. He wrote two
banal novels.

Life to Conway was a pilgrimage—expressed in *The Earthward
Pilgrimage* (1874) and *My Pilgrimage to the Wise Men of the East*
(1906). He was constantly a seeker and a reformer: an abolitionist,
a humanitarian, a freethinker in religious faith, and a spokesman
for world peace. His pilgrimage was to make life beautiful and the
world a better place to live.

WORKS: *Free-schools in Virginia: A Plea of Education, Virtue and Thrift,
vs. Ignorance, Vice and Property* (1850). *The Rejected Stone: or, Insurrection against Resurrection in America* (1861). *The Golden Hour* (1862).
"Benjamin Banneker: The Negro Astronomer," *Atlantic Monthly*, XI
(January, 1863), 79–84. *Testimonies Concerning Slavery* (1864). Pamphlet, *Mazzini* (1872). "Introduction" to *Passages from the Note-books
of the Late Nathaniel Hawthorne* (1869). *Republican Superstitions as
Illustrated in the Political History of America* (1872). *The Earthward
Pilgrimage* (1874). Ed., *The Sacred Anthology: A Book of Ethnical Scrip-
tures* (1874). *Christianity* (1876). *Idols and Ideals* (1877). *Demonology
and Devil-Lore*, 2 vols. (1879; rev., 1880, 1881, 1889). *A Necklace of
Stories* (1880). *Thomas Carlyle* (1881). *The Wandering Jew* (1881).
Chronicles of Christopher Columbus. A Poem in Three Cantos (1882).
Emerson at Home and Abroad (1882). *Lessons for the Day*, 2 vols. (1882;
rev., 1907). *Travels in South Kensington with Notes on Decorative Art
and Architecture* (1882). *Farewell Discourses* (1884). *Three Lyrical
Dramas. Sintram, The Friends of Syracuse, The Lady of Kynast* (1886).
Passages from Some Journals and Other Poems (1886). *Pine and Palm*
(1887). *Omitted Chapters of History Disclosed in the Life and Papers
of Edmund Randolph* (1888). "Historical and Genealogical Introduction"
to *George Washington and Mount Vernon: A Collection of Washington's
Unpublished Agricultural and Personal Letters* (1889). *George Washington's Rules of Civility* (1890). *Life of Nathaniel Hawthorne* (ca. 1890).
Prisons of Air (1891). *Barons of the Potomack and the Rappahannock*
(1892). *The Life of Thomas Paine*, 2 vols. (1892). *Centenary History of
the South Place Society* (1894). *The Writings of Thomas Paine: Collected
and Edited*, 4 vols. (1894–96). "Biographical Introduction" to John L.
Motley, *The Rise of the Dutch Republic* (1896). "Introductions" to *Works*

of Nathaniel Hawthorne (1897–99). *Solomon and Solmonic Literature* (1899). "Introduction" to James A. Froude, *The Nemesis of Faith* (1903). *Autobiography, Memories, and Experiences* (1904). *My Pilgrimage to the Wise Men of the East* (1906). *Addresses and Reprints, 1850–1907* (1909).

LOUISE CALLISON
Alderson-Broaddus College
Phillipi, W.Va.

J[AMES] GORDON COOGLER (1865–1901). The literary reputation of J. Gordon Coogler, poetaster and unintentional humorist, rests on a series of little books which he titled *Purely Original Verse*, printing and selling them himself, and a widely quoted couplet: "Alas! for the South, her books have grown fewer—She never was much given to literature."

Coogler was born near Blythewood, Richland County, S.C. His forebears, who settled in central South Carolina before the Revolution, were of German and British origin. The death of his father in 1880 left his family impoverished. Coogler was apprenticed to a newspaper in Columbia, S.C., to learn the printing trade, and worked as a journeyman printer, mostly for religious periodicals, in Columbia where eventually he had his own small shop. He appears to have dutifully supported his mother and two spinster sisters. His life seems adequately summarized by an excerpt from the heading of his obituary in the Charleston *News and Courier*: "an Excellent Young man, who Unfortunately thought he was a poet."

Coogler displayed a sign at his printing office, "Poems Written While You Wait," and in the early 1890s put together a little booklet of effusive verse which he proffered for 50 cents a copy and sent out widely for review. The obvious seriousness with which he took himself, his ludicrous rhyme and syntax, and the unoriginality of his *Purely Original Verse* made him a popular joke in the newspapers and magazines, among them *Munsey's*, the *Literary Digest*, and *Puck*. There were Coogler fan clubs. "Stanza 1, of Atlanta, Ga.," was headed by Henry W. Grady.

Beginning in the 1890s Coogler issued paper-bound collections of his verse. By 1895 he had published four such collections and a one-volume "Complete Works," in cloth. A sixth edition was published in 1901. In its obituary notice the Columbia *State* estimated that Coogler had sold more than 5,000 copies in various formats which he put together as the market required. Coogler was a canny promoter and seems, though perhaps in innocence, to have allowed himself to be exploited humorously.

WORKS: *Purely Original Verse* (*ca.* 1891, *ca.* 1893, 1894, 1895, 1897). *Purely Original Verse. Complete Works, and a number of new productions, in one volume* (1897, 1901).

HENNIG COHEN
University of Pennsylvania
Philadelphia

EBENEZER COOKE (1667?–post-1732). Ebenezer Cooke, poet laureate of early Maryland, remains one of the most shadowy colonial authors; though his life was given a certain zany plausibility in John Barth's *The Sot-Weed Factor* (1960), we are not even sure whether the poet's title was self-assumed or playfully or seriously bestowed by others. He first signed himself poet laureate in October, 1726, but there is evidence—notably a versified letter from the Virginia lawyer John Fox to Thomas Bordley, attorney general of Maryland—that the title had been familiarly applied to him before 1724.

The son of a Maryland merchant and his wife, Andrew and Anne Bowyer Cooke, Ebenezer was born in St. Michael's Parish, Bassingshawe, London, sometime in the late 1660s; his name first appears in Maryland records in 1694, when he signed a petition protesting the removal of the colonial capital from St. Mary's City to Annapolis. Apparently he returned to London shortly thereafter, possibly to oversee publication of his satire, *The Sot-weed Factor*, which came out in 1708. He remained long enough to probate his father's will on January 2, 1712, by the terms of which he and his sister Anna each received half of the family estate, Malden, at Cooke's Point, Md. By 1717 he was back in the colony and, hard pressed for cash, had sold his share of Malden. From then on through the 1720s, he attempted to support himself by becoming a lawyer, by acting as a land agent for the proprietors' receivers-general Henry and Bennett Lowe, and by turning once again to the poet's trade he seems to have relinquished between 1708 and 1726, the year of his *ELOGY* on the death of Thomas Bordley. The first belletristic writing published in the colonial South, Cooke's *ELOGY* initiated his association with the printer William Parks, who was also to publish *Sotweed Redivivus* and "The History of Bacon's Rebellion" in the next several years. But if Cooke's frequent complaints to his empty purse can be trusted, the venture with Parks seems to have brought in little money, and the impoverished poet lived just long enough after the second of these pieces to mourn the passing of two friends, Justice William Lock and Benedict Leonard Calvert, in 1732. The rest, so far as history is concerned, is silence.

Although Cooke favored Samuel Butler's hudibrastic verses and lifted more than one line from *Hudibras*, he possessed a significant comic talent of his own and was more than merely an imitator. His treatment of Maryland's drunken rabble, his creation of a snobbish foreign persona who is himself the object of the poet's satire, and his attempt to maintain the point of view of a gentleman even while appreciating the vitality of backwoods language make him an important innovator in, if not indeed the founder of, the southern comic tradition.

WORKS: *The Sot-weed Factor* (1708). *An ELOGY on the Death of Thomas Bordley* (1726). "An Elegy on the Death of the Honourable Nicholas Lowe" (1728). *Sotweed Redivivus* (1730). "The Sot-Weed Factor" (3rd. ed.?), and "The History of Colonel Nathaniel Bacon's Rebellion in Virginia," in *The Maryland Muse* (1731). "An Elegy on the Death of the Honourable William Lock" (1732). "A Poem in Memory of the Hon[ble] Benedict Leonard Calvert" (1732).

ROBERT D. ARNER
University of Cincinnati
Cincinnati, Ohio

JOHN ESTEN COOKE (1830–1886). John Esten Cooke, novelist and historian of Virginia, occupies a unique position among southern writers as the only significant figure whose literary career spanned the last decade of the Old South, the Civil War and Reconstruction era, and the early years of the New South. One of thirteen children of Maria Pendleton (1792–1850) and John Rogers Cooke (1788–1854), he was born on November 3, 1830, in Winchester, Va. Following his childhood years in the Upper Valley, while his oldest brother, Philip Pendleton (1816–1850) launched his promising literary career, financial reverses compelled his father to relocate his legal practice in Richmond. From 1840 until the Civil War, Cooke lived in the capital city, where he attended the Richmond Academy until he was seventeen. Ambitious, though financially unable, to attend the University of Virginia, he read law with his father and was admitted to practice in 1851. With the publication of four volumes in 1854 his legal career was permanently eclipsed by his literary preoccupation.

In concentrating on Virginia, past and present, by 1861 Cooke was generally recognized as the literary apostle of the Old Dominion. *The Virginia Comedians* (2 vols., 1854) and the sequel, *Henry St. John* (1859), which are his best historical novels, focus upon the class conflict inherent in Virginia's sectional tensions on the eve of the Revolution, with "the aristocracy whom I don't like, getting the worst of it," Cooke insisted.

During the Civil War, as the most notable novelist to serve in either army, Cooke was engaged in every campaign of importance in the Virginia theater of the war, serving the greater part of his time as ordnance officer on the staff of his kinsman, General J. E. B. Stuart. In 1863 he published his first biography of "Stonewall" Jackson, while his numerous accounts of the battlefield and camp life, printed in southern newspapers (*Outlines from the Outpost* [1961]), became the basis of his Confederate classic, *Wearing of the Gray* (1867). Blending history with romance, *Surry of Eagles'-Nest* (1866) and its sequel, *Mohun* (1869), are the fictional counterparts of his biographies of Jackson (1866) and Lee (1871).

From his marriage to Mary Frances Page of Saratoga in 1867 until his death from typhoid fever on September 27, 1886, Cooke lived at The Briars near Millwood in his beloved Upper Valley.

Supplementing his substantial literary income, he endeavored to practice his gospel of diversified farming which he had espoused as the economic salvation of the New South in his Reconstruction novel, *The Heir of Gaymount* (1870).

After 1871 Cooke resumed his earlier absorption with the cavalier culture of the Old Dominion. Reversing his initial position, to portray the aristocracy in heroic stature, Cooke became the transitional figure between the antebellum and postwar plantation romance. Later, struggling to keep abreast with modern trends, he attempted to adapt his romantic style to contemporary realism; his more successful efforts resulted in the blending of romance and realism in local color stories, and *The Virginia Bohemians* (1880). As a historian, Cooke's most enduring work is *Virginia* (1883), for years a popular text in the public schools of the Old Dominion.

WORKS: *Leather Stocking and Silk* (1854). *The Virginia Comedians*, 2 vols. (1854); Vol. I reissued as *Beatrice Hallam* (1893); Vol. II as *Captain Ralph* (1893). *The Youth of Jefferson* (1854). *Ellie* (1855). *The Last of the Foresters* (1856). *Henry St. John, Gentleman* (1859); reissued as *Bonnybell Vane*, also as *Miss Bonnybell* (1892). *The Life of Stonewall Jackson* (1863). *Stonewall Jackson: A Military Biography* (1866). *Surry of Eagles'-Nest* (1866). *Wearing of the Gray* (1867). *Fairfax* (1868). *Hilt to Hilt* (1869). *Mohun* (1869). *Hammer and Rapier* (1870). *The Heir of Gaymount* (1870). *A Life of Gen. Robert E. Lee* (1871). *Out of the Foam* (1872). *Dr. Vandyke* (1872). *Her Majesty the Queen* (1873). *Pretty Miss Gaston and other stories* (1874). *Justin Harley* (1875). *Canolles* (1877). *Professor Pressensee* (1878). *Mr. Grantley's Idea* (1879). *Stories of the Old Dominion* (1879). *The Virginia Bohemians* (1880). *Franchett* (1883). *Virginia: A History of the People* (1883). *My Lady Pokahontas* (1885). *The Maurice Mystery* (1885), reissued as *Colonel Ross of Piedmont* (1893). *Outlines From the Outpost* (1961).

MARY JO BRATTON
East Carolina University
Greenville, N.C.

PHILIP PENDLETON COOKE (1816–1850). Philip Pendleton Cooke was the eldest son of John Rogers and Maria Pendleton

Cooke and the brother of John Esten Cooke, the novelist. He was born in Martinsburg, Va. (now. W.Va.) on October 26, 1816. In 1828 the family moved to Winchester and finally settled on an estate called Glengary. After graduating from Princeton in 1834, Cooke returned to this home. For the next three years he studied law, enjoyed landed gentry living, and wrote some poetry and critical essays which were published in the *Southern Literary Messenger*. During this time he unsuccessfully courted his cousin, Mary Evalina Dandridge, a situation that provided the basis for his most famous poem, "Florence Vane." In 1837 he married Willie Anne Burwell; they were to have five children before his untimely death. By age 21 he had been admitted to the bar and had acquired local fame for both his writing and his hunting skills.

In the financial panic of 1837, Cooke's father lost the family fortune, and Cooke became obligated for some of his father's debts. The situation worsened in 1839 when Glengary burned. Cooke established his law practice in Martinsburg, but success came slowly. He frequently had to borrow money from his father who had reestablished his own practice in Richmond. In 1841 Cooke made a trip to Palmyra, Mo., but plans to emigrate there were abandoned as prospects improved in Virginia. The biggest improvement occurred in 1845 when part of his wife's inheritance (1,000 acres and a new house twelve miles from Winchester) finally came into their possession. This estate was called Vineyard, and Willie Anne lived there until her death in 1899. Cooke had a resurgence of literary effort after the move to Vineyard, but he died on January 20, after contracting pneumonia while on a hunting trip.

Cooke's writing career began with poetry. While at Princeton, three of his poems, including "Song of the Sioux Lovers," were published in the *Knickerbocker Magazine*. Many of his poems first appeared in the *Southern Literary Messenger* which, in 1835, published his essay on English poetry and his first widely popular poem, "Young Rosalie Lee." However, the study of law and the financial reverses made increasing demands on Cooke's time, and he began restricting both of his favorite activities, hunting and poetry. In 1839 Cooke received a request from Edgar Allan Poe to contribute to Burton's *Gentleman's Magazine*. Cooke sent him "Florence Vane," which was published in the spring of 1840. This sentimental poem brought Cooke fame. A more skillful poem, "Life in the Autumn Woods," appeared in the *Southern Literary Messenger* in 1843. Shortly after Cooke settled at Vineyard, he renewed his interest in poetry. Poe highly praised "Florence Vane" in a New York lecture and reprinted it in the *Broadway Journal*. Inclusion in Rufus Griswold's new edition of *Poets and Poetry of America* and encouragement by his cousin, John Pendleton Kennedy, prompted Cooke to bring out his only book, *Froissart Ballads and Other Poems* (1847). It received good reviews but failed commercially.

Prose replaced poetry in the last development of Cooke's brief career. The *Southern Literary Messenger* published all of his later critical essays (including "Living Novelists" in 1847) and the most important of his longer tales. The first of these was *John Carper, the Hunter of Lost River* (1848), a realistic presentation of Indians and Mountaineers in western Virginia during the Revolutionary War. *The Two Country Houses. The Gregories of Hackwood*, and *The Crime of Andrew Blair* are fictional, contemporary accounts of the aristocracy of the Shenandoah. Another work, in progress at the time of his death, was a historical romance, *The Chevalier Merlin*.

WORKS: *Froissart Ballads and Other Poems* (1847).

V. L. THACKER
U.S. Air Force Academy
Colorado Springs, Colo.

JOHN WILLIAM CORRINGTON (1932–). Born on October 28, in Memphis, Tenn., son of John and Viva Shelley Corrington, John William Corrington was raised in Shreveport, La., graduating from Centenary College there in 1956. He received an M.A. from Rice University in 1960, a Ph.D. from the University of Sussex in 1964, and a J.D. from Tulane Law School in 1976. After two years in Europe as a correspondent Corrington taught in the English departments of Louisiana State University (1960–1966) and

Loyola University of the South (1966–1973), where he was professor and chairman, and he served as visiting professor at the University of California, Berkeley in 1968. Recently he entered law practice in New Orleans. He married Joyce E. Hooper, a chemistry professor, in 1959; they have four children.

His publications include poetry, fiction, screenplays, and literary criticism. He edited (with Miller Williams) the two-volume anthology, *Southern Writing In The Sixties* (1966); he also has contributed literary and philosophical essays to many journals, anthologies, and symposia.

His first book of poetry, *Where We Are* (1962), won the Charioteer Poetry Prize. His short stories, most of which concern traditional southern subjects, have been published in leading periodicals, and several were collected in *The Lonesome Traveller* (1968). His stories won a National Endowment for the Arts Award for 1973 and for 1976, and the O. Henry Award for 1976. He has published three novels. His several screenplays were written in collaboration with his wife, Joyce Hooper Corrington.

WORKS: *Where We Are* (1962). *The Anatomy of Love* (1964). *And Wait For Night* (1964). *Mr. Clean and Other Poems* (1964). *Lines to the South and Other Poems* (1965). *The Upper Hand* (1966). Ed., *Southern Writing in the Sixties*, with Miller Williams, fiction (1966), poetry (1967). *The Lonesome Traveller and Other Stories* (1968). *The Bombardier* (1970).

JOSEPH R. MILLICHAP
University of Tulsa
Tulsa, Okla.

JOHN COTTON OF QUEEN'S CREEK, VA. (1643?–post-1680).
John Cotton's modest literary reputation rests upon a single work, a fragmentary narrative of Nathaniel Bacon's Rebellion discovered in the Burwell Manuscripts and first published in the *Massachusetts Historical Society Collections* in 1814 and again in 1866. The second son of William Cotton, minister of Hungars Parish, Va., Cotton was probably born early in 1643 and may have lived on well into the eighteenth century. A planter of modest com-

munity standing, he married Ann (or Hannah) Harrison (or Bernard) and continued to reside in Hungars Parish, where his daughter Mary (October 21, 1660) and son John (December 8, 1661) were born, until 1665 or so; on December 31, 1666, he purchased a tract of land lying between Queen's and Townsend (later Yorktown) Creeks, York County. This new plantation adjoined Ringfield, the estate of the elder Colonel Nathaniel Bacon, and so Cotton had ample opportunity to observe and may even have participated in the insurrection that Colonel Bacon's nephew and namesake headquartered at Ringfield ten years later. Himself a nephew of the Maryland rebel William Stone, Cotton appears from some remarks in his narrative to have aligned himself with Governor Sir William Berkeley's cause but may also have sympathized with some of the aims of the rebellious Bacon. He was not, however, a politically active member of the merchant-planter class, and after this one brush with history he virtually disappears from colonial records.

By far the most vivid of all contemporary accounts of the rebellion, Cotton's narrative is marked by a sense of humor and spiced with comic metaphors; it features two contrapuntal verses, "Bacons Epitaph, made by his Man" and "Upon the Death of G. B.," which have been called the best poems to come out of seventeenth-century Virginia. Their balanced images perhaps reflect Cotton's own ambivalent feelings about the governor and the rebel.

WORKS: "A History of Bacon's and Ingram's Rebellions" (1676). "To his Wife A. C. at Q. Creek" (1676).

ROBERT D. ARNER
University of Cincinnati
Cincinnati, Ohio

ALFRED LELAND CRABB (1884–). The son of James Wade and Annie Arbuckle Crabb, Alfred Leland Crabb, was born in Warren County, Ky., near Bowling Green, on January 22, 1884. He taught in the public schools from 1901 until he joined the faculty of Western Kentucky State College in 1916. Before receiving his degree from George Peabody College for Teachers in that year, he had attended Bethel College, Southern Normal School, and Western Kentucky State Normal School. He stayed at Western Kentucky until 1927 when he became professor of education at Peabody, teaching there until 1950 when he became professor emeritus. He received his M.A. from Columbia University and his Ph.D. from Peabody. He married Bertha Gardner; they have one son.

Crabb's writing reflects his vocation and his avocation of history and biography. Nine of the novels draw heavily upon the Civil War, the years leading to the war, and the Reconstruction period. Of these, six are set in his adopted home, Nashville; two are laid in nearby Chattanooga; another depicts a family's life in Bowling Green, Ky. The remaining fictional works are biographical novels of the area's historical and political figures, one of Andrew Jackson and the other of Henry Clay. All are firmly based in the history of his region and are characterized by such local color elements as dialect and custom.

After these works of fiction, Crabb turned to history with two accounts of Nashville followed by one of the Nashville Baptist Church. His latest work is a fictional biography, intended primarily for children, of the young Andrew Jackson.

WORKS: *Standard Speller*, with A. C. Fergurson and August Dvorak (1931–34). *The Genealogy of George Peabody College for Teachers*, with Altstetter and Newton (1935). *America Yesterday and Today*, with L. E. Broaddus and J. P. Cornette (1937). *Modern English Handbook with Exercises* (1941). *Dinner at Belmont* (1942). *Supper at the Maxwell House* (1943). *Breakfast at the Hermitage* (1945). *Lodging at the Saint Cloud* (1946). *Home to the Hermitage* (1948). *A Mockingbird Sang at Chickamauga* (1949). *Reunion at Chattanooga* (1950). *Home to Tennessee* (1952). *Home to Kentucky* (1953). *Peace at Bowling Green* (1955). *Journey to Nashville* (1957). *Nashville: Personality of a City* (1960). *Andrew Jackson's Nashville* (1966). *Acorns to Oaks*, with J. Tresch, H. D. Gregory, J. D. Freeman, and Guard Green (1972?). *A Cannon for General Marion* (1975).

ARTHUR H. BLAIR
The Citadel
Charleston, S.C.

CHARLES EGBERT CRADDOCK. See Mary Noailles Murfree.

THOMAS CRADOCK (1718–1770). Son of a Staffordshire tailor, Thomas Cradock was raised at the Trentham estate of the first Earl Gower, from whom his father leased small parcels of land. Apparently with Lord Gower's encouragement, he matriculated at Magdalen Hall, Oxford, in 1737, but never took the examinations for a degree. Ordained to the diaconate in 1741 and to the priesthood in 1743, Cradock secured license to preach in Maryland in 1744. The following year he became the first rector of the newly created St. Thomas Parish in western Baltimore County where he remained until his death. At his home, Trentham, he established a school in 1747 where he taught the sons of the local gentry.

During his lifetime he published only two religious poems; a few hymns were printed in 1854. More important were his two metrical versions of the psalms printed in London and Annapolis. An honorary member of the Tuesday Club of Annapolis, he composed at least one bawdy poem for that group. The remainder of his poetry and approximately 100 manuscript sermons survive in Maryland Historical Society collections. Of the verse, most significant are the nine satirical "Maryland Eclogues in Imitation of Virgil's," the apologetical "Crurulia, Part the 2nd" and a 76-page fragment of a neoclassical play on the trial and death of Socrates. He published only two sermons early in his pastorate and his most famous homily on the immorality of many of his fellow Anglican clergymen was not printed until 1970. Richard Beale Davis described this latter effort, preached before the Maryland General Assembly in 1753, as "perhaps the most courageous sermon of colonial America." A stroke about 1763 necessitated an amanuensis until his death and reduced his literary efforts. Cradock's career demonstrates the extent to which both the neoclassical tradition and the homiletic style of Archbishop John Tillotson permeated the Chesapeake frontier.

WORKS: *Two Sermons, with a Preface* . . . . (1747). *A Poetical Translation of the Psalms* . . . . (1754). *A New Version of the Psalms* . . . . (1756). "A Poem Sacred to the Memory . . . ," *Maryland Gazette* (Annapolis), March 15, 1753. "To Thyrsis," *American Magazine*, I (1757–58), 605–607. Ethan Allen, ". . . Thomas Cradock," *American Church Review*, VII (July, 1854), 308–11. "Sermon on the Governance of Maryland's Established Church," *William and Mary Quarterly*, 3rd ser., XXVII (1970), 629–53.

DAVID CURTIS SKAGGS
Bowling Green State University
Bowling Green, Ohio

WILLIAM CRAFTS (1787–1826). The son of a Boston merchant who settled in Charleston, S.C., and married a native of Beaufort, S.C., William Crafts, a handsome, popular man with a reputation for wit, was a minor poet and essayist. He was born in Charleston, on January 24, 1787. As a boy he studied under tutors, and entered Harvard as a sophomore, being graduated in 1805. For three years he read law in Charleston but seemingly learned little. He returned to Harvard in 1807 to work for a master's degree, and established a name for himself, particularly for a famous lecture he delivered in "execrable Latin." Admitted to the South Carolina bar in 1809, his ignorance of the law forced him into criminal practice, where his ability to dazzle juries proved useful. He entered politics as a Federalist in 1810, being elected to the state lower house. He was defeated for reelection, but was elected again two years later. The last six years of his life he was a member of the South Carolina senate.

A popular occasional speaker, Crafts was the author of numerous essays that faintly echoed Addison in the Charleston *Courier*. He wrote occasional verse, imitative of Pope, and later of Moore. In 1810 he published *The Raciad and Other Occasional Poems*; the title poem, along with his Anacreontics, is his best work, an amusing account of Charlestonians at Race Day. *The Sea Serpeant* was published in 1819, and *Sullivan's Island, The Raciad, and Other Poems* in 1820. Always torn between New England, which he treasured, and the South, which he loved, he bound the two together by marriage to a Boston cousin in 1823. He died in Lebanon Springs, N.Y., on September 23, 1826, and was buried in Boston.

A posthumous collection of his work appeared in 1828. He is well summed up by Vernon L. Parrington as "a graceful imitator of doubtful models."

WORKS: *The Raciad and Other Occasional Poems* (1810). *The Sea Serpeant; or Gloucester Hoax, a Dramatic Jeu d'Esprit in Three Sets* (1819). *Sullivan's Island, The Raciad, and Other Poems* (1820). *A Selection, in Prose and Poetry, from the Miscellaneous Writings of the Late William Crafts*, ed. with a Memoir, by Samuel Gilman (1828).

C. HUGH HOLMAN
University of North Carolina
Chapel Hill

PORTE CRAYON. See David Hunter Strother.

HUBERT CREEKMORE (1907–1966). Born on January 16, 1907, in Water Valley, Miss., Hubert Creekmore began writing poems and stories while attending the local schools. Graduating from the University of Mississippi in 1927, he then studied drama at the University of Colorado and playwriting at Yale. His first real publication came in 1934 with poems in *Poetry* and fiction in *Story*. In 1940 he received a master's degree in American literature from Columbia and published his first volume of poetry, *Personal Sun*.

Creekmore served in the Navy from 1942 to 1945. His second collection of verse, *"The Stone Ants,"* was published in 1943, while he was stationed in the Pacific. During a sojourn in New Caledonia, he composed most of the poems which were published in 1946 in *The Long Reprieve*. Following World War II, he worked at various times as an editor, free-lance writer, teacher, lecturer, and translator.

Creekmore's first published novel, *The Fingers of Night*, appeared in 1946. Set against a background of Mississippi hill farming, it deals with an ignorant, inexperienced girl's emergence from a life ruled by the religious fanaticism of her father. Creekmore published *Formula*, his fourth collection of poetry, in 1947. The following year saw the appearance of his second novel, *The Welcome*. Set in a small Mississippi town, this work examines the necessity of marriage, its usefulness, and its possibilities for success in the light of modern neurotic life, the modern woman, and divorce.

Creekmore's last novel, *The Chain in the Heart*, which appeared in 1953, is a three-generation chronicle of a southern black family's attempts to survive and advance in a white-dominated society. A southern expatriate who understood well the region and the people he portrayed in his fiction, Hubert Creekmore died in New York on May 23, 1966.

WORKS: *Personal Sun* (1940). *"The Stone Ants"* (1943). *The Long Reprieve* (1946). *The Fingers of Night* (1946). *Formula* (1947). *The Welcome* (1948). Trans., *No Harm to Lovers* (1950). Ed., *A Little Treasury of World Poetry* (1952). *The Chain in the Heart* (1953). Ed. and trans., *Lyrics of the Middle Ages* (1959). Ed. and trans., *Satires of Decimus Junius Juvenalis* (1963). *Daffodils Are Dangerous* (1966).

L. MOODY SIMMS, JR.
Illinois State University
Normal

DAVID CROCKETT (1786–1836). David Crockett was born on August 17, 1786, near the present Rogersville, Hawkins County, Tenn., the son of a tavern operator. He received very little formal education. He enjoyed frontier life but failed at almost all other endeavors: farming, managing a gristmill, a gunpowder manufactory, and a distillery. He achieved some success in the military, fighting under Jackson in the Creek Wars of 1813, and in politics, losing after he opposed Jackson on land policies. Crockett served in the Tennessee legislature and for two terms as United States Congressman. He went westward, twice moving to the frontier in Tennessee and finally to Texas, where, disillusioned after his losses in politics, he was killed at the Alamo, on March 6, 1836.

It was through politics that Crockett's writing abilities were discovered. His backwoods ways were celebrated and recorded in newspapers, almanacs, a prize play, and an unauthorized biography. Because the latter work had done him "much injustice" and had damaged him politically, Crockett wrote his autobiography

(1834). Immensely popular, it was the only work of several attributed to Crockett of which he had a major part as author.

In reality a sober, genteel person, Crockett in his autobiography feigned crudeness as an uncouth backwoodsman. He did not set the record straight as he claimed he would do, but he revealed his greatest gift—telling humorous anecdotes. The autobiography should be read not so much as biography but as fiction by an oral storyteller. Characterized by loose grammar, "natural" spelling and unconventional punctuation, the biography is alive with earthy metaphors, forceful language, and a strong sense of humor. Had a tape recorder been available, it is doubtful that we would have a more authentic transcript of the dialect of the frontier. Among the earliest writings of the southwest humorists, Crockett's prose employed a colloquial style that reached its peak in the works of Mark Twain.

WORKS: *A Narrative of the Life of David Crockett, of the State of Tennessee*, with Thomas Chilton (1834).

JOE ROSS
University of Alabama
Birmingham

GEORGE WASHINGTON PARKE CUSTIS (1781–1857). George Washington Parke Custis was born on April 30, 1781, at Mt. Airy, Md., the son of John Parke Custis, who was the stepson of George Washington. After his father's death, Custis came under the charge of George and Martha Washington at Mount Vernon. He was educated at Princeton and Annapolis. Following Mrs. Washington's death, he built the residence now known as the Custis-Lee Mansion (Arlington), where he died October 10, 1857. After marrying Mary Lee Fitzhugh in 1804, he managed his large estate. In the War of 1812 he served as a volunteer. He wrote prose, verse, and was a speaker of ability, but his main efforts involved drama.

Custis' first play was *The Indian Prophecy* (1827), which presents Washington's exploration of western Virginia. Based on an actual incident, an Indian chief predicts that he will be the founder of a great empire. The next play, *Pocahontas, or The Settlers of Virginia* (1830), is his most notable work and helped start the vogue of Pocahontas plays. Custis' popularity reached its climax with a gala performance of this play at the National Theatre of Washington in 1836. Other plays performed but not published include *The Railroad* (1830), *North Point or Baltimore Defended* (1833), and *The Eighth of January* (1834), celebrating Jackson's victory at New Orleans. Six plays by Custis were produced. Besides plays Custis published "Conversations with Lafayette" in the Alexandria *Gazette* and starting in 1826 published his recollections of Washington's private life in the *United States Gazette*; this work was later published by his daughter along with a memoir of Custis in 1860. Succeeding where previous Virginia dramatists had failed, Custis achieved production of a large number of plays because of close contacts with large northern cities, his name, and actable plays. His popular dreams stimulated American nationalism during this period.

WORKS: *The Indian Prophecy: A National Drama in Two Acts* (1827). *Pocahontas, or The Settlers of Virginia* (1830).

CHARLES S. WATSON
University of Alabama
Tuscaloosa

JAMES McBRIDE DABBS (1896–1970). The parents of James McBride Dabbs came from, and represented, two distinct types of South Carolina families—the plantation through his mother, Maude McBride, and the small farmer through his father, Eugene Whitefield Dabbs. Their son James, born on May 8, 1896, in Mayesville, was one day to study the positions held by these two competing and cooperating forces in relation to the churches, soil, politics, industry, education, history, laws, and black citizens of the South.

Dabbs attended public schools near the family plantation, Rip Raps, before enrolling at the University of South Carolina, from which he received an A.B. in 1916. He pursued his graduate studies at Clark University, M.A., 1917, and Columbia University, 1924–1925, 1929–1930. Before beginning a career in teaching, he served in the United States Army (1917–1919).

His teaching career started at the University of South Carolina as an instructor in English (1921–1924) and ended at Coker College in Hartsville, S.C., in 1942. From 1925 until 1937 he was head of Coker's English department. He stopped teaching to become a farmer and free-lance writer, carrying out both aims at the family plantation, now his to manage. His concern for personal, community, and regional relations led him to assume many civic and religious posts, among them the South Carolina Council on Human Relations, the Southern Regional Council, of which he was president (1957–1963), Penn Community Services, and the Fellowship of Southern Churchmen.

He was twice married, first to Jessie Armstrong on May 11, 1918, and following her death to Edith Mitchell on June 11, 1935.

His writings provide a definition of southern character, giving explanations of the forces shaping that character. Numbering more than 100, his essays appeared in many American journals and in such collections as *The Lasting South*, *This Is the South*, and *We Dissent*.

Dabbs died on May 30, 1970, in Mayesville.

WORKS: *Pee Dee Panorama*, with Carl Julien (1951). *The Southern Heritage* (1958). *The Road Home* (1960). *Who Speaks for the South?* (1964). *Civil Rights in Recent Southern Fiction* (1969). *Haunted by God* (1972).

JOHN L. IDOL, JR.
Clemson University
Clemson, S.C.

RICHARD DABNEY (1787–1825). One of twelve children born to Samuel and Jane Meriwether Dabney, Richard Dabney was reared on a plantation in Louisa County, Va. The family was distinguished (the explorer Meriwether Lewis was Richard's first cousin) but not wealthy, and Dabney was sent to a classical school in Richmond rather than to college. In school he apparently excelled in Latin and Greek, and before he was 20 he was teaching these languages in a Richmond academy.

Dabney sustained injuries when the Richmond Theatre burned in 1811, and he became addicted to the opium that had been prescribed for his pain. He was already fond of alcohol, and the use of both drugs affected his health and productivity. In 1812 at Richmond he published *Poems, Original and Translated*, but this work elicited little interest, and he soon moved to Philadelphia where he worked for the publisher Mathew Carey. In 1815 Carey published a revised and enlarged edition of Dabney's *Poems*, but this volume too went largely unnoticed.

Returning to Louisa County in 1815, Dabney continued his reading, participated in the social life of the community, and for a while taught at a country school. His reputation locally as a classical scholar may have prompted a reviewer to attribute *Rhododaphne*, an admired classical poem by Thomas Love Peacock, to Dabney. Though he denied writing it, the rumors persisted. His last years were not creatively productive, and he died on November 25, 1825, unmarried at 38, and after considerable mental and physical suffering.

Dabney's verse is generally regarded as didactic and derivative, less effective than his translations. About half of *Poems* consists of translations of minor Greek, Latin, and Italian poets. The rest consists of his own poems, accompanied in the 1815 revision by "Preliminary Remarks," which reveals Dabney's interest in poetic theory. Although some readers have believed that elements in his work anticipate Poe and Emerson, Dabney must be regarded as a poet and translator of modest ability who did not realize his early promise.

WORKS: *Poems, Original and Translated* (1812, 1815).

WILLIAM OSBORNE
Memphis State University
Memphis, Tenn.

THOMAS DALE (1700–1750). Little is known of the circumstances of the birth or death of Thomas Dale—"Doctor of Physic," man of letters, assistant judge—other than that he was the son of an English apothecary. Dale graduated at Leyden in 1723, published translations of medical works in London between 1729–1732, arrived in Charleston, S.C., perhaps as early as 1725 but at least by the time of his first marriage, where he lived until his death, sometime near the end of 1750. He married (1) Mary Brewton on March 28, 1733, (2) Anne Smith on November 26, 1738, and (3) Hannah Simons on June 30, 1743. Thomas Simons Dale, son of the third marriage, received his medical degree at Edinburgh in 1775.

Dale wrote an Epilogue for the first production in Charleston (January, 1736) of George Farquhar's *The Recruiting Officer* to be spoken by Silvia "in Man's Cloaths," too ribald for a Charleston lady to print in full in 1924. A man of choleric temper, Dale accused James Kilpatrick of negligence in his inoculation and care of a child, which accusation stimulated an exchange of pamphlets. In the *Puff* Dale tried to have the last word, which pamphlet he considered would be "a proper reply/ to Skimmington's last crudities/ Mad with revenge, he gathered all/ his wind,/ And bounc'd like Fifty Bladders/ from behind." Kilpatrick, not deflated, went on to a notable career in England as the writer James Kirkpatrick who published defenses of inoculation, poems, and translations of medical treatises.

Dale was appointed one of the justices of the court of common pleas on March 17, 1746. He represented the parish of St. Peter in the commons house of assembly (1749–1750). In his will he ordered "my Study of Books"—the inventory of his estate recorded 2,273 items in ten categories valued at £810 in South Carolina currency—to be sold at a private sale and that his "Collection of Dryed Plants as well as other Natural Rarities . . . be packed up in a box and be Sent to my good friend Dr. John Frederick Gronovius at Leyden in Holland."

WORKS: *Dissertatio medico-botanica inauguralis de pareira brava et serapia off., etc.* (1723). Trans., John Freind, *Emmenologia* (1729). Trans., John Freind, *Nine Commentaries upon Fevers* (1730). Trans., H. F. Le Dran, *Methods of Extracting the Stone* (1731). Trans., N. Regnault, *Philosophical Conversations*, 2 vols. (1731). Trans., Jodocus Lommius, *A Treatise of Continual Fevers* (1732). Epilogue, "The Recruiting Officer," *Gentleman's Magazine*, VI (1736), 288. *An Epistle to Alexander Pope, Esq.; from South Carolina* (1737). *The Case of Miss Mary Roche, more fairly related, &C* (1738). *The Puff* (1739).

GEORGE C. ROGERS, JR.
University of South Carolina
Columbia

DANSKE DANDRIDGE (1854–1913). At least four different published dates designate the birth of Caroline Lawrence Bedinger Dandridge, who was called by her parents "Danske," or "little Dane"; however, family records conclusively state 1854. She was born in Copenhagen, Denmark, where her father, Henry Bedinger, was serving as the first American minister to that country. After his death in 1858, her mother bought an estate near Shepherdstown, Va. (now W.Va.), which Danske named Rose Brake. Following the Civil War, and the subsequent death of her mother, Danske lived for a time with her grandparents in Flushing, Long Island, and attended Miss Williams' Young Ladies School there.

In 1877 she married Adam Stephen Dandridge, Jr. Beginning in 1880 the Dandridges and their three children enjoyed a residence at Rose Brake that extended to almost three decades. Here Danske developed an intense interest in horticulture by cultivating the garden started by her mother; it contained more than 100 varieties of roses and 60 of spirea. This activity formed the basis of her numerous articles on gardening that appeared both in American publications (*e.g.*, *Forest and Stream*, *Garden and Forest* and *Gardening*) and English (*e.g.*, *The Garden* and *Flora and Silva*).

Her horticultural activities likewise inspired numerous poems. Many of the selections in *Joy and Other Poems* (1888), most of which had appeared in such periodicals as the *Independent*, *Harper's* and *Century*, reflect a love of nature and contain much natural imagery. The same can be said for *Rose Brake* (1890). It is, however, for *Joy* that she is best remembered. This collection enjoyed two editions and has been generally praised by her critics.

After the death of her only son (a student at the University of Virginia), Danske Dandridge stopped writing poetry and concentrated on history. Among her works in this area are *George Michael Bedinger: A Kentucky Pioneer* (1909) and *Historic Shepherdstown* (1910). Having been ill during most of her married life, and saddened in her later years by the deaths of two of her children and her husband's business problems, she committed suicide in 1913. Because of her dozens of articles on the flora of West Virginia and her poetry, she continues to attract the attention of readers interested both in botany and literature.

WORKS: *Joy and Other Poems* (1888; 2nd enl. ed., 1900). *Rose Brake* (1890). *George Michael Bedinger: A Kentucky Pioneer* (1909). *Historic Shepherdstown* (1910). *American Prisoners of the Revolution* (1911).

WELFORD DUNAWAY TAYLOR
University of Richmond
Richmond, Va.

OLIVE TILFORD DARGAN (1869–1968). Olive Tilford Dargan was born on January 11, 1869, in Grayson County, Ky., of schoolteaching parents. When she was ten, the family moved to Missouri, and at thirteen she was assisting her mother and father in the classroom. From Peabody College in Tennessee she earned a degree in two years, and thereafter taught in Arkansas, Texas, and Nova Scotia. During 1893–1894 she studied at Radcliffe and there met a Harvard senior, Pegram Dargan of South Carolina, whom she married in 1898. From New York City, the couple moved in 1906 to a mountain farm near Almond in Swain County, N.C., where Mrs. Dargan was a secretary in the office of the Boston Rubber Company. Her sympathies for the underprivileged, aroused by her observations of industry's indifference to underpaid workers, became centered on her mountain neighbors. After several volumes of closet dramas, mostly in blank verse on a variety of subjects, came the poetry of *Pathflower* and *The Cycle's Rim*, the latter a series of 53 sonnets in memory of her husband, who was drowned in 1915. The poems in *Lute and Furrow* and the stories in *Highland Annals* foreshadowed two impassioned proletarian novels inspired by the shabby treatment of the hill people during the Gastonia textile strike of 1929. *Call Home the Heart* and *A Stone Came Rolling* were published under the pseudonym of Fielding Burke. Though she had made frequent trips to Europe and extended visits elsewhere, Mrs. Dargan, from 1925 until her death on January 22, 1968, lived in a rustic cottage in West Asheville. *Sons of the Stranger*, a novel of western miners published when she was 78, was followed by collections of poetry and short stories.

WORKS: *Semiramis and Other Plays* (1904). *Lords and Lovers, and Other Dramas* (1906). *The Mortal Gods and Other Plays* (1912). *The Welsh Pony* (1913). *Pathflower* (1914). *The Cycle's Rim* (1916). *The Flutter of the Gold Leaf and Other Plays*, with Frederick Peterson (1922). *Lute and Furrow* (1922). *Highland Annals* (1925). *Call Home the Heart* (1932). *A Stone Came Rolling* (1935). *From My Highest Hill* (1941). *Sons of the Stranger* (1947). *The Spotted Hawk* (1958). *Innocent Bigamy and Other Stories* (1962).

RICHARD WALSER
North Caroline State University
Raleigh

DONALD GRADY DAVIDSON (1893–1968). The descendant of Scottish pioneers, and the son of a rural schoolmaster and a music teacher, Donald Davidson was born in Campbellsville, Tenn., on August 18, 1893. After attending Lynnville Academy and the Branham and Hughes School, he enrolled in Vanderbilt University in Nashville at age sixteen but because of a lack of funds left after one year to teach in several small Tennessee towns. In 1914 he returned to Vanderbilt and finished his undergraduate degree just as he entered the U.S. Army in 1917 to fight as an infantryman in some of the last but toughest battles in France. Just before leaving for Europe, he had married Theresa Sherrer, an artist and later lawyer and classical scholar.

Following his discharge, he taught at Kentucky Wesleyan College. In 1920 he began graduate studies for an M.A. at Vanderbilt and at the same time served as an instructor in the English department. Except for his adjunct position as book-page editor for the Nashville *Tennessean* (1924–1930) and his summers teaching as a faculty member at the Bread Loaf School of English at Middlebury College in Vermont (beginning in 1931), Davidson was to spend his entire professional career at Vanderbilt until his retirement in 1964. After purchasing a home near that of Robert Frost, Davidson spent his summers in Vermont and the academic year in Nashville, where he died on April 25, 1968.

Davidson fell in with a group of young scholars and students who met regularly to discuss philosophy, art, and literature in Nashville in 1920. This group, which evolved into the Fugitives, included John Crowe Ransom, Allen Tate, and Robert Penn Warren, among others. In 1922 the first issue of the *Fugitive* appeared under their editorship, which in the three and one-half years of its existence became an influential outlet for the regional voice in American poetry. It has been said that the *Fugitive* inaugurated the Southern Literary Renaissance which dominated the national scene in writing for several decades.

The same four young poets, with Davidson serving as the cohesive force, became interested in the encroachments of the technological society on the southern culture in the 1920s and led a second group of thinkers to make an appeal for an agrarian-based economy in America through a symposium published as *I'll Take My Stand* (1930). While the other central figures modified their philosophies with the passage of time, only Davidson stood behind his carefully formulated beliefs and steadily developed them through a series of essays which remain admirable for their rhetorical facility. Many of these essays were collected in *The Attack on Leviathan* (1938) and *Still Rebels, Still Yankees* (1957).

From his early contributions to the *Fugitive* through his retirement, Davidson continued to write and to develop as a poet, moving from a romantic, experimental stance towards the use of regional experience and history in poetic forms based on the ballad and narrative verse. His best works are considered to be *The Tall Men* (1927), a probing analysis of modern man torn between his traditional past and the coming technological apocalypse, and "Lee in the Mountains" (1934), a partisan but historically accurate analysis of Robert E. Lee's reflections on the Civil War, a stream-of-consciousness poem that brings Lee's fate to the level of Christian tragedy. Davidson also taught and influenced several generations of younger southern writers and scholars, wrote a quantity of literary criticism and historical studies, and produced several successful textbooks in teaching composition.

WORKS: *An Outland Piper* (1924). *The Tall Men* (1927). *British Poetry of the Eighteen-Nineties* (1937). *The Attack on Leviathan* (1938). *American Composition and Rhetoric* (1939). *Readings for Composition from Prose Models* (1942). *The Tennessee*, 2 vols. (1946, 1948). *Twenty Lessons in Reading and Writing Prose* (1955). *Still Rebels, Still Yankees* (1957). *Southern Writers in the Modern World* (1958). *The Long Street* (1961). *The Spyglass: Views and Reviews* (1963). *Poems 1922–1961* (1966). *Selected Essays and Other Writings of John Donald Wade* (1966).

M. Thomas Inge
Virginia Commonwealth
University
Richmond

SAMUEL DAVIES (1723–1761). Samuel Davies, southern evangelist during the Great Awakening, spokesman for religious toleration, fourth president of Princeton University, and author of *Miscellaneous Poems*, was born in New Castle County, Del., on November 3, 1723. He attended Samuel Blair's school at Fagg's Manor, Pa., where he was trained as a New Light Presbyterian. In 1747 he was ordained and sent to Virginia where he began a long struggle to establish the Presbyterian faith among the Anglican aristocracy. After the death of his first wife, he married Jean Holt of Hanover County, who was related to the editor of the *Virginia Gazette*, William Hunter, who published Davies' poems. In 1753 he was sent to England by the trustees of the College of New Jersey (now Princeton) to raise funds, a task he performed with great success. During his fourteen months abroad he kept a diary which contains interesting facts and observations as well as a record of his travels. In 1759, after having helped to establish the Presbyterian faith in the Old Dominion, Davies was persuaded to succeed Jonathan Edwards as president of the College of New Jersey. He died of pneumonia February 4, 1761, after only eighteen months, during which time he left a good record and raised the standards for the Bachelor's degree.

Davies is remembered primarily as perhaps the finest pulpit orator of his time and as a writer of many published sermons. Written from an orthodox Calvinist point of view, his sermons— as well as many of his poems—are similar in subject to those of his friend, Jonathan Edwards. Davies' poems are in the meditative tradition, and, as their subtitle indicates, "Chiefly on Divine Subjects." In a famous controversy, he defended them successfully against attacks in the *Virginia Gazette* by the Anglican "Walter Dymocke." The poems exhibit characteristics of the sublime, and the influence of Milton and Pope as well as hymnists like Isaac Watts is clear. Many were composed as hymns to accompany his sermons. Although not considered great poetry, his verse, avoiding the extremes of rationalism and emotionalism, is interesting for its moderate position in writing of the Great Awakening.

WORKS: *Miscellaneous Poems, Chiefly on Divine Subjects* (1752). *The Reverend Samuel Davies Abroad: The Diary of a Journey to England and Scotland, 1753–55* (1967). For a bibliography of Davies' numerous published sermons and essays, see George W. Pilcher, *Samuel Davies: Apostle of Dissent in Colonial Virginia* (1971), 196–202.

PETER L. ABERNETHY
Texas Tech University
Lubbock

OSSIE DAVIS (1917–). Ossie Davis was born in Cogdell, Ga., on December 18, 1917, the son of Charles and Laura Cooper Davis and the eldest of five children. He attended high school in Waycross, Ga., and upon graduation entered Howard University where he was encouraged by Dr. Alain Locke, black philosopher and drama critic. Davis dropped out of Howard at the end of his junior year, went to New York City, and joined the Rose McClendon Players, a Little Theater group, where he did the usual chores of an apprentice, but also played bit parts.

In 1942 Davis was inducted into the United States Army, and after his discharge in 1945, he rejoined the Rose McClendon Players. He was given the title role in *Jeb*. His costar in the play was Ruby Dee, whom he married on December 9, 1948.

In 1949 Davis took a course in playwriting at Columbia University and soon branched out to small parts in the Broadway theater. In the 1950s he also began to play in films.

Although he had a one-act play, *Alice in Wonder*, produced (1953), it was not until the opening of *Purlie Victorious* in 1961 that Davis came into his own as a playwright. *Purlie Victorious* is a comedy about a southern black minister, who is little more than a con man, and his efforts to regain control of a black Baptist church that has fallen into the hands of a cruel white landowner. Some critics were struck by Davis's use of stereotypes, both black and white, but particularly black stereotypes. *Purlie Victorious* was made into a film, *Gone are the Days* (1963). Later it became the musical *Purlie!* which opened in New York City in 1970. Davis also served as writer, director, or producer of several black movies: *Cotton Comes to Harlem* (1970); *Grodon's War* (1973); and *Countdown at Kusini* (1976). He and his wife live in New Rochelle, N.Y.

WORKS: *Purlie Victorious* (1961).

MARY MEBANE
University of South Carolina
Columbia

REBECCA HARDING DAVIS (1831–1910). Rebecca Blaine Harding Davis, daughter of Richard and Rachel Harding, was born on June 24, 1831, in Washington, Pa. The Harding family lived in Big Spring, Ala., until 1837, when they moved to Wheeling, W.Va. Rebecca attended Washington Female Seminary, graduating in 1848 with highest honors. A life of uneventful spinsterhood seemed her destiny when, at age 30, she published anonymously "Life in the Iron Mills" in the *Atlantic Monthly*. This short story became a landmark of American realism. The narrative recounts the sordid details of a frustrated iron mill worker who aspires to become an artist, but ends his life by suicide. Davis' next work, a novel, is just as grim. Published serially in the *Atlantic Monthly* as "A Story of Today," *Margret Howth* (1862) depicts the degrading conditions of mill workers and the evils of social inequality. Davis considered it as an attempt "to dig into this commonplace, this vulgar American life, and see what it is."

In 1863 she married Clarke Davis and moved to Philadelphia where Clarke became a prominent journalist. Rebecca herself was an associate editor for the New York *Tribune* from 1869 to 1875. The couple had three children, one of whom, Richard Harding Davis, became one of the most popular journalists of his generation. Rebecca Harding Davis remained a crusader for the poor and the dispossessed in her nonfiction social criticism, but her voluminous fictional output never fulfilled the promise of her early work. Her stories, many published in the *Atlantic Monthly*, *Lippincott's*, and *Scribner's*, became repetitious, sentimental, and didactic. Nevertheless, two more of her novels did show potential: *Waiting for the Verdict* (1868), a Reconstruction story about miscegenation, and *John Andross* (1874), an indictment of corrupt politics and the Whiskey Ring scandal.

Rebecca Harding Davis died at her son Richard's home at Mount Kisco, N.Y., on September 29, 1910.

WORKS: "Life in the Iron Mills" (April, 1861; repr., 1972). *Margret Howth* (1862; repr. as *Margaret*, 1970). *The Second Life* (ser. in *Peterson's*, January–June, 1863). *Atlantic Tales* (1866). *Waiting for the Verdict* (1868; repr., 1968). *Dallas Galbraith* (1868). *Kitty's Choice* (1873). *Pro Aris et Focis* (1869 in England; 1870 in U.S.). *Earthern Pitchers* (ser. in *Scribner's Magazine*, November, 1873–April, 1874). *John Andross* (1874). *A Law unto Herself* (1878). *Natasqua* (1878). *Gleanings from Merrimac Valley* (1881). *Silhouettes of American Life* (1892; repr., 1968). *Kent Hampden* (1892). *Stories of the South* (1894). *Doctor Warrick's Daughters* (1896). *Frances Waldeaux* (1897). *Bits of Gossip* (1904).

HAROLD WOODELL
Clemson University
Clemson, S.C.

WILLIAM DAWSON (1704–1752). William Dawson is a rare kind of writer; he achieved a place in American literary history with a book of English poems. That thin 30-page book, the only known volume and once the personal property of George Washington, is now lodged in the Boston Athenaeum library. See Ralph L. Rusk's reprint edition (N.Y.: Facsimile Text Society, 1930).

Poems on Several Occasions by a Gentleman of Virginia (Williamsburg: William Parks, 1736) is a beautifully printed little book, containing "the casual Productions" of Dawson's youth. He probably wrote these poems while a student at Queen's College in Oxford, which he entered at the age of fifteen and where he remained (until 1728 or 1729) before coming to America. Dawson imitated Anacreon and Horace and also Shakespeare, Milton, and James Thomson. Yet his poetry has some originality and spontaneity. He avoids the mannered style of some contemporary English neoclassical verse. Brooks and rills, for example, don't "babble" in Dawson's poetry—they "gurgle." He also had a touch of the Cavalier, at times reminding one of Herrick or Waller—particularly in his addresses to Sylvia, that paragon of her sex and object of his desire. He wrote in a variety of forms—epistles, epigrams, fables with morals, hymns, songs, light satires—but all of it is pure English poetry, far removed from our native American tradition.

Little is known of Dawson's life in England. He was born in Cumberland County, spent nine years at Oxford, taking his M.A. there in 1728, and leaving to become Professor of Moral Philosophy at William and Mary in 1729. In a letter to the bishop of London (June 2, 1740) he mentions being elected a Fellow at Oxford in 1733—after he had left.

In Virginia the Reverend Dawson married Mary Randolph Stith, a niece of Sir John Randolph. In succession to James Blair, he became second president of William and Mary, receiving a D.D. there in February, 1747. His papers are in the Library of Congress.

WORKS: *Poems on Several Occasions by a Gentleman of Virginia* (1736).

RICHARD E. AMACHER
Auburn University
Auburn, Ala.

JAMES DUNWOODY BROWNSON DE BOW (1820–1867).

Born on July 10, 1820, in Charleston, De Bow attended Cokes-
bury Institute and was graduated from the College of Charleston
(1843). He practiced law briefly and then launched his career as a
magazinist with the *Southern Quarterly Review*, publishing essays
on history and law and performing minor editorial work. As a delegate to the Southern Commercial Convention of 1845, he took an
interest in regional economic problems and subsequently moved to
New Orleans to found a monthly devoted to "trade, commerce,
commercial polity, and manufacturers." First appearing in January, 1846, *De Bow's Review* regularly featured articles on agricultural commodities, transportation and communication, commercial
conventions, industrialization, and trade laws. The editor envi-
sioned a southern prosperity based upon education, economic
diversification, and slavery. In 1848 De Bow became head of the
Louisiana Bureau of Statistics and lectured on commerce at the
University of Louisiana. He published a collection of essays from
the *Review* in 1852–1853 and then moved to Washington, where
he became superintendent of the Census Bureau. He oversaw the
tabulation of the important 1850 census and published the results
in three major works.

Meanwhile his *Review* had become the main repository of arguments for slavery and sectional rights. As president of the Southern
Commercial Convention of 1857, De Bow preached regional loyalty, spoke of a possible "separate confederation," and urged the
reopening of the African slave trade. During the war he acted as
general agent for the Confederate Produce Loan Agency. The fall
of New Orleans in 1862 curtailed publication of the *Review*, which
De Bow could not resume regularly until 1866. In the face of Reconstruction, he continued to champion southern causes and encourage economic development; he became president of the
Tennessee and Pacific Railroad in 1866. After De Bow's death on
February 27, 1867, the influential *Review* survived only a few
years, but its place in the cultural history of the South was already
secure.

WORKS: *Political Annals of South Carolina* (1845). *De Bow's Review*
(1846–62; 1866–67). *The Industrial Resources, etc., of the Southern*

and Western States (1852–53). *The Seventh Census of the United States: 1850* (1853). *Statistical View of the United States* (1854). *Mortality Statistics of the Seventh Census of the United States, 1850* (1855). *The Interest in Slavery of the Southern Non-slaveholder* (1860).

J. GERALD KENNEDY
Louisiana State University
Baton Rouge

EDWIN DE LEON (1818–1891). Writer and diplomat, Edwin De Leon was born in Columbia, S.C., on May 4, 1818. He was the second son of Dr. Mardici Heinrich and Rebecca Lopez-y-Nuñez De Leon, and the elder brother and guardian of the journalist and author, Thomas Cooper De Leon. De Leon graduated from South Carolina College in 1837 and in 1840 was admitted to the South Carolina bar. From 1842 to 1848 he worked as coeditor of the *Republican* of Savannah, Ga., and in 1850, by request of the southern wing of Congress, he moved to Washington, D.C., where he and Ellwood Fisher founded the *Southern Press*, a mouthpiece for the southern cause.

In 1854 De Leon embarked on a diplomatic career as consul general and diplomatic agent to Egypt and its dependencies where he distinguished himself in a dramatic confrontation with Abbas Pasha, the Egyptian ruler who threatened to murder the Greeks in Alexandria. In 1861, at the outbreak of the Civil War, De Leon's southern allegiances forced him to resign his position. In the following year Jefferson Davis appointed him the Confederate diplomatic agent to Europe, a post which he held until 1867 when he returned to the South. After the war De Leon went back to Egypt and Europe, returning briefly in 1879 to negotiate arrangements for introducing a telephone system to Egypt. This he accomplished in 1881.

Throughout his life De Leon demonstrated a talent and interest in writing. He edited his college journal, and after graduation made frequent contributions to magazines and periodicals. Later in life he cultivated the friendship of such literary figures as Hawthorne, Longfellow, Dickens, Tennyson, and Thackeray. Most of

De Leon's writings draw on his experiences abroad, especially those of Egypt. He died in New York City on December 1, 1891, shortly after returning to the United States where he planned to give a series of lectures on his experiences in foreign lands.

WORKS: *Three Letters from a South Carolinian, Relating to Secession, Slavery, and the Trent Case* (1862). *La Vérité sur les États Confédérés d'Amérique* (1862). *Askaros Kassis, the Copt* (1870). *The Khedive's Egypt* (1877, 1882). *Under the Stars and Under the Crescent* (1879). *Thirty Years of Life in Three Continents* (1890).

JAMES A. LEVERNIER
University of Arkansas
Little Rock

THOMAS COOPER DE LEON (1839–1914). Alabama's first professional man of letters was born in Columbia, S.C., on May 21, 1839, the son of Dr. Mardici Heinrich and Rebecca Lopez-y-Nuñez De Leon. De Leon began his formal education at Fort Prevel, Me., attended Rugby Academy in Washington, D.C., and was graduated from Georgetown College in Washington in 1858 with a degree in engineering. From 1858 until 1861 he was an audit clerk in the Bureau of Topographical Engineering, Washington, D.C. In 1862 he was commissioned a captain in the Confederate Army and served throughout the war as secretary to President Davis.

After the war De Leon turned to literature as a professional, first in New York and then in Baltimore, where he edited a magazine, the *Cosmopolite* (1866), and published his first book, *South Songs* (1866), a collection of Confederate poems and songs. In Mobile, where he became managing editor of the *Register* in 1867 and lived 47 years thereafter, he found outlets for his boundless energies. Among numerous other activities, he managed the Mobile Theatre, 1873–1885, and organized in 1873 the Mobile Mardi Gras as a public celebration and managed the carnival for 25 years. In 1878 he edited a literary periodical, the *Gulf Citizen*; and from his own press, the Gossip Printing Company, 1885–1897, he reprinted a number of his books and issued at irregular intervals a spicy little journal, the *Gossip*.

As a poet, De Leon paid tribute in his best verses to leaders of the Confederacy; and after becoming blind in 1903, he was called "The Blind Laureate of the Lost Cause." A few of his novels focused upon the Civil War and featured intersectional love plots, though De Leon himself always remained a bachelor. He is best remembered for his reminiscences and biographical sketches published in *Four Years in Rebel Capitals* (1890) and *Belles, Beaux and Brains of the 60's* (1909). Despite his blindness, he learned to type and continued to write until his death on March 19, 1914.

WORKS: *South Songs* (1866). *Cross Purposes* (1871). *Coqsureus* (1887). *The Soldiers' Souvenir* (1887). *The Rock or the Rye* (1888). *Creole and Puritan* (1889). *Four Years in Rebel Capitals* (1890). *Juny* (1890). *Our Creole Carnivals* (1890). *Society As I Have Foundered It* (1890). *A Fair Blockade-Breaker* (1891). *The Puritan's Daughter* (1891). *Sybilla* (1891). *John Holden, Unionist*, with Erwin Ledyard (1893). *Schooners That Bump on the Bar* (1894). *Out of the Sulphur* (1895). *The Rending of the Solid South* (1895). *East, West and South* (1896). *Crag-Nest* (1897). *A Novelette Trilogy* (1897). *Creole Carnivals* (1898). *An Innocent Cheat* (1898). *The Pride of the Mercers* (1898). *War Rhymes, Grave and Gay* (1898). *Confederate Memories* (1899). *Joseph Wheeler* (1899). *Inauguration of President Watterson* (1902). *Tales from the Coves* (1903). *The Passing of Arle Haine* (1905). *Belles, Beaux and Brains of the 60's* (1909).

RAY M. ATCHISON
Samford University
Birmingham, Ala.

JAMES DICKEY (1923–). James Dickey was born in Atlanta, Ga., on February 2, 1923. His Georgia origins are important, for a large number of his poems as well as for his first novel, *Deliverance*.

After a year at Clemson University, where he participated in several athletic programs, Dickey became a fighter pilot in the Pacific during World War II. He completed 87 missions and was awarded a Silver Star and two Distinguished Flying Crosses. During those war years, Dickey reports, he became interested in poetry. After the war Dickey resumed his education at Vanderbilt University, and graduated in 1948, magna cum laude. He stayed on at Vanderbilt for graduate work, taking his M.A. in 1950.

The 1950s were itinerant years for Dickey. He taught freshman English at Rice University and later at the University of Florida. Between those assignments, he returned to active duty with the Air Force during the Korean War, followed by a year of travel in Europe. In 1956 he temporarily abandoned his teaching duties to become an advertising writer for Coca-Cola in New York, contributing material for Eddie Fisher's television series, *Coke Time*. Returning to Atlanta, he continued his advertising work. His first volume, *Into the Stone*, was published in 1960; his second volume, *Drowning with Others*, appeared two years later.

In 1961 Dickey left the Atlanta business world. Boosted by a Guggenheim Fellowship, he and his wife Maxine spent a year in Italy, France, and Germany. He wrote many of the poems of his next volume, *Helmets*, during that year. Teaching positions at Reed College, San Fernando State College, and, briefly, at the University of Wisconsin provided further occasions for reviews, criticism, fiction, and especially poetry. *Buckdancer's Choice* won the National Book Award for poetry in 1966. With the publication of *Poems 1957–1967*, while he was serving a two year appointment as poetry consultant to the Library of Congress, Dickey established his reputation as a major American poet. When his novel *Deliverance* appeared in 1970, it became a best seller and was made into a successful motion picture.

Dickey followed *Deliverance* with poetry volumes in 1970 and 1976. After his wife's death in 1976, Dickey married Deborah Dodson, a former student, early in 1977. He composed the poem "The Strength of the Fields" for the occasion of the inauguration of his fellow Georgian Jimmy Carter and recited it during the festivities in Washington. The father of two sons, poet-in-residence and professor of English, Dickey lives in Columbia, S.C., and teaches at the University of South Carolina.

WORKS: *Into the Stone* (1960). *Drowning with Others* (1962). *The Suspect in Poetry* (1964). *Helmets* (1964). *Buckdancer's Choice* (1965). *Poems*

1957–1967 (1967). *Babel to Byzantium* (1968). *Deliverance* (1970). *The Eye-Beaters, Blood, Victory, Madness, Buckhead and Mercy* (1970). *Self-Interviews* (1970). *Sorties: Journals and New Essays* (1971). *The Zodiac* (1976). *God's Images*, with Marvin Hayes (1977).

GEORGE S. LENSING
University of North Carolina
Chapel Hill

SAMUEL HENRY DICKSON (1798–1872). Samuel Henry Dickson was born on September 20, 1798, in Charleston, S.C. His parents were Scottish Presbyterians; his father, a schoolmaster. He was educated at Yale and studied medicine at the University of Pennsylvania. A founder of the Medical College of South Carolina in 1833, he taught there till 1858, except for three years at the University of the City of New York (1847–1850). In 1858 he went to teach at the Jefferson Medical College in Philadelphia, where he remained until his death on March 31, 1872.

An amateur poet, Dickson's literary reputation rests solely on his popular poem composed in 1830, "I Sigh for the Land of the Cypress and the Pine," which was set to music. A collection of his verses, *Poems*, was printed for the author in 1844 and included his best-known poem. It was reviewed in the *Southern Literary Messenger* (July, 1844). His poems are frequently plaintive or mournful. Dickson was a friend of William Gilmore Simms, to whom he lent money. Simms dedicated *The Yemassee* to Dickson in 1835, included a composition by him in *The Charleston Book* (1845), and met with him in the 1850s at Russell's Bookstore in Charleston.

A popular occasional speaker and author of varied compositions (many medical books and pamphlets), Dickson published in 1830 one of the first lectures on temperance in the South. He delivered the Phi Beta Kappa address at Yale in 1842, "Pursuit of Happiness." In 1845 he published a proslavery pamphlet, *Essays on Slavery*. Besides numerous monographs on medicine, he contributed articles to such journals as the *Southern Literary Messenger* and the *Southern Quarterly Review*. Combining poetic composition, support of literature, and his medical activities, Dickson stands as a worthy example of the literary amateur in the Old South.

WORKS: *Poems* (1844).

CHARLES S. WATSON
University of Alabama
Tuscaloosa

THOMAS DIXON (1864–1946). Born in a farmhouse near Shelby, N.C., on January 11, 1864, Thomas Dixon was one of five children of Thomas Dixon, a Baptist minister and farmer, and Amanda Elizabeth McAfee, the daughter of a South Carolina planter. Reared in post–Civil War poverty, Dixon later portrayed in his novels many of the events he had witnessed during Reconstruction.

Farm work prevented Dixon from attending school regularly, but when he was thirteen (1877), he entered Shelby Academy and spent the next two years mastering the curriculum. At the age of fifteen, he entered Wake Forest College, earning his M.A. in four years (1883) and winning more awards than anyone in the history of the college. He earned a scholarship to Johns Hopkins University to study history and politics; there he became a close friend of Woodrow Wilson, who helped Dixon gain part-time work as a drama critic for the Baltimore *Mirror*. Drawn by his love of the theater, Dixon left Johns Hopkins without completing his graduate work for an unsuccessful stint as an actor in New York.

He returned to North Carolina, and though only 20 years old, ran successfully for the state legislature in 1884. Before beginning his term, he enrolled in the Greensboro, N.C., Law School and completed his LL.B. in 1885. On March 3, 1886, he eloped with Harriet Bussey of Columbus, Ga.; they had three children. Disillusioned with government and law, Dixon was ordained a Baptist minister on October 6, 1886. His reputation as a fearless, persuasive speaker soon carried him to large pastorates in Boston and New York.

In March of 1895 Dixon left the ministry and gave his full attention to lecturing, which brought him a meteoric fame and financial success. While on a lecture tour in the Midwest in the spring of 1903, he wrote *The Leopard's Spots*, which glorified the Reconstruction South. The novel was an immediate sensation.

During the following 20 years, Dixon wrote many popular novels dealing with the issues of the day. Always taking the conservative, even reactionary view, Dixon became the center of much controversy. He also wrote a number of highly successful plays and was a compelling actor in several of them.

In 1915, after several unsuccessful years of effort to sell a scenario based on his sensationally popular novel *The Clansman* (1905), Dixon found a producer in the newly formed Epoch Producing Corporation. Under the direction of D. W. Griffith, the movie, *The Birth of a Nation*, became a landmark in the history of motion picture art and made the producers and Dixon millionaires.

Dixon moved in the summer of 1915 to California and built the Dixon Studios, Laboratory, and Press, where he produced several motion pictures. Although Dixon introduced several innovations in motion picture art, he was not notably successful in this venture and returned to New York in 1923.

The remainder of Dixon's career was given to writing novels that, as social values changed, had less appeal. He gave strong support to President Roosevelt's New Deal but finally attacked Roosevelt's policies.

On February 26, 1939, Dixon suffered a cerebral hemorrhage in his hotel suite in Raleigh, N.C. Madelyn Donovan, his secretary and a former actress in his motion pictures, married him at his bedside in March. His first wife, Harriet Bussey Dixon, had died in 1937. For the remaining seven years of his life, Dixon was bedridden at his home in Raleigh. Although he had made two fortunes, he died nearly penniless on April 3, 1946. At the height of his career his name appeared in every newspaper in the land; today he is virtually unknown.

WORKS: *What is Religion? An Outline of Vital Ritualism* (1891). *Dixon on Ingersoll: Ten Discourses Delivered in Association Hall, New York*

(1892). *The Failure of Protestantism in New York and Its Causes* (1896). *Dixon's Sermons, Delivered in the Grand Opera House, 1898–1899* (1899). *Living Problems in Religion and Social Science* (1899). *The Leopard's Spots: A Romance of the White Man's Burden—1865–1900* (1903). *The One Woman: A Story of Modern Utopia* (1903). *The Clansman: An Historical Romance of the Ku Klux Klan* (1905). *The One Woman: A Drama* (1906). *The Traitor: A Story of the Fall of the Invisible Empire* (1907). *Comrades: A Story of Social Adventure in California* (1909). *The Root of Evil: A Novel* (1911). *The Sins of the Father: A Romance of the South* (1912). *The Southerner: A Romance of the Real Lincoln* (1913). *The Victim: A Romance of the Real Jefferson Davis* (1914). *The Life Worth Living: A Personal Experience* (1914). *The Foolish Virgin: A Romance of Today* (1915). *The Fall of a Nation: A Sequel to The Birth of a Nation* (1916). *The Way of a Man: A Story of the New Woman* (1919). *A Man of the People: A Drama of Abraham Lincoln* (1920). *The Man in Gray: A Romance of North and South* (1921). *The Black Hood* (1924). *The Love Complex* (1925). *The Hope of the World: A Story of the Coming War* (1925). *Wildacres: In the Land of the Sky* (1926). *The Sun Virgin* (1929). *Companions* (1931). *A Dreamer in Portugal* (1934). *The Flaming Sword* (1939).

RAYMOND A. COOK
Valdosta State College
Valdosta, Ga.

J[AMES] FRANK DOBIE (1888–1964). J. Frank Dobie was born on a ranch in Live Oak County, Tex., on September 26, 1888. He received an A.B. from Southwestern University in 1910, and an M.A. from Columbia University in 1914. He was principal of a high school in Alpine, Tex., 1910–1911; teacher of English and secretary to the president of Southwestern University, 1911–1913; instructor in English at the University of Texas, 1914–1917, 1919–1920, 1921–1923; field artillery lieutenant in World War I; ranch manager, 1920–1921, head of the English Department, Oklahoma A&M College, 1923–1925; adjunct professor of English, University of Texas, 1925–1926; associate professor, 1926–1933; professor, 1933–1947; and visiting professor of American history, Cambridge University, 1943–1944. Dobie became editor of the Texas Folklore Society in 1922 and remained in that position until 1942.

In 1929 he introduced the course that made him a famous teacher: "Life and Literature of the Southwest." A highly vocal defender of unpopular causes in a conservative state, he left the University of Texas in 1947 when the regents refused to extend a leave of absence. "Pancho" Dobie and his close friends, naturalist Roy Bedichek and historian Walter Prescott Webb, formed a unique Texas triumvirate. He died September 18, 1964.

Dobie loved and understood his hard land and the people who struggled for a living on it; and his life's task was to interpret the southwestern heritage in books, pamphlets, articles and tales contributed to magazines, and a Sunday newspaper column. *A Vaquero of the Brush Country* (1929) sparked a regional literary renaissance. *Coronado's Children* (1930), and *Apache Gold and Yaqui Silver* (1939), contained the treasure stories that he loved so well. *The Longhorns* (1941) was his most popular book; to Dobie the longhorn represented strength, vitality, freedom, and endurance. Never a narrow regionalist, he found in the pioneers, hunters, cow people, treasure seekers, and wild animals of the Southwest and Mexico symbols of universal human values.

WORKS: *A Vaquero of the Brush Country* (1929). *Coronado's Children* (1930). *On the Open Range* (1931). *Tongues of the Monte* (1935). *Tales of the Mustang* (1936). *The Flavor of Texas* (1936). *Apache Gold and Yaqui Silver* (1939). *John C. Duval: First Texas Man of Letters* (1939). *The Longhorns* (1941). *Guide to Life and Literature of the Southwest* (1942, 1952). *A Texan in England* (1945). *The Voice of the Coyote* (1949). *The Ben Lilly Legend* (1950). *The Mustangs* (1952). *Tales of Old-Time Texas* (1955). *Up the Trail From Texas* (1955). *I'll Tell You a Tale* (1960). *Cow People* (1964). *Rattlesnakes*, ed. Bertha McKee Dobie (1965). *Some Part of Myself*, ed. Bertha McKee Dobie (1967). *Out of the Old Rock*, ed. Bertha McKee Dobie (1972). *Prefaces*, ed. Bertha McKee Dobie (1975).

NORMAN D. BROWN
University of Texas
Austin

ELLEN DOUGLAS (1921–). Mississippi novelist "Ellen Douglas," Josephine Ayres Haxton, was born in Natchez on July 12, 1921, the daughter of Richardson and Laura Davis Ayres. After attending schools in Hope, Ark., and Alexandria, La., she went first to Randolph-Macon Woman's College in Virginia and then to the University of Mississippi. While a student at Ole Miss, from which she was graduated in 1942, she met her future husband, Kenneth Haxton, Jr., of Greenville, Miss., who in addition to his achievements as a businessman, composer, and organizer of the Greenville Symphony Orchestra, was a member of the Levee Press, which during its brief existence published limited editions of works by Faulkner and Welty. The Haxtons have three sons— Richard, Ayres, and Brooks.

Douglas' first novel, *A Family's Affairs* (1962), was awarded the Houghton Mifflin Fellowship and was named by New York *Times* critic Orville Prescott as one of the five best novels of the year. Her story "On the Lake," which became part of the novella "Hold On" included in her second book, *Black Cloud, White Cloud*, was first published in the *New Yorker* and received recognition by being included in the O. Henry collection for 1963. Her second novel, *Where the Dreams Cross*, was followed by a third, *Apostles of Light* (1973), which was nominated for the National Book Award. Her study of Walker Percy's *The Last Gentleman* was published by the Seabury Press in its series *Religious Dimensions in Literature*.

At present Douglas divides her time between Greenville and Monroe, La., where she is writer-in-residence at Northeast Louisiana University. In June, 1976, she received one of the grants from the National Endowment for the Arts awarded to "published writers of exceptional talent."

WORKS: *A Family's Affairs* (1962). *Black Cloud, White Cloud* (1964). *Where the Dreams Cross* (1968). *Commentary on Walker Percy's* "The Last Gentleman" (1969). *Apostles of Light* (1973).

> ROBERT L. PHILLIPS, JR.
> Mississippi State University
> Starkville

CLIFFORD DOWDEY (1904–). Clifford Dowdey was born in Richmond, Va., on January 23, 1904. He graduated from John Marshall High School in Richmond and attended Columbia Uni-

versity from 1921 to 1922 and from 1923 to 1925. In 1925 he returned to Richmond to work for a few months on the Richmond
News Leader, but by 1926 he was back in New York. There for
the next ten years he worked as an editor of various pulp magazines and, as a free-lance writer, contributed large numbers of
westerns and confession romances to these magazines.

Through the worst of the depression years Dowdey gave his
days to free-lance and editorial duties, but many of his nights were
spent researching Civil War history. Out of this research came a
short story which the *Atlantic Monthly* immediately accepted,
with an option for a novel dealing with a similar Civil War background. The result was *Bugles Blow No More* (1937), an account
of Richmond under siege which won Dowdey a Guggenheim Fellowship. Over the next eight years he combined writing with
travel, living in such diverse places as Vermont, Hollywood, and
Texas. During this period he published four more historical novels.

In 1945 Dowdey returned to Richmond, where he eventually
established permanent residence in his boyhood home. Here he
researched his first nonfictional history, *Experiment in Rebellion*
(1946). This account of the Confederacy in Richmond, the initial
choice of the History Book Club, was well received by both readers and critics and marked the beginning of Dowdey's career as
a distinguished historian. He wrote four novels after *Experiment in
Rebellion*, but by 1960 he was best known for a series of Civil
War histories that have made him an authority on the background
and the events of the war, on the Army of Northern Virginia, and
on the men who profoundly influenced the Virginia campaigns—
Robert E. Lee and "Stonewall" Jackson. More recently Dowdey
has published two histories of colonial Virginia.

WORKS: *Bugles Blow No More* (1937). *Gamble's Hundred* (1939). *Sing for
a Penny* (1941). *Tidewater* (1943). *Where My Love Sleeps* (1945). *Experiment in Rebellion* (1946). *Weep for My Brother* (1950). *Jasmine Street*
(1952). *The Proud Retreat: A Novel of the Lost Confederate Treasure*
(1953). *The Land They Fought For: The Story of the South as the Confederacy, 1832–1865* (1955). *The Great Plantation: A Profile of Berkeley
Hundred and Plantation Virginia from Jamestown to Appomattox* (1957).

Death of a Nation: The Story of Lee and His Men at Gettysburg (1958). *Lee's Last Campaign: The Story of Lee and His Men Against Grant— 1864* (1960). Ed., *The Wartime Papers of R. E. Lee*, with Louis Manarin (1961). *Last Night the Nightingale* (1962). *The Seven Days: The Emergence of Lee* (1964). *Lee* (1965). *The Virginia Dynasties: The Emergence of "King" Carter and the Golden Age* (1969). *The Golden Age: A Climate for Greatness, Virginia, 1732–1775* (1970).

RITCHIE D. WATSON, JR.
Randolph-Macon College
Ashland, Va.

HARRIS DOWNEY (1907–). Born on May 12, 1907, in Baton Rouge, La., the son of Lawrence and Florence Chiek Downey, Harris Downey was educated at local schools and at Louisiana State University where he received a B.A. (1929) and an M.A. (1930). After further graduate study at New York University he returned to Baton Rouge where he was an assistant professor of English at Louisiana State. From 1941 to 1945 he served in Europe with the U.S. Air Force. After the war he again taught at Louisiana State, but later became a free-lance writer. Since his retirement from the Louisiana State faculty, he has continued to live in Baton Rouge.

In 1951 Downey received the first prize in the O. Henry memorial awards for his story "The Hunters." Other stories appeared in a number of periodicals, and his first novel, *Thunder in the Room*, was published in 1956. The novel received mixed reviews, as did his two other books, *The Key to My Prison* (1964) and *Carrie Dumain* (1966). Harris Downey has produced a small body of uncompromising fiction which has not met with widespread critical or commercial success, but which merits serious consideration.

WORKS: *Thunder in the Room* (1956). *The Key to My Prison* (1964). *Carrie Dumain* (1966).

JOSEPH R. MILLICHAP
University of Tulsa
Tulsa, Okla.

DANIEL DULANY, THE ELDER (1685–1753). Daniel Dulany the Elder, born in Queens County, Ireland, attended the University of Dublin before embarking for Maryland as an indentured servant in 1703. His services were bought by a prominent lawyer, who turned Dulany toward the law. After his term of service he rapidly established himself as a leading attorney.

Honors and wealth came his way in such plenitude that his life is an almost unparalleled example of the American success story. He first held elective offices but soon began accumulating the lucrative appointive posts possible in an age that tolerated plural office holding: the posts of attorney general, receiver general, chief judge in admiralty, chief probate judge, and councilor of state. In his private capacity he simultaneously practiced law, ran a mercantile business, engaged in iron manufacturing, and speculated in land. In all of these he prospered, but his land speculations proved a bonanza, raising a "handsome" fortune to a fabulous one before his death on September 6, 1753.

Dulany's literary work came early in his career. He wrote *The Right of the Inhabitants of Maryland to the Benefit of the English Laws* in the autumn of 1728 when the popularly elected house of the assembly battled the lord proprietor over the question of the extension of English statute law to the province. As a leader in the lower house Dulany supported the popular view in this pamphlet, notable for its early use of fundamental or natural law and its novel legal argument. Dulany premises the right of Englishmen to the rule of law, the common law compounded of the "Law of Nature, the Law of Reason, and the revealed Law of God." But, he argues, the depravity of men over the years necessitated the passage of statutes which declared, altered, and strengthened the common law. Accordingly, denial of this essential statute law rendered "Life, Liberties, and Properties Precarious."

WORKS: *The Right of the Inhabitants of Maryland to the Benefit of the English Laws* (1728).

AUBREY C. LAND
University of Georgia
Athens

DANIEL DULANY, THE YOUNGER (1722–1797). Eldest son of Daniel the Elder, Daniel Dulany the Younger was born in Annapolis, Md., June 28, 1722. As heir of a well-to-do social and political leader, Dulany went to England for the most complete education available to a colonial: Eton, Cambridge, and the Inns of Court, where he was called to the bar of the Middle Temple. On his return to the province in 1747 he embarked in law practice that won him even greater acclaim than his father's, and his marriage in 1749 to Rebecca Tasker brought him into kinship with the squirearchy of Maryland and Virginia.

As a benefactor of his father's wealth, young Dulany encountered few obstacles to his political advancement. Even his opponents admired his astute dealings with the tight but highly competitive elite that ruled Maryland. Within half a decade Dulany rose to the top in the political scramble. Curiously he managed to command the respect of both leading political factions in Maryland.

During the Stamp Act troubles, Dulany presented the case for American rights in a brilliant pamphlet, *Considerations on the Propriety of Imposing Taxes in the British Colonies* (1765), instantly reprinted throughout the colonies and in London. His reputation suffered no ill effects from a second pamphlet later in the same year, *The Right to the Tonnage*, which argued the Lord Proprietor's legal right to collect the unpopular ship taxes in the province. Dulany became such a power in the politics of equilibrium that the governor sarcastically dubbed him "the patriot councillor."

During the decade of his ascendancy Dulany added considerably to the family fortune and enhanced his reputation as "oracle of the law," quoted admiringly by Lord Chief Justice Camden. But the Revolution shattered his world forever. His two sons divided in loyalty, one to the crown and one to the patriot cause. Dulany himself became a neutral and went into permanent retirement until his death in Baltimore on March 17, 1797.

WORKS: *Considerations on the Propriety of Imposing Taxes in the British*

Colonies, For the Purpose of Raising a Revenue, By Act of Parliament (1765). *The Right to the Tonnage* (1765).

AUBREY C. LAND
University of Georgia
Athens

JOSEPH DUMBLETON (fl. 1740). Biographical information about Joseph Dumbleton, colonial writer of newspaper verse between 1740 and 1750, is nonexistent. Dumbleton's full name would not even be known had he not foregone his customary signature, "J. Dumbleton," when signing his "Ode for St. Patric's Day." Although his early poems appear in the *Virginia Gazette*, and he seems to have been associated with William Parks, its editor, his signature to "A Rhapsody on Rum" published in *Gentleman's Magazine* indicates that he was a resident of South Carolina by 1749. That he had some classical background is evident from his poems' epigraphs from Ovid and Vergil and from the poems' allusions to Greek and Roman deities. The five poems by which Dumbleton is known reveal further an irrepressible sense of humor which could leap from the whimsical in "The Paper Mill" to the Rabelaisian in "The Northern Miracle," the only original narrative poem of any length published in the *South Carolina Gazette* during its four decades.

WORKS: "A Transient View of Solomon's Pursuit after Content," *Virginia Gazette*, ca. 1740, credited to the *Virginia Gazette* by *General Magazine and Historical Chronicle*, I (April, 1741), 276–78. "The Paper Mill. Inscribed to Mr. Parks," *Virginia Gazette*, July 26, 1744, repr. in *Virginia Magazine of History and Biography*, VII (April, 1900), 442–44. "Ode for St. Patric's Day. Humbly Inscribed to the President and Members of the Irish Society," *South Carolina Gazette*, March 20, 1749, p. 1. "A Rhapsody on Rum," *South Carolina Gazette*, March 20, 1749, p. 1; also printed in *Gentleman's Magazine*, XIX (September, 1749), 424. "The Northern Miracle. A Tale," *South Carolina Gazette*, January 8, 1750, pp. 1–2.

ROBERT BOLICK
University of Pennsylvania
Philadelphia

WILLIAM EDDIS (1738–1825). William Eddis was born February 6, 1738, at Northleach, England. The records yield hardly a shred of evidence about his early years and education. At 26 he married and soon left for London, where he supported his family on his income as a petty clerk. His companions included his boyhood friend, William Powell, idol of the London stage, and miscellaneous aspiring painters and writers, among them Hannah More, then on the threshold of her famous career.

In 1769 Eddis came to Maryland as a minor customs official in Annapolis. He entered with zest the social life of Annapolis: the theatricals, balls, horse races, and the exclusive Homony Club, which included the elite among its members. In 1772 he acquired an additional patronage post in the paper currency office and shortly after still a third position. On these three salaries Eddis lived comfortably, almost as a gentleman, contributing short prose pieces and verse to the Annapolis *Gazette* and above all writing to friends back home the letters that later preserved his memory.

The *Letters from America*, collected and published in London (1792), belong to a great eighteenth-century tradition. The earliest letters dated before 1773 comment with wit and insight on the local scene in the provincial capital, its manners, institutions, and personalities. Then, in 1774 his world of beautiful people began falling apart. Thereafter his letters are a running commentary on the coming of the Revolution through the eyes of a true Briton who loved America.

In June, 1777, Eddis left the colonies permanently. As compensation for his losses a royal commission awarded him a pension of £180 a year for life. On this modest income, and, doubtless, memories of brighter days, Eddis lived on uneventfully until December 14, 1825, just short of his 88th birthday.

WORKS: *Letters from America: Historical and Descriptive, Comprising Occurrences from 1769 to 1777 Inclusive* (1792).

AUBREY C. LAND
University of Georgia
Athens

RANDOLPH EDMONDS (1900–). Widely known as the "Dean of the Black Academic Theatre," Randolph Edmonds was born in Lawrenceville, Va. After graduating from the high school department of St. Paul's Normal and Industrial School, he received degrees from Oberlin College and Columbia University. He received a Rockefeller Fund Fellowship and studied at the Yale University School of Drama. Subsequently, he studied drama in England, Ireland, Scotland, and Wales on a Rosenwald Fund Fellowship. He took courses at Dublin University and at the London School of Speech Training and Dramatic Arts.

For more than 40 years Edmonds was associated with predominantly black colleges as a teacher of English and drama and as a director of drama. These institutions included Morgan College, Dillard University, and Florida Agricultural and Mechanical College.

Edmonds founded the two most outstanding drama organizations among black colleges and universities: The Negro Intercollegiate Drama Association and the National Association of Dramatic and Speech Arts. He organized high school associations in Louisiana and served as chief consultant for associations throughout the South. He received a Doctor of Letters from Bethune-Cookman College.

Edmonds' works are chiefly of three types: folk plays, problem plays, and plays of fantasy. His many short plays appear in numerous anthologies. Edmonds now resides in Lawrenceville, Va. He travels, appears at workshops, and is revising his history of the black theater.

WORKS: *Shades and Shadows* (1930). *Six Plays for a Negro Theatre* (1934). *The Land of Cotton and Other Plays* (1942).

ELAINE MITCHELL NEWSOME
Fayetteville State University
Fayetteville, N.C.

[THOMAS] MURRELL EDMUNDS (1898–). Murrell Edmunds was born in Halifax, Va., on March 23, 1898, the son of John Richard and Willie Thurman Murrell Edmunds. Educated in the public schools of Lynchburg, Edmunds completed both undergraduate and law degrees at the University of Virginia; he was vice-president of his law class and a member of the editorial staff of the *Virginia Law Review*. After serving in the U.S. Army during World War I, he was admitted to the Virginia bar in 1920.

Edmunds spent a year as English teacher and head varsity basketball coach at a private boarding school for boys (1921–1922) before entering law practice. He abandoned what seemed to be a promising law career, including a stint as an assistant commonwealth's attorney (1922–1926), to devote all his energies to creative writing. Edmunds has written a dozen books of fiction, drama, or verse, and has contributed to numerous magazines and anthologies. Several of his stories have earned mention on the annual Honor Rolls of American Short Stories, and in 1963 Edmunds was awarded the annual poetry prize by the *Arizona Quarterly*. His 1942 novel, *Time's Laughter in Their Ears*, has been translated into Danish. A Unitarian, Edmunds has lived in New Orleans for the past several decades, where he completed a novella, *Reservoir*.

The thrust of Edmunds' work is away from what he considers to be traditional southern stereotypes moving "toward a more philosophically revolutionist stance, carefully attuned to history's evolving mandate." Throughout his work emerges a passionate commitment to individual freedom, brotherhood, and racial harmony, carefully articulated with a complex awareness of the tragedy and blasted hope of his homeland. A large volume of unpublished materials—proofs, manuscripts, notes, letters—is available in the Murrell Edmunds Collection at the University of Virginia library.

WORKS: *Music-makers* (1927). *Earthenware* (1930). *Sojourn Among Shadows* (1936). *Between the Devil* (1939). *Time's Laughter in Their Ears* (1942). *Red, White and Black* (1945). *Behold, Thy Brother* (1950). *Moon of My Delight* (1961). *Passionate Journey to Winter* (1962). *Laurel for the Undefeated* (1964). *Beautiful Upon the Mountains* (1966). *Shadow of a Great Rock* (1969). *Dim Footprints Along a Hazardous Trail* (1971).

JAMES D. WILSON
Georgia State University
Atlanta

HARRY STILLWELL EDWARDS (1855–1938). Born on April 23, 1855, in Macon, Ga., Harry Stillwell Edwards spent all of his life there, except for three years in Washington, D.C. He attended private schools, began writing newspaper sketches, studied law at night, and at age 21, received his Bachelor of Laws from Mercer University. Then he began practicing law and increased his writing in the Macon *Telegraph* and the Macon *Evening News*.

Two of Edwards' early newspaper sketches, "Dooly County Safe" and "The Man on the Monument," immediately became popular, and in 1881 he married Mary Roxie Lane, who herself wrote children's stories and greatly encouraged him. It was with her urging that he submitted his first story "Elder Brown's Backslide" to *Harper's Magazine* and received immediate acceptance. Then "Two Runaways" followed in the *Century*, and showed, as few stories had ever done before, a genuine understanding of the Negro and of his dialect.

Edwards' realistic depiction of the Negro is the most striking characteristic of his approximately 100 stories, and this is particularly true of the best known of all: *Eneas Africanus*. With approximately 2,000,000 copies sold, it is still selling. In this story, Edwards wrote, as he did in many others, of a real, living person.

Edwards wrote two novels: *Sons and Fathers*, for which he won a $10,000 prize and which some refer to as the best mystery novel ever written by an American, and *The Marbeau Cousins*, which he thought better of and which centered on Holly Bluff, his home near Macon. Also, he wrote poems, of which "The Vulture and His Shadow," "At the Crossing," and "Toast to the Georgia Girl" are among his best.

Page for page, the greatest amount of Edwards' writing was in newspapers, particularly the column "Coming Down My Creek" in the Atlanta *Journal*; in these pages, as throughout all that he wrote, are found the salient characteristics of regionalism and love of the legends and traditions of the South. He died on October 22, 1938.

WORKS: *Two Runaways and Other Stories* (1889). *Sons and Fathers* (1896). *The Marbeau Cousins* (1898). *His Defense and Other Stories*

(1899). *Eneas Africanus* (1919). *Isam's Spectacles* (1920). *The Blue Hen's Chicken* (1924). *The Tenth Generation* (1928). *Little Legends of the Land* (1930).

JOHN O. EIDSON
University System of Georgia
Atlanta

GEORGE CARY EGGLESTON (1839–1911). Eggleston was a novelist, historian, writer of juvenile books, lawyer, and journalist. The Egglestons and Carys settled in Virginia in 1635 and 1750, respectively. Born at Vevay, Ind., on November 26, 1839, Eggleston came to Amelia County, Va., in 1856 and stayed until 1865: attended Richmond College, 1856–1857; studied law; and fought for the Confederacy.

Disillusioned, he fled to Cairo, Ill., at war's end. Since employment there and in Mississippi was unsatisfactory to him, he moved to New York. His employment for the ensuing years included the Brooklyn *Daily Union*, 1870–1871; *Hearth and Home* and *American Homes* magazines, 1872–1875; literary editor, *Evening Post*, 1875–1881; reader for Harper publishing house, 1881–1885; editor of the *Commercial Advertiser*, 1885–1889; the New York *World*, 1889–1900. Retiring from the *World* in 1900, he continued writing books and magazine articles. He died on April 14, 1911.

A Rebel's Recollections, *The History of the Confederate War*, and some of his novels deal with his interpretation of the "irrepressible conflict." Defending the southern viewpoint clearly, he portrayed the courage of leaders and soldiers of both the Union and the Confederacy. Too easily inclined to sentimentality in his novels, Eggleston lamented the passing of the leisurely southern life of antebellum days and the changing of values everywhere. He also portrayed greed, speculation, political corruption, and man's inhumanity to man. Although always an advocate of state rights, he extolled the principles of equality, free institutions, and freedom with responsibility.

Eggleston believed literature had the power to reform: his writings propound integrity, courage, kindness, and ingenuity. The necessity of struggle for a meaningful life was basic in his philosophy. He stressed that the literary artist must be true to human nature even dealing "wholesomely with the unwholesome things of life." Ultimately, his life and his work reflect his deep love and respect for his country and his southern heritage.

WORKS: *How To Educate Yourself With or Without Masters* (1872). *A Man of Honor* (1873). *The Big Brother* (1875). *How To Make a Living* (1875). *A Rebel's Recollections* (1875). "The Old Regime in the Old Dominion," *Atlantic Monthly* (November, 1875), 603–16. *Captain Sam* (1876). *The Signal Boys* (1877). *Red Eagle and the Wars with the Creek Indians of Alabama* (1878). *The Wreck of the Red Bird* (1882). *Strange Stories from History for Young People* (1885). "The American Idea," *New Princeton Review* (November, 1887), 317–27. Ed., *American War Ballads and Lyrics* (1889). *Juggernaut, a Veiled Record*, with Dolores Marbourg (1891). Ed., with Rossiter Johnson and John Champlin, *Liber Scriptorum I* (1893). "The Literary Disadvantages of Living Too Late," *Liber Scriptorum, The First Book* (1893). *Southern Soldier Stories* (1898). *The Last of the Flatboats: A Story of the Mississippi and Its Interesting Family of Rivers* (1900). *American Immortals* (1901). *Camp Venture: A Story of the Virginia Mountains* (1901). *A Carolina Cavalier: A Romance of the American Revolution* (1901). *The Bale Marked Circle X: A Blockade Running Adventure* (1902). *Dorothy South: A Love Story of Virginia Just Before the War* (1902). *The First of the Hoosiers, Edward Eggleston* (1903). *The Master of Warlock: A Virginia War Story* (1903). *Captain in the Ranks* (1904). *Evelyn Byrd* (1904). *Running the River: A Story of Adventure and Success* (1904). *A Daughter of the South: A War's End Romance* (1905). *Life in the Eighteenth Century* (1905). *Our First Century* (1905). *Blind Alleys: A Novel of Nowadays* (1906). *Jack Shelby: A Story of the Indiana Backwoods* (1906). *Long Knives: The Story of How They Won the West* (1907). *Love Is the Sum of It All: A Plantation Romance* (1907). *Two Gentlemen of Virginia: A Novel of the Old Regime in the Old Dominion* (1908). *The Warrens of Virginia* (1908). *Irene of the Mountains: A Romance of Old Virginia* (1909). *The History of the Confederate War, Its Causes and Its Conduct: A Narrative and Critical History*, 2 vols. (1910). *Recollections of a Varied Life* (1910). *What Happened at Quasi: The Story of a Carolina Cruise* (1911).

LOUISE CALLISON
Alderson-Broaddus College
Philippi, W.Va.

SARAH BARNWELL ELLIOTT (1848–1928). The Georgia-born daughter of Protestant Episcopal Bishop Stephen Elliott and his wife Charlotte Bull Barnwell, Sarah Barnwell Elliott was well imbued with religious doctrine and concern. She was born in Georgia in 1848. In the early 1870s she moved, with her family, to Sewanee, Tenn., the site of the University of the South, an institution her father had helped to found. Much of the remainder of her life was spent there on the Cumberland Plateau.

Except for a year at Johns Hopkins University in 1886, her education was derived from the home. Her writing and its emphases derive similarly from her upbringing and familiar surroundings.

Her first three novels, *The Felmeres* (1879), *A Simple Heart* (1889), and *John Paget* (1893), all center on church-related and inspirational themes. It was, however, through a serial entitled "Jerry" and published in *Scribner's Magazine* during 1890–1891 that her most significant literary impact would be made. She chose as her subject matter the difficulties of progress and development for a Tennessee mountain boy, a story of both local color and sociological interest. Only Charles Egbert Craddock could rival her descriptions of southern mountaineer life and existence. Her treatment of such topics and later influence as vice-president of the Association of Southern Writers helped to lead authors away from overly sentimentalized looks at southern life.

During her residence in New York (1895–1902), she wrote and published two more novels, *The Durket Sperret* (1898) and *The Making of Jane* (1901); a collection of short stories, *An Incident and Other Happenings* (1899); and a biography, *Sam Houston* (1900).

Following her return to Sewanee in 1902, Sarah Elliott became extremely active in the women's suffragist movement, becoming president of the Tennessee State Equal Suffrage Association, vice-president of the Southern States Woman Suffrage Conference, and vice-president of the Civic League of Sewanee. She died on August 30, 1928.

WORKS: *The Felmeres* (1879). *A Simple Heart* (1887). *Jerry* (1891). *John*

Paget (1893). *The Durket Sperret* (1898). *An Incident, and Other Happenings* (1899). *Sam Houston* (1900). *The Making of Jane* (1901).

ROBERT M. WILLINGHAM, JR.
University of Georgia
Athens

WILLIAM ELLIOTT (1788–1863). The eldest son of William and Phoebe Waight Elliott was born in Beaufort, S.C., on April 27, 1788. He received his education in the schools at Beaufort and at Beaufort College. He also attended Harvard University and received his A.B. and A.M. there. At an early age he acquired a sportsman's taste for hunting and fishing. The broad waters of Port Royal Sound became the scene for his extraordinary tales of harpooning the devil-fish. These colorful sketches were to provide him with a reputation as a writer on rural sports.

Elliott served for eighteen years as representative and senator in the state legislature. He aligned himself with the Unionists against nullification and secession. In 1832 he resigned from the state senate rather than bow to a mandate from his constituents who had instructed him to vote for nullification of the federal tariff laws.

Following his father and grandfather, Elliott became a planter in the Beaufort area. His plantations produced large crops of rice and cotton. Elliott became widely known for his leadership and influence in agricultural circles and spoke frequently to agricultural societies. He wrote articles on agriculture, advocating better farming practices and crop diversification.

Elliott is best known as a writer of sporting sketches, which were collected and published in 1846 as *Carolina Sports by Land and Water Including Incidents of Devil-Fishing, Wild Cat, Deer and Bear Hunting, Etc.* The sketches, many of which had been published in Charleston newspapers, are lively accounts of his own hunting and fishing experiences. The book has been published in six separate editions and one reprint edition. Elliott also wrote a five-act drama based on the sixteenth-century conspiracy of John Lewis de Fiesco, a Genoese nobleman, against the Dorias, the ruling family of Genoa. The drama, entitled *Fiesco: A Tragedy*, was privately published in 1850.

Elliott died in Charleston, S.C., on February 3, 1863.

WORKS: *Address to the People of St. Helena Parish* (1832). *Examination of Mr. Edmund Rhett's Agricultural Address: On the Question "Who is the Producer?"* (1841). *The Planter Vindicated: His Claims Examined—To Be Considered a Direct Producer: The Chief Producer: And Chief Tax-Payer of South Carolina* (1842). *Carolina Sports by Land and Water Including Incidents of Devil-Fishing, Wild Cat, Deer and Bear Hunting, Etc.* (1846). *Anniversary Address of the State Agricultural Society of South Carolina, Delivered in the Hall of the House of Representatives, November 30, 1848* (1849). *Address Delivered by Special Request Before the St. Paul's Agricultural Society* (1850). *Fiesco: A Tragedy* (1850). *Letters of Agricola* (1852). *Report of the Honorable William Elliott, Commissioner of the State of South Carolina to the Universal Exhibition of Paris* (1856). *Address to the Imperial and Central Agricultural Society of France, Read Before Them at Paris, July 4, 1855* (1857). "A Trip to Cuba," *Russell's Magazine*, II, III (October–December, 1857, January–February, April, 1858).

B. N. SKARDON
Clemson University
Clemson, S.C.

RALPH WALDO ELLISON (1914–). Ralph Ellison, one of America's most significant black writers, was born on March 1, 1914, in Oklahoma City, Okla. His father, Lewis Alfred Ellison, was a construction worker and a tradesman. His mother was a political activist who canvassed for the Socialists and was jailed on several occasions for violating segregation laws. Ellison has emphasized, however, that his childhood was not any sort of stereotyped hell because of white racism. In an interview published in a collection of essays entitled *Shadow and Act*, he talked about "the communion, the playing, the eating, the dancing and the singing" that were part of his youth in Oklahoma. Although segregation existed, he noted that there was "no tradition of slavery, and . . . relationships between the races were more fluid and thus more human than in the old slave states."

Ellison's is a rich literary background. As a child he first read fairy tales, then westerns and detective fiction as well as magazines like *Vanity Fair*. His mother, he recalled, brought home the *Literary Digest* from her job, and through friends he got copies of various of the Harvard Classics and of the works of George Bernard Shaw and Maupassant. He wrote in another essay that he learned a "rich oral literature" in "the churches, the schoolyards, the barbershops, the cotton-picking camps; places where folklore and gossip thrived." And he learned during these early years the rhythms, idioms, and lifestyles of a wide variety of people—blacks, Indians, Mexicans, Jews, and many others who lived in or passed through Oklahoma City.

In elementary school one of his teachers instructed him about the history of blacks in the United States. He learned of the New Negro, and of Langston Hughes, Countee Cullen, Claude McKay, and James Weldon Johnson, among others. While still in secondary school he began to study music seriously. But more influential than any courses were the jazz groups, blues singers, and orchestras with which he came in contact.

In 1933 Ellison went to Tuskegee Institute to continue his musical education. He remained there three years, studying music but also beginning what he termed his "conscious education in literature" after being profoundly affected by *The Waste Land*. As he investigated the sources of Eliot's literary allusions, he turned to criticism, which in turn led him to "Pound and Ford Madox Ford, Sherwood Anderson and Gertrude Stein, Hemingway and Fitzgerald," and thence back to Melville and Mark Twain.

While still at Tuskegee he became interested in politics and art, and after moving to New York in 1936 and there meeting Langston Hughes, he began reading André Malraux's work, the while searching among black authors for their expression of a modern sensibility. Hughes introduced him to Richard Wright, whom Ellison credits with guiding him toward fiction. Wright had Ellison read Henry James's prefaces to his novels, as well as Conrad's work, Dostoievsky's letters, and the criticism of Joseph Warren Beach. Langston Hughes also guided him; and a combination of circumstances—artistic and political—led Ellison to choose Malraux as his "literary ancestor," because the French author's fiction of engagement was what Ellison wanted his own to be. "Malraux," he later declared in an interview for the *Paris Review*, "was the artist-revolutionary rather than a politician when he wrote *Man's Fate*, and the book lives not because of a political position embraced at the time, but because of its larger concern with the tragic struggle of humanity."

Ellison did research for the New York Federal Writers' Project from 1938 to 1942, in 1939 settling down to a writing career. A small portion of what would become *Invisible Man* appeared in 1940. From then on he has had short stories, articles, and essays published regularly, if not with great frequency. He applied himself to his novel in 1945, which was finally published in 1952. In *Invisible Man* Ellison wrote about the black culture he knew, about the initiation of a young man, and about the problem all Americans face who try to achieve recognition in a mass society. The novel earned immediate critical praise, and Ellison was awarded a National Book Award in 1953. His reputation was established; from that point on he has been honored repeatedly with awards and has served as lecturer or professor at numerous institutions.

In 1964 Ellison's only other book was published, the collection of essays entitled *Shadow and Act*. Portions of a second novel have been appearing since 1960, when "And Hickman Arrives" was published in *Noble Savage*; but Ellison has yet to complete the book.

WORKS: *Invisible Man* (1952). *Shadow and Act* (1964).

TOWNSEND LUDINGTON
University of North Carolina
Chapel Hill

AUGUSTA JANE EVANS. See Augusta Jane Evans Wilson.

WILLIAM CLARK FALKNER (1825–1889). William Clark Falkner was born on July 6, 1825, in Knox County, Tenn. His parents thereafter resumed their journey from North Carolina to Missouri, where they settled in Ste. Genevieve. About 1840, fleeing punishment or seeking means to support his widowed mother, the boy made his way to Ripley, Miss., where he had relatives. An energetic worker, studying law and profitably serving as amanuensis for a condemned ax murderer, Falkner made his way.

His equivocal service in the Mexican War provided the substance for an autobiographical poem, *The Siege of Monterey* (1851). Later the same year he published an adventure novel called *The Spanish Heroine*. In the ten years before the outbreak of the Civil War he prospered at law and farming, killed two men in affrays, and was widowed and rewed. (John Wesley Thompson Falkner, the only child of his first marriage, would become William Faulkner's grandfather.)

After leading with distinction at the First Manassas, Colonel Falkner was defeated for reelection as commander of his regiment. Raising a regiment of Partisan Rangers, he waged guerilla warfare until that command was destroyed and he was forced to go underground.

After the war he wrote an eight-scene play, *The Lost Diamond*, whose proceeds helped to reopen a local school renamed Stonewall College. Although preoccupied with expanding the Ripley Railroad, Falkner found time to write a serial for the Ripley *Advertiser* called *The White Rose of Memphis*. With a Mississippi riverboat journey for a frame setting, Falkner's characters—costumed for a masquerade ball—took turns telling stories, but a central plot involved violence, betrayal, and true love rewarded. Published in 1881, it went through many editions. *The Little Brick Church* of the next year was set partly on the Hudson but showed a number of similarities to its predecessor, sharing many of the same faults without the compensating vitality and ingenuity. A trip to Europe produced *Rapid Ramblings in Europe*, a book of travel sketches distinguished by clear narration and exposition and good handling of dialect. This was Falkner's last work, as railroad-building and politics occupied him until his death at the hands of a former partner on November 6, 1889.

WORKS: *The Siege of Monterey* (1851). *The Spanish Heroine* (1851). *The*

Lost Diamond (1867). *The White Rose of Memphis* (1881). *The Little Brick Church* (1882). *Rapid Ramblings in Europe* (1884).

JOSEPH BLOTNER
University of Michigan
Ann Arbor

JOHN WESLEY THOMPSON FAULKNER III (1901–1963).

Engineer, Navy pilot, farmer, teacher, writer, and painter—John Faulkner III was born in Ripley, Miss., on September 24, 1901, and moved with his parents to Oxford when he was a year old. Here he grew up with his three brothers, William, Murry, and Dean. Throughout his life he exhibited much of the versatility of his great-grandfather, Colonel W. C. Falkner, in his varied interests and accomplishments.

In September, 1922, he was married to Lucille Ramey of Oxford. They had two sons—James Murry and Murry Cuthbert (Chooky).

Experiences and accomplishments in the life of John Faulkner include an attempt to join the U.S. Army during World War I at the age of sixteen, working in a munitions plant at Muscle Shoals, operating a dry cleaning business, working with Boy Scouts, taking flying lessons, barnstorming, crop dusting, serving as city engineer for the town of Oxford, engineering projects in building highways and bridges for the Mississippi Highway Department, and serving as manager for the Mid-South Airways in Memphis. Along the way, Faulkner earned a degree in engineering at Ole Miss, joined the U.S. Navy and retired in 1946 as Lieutenant Commander, took graduate work in history and later taught a course in creative writing at the University of Mississippi. He died on March 28, 1963.

For posterity John Faulkner has left a number of books, short stories, and paintings. His short stories were published in *Collier's* and other magazines. His paintings in water color and in oil were calculated to capture the scenes of his region. He had finished at his death about half of a planned series of 30 paintings under the general subject "The Vanishing South."

WORKS: *Men Working* (1941). *Dollar Cotton* (1942). *Chooky* (1950). *Cabin Road* (1951). *Uncle Good's Girls* (1952). *Sin Shouter of Cabin*

Road (1955). *Ain't Gonna Rain No More* (1959). *Uncle Good's Week-End Party* (1960). *My Brother Bill* (1963).

JAMES W. WEBB
University of Mississippi
Oxford

WILLIAM CUTHBERT FAULKNER (1897–1962). William Cuthbert Faulkner was born in the north Mississippi town of New Albany on September 25, 1897. Fifteen months later his parents moved to nearby Ripley where his great-grandfather had settled about 1840. A lawyer and a planter, William Clark Falkner had led a regiment north in 1861 to fight valiantly at First Manassas, and later he had served near home as colonel of his regiment of partisan cavalry. A successful novelist and railroad builder in the postwar years, he was fatally shot by a onetime business rival the day he was elected to the legislature. Precocious as Billy Falkner was, he may well have absorbed some of this family lore before his parents moved southwest to Oxford just before his fifth birthday.

There with his three younger brothers he enjoyed a comfortable small-town boyhood. He was a bright student but eventually lost interest and dropped out during high school. He quit a job in his grandfather's bank to pursue his real interest: writing verse. Encouraged by Phil Stone, an older and better-educated friend, he remained in Oxford until the spring of 1918 when, his sweetheart about to be married to a successful lawyer, he traveled north to share Stone's student lodgings at Yale. That July, spelling his name Faulkner, he began pilot training in Toronto with the RAF-Canada. Although this experience ended with the war, it profoundly affected his imagination and supplied material for future writing.

At home again, he led an existence deceptive in appearance. Roaming the countryside, taking odd jobs when he chose, he was still reading widely and experimenting in verse and prose. A brief taste of New York in 1921 and nearly three onerous years as postmaster at the University of Mississippi whetted his appetite for Europe. He planned to travel there via New Orleans, where he visited late in 1924 just before the appearance of *The Marble Faun*, a sequence of pastoral verses financed by himself and Stone.

He had met Sherwood Anderson in New Orleans, and in the genial company of the older writer and his circle he settled in for half a year, writing prose and verse, much of it published in the *Times-Picayune*. After sending a novel manuscript to Anderson's publisher, Faulkner sailed for Europe in July with his friend, architect William Spratling. From Genoa they journeyed through Switzerland to Paris, where Faulkner spent the rest of the year but for brief trips into the French countryside and to England. He worked on stories and novels, elements of which he would salvage later.

On February 25, 1925, Boni & Liveright published *Soldiers' Pay*, Faulkner's Lost Generation novel of postwar disillusionment. Returning to New Orleans, he worked on a novel set there called *Mosquitoes* (1927), which suggested Huxleyan bohemians and dilettantes. Faulkner found his unique metier and voice in *Flags in the Dust*, a novel of the north Mississippi Sartoris clan (based on the Falkners). Several times rejected, it was published as *Sartoris* by Harcourt, Brace in 1929, when Faulkner was completing a highly experimental book called *The Sound and the Fury*, which Cape & Smith issued that October. Fusing poetic imagery with stream-of-consciousness narration, Faulkner used the disintegrating Compson family in both a realistic and a symbolic manner. Some reviewers recognized the novel as a masterpiece.

These two works of 1929 signaled the beginning of more than a decade of productivity and brilliance unmatched by any other American novelist. Pushing into other regions of his mythic Yoknapatawpha County, Faulkner extended his use of the stream-of-consciousness technique in a story of country people called *As I Lay Dying* (1930), which operated on a realistic level yet also suggested symbolic Christian and pagan analogues as *The Sound and the Fury* had done. *Sanctuary* (1931) was a shocking novel of violence which brought Faulkner notoriety, sales, and a Hollywood offer. Married to his divorced childhood sweetheart, and now owner of a big antebellum house much in need of repair, he went to Hollywood as a screenwriter the next spring, beginning a remunerative but costly second career that would continue intermittently for more than two decades.

He was at the height of his powers, as he showed in *Light in August* (1932), a massive contrapuntal novel portraying self-isolated characters against the complex Yoknapatawpha society. But he was far from financially secure, and he now spent much energy on short stories in the hope of quick returns from major magazines. He was publishing a book a year now, culminating in 1936 in *Absalom, Absalom!* issued by Random House, his publisher thenceforward. Here Quentin Compson, of *The Sound and the Fury*, tried to understand, through the life of Colonel Thomas Sutpen, larger meanings extending into the realms of southern history and human values. He fashioned short stories into novels with *The Unvanquished* (1938) and *Go Down, Moses* (1942), exploring the quintessentially southern matter of the war and race relations. *The Hamlet* (1940) had employed similar reworkings to begin in novel form the Snopes saga which would engage Faulkner during two decades in a fictional view of sweeping historical and socioeconomic change.

Gaining increasing recognition but modest sales, Faulkner had worked for three other studios before going to Warner Brothers in 1942. Much of the next three years was spent there on ephemeral scenarios, but *Intruder in the Dust*, a popular novel of detection and race relations, brought him financial security and renewed popularity in 1948.

Faulkner's international stature was confirmed by the Nobel Prize in 1950. During this decade he traveled extensively on State Department cultural missions, but he worked intensively to complete *A Fable* (1954), his recasting of the Christ story set in 1918, and his Snopes trilogy. In *The Town* (1957) he followed the incursion of the Snopeses into Jefferson, the seat of Yoknapatawpha County, and in *The Mansion* (1959) he brought the triumph and fall of Flem Snopes into the contemporary period.

Residing in Charlottesville half the year, where he was associated with the University of Virginia, he lived the life of a venerated artist and fox-hunting country gentleman. *The Reivers* (1961) was a grandfather's mellow reminiscence of a boy's coming of age in the early years of the century. The most honored of living writers, secure as one of America's greatest artists, he died in Mississippi on July 6, 1962, just short of his 65th birthday.

WORKS: *The Marble Faun* (1924). *Soldiers' Pay* (1926). *Mosquitoes* (1927). *Sartoris* (1929). *The Sound and the Fury* (1929). *As I Lay Dying* (1930). *Sanctuary* (1931). *These 13* (1931). *Light in August* (1932). *A Green Bough* (1933). *Doctor Martino and Other Stories* (1934). *Pylon* (1935). *Absalom, Absalom!* (1936). *The Unvanquished* (1938). *The Wild Palms* (1939). *The Hamlet* (1940). *Go Down, Moses* (1942). *Intruder in the Dust* (1948). *Knight's Gambit* (1949). *Collected Stories of William Faulkner* (1950). *Requiem for a Nun* (1951). *A Fable* (1954). *Big Woods* (1955). *The Town* (1957). *The Mansion* (1959). *The Reivers* (1961). *Selected Letters of William Faulkner*, ed. Joseph Blotner (1977).

JOSEPH BLOTNER
University of Michigan
Ann Arbor

JESSIE REDMON FAUSET (1886–1961). Daughter of a minister, Jessie Fauset grew up in upper middle-class Negro society in Philadelphia—"O.P.'s," as these Old Philadelphians were called. She attended Cornell University (B.A., 1905) and the University of Pennsylvania (M.A., 1906). She then taught Latin and French at Douglass High School in Baltimore, later moving to Dunbar High School in Washington, D.C. She left the public school system in 1919 to serve as literary editor for the *Crisis*, official publication of the NAACP. In this capacity, according to Langston Hughes, she helped to midwife the Negro renaissance of the 1920s. She herself wrote stories, poetry, articles, and book reviews for the magazine before she began her major career as a novelist.

In 1920 she and W. E. B. DuBois put together the *Brownies' Book*, a children's periodical; and in 1921 DuBois sent her to Europe to cover the second Pan-African Congress for the *Crisis*. Infatuated with Paris, she spent the entire year of 1924 studying French at the Sorbonne. She gave up her position of literary editor in 1926 and returned to teaching, accepting a post at DeWitt Clinton High School in New York City, which she held until 1944. She married Herbert E. Harris in the late 1920s and continued her education by attending Columbia University in 1931. She became a visiting professor of English at Hampton Institute in 1949, and late in her life she taught Latin and French at Tuskegee Institute. She died in Philadelphia on April 30, 1961.

Jessie Fauset wrote four novels, all dealing with the social milieu of upper middle-class black life. William Stanley Braithwaite called her the "potential Jane Austen of Negro literature," yet it would be a mistake to take this analogy too seriously. Her characters are haunted by ghosts from their racial past, and in this respect she is closer to Hawthorne and Faulkner than she is to Jane Austen. All four of her heroines try in various ways to escape the burdens of history, and they are judged in terms of how honestly they accept their blackness. The curse of America, as Fauset sees it, is that racial hostility keeps black people from living normal American lives.

WORKS: *There is Confusion* (1924). *Plum Bun* (1929). *The Chinaberry Tree* (1931). *Comedy: American Style* (1933).

CHARLES SCRUGGS
University of Arizona
Phoenix

PETER STEINAM FEIBLEMAN (1930–). Born in New York City, Peter Feibleman was raised in New Orleans where his father, James K. Feibleman, was professor of philosophy at Tulane University and a widely published writer of philosophy, poetry, and fiction. Professor Feibleman divorced Peter's mother Dorothy Steinam Feibleman, and later married the novelist Shirley Ann Grau. Peter Feibleman was educated in New Orleans and later at Carnegie Tech and Columbia, where he studied drama. From 1951 to 1958 he lived in Spain, working as an actor and theatrical manager.

In Spain he completed his first novel, *A Place Without Twilight* (1958), and then returned to the United States where he has been a free-lance writer residing in many places. In 1959 he held a Guggenheim Fellowship. His other novels are *The Daughters of Necessity* (1959) and *The Columbus Tree* (1972). A collection of four short novels, *Strangers and Graves*, appeared in 1966. Feibleman dramatized his first novel as *Tiger, Tiger, Burning Bright*; it opened on Broadway in 1962, and the play was published in 1963. He also wrote books in the Time-Life Series.

WORKS: *A Place Without Twilight* (1958). *The Daughters of Necessity* (1959). *Tiger, Tiger, Burning Bright* (1963). *Strangers and Graves* (1966). *American Cooking: Creole and Acadian* (1971). *The Cooking of Spain and Portugal* (1971). *The Columbus Tree* (1972). *The Bayous* (1973).

JOSEPH R. MILLICHAP
University of Tulsa
Tulsa, Okla.

JULIA FIELDS (1938–). Julia Fields was born in Uniontown, Ala., on January 21, 1938, one of eight children of Winston and Maggie Johnson Fields. She grew up on a farm and, while attending school in Uniontown, also did factory work, sold vegetables, washed dishes, and waited on tables. She entered Knoxville College from which she was graduated in 1961. Already a writer, she had had a play presented by a drama group at Knoxville College, and in 1962 two of her poems were included in a pioneering anthology of black poetry, *Beyond the Blues*. She returned to Alabama to teach in a high school in Birmingham but spent the following two summers at the Bread Loaf Writers' Conference (1962) in Vermont and the University of Edinburgh (1963). She also lived in New York City and taught in a public high school there. In 1968 her first book, *Poems*, was published; in the same year she was appointed a Woodrow Wilson Teaching Fellow at Miles College in Alabama and was awarded a grant by the National Endowment for Arts and Humanities. Fields went on to earn an M.A. at Middlebury College, awarded in 1972. Although Scotland Neck, N.C., was by this time her home base, from 1969–1974 she taught or was poet-in-residence at Hampton Institute, Saint Augustine's College, East Carolina University, and North Carolina State University. Recently she has been teaching at Howard University. In 1973 her second book of poems, *East of Moonlight*, appeared. She is the mother of two daughters.

Frequent themes of Fields's poetry are nature, especially natural beauty and renewal, and the black experience. She has written poems about notable black figures such as Malcolm X, Langston Hughes, and Moms Mabley. She has read her poetry widely and has been published in a number of anthologies.

WORKS: *Poems* (1968). *East of Moonlight* (1973).

MARY C. WILLIAMS
North Carolina State University
Raleigh

GEORGE FITZHUGH (1806–1881). George Fitzhugh, the son of Dr. George Fitzhugh and Lucy Stuart, was born on November 4, 1806, at Brent Town Tract, Prince William County, Va. In 1812 his family removed to the Chotank area of King George County. In boyhood Fitzhugh attended a field school, but he largely educated himself through reading in belles lettres, economics, and law. Adopting the law as his profession, he married Mary Metcalf Brockenbrough in 1829 and took up residence with his bride in the "somewhat decayed" but pleasant classical mansion of the Brockenbroughs in Port Royal, Carolina County, Va. Like the late John Taylor of Caroline, Fitzhugh developed a great affection for the Port Royal region and regarded it as the ideal embodiment of an anticapitalistic agrarian philosophy. In the late 1840s Fitzhugh began the career he is remembered for, that of the southern man of letters as proslavery advocate, publishing in 1849 a pamphlet called *Slavery Justified* and in 1851 another pamphlet entitled *What Shall Be Done with the Free Negroes?* These small efforts were preparatory to two major works of the proslavery literature: *Sociology for the South: or, The Failure of Free Society* and *Cannibals All! or, Slaves Without Masters*. Fitzhugh subsequently became a prolific contributor of essays on slavery and other subjects to *De Bow's Review*.

In the ironic aftermath of the Civil War he was employed as an associate judge of the Freedman's Court in Richmond (1865–1866). Returning to Port Royal he lived in semipoverty at Brockenbrough, which had been damaged by shell fire during the war years. Following the death of his wife in 1877, his own health badly depleted, Fitzhugh lived for a year with a son in Frankfort, Ky., and subsequently with a daughter in Huntsville, Tex., where he died on July 30, 1881.

Seeing the South (as Eugene D. Genovese says) in the "ideal of the patriarchal slave plantation recapitulated in the large," Fitzhugh, with something like the visionary force of a Carlyle, described southern civilization as a necessary reaction against the corruption of the human community founded in feeling and experience by the ideological forces of capitalism and democracy.

WORKS: *Slavery Justified* (1849). *What Shall Be Done with the Free Negroes?* (1851). *Sociology for the South: or, The Failure of Free Society* (1854). *Cannibals All! or, Slaves Without Masters* (1857).

LEWIS P. SIMPSON
Louisiana State University
Baton Rouge

WILLIAM FITZHUGH (1651–1701). The son of a wealthy woolen draper, William Fitzhugh was born in Bedford, England, and baptized January 10, 1651. Little is known of his early life, but when he arrived in Virginia about 1670 he was an educated lawyer. He had fortune enough to purchase certain lands, or he received them on August 26, 1674, as part of the dowry of Sarah Tucker, the eleven-to-thirteen-year-old daughter of influential Virginians. Family tradition insists that she was sent to Europe for two years before the marriage was consummated. By 1676 Fitzhugh had settled on a large Stafford County estate and prospered as a lawyer, member of the House of Burgesses, and gentleman farmer who grew and exported tobacco. A recognized authority on colonial law, he earned fame for his defense of Major Robert Beverley, who had refused to supply the royal governor copies of the house's journals without that body's permission (1682–1684/85). The lawyer also became a lieutenant colonel of Stafford's militia and a justice of the peace (1684), and one of two resident agents for the Culpeper heirs and Lord Fairfax in the Northern Neck Proprietary

(1693). Fitzhugh's agency set a pattern of land grant and patenting that significantly influenced future American land speculation and development.

Fitzhugh's literary importance derives from a collection of 212 letters, which together with William Byrd I's, give the clearest picture of seventeenth-century Virginia life. Through these letters (May 15, 1679–April 26, 1699) Fitzhugh chronicles colonial economic and governmental development. He reveals his self-made success, personal piety, emphasis upon moderation in all things, his introduction of large-scale slave labor, fear of Indian attack, a fairly sophisticated social life, and gives the best physical description of a seventeenth-century plantation. Fitzhugh completed a short history of Virginia as a preface to his edition of its laws (1693 —never published, not extant), and projected a longer history to encourage settlement (1697). The final two years of Fitzhugh's life escape record except for a trip to England (1699–1700) and his death on October 21, 1701.

WORKS: *William Fitzhugh and His Chesapeake World, 1676–1701: The Fitzhugh Letters and Other Documents*, ed. Richard Beale Davis (1963).

MICHAEL A. LOFARO
University of Tennessee
Knoxville

INGLIS FLETCHER (1879–1969). Inglis Fletcher, daughter of Maurice William and Flora Deane Chapman Clark, was born on October 20, 1879, in Alton, Ill., and grew up listening to captivating stories of her North Carolina great-grandfather. At the School of Fine Arts of Washington University in St. Louis, she withdrew from classes in sculpture to marry John G. Fletcher, mining engineer, and for five years followed him to camps in Alaska and along the West Coast before residing for more settled periods in Spokane and San Francisco. After a visit to Africa in 1928, she wrote two novels based on her travels there.

A genealogical curiosity about her North Carolina forebears led to the rich materials used in *Raleigh's Eden*, first of twelve novels in her Carolina Series, which, their author explained, attempted to depict, over a period of two hundred years from the first Roanoke Island colony of 1585 to the ratification of the Constitution in 1789, the joint struggle of the gentle born and the common man to establish sound government in the North Carolina wilderness. But whatever their serious purpose, they were among the most popular and widely read historical novels of their day.

During and after the writing of *Raleigh's Eden*, Mrs. Fletcher often visited North Carolina, and in 1944 she and her husband bought and repaired Bandon Plantation on the Chowan River near Edenton and there she lived until it burned in 1963. Thereafter she lived in Greenville, N.C. She died on May 30, 1969, and was buried in the National Cemetery in Wilmington, N.C.

The Carolina Series, not written in historical sequence, was groomed, as intended, less as belles lettres than as an unlabored blending of solid history and exciting romance.

WORKS: *The White Leopard* (1931). *Red Jasmine* (1932). *Raleigh's Eden* (1940). *Men of Albermarle* (1942). *Lusty Wind for Carolina* (1944). *Toil of the Brave* (1946). *Roanoke Hundred* (1948). *Bennett's Welcome* (1950). *Queen's Gift* (1952). *The Scotswoman* (1955). *The Wind in the Forest* (1957). *Cormorant's Brood* (1959). *Pay, Pack, and Follow* (1959). *Wicked Lady* (1962). *Rogue's Harbor* (1964).

RICHARD WALSER
North Carolina State University
Raleigh

JOHN GOULD FLETCHER (1886–1950). John Gould Fletcher was born in Little Rock, Ark., on January 3, 1886, the son of a Confederate veteran whose Scotch-Irish pioneer family had settled in Tennessee before the Revolution and migrated westward to Arkansas early in the nineteenth century. His mother was a gifted woman of German-Danish extraction, who educated him, in his early youth, at home. Fletcher went to high school in Little Rock, then spent a year at Phillips (Andover) Academy. Although an avid student who read widely in Latin, French, and German as well as English, he dropped out of Harvard in his senior year, when his father's death left him financially secure for life, and allowed him to pursue an independent career as a writer. He lived in Boston for a year after leaving Harvard, then went west with an archeological team from the Peabody Museum to study the Mesa Verde civilization of the American Indians. In the summer of 1908, he sailed for Italy, living there for a time, and then in Paris, before settling in London in 1913, where in that one year he published his first five volumes of poetry.

Fletcher's first poems were in a conventionally Romantic manner, but in London he became acquainted with the Imagist group of poets who had started a movement toward a new poetic style. In 1915 he contributed poems to the first volume of *Some Imagist Poets*, edited by Amy Lowell, and published a new collection called *Irradiations, Sand and Spray*, his most distinctive volume. Fletcher became known as an innovator in poetic style, and an exponent of what he called "polyphonic prose."

After 1922, though still living in London, Fletcher became attracted to the Fugitive poets in his native South and contributed poems to the *Fugitive* magazine. In 1930, when the leading Fugitives became Agrarians, Fletcher contributed an essay to their symposium, *I'll Take My Stand: The South and the Agrarian Tradition*. He returned to the United States in 1933 to accept an honorary doctorate at the University of Arkansas, and took up residence again in his native state, remaining there until his death in 1950. In his reflective autobiography, *Life Is My Song* (1937), Fletcher gave an engaging personal account of his years as a participant in two of the major American poetic groups of the twentieth century, the Imagists and the Fugitives, a dual association which no other poet enjoyed. His *Selected Poems* (1938) won the Pulitzer Prize for Poetry. Always a serious and gifted writer, Fletcher was more the follower than the leader in poetic developments, but his reconciliation of a strong literary internationalism and modernism with an equally strong southern regionalism and conservatism gives him special importance in twentieth-century literature.

WORKS: *The Book of Nature, 1910–12* (1913). *Fool's Gold* (1913). *Visions of the Evening* (1913). *Fire and Wine* (1913). *The Dominant City* (1913).

Irradiations, Sand and Spray (1915). *Goblins and Pagodas* (1916). *Japanese Prints* (1918). *The Tree of Life* (1918). *Breakers and Granite* (1921). *Paul Gauguin, His Life and Art* (1921). *Preludes and Symphonies* (1922). *Parables* (1925). *Branches of Adam* (1926). *The Black Rock* (1928). *John Smith—Also Pocahontas* (1928). *I'll Take My Stand: The South and the Agrarian Tradition*, contributor (1930). *The Two Frontiers: A Study in Historical Psychology* (1930). *XXIV Elegies* (1935). *The Epic of Arkansas* (1936). *Life Is My Song: The Autobiography of John Gould Fletcher* (1937). *Selected Poems* (1938). *South Star* (1941). *The Burning Mountains* (1946). *Arkansas* (1947).

WILLIAM PRATT
Miami University
Oxford, Ohio

SHELBY FOOTE (1916–). Born on November 17, 1916, in Greenville, Miss., son of Shelby Dade and Lillian Rosenstock Foote, grandson of Huger Lee Foote, early planter near Greenville, whose father was a cavalry officer at Shiloh, Shelby Foote grew up in Greenville, where he was influenced by William Alexander Percy and was a friend and schoolmate of Walker Percy.

He attended the University of North Carolina (1935–1937) and joined the Mississippi National Guard in 1939. In 1940 he was mobilized into the army (artillery) as sergeant and rose to captain before being "kicked completely out" during service in Northern Ireland for leaving to see the girlfriend who became his first wife in 1944. Foote worked as an Associated Press reporter at the New York desk in the fall and winter of 1944, then enlisted in the Marine Corps (January–November, 1945) in the combat intelligence branch. After the war he held various jobs, including construction work, radio copywriting, and reporting for the *Delta Democrat-Times*. Foote began his first novel, *Tournament*, before the war, but did not complete it until 1949. In the next five years, he published four novels, which he wrote in a garage behind his mother's home. Foote was praised as one of America's finest young authors in the years following World War II.

He moved to Memphis in 1953 where he married Gwyn Rainer.

In 1956 he wrote a story for Stanley Kubrick but refused to travel to Hollywood to pursue a career.

From boyhood he had been interested in the Civil War, and in 1954 he began his three-volume history of the war, a masterpiece that would require 20 years work. The actual writing of Volume I took eight hours a day, seven days a week, culminating in publication in 1958. The second volume appeared in 1963, the last in 1974.

Foote has been three times a Guggenheim Fellow and once a Ford Fellow. He has served as lecturer at the University of Virginia (1963) and Memphis State (1966–1967), and as writer-in-residence at the Arena Stage in Washington (1963–1964) and at Hollins College (Spring, 1968).

In 1964 he and his family moved to the Alabama coast, but his stand against racial discrimination raised the ire of Klansmen. He returned to Raleigh, Tenn., in 1965, before moving back to Memphis in July, 1965, where he still lives. He recently completed a sixth novel, *September, September*, and has begun work on a seventh, "Two Gates to the City," which will treat a struggle for values in the modern South. Its setting is his mythical Delta town of Bristol in the late 1940s.

All his novels except *Shiloh* are set in and around Bristol. *Tournament* (1949) outlines the rise and fall of a Delta family from 1887 to World War I. Hugh Bart, the main character, is said to be modeled after the novelist's grandfather. *Follow Me Down* (1950), perhaps the best of the novels, centers on a crime of passion. It is based on a Delta trial which Foote attended. *Love in a Dry Season* (1951) outlines the lives of two Bristol families from the Depression to World War II. *Jordan County* (1954) moves from a contemporary setting and an act of violence, back in time to the 1700s and another act of violence. Man does not change much during the process; and here, as in the Foote canon generally, the failure of love and the desire for exploitation are the chief causes of violence. One of Foote's primary themes is the inescapable loneliness of the human situation.

WORKS: *Tournament* (1949). *Follow Me Down* (1950). *Love in a Dry Season* (1951). *Shiloh* (1952). *Jordan County* (1954). Ed., *The Night*

Before Chancellorsville and Other Civil War Stories (1957). *The Civil War: A Narrative*, I–III (1958, 1963, 1974). *September, September* (1978).

JAMES E. KIBLER, JR.
University of Georgia
Athens

JESSE HILL FORD (1928–). Born in Troy, Ala., on December 28, 1928, Jesse Hill Ford received his B.A. from Vanderbilt University (1951) and his M.A. from the University of Florida (1955). He married Sarah Anne Davis, of a prominent Humboldt, Tenn., family, on July 20, 1951, and served in the United States Navy for two years. The Fords have two sons and two daughters.

Ford's jobs range from reporter for the Nashville *Tennessean* (1950–1951) to writer-in-residence, Memphis State University (1969–1971). Best known for his fiction, Ford has also written two screenplays, CBS-TV's *The Conversion of Buster Drumwright* and, with Sirling Silliphant, the 1970 movie version of *The Liberation of Lord Byron Jones* (a Book-of-the-Month Club Selection).

For his fiction Ford has been recognized through a Fulbright Scholarship (1961), a Guggenheim Fellowship (1966), and an honorary D. Litt., Lambuth College, Jackson, Tenn. (1968). The movie *The Liberation of Lord Byron Jones*, however, led to less desirable recognition. Its characters bear similarity to certain citizens of Humboldt; racial tension which it apparently provoked climaxed in an incident in November, 1970, after which Ford was charged with the murder of a black soldier. In July, 1971, he was acquitted by a jury of eleven whites and one black.

Ford's fiction is filled with conflict, with violence, with hate. Yet often his characters are vulnerable, unable to cope with the complexities of their world and the changing country, from the settlement of the wilderness and the Civil War (*The Raider*) to the upheaval of the 1960s (*The Liberation of Lord Byron Jones* and *The Feast of Saint Barnabas*). All of Ford's novels except *Saint Barnabas* and many of his short stories are set in his fictional west Tennessee town of Somerton or surrounding Sligo County. Ford is noted as an oral storyteller, and his fiction is distinguished by gifted narration and concrete images through which he has explored the southern consciousness.

WORKS: *Mountains of Gilead* (1961). *The Conversion of Buster Drumwright: The Television and Stage Scripts* (1964). *The Liberation of Lord Byron Jones* (1965). *Fishes, Birds and Sons of Men: Stories* (1967). *The Feast of Saint Barnabas* (1969). *The Raider* (1975).

MARTHA E. COOK
Longwood College
Farmville, Va.

ALCÉE FORTIER (1856–1914). Author, historian, and educator, Alcée Fortier was one of the most accomplished scholars of Louisiana in his time and a leader in programs to record and preserve the French culture of the state. He was born on June 5, 1856, in St. James Parish, son of Florent Fortier, whose ancestors had been prominent since the early French settlements, and Edwige Aime, daughter of a sugar planter. After preparatory schooling in New Orleans, Fortier attended the University of Virginia. He studied law and began work as a bank clerk, but soon turned to teaching, first in the New Orleans Boys' High School and afterward in the preparatory department of the University of Louisiana, of which he became principal. In 1880 he was appointed professor of French in the university (which soon became Tulane University); in 1894 professor of romance languages; in 1913 dean of the graduate department. In 1881 he married Marie Lanauze, and they had eight children, five of whom survived him. He died on February 14, 1914.

Fortier was one of the first to study the French dialects of Louisiana and to collect and print the lore of the region. In 1904 appeared his major work, a four-volume *History of Louisiana*. He lectured at major universities in the United States, received honorary degrees from Washington and Lee University and from Laval University, and was twice decorated by the French government. He served as president of the Modern Language Association of America, the American Folklore Society, and the Federation de l'Alliance Française; filled long terms as the chief officer of the Louisiana Historical Society and of l'Athéné Louisianais; and served as curator of the Louisiana State Museum and on the Louisiana State Board of Education and the Civil Service Commission.

WORKS: *Sept grands auteurs du XIXe siècle* (1889). *Histoire de la littérature française* (1893). *Louisiana Folk Tales* (1894). *Louisiana Studies* (1894). *Précis de l'histoire de France* (1899). *A History of Louisiana*, 4 vols. (1904). *Central America and Mexico*, with John Rose Ficklen (1907).

ARLIN TURNER
Duke University
Durham, N.C.

JOHN WILLIAM FOX, JR. (1863?–1919). John Fox, Jr., son of John William Fox, Sr., and his second wife, Minerva Carr Fox, attended the boys' school taught by his father in bluegrass Kentucky, and graduated from Harvard, the youngest in his class (1883). His family attributed his lifelong ill health to a college wrestling injury, but his letters indicate tuberculosis. After a semester at Columbia University law school (1883) and six months as reporter on the New York *Sun* (1884), he was sent home to Kentucky to die. Working with his father and brothers to open up mining and timber lands in the Virginia mountains (1885 on), he developed a respectful understanding of the isolated mountain folk, who in turn accorded him respect and affection.

After 1890 Fox continued interest in mining and timber options and, in spates of activity, wrote through the night at the family's new home in Big Stone Gap, Va., going out at intervals to give readings and to visit affluent friends. In addition he reported the Spanish-American War from Cuba (1898), tried unsuccessfully to report the Russo-Japanese War from the front lines (1904), and wooed Mme. Fritzi Scheff through the fashionable summer colonies of New England. From marriage (1908) to divorce (1913) they lived with the Fox family in Big Stone Gap. Fox died of pneumonia, July 8, 1919, an after-effect of the 1918 influenza epidemic.

Personable, affable, sometimes flamboyant, he was welcome in

mountain cabin, Bar Harbor, Newport, and the White House. He
counted Thomas Nelson Page, Richard Harding Davis, and Theodore Roosevelt among his friends, and through Roosevelt was instrumental in distributing federal patronage in Virginia.

Family reluctance to release papers after his death combined
with new national preoccupations after World War I hastened the
decline of his reputation. Sketches of isolated Cumberland mountaineers in his own day placed him among local-color realists, but
Fox's reputation 50 years after his death derives from his more
sentimental historical fiction and from the best-selling *The Little
Shepherd of Kingdom Come* and *The Trail of the Lonesome Pine*.

WORKS: *A Cumberland Vendetta and Other Stories* (1896). *"Hell fer
Sartain" and Other Stories* (1897). *The Kentuckians: A Novel* (1898). *A
Mountain Europa* (1899). *Crittenden: A Kentucky Story of Love and War*
(1900). *Blue-Grass and Rhododendron: Out-Doors in Old Kentucky*
(1901). *The Little Shepherd of Kingdom Come* (1903). *Christmas Eve on
Lonesome and Other Stories* (1904). *Following the Sun-Flag: A Vain Pur-
suit through Manchuria* (1905). *A Knight of the Cumberland* (1906).
The Trail of the Lonesome Pine (1908). *The Heart of the Hills* (1913).
In Happy Valley (1917). *Erskine Dale, Pioneer*, completed by Minnie
Fox (1920). *John Fox and Tom Page as They Were: Letters, an Address,
and an Essay* (1969).

HARRIET R. HOLMAN
Clemson University
Clemson, S.C.

WILLIAM PRICE FOX, JR. (1926–). William Price Fox, Jr., was
born in Waukegan, Ill., on April 9, 1926, one of four sons of William Price and Annette Fanta Fox, Sr. At the age of two he and
his family moved to Columbia, S.C., where Fox attended public
schools, Logan, Wardlaw, and Columbia High School. After leaving school in the tenth grade, he joined the Army Air Corps at the
age of sixteen, but he qualified as a navigator/bombardier and became a second lieutenant before leaving the service in 1946. Fox
then returned to Columbia, completing his high school work in
five months, and entered the University of South Carolina, gradu-

ating with a degree in history in 1950. He taught at Miami Military Academy in 1951, but soon left, and subsequently hitchhiked to New York City.

While working in sales positions in the late 1950s, Fox began his literary career in earnest by attending the New School For Social Research, where he studied under Caroline Gordon, and by publishing his first short stories. In 1962 he began to receive national recognition with the publication of a 40-cent paperback entitled *Southern Fried*. This collection of sixteen short stories, only three of which had been published previously, established Fox as a perceptive observer of character types in the southern scene, particularly in and around Columbia. In both his fiction and his personal essays, he displays an appreciation for the humorous, the idiosyncratic, and the courageous in the human condition.

During the 1960s Fox continued his writing career with two novels, through television and movie scriptwriting in Hollywood (1964–1965), and by publishing several short stories and personal essays, many of which appeared in the *Saturday Evening Post*, *Holiday*, and *Sports Illustrated*. In 1968, at the request of Kurt Vonnegut, Jr., Fox became a teacher at the Writer's Workshop at the University of Iowa, and in 1975 he returned with his wife and two children to his hometown of Columbia as a writer-in-residence at the University of South Carolina.

WORKS: *Southern Fried* (1962). *Dr. Golf* (1963). "The Beverly Hillbillies," television (1964–65). *Moonshine Light, Moonshine Bright* (1967). *Southern Fried Plus Six* (1968). *Cold Turkey*, movie (1968). *Ruby Red* (1971).

HAROLD WOODELL
Clemson University
Clemson, S.C.

EDWIN WILEY FULLER (1847–1876). Poet and novelist, Edwin Wiley Fuller was born on November 30, 1847, and lived his entire life in Louisburg, seat of Franklin County, N.C. He was the only son of Jones Fuller, a cotton broker and merchant, and of

Anna Long Thomas, great-granddaughter of Colonel Nicholas Long, commander of the Halifax military district during the American Revolution.

A small man physically, Fuller was a skillful hunter and horseman and was known for quick wit, droll humor, and conversational ability. Letters from schoolmates speak of his strong character. Later in life he taught Methodist Sunday school and was active in the Friends of Temperance. Entering the University of North Carolina in 1864, he was Delta Psi fraternity anniversary orator as a freshman and a sophomore declaimer at commencement his second year. The next year he worked in his father's store and decided to study law. Fuller entered the University of Virginia in October, 1867, and graduated in 1868. His father's ill health forced a return home to manage the family business until his own death, of pneumonia, on April 22, 1876. In 1871 he married Mary Elisabeth Malone. They had two daughters, Ethel Stuart Fuller, who died at sixteen months, and Edwina Sumner Fuller.

Fuller's two books had made him the best-known writer in the state when he died at age 28. *The Angel in the Cloud* (1871), a long philosophical poem, received favorable reviews in northern newspapers. *Sea-Gift* (1873), his autobiographical novel of student life, was published while he was mayor of Louisburg. It became known as the "Freshman's Bible" at the University of North Carolina and contains folktales, Dickensian humor, and an adaptation of the state's "Dromgoole Legend" about a campus duel.

WORKS: *The Angel in the Cloud* (1871). *Sea-Gift* (1873).

E. T. MALONE, JR.
North Carolina Central University
Durham

CHRISTOPHER GADSDEN (1724–1805). Christopher Gadsden was born on February 6, 1724, at Charleston, S.C., the son of Thomas and Elizabeth Gadsden. After schooling in England, he returned to Charleston when he was sixteen and was then apprenticed to Philadelphia merchant Thomas Lawrence. Gadsden completed his apprenticeship at 21, went again to England, returned to Charleston, served two years as purser of the ship *Aldborough*, and was at the siege of Louisbourgh. When his father died on August 16, 1741, Gadsden and his two brothers inherited his estate. He was thrice married—to Jane Godfrey, who died in May, 1755; to Mary Hasell, who died in January, 1768; and to Anne Wragg, who survived him. Four children from the first two marriages reached maturity.

From 1748 to 1757, Gadsden built a thriving business in wholesaling, retailing, factorage, money-lending, and land speculation. He entered the South Carolina Commons House of Assembly in 1757, and thereafter devoted much of his energy to public service as well as business. Early in his political career, he won favor with the Charleston mechanics and helped lead them in opposition to the British. He opposed the Stamp Act, spoke and wrote early for independence, served in the Second Continental Congress, and helped write the South Carolina Constitution. But disputes with "the old leaven" Charlestonians caused his power to decline in 1778. As lieutenant governor he surrendered Charleston to the British in 1780 and was imprisoned for eleven months in Florida. He declined his election as governor in 1782 and grew increasingly disillusioned and more conservative. A Federalist, he supported the new Constitution and opposed Jefferson and the Republicans. He died in Charleston on August 28, 1805.

A prolific writer, Gadsden contributed chiefly to newspapers and pamphlets published by the Timothys of Charleston. He was a skillful polemicist for independence and later for order in the republic based on constitutional rights. His writings reveal an economic nationalist. He wanted limited democracy, not leveling. He hated and feared slavery but offered no panacea to the disease, and he supported the plantation rather than the manufacturing system, a fact that contributed to the break with the Charleston mechanics. Many of his letters and papers have been lost.

WORKS: *The Writings of Christopher Gadsden*, ed. Richard Walsh (1961). "A Defense of the Houses," *South Carolina Gazette*, December 3, 24, 1764.

RICHARD WALSH
Georgetown University
Washington, D.C.

ERNEST J. GAINES (1933–). The son of Manuel and Adrienne
Colar Gaines, Ernest J. Gaines was born in Oscar, La., on February 15, 1933. As a boy Gaines worked in the plantation fields near
Baton Rouge; he spent most of his free time either alone or with
his aunt, Miss Augusteen Jefferson. Although Gaines wrote and
directed a church play when he was about twelve years old, his
early interest in literature was not nurtured until he moved to
Vallejo, Calif., in 1948, to live with his mother and his stepfather,
who was indirectly responsible for Gaines's reading widely as a
teenager. A merchant marine with a strict code of behavior, his
stepfather instructed him to find something better to do with his
time than to waste it loitering on the streets, and Gaines began
reading in the Vallejo public library. He wanted to learn about the
South and its people, especially about rural blacks, the people who
would later populate his fiction. He found few works which he
thought portrayed blacks or the rural South positively. The lack
of these materials motivated his first extended writing effort. At
age sixteen he wrote in a few weeks a novel. He knew nothing
then about the techniques of fiction writing, and the publisher
immediately rejected it.

Gaines completed high school and then attended a junior college
in Vallejo before he was drafted into the Army in 1953. He entered
San Francisco State College on the G.I. bill in 1955 and graduated
with a B.A. in 1957. While an undergraduate, Gaines wrote a few
short stories, some of which were published in a college magazine.
Two stories helped to gain him a Wallace Stegner Creative Writing
Fellowship in 1958 for graduate study at Stanford, where he concentrated in fiction writing. In 1959 he received the Joseph Henry
Jackson Literary Award for a short story titled "Comeback."

At Stanford Gaines worked on the novel he had tried to write at
age sixteen. In 1964 he published it under the title *Catherine
Carmier*. In 1966 he received a grant from the National Endowment for the Arts. The following year he published *Bloodline*, a
collection of five stories told from the point of view of children of
varying ages.

Gaines has expressed admiration for works by Chekhov, Turgenev, Zora Neale Hurston, Ellison, and Baldwin, among others, and for short fiction by Hemingway and James Alan McPherson. He has admitted the influence of Faulkner's *The Sound and the Fury*. But the substance of his fiction derives from the rural Louisiana South, and it is out of this background that he produced his most critically successful work, *The Autobiography of Miss Jane Pittman* (1971), a novel he described as "folk autobiography." Gaines has nearly perfected his art in this novel, and the title character (who is based on his aunt Augusteen Jefferson) will likely become one of the most memorable characters in American literature.

In 1971 he was writer-in-residence at Denison University in Granville, Ohio. He has lived near or in San Francisco for almost 30 years, but periodically he travels to rural Louisiana.

WORKS: *Catherine Carmier* (1964). *Of Love and Dust* (1967). *Bloodline* (1968). *The Autobiography of Miss Jane Pittman* (1971).

J. LEE GREENE
University of North Carolina
Chapel Hill

FRANCES GAITHER (1889–1955). Frances Ormond Jones Gaither was born on May 21, 1889, in Sommerville, Tenn., to Annie Smith and Paul Tudor Jones. Her father, a doctor and son of a substantial antebellum planter, moved his family to Corinth, Miss., soon after "Frankie" was born. In 1909 Frances was graduated with highest honors from Mississippi State College for Women (now Mississippi University for Women) where she had been student body president. After teaching senior high school English for a brief period in Corinth, she married journalist Rice Gaither, who had been her childhood sweetheart, on April 25, 1912. The couple lived first in Fairhope, Ala., and then in 1929 moved to New York City where Rice Gaither was a reporter and feature writer for the New York *Times* until his death in 1953. Frances Gaither died in Cocoa, Fla., on October 28, 1955.

She began her career by writing ceremonial pageants and

masques; among these are *The Commencement Play of the Class of
1915* (including "The Pageant of Columbus"), "The Book of
Words," and "The Clock and the Fountain" which she wrote for
her alma mater, and "The Shadow of the Builder" and "Shores
of Happiness" for the University of Virginia, the former celebrating that university's centennial. During the 1930s she wrote four
children's books (three stories, *The Painted Arrow*, *The Scarlet
Coat*, and *Little Miss Cappo*, and one biography, *The Fatal River*,
about La Salle). Turning to adult fiction in 1940 with *Follow the
Drinking Gourd*, she found the antebellum plantation setting and
theme upon which her reputation as a serious novelist rests. It was
a world she knew through the tales told in Corinth and Sommerville. Her last novel, *Double Muscadine*, was a Book-of-the-Month
Club selection for March, 1949.

WORKS: *The Painted Arrow* (1931). *The Fatal River: The Life and Death
of La Salle* (1931). *The Scarlet Coat* (1934). *Little Miss Cappo* (1937).
Follow the Drinking Gourd (1940). *The Red Cock Crows* (1944). *Double
Muscadine* (1949).

ROBERT L. PHILLIPS, JR.
Mississippi State University
Starkville

ALEXANDER GARDEN (ca. 1730–1791). Alexander Garden, a
native of Aberdeen, was a product of the Scottish parochial system
of education and the University of Edinburgh. Upon his arrival in
Charleston, S.C., in April, 1752, he became the central figure in a
circle of doctors from North Britain: John Lining, Lionel Chal-
mers, David Olyphant, John Moultrie, George Milligen, John and
William Murray, and David and Lewis Caw. With Dr. Lining he
corresponded with Doctors Charles Alston and Robert Whytt of
Edinburgh, the description, history, and account of "our Pink
Root" being the literary effort which introduced him to the Philosophical Society of Edinburgh.

The second circle in which he moved consisted of Cadwalader
Colden of New York and John Bartram of Philadelphia, contacts

that brought him in touch with John Ellis and the members of the Society of Arts in London.

For his British and American friends he became a collector. In 1756 he made a journey with Governor James Glen to the Saluda River. The journal he kept was to have been a report to the Royal Society of London, but *"Iter Saludiense"* was never published. In 1771, upon the death of Dr. John Moultrie, he purchased the Moultrie plantation at Goose Creek, renamed it Otranto, and established a botanical garden. George Roupell and later young John Laurens made drawings of flora and fauna which were sent to his friends. Perhaps if he had been less busy in his practice and in his instruction of the young, he would have completed more reports. A few brief papers were published in the *Essays and Observations, Physical & Literary* of the Philosophical Society of Edinburgh and in the *Transactions* of the Royal Society of London.

In the 1750s he acted as literary agent for one ambitious young Scotsman in Carolina who had written an essay on love. During the American Revolution he retired to England as a Loyalist where he lived out the remainder of his days. He died from tuberculosis on April 15, 1791.

WORKS: "The Description of a New Plant," *Essays and Observations, Physical & Literary*, II (1756), 1–7. *An Account of the Medical Properties of the Virginia Pink-Root* (1764). Description of the "Siren Lacertina" in Abraham Oester, *Amoenitates Academiae*, VII (1766), 311–21. "Account of the Indian Pink," *Essays and Observations, Physical & Literary*, III (1771), 145–53 and plate. Description of a soft-shelled turtle in Thomas Pennant, "An Account of two new Tortoises; in a letter to Matthew Maty," *Transactions of the Royal Society of London*, LXI (1771), 267–71. "An Account of the *Gymnotus Electricus*, or Electrical Eel, In a Letter from Alexander Garden, M.D., F.R.S., to John Ellis, Esq., F.R.S.," *Transactions of the Royal Society of London*, LXV (1775), 102–10. Description of a tornado in Thomas Pennant, *Arctic Zoology: Supplement* (London, 1788), 41–44.

GEORGE C. ROGERS, JR.
University of South Carolina
Columbia

GEORGE PALMER GARRETT (1929–). Son of George Palmer, Sr., and Rosalie Toomer Garrett, George Garrett was born on June 11, 1929, in Orlando, Fla. He attended Sewanee Military Academy, the Hill School, and Princeton University, from which he graduated in 1952. After three years in the army, he returned to Princeton, receiving, in 1956, a master's degree in English. From 1957 to 1960, when he taught at Wesleyan University and spent a year in Rome on the American Academy's Prix de Rome and a *Sewanee Review* fellowship, he established a remarkably productive writing career, publishing two volumes of poetry, a collection of short stories, and a novel about Florida politics entitled *The Finished Man*. He then moved to Houston, Tex., where he taught at Rice University and worked with the Alley Theatre on a Ford Foundation Fellowship. While in Houston he produced another collection of stories, a third book of poems, two plays (one of which was published), and *Which Ones Are the Enemy?* a novel about military life in Trieste.

Resuming his teaching career at the University of Virginia (1963–1967) and Hollins College (1967–1971), he continued to write in several genres. He worked on screenplays for Hollywood films and completed two more collections of stories, another book of poems, and the novel *Do, Lord, Remember Me*. In 1971, when he joined the faculty of the University of South Carolina, his highly praised novel *Death of the Fox*, based on the execution of Sir Walter Raleigh, appeared. After publishing three shorter works of fiction under the title *The Magic Striptease*, he returned to Princeton University in 1974 as lecturer in creative writing. He has also written literary criticism, compiled several anthologies, and served as an editor of the *Hollins Critic*, *Contempora*, and the *Transatlantic Review*.

WORKS: *The Reverend Ghost: Poems* (1957). *King of the Mountain* (1957). *The Sleeping Gypsy and Other Poems* (1958). *The Finished Man* (1959). *Abraham's Knife and Other Poems* (1961). *In the Briar Patch: A Book of Stories* (1961). *Which Ones Are the Enemy?* (1961). *Sir Slob and the Princess* (1962). *Cold Ground Was My Bed Last Night* (1964). *Do, Lord, Remember Me* (1965). *For a Bitter Season: New and Selected Poems*

(1967). *A Wreath for Garibaldi and Other Stories* (1969). *Death of the Fox* (1971). *The Magic Striptease* (1973).

C. MICHAEL SMITH
Winthrop College
Rock Hill, S.C.

CHARLES GAYARRÉ (1805–1895). On January 9, 1805, Charles Étienne Arthur Gayarré was born into one of Louisiana's most prominent families. In 1830, his legal education completed, the young lawyer published *Essai historique sur la Louisiane*, essentially a translation of Martin's *History of Louisiana* (1827). Gayarré rose from state senator (1830) to assistant attorney general (1831) to attorney general (1832) to presiding judge of the City Court of New Orleans (1832–1835). Although he was elected to the U.S. Senate in 1835, poor health forced him to resign, and he spent most of the next eight years in France. After returning to New Orleans, he served as state senator and as Louisiana's secretary of state. Defeat in the 1853 election prompted him to attack political corruption in pamphlets and a "dramatic novel," *The School for Politics* (1854).

The time spent in Europe and his political positions enabled Gayarré to collect documents from European archives which he cited at great length in *Histoire de la Louisiane* (1846–1847). Desiring a larger readership he abandoned French for English in *Romance of the History of Louisiana* (1848), a series of lectures that grew into the four-volume *History of Louisiana* (1866), his major work. Influenced by Scott, he at first tended to sacrifice fact to romance, but beginning with his coverage of the Spanish administration, the history became accurate as well as vivid.

His fortune lost during the Civil War, Gayarré lived in near poverty until his death on February 11, 1895. He was a dominant figure in Louisiana's literary circles and the author of a psychological study, *Philip II of Spain* (1866), an autobiographical novel, *Fernando de Lemos* (1872), other fiction, a comedy, and many essays and pamphlets.

WORKS: *Essai historique sur la Louisiane* (1830). *Histoire de la Louisiane* (1846–47). *Romance of the History of Louisiana* (1848). *Louisiana:*

Its Colonial History and Romance (1851). *Louisiana: Its History as a French Colony* (1852). *History of Louisiana: The French Domination* (1854). *History of Louisiana: The Spanish Domination* (1854). *The School for Politics: A Dramatic Novel* (1854). *Dr. Bluff in Russia, or The Emperor Nicholas and the American Doctor: A Comedy in Two Acts* (1865). *History of Louisiana: The American Domination* (1866). *History of Louisiana* (1866, 1879, 1885, 1903). *Philip II of Spain* (1866). *Fernando de Lemos: Truth and Fiction* (1872). *Aubert Dubayet, or The Two Sister Republics* (1882).

ALFRED BENDIXEN
University of North Carolina
Chapel Hill

CAROLINE HOWARD GILMAN (1794–1888). The youngest daughter of Samuel Howard, an "Indian" of the Boston Tea Party, Caroline Gilman was born on October 8, 1794, in Boston. Reared by an older sister, Ann Marie White, whose own daughter married James Russell Lowell, Caroline wrote poetry, visited her brothers who were merchants in Savannah, and in 1819 married the Reverend Samuel Gilman. The Reverend Gilman and his new bride moved immediately to Charleston, S.C., where he served as a famous Unitarian minister for almost 40 years. After his death in 1858, Gilman continued to live in Charleston and the South until 1873, when she moved to her married daughter's in the North. She died on September 15, 1888.

Her Boston upbringing was conducive to her conservatism, modesty, and piety, traits furthered by her marriage to a minister. Her love of Charleston and southern ways was a natural response to her years of active social and cultural involvement in her new home. Perhaps the only characteristic not predicated by her cultural environment was her delightful sense of humor revealed throughout her life in her best writing and especially in her family letters.

An early interest in providing suitable reading for her own and other children led her in 1832 to found and to edit the *Rose Bud*, later the *Southern Rose Bud*, and for the final four years, as a magazine for adults, the *Southern Rose*. It published some leading contemporaries, including Hawthorne and Simms, and was also the source for her own later books. Notable were her editing of the *Letters of Eliza Wilkinson* (eye witness accounts of the Revolutionary War in Charleston) and her own lively *Recollections of a Housekeeper*, *Recollections of a Southern Matron*, and *Poetry of Travelling in the United States*. If her writing, especially her poetry, seems overly didactic now, her contemporary popularity was not thereby weakened. Indeed, she was clearly the best-known southern woman writer in the quarter century, 1833–1858. An overlooked resource for social histories is her lifelong effort to educate the North to the ways of life in the South, for she felt that as a daughter of New England she was in the best position to explain her adopted region.

WORKS: *The Rose Bud, or Youth's Gazette* (1832–33). *Southern Rose Bud*, II–III (1833–35). *The Southern Rose*, IV–VII (1835–39). *The Lady's Register and Housewife's Memorandum-Book* (1839–41). *Recollections of a Housekeeper* (1834, 1836, 1838, 1842). *Tales and Ballads* (1834, 1838, 1839, 1844). *Recollections of a Southern Matron* (1837, 1838, 1839, 1852, 1854). *The Poetry of Travelling in the United States* (1838). Ed., *Letters of Eliza Wilkinson, During the Invasion and Possession of Charleston, S.C. by the British in the Revolutionary War* (1839, 1969). *Love's Progress* (1840). *The Rose-Bud Wreath* (1841). *Oracles from the Poets: A Fanciful Diversion for the Drawing-Room* (1844, 1845, 1847, 1848, 1849, 1852, 1853, 1854). *Stories and Poems for Children* (1844, 1845). *The Little Wreath of Stories and Poems for Children* (1846). *The Sibyl, or, New Oracles from the Poets* (1848, 1849, 1852). *Verses of a Life Time* (1849). *A Gift Book of Stories and Poems for Children* (1850, 1854). *Oracles for Youth. A Home Pastime* (1852, 1853). "My Autobiography," *The Female Prose Writers of America*, ed. John S. Hart (1852), 49–57. *Recollections of a New England Bride and of a Southern Matron* (1852, 1854). *Recollections of a Southern Matron, and a New England Bride* (1859, 1867, 1889). *Record of Inscriptions in the Cemetery and Building of the Unitarian, Formerly Denominated the Independent Church, Archdale Street, Charleston, S.C., from 1777 to 1860* (1860). *Stories and Poems by Mother and Daughter*, with Caroline Howard Jervey (1872). *The Young Fortune Teller; Oracles for Youth* (1874). *The Poetic Fate Book: New Oracles from the Poets* (1874). *Recollections of the Private Centennial Celebration of the Overthrow of the Tea, At*

Griffin's Wharf, in Boston Harbor, December 16, 1773, in Honor of Samuel Howard, One of the Actors, at Cambridge, Mass., December, 1873 (1874). "Letters of a Confederate Mother: Charleston in the Sixties," *Atlantic Monthly*, CXXXVII (April, 1926), 503–15.

JANICE JOAN THOMPSON
Raleigh, N.C.

FRANCIS WALKER GILMER (1790–1826). The tenth child of Dr. George Gilmer, Francis Walker Gilmer was born on October 9, 1790, at Pen Park, an estate across the river from Monticello. Christened Francis Thornton Gilmer, he assumed the name of his uncle Francis Walker after the latter's death in 1806. After his father's death in 1795, Gilmer remained in Albemarle County, Va., until he was eighteen as a guest-ward of his neighbors. He entered William and Mary College in 1809 and by January, 1811, he was practicing law in Richmond under the tutelage of William Wirt. After moving to Winchester in July, 1814, he returned to Richmond in 1818 to take over Wirt's substantial practice. Here Gilmer also served as the court reporter for the Virginia Court of Appeals (1820–1821) and laid the foundation for an eminent legal career.

The extraordinary achievements predicted for Gilmer, whom his friend Jefferson called "the best educated subject we have raised since the Revolution," were never fully realized. Yet, despite his weak constitution, he became an accomplished lawyer, as well as an author, geologist, economist, botanist, and social scientist. He was elected the first professor of law at the University of Virginia and was entrusted by Jefferson to travel to Europe in 1824 to select and hire the institution's future faculty.

The range of Gilmer's erudition is mirrored by his writings. His claim to literary fame is founded upon his *Sketches of American Orators* (1816), one of the first evaluations of the finest practitioners of America's then most widespread literary endeavor. His "On the Geological Formation of the Natural Bridge of Virginia" (1816) was the first treatise to suggest the still accepted theory of formation by erosion due to an underground stream. Gilmer's interest in Virginiana also led to his publishing the first scholarly

American editions of John Smith's *General Historie of Virginia* and Smith's *Memoirs* (1819). Although somewhat a preromantic in taste, Gilmer, in his "Reflections on the Institutions of the Chero- kee Indians" (1818), a result of his excursion to Georgia (1815), describes the Indians not as noble savages but as a "mixture of insensibility, vulgarity, and vice." In economics, his *Vindication* (1820) was a highly esteemed rebuttal of Jeremy Bentham's classic *Defense of Usury*. Gilmer's busy legal career and subsequent ill- nesses precluded any further publication. He died a bachelor on February 25, 1826, a victim of pulmonary consumption.

WORKS: *Sketches of American Orators* (1816). "On the Geological Forma- tion of the Natural Bridge of Virginia," *Publications of the American Philosophical Society*, n.s., I (February, 1816). "Reflections on the Insti- tutions of the Cherokee Indians, from Observations Made During a Recent Visit to That Tribe: In a Letter from a Gentleman of Virginia to Robert Walsh, Jan.–June 1st. 1817," *Analectic Magazine*, XII (July, 1818). Editions of *The General Historie of Virginia, New England, and the Summer Iles . . .* and *The True Travels, Adventures and Observa- tions of Captaine John Smith . . .* (1819). *A Vindication of the Laws, Limiting the Rate of Interest on Loans; from the Objections of Jeremy Bentham, and the Edinburgh Reviewers* (1820). *Reports of Cases De- cided in the Court of Appeals of Virginia* (from Apr. 10, 1820, to June 28, 1821) (1821). *Sketches, Essays and Translations* (1828).

MICHAEL A. LOFARO
University of Tennessee
Knoxville

NIKKI GIOVANNI (1943–). Yolande Cornelia Giovanni, Jr. (Nikki) was born on June 7, 1943, in Knoxville, Tenn., to black middle-class parents. Her father, Jones, and her mother, Yolande, both graduated from Knoxville College. Her maternal grandfather, Thomas "Book" Watson, was also a college graduate and taught Latin, first in Albany, Ga., then later in Knoxville.

At an early age, Giovanni moved to Cincinnati, Ohio, her fa- ther's home, with her parents and Gary, her older sister. They set- tled in Lincoln Heights, a black middle-class suburb. Giovanni

attended school in Cincinnati, first in public school, later in parochial school. She attended high school in Knoxville. At Fisk University where she went as an early entrant in 1959, Giovanni was
expelled for exhibiting "attitudes unbecoming a Fisk woman." She
was later reinstated and received her degree in history in 1967. At
Fisk she was active politically and was also a student in the writing
classes of John Oliver Killens, the black novelist, who was writer-
in-residence.

After her graduation Giovanni entered the Pennsylvania School
of Social Work, intending to become a social worker. But the work
palled on her, and she left without completing the program. In
1968 she enrolled in Columbia University seeking a master's degree in the School of Fine Arts. She had proposed a novel as a
thesis, but she completed neither the master's degree nor the
novel.

With the publication of *Black Feeling, Black Talk* (1968), Giovanni became one of the new wave of black poets. By the early
1970s, she had become a major media person. She employed a
publicist and made innumerable appearances on television talk
shows, and was and is a major figure on the college lecture circuit.

Giovanni lives in New York City and has a son, Thomas, whose
father's name she declines to reveal. Since 1969 she has been a
member of the faculty of Livingston College of Rutgers University.

WORKS: *Black Feeling, Black Talk* (1968). *Black Judgment* (1969). *Re:
Creation* (1970). *Broadside Poem of Angela Yvonne Davis* (1970). Ed.,
Night Comes Softly: Anthology of Black Female Voices (1970). *Black
Feeling, Black Talk/Black Judgment* (1970). *Spin a Soft Black Song:
Poems for Children* (1971). *Gemini* (1971). *My House* (1972). *James Bald-
win and Nikki Giovanni: A Dialogue* (1973). *Ego Tripping and Other
Poems for Young People* (1973). *A Poetic Equation: Conversation Between
Nikki Giovanni and Margaret Walker* (1974).

MARY MEBANE
University of South Carolina
Columbia

ELLEN GLASGOW (1873–1945). Although modern southern literature grew out of ground cleared, and for the most part tended,

by Ellen Glasgow, traditional attitudes about women have left important episodes of her life distorted by rumor and speculation. No official record exists to show whether she was born April 21, 1874, or April 22, 1873. In either case, she was the eighth of ten children (eight lived to maturity) of Francis Thomas Glasgow, who managed Tredegar Iron Works in Richmond and whose roots ran back to the Scotch Presbyterians of the Shenandoah Valley. Her mother was the orphaned daughter of an orphaned mother, although her ties were to many of the oldest families of Tidewater Virginia. Ellen Glasgow received almost no formal education, but relatives and tutors taught her to read and write.

In her late teens she started a novel, and shortly thereafter fell under the guidance of Walter McCormack of Charleston, her sister Cary's husband-to-be, who directed her attention to Charles Darwin and to the other thinkers who shaped her views of man and society. Her interest in critical realism hardened to pessimism when, within the period of a few years, she experienced difficulty hearing, rebelled against her father's inflexible religion, watched her mother die (1893), failed to conclude either of two novels satisfactorily, and, finally in 1894, learned that McCormack, for whom she had developed a deep respect, had committed suicide under sordid circumstances.

To work out her bitterness she finished the second of the novels she had begun, a Darwinian study of New York's Bohemia called *The Descendant* (1897), which she followed with a second bohemian study before choosing her native state as the scene of *The Voice of the People* (1900), the first of the novels eventually to compose her social history of Virginia. By 1905 this series included a Civil War novel and a powerful exploration of tensions that beset agrarian classes after the war.

During this fruitful period (1899–1905), she found herself involved in the most devastating of her three important affairs, a sometimes ecstatic romance with a married man she later called "Gerald B." "Gerald B." has been variously identified as a figment of her imagination, as another woman, as a middle-aged New York aurist, H. Holbrook Curtis (1856–1920), as an important New York neurologist, Pearce Bailey (1865–1922), and as the fiction editor of

Bobbs-Merrill, Hewitt Hanson Howland (1863–1944). While some
of these possibilities need not exclude one another, recent evidence points toward Howland, whose wife of fifteen years sued for
divorce in 1903 on grounds that he had failed to provide. Glasgow
was later engaged twice: between 1906 and 1909 to Frank Ilsley
Paradise, a roving Episcopal minister and author, and from 1917,
off and on, to Henry Watkins Anderson, a prominent Richmond
lawyer, adventurer, and experimental politician, who remained
her frequent visitor long after their engagement wore itself out.

Each of the latter two romances spanned a fallow phase in the
career of Glasgow, who reached her full power with *Virginia*
(1913), the best of her books before 1925. After her closest brother
committed suicide in 1909 and her sister Cary died in 1911, Glasgow, now a feminist, took an apartment in New York, where she
lived for the most part until her father, from whom she still felt
estranged, died in 1916; then she returned to the family home
in Richmond, to live with a nurse-secretary. Her poorest work fell
around 1918, when Howland remarried, Walter Hines Page her
early publisher died, and rumors of Anderson's wartime flirtation
with Queen Marie of Rumania caused the author to attempt suicide. After these troubles forced her to confront deeper levels of
herself, she exceeded her former powers in the lacerating *Barren
Ground* (1925) and the two scintillant comedies of manners that
preceded her finest book, *The Sheltered Life* (1932). During this
period many writers formed friendships with her, but her special
confidant was notorious James Branch Cabell. As woman of letters
she reached her height in 1931, when she presided in spirit and
flesh at the first modern Southern Writers Conference, held at the
University of Virginia.

With *Vein of Iron* (1935) the intensity of her characterization
began to fail, and *In This Our Life* (1941), written despite two
heart attacks, revealed a weakening of stylistic control, although it
brought her the Pulitzer Prize (1942). Her exceptional contribution
to regional and national letters had previously earned special
recognition from four universities, the National Institute of Arts
and Letters (1932), the American Academy of Arts and Letters
(1938 and 1940), and the *Saturday Review of Literature* (1941). Her

collected prefaces (1943) presented Ellen Glasgow as master of the novel, the mask she wore for her public. When she died on November 21, 1945, she left in manuscript a sequel to *In This Our Life*, plus her autobiography in which she exposed the victim's mask she wore for her intimates and, it seems, for herself.

WORKS: *The Descendant* (1897). *Phases of an Inferior Planet* (1898). *The Voice of the People* (1900). *The Battle-Ground* (1902). *The Freeman and Other Poems* (1902). *The Deliverance* (1904). *The Wheel of Life* (1906). *The Ancient Law* (1908). *The Romance of a Plain Man* (1909). *The Miller of Old Church* (1911). *Virginia* (1913). *Life and Gabriella* (1916). *The Builders* (1919). *One Man in His Time* (1922). *The Shadowy Third and Other Stories* (1923). *Barren Ground* (1925). *The Romantic Comedians* (1926). *They Stooped to Folly* (1929). *The Sheltered Life* (1932). *Vein of Iron* (1935). *In This Our Life* (1941). *A Certain Measure* (1943). *The Woman Within* (1954). *Letters of Ellen Glasgow*, ed. Blair Rouse (1958). *The Collected Stories of Ellen Glasgow*, ed. Richard K. Meeker (1963). *Beyond Defeat*, ed. Luther Y. Gore (1966).

JULIUS R. RAPER
University of North Carolina
Chapel Hill

CAROLINE GORDON (1895–). Caroline Gordon, writer of novels and short fiction, was born on October 6, 1895, at Merry Mont farm, Todd County, Ky. Her mother's family, whose name was Meriwether, had come to southwestern Kentucky from Virginia in the eighteenth century to set up as tobacco planters. Her father, James Morris Gordon, was a Virginian who went to Kentucky as a tutor for the Meriwether connection. He was the original for the central figure of the novel *Aleck Maury, Sportsman* (1934) and a related group of stories. Caroline Gordon was not required to attend formal classes until she was fourteen because her father, who conducted a classical school for boys in nearby Clarkesville, Tenn., felt it was only necessary to learn Greek, Latin, and mathematics.

Gordon attended Bethany College in West Virginia; she was graduated in 1916 (30 years later her alma mater awarded her an honorary Litt. D.). After college she taught high school for three years and then worked as a journalist on the Chattanooga *News* from 1920 to 1924. At this time the Fugitive poets in Nashville were attracting attention in southern literary circles; Gordon was one of the first to recognize them, and in fact she was acquainted with Robert Penn Warren, who was also from Todd County. Through him she met Allen Tate, whom she married on November 2, 1924. The marriage was ended by divorce in August, 1959.

From 1924 to 1928 the Tates lived in New York, where they were on close terms with Hart Crane and many other writers of their generation. In her later novels, beginning with *The Women on the Porch* (1944), Gordon often draws on this phase of their life. Of special importance to her was her friendship with the British novelist Ford Madox Ford. In 1928 the Tates went to France for almost two years on a Guggenheim Fellowship which he had been awarded. During this period she published her first stories in *Gyroscope*, a little magazine edited by Yvor Winters in California, and she worked on her novel, *Penhally*, which was published in 1931.

In 1930 the Tates returned to Tennessee with their daughter, Nancy (born 1925), and settled in an old house which they called Benfolly, located only a few miles from Clarksville. They lived here most of the time until 1938. Gordon published four novels and a number of stories during these years, most of them concerned with the history of families very much like her own. Many years later she recreated the Benfolly of the 1930s in *The Strange Children* (1951).

Gordon held her first academic appointment in 1938–1939 at the Woman's College of the University of North Carolina, and since then she has been writer-in-residence or lecturer at many universities. She has been a critic as well as a teacher. *The House of Fiction* and *How to Read a Novel* are an important part of her ouevre. But the practice of fiction continues to be her central work. In 1956 she published a novel, *The Malefactors*, which examines the life of her literary generation from the viewpoint of the Roman Catholic faith, which she had adopted in the late 1940s. *The Glory of Hera* (1972) is the first part of a two-volume novel to be called *Behold My Trembling Heart*. Gordon is head of the creative writing program at the University of Dallas in Irving, Tex., where she has lived since 1973.

WORKS: *Penhally* (1931). *Aleck Maury, Sportsman* (1934). *None Shall Look Back* (1937). *The Garden of Adonis* (1937). *Green Centuries* (1941). *The Women on the Porch* (1944). *The Forest of the South* (1945). *The House of Fiction: An Anthology of the Short Story*, with Allen Tate (1950). *The Strange Children* (1951). *The Malefactors* (1956). *How to Read a Novel* (1957). *Old Red and Other Stories* (1963). *The Glory of Hera* (1972).

ASHLEY BROWN
University of South Carolina
Columbia

FRANCIS ROBERT GOULDING (1810–1881). In a sermon upon Goulding's death on August 22, 1881, the Reverend John Jones said of him, "His active mind ranged over a vast field with intelligence and marked originality. As a writer for the young he stood in the forefront of the best authors of the age."

Francis Robert Goulding was born in the Midway Community of Liberty County, Ga., on September 28, 1810. Midway had been settled in the 1750s by New England Puritan descendants. Goulding's father Thomas, a Presbyterian clergyman, was educated at New Haven, and his mother, Ann Holbrook, was a native of Wolcott, Conn. At nineteen Francis Goulding was graduated from the University of Georgia and at 22 received his degree from the Columbia (S.C.) Theological Seminary of which his father was president. He married Mary Wallace Howard in 1833, and they had six children, the eldest Charles Howard Goulding dying in December, 1862, in camp during the Civil War. After his first wife's death, he married Matilda Rees in 1855. They became the parents of two daughters.

In 1842, while serving a pastorate in Eatonton, Ga., Goulding developed a sewing machine four years before Howe's patent, although he himself did not apply for a patent. His literary career began inauspiciously with the publication of a pious children's book, *Little Josephine*. By 1852, after much toil and refinement, Goulding published the work on which his fame rests, *Robert and*

Harold; or, The Young Marooners on the Florida Coast. This juvenile proved immensely popular going through over ten editions in America and England, as well as being translated into several foreign languages. During the Civil War he compiled the *Soldiers Hymn Book* and also served unofficially as a Confederate chaplain. In the years following the war he continued work on stories for youth. *Marooners Island* (1867) gained some popularity, but the three novels in his "Woodruff Stories" (1870–1871) received little notice.

Goulding's life was spent ministering and teaching the citizens of Georgia. His pastorates included Greensboro, Washington, Eatonton, and Bath in north Georgia and Darien in the south. He operated schools in Kingston, near Atlanta, and in Macon. His last years were spent in ill health and in near poverty, at Roswell, but, to his death, he remained compassionately concerned about the spiritual and educational development of southern youth.

WORKS: *Little Josephine* (1844). *Robert and Harold: or, The Young Marooners on the Florida Coast* (1852). *Soldiers Hymn Book* (1864). *Marooners Island* (1868). *Frank Gordon* (1869). *Life Scenes from the Gospel History* (1870). *Sal-o-quah* (1870). *Tah-le-quah* (1870). *Nacoochee* (1871). *Sapelo; or Child Life in the Tide Waters* (1888).

ROBERT M. WILLINGHAM, JR.
University of Georgia
Athens

WILLIAM GOYEN (1915–). William Goyen was born on April 24, 1915, in Trinity, Tex., to Charles Provine and Mary Inez Trow Goyen. In 1922 the Goyens moved to Shreveport, and within a year moved again, this time to Houston, Tex. After graduating from Sam Houston High School, Goyen entered Rice University. Until he discovered literature he found college life intolerable; then he wanted to be an actor, or composer, or dancer, or singer. He won every prize offered in both fiction and drama during his junior and senior years, and went on to earn a B.A. in 1932 and an M.A. in comparative literature in 1939.

Goyen enlisted in the Navy in 1940 and served three and a half years on an aircraft carrier in the South Pacific. To pass the time, he wrote. In 1945 he moved to El Prado, N.Mex., and two years later had the first of the pieces written during the war published in the *Southwest Review*, a little magazine which would publish most of his short fiction and which awarded him its Literary Fellowship in 1948. His first novel, *House of Breath*, appeared in 1950 and won him the Texas Institute of Arts & Letters Award for Fiction and the McMurray Bookship Award for the best first work by a Texan. Two Guggenheim fellowships in the early 1950s and an editorial position at McGraw-Hill helped provide income after he moved to New York. In 1953 his dramatic adaptation of his first book appeared at The Circle in the Square. From 1955 to 1960 Goyen taught at the New School for Social Research. During 1963–1964 he worked at Lincoln Center Repertory Theatre under a grant from the Ford Foundation, and on November 10, 1963, married the actress Doris Roberts.

Goyen has alternated between drama and prose fiction. His work, tending toward the gothic or surrealistic, became "classic" in 1974 when his *Selected Writings* appeared, followed by his *Collected Stories* and reissue of his first novel, *House of Breath*, in 1975.

WORKS: *The House of Breath*, novel (1950). *Ghost and Flesh: Stories and Tales* (1952). *In a Farther Country: A Romance* (1955). *The House of Breath*, play (1956). *The Faces of Blood Kindred: A Novella and Ten Short Stories* (1960). *The Bite of the Diamond Rattler* (1960). *The Fair Sister* (1963). *Christy* (1964). *The House of Breath Black/White* (1972). *A Book of Jesus* (1973). *Come the Restorer: A Novel* (1974). *Aimée* (1974). *Selected Writings of William Goyen* (1974). *Collected Stories of William Goyen* (1975).

E. BRUCE KIRKHAM
Ball State University
Muncie, Ind.

HENRY WOODFIN GRADY (1850–1889). Henry Woodfin Grady was born on May 24, 1850, in Athens, Ga., to Ann Gartrell and William Sammons Grady, a substantial merchant. Graduated from the University of Georgia in 1868, Grady attended the University of Virginia the following year, where he excelled in oratory and showed journalistic talent.

Returning to Georgia, Grady married Julia King in 1871 and began a career in journalism, working for various newspapers, including the Atlanta *Constitution*, during the 1870s. In 1880 he bought a quarter interest in the *Constitution*. Under his lead as managing editor, the paper soon became the preeminent organ of the New South movement, an attempt to effect regional prosperity mainly through industrialization.

Not only in press but also at podium, Grady, the foremost spokesman of the movement, hailed what he perceived to be the matchless material progress of the postbellum South. To sustain this progress he entreated the North and the South to surmount sectional animosity so that northern capital might more readily move south. To insure the social stability prized by northern investors, he proposed that the race problem be solved to the satisfaction of all. Granted northern restraint and trust, white southerners would respect the civil and political rights of black southerners but would maintain white supremacy and segregation, an arrangement merely reflecting the instinct of both races. These matters settled, nothing could hinder the South, with its abundant resources, from achieving the prosperity ordained by Providence. Late in his life, though, Grady began to view concentrated capital selfishly used as a threat to regional progress.

Throughout his writings and speeches, Grady prefaced his tribute to the new order with encomiums to the legendary Old South and the "hero in gray" of the Lost Cause. The emotional appeal of his addresses made him a figure of national stature.

After a speaking engagement in Boston late in 1889, Grady developed pneumonia and died in Atlanta on December 23. The dream of a prosperous New South, his own claims notwithstanding, remained far from fulfillment.

WORKS: *Life and Labors of Henry W. Grady: His Speeches, Writings, etc.* (1890). *The New South*, six articles first published in the New York *Ledger*, November 16–December 21, 1889 (1890). "Writings and Speeches," in Joel Chandler Harris, *Life of Henry W. Grady* (1890). *The*

Speeches of Henry W. Grady (1895). *The New South and Other Addresses* (1904). *The Complete Orations and Speeches of Henry W. Grady*, ed. Edwin DuBois Shurter (1910). *The New South: Writings and Speeches of Henry W. Grady* (1971).

WAYNE MIXON
Mercer University
Macon, Ga.

EDWIN GRANBERRY (1897-). Although a native Mississippian, Edwin Granberry is more closely identified with the backwoods of southern Florida. He was born in Meridian, Miss., on April 18, 1897, but moved to Florida with his family at age ten. He attended the University of Florida, obtained his A.B. from Columbia University, and did postgraduate work at Harvard where he was a member of George Pierce Baker's 47 Workshop from 1922 to 1924. Originally trained as a concert pianist, he later returned to teaching romance languages at various places and in 1933 was appointed associate professor of creative literature at Rollins College, Winter Park, Fla., where he still resides.

Granberry's work includes three translations from the French, two plays, numerous articles and short stories, and four novels. Much of his fame, however, rests on one short story, "A Trip to Czardis," which he says "has so overshadowed all my other writings that one might suppose it to be the only thing I have written." Since publication in *Forum* in 1932 and receipt of the O. Henry Memorial Prize, the story has been anthologized over 30 times and adapted for both radio and television.

All four of Granberry's novels demonstrate a sustained atmosphere of regional scene with exalted characters set against an elemental landscape. His second novel, *Strangers and Lovers*, a story of two young ill-fated lovers, was the first writing to introduce the Florida "cracker" into American literature and attracted wide critical acclaim. *A Trip to Czardis*, the only one of his books which he considers mature, appeared 36 years after his third novel. Hailed by many reviewers as a masterpiece, the book, which derived from the story, is a powerful and highly sensitive portrayal of the irra-

tional forces that drive ordinary human beings. He is presently at
work on a novel based on his play *The Falcon*, which was produced
at Rollins College in 1951. Another play, *Hitch Your Wagon to a
Star*, had been produced at 47 Workshop, Harvard University,
in 1924. For the past 30 years Granberry has coauthored, with Roy
Crane, the comic strip *Buz Sawyer*.

WORKS: *The Ancient Hunger* (1927). *Strangers and Lovers* (1928). *The
Erl King* (1930). Trans., *A Lover Returns*, by Dominique Dunois (1931).
Trans., *A Man's Life*, by Jacques de Lacretell (1931). Trans., *The Moun-
tain Tavern*, by André Chamson (1933). *A Trip to Czardis* (1966).

ELAINE HUGHES
Hinds Junior College
Raymond, Miss.

SHIRLEY ANN GRAU (1929–). Born on July 8, 1929, in New
Orleans, Shirley Ann Grau was the daughter of Adolph Eugene
Grau, a dentist, and Katherine Onions Grau. Her paternal grandfather, a Prussian soldier, came to New Orleans, by way of Cuba,
shortly after the Civil War, and later married a Prussian-English
girl of similar background. Her mother's family, seventeenth- and
eighteenth-century immigrants of English, Scottish, Welsh, and
"a dash of Delaware Indian" descent, included branches in North
Carolina and Virginia as well as Massachusetts and Rhode Island.
Usually poor and prolific but literate, they kept written accounts
of their times and experiences. Grau recognizes in her ancestry
"the two strains—New England and Southern—that were careful
to preserve a sense of family continuity." Her novels reveal a
southern concern with family history, though not particularly her
own. Like other southern children, she was raised with "family
stories of births and wars and killing, of Indians and feuds," and
her fiction, especially that which deals with primitive people, presents a cultural milieu in which violence seems a natural part
of life.

Grau was educated at Booth School in Montgomery, Ala., and
Newcomb College, Tulane University, where she received her
B.A. with honors in 1950. This was followed by a year of graduate

work, which she used primarily to write her first book. In 1955 she married writer and Tulane philosophy professor James Kern Feibleman; they have two sons and two daughters. Her first book, *The Black Prince* (1955), a collection of stories about black and white people from bayou country, received wide critical acclaim and is still thought by many to contain her finest work. The two novels that followed were less highly regarded, but the third, *The Keepers of the House* (1964) won her a Pulitzer Prize, together with renewed critical interest and a recognition of her powers as a novelist. The novel, which deals candidly with the personal, racial, and political conflicts of a southern family, was acclaimed for its craftsmanship, vivid characterization, and dramatic effectiveness. Two subsequent volumes, a novel and a collection of stories, have shown her painstaking dedication to the art of fiction. She describes her varied life as "conventional, and very comfortable," even "happy and contented." She enjoys music, painting, sculpture, and sports; she and her husband have a large personal library of the classics and philosophy. If she fulfills her expressed aim of producing a novel and a few stories every three years, readers may look forward to several more works from this modest and accomplished writer.

WORKS: *The Black Prince and Other Stories* (1955). *The Hard Blue Sky* (1958). *The House on Coliseum Street* (1961). *The Keepers of the House* (1964). *The Condor Passes* (1971). *The Wind Shifting West* (1973). *Evidence of Love* (1977).

RUTH M. VANDE KIEFT
Queens College
Flushing, N.Y.

WILLIAM JOHN GRAYSON (1788–1863). William J. Grayson was born in Beaufort, S.C., on November 10, 1788, the son of William Grayson who served with Washington and was a member of the U.S. Senate. The father died before William reached ten; and shortly after, his mother and step-father sent him north for his secondary education. Returning to South Carolina, he graduated from South Carolina College in 1809 and took up what he called

a life of idleness until 1814 when he married Sara Somarsall and
became an assistant teacher at Beaufort College. After a trip to the
North, 1817–1818, Grayson turned to law, passed the bar exam,
and commenced practice in Beaufort. Uneasy in this profession, he
began a political career marked throughout by moderation. He first
served as state representative from 1822 to 1826, then as state
senator until 1831, then as commissioner of equity in 1831, then as
the Beaufort and Colleton districts representative in the U.S. Congress from 1833 to 1837, and finally as the Charleston port collector of customs from 1841 to 1853.

In 1853 Grayson embarked on a literary career, becoming a
frequent contributor to the *Southern Quarterly Review* and, later,
to *Russell's Magazine*. His arrival in the literary world was marked
by the publication of *The Hireling and the Slave* (1854), a response
to *Uncle Tom's Cabin*, which contrasts in heroic couplets the
northern wage earner's desperate situation with the happy, pastoral circumstance of the southern slave. Although graced with
vehement antiabolitionist invective, the poem does not advocate
secession. Such moderation also colored Grayson's views on poetry, leading him to prefer Dryden, Pope, and Cowper to the
romantics. He debated his predilections with Paul Hamilton
Hayne, Henry Timrod, and other members of the literary group
that regularly met at Russell's Bookshop in Charleston. Nourished
by this literary ambiance, Grayson published three more volumes
of poetry, all reflecting his preference for eighteenth-century
poetics.

Many consider Grayson to have been more successful at prose
than at verse, and his last two works were his *Autobiography*
and what is thought to be his best piece of prose, *James Louis
Petigru: A Biographical Sketch*. With these two works completed,
though unpublished, Grayson died on October 4, 1863, in New-
berry, S.C.

WORKS: *Letter to His Excellency, Whitemarsh B. Seabrook, Governor of
the State of South Carolina, on the Dissolution of the Union* (1850).
The Hireling and the Slave (1854). *The Hireling and the Slave, Chicora,
and Other Poems* (1856). *The Country* (1858). *Marion* (1860). *James Louis*

Petigru: A Biographical Sketch (1866). *The Autobiography of William John Grayson*, ed. S. G. Stoney, *South Carolina Historical and Genealogical Magazine*, XLVIII–LI (July, 1947–April, 1950).

ROBERT BOLICK
University of Pennsylvania
Philadelphia

PAUL GREEN (1894–). Paul Green was born March 17, 1894, in Lillington, N.C., the son of William Archibald and his second wife, Betty Byrd Green. He attended Buies Creek Academy, then served as principal of the country school in Olive Branch. After one year at the University of North Carolina, he served two years in the army engineers, returned to the university and, upon graduation in 1921, received a fellowship to study philosophy at Cornell. He began teaching philosophy at the University of North Carolina at Chapel Hill in 1922. In the same year, he married Elizabeth Lay; they have four children. Except for occasional years in Hollywood and extended trips abroad, he has lived in Chapel Hill.

Green's one-act folk plays served apprenticeship for his overnight success in New York with three full dramas: *In Abraham's Bosom* (1926), winner of a Pulitzer Prize, *The Field God* (1927), and *The House of Connelly* (1928). Critical acclamation ranked him then second only to O'Neill among American playwrights. A Guggenheim Fellowship took him to Europe in 1928–1929 where he met Alexis Gronowsky and Bertholt Brecht. He wrote four plays in their experimental form—a blend of dialogue, music, film, dance, chorus, and commentary; but except for *Johnny Johnson's* modest success, all were failures. But they readied him for his outdoor "symphonic dramas." This form fuses music, stylized movement, and dialogue to stimulate ritual participation. Green's subjects are from American history. The first, *The Lost Colony*, appeared in Roanoke Island in 1937 and, except for the World War II years, has continued for 35 summers.

Green's work attests to his belief in the heroic possibility of all men: humanity's value lies in the continuous reaffirmation of its own greatness. The heroes are Negro and white, for Green sees no distinction between them in potential and achievement. His writing is a profile of democracy, from his early short stories and novels on the land and those who love and hate it, to the "heritage dramas" that recount the pain and glory in the making of America.

WORKS: *Salvation on a String* (1924). *Contemporary American Literature*, with Elizabeth Lay Green (1925). *The Lord's Will and Other Carolina Plays* (1925). *Lonesome Road: Six Plays for the Negro Theater* (1926). *The Field God* and *In Abraham's Bosom* (1927). *In the Valley and Other Carolina Plays* (1928). *Wide Fields* (1928). *The House of Connelly and Other Plays* (1931). *The Laughing Pioneer* (1932). *Fixin's*, with Erma Green (1934). *This Body the Earth* (1935). *Shroud My Body Down* (1935). *Johnny Johnson* (1937). *The Lost Colony* (1937). *The Southern Cross* (1938). *The Lost Colony Song-Book* (1938). *The Critical Year* (1939). *Franklin and the King* (1939). *Out of the South*, 15 plays revised (1939). *The Enchanted Maze* (1939). *Native Son*, adapt. with Richard Wright (1941). *The Highland Call* (1941). *The Hawthorne Tree* (1943). *Forever Growing* (1945). *Song of the Wilderness*, music by Charles Vardell (1947). *The Common Glory* (1948). *Dog on the Sun* (1949). *Peer Gynt*, adapt. (1951). *The Common Glory Song-Book* (1951). *Dramatic Heritage* (1953). *Wilderness Road* (1956). *The Founders* (1957). *Drama and the Weather* (1958). *The Confederacy* (1959). *Wings for to Fly: Three Plays of Negro Life* (1959). *The Stephen Foster Story* (1960). *Five Plays of the South*, five plays revised (1963). *Plough and Furrow* (1963). *Cross and Sword* (1966). *Texas* (1967). *Texas Song-Book* (1967). *Words and Ways* (1968). *Home to My Valley* (1971). *Honeycomb* (1972). *Trumpet in the Land* (1972). *The Land of Nod* (1976).

VINCENT S. KENNY
Marymount College
Tarrytown, N.Y.

JOHN HOWARD GRIFFIN (1920–). A novelist and nonfiction writer, John Howard Griffin was born in Dallas, Tex., on June 16, 1920, to Jack Walter and Lena Mae Young Griffin. His education is European: a certificate of studies from the Institut de Tours, France, in 1937 and studied at the University of Poitiers from 1938 to 1939. During World War II he served in the Army Air Corps—losing his sight from an injury; he regained it ten years later. After the war he entered the Conservatory of Fontainebleau, Abbey of Solesmes, from which he received certificates in piano and composition in 1947. Griffin's wide range of interests from music to his Catholicism is reflected in his first novel, *The Devil Rides Outside* (1952). Here a young American, a sexually obsessed miscreant, lives in a French monastery as he pursues the study of Gregorian music. The novel suggests a debate between the body and the soul. His second novel, *Nuni*, published in 1956, indicates Griffin's increased consciousness of form, for it is narrated in the first person and completely in the present tense. The situation is stock: a professor survives a plane crash on a South Pacific island inhabited by savages. What lifts the narrative is that it effects an allegory toward a "spiritual evolution." The emphasis on anthropological detail is a prelude to the author's social interest in his nonfiction and journalism.

Griffin, noted for his odyssey through the South in the disguise of a Negro, wrote about the venture in *Sepia*. Since 1956 his writing has turned toward autobiography, biography, and sociology with works like *Mansfield, Texas*; *Black Like Me*; and *Jacque Maritain*. The winner of several humanitarian awards, including the Pacem in Terris in 1963, Griffin, a prolific writer, published *The Biography of Thomas Merton* in 1976.

WORKS: *The Devil Rides Outside* (1952). *Nuni* (1956). *Mansfield, Texas* (1957). *Land of the High Sky* (1959). *Black Like Me* (1961). *Scattered Shadows* (1963). *John Howard Griffin Reader* (1968). *The Church and the Black Man* (1969). *A Hidden Wholeness: The Visual World of Thomas Merton* (1972). *Twelve Photographic Portraits* (1973). *Jacque Maritain: Homage in Words and Pictures* (1975). *The Biography of Thomas Merton* (1976). *The Problems of Racism* (1976).

THOMAS BONNER, JR.
Xavier University
New Orleans, La.

ALEX HALEY (1921–). The first of three sons born to Bertha Palmer and Simon Haley, Alexander Palmer Haley was born in Ithaca, N.Y., on August 11, 1921. His parents were in their first

year of graduate study, Bertha at Ithaca Conservatory of Music
and Simon at Cornell University. Six weeks after Alex' birth, they
returned to the Palmer family home in Henning, Tenn., where
Bertha and Alex remained while Simon returned to Cornell to continue graduate studies in agriculture.

During his childhood in Henning, Haley formed a close bond
with his grandparents, Will and Cynthia Palmer. The death of
Will Palmer when Haley was about four brought Simon back to
Henning where he managed his mother-in-law's lumber business
until she sold it in 1929. For the next several years Simon moved
his family frequently while he taught agriculture at various black
colleges in the South.

Graduated from high school when he was fifteen, Haley completed two years of college before enlisting in the United States
Coast Guard in 1939 as a mess boy on a cargo-ammunition ship in
the South Pacific. To alleviate his boredom, Haley wrote countless
letters, read everything he could find, and wrote adventure stories,
modeled on those he had read in the ship's library. In 1949 he
became the first chief journalist of the Coast Guard.

Retiring from the service in 1959, Haley moved to Greenwich
Village, determined to support himself as a free-lance writer. The
next three years were lean, but in 1962 he landed a job with *Playboy* where he began the magazine's now famous interviews. His
interview with Malcolm X was the germ for the best seller *The
Autobiography of Malcolm X*, which Haley was commissioned to
write and for which he is now credited as the book's author rather
than ghostwriter. Shortly after *Malcolm X* appeared in 1965, Haley
began his work on *Roots*, a twelve-year search into his family background, sustained by income from *Malcolm X*, from his magazine
writings, and from lectures. Highly publicized before it appeared
and boosted by a television drama weeks after it was issued, *Roots*
gave Haley instantaneous fame and fortune.

In 1964, after 23 years of marriage, Haley was divorced from
Nannie Branch, with whom he had two children, Lydia and William. That same year he married Juliette Collins, from whom he
was later divorced. They had one child, Cynthia.

WORKS: *The Autobiography of Malcolm X* (1965). *Roots: The Saga of an American Family* (1976).

> J. LEE GREENE
> University of North Carolina
> Chapel Hill

ALEXANDER HAMILTON (1712–1756). Dr. Alexander Hamilton was born on September 26, 1712, in Edinburgh, Scotland, the sixth son of the Reverend William Hamilton, principal of the University of Edinburgh. In 1737 he graduated M.D. from Edinburgh, and in 1739 followed his older brother John to Maryland, where he was to become a leading physician of Annapolis.

Evidently the climate of Maryland did not agree with Hamilton, for he soon contracted consumption, an illness that worsened over the years. In 1743 he took a four-month tour of the northern colonies. His record of this 1,624-mile journey by horseback, entitled *The Itinerarium*, is the only book-length work of Hamilton that has been published. *The Itinerarium* records the manners and characters Hamilton observed in mid-eighteenth-century America. The style is basically neoclassic, but also includes dialect, proverbs, colloquialisms, folk sayings, and nature descriptions.

In 1745 Hamilton organized the Tuesday Club, a literary and social organization of distinguished Annapolis citizens. About the activities of the club, which included drinking, music, and composing belletristic pieces, Hamilton wrote two works, which remain in manuscript.

Hamilton married Margaret Dulany in May, 1747. His political activities included serving as a common-councilman for Annapolis from 1743 until 1756, and a one-year term as a representative to the state assembly. He died May 11, 1756, at Annapolis.

His wit and learning, and his support of letters and literature, made Hamilton one of Maryland's leading colonial figures.

WORKS: Miscellaneous poems and satiric essays published in the *Maryland Gazette*. *A Defence of Dr. Thomson's Discourse* . . . (1751). *Hamilton's Itinerarium*, ed. Albert Bushnell (1907). *Gentleman's Progress: The Itinerarium of Dr. Alexander Hamilton*, ed. Carl Bridenbaugh (1948).

"The Record of the Tuesday Club," MS (*ca.* 1749). "The History of the Tuesday Club," MS (*ca.* 1754).

REED SANDERLIN
University of Tennessee
Chattanooga

JOHN HAMMOND (d. 1663). We know little of John Hammond's life before his emigration to Virginia. The suggestion that his father was Dr. John Hammond, physician to Henry, Prince of Wales seems doubtful because Dr. Hammond's genealogy lists no descendant named John. Hammond tells us in his promotional tract, *Leah and Rachel, or, The Two Fruitfull Sisters Virginia and Mary-Land* (London, 1656), that he had lived in those colonies for 21 years. That statement places him in Virginia by 1634.

He and his wife, Ann, had four children: Mordecai, Bernard, Ann, and Daniel. In 1652 Hammond was elected burgess from Isle of Wight. The House of Burgesses, however, expelled him because of his "scandalous" reputation. This rejection apparently led Hammond to move his family to Maryland where he purchased a plantation in Newton, St. Mary's County. During the next two years, Hammond ran his plantation, acted as attorney before the Provincial Court of Maryland, and established an inn where the court of St. Mary's County met. Hammond joined Lord Baltimore's forces in the Maryland wars, and after the Puritan victory at the Battle of the Severn (March 25, 1655), he escaped to England. While in London, Hammond wrote the political pamphlet *Hammond vs. Heamans* (1655) and *Leah and Rachel*. Hammond was back in Maryland by the spring of 1661. He died there in February or March, 1663.

Hammond vs. Heamans counters with wit and invective the accusations of Captain Roger Heamans, a participant on the Puritan side in the Battle of the Severn. *Leah and Rachel*, Hammond's one important work, presents the vigorous and realistic attitudes of a citizen of the New World. His close observation of the London poor shows him that they live "far below the meanest servant in *Virginia*." He frankly recommends emigration to those sister colonies "wherin is plenty of all things necessary for Humane subsistance."

works: *Hammond vs. Heamans* (1655). *Leah and Rachel: or, The Two Fruitfull Sisters Virginia and Mary-Land* (1656).

FREDA F. STOHRER
Old Dominion University
Norfolk, Va.

CHARLES HANSFORD (1685–1761). Little is known about this colonial primitive poet except for a memoir by his friend Benjamin Waller of Williamsburg, appended in 1765 to Waller's manuscript copy of Hansford's poems. He was a second-generation Virginian, his grandfather having emigrated to the colony before 1644, and he lived and died in York County, Va. The Hansfords were substantial yeomen or tradesmen. The poet is thus unique among early southern writers as a representative of the colonial middle classes.

According to Waller, the poet "was bred a blacksmith, and worked at his trade as long as his strength would permit." Largely self-educated, he seems to have read voraciously "from borrowed books when he could obtain leisure," thus acquiring sufficient learning to be able to teach school for a time. A man of pious orthodoxy, he was a lay reader in Yorkhampton Parish. Richly detailed descriptions of life at sea in one of his autobiographical poems ("Barzillai") suggest nautical experience. From his brother he inherited an ordinary between Yorktown and Williamsburg, which he ran between 1755 and 1759, and it is clear from his will, probated June 15, 1761, that he owned five or six slaves and at least 200 acres of land.

Hansford's extant verses date from about 1745–1752 when, losing his hearing and unable to enjoy the "cheerful conversation," he indulged himself in what he described as "A Clumsey Attempt of an Old Man to turn Some of his Serious Thoughts into Verse." The results of this attempt were 1,862 rough-hewn heroic couplets and triplets composing four untitled poems of varying lengths. A fifth poem, reprinted anonymously in 1745 in the *Boston Post Boy* from a now lost issue of the *Virginia Gazette*, has been convincingly claimed as Hansford's.

WORKS: *The Poems of Charles Hansford*, ed. J. A. Servies and C. Dolmetsch (1961). J. A. Leo Lemay, "A Poem Probably by Charles Hansford," *Virginia Magazine of History and Biography*, LXXIV (1966), 445–47.

CARL DOLMETSCH
The College of William and Mary
Williamsburg, Va.

WILL[IAM] N[ATHANIEL] HARBEN (1858–1919). Born on July 5, 1858, and reared in Dalton, Ga., Will N. Harben was educated locally and worked as a merchant until he was 30. He began to write in 1888, moved to New York, and published his first novel, *White Marie* (1889), an antebellum tragedy with implied criticism of traditional southern values. He next experimented with detective fiction and a utopian novel. From 1891 to 1893 he was assistant editor of the *Youth's Companion*. In 1896 he married Maybelle Chandler, who survived him. He died on August 7, 1919.

In the late 1890s Harben began to exploit his own background successfully and produced his most characteristic work. In his sole volume of stories, *Northern Georgia Sketches* (1900), he wrote realistically about the poor yeoman farmers and Negroes of antebellum times and after. Impressed by the volume, William Dean Howells asked for a novel from Harben to be published by *Harper's*. Harben sent them "Westerfelt" (1901), a manuscript they had already rejected. The story is of a common man dogged by guilt after the suicide of a girl who loved him hopelessly. Harben wrote at the rate of a novel a year for the remainder of his career, creating a valuable social history of the rise of the humble white man as he aspires to middle-class status. In *Pole Baker* (1905) Harben created the character of a whiskey-drinking poor white who is a man of firm decision and as a symbol suggests the hope for the rise of the common man. *Ann Boyd* (1906), Harben's most powerful novel, rises above the regional in dealing with the suffering that stems from calumny. The hero of *Gilbert Neal* (1908) illustrates again the author's optimism for the poor, in whom he sees reserves of energy and honesty for the future of the South.

WORKS: *White Marie: A Story of Georgia Plantation Life* (1889). *Almost Persuaded* (1890). *A Mute Confessor: The Romance of a Southern Town* (1892). *The Land of the Changing Sun* (1894). *The Caruthers Affair* (1898). *The North Walk Mystery* (1899). *Northern Georgia Sketches* (1900). *Westerfelt* (1901). *The Woman Who Trusted: A Story of Literary Life in New York* (1901). *Abner Daniel* (1902). *The Substitute* (1903). *The Georgians* (1904). *Pole Baker* (1905). *Ann Boyd* (1906). *Mam' Linda* (1907). *Gilbert Neal* (1908). *The Redemption of Kenneth Galt* (1909). *Dixie Hart* (1910). *Jane Dawson* (1911). *Paul Rundel* (1912). *The Desired Woman* (1913). *The New Clarion* (1914). *The Inner Law* (1915). *Second Choice* (1916). *The Triumph* (1917). *The Hills of Refuge* (1918). *The Cottage of Delight* (1919). *The Divine Event* (1920).

ROBERT BUSH
Herbert Lehman College
Bronx, N.Y.

ISAAC HARBY (1788–1828). Isaac Harby was born on November 7, 1788, in Charleston, S.C., the son of an immigrant from England. After trying law and teaching he began editing the *Quiver*, a weekly periodical in 1807. He next edited the *Southern Patriot*, expressing strong Democratic-Republican sentiments. He also wrote for the *City Gazette* after 1822 and the *Mercury*. A leader in the Jewish Reform Movement, he helped establish a new congregation in 1824 called "The Reformed Society of Israelites." He moved to New York in June, 1828, where he wrote briefly for the *Evening Post*, before his death on December 14, 1828.

Harby's writings consist mainly of dramatic criticism and plays. In his dramatic essays he emphasized the theater's moral purpose, and praised Shakespeare, but regretted that he bowed to the prejudice of his age in Shylock. He discussed the acting of such famous figures as Edmund Kean in Charleston. His first play, "Alexander Severus," was rejected by the Charleston manager, Alexander Placide, who, however, produced his next, *The Gordian Knot*, in 1810. Sharing a contemporary objection to Gothic excesses, he attempted to come closer to probability in this play. *Alberti* (1819) is a melodrama set in fifteenth-century Florence. It presents the relinquishment of revenge by Alberti, a military hero, and the discovery of his lost son. Its democratic sentiments would have pleased President James Monroe, who attended its performance while in Charleston. This play was published along with examples of his dramatic criticism and a memoir of Harby in *Selections from the Miscellaneous Writings of the Late Isaac Harby* (1829). Because of his versatility as a critic-dramatist and close relations with the actors and managers of the Charleston theater, Harby represents well the vitality of drama in Charleston during the first quarter of the nineteenth century.

WORKS: *The Gordian Knot* (1810). *Selections from the Miscellaneous Writings of the Late Isaac Harby* (1829).

CHARLES S. WATSON
University of Alabama
Tuscaloosa

ELIZABETH HARDWICK (1916–). Born in Lexington, Ky., on July 27, 1916, Elizabeth Hardwick grew up there and received both her B.A. and M.A. from the University of Kentucky in 1938 and 1939, respectively. She moved to New York and did postgraduate work at Columbia University. In 1949 she married Robert Lowell, the poet. She is best known for her far-ranging and keenly phrased essays about literature and culture contributed to the *Partisan Review*, *Harper's*, the *New Yorker*, and the *New York Review of Books*, many of which are collected in *A View of My Own* (1962) and *Seduction and Betrayal: Women and Literature* (1974). She was a Guggenheim Fellow in 1947 and has served as an advisory editor for the *New York Review of Books*.

Hardwick's first novel, *The Ghostly Lover* (1945), explores with delicate sensitivity and psychological insight the frustrations of a young woman who is just beginning to comprehend the import of her relationships with her middle-class Kentucky family. Its quiet surface and subtle portrayal of the hidden corners of the spirit led several reviewers to overlook its craftsmanship and thematic depth. Her second novel, *The Simple Truth* (1955), is not set in the South but deals with a murder trial in an Iowa university town. Several of the uncollected short stories are set in Kentucky and a novel is in progress which will draw upon her youth in the South. Hardwick feels that her experience as a southerner has been significant in her work and has written (in a letter to this writer dated May 17, 1976), "I feel that as a writer I have been formed by the union in myself of my Kentucky background and my skeptical intellectual temperament—what might be called 'the New York' part of my interests and themes."

WORKS: *The Ghostly Lover* (1945). *The Simple Truth* (1955). Ed., *The Selected Letters of William James* (1960). *A View of My Own* (1962). *Seduction and Betrayal: Women and Literature* (1974).

M. THOMAS INGE
Virginia Commonwealth
University
Richmond

THOMAS HARRIOTT [HARIOT] (1560–1621). Born at Oxford, Thomas Harriott entered St. Mary Hall, graduating B.A., 1580. Tutor to Sir Walter Ralegh by 1583–1584, he taught Ralegh and his friends how to follow a course by the use of instruments and charts and how to make charts at sea. Harriott served as a surveyor with Sir Richard Grenville's expedition to Virginia in 1585, returning to England in July, 1586. In 1598 he became the Earl of Northumberland's pensioner. He died on July 2, 1621. Ill throughout his life, he complained that he was unable to write or think accurately on any subject; but recognized by his contemporaries as England's most profound mathematician and a leading experimental scientist, he took volumes of notes and left behind thousands of pages of mathematical calculations and scientific observations. Among his other achievements, he was the first Englishman to train a telescope on the heavens; he is credited with having given algebra its modern form, his particular discovery being the "greater than" and "less than" signs. Recently, he has been cited as the discoverer of the fundamental elements of the binary notation.

Harriott is best known today as the author of *A Briefe and True Report of the New Found Land of Virginia* (1588). Probably written during 1586–1587, *A Briefe and True Report* is a firsthand account of the 1585–1586 voyage to America. Designed as a promotional tract to gain support for colonization in the New World, it is the first original book about the colonizing of America. In it, Harriott discusses three major topics: (1) commodities found in the New World which might ultimately be produced for export; (2) commodities grown and used by the natives; (3) building techniques and materials, together with a description of the nature and customs of the people. Immediately popular, the treatise was translated into several languages and merited for its author a reputation as surveyor, colonizer, and authority on the American Indians.

WORKS: *A Briefe and True Report of the New Found Land of Virginia* (1588). *Artis Analyticae Praxis* (1631).

DENNIS G. DONOVAN
University of North Carolina
Chapel Hill

BERNICE KELLY HARRIS (1892–1973). Bernice Kelly Harris was born twelve miles east of Raleigh in Wake County, N.C., on October 8, 1892, third of seven children of William Haywood Kelly. It was an area of right-thinking Baptists and small, independent farmers. After graduating from Meredith College in 1913, she taught in Beulaville, Maiden, Rich Square, and for ten years in Seaboard, where she met Herbert Kavanaugh Harris, a farmer with numerous other agricultural interests. They were married in 1926, built a home in the small town, and there Harris lived until her death.

From childhood, she had written poems and stories. Then during a 1919 summer term at the University of North Carolina at Chapel Hill, a playwriting course under Frederick H. Koch inspired her to return to Seaboard and spread the "gospel" of the folk play. As an example to her students and friends, she wrote a number of plays herself. When her human-interest dispatches, printed in the Raleigh and Norfolk newspapers, were noticeably more than routine journalese, she was encouraged to write in a more expanded form. *Purslane*, based on events of her childhood, was the first of seven novels set among the farms and small towns of eastern North Carolina. Nostalgic and romantic in mood and approach, they reflected Harris' view that men and women are creatures whose basic quality is one of goodness, an attitude which pervades everything she wrote. In 1963 she began teaching creative writing at Chowan College, and from her classes came two collections of short selections which she edited and to which she contributed. She died on September 13, 1973.

WORKS: *Purslane* (1939). *Folk Plays of Eastern Carolina* (1940). *Portulaca* (1941). *Sweet Beulah Land* (1943). *Sage Quarter* (1945). *Janey Jeems* (1946). *Hearthstones* (1948). *Wild Cherry Tree Road* (1951). *The Very Real Truth About Christmas* (1961). *The Santa on the Mantle* (1964). *Southern Savory* (1964). *Southern Home Remedies* (1968). *Strange Things Happen* (1971).

RICHARD WALSER
North Carolina State University
Raleigh

CORRA HARRIS (1869–1935). Corra Mae White was born on May 17, 1869, in Elbert County, Ga. She was educated at home, at the Elberton Female Academy, and at the Old Salem School in Banks County. At the latter institution, she met Lundy Howard Harris (1858–1910), an educator and Methodist clergyman, whom she married in 1887. The next twelve years were devoted to her family. Harris' literary career began in 1899 when a nervous collapse forced her husband to give up his professorship of Greek at Emory College. An editorial in the *Independent* on lynching drew from her a reply which aroused wide interest. At the invitation of the editors, she became a regular contributor to the *Independent*, writing numerous articles, book reviews, and editorials.

Harris' first book and first piece of fiction was *The Jessica Letters* (1904), written in collaboration with Paul Elmer More. A perceptive commentator on southern literature, she was especially outspoken in her criticism of the literary achievements of her native region since the Civil War (*The Critic*, September, 1903, and June, 1904). Harris' first great literary success was her novel *The Circuit Rider's Wife*, which drew on her experiences as a minister's wife in the hills of Georgia. Published first as a serial in the *Saturday Evening Post* and then in book form (1910), this work was followed by thirteen more novels during the next sixteen years.

All of Harris' novels are basically didactic. The shortcomings of Methodism are exposed in the circuit rider series; the backwardness of an entire town in *The Recording Angel*; and small-town political corruption in *The Co-Citizens*. The remaining novels deal with the problems of marriage. Very popular in her day, Corra Harris died in Atlanta, on February 7, 1935.

WORKS: *The Jessica Letters*, with Paul Elmer More (1904). *A Circuit Rider's Wife* (1910). *Eve's Second Husband* (1911). *The Recording Angel* (1912). *In Search of a Husband* (1913). *Justice* (1915). *The Co-Citizens* (1915). *A Circuit Rider's Widow* (1916). *Making Her His Wife* (1918). *From Sun-up to Sun-down*, with Faith Harris Leech (1919). *Happily Married* (1920). *My Son* (1921). *The Eyes of Love* (1922). *A Daughter of Adam* (1923). *The House of Helen* (1923). *My Book and Heart* (1924). *As a Woman Thinks* (1925). *Flapper Ann* (1926). *The Happy Pilgrimage* (1927).

L. MOODY SIMMS, JR.
Illinois State University
Normal

GEORGE WASHINGTON HARRIS (1814–1869). George Washington Harris was born on March 20, 1814, in Allegheny City, Pa. In 1819 he moved to Knoxville, Tenn., with Samuel Bell, his half-brother. Bell became a successful metalworker in Knoxville, and Harris learned the trade from him. Harris was an apt pupil: by the age of twelve he was skilled enough to fashion and exhibit a working miniature steamboat. His early training in metalworking and jewelrymaking seems to have given him a sense of craftsmanship that would later be evident in his writings.

Harris had almost no formal schooling, but he was mature and responsible beyond his years. At fifteen he was traveling as Bell's representative on business trips, and by the age of 21, he was captain of a Mississippi steamboat. In 1835 he married Mary Emeline Nance. Four years later Harris left steamboating and attempted to establish himself as a gentleman landowner, but he was unsuccessful and was forced by debt to give up his farm. By 1843 he was back in Knoxville and had opened his own metalworking shop there.

In that same year, Harris began contributing epistles and reportage to the New York *Spirit of the Times*, a sporting, racing, and literary journal whose editor, William Trotter Porter, fostered much antebellum southern humorous writing. With Porter's encouragement, Harris wrote a number of realistic and humorous items for the *Spirit* under the pseudonyms "Mr. Free" and "Sugartail." Harris' most famous creation, Sut Lovingood, made his first appearance on November 4, 1854, in the *Spirit*.

In the 1850s Harris became deeply involved in politics as a Democrat and a secessionist. During this period he held a number of jobs, most of them connected with metalworking, glassworking, mining, or railroading. He also served as an alderman and later as postmaster in Knoxville. (Harris was not a good businessman; during his adult life he moved from one venture to another, always ready to make a new start but never able to establish himself in any profession.) In a literary sense, though, these years were productive: he published numerous sketches in the Nashville *Union and American* and in other newspapers and periodicals. In 1858 he made plans to collect some of his writings in a volume, but he was unable to find a publisher.

During the Civil War, Harris was forced to move from city to city with his wife and children. These troubled years of wandering, during which he saw the South crumble, disillusioned and embittered him. After the war, Harris worked for the Wills Valley Railroad and turned his pen increasingly to vicious and even scurrilous antinorthern satire. His wife died in 1867; two years later (just two months before his own death) Harris remarried. There was one bright spot after the war: in April, 1867, the New York publisher Dick & Fitzgerald brought out Harris' now-famous collection *Sut Lovingood. Yarns Spun by a "Nat'ral Born Durn'd Fool.["]* Harris continued to write and publish sketches during the next two years, and by December, 1869, he had assembled the manuscript of a second collection, this one entitled *High Times and Hard Times*. He took the manuscript to Lynchburg, Va., to negotiate with a printer, but on the train trip home he fell ill. He died the night of December 11, 1869. Harris is reputed to have uttered the word *poisoned* on his deathbed; perhaps he was the victim of foul play, but it is more likely that he died of apoplexy. The manuscript that he carried has never been recovered.

WORKS: *Sut Lovingood. Yarns Spun by a "Nat'ral Born Durn'd Fool ["]* (1867). *Sut Lovingood*, ed. Brom Weber (1954). *High Times and Hard Times*, ed. M. Thomas Inge (1967).

JAMES L. W. WEST III
Virginia Polytechnic Institute and
State University
Blacksburg

JOEL CHANDLER HARRIS (1848–1908). Joel Chandler Harris was born on December 8, 1848, at Eatonton, Ga. The area had already been memorialized by some middle Georgia humorists (A. B. Longstreet, William Tappan Thompson, Richard Malcolm Johnson, Bill Arp) who provided a tradition for Harris. Harris was an illegitimate child, the son of an Irish laborer who deserted his mother either before or shortly after his birth. His mother was treated kindly by the people of Eatonton, who gave her sewing work and took an interest in her son. Still, his early life seems to have left Harris with some scars; later he spoke of a childhood that had been "sad and unfortunate." His small stature, his red hair, and his bad stammer were sources of lifelong embarrassment.

In 1862, at age thirteen, Harris left his mother to become a type-setter for a weekly paper published on Turnwold plantation by a remarkable planter-writer-editor, Joseph Addison Turner. Turner provided a father image for Harris, instilled in him a respect for literature, and taught him the arts of printing and publishing. At Turnwold, Harris learned firsthand the plantation lore that he would use later. At the end of the Civil War, Turner no longer had the resources to continue his newspaper; Harris moved on to increasingly important editorial positions in Macon, New Orleans, Forsyth, and finally Savannah. On the Savannah *Morning News* Harris had a popular humor column on current events and local personalities. During this period he also developed a horror of strangers, an extreme sensitivity, and a habit of brooding that contrasted sharply with his image as an easy-going jokester.

In 1873 Harris married Esther La Rose, with whom he had eight children. Three years later, Harris left Savannah with his young family to avoid a yellow fever epidemic. He accepted an offer to join the staff of the South's most progressive newspaper, the Atlanta *Constitution*. With Henry Grady and Evan P. Howell, he began to shape editorial policies that would assist the revitalization of the South. While Grady pushed for a revolutionized econony, Harris stressed the need for reconciliation between North and South. Grady captivated the nation with the New South speech that he delivered in New York City in December, 1886; Harris had a quieter but equally significant impact on opinion through an old black character that he began developing as a narrator in sketches for the *Constitution* in 1876. In the early years Uncle Remus was often a "shufflin'" clown, sometimes a venerable advisor of his race. Between 1876 and 1880 Harris gradually turned Remus into a sharp-witted, articulate teller of folktales who recalled with affection the "old times" of the plantation.

Uncle Remus' tales were first published in book form in November, 1880, as *Uncle Remus: His Songs and His Sayings*. Ten thousand copies sold by the following March, and Harris' career both as writer and as respected "expert" on the Old South and the "Negro Question" was dramatically launched. Many readers, Mark Twain included, believed that the plantation backgrounds that Harris provided for the telling of the tales were the most important part of the book. The descriptions of the loving relationships maintained through the plantation system enchanted northern as well as southern readers. Twain invited Harris to join him on the lecture circuit; aghast, Harris declined.

Four more collections of Uncle Remus material appeared during Harris' lifetime: *Nights With Uncle Remus* (1883), *Uncle Remus and His Friends* (1892), and *Told By Uncle Remus* (1905). In these volumes, Remus, from his position as a slave, identified with the difficult situations that faced the disadvantaged Brer Rabbit.

Harris published more than 20 other books dealing with different types of southerners. *Mingo and Other Sketches* (1884) was his first book without Uncle Remus, and in it he widened his range to include poor whites, northern Georgia mountaineers, and greedy plantation owners. In *Free Joe and the Rest of the World* (1887), the title story illustrated injustices of the plantation system. In *Balaam and His Master* (1891), the story "Where's Duncan" approached tragedy as it dealt with the revenge of the rejected son of a planter and his mulatto slave. Many of Harris' books were autobiographical. Particularly interesting is *Sister Jane: Her Friends and Acquaintances* (1896) in which Harris touched on his mother's problems and romanticized the issue of his illegitimacy.

Harris retired from the *Constitution* in 1900 after 24 years. At his residence, the Wren's Nest, in a suburb of Atlanta, he tried to escape the complexities of a New South that had grown beyond his own concepts of how it should progress. His most important book after his retirement was his novel, *Gabriel Tolliver* (1902), in which he tackled with moderate success the subject of Reconstruction. Harris seems to have felt at the last that he was out of touch with the times. Throughout the years of his greatest productivity he had suffered from illness and bouts of heavy drinking, and in retirement he had little energy to take on new ways.

Harris received several honors in his last years. Emory College conferred on him the honorary Doctor of Literature in 1902; he was elected to membership in the American Academy of Arts and Letters in 1905; and in the same year President Theodore Roosevelt insisted upon appearing with him in ceremonies in Atlanta. From 1906 to 1908 he directed his failing energies to editing the *Uncle Remus Magazine* and to writing stories and folklore material that would be collected into several books after his death. Harris died of complications caused by cirrhosis of the liver on July 2,

1908, at the age 59. One week before his death he was baptized into the Catholic faith.

WORKS: *Uncle Remus: His Songs and His Sayings* (1880). *Nights with Uncle Remus* (1883). *Mingo and Other Sketches in Black and White* (1884). *Free Joe and Other Georgian Sketches* (1887). *Daddy Jake, the Runaway, and Short Stories Told After Dark* (1889). *Life of Henry W. Grady* (1890). *Balaam and His Master* (1891). *On the Plantation* (1892). *Uncle Remus and His Friends* (1892). *Little Mr. Thimblefinger and His Queer Country* (1894). *The Story of Aaron* (1895). *Mr. Rabbit at Home* (1895). *Stories of Georgia* (1896). *Sister Jane: Her Friends and Acquaintances* (1896). *Aaron in the Wildwoods* (1897). *Tales of the Home Folks in Peace and War* (1898). *Plantation Pageants* (1899). *The Chronicles of Aunt Minervy Ann* (1899). *On the Wing of Occasions* (1900). *Qua: A Romance of the Revolution* (ca. 1900). *The Making of a Statesman, and Other Stories* (1902). *Gabriel Tolliver* (1902). *Wally Wanderoon and His Story-Telling Machine* (1903). *A Little Union Scout* (1904). *The Tar-Baby and Other Rhymes of Uncle Remus* (1904). *Told by Uncle Remus* (1905). *Uncle Remus and Brer Rabbit* (1906). *The Shadow Between His Shoulder-Blades* (1908). *The Bishop and the Boogerman* (1909). *Uncle Remus and the Little Boy* (1910). *Uncle Remus Returns* (1918). *Favorite Uncle Remus* (1948). *Seven Tales of Uncle Remus* (1948). *The Complete Tales of Uncle Remus* (1955).

LUCINDA H. MACKETHAN
North Carolina State University
Raleigh

CONSTANCE CARY HARRISON [MRS. BURTON HARRISON] (1843–1920). Born in Lexington, Ky., on April 25, 1843, Constance Cary was the daughter of Monimia Fairfax and Archibald Cary. She was connected to many of the most distinguished families of Virginia. After her father's death in Cumberland, Md., in 1854, his widow and three children returned to Vaucluse, the family home in Virginia.

Educated by a French governess at home and then at Mr. Le-Febvre's boarding school in Richmond, she later spent the Civil War years as a refugee in Richmond with her family. Clever and beautiful, the auburn-haired Constance experienced firsthand the horrors of the war. She knew many of the Confederate leaders during the war. After studying in Europe for a year, she returned home to marry Burton Harrison, Jefferson Davis' secretary during the war years. The Harrisons lived in New York City, where he was a successful lawyer and she a prolific writer. They had three sons. After his death in 1904, she moved to Washington, D.C., where she remained until her death on November 21, 1920.

Her literary career began during the war when she wrote for Richmond newspapers under the pseudonym Refugitta. Later she began publishing pieces in magazines, drawing on her own background for material on William Byrd, George Washington, and Lord Fairfax. She then published short stories, novels, fairy tales, and plays. She drew on both her knowledge of New York City (*The Anglomaniacs*) and her Virginia past (*Flower de Hundred*) in her fiction, but her most valuable work is undoubtedly the autobiographical *Recollections Grave and Gay*, which includes a full account of life in Richmond during the Civil War.

WORKS: *Golden-Rod: An Idyl of Mount Desert* (1879). *The Story of Helen of Troy* (1881). *Woman's Handiwork in Modern Homes* (1881). *The Old Fashioned Fairy Book* (1884). *Bric-a-brac Stories* (1885). *Folk and Fairy Tales* (1885). *Bar Harbor Days* (1887). *Short Comedies for Amateur Players* (1889). *Alice in Wonderland: A Play for Children in Three Acts Dramatized by Mrs. Burton Harrison* (1890). *The Anglomaniacs* (1890). *Flower de Hundred* (1890). *A Russian Honeymoon*, adapted from the French of A. E. Scribe (1890). *Belhaven Tales* (1892). *A Daughter of the South, and Shorter Stories* (1892). *An Edelweiss of the Sierras: Goldenrod, and Other Tales* (1892). *The Mouse Trap: A Comedietta in One Act* (1892). *Tea at Four O'Clock: A Drawing Room Comedy in One Act* (1892). *Two Strings to Her Bow: A Comedy in Two Acts* (1892). *Weeping Wives*, trans. and adapted from the French of P. Siraudin (1892). Ed., *Short Stories* (1893, 1969). *Sweet Bells Out of Tune* (1893). *A Bachelor Maid* (1894). *An Errant Wooing* (1895). *A Virginia Cousin, & Bar Harbor Tales* (1895). *The Merry Maid of Arcady, His Lordship, and Other Stories* (1897). *A Son of the Old Dominion* (1897). *Good Americans* (1898). *The Well-Bred Girl in Society* (1898). *The Carcellini Emerald* (1899). *The Circle of a Century* (1899). *A Triple Entanglement* (1899). *A Princess of the Hills* (1901). *The Unwelcome Mrs. Hatch* (1901). *Sylvia's*

Husband (1904). *The Carlyles* (1905). *Latter-day Sweet-hearts* (1906). *The Count and the Congressman* (1908). *Recollections Grave and Gay* (1911).

DOROTHY MCINNIS SCURA
University of Richmond
Richmond, Va.

HENRY SYDNOR HARRISON (1880–1930). Henry Sydnor Harrison, journalist, popular novelist and short-story writer, was born on February 12, 1880, at Sewanee, Tenn. His family settled in Brooklyn, N.Y., in 1885, where his father, of Virginian descent, and who had been a professor of Greek and Latin at the University of the South, founded a Latin school. Harrison received a B.A. from Columbia University in 1900 (M.A., 1913). He was a member of Phi Beta Kappa. By 1908 he had become the leading editorialist for the *Times-Dispatch* in Richmond, Va.

In 1910 his first novel (written under the pen name Henry Second), *Captivating Mary Carstairs*, was well received. He then turned from newspaper work to a career as a writer of fiction, moving to Charleston, W.Va. *Queed*, his best and most popular novel, was a quick success in 1911. Its absentminded, charming hero had several love affairs, took boxing lessons, and did newspaper work. The novel exploited the local color of a southern city. Harrison's next novel, *V. V.'s Eyes* (1913), also succeeded. Its setting was similar to that of *Queed*, and it involved reform in the tobacco industry. This was followed by *Angela's Business* (1915).

In that year he became a member of the American Ambulance service in France, and he served in the U.S. Navy during 1917–1919. He then settled permanently in New York City. A nonfiction tribute to his brother, who was lost in World War I, *When I Come Back*, appeared in 1919. The fictional works *Saint Teresa* (1922) and *Andrew Bride of Paris* (1925) ended his writing of novels.

A lifelong bachelor, a member of the National Institute of Arts and Letters, and a best seller in the prewar years, he died on July 14, 1930, and was buried at Richmond.

WORKS: *Captivating Mary Carstairs* (1910). *Queed* (1911). *V. V.'s Eyes* (1913). *Angela's Business* (1915). *When I Come Back* (1919). *Saint Teresa* (1922). *Andrew Bride of Paris* (1925).

WILLIAM K. BOTTORFF
University of Toledo
Toledo, Ohio

MILDRED EUNICE HAUN (1911–1966). Born in Hamblen County, Tenn., on January 6, 1911, Mildred Haun grew up in Haun Hollow, Hoot Owl District, Cocke County, in a typical Appalachian community rich in folklore, proverbs, music, and tall tales. At the age of sixteen, she moved to Franklin, near Nashville, to attend high school with the intention of studying medicine and returning to her community as an educated "granny-woman," who traditionally tended the sick and acted as a midwife. She entered Vanderbilt University in 1931, and under the encouragement of John Crowe Ransom, and later Donald Davidson, Haun wrote her first fiction. For her master's thesis in 1937, she compiled a collection of "Cocke County Ballads and Songs," which has been of inestimable value to southern ballad specialists.

After studying with Wilbur Schramm at the University of Iowa, she gathered her stories together as a fictionalized chronicle of Cocke County. Bobbs-Merrill published it as *The Hawk's Done Gone* in 1941. Although she continued to write after 1941, she published only one story, but during the last 25 years of her life, she did other professional writing as the book review editor of the Nashville *Tennessean*, an editorial assistant to Allen Tate on the *Sewanee Review*, an information specialist at the Arnold Engineering Development Center in Tullahoma, and for thirteen years a public relations editor and author of technical manuals for the Department of Agriculture in Memphis and Washington, D.C. Haun died in Washington on December 20, 1966. After her death Herschel Gower collected ten additional pieces and published them along with the text of her only book as *The Hawk's Done Gone and Other Stories* (1968).

WORKS: *The Hawk's Done Gone* (1941). *The Hawk's Done Gone and Other Stories* (1968).

M. THOMAS INGE
Virginia Commonwealth
University
Richmond

JOSEPHINE AYRES HAXTON. See Ellen Douglas.

PAUL HAMILTON HAYNE (1830–1886). Paul Hayne was born in Charleston, S.C., on January 1, 1830, the only child of Paul Hamilton (1803–1831) and Emily McElhenny Hayne (1806–1879). Hayne's father, a naval officer and member of a prominent South Carolina family, died shortly thereafter, and his uncle, Senator Robert Y. Hayne, became his guardian and a lifelong influence. Hayne was educated at Christopher Cotes's school (Henry Timrod was a schoolmate) and at the College of Charleston (1847–1850). A publishing poet from 1845, he nevertheless studied law with James Louis Petigru and in 1852 married Mary Middleton Michel, daughter of a well-known physician. In the same year he was admitted to the bar and served as assistant editor and then as editor of the *Southern Literary Gazette*. He sold his interest in this weekly in 1854 and thereafter devoted himself to literature, editing *Russell's Magazine* (1857–1860) and publishing three volumes of poems by 1860. An early espouser of secession, Hayne embraced his state's cause, and though frail in health since youth, served actively for four months in 1861–1862 as aide-de-camp to Governor Francis Pickens. When his health failed, he continued to support the Confederacy with his pen.

The end of the Civil War brought not only defeat but near economic ruin, and Hayne moved his family (wife, son, and mother) to eighteen acres in Columbia County, Ga. (later called Copse Hill), and committed himself anew to literature. Struggling for bread, he served in various editorial capacities on several southern periodicals and contributed to southern magazines and any northern journals—*The Old Guard, Round Table, Appletons' Journal*,

Lippincott's, and the *Galaxy*—that would print his work. By the early 1870s his poems were appearing in the *Atlantic Monthly*, *Scribner's Monthly*, *Harper's New Monthly* and *Weekly*, and in most major northern literary magazines, and he was able to make a modest living. He collected new poems in 1872 and 1875, and in 1882 a misnamed "complete edition" came out.

During this period, particularly after the death of Simms in 1870, Hayne was widely known as the "representative poet of the South," and he took seriously the duties associated with such a reputation. He corresponded with many prominent American and British writers, including Longfellow, Whittier, Holmes, Whipple, Howells, Stedman, Taylor, Gayarré, Cooke, Lanier, Margaret Preston, and Constance Woolson among the American, and Swinburne, Charles Reade, R. D. Blackmore, Jean Ingelow, William Black, and Wilkie Collins among the British. His letters, indeed, may be his most important contribution to literature. As a poet, Hayne generally accepted the Anglo-American tradition, and despite his role as southern laureate, his verse suggests his background only in its stress on verbal melody and in its occasional treatment of nature and politics. His prose is a different matter, and his essays and letters at times demonstrate his Carolina temperament and unreconstructed political views. His postwar experience illustrates more fully than that of his contemporaries the plight of a dedicated man of letters in the South.

WORKS: *Poems* (1855). *Sonnets, and Other Poems* (1857). *Avolio: A Legend of the Island of Cos. With Poems, Lyrical, Miscellaneous, and Dramatic* (1859). *Legends and Lyrics* (1872). Ed., *The Poems of Henry Timrod* (1873). *The Mountain of the Lovers; With Poems of Nature and Tradition* (1875). *Poems*, complete ed. (1882).

RAYBURN S. MOORE
University of Georgia
Athens

LAFCADIO HEARN (1850–1904). Lafcadio Hearn's life, like his work, was exotic and varied. Born on June 27, 1850, on the Isle of Santa Maura (Leucadia), off the west coast of Greece, the second son of Charles Hearn, a British army physician, and Rosa Cassimati, a native Ionian, Hearn was educated in Ireland, England, and France. The financial ruin of his father's family ended his prospects among them, and in 1869 he went to America.

In Cincinnati, Hearn began an apprenticeship in journalism, doing sensationalist night reporting for weekly newspapers. He began translations of Gautier and Flaubert. In 1877 Hearn went South on a vacation journey and resolved never to go back North, a decision he said later he never regretted. In New Orleans he became associate editor of the *Item* and later joined the editorial staff of the *Times-Democrat*. He published *One of Cleopatra's Nights* (1882), a translation of Gautier's short stories. He continued his study, begun in Ohio, of Oriental literature, rewriting myths in what he called poetic prose and collecting them in *Stray Leaves from Strange Literature* (1884) and *Some Chinese Ghosts* (1887). In 1884 Hearn vacationed at Grand Isle, La., which became the setting for his impressionistic novelette, *Chita* (1889).

Hearn spent 1887 to 1889 in Martinique, which he described as a younger, fresher New Orleans. His sketches of island life appear in *Two Years in the French West Indies* (1890) and *Youma* (1890).

In 1890 he was sent to Japan by Harper Brothers. The remainder of his life was spent in Japan where he married and eventually became a lecturer on English literature at Tokyo Imperial University and the author of twelve books about Japan.

Physically disfigured by an eye injury in childhood, Hearn was an unusual man who lived on the margins of society, continually questing for the novel and exotic in life. His contributions to literature, however, are by no means slight. His stylistic experiments, criticisms of American literature, and interpretations of Japanese life and literature, with a plea for an integration of East and West in a world literature, reveal the extensive range of his work. He died on September 26, 1904.

WORKS: Trans., *One of Cleopatra's Nights and Other Fantastic Romances* by Théophile Gautier (1882). *Stray Leaves from Strange Literature* (1884). *La Cuisine Créole: A Collection of Culinary Recipes* (1885). *"Gombo Zhebes": A Little Dictionary of Creole Proverbs, Selected from*

Six Creole Dialects (1885). Ed., *Historical Sketch Book and Guide to New Orleans*, with others (1885). *Some Chinese Ghosts* (1887). *Chita: A Memory of Last Island* (1889). Trans., *The Crime of Sylvestre Bonnard* by Anatole France (1890). *Two Years in the French West Indies* (1890). *Youma* (1890). *Glimpses of Unfamiliar Japan*, 2 vols. (1894). *Out of the East: Reveries and Studies in New Japan* (1895). *Kokoro: Hints and Echoes of Japanese Inner Life* (1896). *Gleanings in Buddha-Fields: Studies of Hand and Soul in the Far East* (1897). *Exotics and Retrospectives* (1898). *Japanese Fairy Tales*, 5 vols. (1898–1903). *In Ghostly Japan* (1899). *Shadowings* (1900). *A Japanese Miscellany* (1901). *Kotto: Being Japanese Curios, with Sundry Cobwebs* (1902). *Kwaidan: Stories and Studies of Strange Things* (1904). *Japan: An Attempt at Interpretation* (1904). *Romance of the Milky Way, and Other Studies and Stories* (1905). *Leaves from the Diary of an Impressionist*, ed. Ferris Greenslet (1911). *The Writings of Lafcadio Hearn*, 16 vols. (1922).

ANNE ROWE
Florida State University
Tallahassee

LILLIAN HELLMAN (1905–). One of the most important American playwrights, ranking just below the top three or four, Lillian Hellman was born in New Orleans on June 20, 1905, the only child of Max Hellman, also New Orleans born, and Julia Newhouse from Alabama. Several of her plays draw upon her parents' families for material. When she was five, her father moved his family to New York, and she spent portions of her early years in both cities. After attending New York University and Columbia, she held various jobs relating to publishing and to the theater. Her marriage to Arthur Kober in 1925 ended in divorce in 1932. In 1934 came the highly successful production of her *Children's Hour*, a play notable for its treatment of an unusually frank subject for the period, lesbianism, and for other qualities which have become Hellman hallmarks: sharply drawn characters, taut plot, outspoken themes, and firm, lifelike dialogue.

From then through 1960, Hellman wrote seven more original plays, most of which met success with both critics and audiences, especially *The Little Foxes* (1939), *Watch on the Rhine* (1941; won

Drama Critics' Circle Award), *Another Part of the Forest* (1946), *The Autumn Garden* (1951), and *Toys in the Attic* (1960; won Critics' Award). Of these, *The Little Foxes*, trenchant study of the Hubbards, a rapacious entrepreneurial Alabama family, is likely to remain her best-known and most frequently revived work. (*Another Part of the Forest* is about the same family 20 years earlier.) All her original plays except *The Children's Hour* and the unsuccessful *Days to Come* (1936) are laid in the South: small-town Alabama, the Gulf Coast, New Orleans, the environs of Washington. The two Washington plays, *Watch on the Rhine* and *The Searching Wind* (1944), are probably too closely related to attitudes connected with World War II for frequent revival, though the first may well be the finest American play concerned with that war.

Hellman also adapted two French plays; wrote the book for a musical adaptation of Voltaire's *Candide*; wrote an original film script, *The North Star* (1943), concerned with World War II Russia; wrote an unsuccessful play, *My Mother, My Father and Me* (1962), based on a novel; edited a volume of Chekhov's letters; and wrote three highly acclaimed autobiographical studies, *An Unfinished Woman* (1969), *Pentimento* (1973), and *Scoundrel Time* (1976), which display her continued mastery of prose and of storytelling.

Aside from her work for the theater, a world in which she has never felt at home, Hellman's life centered for many years on her association with the novelist Dashiell Hammett, who died in 1959; and both were strongly affected by the Cold War politics of the 1950s, which led to Hammett's six-month imprisonment for contempt of court, his appearance before Senator Joseph McCarthy's investigating committee, and her appearance before the House UnAmerican Activities Committee. As a result, both were blacklisted and suffered severe financial losses. With the fading of the McCarthy era, Hellman recovered her rightful place in the world of letters and is now considered among the most distinguished of living American writers.

WORKS: *The Children's Hour* (1934). *Days to Come* (1936). *The Little Foxes* (1939). *Watch on the Rhine* (1941). *Four Plays*, with intro. (1942).

The North Star (1943). *The Searching Wind* (1944). *Another Part of the Forest* (1946). *Montserrat*, adapted from the French play by Emmanuel Roblès (1950). *The Autumn Garden* (1951). Ed., *The Selected Letters of Anton Chekhov* (1955). *The Lark*, adapted from the French play by Jean Anouilh (1956). *Candide* (1957). *Toys in the Attic* (1960). *My Mother, My Father and Me*, based on the novel *How Much?* by Burt Blechman (1963). Intro., *The Big Knockover* by Dashiell Hammett (1966). *An Unfinished Woman* (1969). *Pentimento* (1973). *Scoundrel Time* (1976).

JACOB H. ADLER
Purdue University
Lafayette, Ind.

JOHN BELL HENNEMANN (1864–1908). John Bell Hennemann was born in Spartanburg, S.C., on January 2, 1864. Educated at the University of Virginia and at the University of Berlin, he was professor of English at the University of Tennessee (1893–1900), where, on September 7, 1897, he married Marion Hubard. In 1900 he moved to Sewanee, Tenn., where he became dean of the School of Arts and Sciences and professor of English at the University of the South (1900–1908). There he assumed the editorship of the *Sewanee Review* (1907–1908), which had been founded in 1892 by his friend and colleague, W. P. Trent.

Hennemann's career as educator, editor, literary historian and critic is closely aligned with Trent's. In "The National Element in Southern Literature," *Sewanee Review* (July, 1903), he praises Trent's *Life of William Gilmore Simms* (1892) as an example of a seminal school of criticism then forming in the South—a school that included such scholars as William M. Baskervill of Vanderbilt and himself and which, he felt, was germinated by Sidney Lanier's literary lectures at Johns Hopkins (1880). Hennemann believed that romantic southern local color was more indicative of a national literary heritage and point of view than the realism of Howells and James, but in "The Modern Spirit in Literature," *Sewanee Review* (August, 1894) he had maintained that all regional and national literatures would shortly lose identities in world literature. His entry on Trent in *The Library of Southern Literature* (1907) is a defense of this critical movement and of academic freedom. Here he again defends Trent's *Simms* and congratulates the University of the South for supporting Trent against irate Charlestonians.

While at Sewanee, Hennemann became a prominent editor whose interests ranged from Shakespeare to American short fiction. He died at Richmond, Va., November 26, 1908.

WORKS: Ed., *Johnson Series of English Classics* (1900–03). Ed., *The Complete Works of Thackeray*, with W. P. Trent (1904). Ed., *Shakespeare's Twelfth Night* (1906). Ed., *Antiphon to the Stars* by Kemper Bocock (1907). Ed., *Best American Tales*, with W. P. Trent (1907).

JOHN T. HIERS
Valdosta State College
Valdosta, Ga.

O. HENRY. See William Sydney Porter.

CAROLINE LEE HENTZ (1800–1856). Novelist Caroline Lee Hentz was born in Lancaster, Mass., on June 1, 1800, the eighth and youngest child of John and Orpah Whiting. The Whitings had lived in Massachusetts for six generations, and Caroline's father and three of her brothers were career army officers. At the age of 24 she married Nicholas Marcellus Hentz, a native of Metz, France, who had come to America for political reasons. Hentz was teaching at George Bancroft's Round Hill School in Northampton when he married Caroline; but in 1826 he moved south to teach modern languages at the University of North Carolina. Mrs. Hentz's remaining years were lived in southern and border states, in which she and her husband established and conducted girls' schools. The Hentzes taught successively in Covington, Ky. (1830–1832); in Cincinnati (1832–1834); in Florence, Ala. (1834–1843); in Tuscaloosa, Ala. (1843–1845); in Tuskegee, Ala. (1845–1848); and in Columbus, Ga. (1848–1849).

During the years in which she raised four children and helped her husband teach, Hentz also found the time to write. She composed poetry, three plays, a novel, and a popular collection of short stories, *Aunt Patty's Scrap-Bag* (1845). The breakdown of

her husband's health in 1849 and the closing of their school in
Columbus forced Hentz to write full time to support her family.
Over the next seven years she completed an astonishing total of
seventeen novels and short story collections. A number of these
works were popular and were reprinted well into the 1880s.

Hentz's novels and stories are sentimental and melodramatic.
They project a romantic vision of southern plantation life—of refined ladies and gentlemen, contented slaves, and rustic backwoods farmers. Two of her novels, *The Planter's Northern Bride*
(1851) and *Marcus Warland* (1852), were written to refute the view
of the South and of slavery presented in *Uncle Tom's Cabin*.
Hentz died on February 11, 1856, in Marianna, Fla., where she
had moved to live with her grown children.

WORKS: *Lovell's Folly, a Novel* (1833). *De Lara: or, The Moorish Bride*
(1843). *Aunt Patty's Scrap-Bag* (1845). *Ugly Effie: or, The Neglected One
and the Pet Beauty, and Other Tales* (1850). *Linda: or, The Young Pilot
of the Belle Creole* (1850). *The Mob Cap and other Tales* (1850). *The
Planter's Northern Bride* (1851). *Rena: or, The Snowbird* (1851). *The
Banished Son, and Other Stories of the Heart* (1852). *Eoline: or, Magnolia Vale* (1852). *Marcus Warland: or, The Long Moss Spring* (1852).
Wild Jack: or, The Stolen Child, and Other Stories (1852). *Helen and
Arthur: or, Miss Thusa's Spinning Wheel* (1853). *The Victim of Excite-
ment, The Bosom Serpent, etc., etc., etc.* (1853). *The Flowers of Elocu-
tion: A Class Book* (1855). *Robert Graham, a Novel* (1855). *Courtship
and Marriage: or, The Joys and Sorrows of American Life* (1856). *Ernest
Linwood, a Novel* (1856). *The Lost Daughter and Other Stories of the
Heart* (1857). *Love after Marriage, and Other Stories of the Heart* (1857).
The Planter's Daughter: A Tale of Louisiana (1858).

RITCHIE D. WATSON, JR.
Randolph-Macon College
Ashland, Va.

SOPHIA BLEDSOE HERRICK (1837–1919). Sophia Bledsoe was
born on March 26, 1837, in Gambier, Ohio, where her father,
Albert Taylor Bledsoe, was both student of theology and teacher
of mathematics at Kenyon College. Later, at the universities of

Mississippi and Virginia, where he was professor of mathematics, she studied in his field, but also in drawing and geology and other sciences. She married the Reverend James B. Herrick in 1860 and moved to New York, where in addition to rearing a son and two daughters she made a thorough study of Darwin and other evolutionary scientists.

In 1868 her husband renounced his Episcopalian ministry in order to join the Oneida Community. She could not follow him in this venture and moved to Baltimore, where her father was editing the *Southern Review*. She conducted a school for girls for a year, while contributing occasional scientific articles and reviews to the journal. As her work with the magazine grew in amount and quality, her father turned over many of the editorial and business matters to her capable guidance. After studying biology at Johns Hopkins she wrote a series of articles, with her own illustrations, for *Scribner's Magazine*. She was encouraged to write more and did so. After her father's death in 1877 and failure of the *Southern Review* in 1878, she became a favorite contributor on popular science for both *Scribner's* and *Century*. She became assistant editor of *Century* during the term of Richard Watson Gilder, and retired when he died in 1909. In her last years she continued to write and illustrate works on travel and observations of nature. She died on October 9, 1919.

works: *The Wonders of Plant Life under the Microscope* (1883). *Chapters on Plant Life* (1885). *The Earth in Past Ages* (1888). *A Century of Sonnets* (1902).

C. Carroll Hollis
University of North Carolina
Chapel Hill

DUBOSE HEYWARD (1885–1940). The most celebrated of the South Carolina Poetry Society founders, Edwin DuBose Heyward, was born in Charleston, August 31, 1885, to Edward Watkins and Janie Screven DuBose Heyward. He was a direct descendant of a signer of the Declaration of Independence.

After attending Susan Hayne's, Craft's, and Boy high schools, Heyward abandoned formal education at fourteen in order to work in a hardware store to support his family. His father had died in a mill accident when Heyward was two. At eighteen Heyward was stricken with polio, then with typhoid and pleurisy. At 20, he worked for a time as a wharf checker. In 1908 he entered an insurance and real estate partnership.

Heyward took up painting in Hendersonville, N.C., in 1917 and bought a summer cottage. (Later he built a home, Dawn Hill, there.) Under the influence of John Bennett and Hervey Allen, both published writers, Heyward turned in 1920 from unimpressive attempts at short-story writing to poetry. Their "fangfest" discussions of one another's work and H. L. Mencken's ridicule of southern culture led Heyward to propose a South Carolina poetry society in the fall of 1920. He became secretary and edited yearbooks until 1924 when he was elected president. His first volume of poems, with Allen, *Carolina Chansons*, was published in 1922, his second in 1924.

Heyward spent summers at MacDowell Colony in 1922 and 1923 where he met Dorothy Hartzell Kuhns, a playwright; they were married on September 22, 1923. They had one child, Jennifer, born in 1930. In 1924 Heyward gave up his business and committed himself full-time to lecturing on southern literature and writing his first novel, *Porgy* (1925).

Subsequently, Heyward completed eleven additional volumes of fiction, poetry, or drama, as well as two movie scenarios (*The Emperor Jones* and *The Good Earth*) and the libretto and most of the lyrics for George Gershwin's opera, *Porgy and Bess*, which appeared in 1935. He died in Tryon, N.C., on June 16, 1940.

In *Porgy* and *Mamba's Daughters*, his second Charleston novel, Heyward defined the major theme of his work and made his chief contributions to literature: a realistic and human treatment of urban southern black characters. The characters of Catfish Row are flawed by primitivism, innocence, and lack of discipline, yet they must face the pressures of white society and the demands of fate. They meet these challenges with what Heyward later called "the secret rhythm of life," defined by faith, community, and a common history of suffering.

WORKS: *Carolina Chansons: Legends of the Low Country*, with Hervey Allen (1922). *Skylines and Horizons* (1924). *Porgy* (1925). *Angel* (1926). *Porgy: A Play in Four Acts*, with Dorothy Heyward (1927). *The Half-Pint Flask* (1929). *Mamba's Daughters* (1929). *Jasbo Brown and Selected Poems* (1931). *Brass Ankle* (1931). *Peter Ashley* (1932). *Porgy and Bess*, with music by George Gershwin, libretto by Heyward, lyrics by Heyward and Ira Gershwin (1935). *Lost Morning* (1936). *Mamba's Daughters*, with Dorothy Heyward (1939). *Star Spangled Virgin* (1939). *The Country Bunny and the Little Gold Shoes* (1939).

WILLIAM H. SLAVICK
University of Maine
Gorham

LESLIE PINCKNEY HILL (1880–1960). Leslie Pinckney Hill was born in Lynchburg, Va., on May 14, 1880. He was educated in a Lynchburg elementary school, in an East Orange, N.J., high school, and at Harvard University where he earned an A.B. (Phi Beta Kappa, 1903) and an A.M. (1904). He then taught at Tuskegee Institute (1904–1907); served as principal of the Manassas, Va., Industrial Institute (1907–1913); and as head of the Cheyney, Pa., Institute for Colored Youth, a school which he guided toward full recognition and state support by 1920. During his administration (1913–1951), the Institute became Cheyney Training School for Teachers (1914), State Normal School (1920), and Cheyney State Teachers College (1951).

Besides being an educator and administrator, Hill was a poet, dramatist, lecturer, and an essayist. The role which appears to have informed most of his efforts, however, is that of educator, a role reflected in the Foreword to both of his published works. In his 1921 volume of poetry, *The Wings of Oppression*, he announced his hope that some poems would exhibit the "indestructible spiritual quality of my race." Similarly, he stated that his blank-verse drama, *Toussaint L'Ouverture* (1928), together with other creative literature of Negro America, "must correct and counterbalance this falsehood" that Negroes have made no substantial contributions. Not all of Hill's works, however, are "correctives" on behalf of black Americans; some of his poems are pure lyric expressions having no didactic quality.

Both creative and civic-minded, Hill was founder and president of Chester Community Center, founder and president of the Pennsylvania State Negro Council, and member of many boards and committees. For his contributions, he was awarded honorary degrees by Lincoln University, Morgan State College, Haverford College, and the Rhode Island College of Education. Hill died on February 5, 1960, in Philadelphia.

WORKS: *The Wings of Oppression and Other Poems* (1921). *Toussaint L'Ouverture: A Dramatic History* (1928).

PATSY B. PERRY
North Carolina Central University
Durham

CHESTER BOMAR HIMES (1909–). Chester Himes was born in Jefferson City, Mo., on July 29, 1909, to middle-class, schoolteacher parents. Because his father changed positions frequently, Himes attended school in several southern and midwestern cities before graduating from a Cleveland, Ohio, high school in 1926. He was enrolled at Ohio State University for approximately seven months; his failure to adjust academically and socially resulted in his dismissal before the second quarter ended in the spring of 1927. Following his brief college experience, he became involved with small-time racketeers in Cleveland and, by December, 1928, had drawn a 20-to-25-year sentence in the Ohio State Penitentiary for armed robbery. Himes began writing while in prison and published his first story, "Crazy in the Stir," in *Esquire* (August, 1934). By the time he was paroled in 1936, he had published stories in *Abbott's Monthly* and the *Bronzeman*. He returned to Cleveland following his release, worked on numerous nonliterary jobs, and, for a short time, for the Ohio Writers Project before moving to California and, then, to New York. Since 1953 Himes has lived in France and Spain.

A prolific writer, he published five social protest novels from 1945 to 1955. Often classified in the Richard Wright school of naturalism, these novels explore the emasculating effect of American racism on black men. Since 1957, in addition to *Pinktoes*, his 1965 satire, Himes has written detective novels which have been highly popular in France, where he was presented the 1958 Mystery Writers' Award, the Grand Prix Policier. One detective thriller, *Cotton Comes to Harlem* (1965), was made into a successful American movie, but, generally, these novels have not been applauded in America. When one examines Himes's short stories, protest works, *and* detective novels, he finds many diverse characters who picture colorfully, and sometimes humorously, several aspects of black American life.

WORKS: *If He Hollers Let Him Go* (1945). *Lonely Crusade* (1947). *Cast the First Stone* (1952). *The Third Generation* (1954). *The Primitive* (1955). *For Love of Imabelle* (1957); also published as *A Rage in Harlem* (1965). *The Crazy Kill* (1959). *The Real Cool Killers* (1959). *All Shot Up* (1960). *The Big Gold Dream* (1960). *Cotton Comes to Harlem* (1965). *Pinktoes* (1965); original title, *Mamie Mason*, published in Paris and London in 1961. *The Heat's On* (1966); also published as *Come Back, Charleston Blue*, 1972. *Run, Man Run* (1966). *Blind Man With a Pistol* (1969); also published as *Hot Day, Hot Night*, 1970. *The Quality of Hurt*, I (1972). *Black on Black: Baby Sister and Selected Writings* (1973).

PATSY B. PERRY
North Carolina Central University
Durham

CARL WENDELL HINES, JR. (1940–). Carl Wendell Hines, Jr. was born September 1, 1940, in Wilson, N.C., to middle-class black parents. His father, a graduate of North Carolina Agricultural and Technical College, was first a mathematics teacher and later an elementary school principal in the Wilson city schools. His mother, Ruth Johnson Hines, a graduate of Bennett College, Greensboro, taught in the Wilson public school system until her retirement. The Hineses had two children besides Carl, Jr.: Brenda Carol and Edwin Harold.

Hines attended public school in Wilson, where he developed an interest in music and became a jazz pianist. After graduation from high school in 1958, Hines enrolled in Tennessee Agricultural and Industrial State University, pursuing a major in science and mathematics education. He went one night to neighboring Fisk University to hear Langston Hughes read his poetry. He came away resolved to be a poet. In college Hines started writing a column for the *Meter*, the campus newspaper. These columns reflected his interest in music and literature. Hines had his first success as a published poet when Arna Bontemps accepted two "Jazz Poems" for inclusion in an anthology that he was editing called *American Negro Poetry* (1963).

After graduation from Tennessee A and I, Hines enrolled at the University of Tennessee, Knoxville, and received his master's degree in science and mathematics education in 1966.

In 1963 Hines went to the small town of Alcoa, Tenn., to teach, but he left after one year. He joined a college classmate in the public school system of Indianapolis, Ind. There he continued his interest in jazz, playing with a combo that is sometimes called The Carl Hines Jazz Quartet. He is divorced and has a small son.

WORKS: "Two Jazz Poems," in *American Negro Poetry*, ed. Arna Bontemps (1963). "Now That He Is Safely Dead," in *Hold Fast to Dreams*, ed. Arna Bontemps (1969).

MARY MEBANE
University of South Carolina
Columbia

[HENRY] **WILLIAM HOFFMAN** (1925–). Although born in Charleston, W.Va., on May 16, 1925, William Hoffman's fiction concerns, for the most part, Virginia and Virginians. Reared by his grandmother in Charleston, he was graduated from Kentucky Military Institute in 1943 and was drafted into the army immediately. After the army he attended Hampden-Sydney College, receiving a B.A. in 1949, and he continued his education in law school at Washington and Lee University for one year—1949–1950. While at Washington and Lee he took a creative writing course "just as a lark," he said to a *McCall's* interviewer, but was "trapped" by writing.

With his first story appearing in *Shenandoah* in 1950, Hoffman's interest in writing took him to the University of Iowa and the Writers' Workshop for a year—1950–1951. He worked briefly for a newspaper in Washington, D.C., and for the Chase National Bank in New York, finally becoming an instructor in English at Hampden-Sydney College in 1952. His first two novels were published during his instructorship there from 1952 to 1959. During this time, too, he met and later married Alice Sue Richardson on April 17, 1957. They have two daughters—Ruth Beckley and Margaret Kay.

Between his leaving Hampden-Sydney in 1959 and his return as writer-in-residence in 1966, Hoffman published three more novels. Two additional books appeared during his latter tenure at Hampden-Sydney, and Hoffman was playwright-in-residence at the Barter Theatre in Abingdon, Va., during the summer of 1967. His only play, "The Love Touch," also was published in 1967. He resigned from Hampden-Sydney in 1973, the year of his last book. He is presently at work on his eighth novel at his home in Charlotte Court House, Va.

Hoffman's other occupations include breeding horses and serving as director of the Elks Grocery Company, the Elk Storage and Warehouse Company, and the Kay Company. His numerous stories, though uncollected, may be found in such periodicals as *McCall's, Playboy, Cosmopolitan, Gentleman's Quarterly, Scholastic, Virginia Quarterly Review, Sewanee Review, Transatlantic Review, Carelton Miscellany,* and *Saturday Evening Post.*

WORKS: *The Trumpet Unblown* (1955). *Days in the Yellow Leaf* (1958). *A Place for My Head* (1960). *The Dark Mountains* (1963). *Yancey's War* (1966). *A Walk to the River* (1970). *A Death of Dreams* (1973).

JEANNE R. NOSTRANDT
James Madison College
Harrisonburg, Va.

GEORGE FREDERICK HOLMES (1820–1897). Born on August 21, 1820, in British Guiana and briefly educated in England at the University of Durham, George Frederick Holmes, at the age of sixteen, sailed for Canada. Coming then to the United States, he moved about in Virginia, Georgia, and South Carolina for four years, finally being admitted to the practice of law, which he found unsatisfactory. Although as early as 1839 he had published a short story in the *Southern Literary Messenger*, his first creative efforts ultimately were supplanted by the periodical review, which was to become his literary forte. He accepted a professorship in classical languages at Richmond College in 1846; the following year he taught at the College of William and Mary. His election to the presidency of the newly created University of Mississippi did not provide the academic security he urgently needed: his short tenure was a virtual fiasco.

From 1849 to 1857 Holmes resided in self-imposed exile at his wife's western Virginia plantation. Although he was perpetually plagued by ineptitude in practical matters—principally financial—during these years he produced his most significant intellectual accomplishments, represented by a ponderous bibliography of reviews and articles for contemporary periodicals. Following the years of rustification, Holmes secured a position in the School of History and Literature at the University of Virginia, where he remained until his death on November 4, 1897.

WORKS: *Address Delivered Before the Beaufort District Society* (1845). *Inaugural Address Delivered on Occasion of the Opening of the University of the State of Mississippi, November 6, 1848* (1849). *The Southern Elementary Spelling-Book for Schools and Families* (1866). *Holmes' Pictorial Primer, for Home or School* (1867). *An Elementary Grammar of the English Language* (1868). *Holmes' First (-Sixth) Reader* (1870–72). *A Grammar of the English Language* (1871). *A School History of the United States of America, from the Earliest Discoveries to the Year 1870* (1871). *The Science of Society* (1883). *New School History of the United States* (1883, 1886).

LEONIDAS BETTS
North Carolina State University
Raleigh

JOHNSON JONES HOOPER (1815–1862). The creator of Simon Suggs, one of the most vividly drawn characters in the antebellum humor of the Old Southwest, was born on June 9, 1815, in Wilmington, N.C. His father, Archibald Maclaine Hooper, was related to several prominent North Carolina families, and his mother, Charlotte DeBerniere, was descended from the English divine Jeremy Taylor and from an eminent Huguenot who had fled France after the revocation of the Edict of Nantes. Johnson was the youngest of six. The father, a competent journalist but a poor business manager, could ill support the large family, and Johnson went to work, as a printer's devil, instead of to college. At 20 he began reading law in the frontier town of La Fayette, Ala., though his studies were interrupted by trips to Louisiana and South Carolina as well as by a stint as census taker in 1840—experiences of which he later made humorous capital. In 1841 he started a law practice in Dadeville, Ala., and the next year married Mary Mildred Brantley, daughter of an Alabama merchant; they had three children: William (1844–1875), Annie (1845–1847), and Adolphus (1849–1895).

In 1842 Hooper founded the La Fayette *East Alabamian*, for which newspaper he wrote humorous and realistic sketches and tales of frontier life published as *Some Adventures of Captain Simon Suggs* (1845). Actively promoted by William T. Porter, editor of the *Spirit of the Times*, a sporting weekly which first introduced many of Hooper's pieces to a nationwide readership, *Suggs*, with the motto, "It is good to be shifty in a new country," made its author immediately famous; yet because of his law practice, his editorship of the *Alabama Journal* in Montgomery (1846–1849), and his political ambitions, his creative output declined in quantity. However, by 1849, after resuming the practice of law in La Fayette and despite new duties as editor of the *Chambers County Tribune*, he had written the pieces collected in *A Ride with Old Kit Kuncker* (1849).

In the same year Hooper, a Whig, was elected solicitor of Alabama's Ninth District, but was defeated for reelection in 1853 and the next year cofounded the Montgomery *Mail*, a paper nominally independent but with cautious Know-Nothing inclinations despite

Hooper's disapproval of that party's religious intolerance. He remained associated with the *Mail* until 1861, when he became secretary to the Provisional Congress of the new Confederacy and removed with that body to Richmond. When the unicameral Congress reorganized as a Senate and House, Hooper was defeated for election as secretary of the Senate but soon gained a position as editor of the Provisional Congress records. His new labors were cut short by death, probably from tuberculosis, on June 7, 1862.

Hooper left a number of pungent, realistic sketches and tales that rank with the best work of the humorists of the Old Southwest. Especially significant are the Simon Suggs pieces, which constitute the only effective picaresque novel by any of the Southwest writers. In creating Suggs and his victims, Hooper broke out of regional humor and made a permanent contribution to the international literature of roguery.

WORKS: *Some Adventures of Captain Simon Suggs, Late of the Tallapoosa Volunteers; Together with "Taking the Census," and Other Alabama Sketches* (1845). *A Ride with Old Kit Kuncker, and Other Sketches and Scenes of Alabama* (1849). *The Widow Rugby's Husband, A Night at the Ugly Man's, and Other Tales of Alabama* (1851). *Read and Circulate: Proceedings of the Democratic and Anti–Know-Nothing Party in Caucus; or the Guillotine at Work, at the Capital, during the Session of 1855–'56* (1855). *Dog and Gun; A Few Loose Chapters on Shooting. Among Which Will Be Found Some Anecdotes and Incidents* (1856).

NORRIS YATES
Iowa State University
Ames

GEORGE MOSES HORTON (1797?–1883?). One of ten children of a slave woman belonging to William Horton, George Moses Horton was born in Northampton County, N.C. When a child, he moved upstate with his master to Chatham County, began to teach himself to read, and started composing lines in his head based on the meter and rhyme of Wesley hymns. At nearby Chapel Hill, where he was sent to sell farm produce, he proudly recited his poems to the startled university students, who, serving as his amanuenses, thereafter commissioned him for a fee to write acrostics on their sweethearts' names. Caroline Lee Hentz, novelist, married to a professor of French, tutored him in poetic composition, and 21 of his poems were published in 1829 to raise money to send him to Liberia. This first book by a southern black contained verses decrying his slave's condition, but profits from its sale were meager.

Slowly he learned to write, and for the next 30 years, he was employed in and around Chapel Hill, "buying his time" from several Horton masters with money earned from the well-paying acrostics. As he went about gathering subscriptions for a new book of poems, he was indulged by townspeople, faculty members, university presidents, students, freedom-loving newspaper editors in both North and South, and at least one governor of North Carolina. In 1865 he attached himself to a Michigan captain in the occupation forces, published his third book in Raleigh, then went to Philadelphia, where he worked for old North Carolina friends living in the city. The circumstances of his death are unknown. Horton's poems are for the most part academic and conventional, the most admirable ones being those about himself and the rural scene he loved.

WORKS: *The Hope of Liberty* (1829). *Poetical Works of George M. Horton, the Colored Bard of North-Carolina, To Which Is Prefixed the Life of the Author, Written by Himself* (1845). *Naked Genius* (1865).

RICHARD WALSER
North Carolina State University
Raleigh

JAY BROADUS HUBBELL (1885–1979). Jay Hubbell, the son of the Reverend David Shelton and Ruth Eller Hubbell, was born in Smyth County, Va., and educated at Richmond College (B.A., 1905), Harvard (M.A., 1908) and Columbia (Ph.D., 1922). He taught at Wake Forest, North Carolina, Southern Methodist, and served as an officer in World War I. He married Lucinda Smith in 1918 and became the father of two boys—Jay, Jr., and David. Subsequently he became chairman of the department and E. A. Lilly Professor at Southern Methodist and edited the *Southwest*

Review. In 1927 he went to Duke and remained, with occasional breaks for exchange professorships at Vienna, Athens, and Hebrew University, until he retired in 1954.

At Duke, Hubbell became a pioneer in the study of American literature. He was an early member and chairman (1924–1927) of the American Literature Group of the Modern Language Association and in 1928 became the founding editor of *American Literature*, the first scholarly journal in the field. His anthology, *American Life in Literature* (1936), was chosen to be reprinted in armed services editions in World War II, and his position as a leader was affirmed by his election to the executive council of MLA (1946–1949) and to the vice-presidency in 1951. His articles, his direction of theses and dissertations, and his magisterial *The South in American Literature* (1954) established him as dean among scholars in southern literature. His most recent books, *South and Southwest* (1965) and *Who Are the Major American Writers?* (1972), testify anew to his stature in both fields, a stature exemplified by the Hubbell Medallion awarded by the American Literature Group for important contributions to the field and by the Jay B. Hubbell Center for American Literary Historiography at Duke. Hubbell died on February 13, 1979.

WORKS: *Virginia Life in Fiction* (1922). *An Introduction to Poetry*, with John O. Beaty (1922). *An Introduction to Drama*, with John O. Beaty (1927). Ed., *Treasure Island*, by Robert Louis Stevenson (1927). *The Enjoyment of Literature* (1929). Ed., *Swallow Barn*, by John Pendleton (1929). Ed., *American Life in Literature*, 2 vols. (1936, 1949). *The Last Years of Henry Timrod, 1864–1867* (1941). Ed., with Douglass Adair, *The Candidates*, by Robert Munford (1948). *The South in American Literature, 1607–1900* (1954). "Edgar Allan Poe" in *Eight American Authors: A Review of Research and Criticism*, ed. James Woodress (1956, 1971). *Southern Life in Fiction* (1960). *South and Southwest: Literary Essays and Reminiscences* (1965). *Who Are the Major American Writers? A Study of the Changing Literary Canon* (1972).

RAYBURN S. MOORE
University of Georgia
Athens

LANGSTON HUGHES (1902–1967). Born February 1, 1902, in Joplin, Mo., James Mercer Langston Hughes lived with relatives and family after his parents separated, spending most of his childhood with his grandmother in Lawrence, Kan., before joining his mother and stepfather in Lincoln, Ill., in 1914. His family were college educated, and at an early age Hughes was introduced to books and theatrical performances.

In 1916 Hughes and his mother joined his stepfather in Cleveland, Ohio, where at Central High School he came into contact for the first time with large numbers of blacks. In his high school English classes he read the poetry of Sandburg, Masters, and other popular poets. He had written his first poem when he was thirteen, and published several poems in his high school's literary magazine.

After graduating from high school in 1920, Hughes spent an unhappy year in Mexico with his father, James Nathaniel Hughes, who was a financial success and urged his son to study engineering at a major European university. The two compromised, agreeing that Langston would study engineering at Columbia University. But his interest in engineering was slight, and after one year he abandoned his studies and worked at odd jobs in New York before signing on as a mess boy on a ship that took him to Africa and Europe.

The year he entered Columbia (1921) was eventful in Hughes's life. When the NAACP's *The Brownie's Book*, in which he had published some works, ceased publication, the *Crisis*, another organ of the NAACP, published what has become one of his best-known poems, "The Negro Speaks of Rivers." By 1930 he had won several awards for his poetry, had helped organize a short-lived literary magazine, *Fire*, and had become an important member of the literary coterie that helped form the Harlem Renaissance.

In 1924 Hughes returned from Europe and lived for a few months with his mother in Washington, D.C. He completed a poem he had begun at Columbia, in which he artistically captured that musical, rhythmic aspect of black urban life which was to distinguish many of his poems. This poem became the title of his first volume, *The Weary Blues* (1926). The enthusiastic critical acceptance of this book launched his successful career as a poet.

Hughes obtained a scholarship to Lincoln University (Pennsylvania), graduating in 1929. At Lincoln he worked on his first novel, *Not Without Laughter*. His most memorable work in prose fiction came in 1950 with publication of *Simple Speaks His Mind*. This book features the highly original character Jesse B. Simple, whom Hughes first introduced in 1942 in the Chicago *Defender*.

Hughes lived most of his last 25 years in New York, writing more lightly and more humorously. When he died on May 22, 1967, he left more than 60 books which he had written, edited, translated, and compiled, and numerous uncollected works in prose, poetry, drama, and song.

WORKS: *The Weary Blues* (1926). *Fine Clothes to the Jew* (1927). *Not Without Laughter* (1930). *Dear Lovely Death* (1931). *The Negro Mother* (1931). *The Dream Keeper and Other Poems* (1932). *Scottsboro Limited* (1932). *Popo and Fifina*, with Arna Bontemps (1932). *The Ways of White Folks* (1934). *A New Song* (1938). *The Big Sea* (1940). *Shakespeare in Harlem* (1942). *Freedom's Plow* (1943). *Jim Crow's Last Stand* (1943). *Lament for Dark People and Other Poems* (1944). *Fields of Wonder* (1947). *Street Scene: An American Opera Based on Elmer Rice's Play* (1948). *Troubled Island* (1949). *One-Way Ticket* (1949). *Simple Speaks His Mind* (1950). *Montage of a Dream Deferred* (1951). *Laughing to Keep from Crying* (1952). *The First Book of Negroes* (1952). *Simple Takes a Wife* (1953). *Famous American Negroes* (1954). *The First Book of Rhythms* (1954). *The First Book of Jazz* (1955). *Famous Negro Music Makers* (1955). *The Sweet Flypaper of Life* (1955). *I Wonder as I Wander* (1956). *A Pictorial History of the Negro in America* (1956). *The First Book of the West Indies* (1956). *Simple Stakes a Claim* (1957). *Famous Negro Heroes of America* (1958). *Tambourines to Glory* (1958). *The Langston Hughes Reader* (1958). *Selected Poems of Langston Hughes* (1959). *Simply Heavenly* (1959). *The First Book of Africa* (1960). *Ask Your Mama: 12 Moods for Jazz* (1961). *The Best of Simple* (1961). *Fight for Freedom: The Story of the NAACP* (1962). *Five Plays of Langston Hughes* (1963). *Something in Common and Other Stories* (1963). *Simple's Uncle Sam* (1965). *Black Magic: A Pictorial History of the Negro in American Entertainment* (1967). *The Panther and the Lash: Poems of Our Times* (1967). *Black Misery* (1969). *Don't You Turn Back* (1969).

J. LEE GREENE
University of North Carolina
Chapel Hill

WILLIAM HUMPHREY (1924–). Essayist, short story writer, and novelist, William Humphrey was born in Clarksville, Tex., on June 28, 1924. Clarksville is the setting for his best fiction. In 1938, after his father was killed in an automobile accident, Humphrey and his mother moved to Dallas, where Humphrey attended public school and later Southern Methodist University. Also in 1941–1942 he attended the University of Texas.

In 1969 he was awarded a Doctor of Letters from Southern Methodist University. In addition to his writing Humphrey has taught at Bard College (1949–1958), Washington and Lee (1963–1964), Massachusetts Institute of Technology (1965–1966), and at Smith College (1976–1977). At Washington and Lee he held the Glasgow Professorship, and at Smith College he presently holds the Elizabeth Drew Professorship. He received awards from the Texas Institute of Arts and Letters in 1958 and again in 1965 and from the National Institute of Arts and Letters in 1962. His nonfiction essays include "Ditches Are Quicker," which appeared in *Life* in 1970, and "Bonefishing," which appeared in *True* in 1971.

Humphrey's first book, *The Last Husband and Other Stories*, appeared in 1953. It is a collection of ten short stories, six of which had been previously published. Critical reaction to the volume praised Humphrey for his ability to render accurately the idiom and life of east Texas. *Home from the Hill*, Humphrey's first novel, appeared in 1958. Its principal fault is Humphrey's inability to free himself from Faulkner's milieu and to write in terms of his own experience. Rights to *The Ordways*, Humphrey's second novel, were sold to Columbia pictures. Since 1968, when *A Time and a Place* was published, Humphrey has not published any short stories, devoting his time primarily to writing novels and nonfiction. His works have been translated into French, German, Spanish, and Swedish.

WORKS: *The Last Husband and Other Stories* (1953). *Home from the Hill* (1958). *The Ordways* (1965). *A Time and a Place* (1968). *The Spawning Run* (1970). *Proud Flesh* (1973).

MARION C. MICHAEL
Texas Tech University
Lubbock

DANIEL ROBINSON HUNDLEY (1832–1899). Daniel Robinson Hundley was born in Madison County, Ala., on December 11, 1832, to John Henderson and Melinda Robinson Hundley, both of Virginia. He graduated from Bacon College, Harrodsburg, Ky., in 1850 and entered law school at the University of Virginia. Continuing his study at Harvard, he received an LL.B. there in 1853.

After marrying his first cousin, Mary Ann Hundley, of Charlotte County, Va., in 1853, he moved, in 1856, to Chicago, where his father-in-law had real estate interests. There he practiced law, contributed to periodicals, and wrote *Social Relations in our Southern States*.

An ardent Unionist, Hundley opposed both abolition and secession and urged southern support of Douglas in 1860. After Fort Sumter, however, and leaving considerable property in Illinois, he returned to Alabama, where he was elected colonel of the 31st Alabama Infantry Regiment.

Hundley's regiment fought in Tennessee, and in the defense of Vicksburg he was wounded and captured at Port Gibson, Miss. Exchanged after Vicksburg's surrender, he commanded his regiment in the Army of Tennessee until captured at Big Shanty, Ga., in June, 1864. While imprisoned at Johnson's Island, Ohio, he escaped but was recaptured in January, 1865.

After the war he settled in Lawrence and Limestone counties, Ala., as a planter and attorney and, for a time, edited a newspaper. In 1874 he published his journal of prison experiences. Hundley died in Mooresville, Ala., on December 27, 1899, without completing a planned work on the results of war and Reconstruction.

Social Relations in Our Southern States is notable for its candid delineation of classes in southern society. Hundley insisted that southerners descended from the cavaliers were far outnumbered by those of middle- and lower-class origins. Although he stoutly defended slavery, he admitted extreme abuse of slaves by some, such as the "Cotton Snobs," whom he satirized severely.

WORKS: *Work and Bread: or The Coming Winter and the Poor* (1858).

Social Relations in Our Southern States (1860). *Prison Echoes of the Great Rebellion* (1874).

WILLIAM M. MOSS
Wake Forest University
Winston-Salem, N.C.

ZORA NEALE HURSTON (1903–1960). Zora Neale Hurston, born on January 7, 1903, in all-black Eatonville, Fla., became a major author in the Harlem Renaissance. Recipient of a Rosenwald fellowship (1935) and Guggenheim fellowships (1936, 1938), she earned praise for stories, essays, dramas, four novels, two books of Afro-American folklore, and an autobiography, *Dust Tracks on a Road* (1942), which won an Anisfield-Wolf Award for improving interracial relationships. Yet these achievements neither brought great recognition nor affluence. In early years, a maid, waitress, manicurist, and secretary for Fannie Hurst, and a maid and teacher later, Hurston died penniless in Fort Pierce, Fla., on January 28, 1960.

Seventh of eight children of Lucy Ann and John Hurston—carpenter, minister, and three-term mayor of Eatonville—Hurston, after her mother's death in 1912, migrated among relatives and friends before becoming, at fifteen, an actress' maid. After completing high school four years later at Morgan Academy (now Morgan State University), which subsequently conferred a Litt.D., Hurston studied at Howard University; then, assisted by a scholarship, she was one of the first Afro-American students at Barnard College (1925), where she earned a bachelor's degree (1928). Professor Franz Boas, Columbia's distinguished anthropologist, recommended her for a grant to study Afro-American folklore in Florida and Louisiana. Before releasing her research (*Mules and Men*, 1935), Hurston, who had published stories and essays since 1924, contracted for *Jonah's Gourd Vine* (1934), a novel about her parents. Subsequent books were *Their Eyes Were Watching God* (1937), a black woman's search for individuality in love; *Tell My Horse* (1938), Caribbean folklore; and *Moses, Man of the Mountain*

(1939), a satirical adaptation of the Moses legend to America's black-white interrelationships.

After the novel *Seraph on the Suwanee* (1948), about white Floridians, Hurston, publishing only magazine articles, returned to Florida as a maid and a teacher. Her fifth novel was aborted by a stroke in 1959 and death the following year.

WORKS: *Jonah's Gourd Vine* (1934). *Mules and Men* (1935). *Their Eyes Were Watching God* (1937). *Tell My Horse* (1938). *Moses, Man of the Mountain* (1939). *Dust Tracks on a Road* (1942). *Seraph on the Suwanee* (1948).

DARWIN T. TURNER
University of Iowa
Iowa City

JOSEPH HOLT INGRAHAM (1809–1860). Although Ingraham was a popular and prolific novelist, many details of his life remain obscure. He was born to a wealthy mercantile family in Portland, Me., probably on January 26, 1809. He claimed to have been graduated from Bowdoin College, but the school's records do not show that he ever attended it. In 1830 he left Portland on the sea voyage to New Orleans that he describes in his first book, *The South-West* (1835), and on May 24, 1832, he married Mary Brooks, daughter of a Natchez planter.

He moved frequently between the North and South until 1847. He was in New York when his second book, the first two-volume romantic novel, *Lafitte: The Pirate of the Gulf* appeared in 1836. It was followed by three more historical novels modeled on Sir Walter Scott's novels. Between 1842 and 1847, Ingraham concocted at least 80 more short (100, or fewer, pages), lurid romances, mostly about pirates and the evils of big cities. They were published in paperback pamphlets by various Boston firms. (Full bibliographical details about these are found in Jacob Blanck (ed.), *Bibliography of American Literature*, IV [1963], 458–91.)

Suddenly in 1847 Ingraham's flood of cheap romances ended. He joined the Protestant Episcopal Church and became headmaster of a church school for girls near Nashville, Tenn. In April,

1851, he took charge of St. John's Mission, Aberdeen, Miss.; and on February 8, 1852, he was received into the Episcopal priesthood at Jackson, Miss. In December, 1853, he moved to St. John's Church, Mobile, Ala. During three years there he composed his most famous novel, *The Prince of the House of David* (1855), the first best-selling fictionalization of the life of Christ. *The Sunny South*, a series of letters defending the plantation system, appeared in 1860.

Meanwhile, in 1857, Ingraham had become headmaster of a church school in Riverside, Tenn. Then in September, 1858, he became rector of Christ Church in Holly Springs, Miss. Here he died mysteriously of a self-inflicted gunshot on December 18, 1860. Some have speculated that financial troubles drove him to suicide, but most contemporary accounts affirm that the gun fired accidentally.

WORKS: *The South-West, by a Yankee* (1835). *Lafitte: The Pirate of the Gulf* (1836). *Burton: or, The Sieges* (1838). *Captain Kyd: or, The Wizard of the Sea* (1839). *The American Lounger* (1839). *The Quadroone: or, St. Michael's Day* (1840). *Nobody's Son: or, The Life and Adventures of Percival Mayberry* (1851). *Man: A Sermon Preached at St. John's Church, Aberdeen, Mississippi* (1852). *Pamphlets for the People, in Illustration of the Claims of the Church and Methodism* (1854). *The Prince of the House of David* (1855). *The Pillar of Fire* (1859). *The Throne of David, from the Consecration of the Shepherd in Bethlehem to the Rebellion of Prince Absalom* (1860). *The Sunny South: or, The Southerner at Home* (1860; reissued as *Not "A Fool's Errand,"* 1880, and *Kate's Experiences*, 1891).

WARREN FRENCH
Indiana University-Purdue
University
Indianapolis

WILLIAM IOOR (1780–1850). William Ioor (pronounced yore) was born in St. George's Parish, near old Dorchester, S.C., on January 4, 1780. He was married to Ann Mathewes, a relative of the post-Revolutionary governor of South Carolina. Trained at the University of Pennsylvania, he practiced medicine in St.

George's Parish, Savannah, and Greenville District, S.C. During
the Federalist-Republican controversy, he was a fervent Republican. From 1800 through 1803 he served as a member of the General Assembly of South Carolina. In the last part of his life he
moved to Greenville District, where he died on July 30, 1850.

Ioor was the first South Carolinian known to compose a play and
among the very first dramatists in the South. His first play, *Independence; or Which Do You Like Best, the Peer, or the Farmer?*
was performed at the Charleston Theatre in 1805 and 1806. The
purpose of this play is to present the main tenet of the Jeffer-
sonians: small independent farmers make the best citizens because
of their economic and intellectual independence. Because of its
praise of rural life, this play is an early example of agrarianism.
Ioor's next play, *The Battle of Eutaw Springs*, was presented in
Charleston in 1807, 1808, and afterward in Richmond and Philadelphia. It is the first play to dramatize a Revolutionary battle in
the South. Its purpose is to advocate a defiant stand against Great
Britain in the turbulent years preceding the War of 1812 by showing such a position taken during the Revolution. This play describes the savage Tory-Whig conflict in South Carolina. A comic
Whig farmer, Jonathan Slyboots, is an early example of the humorous southern gentleman. This play provoked a heated argument
between the Federalist *Courier* and the Republican *City Gazette*
in Charleston, the latter defending the work.

WORKS: *Independence* (1805). *The Battle of Eutaw Springs* (1807).

CHARLES S. WATSON
University of Alabama
Tuscaloosa

RANDALL JARRELL (1914–1965). Randall Jarrell was born in
Nashville, Tenn., on May 6, 1914. Shortly thereafter, the family
moved to Long Beach, Calif. When his parents separated in 1925,
Jarrell's mother and younger brother returned to Nashville, and
Randall went to live with his paternal grandparents in Hollywood.
He returned to Nashville a year later. In 1931 Jarrell graduated
from Hume Fogg High School and in 1935 received a B.S. from

Vanderbilt University. Although his undergraduate major was psychology, Jarrell became interested in literature through courses taken under John Crowe Ransom. Jarrell served as an editor of the student literary magazine and, through Ransom, became acquainted with Donald Davidson, Allen Tate, Robert Penn Warren, and Peter Taylor. He went on to do graduate work in English, and received an M.A. from Vanderbilt in 1938.

When Ransom accepted an appointment at Kenyon College in 1937, Jarrell followed as an instructor of English. In 1939 he moved to the University of Texas in Austin where, on June 1, 1940, he married Mackie Langham. Also in 1940, Jarrell's first collection of poems appeared as part of the volume *Five Young American Poets*. *Blood for a Stranger*, Jarrell's first independent book of poems, was issued in 1942. Early that same year, he enlisted in the Army Air Force and eventually served at bases in Illinois and Arizona. His wartime experience was put to good use in *Little Friend, Little Friend* (1945). Upon his release from the army in 1946, Jarrell was awarded a Guggenheim Post-Service Fellowship. That same year he became an instructor at Sarah Lawrence College and poetry editor of the *Nation*. Later, Jarrell was a regular reviewer for the *Partisan Review* and the *Yale Review*. In 1947 the poet began his long association with the University of North Carolina at Greensboro. Jarrell's passion for things German and his distinguished career as a translator began in 1948 when he taught at the Salzburg Summer Seminar in American Civilization. Jarrell's concern with human tragedy, again associated with the war in *Losses* (1948), is given more general treatment in *The Seven League Crutches* (1951). During 1951–1952 Jarrell taught at Princeton, and on November 8, 1952, following his divorce, he married Mary Eloise van Schrader.

Jarrell spent the summer of 1953 at the University of Illinois, and in the fall returned to Greensboro. His first book of criticism, *Poetry and the Age* (1953), was followed in 1954 by *Pictures from an Institution*, a satirical novel apparently based upon the poet's year at Sarah Lawrence. From 1956 to 1958 Jarrell served as consultant in poetry at the Library of Congress. In 1960 Jarrell was awarded the National Book Award in poetry for *The Woman at the*

Washington Zoo. His second volume of criticism, *A Sad Heart at the Supermarket* (1962), was followed by three children's books. Early in 1965 Jarrell was hospitalized for a nervous breakdown. On October 14 he was struck and killed by an automobile in Chapel Hill, N.C.

WORKS: "The Rage for the Lost Penny" in *Five Young American Poets* (1940). *Blood for a Stranger* (1942). *Little Friend, Little Friend* (1945). *Losses* (1948). *The Seven League Crutches* (1951). *Poetry and the Age* (1953). *Pictures from an Institution* (1954). *Selected Poems* (1955). *The Woman at the Washington Zoo* (1960). *A Sad Heart at the Supermarket* (1962). *The Gingerbread Rabbit* (1963). *The Bat Poet* (1964). *Selected Poems*, 2nd ed., including *The Woman at the Washington Zoo* (1964). *The Lost World* (1965). *The Animal Family* (1965). *The Lost World*, repr. including "Randall Jarrell, 1914–1965: An Appreciation" by Robert Lowell (1966). *Complete Poems* (1969). *The Third Book of Criticism* (1969).

PETER STITT
University of Houston
Houston, Tex.

THOMAS JEFFERSON (1743–1826). Thomas Jefferson was born in Shadwell, in the Virginia Piedmont, April 13, 1743. His father, Peter Jefferson, though formally uneducated, was a vigorous and intelligent man—"of strong mind, sound judgement, and eager after information"—Jefferson said of him many years later in his *Autobiography*—who became a surveyor, mapmaker, prosperous landowner, and member of the Virginia House of Burgesses; his mother, Jane Randolph, was a member of one of the most powerful and distinguished Tidewater families. In 1746 Peter Jefferson became executor of the estate of William Randolph of Tuckahoe, where the Jeffersons lived for the next five years. Following their return to Shadwell, Jefferson attended the nearby school of a "correct classical scholar" and in the spring of 1760, three years after his father's death, he entered the College of William and Mary in Williamsburg, where he was profoundly influenced by Dr. William Small. From 1762 to 1767 he studied law under George Wythe, Virginia's most distinguished jurist. He returned to Albemarle County, where he was admitted to the bar, in 1767; a year later he commenced the building of Monticello—to become a lifelong passion—and was elected burgess from Albemarle County to the Virginia Assembly. In 1772 he married Martha Skelton, a young and attractive widow; their first child, Martha, was born the same year.

In these years immediately preceding the American Revolution, Jefferson became increasingly involved with radical younger members of the Virginia Assembly; in 1774, with his first published work, *A Summary View of the Rights of British America*, he moved, as one of his biographers has stated, "in one swift step to the forefront of the great pamphleteers of the Revolution." His authorship of the Declaration of Independence was the culmination of this phase of his career.

For the next 33 years, until his retirement from public life in 1809, Jefferson was actively engaged in political and diplomatic service: he was governor of Virginia (1779–1781), minister to France (1784–1789), secretary of state under George Washington (1789–1793), vice-president under John Adams (1797–1801), and president (1801–1809).

In the midst of such activity, Jefferson's intellectual and creative energies increased rather than diminished. Since childhood he had possessed what later he was to call a "canine appetite" for books and learning, and he pursued knowledge as some men pursue fame or fortune. Like Francis Bacon, whom he greatly admired, he took all fields of knowledge as his province; he was educator, philosopher, book collector, geologist, musician, anthropologist, art collector, linguist.

The many aspects of Jefferson's intellectual career are mirrored in his only full-length book, *Notes on the State of Virginia*; with his thousands of letters, many as yet unpublished, it is his major literary achievement. Begun in the autumn of 1780 as a reply to a questionnaire circulated by François Barbé-Marbois, secretary of the French legation at Philadelphia, and first published in a limited edition in Paris in 1785, the *Notes on Virginia* is perhaps the most important scientific and political book written by an American to that time. In it, along with matter-of-fact accounts of "Productions Mineral, Vegetable and Animal" or "Public Revenue and Expences," Jefferson expounded upon his theories of religious freedom and the separation of church and state, his concepts of art and education, his views on slavery, the Negro, and the American Indian, his ideas concerning evolution and the mysteries of science.

Throughout his career, Jefferson was never concerned solely or primarily with the principles of government or the pursuit of knowledge for their own sakes. His ultimate goal, from which he never really deviated, remained constant: the right of the individual to freedom and happiness under just and equitable law. This quest reached its apex during Jefferson's so-called "retirement years" with the founding of the University of Virginia, one of the first great universities in the American South. Jefferson's "little academical village," his "bantling of forty years growth and nursing"—for which he had sent an emissary abroad to select a faculty, designed the buildings which remain today one of the high achievements of American architecture, chosen the books for the library and drawn up the curriculum—opened in 1825.

He died the following year, at Monticello, on July 4, 1826.

WORKS: *A Summary Review of the Rights of British America* (1774). "A Declaration by the Representatives of the United States of America, in General Congress Assembled" (1776). *Notes on the State of Virginia* (1785). *A Manual of Parliamentary Practice* (1801). *Autobiography* (1814). *The Writings of Thomas Jefferson*, Paul L. Ford, ed., 10 vols. (1892–99). *Essay on Anglo-Saxon* (1851). *The Life and Morals of Jesus of Nazareth* (1902). *The Writings of Thomas Jefferson*, A. A. Lipscomb and A. E. Bergh, eds., 20 vols. (1903). *The Papers of Thomas Jefferson*, ed. Julian P. Boyd *et al.*, 18 vols. to date (1950–72).

WILLIAM PEDEN
University of Missouri
Columbia

GEORGIA DOUGLAS JOHNSON (1886–1965). Born in Atlanta, Ga., Georgia Douglas attended the public schools of that city. She later studied at Atlanta University and Oberlin College. Her early desire was to pursue a career in music composition, but instead she became a teacher in the schools of Alabama. Georgia

Douglas married Henry Lincoln Johnson, who had been appointed Recorder of Deeds by the president of the United States. Following this appointment they moved to Washington, D.C., where she became a government employee. In Washington she was active in civic and literary affairs, working with a Republican women's organization and contributing poetry to black journals and periodicals such as the *Crisis*.

Johnson's interest in black history and biography is evident in such one-act dramas as "Frederick Douglass" and "William and Ellen Craft." Her major achievements, however, were in verse. The first notable black female poet since the antebellum years, she wrote prolifically during and after the Harlem Renaissance. The themes of the poems are frequently, but not always, nonracial. Mood, feeling, and emotional response dominate the short, simple poems, which treat such matters as romantic love, motherhood, and melancholy. Recurrent among the racial themes are bigotry, the black woman, and the black family.

WORKS: *The Heart of a Woman and Other Poems* (1918). *Bronze: A Book of Verse* (1922). *An Autumn Love Cycle* (1938). *Share My World* (1962).

ELAINE MITCHELL NEWSOME
Fayetteville State University
Fayetteville, N.C.

GERALD WHITE JOHNSON (1890–). Born on August 6, 1890, in the rural community of Riverton in eastern North Carolina, Gerald Johnson gained renown in the 1920s and 1930s as a journalist and biographer. His father, Archibald Johnson, was a newspaperman, and Gerald Johnson was educated in a Baptist institution, Wake Forest College. Upon graduation in 1911, he worked briefly for two small North Carolina newspapers before joining the Greensboro *Daily News* in 1913. He served as a reporter and editorial writer for the *Daily News* until 1924, and in 1922 his writing caught the eye of the Baltimore newspaperman H. L. Mencken, who proclaimed Johnson "the best editorial writer in the South." After spending two years (1924–1926) as a professor of journalism at the University of North Carolina, Johnson joined Mencken on the Baltimore Sunpapers as an editorial writer, and he wrote for the *Sun* until 1943. Since 1943 he has been a news commentator and free-lance journalist. He has also written novels and works of history.

Although Johnson became widely respected after 1930 as a national political analyst and a spokesman for the liberal viewpoint, his greatest contribution to southern life was his work as an iconoclastic essayist in the 1920s. He was second only to Mencken in his indictment of southern literary and cultural poverty and in his call for a new southern spirit. He was the boldest of writers for the new southern journals—especially the *Reviewer* of Richmond —and in national magazines such as Mencken's *American Mercury* he reigned as the leading native interpreter of the South. His subjects were religious frenzy, racial prejudice, the poor white, and the subculture of the southern mill town; and his free-wheeling prose style equaled and sometimes surpassed Mencken's own. Johnson's criticism of the South, however, was tempered by a sympathy and an understanding of the South foreign to many southern critics of the 1920s.

WORKS: Essays in the *Reviewer*, the *Journal of Social Forces*, and *American Mercury* (1922–30). *The Undefeated* (1926). *Andrew Johnson: An Epic in Homespun* (1927). *Randolph of Roanoke—A Political Fantastic* (1929). *By Reason of Strength* (1930). *The Secession of the Southern States* (1933). *A Little Night Music* (1937). *The Wasted Land* (1937). *America's Silver Age: The Statecraft of Clay, Webster, and Calhoun* (1939). *Roosevelt: Dictator or Democrat?* (1941). *American Heroes and Hero-Worship* (1943). *Woodrow Wilson* (1944). *An Honorable Titan: A Biographical Study of Adolph S. Ochs* (1946). *The First Captain* (1949). *Liberal's Progress* (1948). *Our English Heritage* (1949). *Incredible Tale: The Odyssey of the Average American in the Last Half Century* (1950). *The American People* (1951). *The Making of a Southern Industrialist: A Biographical Study of Simpson Bobo Tanner* (1952). *Pattern for Liberty: The Story of Old Philadelphia* (1952). *Mount Vernon* (1953). *Lunatic Fringe* (1957). *Peril and Promise: An Inquiry into Freedom of the Press* (1958). *The Lines Are Drawn* (1958). *The Man Who Feels Left Behind* (1960). *The Supreme Court* (1962). *The Congress* (1963). *Hod-*

Carrier (1964). *Communism: An American's View* (1967). *Franklin D. Roosevelt* (1967). *The Imperial Republic* (1972).

FRED HOBSON
University of Alabama
Tuscaloosa

JAMES WELDON JOHNSON (1871–1938). James Weldon Johnson was born on June 17, 1871, in Jacksonville, Fla., to parents whose energy and ambition, coupled with pride of race, set standards of conduct and accomplishment that he would pursue throughout his varied career. His father was headwaiter in Jacksonville's best hotel; his mother, a talented pianist, taught music in all eight grades of the Negro public school. James attended that school and after graduating from the "academy" and college of Atlanta University in the neighboring state of Georgia, returned to it as teacher-principal in 1894.

This was his first job, but it neither satisfied his ambitions nor fully engaged his energies. He read law for two years and was admitted to the Florida bar even while he was upgrading his school to the status of high school. He wrote poetry, including (in 1900) "Lift Every Voice and Sing," which was set to music by his brother and later became famous as the Negro national anthem. Other of Johnson's poems appeared in the weekly newspaper that he founded and edited for Jacksonville's black population. But he had spread himself ambitiously thin, and the paper failed within a year. Meanwhile Rosamond, his older brother, who had settled in New York and was establishing himself as a musician and composer, urged James to join him. And in 1901 he did.

It was an exciting time, which Johnson poetized as "the dawn of a new day," and New York City an exciting place for Negroes to be, especially if they were talented members of the entertainment world. Paul Dunbar, a nationally famous dialect poet, frequented the San Juan Hill section of the city. Sissieretta Jones (popularly called Black Patti) gave concerts there. Bob Cole, George Walker, and Bert Williams provoked storms of laughter in their white audiences at the Winter Garden, the Bijou, and the

New York Theatre in Times Square. These and other popular
Negro performers were constantly in search of new material, and
the Johnson brothers were soon supplying the words (James) and
music (Rosamond) for "coon songs," sentimental ballads, musical
sketches, and plays. In 1903 and 1904, the Johnsons went abroad
with the team of Williams and Walker, and for a total of five years
they collaborated on material for vaudeville and minstrel shows.

But, as James wrote later, the entertainment world did not provide the arena for him to do "the meaningful work . . . for the
benefit of [his] people." He thought politics did, and in 1905 he
campaigned for Theodore Roosevelt. His reward was consulate
appointments, first in Venezuela and then in Nicaragua. During
seven years as consul general, Johnson's creative urge reasserted
itself and what might be called his larger literary career got under-
way. He contributed poems to *Century*, *Atlantic Monthly*, *Harper's* and *Crisis*, which was edited by W. E. B. Du Bois as the
official organ of the NAACP. In 1912 Johnson published his one
novel, *The Autobiography of an Ex-Coloured Man*, which examines, somewhat apologetically, the difficulties of the gifted
Negro who must live in both the white world and the black.

In 1914 James Weldon Johnson was appointed field secretary
of the NAACP, and in 1917 he published *Fifty Years and Other
Poems*. His talent had grown, and probably due to the influence
of Du Bois and others in the NAACP, his temper and tone had
changed radically. Rationalization had given way to exploration and
analysis, apology to defiance, sentimentality to sarcasm, and self-
pity to anger and pride. *God's Trombones: Seven Negro Sermons
in Verse* (1927) confirmed that the introductions to *The Book of
American Negro Poetry* (1922) and *The Book of American Negro
Spirituals* (1925) truly marked the proud return to a racial heritage
once shamefully despised. *Black Manhattan* (1930), a history of
the Negro in New York City, and *Along This Way* (1933), Johnson's
autobiography, are as balanced analyses and nonfictional explorations of being black in America as one can find. And *Saint Peter
Relates an Incident* (1930) is a bitter, angry, and amusing satire
on white racial attitudes.

Vacationing from the professorship that he had held at Fisk Uni-

versity since 1930, James Weldon Johnson was killed in an automobile accident on June 26, 1938.

WORKS: *The Autobiography of an Ex-Coloured Man* (1912, 1927). *Fifty
Years and Other Poems* (1917). *Self-Determining Haiti* (1920). Ed., *The
Book of American Negro Poetry* (1922). Ed., *The Book of American
Negro Spirituals*, with J. Rosamond Johnson (1925). Ed., *Second Book of
Spirituals*, with J. Rosamond Johnson (1926). *God's Trombones: Seven
Negro Sermons in Verse* (1927). *Black Manhattan* (1930). *Saint Peter
Relates an Incident of the Resurrection Day* (1930). *Along the Way*
(1933). *Negro Americans, What Now?* (1934).

SAUNDERS REDDING
Cornell University
Ithaca, N.Y.

MARY JOHNSTON (1870–1936). A popular and prolific writer,
Mary Johnston is now remembered primarily for one of her early
novels, the colonial Virginia romance *To Have and To Hold* (1900).
This book sold over 500,000 copies and was twice made into a
movie. Her principal writings include 23 novels and 38 short
stories.

Born in Buchanan, Va., on November 21, 1870, Johnston was
the eldest of six children. Her health was frail and her education
took place largely at home. Her life was not sheltered because her
father, John William, a former Confederate artillery officer, held
significant public and business posts, requiring travels to Europe
as well as moves to New York City, Birmingham, Ala., and Richmond, Va.

When her mother died in 1889, Mary took charge of the Johnston household. Some of her most successful early books appeared
over the next several years while she strove to assist the family
financially. In 1902 the family moved from Birmingham to Richmond, and this return to the Old Dominion furthered Johnston's
interest in writing about her native state. Notable books of this
period include *The Long Roll* (1911) and *Cease Firing* (1912),
both epic stories of the Civil War.

In the years following her father's death in 1905 Johnston rekindled interests in the Allegheny Mountains of Virginia, and in 1911–1912 she and two of her sisters built a large house, Three Hills, in Warm Springs. Ties to Richmond remained, not only with longstanding friendships with writers such as Ellen Glasgow, but in various causes, such as the suffragist movement. She founded the Equal Suffrage League of Virginia in 1909, with Glasgow and Lila Meade Dalentine. Johnston's novel *Hagar* (1913) reflected many of her strong feminist ideals. As an honorary officer of the league she addressed legislatures in West Virginia and Tennessee and also a governors' conference.

Never strong physically, Johnston contracted Bright's disease late in life and died at her Warm Springs home May 9, 1936, following an extended hospitalization.

WORKS: *Prisoners of Hope* (1898). *To Have and To Hold* (1900). *Audrey* (1902). *Sir Mortimer* (1904). *The Goddess of Reason* (1907). *Lewis Rand* (1908). *The Long Roll* (1911). *Cease Firing* (1912). *Hagar* (1913). *Witch* (1914). *Fortunes of Garin* (1915). *Wanderers* (1917). *Foes* (1918). *Michael Forth* (1919). *Sweet Rocket* (1920). *Pioneers of the Old South* (1920). *1492* (1922). *Silver Cross* (1922). *Croatan* (1923). *Slave Ship* (1924). *The Great Valley* (1926). *Exile* (1927). *Hunting Shirt* (1931). *Miss Delicia Allen* (1933). *Drury Randall* (1934).

WILLIAM W. KELLY
Transylvania University
Lexington, Ky.

RICHARD MALCOLM JOHNSTON (1822–1898). The son of a planter who was also a Baptist minister, Richard Malcolm Johnston was born on March 8, 1822, near Powelton, Ga. Following his graduation from Mercer University in 1841, he taught school for a year, studied and practiced law, married, and returned to teaching. He alternated between law practice and school teaching from 1844 until 1857, when he accepted the chair of rhetoric and belles lettres at the University of Georgia.

When the Civil War began, Johnston, who was no secessionist, resigned his university post and opened a school for boys near Sparta, Ga. In 1867, dissatisfied with conditions in Reconstruction Georgia and pessimistic about the future of his state, he moved to Baltimore and established the Pen Lucy School. Although at first successful, this school gradually declined after Johnston joined the Roman Catholic Church in 1875. Following the breakup of the school in 1883, Johnston's family was largely supported by his daughters, who taught school.

It was the vogue of Augustus Baldwin Longstreet's *Georgia Scenes* that led Johnston to write his first humorous sketches. He published "A Georgia School in the Old Times" (later retitled "The Goosepond School") in 1857 in William T. Porter's *Spirit of the Times*. In 1864 an Augusta firm brought out his first book, *Georgia Sketches from Recollections of an Old Man*, under the pseudonym "Philemon Perch." Johnston's best-known work, *Dukesborough Tales*, appeared in 1871. The sketches in this book preserve Johnston's memories of Powelton and, like many of his others, deal with ordinary people in situations which are awkward, humorous, and sometimes pathetic. Among Johnston's other works are four novels—*Old Mark Langston* (1884), *Ogeechee Cross-Firings* (1889), *Widow Guthrie* (1890), and *Pearce Amerson's Will* (1898)—and numerous stories and essays. Johnston died on September 23, 1898, in Baltimore.

WORKS: *The English Classics* (1860). *Georgia Sketches from Recollections of an Old Man* (1864). *Dukesborough Tales* (1871; enlarged, 1883). *English Literature*, with William Hand Browne (1873). *Life of Alexander H. Stephens*, with William Hand Browne (1878). *Old Mark Langston* (1884). *Two Gray Tourists* (1885). *Mr. Absalom Billingslea, and Other Georgia Folk* (1888). *Ogeechee Cross-Firings* (1889). *Widow Guthrie* (1890). *The Primes and Their Neighbors* (1891). *Studies, Literary and Social*, 1st ser. (1891). *Mr. Fortner's Marital Claims, and Other Stories* (1892). *Mr. Billy Downs and His Likes* (1892). *Studies, Literary and Social*, 2nd ser. (1892). *Little Ike Templin and Other Stories* (1894). *Early Education in Middle Georgia* (1896). *Old Times in Middle Georgia* (1897). *Early Educational Life in Middle Georgia* (1897). *Lectures on Literature English, French, and Spanish* (1897). *Pearce Amerson's Will* (1898). *Autobiography of Col. Richard Malcolm Johnston* (1900).

L. MOODY SIMMS, JR.
Illinois State University
Normal

CHARLES COLCOCK JONES, JR. (1831–1893). Charles Colcock Jones, Jr., has garnered recent interest through the editing of his voluminous correspondence by Robert Manson Myers in *The Children of Pride* (1972) and *A Georgian at Princeton* (1976). His literary talents were not confined to letters, however. He was a noted orator, historian, and archaeologist as well.

Jones was born in Savannah, Ga., on October 28, 1831, the eldest son of a Presbyterian clergyman, the Reverend Dr. Charles Colcock Jones and his wife (and first cousin) Mary Jones. The younger Jones spent his childhood on several Liberty County, Ga., plantations and in Columbia, S.C., where his father served two professorships at Columbia Theological Seminary. Jones attended South Carolina College from 1848 to 1850, graduated from Princeton in 1852, and received a law degree from Harvard in 1855.

He returned to Savannah to join in the practice of law with the Honorable John Elliott Ward. Jones also became actively involved on the local political scene. After serving as city alderman (1859–1860), he was elected mayor of Savannah in 1860. With the outbreak of the Civil War, Jones enlisted in the Chatham Artillery as senior first lieutenant. He was later promoted to lieutenant colonel and served as chief of artillery at the siege of Savannah in December, 1864.

Following the war, he moved to New York City where he practiced law until 1877. In that year Jones returned to Georgia and settled in the Summerville section of Augusta. He died on July 19, 1893, and was buried in Summerville Cemetery beside his second wife, the former Eva Berrien Eve, whom he married in 1863. His first wife, Ruth Berrien Whitehead, whom he married in 1858, had died in 1861.

Jones was perhaps best known for his historical writings. Historian George Bancroft referred to Jones's *The History of Georgia* (1883) as the best state history he knew. His deep interest in Indian culture found its way into three important works, *Indian Remains in Southern Georgia* (1859), *The Monumental Remains of Georgia* (1861), and *Antiquities of the Southern Indians* (1873). His scholarship in the field of Georgia history and biography manifested itself in a number of pamphlets and volumes such as *The Dead Towns of Georgia* (1878) and a masterful dialect and cultural study *Negro Myths from the Georgia Coast* (1888). Perhaps more than any Georgian in the nineteenth century, Jones exemplified the research abilities and penchant for accuracy of the true historian.

WORKS: *Indian Remains in Southern Georgia* (1859). *The Monumental Remains of Georgia* (1861). *Historical Sketch of the Chatham Artillery* (1867). *Historical Sketch of Tomo-chi-chi, Mico of the Yamacraws* (1868). *Antiquities of the Southern Indians* (1873). *The Siege of Savannah in December 1864* (1874). *The Dead Towns of Georgia* (1878). *The Life and Services of Commodore Josiah Tattnall* (1878). *Hernando de Soto* (1880). *The History of Georgia* (1883). *Negro Myths from the Georgia Coast* (1888).

ROBERT M. WILLINGHAM, JR.
University of Georgia
Athens

HUGH JONES (1692–1760). The Reverend Hugh Jones arrived in Williamsburg, Va., in the spring of 1717 to become professor of mathematics at the College of William and Mary. His recently acquired Oxford B.A. and M.A. prepared him for clerical positions which he soon assumed as chaplain to the Virginia House of Burgesses and as minister of a Jamestown church. Jones's active participation in the political, religious, and intellectual affairs of the colony qualified him well for his most famous work, *The Present State of Virginia*, published in London in 1724 while Jones was living there. Returning to America in the same year with a wife and two adopted children, Jones underwent reassignment to a distant parish in King and Queen County, Va. In 1726 he removed to Charles County, Md., where his pastoral and educational labors, particularly among the slaves, were rewarded in 1731 by a more substantial living in Sassafras Parish, Cecil County, in Maryland's upper eastern shore. Here with his family he spent the remainder of his years, defending the Church of England against Catholics and nonconformists alike, working as Lord Baltimore's chief mathematician in the boundary line dispute between Maryland

and Pennsylvania, and continuing to promote scientific investigation and the regulation of arithmetic measurements and methodology.

Intended in some ways as a supplement to and updating of Robert Beverley's *History and Present State of Virginia* (1705, 1722), Jones's 150-page *Present State of Virginia* had descriptive, corrective, and promotional purposes similar to its predecessor. In an appendix, however, Jones went further to recommend improvements for the colony which he eulogized. Noteworthy among these were the modernization of the curriculum and government of the College of William and Mary, the ordination of a "Dean of Virginia" to ensure clerical uniformity in the region, and the relaxation of Britain's restrictive mercantile policy toward the colonies.

WORKS: *The Present State of Virginia* (1724). *An Accidence to the English Tongue* (1724). *The Pancronometer, or Universal Georgian Calendar . . . and The Reasons, Rules, and Uses of Octave Computation, or Natural Arithmetic* (1753).

WILLIAM L. ANDREWS
University of Wisconsin
Madison

MADISON PERCY JONES (1925–). Novelist, short-story writer, and critic, Madison Jones was born in Nashville, Tenn., on March 21, 1925. In the 1940s he spent a few years farming and training horses in Cheatham County, Tenn. From 1945 until 1946 he served as a military policeman in Korea. He received his A.B. from Vanderbilt, where he studied under Donald Davidson, and his M.A. from the University of Florida, where he studied under Andrew Lytle. After studying for two more years at Florida toward a Ph.D., in 1953 Jones accepted a position teaching English at Miami University (Ohio), where he taught for one year. During 1955–1956 he taught English at the University of Tennessee, after which he moved to Auburn University, where he is now a full professor and writer-in-residence. In 1951 he married Shailah McEvilley. They are the parents of five children.

Jones has published several short stories in literary journals, especially the *Sewanee Review*, which also devoted an entire issue in 1966 to the publication of *An Exile*, his fourth novel. "The Homecoming," a short story first published in *Perspective*, was reprinted in Martha Foley's *Best American Short Stories* in 1953. In addition to his fiction, Jones has published critical essays and reviews in, among others, the *Mississippi Quarterly*, Washington *Post*, New York *Times Book Review*, and *South Atlantic Quarterly*. Among the recognitions he has received are a Rockefeller Foundation Fellowship (1968) and a Guggenheim Fellowship (1974–1975).

Jones's first novel, *The Innocent*, was published in 1957. Like much of his fiction it is set in rural Tennessee and involves man's attempts to maintain a sense of dignity and purpose in a society that is disintegrating. In 1967 he published *An Exile*, which in 1970 Columbia Pictures made into a film entitled "I Walk the Line" starring Gregory Peck and Tuesday Weld. His novel *A Cry of Absence* (1971) is one of the best attempts yet to provide a judicious statement of the dilemma of the modern South. All but his most recent novel have been reprinted in England, and *An Exile* and *A Cry of Absence* have been published in Dutch. *An Exile* has also been reprinted in Japanese. In addition to teaching creative writing and a course in the theory of prose fiction at Auburn University, Jones has published a new novel, *Passage Through Gehenna*.

WORKS: *The Innocent* (1957). *Forest of the Night* (1960). *A Buried Land* (1963). *An Exile* (1967); repr. in paperback as *I Walk the Line* in 1970. *A Cry of Absence* (1971). *Passage Through Gehenna* (1978).

MARION C. MICHAEL
Texas Tech University
Lubbock

DONALD JUSTICE (1925–). Poet and teacher, Donald Justice was born on August 12, 1925, in Miami, Fla., where he attended the local schools and the University of Miami, from which he earned his B.A. in 1945. He completed his education at the University of North Carolina (M.A., 1947) and the University of Iowa

(Ph.D., 1954), where he took courses from Karl Shapiro, John Berryman, and Robert Lowell. Justice has taught at various schools, including the University of Missouri, Reed College, Syracuse, Princeton, and the University of Iowa, where he has been a professor of English since 1971. The recipient of many awards, he was twice honored with grants from the National Council on the Arts (1967, 1973); he was a Ford Fellow in both poetry (1954) and theater (1964) and a Guggenheim Fellow (1976). Justice is married and the father of one son, Nathaniel.

Justice has cited his debt to Yvor Winters, who taught him "about meters" during one year at Stanford (1948–1949), and T. S. Eliot, whose theory of depersonalization affected Justice's own writing of poems as "objects of contemplation." Although he now calls his first book "apprentice work," *The Summer Anniversaries* (1960) won the Lamont Award and attracted considerable attention for the poetic deployment of diverse "voices" and for the skillful manipulation of traditional forms, especially the sonnet and sestina. Later work—in the pamphlets *Sixteen Poems* (1970) and *From a Notebook* (1972) and especially the volume *Departures* (1973)— reveals looser, freer structures, a step away, as Justice says, from the "logical steps" and "statement" of his earlier work toward a poetry of open-endedness based on "the principle of uncertainty."

A musician, Justice once studied composition with Carl Ruggles, and since 1973 has written a libretto not yet published. The most recent stage in his development is an interest in "fragments" and epigrams—because their great compression and understatement, though miniaturized, are conducive to "perceptions truly registered."

WORKS: *The Summer Anniversaries* (1960). Ed., *The Collected Poems of Weldon Kees* (1960). Ed., *Contemporary French Poetry: Fourteen Witnesses of Man's Fate*, with Alexander Aspel (1965). *Night Light* (1967). *Sixteen Poems* (1970). *From a Notebook* (1972). *Departures* (1973).

JAMES H. JUSTUS
Indiana University
Bloomington

JOHN PENDLETON KENNEDY (1795–1870). Born in Baltimore, Md., on October 25, 1795, Kennedy was the eldest son of John Kennedy, an Irish immigrant, and Nancy Pendleton Kennedy, descendant of a Tidewater Virginia clan. Following graduation from Baltimore College in 1812, Kennedy served with the Maryland militia in two battles against invading British forces. He studied law with his uncle and was admitted to the bar in 1816. In the same year an early yearning toward literature prompted a series of essays, "The Swiss Traveller," in the Baltimore *Portico*. He practiced law desultorily, devoting much time to a local satirical periodical, the *Red Book* (1819–1821).

Kennedy began a political career as a member of the Maryland House of Delegates in 1820–1823. In 1824 he wed Mary Tenant, who died in childbirth within the year. He married Elizabeth Gray, daughter of a well-to-do local manufacturer in 1829; their union was childless. This marriage secured both his social and financial position, and in 1829 he returned to creative writing with the intent of composing an Irvingesque account of travels in Virginia. The result was *Swallow Barn* (1832), a pioneer contribution to plantation literature which is both respectful toward the Cavalier legend and lightly satirical of the present. Kennedy capitalized on its moderate success by turning to the genre of American historical romance popularized by Cooper. His most considerable achievement, *Horse-Shoe Robinson* (1835), followed the adventures of its titular hero in the Revolutionary struggle in the lower South. The tale was widely praised, notably by Poe, whom Kennedy had helped to place on the *Southern Literary Messenger*. The vogue for native subjects spurred Kennedy to turn next to colonial Maryland, but his active involvement in the Whig party delayed publication of his third romance, *Rob of the Bowl*, until 1838. The story lauds the Cavalier ethic and betrays Kennedy's growing conservatism in the age of Jacksonianism.

In 1838 Kennedy was elected to the House of Representatives and his budding career as romancer ended. His hold on his seat proved precarious, however, and he served as a staunch Whig for only two more terms in 1841–1845. In the meantime he had published *Quodlibet* (1840), a critique of Jackson's policies which he followed up in *Defense of the Whigs* (1844). He served twice more in public office, as Speaker of the Maryland house in 1846 and, briefly, as Fillmore's secretary of the navy in 1852. His last major literary work was the *Life of William Wirt* (1849). During the Civil War period he supported the Union position in *The Border States* (1860) and *Mr. Ambrose's Letters on the Rebellion* (1865). He died on August 18, 1870.

Kennedy was only secondarily a man of letters, always subordinating his creative work to his business and political interests. His maternal ties to Virginia had been strong, but his own commitments to a border state led him to espouse a nationalism that feared the rise of southern sectionalism. What remains viable in his fiction is precisely this portrayal of the dichotomies in the national experience in the decades before the Civil War.

WORKS: *Swallow Barn: or A Sojourn in the Old Dominion* (1832; rev., 1851). *Horse-Shoe Robinson: A Tale of the Tory Ascendency* (1835; rev., 1852). *Rob of the Bowl: A Legend of St. Inigoe's* (1838; rev. 1854). *Quodlibet* (1840). *Memoirs of the Life of William Wirt* (1849). *Collected Works* (1871–72), adds 3 volumes of miscellaneous writings.

J. V. RIDGELY
Columbia University
New York, N.Y.

CHARLES WILLIAM KENT (1860–1917). Noted as an educator, editor, and lecturer, Charles W. Kent was born on September 27, 1860, in Kalona, Louisa County, Va. His parents were Robert Meredith and Sallie Garland Hunter Kent. Educated at schools in Louisa County, Kent entered the University of Virginia in 1878 and graduated in 1882 with an M.A.

After graduation, he and his college friend, Lewis Minor Coleman, founded the University School in Charleston, S.C., where Kent taught from 1882 until 1884. Then, he went to Germany to study English and modern languages at Göttingen, Berlin, and finally Leipsig, where he took a Ph.D. in 1887.

After a year teaching French and German at the University of Virginia, Kent became professor of English and modern languages at the University of Tennessee, where he remained until 1893. That year he accepted the newly established chair at the University of Virginia in the Linden Kent Memorial School of English Literature, named for his older brother.

On June 4, 1895, he married Eleanor Miles. Professor Kent remained on the faculty at the University of Virginia until his death on October 15, 1917.

He was a member of Phi Kappa Psi fraternity, Phi Beta Kappa, and many educational and professional organizations. President of the Young Men's Christian Association, and also president of the Poe Memorial Association, he was a member of the State Board of Education and the executive committee of the Virginia Historical Society.

A Progressive Democrat, Kent was a member of the Disciples of Christ Church. Gifted at oratory and a serious student of the Bible, he taught a Sunday school Bible class with a regular enrollment of 150.

Perhaps the best known of the many volumes edited by Kent is the *Library of Southern Literature*. In addition to serving as literary editor of that project, he contributed pieces on John James Audubon, Lafcadio Hearn, Thomas Nelson Page, and others.

WORKS EDITED: *Cynewulf's Elene* (1889). *Shakespeare Note-book* (1897). *Idyls of the Lawn*, short stories by undergraduate students at the University of Virginia (1899). *The Cotter's Saturday Night* (1901). *The Princess: A Medley by Alfred Tennyson* (1901). *Selected Poems of Robert Burns* (1901). *The Unveiling of the Bust of Edgar Allan Poe in the Library of the University of Virginia* (1901). *Poems of Edgar Allan Poe* (1903). *The Book of the Poe Centenary*, with John S. Patton (1909). *Library of Southern Literature*, with Edwin Anderson Alderman, Joel Chandler Harris, 17 vols. (1909–23). *The Land Where We Were Dreaming, and Other Poems of Daniel Bedinger Lucas*, with Virginia Lucas (1913). *Dramatic Works of Daniel Bedinger Lucas*, with Virginia Lucas (1913). *Southern Poems* (1913).

DOROTHY McINNIS SCURA
University of Richmond
Richmond, Va.

FRANCIS SCOTT KEY (1779–1843). Second of four children of agriculturist John Ross Key of Frederick (now Carroll) County, Md., and the former Anne P. P. D. Charlton, Key was born on August 1, 1779, at the family estate, Terra Rubra, south of Taney-town, Md. Educated at the primary school and college of Saint John's, Annapolis, he graduated salutatorian in 1796. Studying law privately at Annapolis, he commenced practice at Frederick in 1801. In 1802 he married Mary Tayloe Lloyd of Annapolis there and settled at Georgetown, Md.; the couple had eleven children. Key practiced law successfully in Georgetown until about 1835, when he removed to nearby Washington. During 1833–1841 he was United States attorney for the District of Columbia. Originally a Federalist, he became a Jacksonian Democrat and friend of Jackson. In religion he was a devout Episcopalian.

As a prisoner-exchange official Key found himself aboard a cartel sloop below Baltimore harbor witnessing the British fleet's bombardment of Fort McHenry the night of September 13–14, 1814. Long an amateur versifier, Key's lines upon descrying the fort's flag still aloft at dawn were first printed anonymously in handbill form as "Defense of Fort M'Henry," to the British tune of "To Anacreon in Heaven," at Baltimore, September 17. First newspaper publication was in the Baltimore *Patriot*, September 20. The song was first ascribed to Key in the Frederick-Town *Herald*, September 24. By at least October 18 the air was known as "The Star-Spangled Banner," and its first recorded public singing occurred at the Holliday Street Theater, Baltimore, Wednesday evening, October 19. On March 3, 1931, President Hoover proclaimed it the national anthem.

Key died on January 11, 1843, of pleurisy at Baltimore and is buried in Mount Olivet Cemetery, Frederick, Md. His name has been additionally commemorated by a highway, a shopping plaza, a hotel, a postage stamp, an elementary school, four monuments, two bridges, the New York World's Fair (1964) official medal, and a nuclear submarine.

WORKS: *An oration . . . Before the Washington Society of Alexandria* ([1814]). *A discourse on education, delivered in St. Anne's Church,*

Annapolis . . . February 22d, 1827 . . . . (1827). Oration . . . in the rotunda of the Capitol of the U. States, on the 4th of July, 1831 ([1831]). *Speech . . . counsel for Gen. Samuel Houston . . . before the House of Representatives . . . . (1832). The Power of Literature and Its Connexion with Religion: An Oration . . . July 23, 1834 . . . (1834). A Part of a Speech . . . on the Trial of Reuben Crandall, M.D. . . . (1836). Speech . . . Before the Colonization Convention, May 9, 1842* ([1842]). *Poems of the Late Francis S. Key, Esq.* (1857).

CURTIS CARROLL DAVIS
Baltimore, Md.

FRANCES PARKINSON KEYES (1885–1970). Frances Parkinson Wheeler Keyes was born on July 21, 1885, in Charlottesville, Va., where her father was chairman of the Greek department at the University of Virginia. From her earliest years she traveled extensively throughout the world, and her early education was obtained in Boston (where she spent most of her youth), Geneva, Berlin, and from tutors. In 1904 she married Henry Wilder Keyes, who was the Republican governor of New Hampshire from 1917 to 1919 and U.S. senator from 1919 to 1937; they had three sons. Senator Keyes died in 1938.

Her early work, which began to appear when her husband became senator and they moved to Washington, was influenced by her life in the country, her travel, and the political scene in the capital. From 1937 to 1939 she edited the *National Historical Magazine* of the DAR but resigned in 1939 because of a disagreement over policy. In 1939 she became a Roman Catholic and worked extensively to preserve historic shrines and wrote several saints' lives. She received, among several Catholic honors, the Siena Medal in 1946 as outstanding Catholic woman of the year. For many years she lived in Beauregard House in New Orleans and helped in the restoration and preservation of this historic landmark. She received honorary degrees from George Washington University, Bates College, and the University of New Hampshire. She died on July 3, 1970, in New Orleans.

In over 50 volumes of biography, travel, and fiction Keyes made a reputation as a skillful and inventive storyteller of historical material. Her popularity and high sales derived chiefly from an evocation of place and period and the creation of romantic characters and involved plots.

WORKS: *The Old Gray Homestead* (1919). *The Career of David Noble* (1921). *Letters from a Senator's Wife* (1924). *Queen Anne's Lace* (1930). *Silver Seas and Golden Cities* (1931). *Lady Blanche Farm* (1931). *Senator Marlowe's Daughter* (1933). *The Safe Bridge* (1934). *The Happy Wanderer* (1935). *Honor Bright* (1936). *Written in Heaven* (1937; rev. as *Thérèse: Saint of a Little Way*, 1950). *Capital Kaleidoscope* (1937). *Parts Unknown* (1938). *The Great Tradition* (1939). *Along a Little Way* (1940). *The Sublime Shepherdess* (1940; rev. as *Bernadette of Lourdes*, 1953). *Fielding's Folly* (1940). *The Grace of Guadalupe* (1941). *All That Glitters* (1941). *Crescent Carnival* (1942). *Also the Hills* (1943). *The River Road* (1945). *Came a Cavalier* (1947). *Once on Esplanade* (1947). *Dinner at Antoine's* (1948). *Joy Street* (1950). *All This is Louisiana* (1950). *The Cost of a Best Seller* (1950). *Steamboat Gothic* (1952). *The Royal Box* (1954). *Frances Parkinson Keyes Cookbook* (1955). *Mother of Our Saviour* (1955). *The Blue Camellia* (1957). *Land of Stones and Saints* (1957). *Victorine* (1958). *Station Wagon in Spain* (1959). *Mother Cabrini: Missionary to the World* (1959). *Frances Parkinson Keyes' Christmas Gift* (1959). *The Third Mystic of Avila* (1960). *Roses in December* (1960). *The Chess Players* (1960). *The Rose and the Lily* (1961). *Madame Castel's Lodger* (1962). Ed., *A Treasury of Favorite Poems* (1963). *The Restless Lady and Other Stories* (1963). *Three Ways of Love* (1963). *The Explorer* (1964). *I, the King* (1966). *Tongues of Fire* (1966). *The Heritage* (1968). *All Flags Flying* (1972).

JAMES E. ROCKS
Loyola University
Chicago, Ill.

JOHN OLIVER KILLENS (1916–). As a novelist, essayist, screenwriter, playwright, and lecturer, John Killens has had a varied and busy life. Born in Macon, Ga., and educated in the South and the North, Killens' association with academic life has been constant. He attended Edward Waters College, Brown College, and Howard University. He studied law at Columbia University, New York University, and Terrell Law School. Killens was writer-in-residence at Fisk University for three and a half years and currently holds the same position at Howard University. He has also been relatively active in political life; he served on the National Labor Relations Board from 1936 to 1942.

Killens' early novels were set in the South and dealt with the theme of racial injustice. His war novel, *And Then We Heard the Thunder*, had its origins in Killens' war experiences in the Pacific during World War II. More recently in *The Cotillion* Killens explored the hypocrisy of northern black social life. *Black Man's Burden* is a superb collection of essays; but *Great Gittin' Up Morning*, a biographical account of slave insurrectionist Denmark Vesey, is a low water mark in Killens' writing. His scenarios for television and movies have received praise from the black literati but have not been recognized nationally.

Killens is founder and chairman of the Harlem Writers Guild, vice-president of the Black Academy of Arts and Letters, and holds membership in P.E.N., the Author's Guild, and the Dramatist Guild.

WORKS: *Youngblood* (1954). *And Then We Heard the Thunder* (1963). *Black Man's Burden* (1966). *'Sippi* (1967). *Slaves* (1969). *The Cotillion* (1971). *Great Gittin' Up Morning* (1972). *A Man Ain't Nothing But a Man: The Adventures of John Henry*, juvenile (1975).

BARRY H. NATION
Southeastern Community College
Whiteville, N.C.

GRACE (ELIZABETH) KING (1852–1932). Grace King was born on November 29, 1852, in New Orleans, the daughter of William Woodson King, who was a prominent lawyer, and Sarah Ann Miller King. After spending the Civil War years at their remote plantation, the family returned without money to the city, where they lived for several years in a working-class district. Although Presbyterian, King was educated in private Creole schools, chiefly the Institut St. Louis and a school conducted by Heloise Cenas. Her interests were history, literature, and modern languages.

In 1885 she told Richard Watson Gilder that she thought George W. Cable's fiction discredited Creoles and favored Negroes. In

answer to a challenge from Gilder she wrote "Monsieur Motte,"
dramatizing the loyalty of a quadroon in Reconstruction times
toward the child of her former owners. Adding three sequels, she
published her first book, *Monsieur Motte* (1888). After a second
series of stories appeared, *Tales of a Time and Place* (1892), King
was recognized as one of the more interesting new southern regionalists. She was equally successful with her shorter *Balcony
Stories* (1893). Charles Dudley Warner was her first sponsor; visiting him in Hartford, she also became a close friend of Mark Twain.
In Europe (1891–1892) she began a long friendship with Madame
Marie Therese Blanc and completed a biography of Bienville
(1892). During the next decade, as the vogue of local color declined, she wrote Louisiana history, the best volume of which is
New Orleans, the Place and the People (1895). After 1905 she wrote
less, but produced her best novel, *The Pleasant Ways of St.
Medard* (1916), a fictional account of her family's experience during Reconstruction. As she grew older she was forgotten nationally
but honored locally as a symbol of intellectual New Orleans. Tulane University conferred the degree of Doctor of Letters on her
in 1915. She died on January 14, 1932.

works: "Earthlings," *Lippincott's Monthly Magazine*, XLII (November,
1888). *Monsieur Motte* (1888). "The Chevalier Alain de Triton," *Chau-
tauquan*, XIII (July, 1891). *Tales of a Time and Place* (1892). *Jean Bap-
tiste le Moyne, Sieur de Bienville* (1892). *Balcony Stories* (1893). *A History of Louisiana*, with John R. Ficklen (1893). *New Orleans, the Place
and the People* (1895). *De Soto and His Men in the Land of Florida*
(1898). *Stories from Louisiana History*, with John R. Ficklen (1905).
The Pleasant Ways of St. Medard (1916). *Creole Families of New Orleans*
(1921). *Madame Girard, an Old French Teacher of New Orleans* (1922).
La Dame de Sainte Hermine (1924). *The History of Mt. Vernon on the
Potomac* (1929). *Memories of a Southern Woman of Letters* (1932).

ROBERT BUSH
City University of New York
Bronx, N.Y.

HARRY HARRISON KROLL (1888–1967). Harry Harrison Kroll,
son of Darius and Caroline Cripes Kroll, was born on February

18, 1888, near Kokomo, Ind. After his parents moved from Indiana to Kentucky, Arkansas, and Missouri, Kroll spent his boyhood on farms near Dyersburg, Tenn. Here he developed his proletarian identification with tenant farmers and sharecroppers. He had no formal schooling yet became a traveling photographer. In 1909 in Alemeda, Ala., Kroll met Annette Heard, whom he married on May 23, 1911, after he became a teacher.

After teaching in Alabama, Kroll enrolled in George Peabody College in 1919. He graduated in 1923 and was awarded an M.A. in 1925. During this tenure in Nashville, Kroll began to write, at first commercially writing specifically for local juveniles.

Kroll began college teaching in 1926 at Lincoln Memorial University but moved to Iowa Wesleyan College in 1928. He published his first novel, *Mountainy Singer*, in 1928 while at Lincoln Memorial. His creative writing students there included Jesse Stuart, James Still, and Tom Taggart. In 1929 Kroll returned to Nashville to write and was most successful in 1931 with *Cabin in the Cotton*. When the writer's market declined in 1935, Kroll returned to teaching at the University of Tennessee at Martin where he was revered as a teacher of the highest distinction until his retirement in 1960. He died on June 11, 1967.

Although Kroll published numerous novels, he never reached the heights promised by *Cabin in the Cotton*. He continued carrying the banner against class discrimination of the poor white in the New South, but his success with the proletarian novel decreased. His later works became nostalgic and many reflect a romanticism in stark contrast to the vulgar realism of his earlier period. At his death Kroll left four unpublished novels and numerous short stories, most of which are in the Mississippi Valley Collection at Memphis State University Library.

WORKS: *The Mountainy Singer* (1928). *Three Brothers and Seven Daddies* (1931). *The Cabin in the Cotton* (1931). *I was a Sharecropper* (1936). *Keepers of the House* (1939). *The Usurper* (1942). *The Rider on the Bronze Horse* (1943). *Perilous Journey*, with C. M. Sublette (1943). *Rogues Company* (1943). *Waters Over the Dam* (1944). *Fury in the Earth* (1945). *Their Ancient Grudge* (1946). *Darker Grows the Valley* (1947). *Lost Homecoming* (1950). *The Long Quest* (1954). *The Smoldering Fire*

(1955). *Summer Gold* (1955). *My Heart's in the Hills* (1956). *For Chloe with Love* (1959). *The Brazen Dream* (1961). *Riders in the Night* (1965). *Bluegrass, Belles, Bourbon* (1967).

PATRICK D. HUNDLEY
University of Arkansas
Little Rock

MIRABEAU BUONAPARTE LAMAR (1798–1859). Soldier, statesman, and poet, Mirabeau Lamar was born on August 16, 1798, near Louisville, Ga., the son of John and Rebecca Lamar Lamar, and grew to manhood on a plantation near Milledgeville. The lure of the frontier drew him in 1819 to Cahawba, Ala., capital of the new state, where he was first a merchant and later copublisher of the Cahawba *Press*. He then became private secretary to Governor George M. Troup of Georgia, married Tabitha Jordan in January, 1826, and later settled in Columbus as founder of the Columbus *Enquirer*.

Stricken with personal griefs—including the death of his wife—Lamar left his only child, Rebecca Ann, with relatives and fled in 1835 to Texas. Here he won fame in the Battle of San Jacinto, was elected vice-president of the Republic of Texas, and served 1838–1841 as second president, succeeding Sam Houston. Rebecca Ann died in 1843, two years after he temporarily retired from politics to his plantation on the Brazos. In the Mexican War, Lamar was inspector general in the army of Zachary Taylor and led the victory charge at Monterey. In 1851 he married Henrietta, daughter of the Irish-born poet and popular evangelist, John Newland Maffitt. Lamar's second daughter, Loretto Evalina, was born in 1852.

In Central America, where Lamar resided, 1858–1859, as minister to Nicaragua and Costa Rica, he composed his most frequently anthologized poem, "The Daughter of Mendoza." Shortly after his return to Texas, he died on December 19, 1859.

Lamar's only book, *Verse Memorials* (1857), is written in the Cavalier manner complimenting women and celebrating occasions. Many of the poems had first appeared in ladies' albums or newspapers and magazines. Neither these poems nor the additional ones collected by Philip Graham for *The Life and Poems of Mira-*

beau B. Lamar reflect Lamar's politics, his bravado in battle, or the frontier realities of much of his life.

WORKS: *Verse Memorials* (1857).

RAY M. ATCHISON
Samford University
Birmingham, Ala.

SIDNEY LANIER (1842–1881). Born on February 3, 1842, near Macon, Ga., Sidney Lanier was of Scotch-Irish descent on his maternal side and French Huguenot on his paternal. He was the son of Robert Sampson Lanier, who was a lawyer and descendant of a long line of musicians, and Mary Jane Anderson Lanier. Lanier's family was rigidly Presbyterian. But the seriousness of family life was broken by Lanier's rather precocious enjoyment of music, and his home was a cultured one, filled with books and pictures. Receiving his early education at a private academy, he entered Oglethorpe University as a sophomore in 1857. He was much influenced by one of his teachers there, Dr. James Woodrow, a former pupil of Louis Agassiz at Harvard. Lanier graduated at the head of his class in 1860, having lost a year during which he worked as a clerk in the Macon post office. He then spent a year tutoring in English at Oglethorpe.

On July 10, 1861, several months after the outbreak of Civil War, Lanier enlisted in the Confederate cause by joining the Macon Volunteers, the first company to leave Georgia for the battlefields of Virginia. From June 25 through July 1, 1862, he saw action in the Seven Days fighting around Richmond. While stationed at Fort Boykin in 1863, Lanier began to think of literary work as a probable vocation. With his brother, Clifford, he served as a mounted scout along the James River in 1863 and 1864. Transferred to Wilmington, N.C., in August, 1864, Lanier became a signal officer on a blockade runner. Following the capture of his ship on November 2, he was imprisoned at Point Lookout, Md. Even in prison his interest in music and poetry found expression; physically, however, the rigors of prison life greatly weakened him.

Discharged and paroled in February, 1865, Lanier, now seriously ill, returned to Macon on foot, arriving there on March 15. His mother died of tuberculosis shortly thereafter. Lanier then worked as a hotel clerk in Montgomery, Ala., and made several attempts at teaching before entering his father's law office to practice law and act as his father's clerk. In 1867 he married Mary Day of Macon. Their union was a happy one despite Lanier's ill health and the burden of rearing four sons in poverty. Lanier's only novel, *Tiger-Lilies*, was also published in 1867. Written in three weeks, it was based on his war experiences and is an impassioned outcry against war.

By the late 1860s, tuberculosis had a firm hold on Lanier; he suffered his first hemorrhage during his honeymoon. Since neither poetry nor music could support his family, he spent his strength in hack writing. Although he settled in Baltimore, Md., in 1873, his ill health would necessitate trips to Florida, Pennsylvania, Virginia, and North Carolina during the remaining years of his life. In Baltimore, as his health permitted, he played the flute with the newly organized Peabody Orchestra under the direction of Asger Hamerik.

Lanier's career as a published poet began in 1875, when *Lippincott's Magazine* published his poem, "Corn." Praise of this poem strengthened his confidence in himself. In 1876 he was asked to write the words for the official cantata of the Centennial Exposition in Philadelphia. Forgetting that he was writing words to be sung, critics ridiculed his lyrics. Lanier's words for the cantata—which exhibited a strong national spirit—were followed immediately by his "Psalm of the West"; these two works, plus a few short poems, were published in a volume in the fall of 1876 (though the book bore the date of 1877). By 1878 Lanier was writing in the full maturity of his poetic powers. One of his best poems, "The Marshes of Glynn," was published in that year.

Developing an interest in old and middle English and Elizabethan literature, Lanier delivered courses on Elizabethan verse and Shakespeare in private homes and at Baltimore's Peabody Institute. In 1879 he accepted a position as lecturer in English literature at Johns Hopkins University. *The Science of English*

Verse (1880) and *The English Novel and the Principle of Its Development* (1883) were the results of his studies for his university classes. The former work is a permanent contribution to scholarship on the relations of poetry and music.

From 1878 to 1880, a period of constant pain and weakness, Lanier was most prolific as a poet. The poetry he wrote during his last years reveals a depth of spiritual passion rare among modern poets. By the summer of 1880, he was entering his final battle with tuberculosis. In 1881 he went to the mountains of North Carolina, where he died at Lynn on September 7, shortly after completing a characteristic poem, "Sunrise," written when he had a temperature of 104 degrees. Lanier was buried in Greenmount Cemetery at Baltimore.

WORKS: *Tiger-Lilies* (1867). *Florida: Its Scenery, Climate, and History* (1875). *Poems* (1877). *The Science of English Verse* (1880). *The English Novel and the Principle of Its Development* (1883; rev. ed., 1897). *Poems of Sidney Lanier*, ed. Mary Day Lanier (1884; enlarged eds., 1891, 1916). *Music and Poetry*, ed. Henry W. Lanier (1898). *Retrospects and Prospects: Descriptive and Historical Essays*, ed. Henry W. Lanier (1899). *Bob: The Story of Our Mocking-Bird*, ed. Henry W. Lanier (1899). *Letters of Sidney Lanier*, ed. Henry W. Lanier (1899). *Shakespeare and His Forerunners*, 2 vols.; ed. Henry W. Lanier (1902). *Poem Outlines*, ed. Henry W. Lanier (1908). *The Centennial Edition of the Works of Sidney Lanier*, 10 vols. (1945).

L. MOODY SIMMS, JR.
Illinois State University
Normal

HENRY LAURENS (1724–1792). Henry Laurens was born on February 24, 1724, the son of French Huguenot parents John Laurens (1696–1747) and Esther Grasset (1700–1742). He married Eleanor Ball (1731–1770) June 25, 1750, and the couple produced twelve or thirteen children. His father was a Charleston, S.C., saddler and retail merchant. There, Laurens received "the best education" available before joining James Crokatt & Company in London to learn the Atlantic trade in 1744. He returned to Charleston in 1747, and subsequently became a leading merchant in the

1750s. He branched into shipping and planting and was by the Revolution one of the richest merchant-planters.

Laurens' public service mirrored his economic rise. He served in the South Carolina Commons House from 1757 until 1771, when he took his three sons to England to educate them. He returned in December, 1774, and was immediately enlisted by the patriots: he served as president of their first executive body, the General Committee (January–June, 1775); as president of both the Provincial Congress and the new executive, the Council of Safety (June, 1775–March, 1776); as vice-president of South Carolina (March, 1776–July, 1777); as delegate to the Continental Congress (July, 1777–November, 1779). Quickly recognizing his organizational ability, Congress elected him president. He served from November 1, 1777, until December 9, 1778. Congress next commissioned him to negotiate with the Dutch, but he was captured off the Atlantic coast and imprisoned in the Tower of London from October 6, 1780, to December 31, 1781. He then participated in the final peace negotiations and signed the preliminary articles on November 30, 1782. He returned to the states in the fall of 1784. He was elected to the state legislature and to the federal convention of 1787, but declined, preferring to retire at his Mepkin plantation, where he died on December 9, 1792.

A hot-tempered moralist, Laurens produced seven pamphlets reflecting parts of his public career. The more than 12,000 Laurens letters that survive are currently being published by the University of South Carolina Press.

WORKS: "A Letter Signed Philolethes" (1761–63), *The Papers of Henry Laurens*, ed. George C. Rogers, Jr., and David R. Chesnutt (1972), III, 275–355. *A Representation of Facts, Relative to the Conduct of Daniel Moore, Esquire; Collector of His Majesty's Customs at Charles-Town, In South-Carolina, From the Time of his Arrival in March, 1767, to the Time of his Departure in September following. Transmitted By the Merchants of Charles-Town, to Charles Garth, Esquire, in London, Agent for the Province of South-Carolina; and, Recommended in a Letter from the Honourable The Committee of Correspondence* (1767). *Extracts from the Proceedings of the Court of Vice-Admiralty in Charles-Town, South-Carolina; In the Cause, George Roupell, Esq; v. the Ship Ann and Goods:*

With a few Explanatory Remarks. To which is Subjoined, Some General Observations on American Custom-House Officers, and Courts of Vice-Admiralty (1768). *Extracts from the Proceedings of the High Court of Vice-Admiralty, in Charlestown, South-Carolina, upon Six Several Informations. Adjudged by The Honourable Egerton Leigh, Esq; Sole Judge of that Court and His Majesty's Attorney-General in the said Province, In the Years 1767 and 1768. With explanatory Remarks, &c. And Copies of two extraordinary Oaths. To Which Are Subjoined, Recapitulation, Reflections arising from a late Case, and some General Observations on American Custom-House Officers, and Courts of Vice-Admiralty* (1769). *Extracts from the Proceedings of the High Court of Vice-Admiralty, in Charlestown, South-Carolina, upon Six Several Informations . . . Second Edition with an Appendix* (1769). *An Appendix to the Extracts from the Proceedings of the High Court of Vice-Admiralty in Charlestown, South-Carolina, &c. Containing Strictures upon, and proper Answers to, a Pamphlet entitled, The Man Unmask'd, Published by Egerton Leigh. Together with a Full Refutation of Mr. Leigh's Attempts to Vindicate his Judicial Proceedings* (1769). *Mr. Laurens's True State of the Case. By Which his Candor to Mr. Edmund Jenings Is Manifested, and the Tricks of Mr. Jenings are Detected* (1783).

DAVID R. CHESNUTT
University of South Carolina
Columbia

JOHN LAWSON (d. 1711). Little is known of John Lawson's early life, when or where he was born or where he received his education. British records show that John Lawson, son of Andrew Lawson of London, was apprenticed to John Chandler, on February 1, 1675, for eight years. After two years apprenticeship, Chandler died, and Lawson entered the service of James Hayes for the remaining six years. There is no further record until his arrival in America.

He appears in Charleston, S.C., in December, 1700, where he was appointed by the lord proprietors to make a survey of the interior of Carolina. Accordingly, Lawson and five other Englishmen, three Indian men and the Indian wife of the guide, left Charleston in a "large canoe" bound for the mouth of the Santee River.

Lawson kept a daily journal of the 1,000-mile trip, describing the flora and fauna of the region, and the customs and language of the native Indian tribes represented in the sparsely settled country. During a 59-day trip, they followed a horseshoe course from the South Carolina coast through the Piedmont and eastward to the Pamlico River on the North Carolina coast.

In 1709 Lawson returned to England to see about the publication of his book, A New Voyage to Carolina, and his map of Carolina, both based on his travels. While still in England he was appointed with Edward Moseley, to survey the North Carolina–Virginia boundary. The boundary line was not run until nineteen years later.

Lawson played a prominent role in the founding of North Carolina's two oldest towns, Bath and New Bern. He laid out the town of Bath in 1705, made his home there and was active in the political and economic life of the town and county. Lawson was one of the founders of New Bern in 1710. Von Graffenreid authorized Lawson to lay out the town before his arrival.

Lawson's life ended in tragedy. He was the first victim in the Tuscarora War of 1711. On a trip up the Neuse River with Von Graffenreid, the two men were captured by the Indians. Lawson was tried and executed in September, 1711. Von Graffenreid was released unharmed.

WORKS: A New Voyage to Carolina (1709), first appeared in the first volume of John Stevens' A New Collection of Voyages and Travels (1708). See also A New Voyage to Carolina, ed. Hugh T. Lefler (1967).

HUGH T. LEFLER
University of North Carolina
Chapel Hill

LEWIS LEARY. See Dedication.

LEROY LEATHERMAN (1922–). LeRoy Leatherman was born February 10, 1922, in Alexandria, La., the son of LeRoy Sessums and Mary Aline Duggers Leatherman. Leatherman entered Vanderbilt University in 1939 and later spent a year at Kenyon College and a year at the University of Illinois until he entered the U.S. Army Air Force, Intelligence Division, where he served until 1946. He resumed his formal education at Southern Methodist University and received his B.A. in 1948 and his M.A. in 1949, whereupon he became the director of the Films and Recordings Department of the Dallas Public Library until 1953. It was during this period that his first novel, *The Caged Birds*, was published and was well received by critics who generally associated his work with the bizarre but delicate effects achieved by Tennessee Williams, Truman Capote, and Eudora Welty.

Leatherman left Dallas to become the director of the Martha Graham School and Dance Company in New York City, where he remained until 1960. After this time he traveled to Europe and the Orient and became associated with the International Film Foundation as producer and writer. In 1966 he returned to his interest in Martha Graham's art, wrote the text for *Martha Graham: Portrait of the Lady as Artist*, and became the executive director of the Martha Graham Center in New York City. Leatherman has received a MacDowell Colony Fellowship. Huntington Hartford Foundation Fellowship, and the *Sewanee Review* Fellowship (1957–1958).

WORKS: *The Caged Birds* (1950). *The Other Side of the Tree* (1954). *The Springs of Creativity* (1961). *Martha Graham: Portrait of the Lady as Artist* (1966).

ROBERT L. WELKER
University of Alabama
Huntsville

ARTHUR LEE (1740–1792). Arthur Lee, eleventh son of Thomas and Hannah Ludwell Lee and of the fourth generation of the Lees of Virginia, was born on December 21, 1740, in Westmoreland County, Va. After the death of his father, the boy was sent by his elder brother, William, to Eton and then to Edinburgh where he received his academic training in science, literature, and medicine. In 1764 he received an M.D. and in 1766 returned to Williamsburg to begin the practice of medicine.

Having become interested in law and politics, he returned to London in 1768 to study law and was admitted to the bar in 1775. Lee's entrance into political polemics occurred in 1768 with the publication of "The Monitor's Letters," an appeal similar to John Dickinson's "Farmer's Letters." In London he published another series of letters which won him attention and led to his being chosen as agent of Massachusetts in London. In 1774 Lee published an essay entitled *An Appeal to the Justice and Interests of the People of Great Britain*, which he followed up with the *Second Appeal* in 1775.

As the break between America and England neared, Lee was to serve the Continental Congress as a confidential correspondent in London, as one of three commissioners sent to Paris to negotiate peace and solicit assistance, and as emissary to Spain. Involved in incessant bickering and sniping, Lee stirred distrust and discord, finally being dismissed by Congress in 1779.

In 1780 Lee returned to Virginia, where he was elected to the Virginia House of Delegates in 1781, and then in 1785 he was appointed to the treasury board. When the Constitution was proposed, he aligned himself with the anti-Federalist position, opposing the adoption of the Constitution. He died on December 12, 1792.

WORKS: "The Monitor's Letters," Rind's *Virginia Gazette* (February 25–April 28, 1768). *An Appeal to the Justice and Interests of the People of Great Britain* (1774). *Second Appeal* (1775).

REED SANDERLIN
University of Tennessee
Chattanooga

DONALD L. LEE. See Haki R. Mahubuti.

HARPER LEE (1926–). Nelle Harper Lee was born in Monroeville, Ala., on April 28, 1926. She is the daughter of Amasa Coleman and Frances Fincher Lee. After attending public schools in Monroeville, Lee attended Huntington College in Montgomery for one year, 1944–1945. For four years (1945–1949), she attended the University of Alabama where she studied law. She then studied for one year at Oxford University, afterwards moving to New York where she worked during the 1950s as a reservations clerk with Eastern Airlines and British Overseas Airways. She gave up this job to devote full time to her writing.

Her novel, *To Kill a Mockingbird* (1960), has been described as a level-headed plea for interracial understanding. It is set in a small Alabama town, similar to Monroeville, and Lee's father, a lawyer, is believed to be the model for the fictional lawyer who defends a Negro prosecuted on a charge of rape. When the man is convicted and sent to prison, he tries to escape and is shot to death. This shooting is compared to the senseless shooting of songbirds by hunters and children. *To Kill a Mockingbird* won the Pulitzer Prize in 1961. Lee also received the Alabama Library Association Award and the Brotherhood Award of the National Conference of Christians and Jews in 1961. In 1962 she received the *Bestsellers'* paperback of the year award.

To Kill a Mockingbird has been translated into ten languages. The novel was adapted for the motion picture screen by Horton Foote, and it was filmed in 1962. Lee has contributed nonfiction pieces to several national magazines. She lives and writes in Monroeville.

WORKS: *To Kill a Mockingbird* (1960).

LOUISE BLACKWELL
Florida A.&M. University
Tallahassee

RICHARD HENRY LEE (1732–1794). Richard Henry Lee, brother of Arthur Lee, was the seventh child of Thomas and Hannah Ludwell Lee. Born on January 20, 1732, in Westmoreland County, Va., he, like his brother Arthur, was sent to England for his education at Wakefield. He returned to Virginia some time around 1752. Although he did not pursue a professional education, he is thought to have read widely in law, politics, and history before he entered public service in 1757 as a justice of the peace.

In 1757 he married Anne Aylett and established his residence at

Chantilly, an estate near his birthplace. Following the death of his first wife in December, 1768, he married Mrs. Anne Pinckard (widow of Thomas Pinckard) in 1769.

In 1758 Lee entered the House of Burgesses, where his voice was to become more and more influential, opposing as he did the Stamp Act and the Townshend acts in the 1760s. When the call for a convention was issued by Massachusetts, Richard Henry Lee was one of the seven delegates sent to represent Virginia, and was eventually one of the signers of the Declaration of Independence. Because of declining health in 1779, Lee resigned his seat in Congress and returned to Virginia House of Delegates. Elected again to Congress in 1784 (Congress also selected him as its president for a year), he was to serve until his resignation in 1792. He died on June 17, 1794.

When the Constitution was put forth for ratification, Lee aligned himself with the anti-Federalist position. He has been widely credited with having written the two-part "Letters of the Federal Farmer," but this authorship has been convincingly questioned by Gordon S. Wood, "The Authorship of the *Letters from the Federal Farmer*," *William and Mary Quarterly*, 3rd Ser., XXXI (April, 1974), 299–308.

WORKS: *Observations Leading to a Fair Examination of the System of Government Proposed by the Late Convention* (1787). *An Additional Number of Letters from the Federal Farmer to the Republican* (1788).

REED SANDERLIN
University of Tennessee
Chattanooga

HUGH SWINTON LEGARÉ (1797–1843). Born in Charleston, S.C., on January 2, 1797, Hugh S. Legaré has been rightly characterized as perhaps the best linguist and most widely read man in America at the time of his death on June 20, 1843. The auction catalog (1848) for the sale of those books that he had taken to Washington with him in 1841 when he joined Tyler's cabinet lists 573 titles, mostly in history and law but with representations among standard Greek, Latin, French, English, and continental authors.

Legaré's father died in 1799, leaving his young widow to manage a plantation on the Ashley River and to care for Hugh and his two sisters. At four Legaré suffered from an illness that left the lower part of his body stunted, a condition that probably contributed to his bookishness. He studied with tutors, at private schools, at the South-Carolina College, and for more than a year at the University of Edinburgh (1818–1819).

Legaré read and practiced law, served in the state legislature, became attorney-general of South Carolina, was appointed *chargé d'affaires* to Belgium for four years, was elected to Congress, served as attorney-general of the United States, and was for a brief time acting secretary of state. He was a Unionist, against nullification, lost his seat in Congress by opposing Jackson's subtreasury scheme, and had his doubts about slavery. He was also a traditionalist, an empiricist in legal thought, a social elitist, believed in progress through commerce, science, and technology, and feared that the culture of his beloved Charleston was doomed.

He was founder, the chief and most learned contributor, and possibly for a time the editor of the *Southern Review* (1828–1832). He wrote essays on such subjects as Spanish ballads, Sir Philip Sidney, Byron, and Bentham as well as on classical and legal topics. Southerners were pleased to exhibit him and the periodical as evidences of southern culture, but they neither read nor supported the magazine.

WORKS: *Writings of Hugh Swinton Legaré*, 2 vols; ed. Mary S. Legaré Bullen (1845–46).

GUY A. CARDWELL
Cambridge, Mass.

JAMES MATHEWES LEGARÉ (1823–1859). Eldest of three children of the Charleston, S.C., agricultural editor John D. and Mary D. M. Legaré, James Mathewes Legaré was born on November 26, 1823, in Charleston and graduated in 1842 from the municipal college, then for a year attended Saint Mary's College in Baltimore. While there he concocted a spoof on his family genealogy which, when published in the Charleston *Courier* on March 15, 1844, evoked sufficient controversy as to suggest the possibility that Harriet Beecher Stowe, who knew of the family, may have fastened its surname, pronounced "luh-*gree*," upon her villain in *Uncle Tom's Cabin* (1852).

Back at Charleston, Legaré studied law under James L. Petigru. He also published fiction and verse locally and earned praise for landscapes exhibited at Apprentices' Hall. He attracted the sponsorship of John J. Audubon and William G. Simms, but suffered the first of recurring lung hemorrhages. Owing to insolvency John D. Legaré in 1846 removed his family to Aiken, S.C. Here James passed the rest of life, save for occasional trips to New York or Charleston. In March, 1850, he married Anne C. Andrews of Augusta, Ga.; the couple had no children. Legaré supported himself by teaching, painting, serving as postmaster in 1852–1853 under the Fillmore administration, and selling fiction and verse. He intensified his interest in mechanical invention.

Legaré's verse is that of a lyricist of the romantic school, practicing within a marked classical discipline. An outstanding example is his elegy to Attorney-General Hugh S. Legaré, "On the Death of a Kinsman." His fiction, reflective of the sentimental motifs of the period and including a few titles still unidentified, is noteworthy for its attraction to Spanish themes. He cultivated Philadelphia and New York editors and curried the friendship of Henry W. Longfellow, though the two probably never met. His only known piece of criticism, "Magazines of the Day," Charleston *Mercury*, October 11, 1849, offended Simms as a "puff" of the *Knickerbocker Magazine*, but their rift healed; and Simms's interest in Legaré carried past the latter's with a handsome tribute in the *Mercury*, November 29, 1861. This article emphasizes Legaré's inventions, which included experiments with lignin cotton furniture, and earned him gold and silver medals at the Industrial Institute fairs of 1856–1857 at Charleston. (Two Legaré paintings won premiums.) For the cotton process and for an ivory-frame composition Legaré gained United States patents. His elusive magnum opus, a "dual air-engine," has not survived; but two of his paintings, "Fisherman's Cottage" and "Kids in the Cornfield," hang in Charleston.

Legaré politics are unknown. In religion he was a convert to Episcopalianism. His only known likeness appears in *The Knicker-bocker Gallery* (New York, 1855). He died May 30, 1859, in Aiken of tuberculosis and is buried in the cemetery of Saint Thaddeus Episcopal Church there under a monument erected in 1942.

WORKS: *Orta-Undis, and Other Poems* (1848). "Miss Peck's Friend: A Novel in Ten Chapters," *Putnam's Magazine*, I–II (May–July, 1853). "Cap-and-Bells: A Novel in Ten Chapters," *Harper's Magazine*, XXVII–XXVIII (November, 1863–January, 1864).

CURTIS CARROLL DAVIS
Baltimore, Md.

HENRY CLAY LEWIS [MADISON TENSAS] (1825–1850). Henry Clay Lewis' father, David, came to the United States as an adult from Auvergne, France, to fight in the Revolution. His wife, Mary Salomon, was the daughter of a surgeon. Henry was born on June 26, 1825, in Charleston, S.C., where his father kept a furniture store. Before 1829 the family moved to Cincinnati, Ohio, where Mary died in 1831, and Henry went to live with a brother.

Missing the kindness and studious atmosphere of his cultured Jewish parents' home, the child ran away at ten to become a cook's helper and cabin boy on riverboats. At eleven he was taken off a Yazoo River packet by another brother, Joseph, a merchant in Yazoo City, Miss. Joseph promised Henry an education, but, failing in business, he put the boy to hard work in the cotton fields for the next five years. At sixteen Henry was apprenticed to a medical doctor, and in 1844 was sent to Kentucky to the Louisville Medical Institute. He graduated in 1846 and moved to Louisiana to practice in a backwoods community on the Tensas River, treating slaves and their masters on the great plantations and hunters and squatters in the swamps. In 1849 he moved to Richmond, La., where he prospered: he became active in Whig politics; he bought land, new instruments, law books, and a medical library in French, remembering perhaps the European culture of his childhood. Returning home exhausted during the 1850 cholera epidemic, he accidently drowned in a flooded bayou on August 5, 1850.

In 1845 he had begun contributing sketches to the New York *Spirit of the Times*. These are partly picaresque autobiography, and partly accounts of backwoods life, often violent and brutal. Through the use of dialect, the comic folk imagery, folklore, and the form of the mock oral tale, he presents a vigorous, grotesque, demonic vision of the southern backwoods.

WORKS: *Odd Leaves from the Life of a Louisiana Swamp Doctor* (1850; rprt. as *Louisiana Swamp Doctor*, 1962).

MILTON RICKELS
University of Southwestern
Louisiana
Lafayette

RICHARD LEWIS (*ca.* **1700–1734**). Little is known of the early life of this Maryland schoolmaster-poet. From evidence in his poetry he may have been of Welsh extraction. A letter of Governor Benedict Calvert, his patron, mentions his having attended Eton. Possibly he may also have attended, but not graduated from, Oxford, since his name is not listed among the graduates there. He is known to have served in the Maryland Assembly as clerk of a committee considering revision of tax laws (May 26–June 16, 1730). At All Hallows Parish, Anne Arundel County, Md., in "January 1718/19" a Richard Lewis married Elizabeth Batee. He died intestate late in March, 1734, survived by one son, Richard who was apprenticed (by Daniel Dulany) to a saddler, Richard Tootel, in March, 1735.

In the Preface to his translation of Holdsworth's *Muscipula* he writes that he "is engaged in teaching Language" and that he finds it "a very fatiguing Employment." Lewis must also have had some interest in natural philosophy, since he corresponded with Peter Collinson, Fellow of the Royal Society, concerning an unexplained explosion he had witnessed near the present site of Baltimore on

October 22, 1725. In this same letter (October 27, 1732) he also describes "a remarkable Generation of Insects" and "an Earthquake." In another letter to Collinson he discusses the Aurora Borealis and sun spots (Annapolis, December 10, 1730).

Benjamin Franklin printed several of Lewis' poems in the *Pennsylvania Gazette*. Among the most famous of these is an allegory on the life of man entitled "Description of the Spring. A Journey from Patapsco to Annapolis, April 4, 1730," modeled on Thomson's "The Seasons" and reprinted at least five times in England. Other poems of Lewis show in part the influence of Pope's "Windsor Forest"—notably "To Mr. Samuel Hastings (Shipwright of Philadelphia)" and "Food for Critics." Still in the process of discovery, the final canon of Lewis' works has yet to be established. Nevertheless, J. A. Leo Lemay has called Lewis "the finest Augustan poet of the new world" and "a better nature poet than any before Bryant."

WORKS: Trans., Edward Holdsworth's *Muscipula—The Mouse-Trap, or The Battle of the Cambrians and Mice* (1728). "*To Mr.* Samuel Hastings (*Shipwright* of Philadelphia) *on his Launching the* Maryland-Merchant, *a Large Ship Built by Him at* Annapolis," *Maryland Gazette*, December 30, 1729; earliest existing issue is reprinted in *Pennsylvania Gazette*, January 13, 1730. "Description of the Spring. A Journey from Patapsco to Annapolis, April 4, 1730," *Pennsylvania Gazette*, May 21, 1731. "Food for Critics," *Maryland Gazette* (1731); repr. in altered form in *New England Weekly Journal*, June 28, 1731, and the *Pennsylvania Gazette*, July 17, 1732. "A Rhapsody," Annapolis, 1732; repr. in *Maryland Gazette*, February 9, 1733. "Verses, to Mr. Ross, on Mr. Calvert's Departure from Maryland, May 10th, 1732," *Maryland Historical Magazine*, XXXII (June, 1937), 118–20. "Verses: To the Memory of His Excellency Benedict Leonard Calvert; Late Governour of the Province of Maryland who Died at Sea, June—1732," *Maryland Historical Magazine*, XXXII, 121–27. "A Poem. In memory of the Hon. Benedict Leonard Calvert . . . Who Died at Sea on Board the Charles . . . ," *Maryland Historical Magazine*, XXXII, 116–17. "Congratulatory Verses, wrote at the Arrival of our Honourable Proprietary [Thomas Penn]," *Pennsylvania Gazette*, August 21, 1732. "Carmen Seculare," Annapolis, November 25, 1732; repr. in *Gentlemen's Magazine* (April and May, 1733). "Upon

Prince Madoc's Expedition to the Country Now Called America in the 12th [*sic*] Century." by "Philo-Cambrensis" (June 29, 1734).

RICHARD E. AMACHER
Auburn University
Auburn, Ala.

ROMULUS LINNEY (1930–). Romulus Linney, though born on September 21, 1930, in Philadelphia, was descended from western North Carolina people. He was the fifth Romulus Zachariah Linney in a straight line. His childhood was spent in Charlotte and Boone, N.C. and in Madison, Tenn., the summers always reserved for mountain vacations. In 1953 he graduated from Oberlin College, and after two years in the army, received an M.F.A. from Yale University School of Drama in 1958. Thereafter he was involved with television in New York, was stage manager for the Actors Studio, and acted in summer stock. In 1961 he was visiting professor at the University of North Carolina at Chapel Hill, then moved to North Carolina State University as director of fine arts, and later was on the faculty of the Manhattan School of Music and the University of Pennsylvania, intermittently conducting seminars at Brooklyn College and Columbia University. He has held fellowships at Yaddo and the MacDowell Colony. Twice married, to Ann Legett Sims and Margaret Andrews, he has two daughters.

Linney's unusual novels are striking tours de force. *Heathen Valley*, based on Bishop Levi E. Ives's mission at Valle Crucis in the North Carolina mountains during the 1840s, is a Gothic tale of terror and pagan violence, and *Slowly, by Thy Hand Unfurled* is the diary of a semiliterate woman in a small town. *The Sorrows of Frederick* dramatizes the psychological rather than the historical aspects of the German emperor. *The Love Suicide at Schofield Barracks*, an antiwar play, was produced on Broadway. *Democracy and Esther* consolidates ideas from two Henry Adams novels. Unlike his mountain comedies *Holy Ghosts* and *Just Folks*, the bicentennial play *Appalachia Sounding* follows one family through 200 years. Versatility in subjects and themes is the most constant feature of Linney's skillful works.

WORKS: *Heathen Valley* (1962). *Slowly, by Thy Hand Unfurled* (1965). *The Sorrows of Frederick* (1968). *The Love Suicide at Schofield Barracks* (1972, 1973). *Democracy and Esther* (1973). *Holy Ghosts* (prod. 1974). *Appalachia Sounding* (prod. 1976). *Just Folks* (commissioned 1976 by Kennedy Center, prod. 1978). *The Death of King Philip* (opera libretto, prod. 1976). *Old Man Joseph and His Family* (prod. 1978).

RICHARD WALSER
North Carolina State University
Raleigh

AUGUSTUS BALDWIN LONGSTREET (1790–1870). A lawyer, minister, and college president, Longstreet produced a book of short stories entitled *Georgia Scenes*, which was the first significant contribution to southwestern humor. He was the son of Hannah Randolph and William Longstreet (1759–1814), an inventor interested especially in steam engines and steamboats, who migrated to Georgia from New Jersey about 1785.

Augustus Baldwin Longstreet was born in Augusta, Ga., on September 22, 1790. His earliest education was at home, but he attended the academy of Dr. Moses Waddel in Willington, S.C., from 1808 to 1810. He entered Yale College in 1811, following the example of his friend John C. Calhoun. After completing his studies at that school in 1813, he attended Reeve and Gould's Law School at Litchfield, Conn.

In 1814 he returned home and on May 26, 1815, was admitted to the Georgia bar. During his travels to various courts, he met the wealthy Frances Eliza Parke of Greensboro, Ga. They were married in March, 1817, and he moved to Greensboro. He was elected representative to the Georgia legislature from Greene County in 1821, and in 1822 became judge of the Superior Court of Ocmulgee District, a position he held for three years. He moved his family from Greensboro to Augusta in 1827 and continued to practice law. Also he purchased a newspaper, the Augusta *State Rights Sentinel*, and edited it from 1834 to 1836.

Because of intense religious interests, he became a Methodist minister in 1838. His first position as a college president was at the newly founded Emory College from 1839 to 1848. In 1844 he attended a conference of the Methodist Church in New York and actively participated in a discussion about the ownership of slaves, which finally split the Methodist Church into its two branches. He served briefly as president of Centenary College in Jackson, La., in 1849, and then from 1849 to 1856 was president of the University of Mississippi.

Resigning as president of that university because of political pressure, he retired briefly to Abbeville, Miss. In January, 1858, he became president of the University of South Carolina. When the student body joined the Confederate Army in late 1861, he returned to Mississippi. During the war he traveled about and supported, with his writings, the southern cause. He briefly served as a chaplain of the Georgia Militia. His nephew was General James Longstreet, and his son-in-law L. Q. C. Lamar. After the war, he retired to Mississippi, where, though he was not completely impoverished, the family fortune had been considerably reduced. He died at Oxford, Miss., on July 9, 1870.

Although he wrote other books and pamphlets, he is well known for one book, *Georgia Scenes*, published in 1835 in Augusta, Ga., a collection of sketches first printed in the Milledgeville *Southern Recorder* and in the Augusta *State Rights Sentinel*. This work, to be followed in the next several years by an enormous number of other examples of southwestern humor by many writers, had nineteen sketches signed either by Hall (in which men appeared as the principal figures) or Baldwin (in which women were the central characters). Longstreet insisted that for the most part the stories were "fanciful *combinations* of *real* incidents and characters." The purpose was something more than just amusement; he stated that "the aim of the author was to supply a chasm in history which has always been overlooked—the manners, customs, amusements, wit, dialect, as they appear in all grades of society to an ear and eye witness of them" during "the first 50 years of our republic." The popularity of the book was helped by Poe, who in the *Southern Literary Messenger* for March, 1836, stated that the work was "a sure omen of better days for the literature of the South." Later on, after becoming a minister, Longstreet became somewhat disturbed by what he considered the essentially frivolous nature of the sketches.

WORKS: *Georgia Scenes, Characters, Incidents, &c. in the First Half Century of the Republic* (1835). *Master William Mitten: or A Youth of Brilliant Talents Who was Ruined by Bad Luck* (1864). *Stories with a Moral Humorous and Descriptive of Southern Life a Century Ago* (1912).

EDWARD L. TUCKER
Virginia Polytechnic Institute
and State University
Blacksburg

GRACE LUMPKIN (*ca.* **1892–**). Daughter of William Wallace and Annette Morris Lumpkin, Grace Lumpkin was born in Milledgeville, Ga., completed high school in Columbia, S.C., and graduated in 1911 from Brenau College in Gainesville, Ga., with a B.D. She worked for a year in France and then returned to South Carolina, where she taught school and eventually became industrial secretary of the YWCA. Moving to New York City in the mid-1920s, she studied writing at Columbia University and involved herself in left-wing activities. In 1932 her first novel, *To Make My Bread*, was published, winning the Maxim Gorky award as the year's best labor novel. Set in the southern Appalachians, it chronicles the hardships of mountain people forced into mill work, and it concludes with the Gastonia strike in 1929. Albert Bein's stage adaptation, *Let Freedom Ring*, was successfully produced in 1935.

In the same year she finished her second novel, *A Sign for Cain*, which depicts racial injustice and union activity in the South. Both books reflect her commitment to Marxist ideology; however, *The Wedding*, published in 1939, marks a shift away from social protest. This novel and her short story "The Treasure," included in the *O. Henry Memorial Award Stories of 1940*, are concerned more with manners and emotions than with social theory. Partly under the influence of her friend Whittaker Chambers, she embraced a conservative political position and renewed religious conviction in the 1940s, but she lost the inspiration that produced three well-received novels in the previous decade. In 1952, after working on a manuscript for a play, she moved to King and Queen County, Va. It was not until ten years later that she completed her fourth novel, *Full Circle*, which presents a critical view of communism. In 1974 she returned to Columbia, S.C. Her papers are in the University of South Carolina's Caroliniana library.

WORKS: *To Make My Bread* (1932). *A Sign for Cain* (1935). *The Wedding* (1939). *Full Circle* (1962).

C. MICHAEL SMITH
Winthrop College
Rock Hill, S.C.

ANDREW LYTLE (1902–). Andrew Nelson Lytle, novelist, critic, and editor, was born on December 26, 1902, in Murfreesboro, Tenn. His father was Robert Logan Lytle, a farmer; his mother had been Lillie Belle Nelson. His family on both sides had long been prominent in middle Tennessee, and in fact Murfreesboro was founded on land given by his Revolutionary ancestor. His recent family chronicle, *A Wake for the Living* (1975), traces the course of their history for almost two centuries.

Lytle lived in Murfreesboro and north Alabama until he entered Sewanee Military Academy at the age of thirteen. Afterwards he studied for a year in France. But the most important phase of his education occurred at Vanderbilt, where he took his bachelor's degree in 1925. His undergraduate years coincided with the heyday of the Fugitive group, and the friendships he formed with these poets led him into his literary career. His main interest in the 1920s, however, was theater. He went from Tennessee to the Yale School of Drama, where he studied playwriting with George Pierce Baker; and in New York he tried acting.

Lytle's movement into fiction was gradual. Even before he left New York he had begun the research on his first book, *Bedford Forrest and His Critter Company* (1931). He thus followed his friends Allen Tate and Robert Penn Warren, whose first prose works were likewise Civil War biographies. In 1930 these men and nine of their friends, led by John Crowe Ransom, published *I'll*

Take My Stand. This famous symposium inaugurated the Agrarian movement, to which Lytle was passionately committed. He was indeed about the only Agrarian who actually practiced farming in the 1930s, and for a few years he attempted to combine this with the literary profession. His great interest in the history of his region led to his first novel, *The Long Night* (1936), a tragedy of revenge set against the background of the Civil War.

Although Lytle is usually identified with Tennessee, where three of his four novels are set, he is keenly aware of the larger clash of cultures. *At the Moon's Inn* (1941) brings the Spanish explorer de Soto to his fate in North America as he attempts to overcome the vast unknown wilderness through an act of will. Lytle's third novel, *A Name for Evil* (1947), has a modern hero who undergoes somewhat the same experiences in an abortive effort to restore the past; the fictional convention here is the ghost story.

Lytle was married to Edna Langdon Barker in 1938. She is deceased. Their family consists of three daughters: Pamela, Katherine Anne, and Lillie Langdon. Since 1942 he has found a place in the academic world. In that year he acted as professor of history and editor of the *Sewanee Review* at the University of the South. From 1946 to 1948 he lectured at the University of Iowa School of Writing, and he held a similar post at the University of Florida, 1948–1961. Then he returned to Sewanee as professor of English and editor of the *Review*. During his twelve years as editor (1961–1973) he emerged as an important critic; a selection of his essays was published in 1966 as *The Hero with the Private Parts*. He now lives in Monteagle, Tenn. Retired, he continues to write and lecture.

WORKS: *Bedford Forrest and His Critter Company* (1931). *The Long Night* (1936). *At the Moon's Inn* (1941). *A Name for Evil* (1947). *The Velvet Horn* (1957). *A Novel, a Novella and Four Stories* (1958). *The Hero with the Private Parts* (1966). Ed., *Craft and Vision: The Best Stories from the Sewanee Review* (1971). *A Wake for the Living* (1975).

ASHLEY BROWN
University of South Carolina
Columbia

COMAC McCARTHY (1933–). Born in Providence, R.I., on July 20, 1933, the son of Charles Joseph and Gladys McGrail McCarthy, Comac McCarthy attended the University of Tennessee in Knoxville and remains closely associated with the hill and mountain region of east Tennessee, the setting of his novels. His first novel, *The Orchard Keeper* (1965), is distinguished by a keen sense of time and place overlaid with mythic extensions, complexity of presentation, and a highly poetic language. The novel received the Faulkner Foundation Award for 1966 and seemed to place McCarthy as an inheritor of the Faulknerian southern gothic tradition.

His later novels seem to confirm superficially his bent toward grotesquerie as he deals with incest, necrophilia, murder, and general depravity. However, his work also moves deeper into imagined, mythic worlds with metaphysical implications at the same time it evokes even more clearly a land and its people. The prose grows more stark, vivid, compact, and tense, and the themes more cosmically oriented. Prior to the publication of his first novel, McCarthy contributed to the *Sewanee Review* and the *Yale Review* and received the Ingram-Merrill Foundation grant for creative writing in 1960, the American Academy of Arts and Letters traveling fellowship to Europe, 1965–1966. Presently living with his wife, Anne, in the Rockford Community near Maryville, Tenn., Comac McCarthy received a Guggenheim Award for 1976–1977.

WORKS: *The Orchard Keeper* (1965). *Outer Dark* (1968). *Child of God* (1974).

ROBERT L. WELKER
University of Alabama
Huntsville

CARSON McCULLERS (1917–1967). Carson McCullers was born Lula Carson Smith in Columbus, Ga., on February 19, 1917. The first of three children, she was touted by her mother for her precocity and curried for genius. Her maternal great-grandfather —from whom she took the name Carson—had been a slaveowner and landholder of considerable property in Reynolds, Ga., and on both sides she was descended from solid, middle-class families imbued with an aristocratic sense of lineage, place, and southern tradition. Reared on tales of kinsmen who fought and died in the Civil War and the strong-willed women they left behind, young Lula Carson was both repelled and attracted by the paradoxes of life in the South. She spent most of her adult life trying to avoid the South, yet candidly admitted that she had to return home periodically to renew her "sense of horror." Given to ill health, she retreated often to Columbus, where she was succored by her mother until well enough to travel north again.

At thirteen Lula Carson Smith was determined to become a concert pianist, but after four years of study at the piano she turned to another developing obsession: writing. As a child she had scribbled fiction in her Blue Chief notebooks and written plays, which she produced at home for neighborhood audiences. At seventeen, encouraged by her mother, she went alone to New York City to study creative writing under Dorothy Scarborough and Helen Rose Hull at Columbia University. After another illness and recuperation in Georgia, she worked with Sylvia Chatfield Bates at New York University, and at Columbia with Whit Burnett.

On September 20, 1937, she married James Reeves McCullers, Jr., from Wetumpka, Ala. Painfully shy, eccentric in her dress, and unpopular with her peers, she had not seriously dated until courted by her handsome, personable future husband she had met two years earlier while he was a soldier at Ft. Benning. She began her first novel, *The Heart Is a Lonely Hunter*, on her honeymoon in Charlotte, N.C., where they lived for almost a year. Times were difficult during these depression years, but it was the happiest period of their marriage. Although their original intent had been to take turns writing and supporting each other, it soon became apparent that Carson's writing would always come first.

For two lean years they lived in Fayetteville, N.C., where Reeves was transferred as an investigator-manager for a retail credit firm. In the spring of 1939 she finished her first novel, then dashed off a second, *Reflections in a Golden Eye*, in two months.

Upon publication of *The Heart Is a Lonely Hunter* (1940) she and Reeves moved to New York City, determined never to live in the South again. Already their marriage had begun to disintegrate; there were frequent estrangements until their divorce in late 1941. On March 19, 1945, they remarried upon Reeves's return from the European front of World War II. During the next eight years there were traumatic separations and reconciliations which culminated in Reeves's suicide in Paris in November, 1953.

The 1940s were Carson McCullers' most productive years. In New York she aligned herself with artists of all genres. She was a Fellow at the Breadloaf Writers Conference, in August, 1940. In the fall she moved into 7 Middagh Street in Brooklyn Heights with W. H. Auden, *Mademoiselle* editor George Davis, and Gypsy Rose Lee, where they were joined by Richard Wright, Peter Pears, Benjamin Britten, Chester Kallman, Paul and Jane Bowles, and others in a menage that became one of the most eccentric and electric creative atmospheres of the twentieth century. She also worked frequently at Yaddo Artists Colony in Saratoga Springs, N.Y. Here she met, attached herself to, or developed friendships with many other creative people. Identifying with the exiled and the self-estranged, she spent most of her life searching for love and reciprocity and making enormous psychic and physical demands on her friends. Charismatic, fey, and seemingly androgynous, she both attracted and repelled, loving inordinately both men and women in passionate attachments that usually stopped short of the bed.

She was awarded two Guggenheim fellowships, an Arts and Letters Grant, membership in the National Institute of Arts and Letters, and other honors. More than a dozen highly successful short stories and nonfiction prose pieces were published in such magazines as the *New Yorker*, *Harper's Bazaar*, *Vogue*, *Mademoiselle*, *Redbook*, and *Esquire*. Her adaptation of *The Member of the Wedding* opened on Broadway January 5, 1950, ran 501 performances, and won the New York Drama Critics Circle Award, the Donaldson Award, and a Gold Medal. Another play, *The Square Root of Wonderful*, opened on Broadway on October 30, 1957, but closed after 45 performances. *The Ballad of the Sad Cafe*, adapted by Edward Albee, opened on Broadway October 30, 1963, and closed after 123 performances. Screen plays were made of her books *The Heart Is a Lonely Hunter*, *The Member of the Wedding*, and *Reflections in a Golden Eye*.

Plagued by serious illness the last half of her life, Carson McCullers suffered three paralyzing strokes (for which she underwent many operations to relieve her atrophied left limbs), a mastectomy, heart attack, and frequent attacks of pleurisy and other respiratory diseases. She died from a cerebral hemorrhage on September 29, 1967, in Nyack, N.Y., where she is buried.

WORKS: *The Heart Is a Lonely Hunter* (1940). *Reflections in a Golden Eye* (1941). *The Member of the Wedding* (1946). *The Ballad of the Sad Cafe and Other Works* (1951). *The Member of the Wedding*, play (1951). *The Ballad of the Sad Cafe and Collected Short Stories* (1952, 1955). *The Square Root of Wonderful* (1958). *Clock Without Hands* (1961). *Sweet as a Pickle and Clean as a Pig* (1964). *The Mortgaged Heart*, ed. Margarita G. Smith (1971).

VIRGINIA SPENCER CARR
Columbus College
Columbus, Ga.

KATHARINE SHERWOOD BONNER McDOWELL. See Sherwood Bonner.

LARRY MCMURTRY (1936–). Larry McMurtry was born in Wichita Falls, Tex., on June 3, 1936, and grew up in nearby Archer County in the short-grass ranching country of north-central Texas, his "blood's country and his heart's pastureland." Archer City, the county seat, is the Thalia of his fiction. He entered Rice University in Houston in 1954, but left to complete his B.A. degree at North Texas State College (1958). He returned to Rice for an M.A. (1960), and then went to Stanford University for a year on a Wallace Stegner Writing Fellowship. In 1961–1962 he taught at Texas Christian University, and then took a year off while the film "Hud" was being made. He began teaching at Rice in 1963. After the publication of his fourth novel in 1970, McMurtry left Rice and opened a bookstore in Washington, D.C. In addition to his fiction, he writes screenplays, nonfiction pieces for magazines, and lectures on the college circuit.

The son and grandson of cattlemen, McMurtry came to know intimately the romantic myths and harsh realities of cowboy life. In his novels *Horseman, Pass By* ("Hud"), *Leaving Cheyenne*, and *The Last Picture Show*, he portrayed the stark west Texas landscape, the vanishing cowboy, the dust-blown small towns losing their long battle to the cities, and yearning adolescents caught in the uneasy transition from the old way of life to the new. In 1968 he cast a disenchanted eye over his native state in a collection of essays, *In a Narrow Grave: Essays on Texas*. With his trilogy, *Moving On, All My Friends Are Going to Be Strangers*, and *Terms of Endearment*, McMurtry moved from the ranches and small towns to examine Texas urban life (Houston for the most part) through a connected cast of characters; he wrote about the failure of people to let others into their lives—even through marriage.

McMurtry seems well on his way to becoming an ex-native son. *Terms of Endearment* may be his last novel with a Texas setting, at least for a while. "There are only so many stories to tell about Texas," he says, "and now I would like to write about other places." He has California in mind.

WORKS: *Horseman, Pass By* (1961). *Leaving Cheyenne* (1963). *The Last Picture Show* (1966). *In a Narrow Grave: Essays on Texas* (1968). *Moving On* (1970). *All My Friends Are Going to Be Strangers* (1972). *Terms of Endearment* (1975).

NORMAN D. BROWN
University of Texas
Austin

JOHN CHARLES McNEILL (1874–1907). John Charles McNeill, youngest of five children of Duncan and Euphemia McNeill, was born near Wagram in Scotland County, N.C., on July 26, 1874. Many of his poems are nostalgic evocations of a happy boyhood spent roaming the fields and woods, swimming and hunting and fishing, working along the rows with white and black laborers, and attending the "old field" school. Before entering Wake Forest College in 1894, he studied at Whiteville Academy, clerked in a store, and taught in Georgia. At Wake Forest, he was an exemplary student, contributed poems to and edited the literary journal, and took special law courses. Briefly he was on the faculties at Wake Forest and Mercer University.

When 26, he opened a law office in Lumberton, wrote poems and stories for the local newspaper, but after several years moved to Laurinburg to practice, and was elected to the state legislature. He had little interest in deeds and writs, and only the personalities of those involved in courtroom battles intrigued him. Meanwhile, the *Youth's Companion* in 1901 accepted a poem by him, and the *Century Magazine* over a four-year span used eighteen selections, both lyrics and dialect verse. In September, 1904, the Charlotte *Observer* invited him to the staff to write when and what he wished. In the *Observer* over the next three years appeared 467 of his poems, only 134 of them collected in his two published books. Besides the columns of poetry, he wrote anecdotes, fables, reports on fires and funerals, book reviews, and covered special events in North Carolina and South Carolina. His popularity soared, and his byline became regionally famous. "The little loves and sorrows are my song," he said. His dialect verse and his poems on nature and religion are chaste productions of a man who was himself warm-hearted and uncomplicated. He died on October 17, 1907.

WORKS: *Songs Merry and Sad* (1906). *Lyrics from Cotton Land* (1907). *Select Prose of John Charles McNeill* (1936).

RICHARD WALSER
North Carolina State University
Raleigh

DAVID MADDEN (1933–). David Madden published his first short story at eighteen. Since then he has published numerous

poems and stories, several plays and four novels, as well as scores
of critical essays and reviews. His own essays on writing have been
published as *The Poetic Image in Six Genres*.

Madden was born on July 25, 1933, in Knoxville, Tenn., the son
of James and Emile Merritt Madden. He attended Knoxville's
public schools and, beginning in 1951, the University of Tennessee. For the next several years he alternately attended the university, held odd jobs in New York, Boston, and Maine, and went to
sea as a merchant sailor. He spent 1954–1955 in the army. Released from the army, Madden enrolled at Iowa State Teachers
College where he met Roberta Young, a fellow student, whom he
married the next year. They have one son, Blake Dana, born
March 23, 1960. In 1956 David Madden returned to the University
of Tennessee from which he received his B.S. in 1957. He obtained an M.A. from San Francisco State in 1958. During 1959–
1960 he attended the Yale Drama School.

He has taught at Centre College (1960–1962), the University of
Louisville (1962–1964), Kenyon College (1964–1966), Ohio University (1966–1968) and Louisiana State University where he has
been writer-in-residence since 1968.

While at Kenyon, Madden was an assistant editor of the *Kenyon
Review*; he has been associate editor of several magazines. He is
presently associate editor of *Fiction International*, *Appalachian
Heritage*, and editor of *Contemporary Literary Scene*. *The Shadow Knows*, a collection of short stories, won Madden an award
from the National Council on the Arts. "The Day the Flowers
Came" and "No Trace" were selected for inclusion in *Best American Short Stories* of, respectively, 1969 and 1971.

Madden is currently assembling his first collection of poems,
"Venice is Sinking"; he has two novels in progress: "Knoxville,
Tennessee," and "The Sunshine Man."

works: *The Beautiful Greed* (1961). *Wright Morris* (1964). Ed., *Proletarian Writers of the Thirties* (1968). Ed., *Tough Guy Writers of the
Thirties* (1968). *Casandra Singing* (1969). *The Poetic Image in Six Genres*
(1969). Ed., *American Dreams, American Nightmares* (1970). *James M.
Cain* (1970). *The Shadow Knows* (1970). Ed., *Rediscoveries* (1971).

Brothers in Confidence (1972). Ed., *The Popular Culture Explosion*, with Ray B. Browne (1972). Ed., *Nathaniel West: The Cheaters and the Cheated* (1973). *Bijou* (1974). Ed., *Remembering James Agee* (1974). Ed., *Creative Choices* (1975). Ed., *Studies in the Short Story*, with Virgil Scott (1975). *Harlequin's Stick, Charlie's Cane* (1975). *Suicide's Wife* (1978). *Pleasure Dome* (1979).

CHARLES E. BENNETT
Cazenovia College
Cazenovia, N.Y.

JAMES MADISON (1751–1836). The fourth president of the United States, James Madison was born March 16, 1751, the eldest of ten children of James and Nelly Conway Madison, a substantial planter and slaveholding family in Orange County, Va. Following tutoring by local clergymen, Madison entered Donald Robertson's school at age twelve and continued there for five years. Robertson, a Scot, influenced Madison's decision to enroll at the College of New Jersey in 1769. For the first time he traveled beyond the Old Dominion, discovered at Princeton a lively collegiate community, and completed the baccalaureate program in two years. Awarded a B.A. in the fall of 1771, Madison remained for six months studying under President John Witherspoon. There followed a difficult three-year period which found the young graduate at home, uncertain about the choice of a career, abandoning thoughts of the ministry and inclining toward the law, experiencing melancholy and recurring ill health, and concluding that he had but a short time to live. From indecision, introspection, and unhappiness he was suddenly catapulted by the revolutionary crisis into a lifetime of political leadership.

In the 40 years following his election to the Orange County Committee on Safety in December, 1774, Madison moved rapidly from local to state to national levels of influence. Election to the Virginia provisional convention in 1776 was followed by membership on the governor's council in 1778 and selection by the assembly in 1780 as a delegate to the Continental Congress. For the last three years of the Revolutionary War, Madison participated in the critical military, political, and diplomatic decisions made at the continental level. Upon his return to Virginia in December, 1783, he professed a desire for the quiet life of a gentleman-scholar-planter, but he quickly put this aside when opportunities for an active political role presented themselves: election to the Virginia House of Delegates in 1784; attendance at the Annapolis Convention; representation of Virginia in the Confederation Congress in 1787; and selection as a delegate to the Constitutional Convention of 1787.

At Philadelphia in the summer of 1787 Madison led the fight for a strong national government, left his countrymen greatly in his debt by keeping the only detailed notes of the convention debates and proceedings, and through his contributions to *The Federalist*, originally newspaper essays written with John Jay and Alexander Hamilton, in 1787–1788, played a major role in defining republican political theory and interpreting the intent and character of the Constitution. His reputation for political sagacity secured, Madison discovered that the practical tasks of fashioning a new national government afforded opportunities for demonstrating his leadership. As a member of the House of Representatives (1789–1797), he quickly emerged as the spokesman for those opposing Hamilton's economic program and, in the wake of these legislative battles, set about organizing an opposition party, the first in the nation's political history. Next, as secretary of state (1801–1809) during Jefferson's two presidential terms, he played an important role in charting a course designed both to preserve peace and defend American trading rights as Europe was convulsed by war. Finally, as president (1809–1817), the search for peace with honor having failed, he led an ill-prepared nation into a war with Great Britain which brought neither gain nor glory. But it also brought no substantial losses, and while this unhappy event provoked questions then and now about the quality of Madison's statesmanship, the conclusion of the war ushered in an era of dynamic national growth.

Earlier in 1794, at age 43, the shy, sober, dispassionate "Jemmy" Madison married Dolley Payne Todd, a lively young widow who in her own right did much to make the nation's new capital a more tolerable place. Madison died on June 28, 1836, at Montpelier, his Virginia home where he had spent the last two decades of his life entertaining friends and travelers, lending support to public causes, most notably the American Colonization Society, and attempting to discharge the substantial debts accumulated in a lifetime devoted to public service.

The preeminent political theorist in the Revolutionary generation, Madison was no ivory-tower scholar. His delineation of republicanism came in essays, tracts, and articles addressed to immediate problems. His writings are marked by a tough-minded appraisal of human nature, a realistic grasp of the social and economic conditions underlying political issues and ideals, a calm elevated tone, and tightly-reasoned arguments that evinced an abiding faith in reason itself as the source of truth and equity. It is a mark of his genius that these products of the moment have proved timeless in their capacity to instruct and inspire.

WORKS: *Letters and Other Writings of James Madison*, ed. William C. Rives and Philip R. Fendall, 4 vols. (1865). *The Writings of James Madison*, ed. Gaillard Hunt, 9 vols. (1900–10). *The Papers of James Madison*, ed. William T. Hutchinson and William M. E. Rachal, 9 vols. to date (1962–). *The Mind of the Founder: Sources of the Political Thought of James Madison*, ed. Marvin Meyers (1973). *The Federalist [1787–88]*, ed. Jacob E. Cooke (1961). *Notes of Debates in the Federal Convention of 1787. Reported by James Madison [1840]*, ed. Adrienne Koch (1966).

JOHN K. NELSON
University of North Carolina
Chapel Hill

HAKI R. MAHUBUTI (1942–). Haki R. Mahubuti was born Don L. Lee on February 23, 1942, in Little Rock, Ark. While still young, he moved with his family to Chicago where he attended Dunbar Vocational High School. After graduation in 1960, Mahubuti entered the United States Army. Returning to civilian life and to Chicago in 1963, he accepted an apprentice curatorship at the DuSable Museum of African American History. To supplement the curatorship income, he worked as a clerk in the stock department of Montgomery Ward. Mahubuti remained at Du-Sable for four years, and during this time he held jobs as a Chicago post office clerk and as a junior executive at Spiegels.

Mahubuti's first volume of poems, *Think Black*, appeared from Detroit's Broadside Press in 1967. The next year Broadside released three additional Mahubuti volumes: *Black Pride, Back Again, Home*, and *One-Sided Shootout*. When Chicago's Third World Press published *For Black People (And Negroes, Too)* later that same year, Mahubuti firmly established a position as a forceful, innovative, articulate black poet. The increased black presence and militancy on the college campus combined with a general rise in political consciousness characteristic of the late 1960s caused him to be widely sought after as a teacher, lecturer, and reader. He taught at Chicago's Columbia College in 1968; was writer-in-residence at Cornell University during 1968–1969; poet-in-residence, Northeastern Illinois State College, 1968–1969; writer-in-residence, Morgan State College, 1972–1973; writer-in-residence, Howard University, 1971 to the present.

A prolific editor and anthologist as well as poet-essayist, Mahubuti serves on the editorial staff of *Black Books Bulletin, Black Pages Series*, and Third World Press, all of Chicago. In 1969 the National Endowment for the Arts awarded Mahubuti a creative writing grant. He received the Kuumbra Workshop Black Liberation Award in 1973.

By his own account, he writes for and to black people. An effective theorist for the Black Arts Movement, his poetry is intentionally conscious-raising. Mahubuti's concern throughout his work is the radicalization of Negroes into black people. His especial focus is on the form and content of a black life with black institutions and a black value system.

WORKS: *Think Black* (1967). *Black Pride* (1968). *Back Again, Home* (1968). *One-Sided Shootout* (1968). *For Black People (And Negroes, Too)* (1968). *Don't Cry, Scream* (1969). *We Walk the Way of the New World* (1970). *Directionscore* (1971). *Book of Life* (1971). *To Gwen with Love* (1971). "Rappin and Reading," recording (1971). Ed., *Dynamite Voices:*

Black Poets of the 1960's (1971). Ed., *From Plan to Planet: Life Studies: The World for African Minds and Institutions* (1973). Ed., *Enemies: The Clash of Races*, with Patricia L. Brown and Francis Ward (1974).

WALLACE R. PEPPERS
North Carolina A & T
State University
Greensboro

WILLIAM MARCH (1893–1954). The second of eleven children, William March Campbell was born on September 18, 1893, in Mobile, Ala., his parents, John Leonard Campbell and Susy March Campbell, being of Scottish and English ancestry respectively. His boyhood was spent in southern towns, with schooling brief and sporadic. At fourteen he went to work in the office of a lumber mill and at sixteen took a business course. In 1913–1914 he attended the University of Valparaiso, the following year studying law at the University of Alabama. Financially unable to continue at the university, he found employment in a New York law office as clerk and subpoena server.

Accepted in the U.S. Marine Corps on July 31, 1917, he was destined to see much action in France. Severely wounded several times, he received the Navy Cross, the Distinguished Service Cross, and the Croix de Guerre with palm.

Following his discharge from the service on August 31, 1918, he began a successful business career with the Waterman Steamship Company, and in 1938, a wealthy bachelor, he retired to devote himself to the writing. For some time he lived in New York, but in 1953 he bought a home in New Orleans. He died May 15, 1954.

March's fiction is curiously varied; it ranges from novels and stories of war, through tales of the rural South and the interlaced destinies of small-town people, to the descriptions of missionary life in the South Seas, culminating in a detailed dramatization of abnormal psychology. He infused it with an amused observation of humanity, a passionate loathing of religious cant, and a startling sensitivity to both the beauty and ugliness inherent in life. Throughout his entire life he was incapable of writing a dull page.

WORKS: *Company K* (1933). *Come in at the Door* (1934). *The Little Wife and Other Stories* (1935). *The Tallons* (1936). *Some Like Them Short* (1939). *The Looking Glass* (1943). *Trial Balance* (1945). *October Island* (1952). *The Bad Seed* (1954). *A William March Omnibus* (1956). *99 Fables* (1960).

ABIGAIL ANN HAMBLEN
Newton, Mass.

DONALD ROBERT PERRY MARQUIS (1878–1937). The humor of Don Marquis has delighted twentieth-century readers and his characters, archy the cockroach and mehitabel the alley cat, have become part of the American literary heritage.

Marquis was born in Walnut, Ill., on July 29, 1878, the son of James Stuart and Virginia Elizabeth Whitmore Marquis. At the turn of the century he was studying art at the Corcoran Gallery and reporting for the Washington (D.C.) *Times*. He also had begun acting with a traveling stock company.

In 1902 he became affiliated with the Atlanta *News* as associate editor working with John Temple Graves. By 1904 Marquis was serving as editorial writer for the Atlanta *Journal*. And, more important for his future ventures, he was assisting Joel Chandler Harris to edit *Uncle Remus' Magazine* until the publication ceased in 1909. This training gave him a vigorous background in the humor and light social criticism for which he was to become so well known.

Marquis moved to New York in 1910, and, until his death on December 29, 1937, remained in the metropolitan area. It was here, while writing his column "The Sun Dial" for the New York *Sun*, that archy and mehitabel were created. In addition to periodical publication, four archy books were issued, beginning with *archy and mehitabel* in 1927 and concluding with posthumous printing of *the lives of archy and mehitabel* (1940). His character the "Old Soak," created for the New York *Tribune* and inspired by prohibition policies, was also widely enjoyed.

Despite his successes as a journalist and humorist, Marquis remained frustrated because of public refusal to acknowledge his abilities as a serious poet and dramatist. Several volumes of poetry received little notice, and his plays, with the exception of "The Old Soak," suffered either negligible runs or were never produced.

His last years were spent in ill health and, by 1936, total incapacitation.

WORKS: *Danny's Own Story* (1912). *Dreams and Dust* (1915). *The Cruise of the Jasper B* (1916). *Hermione and Her Little Group of Serious Thinkers* (1916). *Prefaces* (1919). *Carter and Other People* (1921). *Noah an' Jonah an' Cap'n John Smith* (1921). *The Old Soak and Hail and Farewell* (1921). *Poems and Portraits* (1922). *The Revolt of the Oyster* (1922). *Sonnets to a Red-Haired Lady and Famous Love Affairs* (1922). *The Old Soak's History of the World* (1924). *The Dark Hours* (1924). *The Awakening and Other Poems* (1925). *The Almost Perfect State* (1927). *archy and mehitabel* (1927). *Love Sonnets of a Cave Man* (1928). *A Variety of People* (1929). *Off the Arm* (1930). *archy's life of mehitabel* (1933). *Chapters for the Orthodox* (1934). *Master of the Revels* (1934). *archy does his part* (1935). *Her Foot Is on the Brass Rail* (1935). *Sun Dial Time* (1936). *Sons of the Puritans* (1939). *the lives of archy and mehitabel* (1940).

ROBERT M. WILLINGHAM, JR.
University of Georgia
Athens

ALEXANDER BEAUFORT MEEK (1814–1865). The son of Anne McDowell and Samuel Mills Meek, who was a physician and Methodist minister, Alexander Beaufort Meek was born on July 17, 1814, in Columbia, S.C. When he was five, his parents moved to Tuscaloosa, Ala., where Meek grew up and attended the university (A.B., 1833; A.M., 1836). He was admitted to the bar in 1835, but he was interested enough in literature to write for a local paper, *Flag of the Union*, and, briefly in 1839, to edit his own magazine, the *Southren*. In the meantime he served in the Indian war in Florida and accepted appointments as attorney general of Alabama in 1836 and later as probate judge of Tuscaloosa County.

In 1841 he published *A Supplement to Aiken's Digest of the Laws of Alabama* and in 1845 went to Washington as assistant secretary of the treasury in the Polk administration. Subsequently he was appointed U.S. attorney for the Southern District of Alabama. In 1849 he became associate editor of the Mobile *Daily Register* and served two terms in the Alabama legislature, first in 1853–1855 when he was responsible for legislation establishing a public school system and again in 1859–1861 when he was speaker of the House. He was married twice—first to Mrs. Emma Donaldson Slatter and following her death in 1863, to Mrs. Eliza Jane Cannon in 1864. He died on November 1, 1865, in Columbus, Miss.

Meek's chief contributions to literature, aside from essays and addresses like "Americanism in Literature" (1844), are *The Red Eagle* (1855), a narrative poem; *Songs and Poems of the South* (1857), his only collection; and *Romantic Passages in Southwestern History* (1857), a miscellany of historical pieces. His failure to contribute more to literature, as *Russell's Magazine* pointed out in 1858, was the result of too much "society" and "partisan politics," factors all too common among gifted southerners.

WORKS: *A Supplement to Aiken's Digest of the Laws of Alabama* (1841). *The Red Eagle* (1855). *Songs and Poems of the South* (1857). *Romantic Passages in Southwestern History; Including Orations, Sketches, and Essays* (1857).

> RAYBURN S. MOORE
> University of Georgia
> Athens

HENRY LOUIS MENCKEN (1880–1956). H. L. Mencken was born on September 12, 1880, in Baltimore, Md., the son of August and Anna Abhau Mencken. His grandfather, Burkhardt Ludwig Mencken, had emigrated from Germany in 1848, and in the late nineteenth century the Menckens were still keenly aware and proud of their German heritage.

H. L. Mencken was educated in private and public schools in Baltimore, worked briefly in his father's cigar factory, and at the age of eighteen became a reporter on the Baltimore *Morning Herald*. In 1906 he joined the Baltimore Sunpapers, the newspapers for which he was to work—as reporter, columnist, and editor—for most of the rest of his life.

During his twenties and while he was a working newspaperman, Mencken produced a volume of verse and books on George Bernard Shaw and Friedrich Nietzsche. In 1908 he became literary editor of the *Smart Set*, and it was his monthly book review essays that first brought Mencken to national attention. He became co-editor of the *Smart Set* in 1914 and remained in that capacity until 1924. During this period Mencken championed such controversial writers as Theodore Dreiser and James Branch Cabell; he also led the fight against censorship and the genteel tradition in American letters and against provincialism, rotarianism, and mediocrity in American life. By the mid-1920s he was the nation's most notorious iconoclast, a role he continued to assume during his editorship of the *American Mercury* from 1924 to 1933. Reading Mencken's *Mercury* became the badge of sophistication to many young Americans, and Walter Lippmann wrote in 1926 that Mencken was "the most powerful personal influence on this whole generation of educated people."

Mencken's career declined after 1930 as he turned from preachers and pedagogues and instead directed his barbs at Franklin D. Roosevelt and the New Deal. He continued to write essays and volumes on many subjects, and continued to expand his philological work, *The American Language*, the first version of which he had published in 1918. Mencken died in Baltimore on January 29, 1956.

Mencken was one of the greatest American essayists and stylists and one of the most original, irreverent, and fearless of American social critics. His best and most representative work is included in the six volumes of *Prejudices* published between 1919 and 1927. One of these essays, "The Sahara of the Bozart," an indictment of southern intellectual and literary sterility, probably occasioned a more hostile response than any other work of Mencken. It also inspired young southerners such as W. J. Cash, Gerald W. Johnson, and Paul Green, who themselves began to echo Mencken.

In social and political thought Mencken was basically a Social Darwinist; he prized individual freedom and was critical of government intervention and reform. He was suspicious of causes and crusaders; yet the irony in Mencken's life is that he himself became a leading crusader for the liberation of American letters and American thought.

WORKS: *Ventures into Verse* (1903). *George Bernard Shaw: His Plays* (1905). *The Philosophy of Friedrich Nietzsche* (1908). *The Artist* (1912). *A Book of Burlesques* (1916). *A Little Book in C-Major* (1916). *A Book of Prefaces* (1917). *In Defense of Women* (1917). *Damn—A Book of Calumny* (1917). *The American Language* (1918 and later revisions). *Prejudices First Series* (1919); *Second Series* (1920); *Third Series* (1922); *Fourth Series* (1924); *Fifth Series* (1926); *Sixth Series* (1927). *Notes on Democracy* (1926). *James Branch Cabell* (1927). *Treatise on the Gods* (1930). *Making a President* (1932). *Treatise on Right and Wrong* (1934). *Happy Days* (1940). *Newspaper Days* (1941). *Heathen Days* (1943). *A Christmas Story* (1946). *A Mencken Chrestomathy* (1949). *Minority Report: H. L. Mencken's Notebooks* (1956).

FRED HOBSON
University of Alabama
Tuscaloosa

CAROLINE MILLER (1903–). Caroline Miller was born Caroline Pafford in Waycross, Ga., on August 26, 1903. Her parents were Elias Moore and Levy Zan Hall Pafford. On August 11, 1921, Caroline Pafford married her high school English teacher, William Dews Miller. The Millers had a son, William Dews, Jr., born on May 20, 1927, and twin boys, George and Harvey, born on March 13, 1929. For a time the Millers lived in Baxley, Ga., where Caroline Miller, in addition to child-bearing and other wifely responsibilities, wrote her prize-winning novel, *Lamb in His Bosom* (1933).

Lamb in His Bosom, the story of rural life in Georgia from revolutionary days to the middle of the nineteenth century, won the Pulitzer Prize for Fiction in 1934. It also won the *Prix Femina Americain* in 1935. The rewards and notoriety of her successful authorship proved to be too much for her marriage, and she and her first husband were divorced in 1936. She later married Clyde H. Ray, Jr., of Waynesville, N.C., where they reside.

Miller continued to write, publishing several short stories in *Pictorial Review* and *Ladies Home Journal*. Her second novel,

Lebanon (1944), is a romance set in the Georgia lowlands in the decades prior to the Civil War.

WORKS: *Lamb in His Bosom* (1933). *Lebanon* (1944).

LOUISE BLACKWELL
Florida A. & M. University
Tallahassee

HEATHER ROSS MILLER (1939–). Heather Ross Miller was born on September 15, 1939, at Albemarle, N.C., the daughter of Fred E. and Geneva Smith Ross. Her family, known as the "writing Rosses," includes her father, a novelist; her sister, Eleanor Ross Taylor, a poet and wife of Peter Taylor; and another sister, Jean Ross Justice, a fiction writer and wife of poet Donald Justice; and an uncle, James Ross, a writer of fiction.

Miller received the B.A. in English and Writing *magna cum laude* in 1961 from the University of North Carolina at Greensboro, where she studied with Randall Jarrell. She earned her M.A. there in 1973 and did postgraduate work in Modern Drama and Cinema at the University of London. Among her awards and honors are a Woodrow Wilson Fellowship (1961); the National Association of Independent Schools Award for her first novel, *The Edge of the Woods* (1964); the Sir Walter Raleigh Prize for Fiction for her second novel, *Tenants of the House* (1966); the Oscar Arnold Young Cup for her first poetry collection, *The Wind Southerly* (1968); and two creative writing fellowships from the National Council on the Arts.

Miller currently resides in Badin, N.C., with her husband Clyde H. Miller, whom she married February 4, 1960, and their two children, Melissa and Kirk. She is writer-in-residence and instructor in English and communications at Stanly Technical Institute, Albemarle, N.C. She also lectures widely, reads her poetry in colleges and universities, and edits *Uhwarrie Review*. She was recently appointed consultant in fiction for Poets and Writers, Inc.

Works in progress include "Children, Gods, and Men," a collection of essays and memoirs, including some pieces on Randall

Jarrell; "California Run-Around," a novel; and "Aluminum," a book-length poem. Miller's popularity in France is indicated by the translations of two of her books and several stories into that language.

WORKS: *The Edge of the Woods* (1964). *Tenants of the House* (1966). *The Wind Southerly* (1967). *Gone a Hundred Miles* (1968). *Horse Horse Tyger Tyger* (1973). *A Spiritual Divorce and Other Stories* (1974). *A Shooting Gallery* (1976). *Confessions of a Champeen Fire-Baton Twirler* (1976).

LOTTIE H. SWINK
Hickory, N.C.

VASSAR MILLER (1924–). Vassar Miller was born on July 19, 1924, in Houston, Tex., the daughter of Jessie Gustavus and Vassar Morrison Miller. When she was a year old, her mother died and her father married Marcelle Loggins. A victim of cerebral palsy, Miller was educated by her parents at home until she entered the sixth grade. She later attended the University of Houston, where she received the B.S. in English in 1947 and an M.A. in 1952.

Miller started writing poetry seriously in high school, most of it religious. (She is an Episcopalian.) She began publishing regularly in the 1950s, and in 1956 her chapbook, *Adam's Footprint*, was published by the *New Orleans Poetry Journal*. Since then she has devoted her time to writing poetry and teaching. She has taught creative writing at St. John's School in Houston. Miller is a member of the Texas Institute of Letters and in 1963 was Poet Laureate of Texas. Three of her books have received awards from the Texas Institute of Letters.

Miller's early poems were all deeply religious in themes, somber in tone, and conventional in form. As a novice she was obviously influenced by John Donne, Gerard Manley Hopkins, and George Herbert—though her work cannot be called derivative. Her approach to poetry can be clearly seen in the following quotation: "Poetry, like all art, has a trinitarian function: creative, redemptive, and sanctifying. It is creative because it takes the raw materials of fact and feeling and makes them into that which is neither fact nor feeling. It is redemptive because it can transform the pain and ugliness of life into joy and beauty. It is sanctifying because it thus gives the transitory at least a relative form and meaning. Hence poetry, whether avowedly so or not, is always religious; it is akin to prayer, an act of love."

Her poetry in the 1960s began to show more variety in tones and themes as she moved away from traditional lyrics into open forms. Although she remains a religious poet, her themes are often humanistic.

WORKS: *Adam's Footprint* (1956). *Wage War on Silence* (1960). *My Bones Being Wiser: Poems* (1963). *Onions and Roses* (1968). *If I Could Sleep Deeply Enough* (1974).

GUY OWEN
North Carolina State University
Raleigh

WILLIAM MILLS (1935–). William Mills was born on June 17, 1935, in Hattiesburg, Miss. His father, William W. Mills, Sr., and his mother, Frances Finney Mills, now reside in Baton Rouge, La., where the poet spent his youth. The eldest of five sons, Mills learned early to revere the family, southern style—that is, to respect his forebears and to honor man's obligation to his fellows. His long poem, "Our Fathers at Corinth," captures this still-vital theme in a manner reminiscent of Allen Tate's "Ode to the Confederate Dead."

From 1955 to 1957 Mills served in the U.S. Army Security Agency, chiefly in Kyoto, Japan. Shortly after his military service, he studied formally and informally in Germany—in Tübingen, in Munich, and at the Goethe Institute in Blaubeuren. In 1961 Mills married Sylvia Richard; that marriage was dissolved in 1973. Mills continued his education at Louisiana State University, receiving the Ph.D. degree in 1972. His doctoral research led to a critical study of the poetry of Howard Nemerov, *The Stillness in Moving Things* (1975).

Mills has had a varied career—serving briefly as an itinerant Methodist preacher, working on pipelines and in refineries both here and in Central America, as well as raising cattle for several years in Louisiana. His poetry immediately informs his readers that these words come from a man who has been attentive to the creature world and who feels a deep kinship with it. Mills has also spent some years teaching in various colleges and universities. On three occasions he has served as visiting poet at the University of Arkansas in Fayetteville.

With James Whitehead, Mills was literary editor of an exhibition, *The Contemporary American South*, sponsored by the U.S. Information Agency. This exhibition, the first American cultural exhibit to enter Red China, toured Europe and the Near and Far East during the 1977–1978 academic year. In the spring of 1978, Mills read and lectured in Hungary, Russia, Lithuania, Latvia, Finland, Turkey—concluding at the American Academy in Rome.

Presently, Mills directs the graduate poetry workshop at Oklahoma State University in Stillwater. His writing career has encompassed both short and long fiction, as well as nonfictional prose, though his chief achievements have been in poetry. His poems have been translated into other languages, and several have been anthologized.

WORKS: *Watch for the Fox* (1974). *The Stillness in Moving Things: The World of Howard Nemerov* (1975). *I Know a Place* (1976). Introduction to photographic collection, *Louisiana Cajuns* (1977). *Stained Glass* (1978).

> BEVERLY JARRETT
> Louisiana State University
> Baton Rouge

EDWIN MIMS (1872–1959). Edwin Mims was born in Richmond, Ark., on May 27, 1872; his parents were Andrew Jackson and Cornelia Williamson Mims, devout Methodists. He attended the Webb School in Bell Buckle, Tenn., before entering Vanderbilt University where he studied under William Malone Baskervill and received an A.B. (1892) and an A.M. (1893). From 1892 to 1894 he was assistant in English at Vanderbilt. In 1894 Mims took a position as professor of English at Trinity College (later Duke University), where he remained until 1909, except for his absence beginning in 1896 when he went to Cornell University to study for his Ph.D., which he received in 1900. Mims married Clara Puryear on June 29, 1898, and they became the parents of two sons and two daughters. While at Trinity, Mims met Walter Hines Page, who became for him the quintessential new southerner. In 1905 Mims published his biography of Sidney Lanier in which he was much more concerned with Lanier the prophet of the New South than Lanier the Confederate soldier. From 1906 to 1909 he was joint editor of the *South Atlantic Quarterly*. In 1909 Mims went to the University of North Carolina at Chapel Hill as professor of English, remaining for three years.

In 1912 Mims went to Vanderbilt University to be chairman of the Department of English (1912–1942), and later chairman of the Division of Humanities (1928–1942). It was in that capacity that he was associated with the Nashville Fugitive-Agrarians, for whom he was often an adversary since his views about the South and its future were quite different from theirs. His ideas were enthusiastically propounded in *The Advancing South: Stories of Progress and Reaction* (1926). Mims's espousal of industrialism was not without qualification, for he insisted that it should not come "at the expense of the grace and charm of life," and throughout his life he was a part-time lay preacher and Sunday school teacher.

During 1935–1936 Mims was Carnegie visiting professor at five British universities. He was named emeritus professor at Vanderbilt in 1942. He remained very active during his later years and was visiting professor at Emory University from 1951 to 1954. He died in his 88th year on September 15, 1959.

WORKS: Ed., Thomas Carlyle, *Essay on Burns* (1903). *The University in the South* (1903). *Sidney Lanier* (1905). Ed., *Southern Prose and Poetry for Schools*, with Bruce R. Payne (1910). Ed., *History of Southern Fiction*, Vol. VIII of *The South in the Building of the Nation* (1910). Ed., *Stevenson's Inland Voyage and Travels with a Donkey* (1911). Ed., *The Van Dyke Book, Selected from the Writings of Henry Van Dyke* (1914). Intro., Thomas Carlyle, *Past and Present* (1918). *A Handbook for Interracial Committees* (1920). *The Advancing South: Stories of Progress and*

Reaction (1926). *God and the New Knowledge*, with Oswald E. Brown and James H. Kirkland (1926). *Adventurous America: A Study of Contemporary Life and Thought* (1929). *Chancellor Kirkland of Vanderbilt* (1940). *Great Writers as Interpreters of Religion* (1945). *History of Vanderbilt University* (1946). *The Christ of the Poets* (1948).

RANDALL G. PATTERSON
Belhaven College
Jackson, Miss.

BENJAMIN BLAKE MINOR (1818–1905). Benjamin Blake Minor, known today chiefly for his editorship of the *Southern Literary Messenger* from 1843 through 1847, was born on October 21, 1818, in Tappahannock, Va. His family was a distinguished one, with plantation gentry on both sides. Unusually well educated for his time, Minor attended the University of Virginia for two years, then the College of William and Mary, where he studied under the famous judge and novelist, Nathaniel Beverley Tucker.

Minor's professional career began with the practice of law, but finding letters more to his taste he purchased the *Southern Literary Messenger* in 1843. In December, 1845, Minor purchased from William Gilmore Simms the *Southern and Western Monthly Magazine and Review* of Charleston, S.C., and merged it with his own journal, but he continued as editor and proprietor only until October, 1847. The most notable feature of Minor's editorship was his encouragement of southern writing, particularly in history.

After selling his magazine to John R. Thompson, Minor became primarily an educator, first as principal of the Virginia Female Institute in Staunton, Va., and then as founder and director of a girls' school in Richmond. On July 4, 1860, he became the president of the University of Missouri, but the university was closed in 1862. After several years as teacher, public lecturer, and life insurance representative in Missouri, Minor returned to Richmond in 1889, where he remained until his death on August 1, 1905.

Although Minor edited George Wythe's *Decisions of Cases in Virginia by the High Court of Chancery*, the only book he wrote was his history of the *Southern Literary Messenger*, a rambling account of the journal's editors, contributors, and contents.

WORKS: The *Southern Literary Messenger 1834–1864* (1905).

> ROBERT D. JACOBS
> Georgia State University
> Atlanta

JOSEPH MITCHELL (1908–). Joseph Mitchell was born on July 27, 1908, on a tobacco and cotton farm near Fairmont, N.C. He traces his ancestry back to English and Scotch-Irish farmers who settled in eastern North Carolina before the Revolutionary War. After graduating from high school, he attended the University of North Carolina for four years, leaving without a degree in 1929. While still a student he wrote for the Durham *Herald* and published his first stories in *American Caravan*. Having published a feature on a tobacco auction in the New York *Herald-Tribune*, he moved to New York City, where he became a newspaper reporter. In 1931 he married Therese Dagny Jacobsen; they have two daughters.

After working as a reporter for the *Herald-Tribune*, he spent seven years on the *World-Telegram*. Since 1938 Mitchell has been on the staff of the *New Yorker*, where he specializes in profiles of misfits and outcasts or unusual groups. For example, he has written about the fishmongers in Fulton market, assorted Bowery characters, a band of gypsies, and a group of Mohawk Indians who became construction workers on the skyscrapers of New York City. His aim has often been to show so-called "little people" as larger-than-life figures. He has depicted, in his words, "the usual in the unusual" in such works as in his graphic book on the New York harbor, containing six of his *New Yorker* profiles.

His first book, *My Ears Are Bent*, was a collection of his best newspaper features. In his most popular work, *McSorley's Wonderful Saloon*, he went beyond reporting, subtly blending reportage with the archetypal and mythic. In the "Black Ankle" stories of this collection—"I Blame It All on Mama," "Uncle Dockery and the Independent Bull" and "The Downfall of Fascism in Black Ankle Country"—he employed tall tales, folk speech, and folk motifs which he learned as a boy in Robeson County. He has continued to deepen each of his later books by the use of poetic symbolism and folk motifs, notably *Old Mr. Flood* and *Joe Gould's Secret*. In his *New Yorker* profiles he has perfected what has been called "the urban tall-tale pastoral." Mitchell was elected to the National Institute of Arts and Letters in 1970.

WORKS: *My Ears Are Bent* (1938). *McSorley's Wonderful Saloon* (1943). *Old Mr. Flood* (1948). *The Bottom of the Harbor* (1959). *Apologies to the Iroquois*, with Edmund Wilson (1960). *Joe Gould's Secret* (1965).

GUY OWEN
North Carolina State University
Raleigh

MARGARET MITCHELL (1900–1949). Margaret Munnerlyn Mitchell Marsh was born on November 8, 1900, in Atlanta. Her Irish Catholic mother, Maybelle Stephens, helped found the woman's suffrage movement in Georgia; her father, Eugene, a lawyer and for a time president of the Atlanta Historical Society, was a fifth-generation Atlantan. As a child Margaret Mitchell read voluminously, listened to the tales of the Civil War and Reconstruction, and wrote stories and plays, keeping a running notebook of ideas.

While attending Atlanta's Washington Seminary (1914–1918), she finished a novel, "The Big Four," about girls in a boarding school, and "Little Sister," the story of a girl who, after hearing her older sister being raped, murders the rapist. Both manuscripts are now lost. In 1918 Mitchell entered Smith College intending to become a doctor, but her mother died of influenza during the epidemic of that year, and in June, Mitchell left college to return to Atlanta and run the family home for her father and her brother, Stephens. Eugene Mitchell wanted his daughter to become a society matron, so she made her debut in 1921, and in 1922 she married Berrien K. Upshaw. They were divorced in 1924.

Mitchell went to work in 1923 as a reporter for the Atlanta *Journal*. During this period she began a novel concerning adolescent life in the 1920s and completed a novelette, "Ropa Carmagin," about the love of a southern white girl for a mulatto man. These manuscripts are also lost.

An advertising executive, John Marsh, who had been best man in her first wedding became her husband in 1925, and soon after their marriage she quit her job at the *Journal*. In 1926, after a year of research, she began writing *Gone with the Wind*, working on it at home for three years. Apparently she did not consider it publishable, and by 1932 she had manila envelopes containing the manuscript stacked in her closets. In April, 1935, at the insistence of a friend at Macmillan's, she showed the novel to Harold S. Latham, editor, who accepted it in July. She spent the following year rewriting, editing, and checking the historical accuracy of the work.

Gone with the Wind sold a million copies during the first six months of its publication. Most of the reviews were favorable, and the novel became a popular sensation. For the rest of her life Margaret Mitchell was absorbed in what she called "cleaning up after *GWTW*." The troubles included international copyright difficulties, contractual misunderstandings, plagiarism cases, thousands of personal letters and calls, impostors, rumors, and requests for articles and appearances. In 1937 she received the annual award of the American Booksellers Association and the Pulitzer Prize; in 1939 Smith College conferred an honorary master's degree upon her, and the movie was released, winning ten Academy awards.

During World War II, Mitchell worked for the war effort; she also nursed her ill father. John Marsh suffered a heart attack in 1945, and she cared for him at home for several months. In 1949 she wrote to *Harper's* to correct a statement that she would never write again, but on August 11 she was struck by an automobile and she died on August 16. She is buried in Atlanta at Oakland Cemetery.

WORKS: *Gone with the Wind* (1936). *Margaret Mitchell's "Gone with the Wind" Letters, 1936–1949* (1976).

ANNE GOODWYN JONES
Allegheny College
Meadville, Pa.

MARION MONTGOMERY, JR. (1925–). Marion Hoyt Montgomery was born in Thomaston, Ga., on April 16, 1925, to Marion Hoyt and Lottie May Jenkins Montgomery. After graduation from Robert E. Lee Institute in Thomaston, he served, 1943–1946, in the field artillery in Europe with the 16th Armored Division and, during occupation, the 1st Division. After his military discharge he attended the University of Georgia, receiving an A.B. in 1950 and an M.A. in 1953. In 1951 he married Dorothy Dean Carlisle of Camilla, Ga., with whom he has five children.

From 1951 to 1953, while completing his M.A., he was assistant director of the University of Georgia Press and business manager of the *Georgia Review*. After one year as instructor at Darlington School for Boys, Rome, Ga., he returned to the university as instructor in English in 1954. On leave from Georgia, he attended the Writers Workshop of the State University of Iowa from 1956 to 1958, on a Sarah Moss Grant for the first year. While there he was assistant editor then managing editor of the *Western Review*. Since then he has taught composition, creative writing, and literature, primarily twentieth-century American poetry and lyric poetry, at the University of Georgia, where he is now professor of English. He lives in nearby Crawford, Ga.

In addition to his books, Montgomery has published over 80 articles on writing, teaching, and literature, principally that of Flannery O'Connor, Eliot, Pound, and Wordsworth, and 27 short stories. His poems have appeared in almost 100 periodicals, and his criticism, poetry, and fiction in numerous anthologies. His awards include Harper and Brothers' Eugene Saxton Memorial Award, the *Carleton Miscellany*'s first Centennial Award for Poetry, the University of Georgia's M. G. Michael Award, the Georgia Writers Association's Award in Fiction and in Poetry, and

Georgia Southern University's Georgia Authors Award. He has lectured and read widely in the South.

WORKS: *Dry Lightning* (1960). *The Wondering of Desire* (1962). *Darrell* (1964). *Stones from the Rubble* (1965). *Ye Olde Bluebird* (1967). *The Gull and Other Georgia Scenes* (1969). *Ezra Pound: A Critical Essay* (1970). *T. S. Eliot: An Essay on the American Magus* (1970). *The Reflective Journey Toward Order: Essays on Dante, Wordsworth, Eliot and Others* (1973). *Fugitive* (1974).

WILLIAM M. MOSS
Wake Forest University
Winston-Salem, N.C.

JOHN TROTWOOD MOORE (1858–1929). John Moore (he added Trotwood after reading Dickens), the son of John and Emily Billingslea Moore, was born in Marion, Ala., on August 26, 1858. Graduating from Howard College in 1878, Moore worked for a newspaper and taught school in Alabama before moving to Columbia, Tenn., in 1885. Here in the bluegrass region of middle Tennessee and at Nashville, where he later moved, Moore lived for the remainder of his life.

In Tennessee, Moore began rearing blooded livestock and, like his neighbors, became interested in the development of a harness racing horse that would pace instead of trot. He became a regular contributor to the Chicago *Horse Review*, patterned after the New York *Spirit of the Times*. By introducing original stories and verse among his comments on the Tennessee pacing horse, Moore moved from magazine columnist to fiction writer. His first collection, *Songs and Stories of Tennessee* (1897), contains accounts of his famous Negro character, Uncle Wash, and his best known racing story, "Ole Mistis."

Between 1897 and 1911 Moore published eight books. The best of these is *The Bishop of Cottontown* (1906), which is one of the early, more realistic portrayals of child labor in the South.

From 1905 through 1910, Moore edited a literary magazine first known as *Trotwood's Monthly* and later as the *Taylor-Trotwood Magazine*. In 1919 he became state librarian for Tennessee, a position he held until his death on May 10, 1929. His best-known historical novel, *Hearts of Hickory: A Story of Andrew Jackson and the War of 1812*, was published in 1926.

Following the death of his first wife, Moore married Mary Brown Daniel on June 13, 1900. On September 11, 1903, their son, Austin Merrill, destined to become a psychiatrist and poet, was born. The Moores became the parents of twin daughters on April 11, 1907.

WORKS: *Songs and Stories from Tennessee* (1897). *A Summer Hymnal: A Romance of Tennessee* (1901). *The Bishop of Cottontown: A Story of the Southern Cotton Mills* (1906). *Ole Mistis, and Other Songs and Stories from Tennessee* (1909). *The Old Cotton Gin* (1910). *Uncle Wash: His Stories* (1910). *The Gift of the Grass: Being the Autobiography of a Famous Racing Horse* (1911). *Jack Ballington, Forester* (1911). *Hearts of Hickory: A Story of Andrew Jackson and the War of 1812* (1926). *Tom's Last Forage* (1926).

CLAUD B. GREEN
Clemson University
Clemson, S.C.

MERRILL MOORE (1903–1957). Austin Merrill Moore was born on September 11, 1903, in Columbia, Tenn. His father, John Trotwood Moore, was a writer, editor, and state librarian of Tennessee; his mother, Mary Brown Daniel Moore, was a music teacher who succeeded her husband as state librarian upon his death in 1929. The family moved to Nashville in 1907, where the father began editing the *Taylor-Trotwood Magazine*. Moore attended Montgomery Bell Academy, a private preparatory school in Nashville, and in 1920 entered Vanderbilt University. He joined the Fugitive group in 1922, while still an undergraduate, and contributed prolifically to its magazine during its four years of publication. He spent the summer of 1923 in Germany, and in 1924, upon graduation from the college, he entered Vanderbilt Medical School, completing his M.D. in 1928. After a year's internship in Nashville, he was appointed in 1929 as neurological house officer at the Boston City Hospital. He lived most of the rest of his life in Boston, except for a period of military service during World War II. He studied psychiatry with Dr. William Herman (1931) and Dr. Hanns Sach (1934–1938). He was awarded a Commonwealth Research Fellowship at Harvard Medical School and in 1950 began teaching there. He also maintained a private psychiatric practice in Boston (Edwin Arlington Robinson was among his patients). Moore died in Boston on September 20, 1957.

Moore successfully combined a professional career as a psychiatrist with an energetic amateur career as a poet. At the Fugitive meetings, Moore often produced a sheaf of poems when other poets were laboring to perfect a single poem; he said he found it easier to write a new poem than to revise an old one. He kept up his sonneteering habit all his life, writing more than 50,000 altogether. His sonnets are outwardly conventional, all in fourteen lines, but otherwise quite unconventional, since he preferred a loose free verse to traditional rhyming patterns. Moore's sonnets are always frank and refreshing, and if few of them are more than momentarily arresting, of these few it can be said, in his friend Allen Tate's words, "They have, at their best, a fluency, an ease, and a subtlety of statement which gives them a definite place in contemporary poetry."

WORKS: *The Noise That Time Makes*, foreword by John Crowe Ransom (1929). *It Is a Good Deal Later Than You Think* (1934). *Six Sides to a Man* (1935). *Poems from the Fugitive, 1922–26* (1936). *Sonnets from the Fugitive, 1922–26* (1937). *15 Poems from the Fugitive, 1922–26, and One Additional Poem: Ego* (1938). *Sonnets from New Directions*, preface by William Carlos Williams (1938). *M: One Thousand Autobiographical Sonnets* (1938). *The Fugitive: Clippings and Comment about the Magazine and the Members of the Group that Published It* (1939). *Clinical Sonnets* (1949). *Illegitimate Sonnets* (1950). *Case Record from a Sonnetorium* (1951). *More Clinical Sonnets* (1953). *Homo Sonetticus Moorensis*, twelve sonnets by Moore with Italian trans. Alexander Bode (1955). *Poems of American Life*, intro. Louis Untermeyer (1958). *The Dance of Death* (1959).

WILLIAM PRATT
Miami University
Oxford, Ohio

VIRGINIA MOORE (1903–). A native Virginian, Virginia Moore was born on July 11, 1903, the daughter of John Fitzallen and Ethel Daniel Moore. She received her education from Brenau School for girls, Hollins College (A.B., 1923), and Columbia University, where she earned an M.A. in English (1924), and a Ph.D. in philosophy of religion (1952). She married Louis Untermeyer, the poet, in 1926, but was divorced two years later; they had one child, a son, John Moore Untermeyer (b. 1928). Moore married John Jefferson Hudgins in 1945. Currently she lives in Scottsville, Va., where she has resided most of her life.

Moore's dozen books demonstrate considerable diversity. Her three volumes of poetry and one novel were all written relatively early in her career, before 1937. These show a pronounced visionary or mystical strain, foreshadowing the affinity which in the foreword to her *The Unicorn: William Butler Yeats' Search for Reality* (1954) she claims to share with "Yeats' belief in a supersensible world and the possibility of true vision." Moore's study of Yeats provides one of the earliest and fullest discussions of Yeats's religious doctrinal sources, calling attention to his lifelong fascination with Eastern and Western philosophy. In her early biography, *The Life and Eager Death of Emily Bronte* (1936), Moore asserts that the ultimate purpose of biography "is not only to relate facts, but to transmit personality . . . to differentiate, as it were, a soul." Such belief likewise controls her numerous books on Virginia history, often anecdotal studies, which capture the unique character of her region.

Moore remains an active writer, currently bringing to completion a study of James and Dolley Madison which is under contract for publication. She also admits to having written in the last few years over 200 unpublished poems.

WORKS: *Not Poppy* (1926). *Girls Who Did: Stories of Real Girls and their Careers*, with H. J. Ferris (1927; rev., 1937). *Rising Wind* (1928). *Sweet Water and Bitter* (1928). *Distinguished Women Writers* (1934). *Homer's Golden Chain* (1936). *The Life and Eager Death of Emily Bronte* (1936). *Virginia is a State of Mind* (1942). *Ho for Heaven! Man's Changing Attitude Toward Death* (1946). *The Unicorn: William Butler Yeats'*

Search for Reality (1954). *Whole World, Stranger* (1957). *Scottsville on the James: An Informal History* (1969).

JAMES D. WILSON
Georgia State University
Atlanta

BERRY MORGAN (1919–). Short story writer and novelist, Berry Morgan was born on May 20, 1919, in Port Gibson, Miss., to John Marshall and Bess Berry Taylor Brumfield. Although she only began writing in her 30s, she recalls telling stories, as a child, to amuse herself and later on feeling the impulse to write. She studied at Loyola University in 1947 and at Tulane University from 1948 to 1949. Married (now divorced) and the mother of four children, she spent her time at Albena plantation (near Port Gibson), a New Orleans home, and a Virginia farm.

Her literary career began in the early 1950s when she completed a long mystery story which was rejected and later abandoned. At 43 she began writing again. In 1966 she won the Houghton Mifflin Fellowship. Her first novel, *Pursuit*, appeared that year as the first of a sequence called *Certain Shadows*, about a cross-section of people in mythical King County, Miss. *Pursuit* depicts Ned Ingles, driven to deter the ruin of his illegitimate son, and the son tortured by the contrary calls of the flesh and the priesthood. Many of her stories have appeared in the *New Yorker*; "Andrew" was included in *The Best American Short Stories of 1967*. Morgan became writer-in-residence at Northeast Louisiana University in 1972. She won another Houghton Mifflin Fellowship in 1974. *The Mystic Adventures of Roxie Stoner* in 1974 presented a series of linked stories told from the point of view of Roxie Stoner, who worked for a while on the Ingles Plantation. The better stories are those describing her activities at the state mental hospital. Berry Morgan is teaching and working on "Fornika Creek," the third volume of the *Certain Shadows* sequence.

WORKS: *Pursuit* (1966). *The Mystic Adventures of Roxie Stoner* (1974).

THOMAS BONNER, JR.
Xavier University
New Orleans, La.

WILLIE MORRIS (1934–). Willie Morris was born on November 29, 1934, in Jackson, Miss., to Henry Rae and Marion Weaks Morris. His father's family had come from Tennessee; his mother's family had played a prominent role in early Mississippi politics.

The Morrises moved in 1935 to Yazoo City, Miss., the Delta town on which Willie Morris drew heavily in his later literary work. After attending the town's public schools, Morris was educated at the University of Texas (A.B. 1956) and, as a Rhodes Scholar, at Oxford University (B.A. 1959, M.A. 1960). He served as editor of the *Texas Observer* from 1960 to 1962, and joined *Harper's Magazine* in 1963. As editor-in-chief of *Harper's* from 1967 to 1971, he particularly cultivated southern writers of promise and published sensitive treatments of southern life during a period of crisis and change.

Morris' most important book has been his autobiography, *North Toward Home* (1967), a story of growing up in the Mississippi Delta, of student days in Texas and at Oxford, and of his early days as an editor in New York. In the book, Morris attempts to come to terms with his southern past and also speaks candidly and often critically of Texas politics and New York literary life. *North Toward Home* is in the broad tradition of southern self-examination, yet is a far more personal and autobiographical account than most works in this tradition.

Morris' lone novel to date has been *The Last of the Southern Girls*, the story of an Arkansas belle in Washington, D.C.

WORKS: Ed., *The South Today: 100 Years After Appomattox* (1965). *North Toward Home* (1967). *Yazoo: Integration in a Deep South Town* (1971). *The Last of the Southern Girls* (1973). *A Southern Album: Recollections of Some People and Places and Times Gone By*, with Irwin Glusker (1975).

FRED HOBSON
University of Alabama
Tuscaloosa

MONTROSE JONAS MOSES (1878–1934). A drama critic and editor, Montrose J. Moses was born in New York City on September 2, 1878, to Montefiore and Rose Jonas Moses. Of Alabama lineage, Moses' parents moved to Montgomery during his childhood, and there Moses received his early education. Later he returned to New York and graduated from the College of the City of New York in 1899. After graduation, Moses first served on the editorial staff of the *Literary Digest,* 1900–1902, and then as dramatic editor of the *Reader,* 1903–1907; the *Independent,* 1908–1918; the *Book News Monthly,* 1908–1918; and the *Bellman,* 1910–1919. From 1919 until his death on March 29, 1934, Moses worked as a free-lance writer.

In addition to his frequent contributions to magazines, Moses wrote, edited, or translated numerous books on drama. He compiled collections of British and continental plays, which illustrated historical developments in drama, and wrote studies of two European playwrights. Especially interested in the history of his own nation's stage, Moses compiled several collections of American plays, helped edit a historical anthology of theater criticism, and wrote biographies of American stage personalities. He also published a survey of American drama which discussed prominent playwrights and the effect social conditions had on the theater of their time. Seeking to interest youngsters in the stage, Moses edited three collections of plays for children. Many of Moses' books appeared in several editions, and some have recently been reissued.

Early in his career, Moses put aside the study of drama long enough to write a historical survey of southern literature. Including oratory, poetry, and fiction, Moses focused on the influence social and economic conditions during each period of the South's history had on its literature. Published in 1910, *The Literature of the South* remained the standard treatment of its subject until succeeded by Jay B. Hubbell's *The South in American Literature* 44 years later.

WORKS: *Famous Actor-Families in America* (1906). *Children's Books and Reading* (1907). *Henrik Ibsen: The Man and His Plays* (1908). *The Litera-*

ture of the South (1910). *The American Dramatist* (1911). *Maurice Maeterlinck: A Study* (1911). *The Life of Heinrich Conried* (1916). *The Fabulous Forrest: The Record of an American Actor* (1929).

GAINES M. FOSTER
University of North Carolina
Chapel Hill

ROBERT MUNFORD III (*ca.* 1737–1783). Robert Munford III was born about 1737, the son of Robert Munford II and Anna Beverley Munford. After the death of his father in 1745 his uncle, William Beverley, took him to Blandfield, then in 1750 to England for his education. In 1756 he returned to Virginia and studied law with his cousin Peyton Randolph in Williamsburg. During the French and Indian War, in 1758, he raised a company to serve with William Byrd III and took part in the capture of Fort Duquesne. In 1761 he married his cousin Anna Beverley and settled down to live as a gentleman planter in Lunenburg (subsequently Mecklenburg) County. He grew tobacco and became a vestryman of the Church of England, a justice of the peace, a member of the county commission, an officer in the county militia, and (in 1765) a member of the House of Burgesses.

From such activities, from his playgoing in England and Williamsburg, and from his reading and observation grew his *The Candidates*, a farce written after 1770 in traditional English style but incorporating colonial materials. Unhappy when the Revolution broke out, he soon devoted his energies to the American cause, commanding the Mecklenburg militia and representing the county in the Virginia House of Delegates in 1779 and 1780. About this time he wrote America's first full-length comedy, *The Patriots*, a play in which he adapted the multiple plot and the comic techniques of the English stage to the Revolutionary scene in Virginia. Late in 1780 he returned to his home, to command the militia of three southside counties in the campaign which culminated at Guilford Court House, in 1781. Soon thereafter Munford resigned most of his responsibilities, made provision for his family, and, in December, 1783, died.

WORKS: *A Collection of Plays and Poems by the late Col. Robert Munford of Mecklenburg County, in the State of Virginia* (1798).

RODNEY M. BAINE
University of Georgia
Athens

MARY NOAILLES MURFREE (1850–1922). Under the pseudonym Charles Egbert Craddock, Mary Noailles Murfree created the foremost body of local color fiction about Tennessee mountaineers. She descended from four generations of pioneers, landed proprietors, lawyers, and legislators who established and lent their patronymic to the towns of Murfreesboro in North Carolina and Tennessee. Born on January 24, 1850, at Grantland, the family plantation on Stone's River, near Murfreesboro, Tenn., Murfree absorbed the cultural advantages of a home rich in books and music. Her father, William Law Murfree, affluent lawyer and landholder, was also a linguist and a published author; her mother, Fanny Priscilla Dickinson, is reputed to have brought the first piano to Tennessee. When she was four she was stricken by a malady which left her partially paralyzed and permanently lame.

Beginning at age five Murfree spent fifteen consecutive summers at the family cottage at Beersheba Springs in the Cumberland Mountains, where she observed minutely the mountain people she later celebrated in her writings. Mr. Murfree moved to Nashville in 1857 to expand his law practice and his children's educational horizons. Mary attended the Nashville Female Academy, excelling in the classical curriculum as in the courses devoted to fashionable refinements. During the Civil War, Grantland, the Murfree home, was overrun and destroyed, a circumstance she reproduced graphically in *Where the Battle Was Fought*. In 1867 she enrolled in Chegary Institute, a Philadelphia finishing school for girls, returning two years later to Nashville. New Grantland, constructed over ruins of the former homestead, was occupied in 1872, and here Murfree began writing with intent to publish.

Her first two printed pieces (*Lippincott's*, 1874, 1875) displayed definite facility for high comedy, but she immediately abandoned this genre, striking the significant vein of her career with "The Dancin' Party at Harrison's Cove" (*Atlantic Monthly*, May, 1878). Thereafter she produced a spate of novels and short stories dealing with the landscapes, characters, and happenings in remote Tennessee mountain communities unsmirched by urban intrusion. Her first collection, *In the Tennessee Mountains*, attracted superlative reviews and assured her a national audience. In the novels *Down the Ravine* and *The Story of Keedon Bluffs*, and in *The Young Mountaineers* (stories from *Youth's Companion*), she rendered these regional materials for juvenile readers.

From 1881 to 1890 she lived in St. Louis. Out of this interlude came her only novel with city background, *The Champion*, a juvenile. When the vogue for local color waned in the mid-1890s, Murfree followed the trend to historical romances, turning out three novels and a volume of short stories on colonial Tennessee, and another Civil War novel, *The Storm Centre*. No longer broadly popular, she published two novels about the Deep South (1908, 1914) and desultory contributions to the magazines until 1921.

Elected state regent of the Daughters of the American Revolution in 1912, she traveled and lectured extensively throughout Tennessee. In 1922 she was awarded an honorary degree by the University of the South. Confined to a wheelchair, and blind, she could not appear at the presentation. She died in Murfreesboro on July 31, 1922.

WORKS: *In the Tennessee Mountains* (1884). *Where the Battle Was Fought* (1884). *Down the Ravine* (1885). *The Prophet of the Great Smoky Mountains* (1885). *In the Clouds* (1886). *The Story of Keedon Bluffs* (1887). *The Despot of Broomsedge Cove* (1888). *In the "Stranger People's" Country* (1891). *His Vanished Star* (1894). *The Mystery of Witch-Face Mountain and Other Stories* (1895). *The Phantoms of the Foot-Bridge and Other Stories* (1895). *The Young Mountaineers* (1897). *The Juggler* (1897). *The Bushwhackers and Other Stories* (1899). *The Story of Old Fort Loudon* (1899). *The Champion* (1902). *A Spectre of Power* (1903). *The Frontiersmen* (1904). *The Storm Centre* (1905). *The Amulet* (1906). *The Windfall* (1907). *The Fair Mississippian* (1908). *The Raid of the Guerilla and Other Stories* (1912). *The Ordeal; A Mountain Romance of Tennessee* (1912). *The Story of Duciehurst; A Tale of the Mississippi*

(1914). *The Erskine Honeymoon* (novel published posthumously in the Nashville *Banner*, December 29, 1930–March 3, 1931).

RICHARD CARY
Colby College
Waterville, Me.

FRANCES NEWMAN (1883–1928). Frances Newman was born in Atlanta, Ga., on September 13, 1883, the daughter of William Truslow and Frances Percy Alexander Newman. Descendants of early Tennessee settlers, her parents moved to Atlanta after the Civil War. Her father, who had been a captain in the C.S.A., became a federal judge in 1888.

Newman's schooling included Washington Seminary, Mrs. Semple's School, and Agnes Scott College. After being graduated from the Atlanta Carnegie Library School in 1912, she served as a librarian at Florida State College for Women in 1913, the Atlanta Carnegie Library from 1913 to 1923, and Georgia Tech University from 1924 to 1926. She studied at the Sorbonne in 1923. She did not marry but raised a nephew, Louis Rucker, with the assistance of her lifelong mammy, Susan Long.

Frances Newman's literary career began with book reviews. James Branch Cabell encouraged her to turn to fiction, and her short story, "Rachel and Her Children," won the O. Henry prize in 1924. The same year *The Short Story's Mutations* was published, 60 pages of succinct and incisive chapters on the development of the genre from Petronius to Paul Morand, illustrated by sixteen stories.

The Hard-Boiled Virgin, her first novel, traces Katherine Faraday's amusing but cynical progress from her breeding to be a southern lady through a succession of beaux and a lover toward the hard disillusionment she finds at the end of all illusions. *Dead Lovers Are Faithful Lovers*, a second novel, offers two similarly self-conscious feminine reflections: aristocratic Evelyn Byrd Page Cunningham's decadent absorption in her erotic relation with her husband, and librarian Isabel Ramsey's erotic anticipations of communications with Cunningham which are mixed with withering notices of library coworkers.

Newman's last work, *Six Moral Tales from Jules Laforgue*, a translation, was published posthumously, following her sudden illness and death on October 22, 1928, in New York City of a brain hemorrhage, pneumonia, and possibly a drug overdose. Newman was almost totally blind before her death and dictated her last work. She had gone to New York to consult specialists when she contracted pneumonia.

WORKS: *The Short Story's Mutations* (1924). *The Hard-Boiled Virgin* (1926). *Dead Lovers Are Faithful Lovers* (1928). *Six Moral Tales from Jules Laforgue* (1928). *Frances Newman's Letters*, ed. Hansell Baugh (1929).

WILLIAM H. SLAVICK
University of Maine
Gorham

CHARLES FENTON MERCER NOLAND (*ca.* 1810–1858). Born in Loudon County, Va., in October, 1810, to William Noland and Catharine Callender, Charles Noland grew up in Aldie, Va. His father served in the Virginia legislature and held federal appointments in Arkansas and in Washington, D.C., under six presidents.

After education at home, Noland was appointed to the U.S. Military Academy at thirteen, but was dismissed in 1825 for deficiency in drawing and mathematics. His father, recently appointed to the land office in Batesville, Ark., desired a rigorous discipline for his son and had him come out to the Arkansas territory in 1826. There he read law under another stern Virginian, and by 1829 was practicing. In a duel in 1831 he killed Governor John Pope's nephew. From 1833–1836 he served with the U.S. Mounted Rangers in Vincennes, Prairie du Chien, and St. Louis before returning to Arkansas. A Whig, he served four terms in the state legislature. In 1840 he married Lucretia Ringgold and, until his death after a lifetime of tuberculosis, held various elective offices and federal and state appointments. He died in Little Rock on June 23, 1858.

Throughout his life he was fond of horse racing, shooting, and the ritualistic bear hunts of the American frontier. His topics for his newspaper sketches were the sports, politics, dances, and brutal fights of the settlements. His best work is a series of mock Pete Whetstone letters written for the New York *Spirit of the Times* from 1837 until 1856. His largely fictional character, carelessly but vigorously conceived, presents, in Noland's version of frontier dialect and perspective, one of our earliest sustained comic re-creations of the Old Southwest frontier.

WORKS: *Pete Whetstone of Devil's Fork*, eds. Ted R. Worley and Eugene A. Nolte (1957).

MILTON RICKELS
University of Southwestern
Louisiana
Lafayette

[MARY] FLANNERY O'CONNOR (1925–1964). An only child, Flannery O'Connor was born on March 25, 1925, in Savannah, Ga., where her father was in the real estate business and where she spent her childhood, attending Catholic schools. In the late 1930s Mr. O'Connor fell fatally ill with lupus, an autoimmune affliction akin to arthritis and the same disease which was later to take his daughter's life at 39, and the family moved to Milledgeville. Here they lived in the antebellum family home of the author's mother, Regina Cline O'Connor, whose forebears were prominent Georgia Catholics and whose father had once been mayor of the town.

O'Connor attended the local Georgia State College for Women, distinguishing herself as a comic artist and a writer, and then the Writers Workshop of the University of Iowa, where she earned her M.A. and also published her first story, "The Geranium," in *Accent*, and in 1949 she went to live with the Robert Fitzgeralds, who were to become her close friends, in their country home in Connecticut. But late in 1950, when O'Connor was 25 and had just completed the initial draft of her first book, the novel *Wise Blood*, she was stricken with lupus. Back home in Georgia, she spent many months undergoing treatment in Emory University Hospital in Atlanta.

That spring she and her mother moved to a dairy farm, which

Mrs. O'Connor owned, on the outskirts of Milledgeville, and it was here that the author spent the remaining thirteen years of her life. With the help of a then new drug, ACTH, she enjoyed periods of relatively good health and was able to continue her writing until a few weeks before her death. *Wise Blood* came out in 1952, and the half decade following were the most productive years of her career, a period in which she wrote many of her best stories (publishing them in such magazines as *Harper's*, the *Sewanee Review*, and *Kenyon Review*), as well as the distinguished opening section of *The Violent Bear It Away*, which was not to appear until 1960.

O'Connor's books were widely reviewed from the beginning, and even though misunderstanding of her religious thought was to continue for some time, her literary career was secure after the appearance of her first collection of stories, *A Good Man Is Hard to Find* (1955). Catholic readers were among the first to perceive that in spite of her rich comic gifts, O'Connor's work was fundamentally of the highest seriousness and that everything she wrote arose from her fierce and uncompromising Christian belief.

She was a writer who worked slowly and with great care for detail, and the highly vivid and meticulous art of her short stories has brought her acclaim in that genre hardly matched by any other writer of her time. Her last collection of stories, *Everything That Rises Must Converge*, appeared a year after her death. She died on August 3, 1964, in Milledgeville.

WORKS: *Wise Blood* (1952). *A Good Man Is Hard to Find* (1955). *The Violent Bear It Away* (1960). *Everything That Rises Must Converge* (1965). *Mystery and Manners: Occasional Prose*, ed. Sally and Robert Fitzgerald (1969). *The Complete Stories* (1971).

MARTHA STEPHENS
University of Cincinnati
Cincinnati, Ohio

EDWIN PHILIP ("PAT") O'DONNELL (1895–1943). E. P. O'Donnell sold his first story at the age of 36. Before his death twelve years later, this late-blooming local colorist introduced the outside world to the heterogeneous *volk* of the Mississippi Delta region. Born in New Orleans, on March 25, 1895, to Edward J., whose people were Galway O'Donnells, and a mother descended from County Clare O'Briens, O'Donnell left school after completing the fourth grade to become a newsboy, the first of 33 jobs he could remember holding. The son of a railroadman, he spent much of his life near his home close by the New Orleans wharves. During World War I, he drove a Red Cross ambulance and served in the Adjutant General's Department.

From a job on the assembly line, he rose to chief publicity man at the Ford Motor Company plant in New Orleans, married, and had two sons. In the late 1920s as he guided Sherwood Anderson on a tour of the plant, he described the operations so vividly that Anderson urged him to become a writer. His first piece appeared in a little magazine called *Blues* in 1929. Two years later, his first commercial story, "Manhood," appeared in *Collier's*. "Jesus Knew" appeared in *Harper's* and helped him win a Houghton Mifflin literary fellowship in 1935. Fifty dollars of the $1000 prize went to buy a one-room shack at Boothville, 90 miles south of New Orleans where he wrote and raised Easter lilies and oranges. There he finished the manuscript for *Green Margins*, a story set in the Delta country, which appeared in 1936 and was a Book of the Month Club selection. His second book, *The Great Big Doorstep*, was also about Delta people.

O'Donnell died in New Orleans on April 19, 1943, following several months of illness and only six weeks after he married his second wife, the author Mary King. The previous November his second novel had been adapted for the stage by Albert and Frances Goodrich Hackett.

WORKS: *Green Margins* (1936). *The Great Big Doorstep, a Delta Comedy* (1941).

E. BRUCE KIRKHAM
Ball State University
Muncie, Ind.

HOWARD WASHINGTON ODUM (1884–1954).

Howard W. Odum, the South's most notable sociologist in the first half of the twentieth century, was born in Walton County, Ga., on May 24, 1884, to William Pleasants and Mary Ann Thomas Odum. "A native of the ruralest of the rural South," as Odum later wrote, and reared among people "from which is [sic] recruited our fundamentalists and often our Ku Klux folk," Odum was educated at Emory College (A.B., 1904), the University of Mississippi (A.M., 1906), Clark University (Ph.D., 1909), and Columbia University (Ph.D., 1910). Between 1904 and 1920 he served as a school principal in Mississippi, an instructor at the University of Mississippi, professor of sociology at the University of Georgia, and dean of the School of Liberal Arts at Emory.

In 1920 Odum became director of the School of Public Welfare at the University of North Carolina, and in 1924 became director of the Institute for Research in Social Sciences. In 1922 he founded the *Journal of Social Forces*, one of the leading organs of southern self-examination in the 1920s. During this period Odum joined with Gerald W. Johnson and other southerners in an attempt to bring about what Odum called a "critical-creative" revival in the South. In the 1930s he was widely identified as the leader of the southern Regionalists, a group concerned largely with defining and attacking southern social and economic ills. He and his philosophy were frequently challenged by the southern Agrarians, who were more concerned with preserving than reforming the South. He died on November 8, 1954, in Chapel Hill.

Odum was also a folk artist, a chronicler of the trials of the southern Negro. His folk trilogy—*Rainbow Round My Shoulder* (1928), *Wings on My Feet* (1929), and *Cold Blue Moon* (1931)—depicted with sympathy and understanding the life of a black laborer he called Black Ulysses. Odum was by discipline a sociologist, but as he showed in his folk trilogy and other work, his sociology was an all-encompassing study of what he called "the folk-regional society."

WORKS: *Social and Mental Traits of the Negro* (1910). Ed., *Southern Pioneers in Social Interpretation* (1929). *The Negro and His Songs* (1925). *Negro Workaday Songs* (1926). *Rainbow Round My Shoulder* (1928). *Wings on My Feet* (1929). *An American Epoch: Southern Portraiture in the National Picture* (1930). *Cold Blue Moon* (1931). *Southern Regions of the United States* (1936). *American Regionalism,* with Harry E. Moore (1938). *American Democracy Anew,* with others (1940). *Alabama, Past and Future* (1941). *Race and Rumors of Race* (1941). *The Way of the South* (1947). *Folk, Region, and Society: Selected Papers of Howard W. Odum,* ed. Katharine Jocher *et al.* (1964).

FRED HOBSON
University of Alabama
Tuscaloosa

THEODORE O'HARA (1820–1867). The son of Kean O'Hara, an immigrant Irish teacher, and Helen Hardy O'Hara, Theodore O'Hara was probably born on February 11, 1820, in Frankfort, Ky., though Danville, Ky., is usually given as the place of his birth. His father's various schools provided his early education. He was graduated with honors from St. Joseph's College in Bardstown, Ky., and later taught Greek there.

Leaving teaching, he studied law and began his career as a journalist, working on the Frankfort *Yeoman* (1843–1844); wrote, in 1845, his first poem, "The Old Pioneer," honoring Daniel Boone; volunteered to fight in the Mexican War; composed an early version of his second elegiac poem, "The Bivouac of the Dead," possibly as early as 1848, to honor the Kentuckians who fell at the battle of Buena Vista in 1847; enlisted in the army led by Narcisco Lopez to fight for Cuban independence (1850); returned to newspaper work as editor of the Louisville *Times* (1852–1853); served in U.S. Army (1855–1856); resumed his editorial career in Alabama as editor of the Mobile *Register* (1857–1860); joined the Confederate Army, holding posts under various generals, and became a cotton factor and planter in Columbus, Ga., and Guerryton, Ala., where he died on June 6, 1867. First interred in Columbus, his body was later (1874) reburied in Frankfort.

Widely known during his lifetime for his oratorical talents, O'Hara was even more famous as the author of "The Bivouac of the Dead," published first in the Mobile *Register* in 1858. The final four lines of the first stanza are inscribed on the gateway of the

Arlington (Va.) National Cemetery. As an editor, O'Hara espoused the principles of the Democratic party and the causes of the South. He perhaps wrote some humorous verses and love lyrics, but no verifiable ascriptions have so far been made.

WORKS: "The Old Pioneer" (1845). "The Bivouac of the Dead" (1858 in first of several printed versions).

JOHN L. IDOL, JR.
Clemson University
Clemson, S.C.

GORONWY [or GRONOW] OWEN (1723–1769). Goronwy Owen spent his last twelve years in Virginia, but he is remembered for his contribution to Welsh literature, not American. Born in Anglesey on January 1, 1723, of a tinker father and an energetic mother, Owen was educated at Welsh schools, and, very briefly, at Jesus College, Oxford. He was ordained a deacon in 1745 and married Ellen Hughes in 1747. For the next several years he served as minister or school teacher to various villages in western England. His interest in Welsh literature was revived and strengthened by Lewis Morris, through whom Owen was in 1755 appointed secretary of the Cymmrodorion Society of London. Under the influence of the Morrises and their circle, Owen brought to fruition his knowledge and skill in Welsh forms and meters, tempering and strengthening his poetry by his familiarity with Greek and Latin classics. But an intemperance similar to his father's plagued him and weakened his ties with the Morrises.

In 1757 Owen was offered mastership of a grammar school attached to William and Mary College. His wife died on the voyage over; he later took as his second wife a widow Clayton, sister to the Reverend Thomas Dawson, president of William and Mary College. In 1760 Owen lost his post at William and Mary, apparently through intemperance and bad conduct, and he became a minister at St. Andrews, Brunswick County, Va. During his years in America, Owen continued to write poetry in Welsh, including his famous "Lament for Anglesey," and a few letters to Welsh friends survive. He died in 1769, his associates apparently unaware of his importance to Welsh literature. In 1913 what is presumed to be his grave was located in Brunswick County, Va.

Owen contributed nothing to American literature, so that his being called "the greatest poet in 18th century America" is at best misleading. Even his importance for Welsh literature is exaggerated.

WORKS: *The Poetical Works of the Rev. Goronwy Owen*, 2 vols.; ed. Robert Jones (1876). *The Letters of Goronwy Owen, 1723–1769*, ed. J. H. Davies (1924).

WELDON THORNTON
University of North Carolina
Chapel Hill

GUY OWEN (1925–). Guy Owen was born on February 24, 1925, in Clarkton, N.C., at the center of what became in his novels the mythical "Cape Fear County." The eldest of four boys, he grew up in Florida, South Carolina, and Clarkton, where on his grandfather's farm he acquired an authentic knowledge of farm chores and tobacco fields. During World War II he served overseas in France and Germany. In 1945 he returned to study at the University of North Carolina at Chapel Hill, receiving a Ph.D. in 1955. While there he married Dorothy Jennings; they have two sons. During 1955–1961 he taught at Stetson University, where he wrote his first novel, *Season of Fear* (1960). Set in "Cape Fear County" during the depression, this is a novel of a lonely God-obsessed man.

Since 1962 Owen has taught modern literature and creative writing at North Carolina State University. Until 1978 he edited *Southern Poetry Review*, a magazine founded as *Impetus* at Stetson in 1958, and for five years coedited *North Carolina Folklore*. Also, he coedited anthologies of southern and North Carolina poetry, including *The White Stallion* (1969) and a number of critical articles.

Owen is best known for Mordecai Jones, the Flim-Flam Man, an engaging con artist who with his young partner follows a comically adventurous path through eastern North Carolina. Introduced in

The Ballad of the Flim-Flam Man (1965), Jones's exploits were continued in another novel and a collection of short stories. A serious novel of the depression, *Journey for Joedel* (1970), nominated for the Pulitzer Prize, tells of the journey from innocence into moral ambiguity of a part Lumbee Indian boy. In his lectures, teaching, and editorial work, Owen has encouraged southern writing; in his novels he has recorded the life of his own region.

WORKS: *Season of Fear* (1960). Ed., *Essays in Modern American Literature*, with Richard Langford and William E. Taylor (1963). *The Guilty and Other Poems* (1964). *The Ballad of the Flim-Flam Man* (1965). *The White Stallion and Other Poems* (1969). *Journey for Joedel* (1970). *The Flim-Flam Man and the Apprentice Grifter* (1972). *The Flim-Flam Man and Other Stories* (1976). Ed., *Modern American Poetry: Essays in Criticism* (1972). Ed., *New Southern Poets: Selected Poems from Southern Poetry Review*, with Mary C. Williams (1975). Ed., *Contemporary Poetry of North Carolina*, with Mary C. Williams (1977).

MARY C. WILLIAMS
North Carolina State University
Raleigh

THOMAS NELSON PAGE (1853–1922). Thomas Nelson Page, son of John and Elizabeth Burwell Nelson Page and descendant of two colonial governors, was born at Oakland plantation north of Richmond, Va., on April 23, 1853. Despite straitened circumstances, he attended Washington College (1869–1872) while Lee was its president, read law and tutored in Kentucky (1872–1873), and studied law at the University of Virginia (1873–1874). After practice in country courts (1874–1876) he established a successful practice in Richmond, with special interest in business, inventions, and mining (1876–1893). Publication of "Marse Chan" (1884) brought him national recognition as local colorist and spokesman for the Old South. Two years later he was happily married to Anne Bruce. After her untimely death (1888), from his modest resources he established in her memory Richmond's first public library, then threw himself into business in Colorado and Europe (1889 and

1891). Delayed in London by worsening business conditions, he enjoyed the social life his reputation as writer opened to him. The panic of 1891 returned him to Richmond, then sent him out on the lyceum circuit to read his stories with F. Hopkinson Smith.

In 1893 upon his marriage to Florence Lathrop Field, widow of Marshall Field's brother Henry, he gave up law to devote full time to writing. With a summer home at York Harbor, Me., and their chief residence in Washington, they entertained frequently, and at Page's "little dinners" men knowledgeable in world events, national affairs, and recent history mingled with artists and writers. Page was, as a result, well informed, though not a systematic scholar. As members of international café society, the Pages regularly visited London, Paris, Rome, and the Riviera, but always on returning he went first to Oakland to see his family there. Habitually generous, Page supported an astounding number of unfortunates and was generous patron to young writers and faltering old ones. Southern writers struggling for recognition found him especially encouraging. He was elected to the American Academy of Arts and Letters (1908).

He wrote steadily—essays, stories, sketches, long fiction, set in Monte Carlo, the Rockies, New England, the inner city—but by 1910 concluded that editors wanted nothing from him except more antebellum Marse Chans. He turned his attention increasingly to backstage politics involving whatever concerned Virginia and causes such as preservation of national forests, recordings for the blind, good roads, and endowment for the University of Virginia. In 1912 he united Virginia's fragmented delegation to help nominate Woodrow Wilson, whose lofty objectives he applauded. Wilson then made Page ambassador to Rome, where the Pages spent themselves freely in official duties and in support of the Italian poor. He served with increasing frustration until Versailles made obvious the chasm between political ideals and the politics of power.

At home again, Page wrote hastily on Italy and the war, prepared an invited series of lectures on Dante for the University of Virginia, and was reworking an antebellum novel when Mrs. Page died suddenly (1921) after nearly 30 years of sharing his interests. Page died at Oakland on October 31, 1922.

WORKS: *Marse Chan: A Tale of Old Virginia* (1885). *In Ole Virginia, or Marse Chan and Other Stories* (1887). *Befo' de War: Echoes in Negro Dialect*, with A. C. Gordon (1888). *Two Little Confederates* (1888). *Unc Edinburg: A Plantation Echo* (1889). *Among the Camps, or, Young People's Stories of the War* (1891). *Elsket and Other Stories* (1891). *On Newfound River* (1891). *The Old South: Essays Social and Political* (1892). *Meh Lady: A Story of the War* (1893). *The Burial of the Guns and Other Stories* (1894). *Pastime Stories* (1894). *Polly: A Christmas Recollection* (1894). *The Old Gentleman of the Black Stock* (1897). *Social Life in Old Virginia Before the War* (1897). *Red Rock: A Chronicle of Reconstruction* (1898). *Two Prisoners* (1898). *The Peace Cross Book, Cathedral of SS. Peter and Paul, Washington* (1899). *Santa Claus's Partner* (1899). *A Captured Santa Claus* (1902). *Gordon Keith* (1903). *Bred in the Bone* (1904). *The Negro: The Southerner's Problem* (1904). *The Coast of Bohemia* (1906). *The Page Story Book* (1906). *Under the Crust* (1907). *The Old Dominion: Her Making and Her Manners* (1908). *Robert E. Lee, the Southerner* (1908). *Tommy Trot's Visit to Santa Claus* (1908). *General Lee, Man and Soldier* (1909). *John Marvel, Assistant* (1909). *Mount Vernon and Its Preservation, 1858–1910: The Acquisition, Restoration and Care of the Home of Washington by the Mount Vernon Ladies' Association for Over Half a Century* (1910). *Robert E. Lee, Man and Soldier*, rev. (1911). *The Land of the Spirit* (1913). *The Shepherd Who Watched by Night* (1913). *The Stranger's Pew* (1914). *Tommaso Jefferson, Apostolo della Libertá (1743–1826)* (1918). *Italy and the World War* (1920). *Dante and His Influence* (1922). *Washington and Its Romance* (1923). *The Red Riders*, completed by Rosewell Page (1924). *The Stable of the Inn* (1959). *John Fox and Tom Page as They Were: Letters, an Address, and an Essay* (1969). *North African Journal, 1912, with Letters Along the Way* (1970). *On the Nile in 1901* (1970). *Mediterranean Winter, 1906: Journal and Letters* (1971).

HARRIET R. HOLMAN
Clemson University
Clemson, S.C.

WALTER HINES PAGE (1855–1918). Born on August 15, 1855, in Cary, N.C., a town founded by his enterprising father, Page was ten years old at the end of the Civil War. The aristocratic tradition and romantic stereotypes of the Confederacy as well as the cruelty of the war were observed closely by the intense young man. The conclusions Page drew became part of his single novel, *The Southerner*, and served as an impetus for the remainder of his life.

Denouncing southerners living in the past as "Mummies," Page fought for the revitalization of the South through social and educational reform. Believing that democracy and the common man were the foundation of a healthy society, Page proclaimed the need for effective public education, worked with the Southern Education Board and the General Education Board, enthusiastically supported sanitation programs like those of the Hookworm Commission, and endorsed the agricultural demonstration work of Dr. Seaman A. Knapp.

It is not surprising that the 21-year-old Page, one of the first 20 fellows at the newly established Johns Hopkins University, did not pursue a scholarly career in Greek, but turned his inquiring mind to a profession more suitable to his missionary zeal: journalism. His distinguished journalistic career included his founding of the Raleigh *State Chronicle*, his editing of the *Forum* and the *Atlantic Monthly*, and his establishing *World's Work*.

Appointed by Woodrow Wilson, his longtime friend, as ambassador to the Court of St. James (1913–1918), Page performed during the war with distinction. His diplomacy, rational approach to problems, patience, and dedication to democracy endeared him to his British counterparts, while his frank assessment of British opinion provided invaluable information to Wilson and his advisors. In failing health Page resigned his ambassadorship returning to his cherished North Carolina to die in Aberdeen on December 21, 1918.

Respected journalist, reformer, and statesman, Page is not a particularly effective novelist. Attacking southern myths, the "ghosts of the Confederacy," and "caste feeling," Page's first-person novel is vigorous and realistic at moments. However, it is marred by rhapsodic passages and editorial comments on the need for educational and political reform.

WORKS: *The Southerner, Being the Autobiography of Nicholas Worth* (1909).

PAMELA GLENN MENKE
St. Mary's Dominican College
New Orleans, La.

FRANKLIN VERZELIUS NEWTON PAINTER (1852–1931).

The son of Israel and Juliana Wilson Painter, F. V. N. Painter was born in Hampshire County, Va. (now W.Va.), April 12, 1852. His father, a millwright, was of German descent; his mother came of Scottish stock. He attended the public schools of Aurora, W.Va., and in 1870 entered Roanoke College, Salem, Va., receiving a B.A. four years later and winning the gold medal for metaphysics and first honor in the graduating class.

In 1878, upon graduation from Lutheran Theological Seminary in Salem, Painter became a Lutheran clergyman. That same year he accepted an appointment to the faculty of Roanoke College, where he was professor of modern languages and literature for many years. In 1906 he retired from the ministry and from his professorship to devote his time to writing, but retained a lectureship in pedagogy and the history of education. In addition to teacher and minister, he was active and outstanding as educator, author, scholar, and poet.

Painter's most notable contribution may be the large number of textbooks he wrote in the field of literature as well as in education and religion. *A History of Education*, for example, went through many editions between 1886 and 1927, as did his *Introduction to American Literature* between 1897 and 1932. He published one volume of Wordsworthian poems, *Lyrical Vignettes*. In addition, he preached sermons, contributed articles to periodicals, and gave literary addresses. He was an ardent spokesman for the teaching of modern foreign languages as opposed to ancient languages in the college curriculum, a position approved by the Modern Language Association in 1885.

Painter married Laura Trimble Shickel on August 9, 1857. Eight children were born to them. He died on January 18, 1931.

WORKS: *A History of Education* (1886; rev., enl., and largely rewritten, 1904). *Luther on Education* (1889). *History of Christian Worship*, with J. W. Richardson (1891). *Introduction to English Literature* (1894; rev. and enl., 1919). *Introduction to American Literature* (1897). *Introduction to English and American Literature* (1899). *A History of English Literature* (1899). *Lyrical Vignettes* (1900). *The Reformation Dawn* (1901). *Elementary Guide to Literary Criticism* (1903). *Poets of the South* (1903). *Great Pedagogical Essays* (1905). *Poets of Virginia* (1907). *Introduction to Bible Study: The Old Testament* (1911).

DOROTHY McINNIS SCURA
University of Richmond
Richmond, Va.

EDD WINFIELD PARKS (1906–1968). Edd Parks was born in Newbern, Tenn., on February 25, 1906, the son of Edward Winfield and Emma Wallis Parks, and educated at Harvard (A.B., 1927) and Vanderbilt (M.A., 1929; Ph.D., 1933). In 1933 he married Aileen Wells and later collaborated with her on several books. He taught at Vanderbilt, at Cumberland University, and in 1935 he went to the University of Georgia at the invitation of John Donald Wade, and, with occasional breaks for tours as Fulbright and Smith-Mundt Professor in Denmark (1955) and Brazil (1949, 1958), he remained there until his death, becoming Alumni Foundation Distinguished Professor in 1964.

Early interested in southern writing, Parks's first contribution to scholarship in the field was his dissertation on Mary Murfree (1941), followed by *Southern Poets* (1936), *Segments of Southern Thought* (1938), and *The Essays of Henry Timrod* (1942). This work was interrupted by service as an officer in military intelligence during World War II, and further contributions to scholarship on southern literature were delayed until the 1960s, when *William Gilmore Simms as Literary Critic* (1961), *Ante-Bellum Southern Literary Critics* (1962), *Henry Timrod* (1964), *Edgar Allan Poe as Literary Critic* (1964), *The Collected Poems of Henry Timrod*, a variorum edition in collaboration with Mrs. Parks (1965), and *Sidney Lanier* (1968) firmly established him as a leading scholar in the field. Honored by his peers, Parks served as president

of the South Atlantic Modern Language Association and the Southeastern American Studies Association, as chairman of the Southern
Humanities Conference, and as a member of the executive coun-
cils of the Modern Language Association and the American Studies
Association. His death on May 7, 1968, deprived the academic
world of a valuable and humane scholar-teacher, a loss acknowledged in the dedication of *A Bibliographical Guide to the Study
of Southern Literature* (1969).

WORKS: Ed., *The Great Critics: An Anthology of Literary Criticism*,
with James H. Smith (1932). Ed., *The English Drama: An Anthology*,
900–1642, with Richmond C. Beatty (1935). Ed., *Southern Poets* (1936).
Segments of Southern Thought (1938). *Charles Egbert Craddock (Mary
Noailles Murfree)* (1941). Ed., *The Essays of Henry Timrod* (1942).
Long Hunter (1942). *Pioneer Pilot* (1947). *Predestinate Iron* (1948). *Little
Long Rifle* (1949). *Safe on Second* (1953). *Teddy Roosevelt All-Round
Boy* (1953). *Backwater* (1957). *William Gilmore Simms as Literary Critic*
(1961). *Ante-Bellum Southern Literary Critics* (1962). *Nashoba* (1963).
Henry Timrod (1964). *Edgar Allan Poe as Literary Critic* (1964). Ed.,
The Collected Poems of Henry Timrod, with Aileen Wells Parks (1965).
Thomas MacDonagh: the Man, the Patriot, the Writer, with Aileen Wells
Parks (1967). *Sidney Lanier: the Man, the Poet, the Critic* (1968).

RAYBURN S. MOORE
University of Georgia
Athens

FRANCES GRAY PATTON (1906–). Born in Raleigh, N.C., on
March 19, 1906, the daughter of a journalist, Frances Gray spent
her youth in North and South Carolina and Virginia. After one year
at Trinity College, she transferred to the University of North Carolina at Chapel Hill but left in her final semester. There she was
active in the Carolina Playmakers, both as actor and playwright.
At 21 she married Lewis Patton, a professor at Duke University.
They had three children, a son and twin daughters.

As her children began to grow up, Patton resumed writing. Her
first published story, "A Piece of Bread" (1944), was reprinted in
the annual *O. Henry Memorial Award Stories*. In the following
years a number of other stories appeared, mainly in the *New*

Yorker. Carefully plotted, sometimes with a clever twist, and written with great care for the precise word, Patton's humorous, ironic, often poignant stories afford insights into such domestic matters as relations between parents and children, husbands and wives, and teachers and pupils; the workings of the childish or the adolescent mind; and the traditions of southern womanhood in an upper-middle-class culture of the first half of the century. There have been three collections of stories: *The Finer Things of Life*, *A Piece of Luck*, and *Twenty-Eight Stories*. The stories have been widely anthologized.

Patton's best-known story, "The Terrible Miss Dove," a sensitive portrayal of a demanding schoolteacher who serves as an inspiration to a soldier in wartime, became the basis for a novel, *Good Morning, Miss Dove*. A bookclub selection, the novel was later made into a film. Patton has three times won the Sir Walter Raleigh Award for excellence in fiction by a North Carolinian. In addition to writing she has taught classes in creative writing.

WORKS: *The Finer Things of Life* (1951). *Good Morning, Miss Dove* (1954). *A Piece of Luck* (1955). *Twenty-Eight Stories* (all but one story reprinted from previous collections, 1969).

MARY C. WILLIAMS
North Carolina State University
Raleigh

LEONIDAS WARREN PAYNE, JR. (1873–1945). Leonidas Warren Payne, Jr., was born on July 12, 1873, in Auburn, Ala., the son of Leonidas Warren and Mary Jane Foster Payne. He married Mary Susan Bledsoe on October 27, 1897, and they were the parents of four children. He received his college education at Alabama Polytechnic Institute (now Auburn University, B.Sc., 1892; M.Sc., 1893) and the University of Pennsylvania (Ph.D., 1904); at the latter he was Harrison Fellow in English (1902–1904). Payne held teaching positions at Southwestern Alabama Agricultural School, Evergreen, Ala. (1894–1901); Jacksonville, Ala., State Normal School (1901–1902), Louisiana State University (1906), and the University of Texas (1906; professor of English, 1919). He was cofounder and the first president of the Texas Folklore Society (1910). He died on June 16, 1945.

In the field of linguistics and language, Payne served as associate editor of Worcester's *Dictionary* (1904–1906), compiled *Word List of Eastern Alabama* (1910) and *Learn to Spell* (1916), and edited a five-volume series, *Using Our Language*, for use in grades three to seven (1935). He also helped to edit three other anthologies for use in secondary schools: *Literature for the Junior High School*, 3 vols. (1929); *Enjoying Literature*, 4 vols. (Grades nine to twelve, 1936); and *Enjoying Literature*, 3 vols. (Grades six to eight, 1942). He was the editor of *Selections from English Literature* (1922).

Payne was the author of *History of American Literature* (1919) and *Readings* (1917), *Selections from American Literature* (1919), and *Selections from Later American Writers* (1927).

Payne's work in southern literature was extensive. He produced *A Survey of Texas Literature* (1928) and edited *Southern Literary Readings* (1913), *Fifty Famous Southern Poems* (1920), and *Texas Poems* (1936). For the biographical Volumes XI and XII of *The South in the Building of the Nation* (1909), Payne contributed sketches of William Gilmore Simms, George W. Cable, Joel Chandler Harris, Paul Hamilton Hayne, Mary Noailles Murfree, and Mary Johnston, among others.

WORKS: Ed., *Hector of Germanie*, by W. Smith (1906). Comp., *Word List of Eastern Alabama* (1910). Ed., *Southern Literary Readings* (1913). Comp., *Learn to Spell* (1916). Ed., *American Literary Readings* (1917). *History of American Literature* (1919). Ed., *Selections from American Literature* (1919). Ed., *Fifty Famous Southern Poems* (1920). Ed., *Selections from English Literature*, with N. Hill (1922). Ed., *Selections from Later American Writers* (1927). *A Survey of Texas Literature* (1928). Ed., *Literature for the Junior High Schools*, 3 vols., with T. H. Briggs and C. M. Curry (1929). Ed., *Using Our Language*, 5 vols., with A. Blount and C. S. Northrup (1935). Ed., *Enjoying Literature*, 4 vols., with M. A. Neville and N. E. Chapman (1936). Ed., *Texas Poems* (1936). Ed., *Enjoying Literature*, 3 vols., with M. A. Neville (1942).

RANDALL G. PATTERSON
Belhaven College
Jackson, Miss.

SAMUEL MINTURN PECK (1854–1938). Alabama's first poet laureate was born in Tuscaloosa, Ala., on November 4, 1854, the son of Judge Elijah Wolsey and Lucy Lamb Randall Peck. His early education was in the Tuscaloosa schools; and he received a master's degree in 1876 from the University of Alabama. He studied medicine to please his parents and in 1879 received his M.D. from Bellevue Hospital Medical College, New York. He never practiced medicine. Later he studied literature and languages at Columbia University and in Paris. A substantial family inheritance afforded him the leisure to travel, study, and write though he remained a bachelor and maintained a permanent residence in Tuscaloosa.

Peck's literary career, spanning over 50 years, began in 1878 when his poem "The Orange Tree" was printed in the New York *Evening Post*. "Mock Orange," appearing in the *Youth's Companion*, was the first poem for which he received pay. In addition to *Independent* and *Century* magazines, his poems were published in numerous northern and southern newspapers. The Boston *Transcript* printed his poems regularly for 30 years.

Although Peck experimented with various types of poems, his reputation rests primarily upon his skill as a writer of vers de société and poems proclaiming the joys of boyhood in Alabama. At the turn of the century Peck's "The Grapevine Swing" was widely acclaimed, especially in the South. A number of his verses were set to music. In the 1890s he published in magazines local color stories with Alabama settings. Eleven were reprinted in *Alabama Sketches* (1902). Peck's four novels were never published.

In 1931 Peck was honored by the Alabama Writers' Conclave, with legislative approval, as Alabama's first poet laureate. He continued to write, though less prolifically, until his death in Tuscaloosa on May 3, 1938.

WORKS: *Cap and Bells* (1886). *Rings and Love-Knots* (1892). *Rhymes and Roses* (1895). *Fair Women of To-day* (1895). *The Golf Girl* (1899). *Alabama Sketches* (1902). *Maybloom and Myrtle* (1910). *The Autumn Trail* (1925).

RAY M. ATCHISON
Samford University
Birmingham, Ala.

WALKER PERCY (1916–). Walker Percy was born on May 28, 1916, in Birmingham, Ala., the oldest son of Leroy Pratt and Martha Phinizy Percy. After his father's suicide, when Percy was eleven, the surviving family lived for a period with Percy's grandmother, in Athens, Ga. Two years after his father's death, his mother died in an automobile accident.

Then Percy and his two brothers were adopted by William Alexander Percy, the lawyer, landowner, and poet, of Greenville, Miss. Best known in literature as the author of *Lanterns on the Levee* (1941), a memoir, William Alexander Percy was a first cousin to Percy's father, but to Percy and his brothers he was known as "Uncle Will."

Percy lived in the Greenville home, observing the traditional southern patrician life and the many writers who came to visit, until he entered the University of North Carolina at Chapel Hill, from which he graduated in 1937, with a B.A. in chemistry. His first attempt (a failure) at publication had been a short short story for *Liberty*, while he was still a boy. At Chapel Hill he served as a reviewer for *Carolina Magazine*.

To please his Uncle Will, Percy entered the College of Physicians and Surgeons, Columbia University. Although he did not particularly care for medicine, he graduated with high honors in 1941. During his years in medical school, he also underwent a three-year period of Freudian analysis.

Throughout the summer of 1941 Percy worked in a Greenville clinic, and that fall he became an intern at Bellevue Hospital, New York City. Working in the pathology laboratory without mask or gloves, he contracted pulmonary tuberculosis in 1942 and had to enter Trudeau Sanitorium, in the Adirondacks. He was released in 1944 and returned to Columbia to teach pathology; but he soon suffered a relapse and had to enter another sanitorium in Connecticut.

When he was released, he decided that he could not actively engage in the practice of medicine and that he would instead study life from the perspective provided by the existentialists, Kierkegaard, Jaspers, Heidegger, Marcel, Camus, and Sartre, whose work he had begun to read during his convalescence.

On November 7, 1946, he married Mary Townsend, a native of Mississippi. Shortly thereafter, the Percys moved to Covington, La., where they still live. During this period both also converted to Catholicism, which, with existentialism, provides the foundation for his thought. The Percys are the parents of two daughters, Mary Pratt and Ann Boyd.

Although his earliest writing consisted of essays about language and the contemporary southern scene, Percy first gained literary prominence with *The Moviegoer* (1961), which won the 1962 National Book Award for fiction. His later novels are *The Last Gentleman* (1967), *Love in the Ruins* (1971), and *Lancelot* (1977). Those essays dealing with language were published in *The Message in the Bottle* (1975). In all of his work thus far, Percy has explored the plight of the individual who attempts to fight the efforts of his culture to define him as a sociological datum and as a consumer without past or future.

WORKS: *The Moviegoer* (1961). *The Last Gentleman* (1967). *Love in the Ruins* (1971). *The Message in the Bottle* (1975). *Lancelot* (1977).

> LEWIS A. LAWSON
> University of Maryland
> College Park

WILLIAM ALEXANDER PERCY (1885–1942). William Alexander Percy was born May 14, 1885, in Greenville, Miss., the son of U.S. Senator Leroy and Camille Bourges Percy. He received his A.B. from the University of the South in 1904 (Litt.D., 1939), an LL.B. from Harvard in 1908, and began the practice of law in Greenville the same year.

In 1916 he was with the Commission for Relief in Belgium and was decorated by King Albert. After the United States entry into the war, he went to France with the 37th Division and was discharged in 1919 a captain with a Croix de Guerre with gold star. Along with his father, he was one of the leaders in 1922 in the successful fight against the Ku Klux Klan in Greenville. In the Mississippi flood of 1927 he acted as chairman of the local Red Cross unit, being responsible for the care and feeding of some 120,000 homeless people. After the death of his father, he took over the management of Trail Lake, a 3,343-acre plantation that employed nearly 600 people; and he found time to travel extensively in England, France, Greece, Japan, and Samoa. He died on January 21, 1942. His immediate heirs were three orphaned cousins whom he had adopted and reared. One of these cousins was Walker Percy.

Percy was what is commonly called an unreconstructed southerner. His autobiography, *Lanterns on the Levee*, is a charming and nostalgic evocation of the Old South, a culture and way of life that he perceived as being in its twilight. Looking out from Greenville on the world, he saw everywhere "the bottom rail on top" and said, "The North destroyed my South; Germany destroyed my world."

WORKS: *Sappho in Levkas and Other Poems* (1915). *In April Once* (1920). *Enzio's Kingdom* (1924). *Selected Poems* (1930). *Lanterns on the Levee: Recollections of a Planter's Son* (1941; with Intro. by Walker Percy, 1974). *Collected Poems* (1943).

EUGENE NOLTE
University of Central Arkansas
Conway

JULIA PETERKIN (1880–1961). The mistress of Lang Syne Plantation, Julia Mood Peterkin, was born on October 31, 1880, in Laurens County, S.C., to Julius Andrew and Alma Archer Mood. At sixteen, she took an A.B. at Converse College and, a year later, an M.A. After teaching for two years in a one-room school at Fort Motte, she married William George Peterkin on June 3, 1903. Their son, William, was born a year later.

For the next decade and a half Peterkin was altogether absorbed in her life as a plantation mistress, a responsibility she sometimes found boring. But, as she once wrote of the self-contained plantation world, she learned to train her senses to appreciate "the great tide of life that flowed about me."

Her escapes from plantation demands were few. Taking up piano again, she found in her teacher, Henry Bellaman, a critic and later novelist, encouragement to write out the stories she told. Carl Sandburg's appreciation of her work led to publication, first in Mencken's *Smart Set*, then in Emily Clark's *Reviewer*, where her Gullan sketches and stories appeared fourteen times in the early 1920s.

Julia Peterkin's fiction treats an exclusively black world in which nature, religious superstition, folklore, and the elemental experiences of the plantation—birth, love, suffering, death—are joined. "I mean to present these people in a patient struggle with fate," she writes; she would "do them as they really are." Donald Davidson called *Black April* "perhaps the first genuine novel in English of the Negro as a human being."

A collection of twelve stories, *Green Thursday*, appeared in 1924. Three novels followed: *Black April*, *Scarlet Sister Mary*, and *Bright Skin*. A nonfiction volume on Lang Syne life, *Roll, Jordan, Roll*, with photographs by Doris Ullman, followed. With a sentimental little book, *A Plantation Christmas* (1934), celebrating "the miracle we call life," Peterkin's literary career ended. She died on August 10, 1961.

WORKS: *Green Thursday* (1924). *Black April* (1927). *Scarlet Sister Mary* (1928). *Bright Skin* (1932). *Roll, Jordan, Roll* (1933). *A Plantation Christmas* (1934). *The Collected Stories of Julia Peterkin*, ed. Frank Durham (1970).

WILLIAM H. SLAVICK
University of Maine
Gorham

ROBERT DEANE PHARR (1916–). Robert Pharr was born on July 5, 1916, in Richmond, Va., the son of the Reverend John Benjamin and Lucie Deane Pharr. He was educated at St. Paul's College, Lawrenceville, Va., 1933; Lincoln University, Pa., 1934; and Virginia Union where he received a B.A. in 1939. He also engaged in graduate study at Fisk University.

Success as a writer came later for Pharr. For many years he was employed as a waiter in New York's resort hotels and private clubs while his ambitions of becoming a successful writer remained in a state of flux. *The Book of Numbers* was published in 1969, receiving general critical acclaim. It was followed by *S.R.O.* in 1971, a more complex and ambitious work considered less successful than *The Book of Numbers*.

The Book of Numbers is a penetrating analysis of black America, emphasizing the nuances and gamesmanship of hustlers in the street world. His protagonists strive for independence and wind up being almost completely dependent themselves. The two waiters do become wealthy after successfully organizing a numbers game. *S.R.O.* expands the locale and impetus of *The Book of Numbers*, developing the nuances of inner city living. *S.R.O.* stands for single-room occupancy, a hotel of Kafkaesque derivatives. Both novels demonstrate Pharr's eye for detail and nuance. Pharr has since published two paperbacks and has been working on "The Welfare Bitch."

WORKS: *The Book of Numbers* (1970). *S.R.O.* (1971). *The Soul Murder Case: A Confession of a Vacation* (1972).

BRIAN J. BENSON
North Carolina A & T University
Greensboro

THOMAS HAL PHILLIPS (1922–).

Born on a farm near Corinth, Miss., on October 11, 1922, Thomas Hal Phillips used his native state in much of his fiction. One of six children of W. T. Phillips and Ollie Fare Phillips, a schoolteacher, he was an all-around student and athlete at Alcorn Agricultural High School. He earned a B.S. in social science from Mississippi State University in 1943 and entered the navy as a lieutenant (j.g.), seeing action in the Mediterranean.

His literary career began after the war at the University of Alabama, where under Hudson Strode, he wrote a novel, *The Bitterweed Path*, as his thesis for the M.A. In 1947 he won a Rosenwald Fellowship in Fiction, followed a year later by the Eugene F. Saxon Award. From 1948 to 1950 he was on the faculty of Southern Methodist University. In 1950 he received a Fulbright Fellowship for study in France. That year his first novel, *The Bitterweed Path*, was published. A novel of sensitivity, it sets the interest of his later fiction, relationships among males, as well as the focus, the boy growing into manhood. *The Golden Lie* (1951) explores father-son and Negro-white conflicts. A story "The Shadow of an Arm" was included in the *O. Henry Prize Stories of 1951*. *Search for a Hero* in 1952 has the romantic theme of a youth's search for self-knowledge. Phillips received a Guggenheim Fellowship in 1953, and the following year *Kangaroo Hollow* appeared in England. In 1955 *The Loved and the Unloved*, an experiment with fiction as autobiography, achieved some measure of critical success. Since then there has been a silence. Phillips' success in handling homosexual themes sensitively is in stark contrast to his weak portrayal of women characters. As one critic noted, there is an "incompleteness."

WORKS: *The Bitterweed Path* (1950). *The Golden Lie* (1951). *Search for a Hero* (1952). *Kangaroo Hollow* (1954). *The Loved and the Unloved* (1955).

THOMAS BONNER, JR.
Xavier University of Louisiana
New Orleans

OVID WILLIAMS PIERCE (1910–). Ovid Williams Pierce was born in Weldon, N.C., on October 1, 1910, one of four children of Ovid Williams, Sr., and Minnie Deans Pierce. For generations his father's family were farmers, doctors, and landowners in northeastern North Carolina. From high school in Weldon he went to Duke University, graduating in 1932. There he edited the *Archive*, undergraduate literary journal. A few years' involvement in the various family businesses was followed by study at Harvard, from which he received a master's degree in 1938. During World War II, he saw service in the Caribbean. He was on the faculty of Southern Methodist University 1945–1949, spent a year teaching at Tulane, 1952–1953, and another year back at Southern Methodist before returning to North Carolina and joining the faculty of the Department of English at East Carolina University in 1956. He retired in 1976.

Four novels, all with settings similar to the rural areas of the author's native Halifax County in North Carolina, are concerned with the disconcerting social and economic conditions of the post-war South. At the turn of the century, the hero of *The Plantation* sacrifices himself to the needs of dependent relatives and retainers. Pierce's second and third novels take place in Reconstruction days, and a fourth looks into the past from a present-day point of view. Six early short stories, written between 1937 and 1951 for the *Southwest Review*, have been collected and published.

WORKS: *The Plantation* (1953; 1975). *On a Lonesome Porch* (1960). *The Devil's Half* (1968). *The Wedding Guest* (1974). *Old Man's Gold and Other Stories* (1976).

RICHARD WALSER
North Carolina State University
Raleigh

ALBERT PIKE (1809–1891). Although he identified passionately with the South through a stormy public career and became a Confederate general, Albert Pike came from old Yankee stock. He was born in Boston on December 20, 1809. Although he passed the class examinations at Harvard, he could not afford tuition and so he became a school teacher. He started writing romantic poetry but left New England in 1831 for the West.

Pike wandered on the prairies, trapping, trading, and dodging Indians and finally settled in Little Rock, Ark., in 1833. In 1835 he became editor and publisher of the *Arkansas Advocate* in which he supported the Whigs and publicized expansionism and slavery. With the decline of the Whigs, Pike became prominent in the Know-Nothing party and was widely known in the border states as a public speaker attacking the federal government and the North. He also made a distinguished reputation as a lawyer before serving with distinction in the Mexican War.

During this period Pike produced his only formally published book, *Prose Sketches and Poems, Written in the Western Country* (1834), and his poetry as well as his accounts of frontier life appeared widely in magazines, notably William T. Porter's *Spirit of the Times*. In 1854 Pike privately distributed his poetry collection *Nagae*, and in 1872 did the same with *"Hymns to the Gods," and Other Poems*. Nearly all the poems in both collections had appeared earlier, "Hymns to the Gods" in *Blackwood's* in 1839.

In 1861 Pike was commissioned a Confederate brigadier general in command of the Indian Territory, where he trained an irregular army of Choctaws and Cherokees. In 1862 he was accused of tactical errors and allowing atrocities by his troops. Pike defended himself in a widely circulated letter to Jefferson Davis who forced his resignation. The end of the war found him impoverished and politically suspect in North and South. Van Wyck Brooks maintains that he was active after the war in the Ku Klux Klan, but there seems to be no firm evidence of it.

In 1868 Pike moved to Washington where he lived the rest of his life in the study of Freemasonry, arcane scholarship, and mysticism. A great power in the Masonic movement, he wrote extensively for private circulation among members of the order. His only major published work in this period (1865–1891) is *Morals and Dogma of the Ancient and Accepted Scottish Rite of Freemasonry* (1871), a massive book blending the principles of Masonic ritual and Pike's own philosophy which drew heavily on Sanskrit religious texts. After Pike's death on April 2, 1891, his daughter, Mrs. L. P. Roome, published much of his poetry, and the Freemasons issued limited editions of a number of his works on Masonry and mysticism.

WORKS: *Prose Sketches and Poems, Written in the Western Country* (1834). *Nugae* (1854). "Letters to the Northern States" (1860). "Letter to the President of the Confederate States" (1862). *Morals and Dogma of the Ancient and Accepted Scottish Rite of Freemasonry* (1871). *"Hymns to the Gods" and Other Poems* (1872). *What Does Freemasonry Teach* (1892). *Masonic Justice* (1893). *The Duties of Freemasonry* (1894). *Lyrics and Love Poems*, ed. Mrs. L. P. Roome (1899). *Albert Pike on Prayer* (1901). *Albert Pike on Blue Lodge Masonry* (1904). *Irano-Aryan Faith and Doctrine as Contained in the Zend-Avesta* (1924). Lengthy extract from MS autobiography in *New Age Magazine* (August, 1929–September, 1930). *Indo-Aryan Dieties and Worship as Contained in the Rig-Veda* (1930). *Lectures of the Arya* (1930).

JACK COBBS
University of North Carolina
Greensboro

ELIZA LUCAS PINCKNEY (1722?–1793). Eliza Lucas was born in the West Indies on December 28, probably in 1722; she died of cancer on May 23, 1793. Christened Elizabeth, sometimes called Betsey, but generally known simply as Eliza, she spent her childhood in the West Indies and then studied in England for a few years. She rejoined the family in 1738 at Antigua and moved the next year to South Carolina, where her father George Lucas took up a plantation at Wappoo outside Charleston.

Although her Carolina contemporaries knew her best for experiments which led to successful indigo production in the 1740s, succeeding generations recognized in her writings a perceptive reflection of eighteenth-century life.

Eliza began to keep a letterbook in 1739 when her father's return to Antigua gave her the responsibility for an ailing mother, a younger sister, and the management of three plantations. (George Lucas was an army officer recalled to service when the War of Jenkin's Ear erupted.) Her letterbook continued until 1746, resumed in 1753, and finally ended in 1762. In the early period she wrote frequently to her father, reporting family news, plantation affairs, and local happenings. She also wrote numerous letters to Charles Pinckney, a leading Carolina planter and politician to whom she turned for advice and encouragement. Eliza eventually married Pinckney in 1744, after the death of his first wife. The three surviving children born of this union were Charles Cotesworth, Harriott, and Thomas. Eliza's letters of 1753–1758 provide a glimpse of the family's sojourn in England, while those of 1758–1762 are largely directed to her two sons who were left in England to continue their education.

No writing of this remarkable woman was published in her lifetime, but portions of her letterbook were privately published in

1850. This edition was succeeded in 1972 by a full letterbook in a modern edition. Eliza's letters reveal her as a lively and literate correspondent whose familiarity with Virgil and Locke distinguished her from her less educated contemporaries. They also reveal a woman of unusual diligence who looked upon an early rising at five in the morning as a virtue, read the classics for behavior models, managed three plantations with aplomb, and taught slave children to read with unperturbed equanimity.

WORKS: *Journal and Letters of Eliza Lucas*, ed. Harriott Pinckney Holbrook (1850). *The Letterbook of Eliza Lucas Pinckney*, ed. Elise Pinckney (1972).

DAVID R. CHESNUTT
University of South Carolina
Columbia

JOSEPHINE PINCKNEY (1895–1957). A descendant of two signers of the Constitution, Josephine Lyons Scott Pinckney was born in Charleston, S.C., on January 25, 1895, to Thomas and Camilla Scott Pinckney. She received her preparatory education at Ashley Hall in Charleston and studied at the College of Charleston, Columbia University, and Radcliffe College. Later the College of Charleston awarded her an honorary LL.D. She traveled widely and lived for a time in the East, though she lived most of her life in Charleston. Her interests included preservation of Charleston architecture and Negro spirituals. She was a trustee of the Charleston Museum. She died in New York City on October 4, 1957, after a brief illness.

Pinckney's verse was already being published when she joined in founding the South Carolina Poetry Society in 1920. Her 1927 volume of poems, *Sea-Drinking Cities*, is evocative of Charleston scenes, people, and moods.

Her greatest fame came as a novelist. In 1941 she published a historical novel, *Hilton Head*, based on accounts of Henry Woodward. The book's protagonist, a resourceful young English surgeon, commits himself to the New World and, after a number of adventures, plays a major role in building a colony on the Ashley

River. *Three O'Clock Dinner*, her next novel, and a best seller in 1945, is an amusing and skillful study of Charleston manners. It was selected by the Literary Guild and bought by a Hollywood producer for $125,000. After *Great Mischief*, a fantasy set in the South of the 1880s, involving a druggist interested in evil spirits, Pinckney located her next novel, one of chance and fate, *My Son and Foe*, on a bewitching Caribbean island. Her final novel, *Splendid in Ashes*, returns to the world of Charleston manners. Pinckney also wrote verse and articles that were published in various journals.

WORKS: *Sea-Drinking Cities* (1927). *Hilton Head* (1941). *Three O'Clock Dinner* (1945). *Great Mischief* (1948). *My Son and Foe* (1952). *Splendid in Ashes* (1958).

WILLIAM H. SLAVICK
University of Maine
Gorham

EDWARD COOTE PINKNEY (1802–1828). Naval officer, lawyer, poet, and editor, Edward Coote Pinkney is rarely mentioned today except as an influence upon Edgar Poe. He was born on October 1, 1802, in London, where his father, William Pinkney, served first as a U.S. commissioner and then as a minister to the Court of St. James. Returning to America in 1811, young Pinkney attended St. Mary's College in Baltimore, but at the age of thirteen he was appointed as a midshipman in the U.S. Navy.

Pinkney's career as a poet appears to have begun in 1822, during a tour of shore duty in Baltimore, but his first publication came in January, 1823, when his poem "Serenade" was set to music and published. He wrote other poems in 1823, and one of them, *Rodolph*, was published as a pamphlet. This same year Pinkney challenged the writer John Neal to a duel for an unflattering description of Pinkney's father that had appeared in Neal's novel *Randolph*. Neal refused the challenge, and Pinkney posted him as a coward.

In 1824 Pinkney resigned from the navy and became a law partner of Robert Wilson, Jr., in Baltimore. He continued to write poems, however, and published a collection in 1825.

When law did not yield adequate financial returns, Pinkney attempted without success to secure a commission in the Mexican navy. After his return from Mexico he was asked in 1827 by a political group to edit the *Marylander*, a paper founded to support John Quincy Adams against the Jacksonians. In this paper he published four of his poems as well as editorials. His editorial activities involved him in a near duel with the editor of the Philadelphia *Mercury*, a Jacksonian newspaper. Pinkney died on April 11, 1828, in Baltimore.

Pinkney's poems are usually described as "Cavalier" lyrics, influenced in expression and subject matter by Thomas Moore and Lord Byron. Although he wrote longer poems in the manner of Byron, he was at his best in lyrics, usually love songs or graceful compliments to women.

WORKS: *Look Out Upon the Stars, My Love* ("Serenade"), a single poem set to music (1823). *Rodolph. A Fragment*, pamphlet (1823). *Poems* (1825).

ROBERT D. JACOBS
Georgia State University
Atlanta

EDGAR ALLAN POE (1809–1849). World famous today for his haunting, musical poems and his masterful short tales of psychological aberration and crime detection, Poe is almost equally well known as a romantic figure whose life was marked by personal tragedy and frustration. Born in Boston, Mass., on January 19, 1809, to Elizabeth Arnold Poe and David Poe, Jr., itinerant actors, Edgar Poe was taken into the household of John Allan, a Richmond, Va., merchant, after the death of his mother on December 8, 1811. He was never legally adopted.

In 1815 young Poe accompanied his foster parents to England, where Allan had business interests, and was sent to private schools, chiefly the Manor House School at Stoke Newington. His memories of this school and its headmaster were later incorporated in his tale "William Wilson." Back in Richmond in 1820, Poe continued his education in private schools until 1826, when he entered the new University of Virginia. Allan sent him with insufficient funds to pay his expenses and brought him back to Richmond at the end of the term, ostensibly because of the heavy gambling and clothing debts the young man had incurred. In March, 1827, Poe left home for Boston, where he brought out a privately printed book entitled *Tamerlane and Other Poems*, now among the most valuable of rare American books. Subsequently he joined the U.S. Army and served until April 15, 1829, when, through Allan's help, he was able to secure a discharge and eventually an appointment to the U.S. Military Academy at West Point.

While awaiting the results of his application to the academy, Poe brought out a second book, entitled *Al Aaraaf, Tamerlane and Minor Poems* (1829) in Baltimore. He reported to West Point in June, 1830, but his stay at the academy was brief. In January, 1831, Poe wrote to Allan that he intended to leave West Point and asked for his guardian's permission. Angered, Allan did not reply, and Poe promptly took steps to insure his own dismissal by court martial. Shortly after he left West Point he published in New York his third book, *Poems by Edgar A. Poe, Second Edition* (1831).

The years following 1831 are obscure. Alienated from his foster father, Poe lived in Baltimore where he tried unsuccessfully for three years to earn a living by writing. His fortune improved when in October, 1833, it was announced that he had won a short-story contest held by a local journal. He also attracted the attention of John Pendleton Kennedy, one of the judges of the contest. Kennedy befriended Poe and got him a position with the *Southern Literary Messenger*, a monthly literary magazine founded in 1834 by T. W. White in Richmond. Poe functioned in 1835–1836 as assistant editor of the magazine and soon gained considerable reputation as a formidable literary critic as well as a writer of fiction and poetry. He was enabled to marry his thirteen-year-old cousin, Virginia Clemm, in 1836, but White never had full confidence in Poe and forced him to resign in January, 1837.

In spite of his reputation as an author and critic, Poe was unable to secure a new post for two years, which were spent first in New York then in Philadelphia. In Philadelphia he joined *Burton's Gentleman's Magazine* as assistant editor in June, 1839, but his tenure was brief. Burton sold the magazine to George R. Graham, who combined it with another to form *Graham's Magazine*. Poe was given an editorial post with this new publication in April, 1841. Between 1837 and 1841 Poe had published some of his most distinctive fiction: a short novel, *The Narrative of Arthur Gordon Pym* (1838), and a collection of short stories entitled *Tales of the Grotesque and Arabesque* (1840); but it was for *Graham's Magazine* that he wrote his best criticism with his classic reviews of Longfellow's *Ballads* and Hawthorne's *Twice-Told Tales*. He resigned from *Graham's* in May of 1842, perhaps because, as he said, his salary did not compensate him for his labor, but more probably because he wished to establish a magazine of his own. Unfortunately, it was at this crucial time that his young wife, Virginia, broke a blood vessel while singing, and her health deteriorated until her death in January, 1847.

Poe sought a political appointment from the Tyler administration in 1843 and tried to get political and financial backing for his projected magazine. Failing in both, he moved once more to New York in April, 1844, gaining a minor editorial position with the New York *Evening Mirror* in October. His most popular poem, "The Raven," appeared in the *Evening Mirror* on January 29, 1845. Also in 1845 Poe published a new edition of his short fiction, entitled *Tales*, and a new edition of his poems, *The Raven and Other Poems*. By October, 1845, he listed himself as "Editor and Proprietor" of the *Broadway Journal*, a weekly paper he acquired for $50 cash and the assumption of debts. His *Broadway Journal* lasted only a few months longer, however, ceasing publication in January, 1846.

Although 1845 had been one of Poe's most successful years, 1846 found him again in desperate circumstances. He was without a regular income, and the health of his wife rapidly declined. They moved to Fordham, N.Y., then a country village, and he endeavored to support them by free-lance journalism. Virginia died in early 1847, and Poe spent the remainder of the year in a state of acute depression. He was able, however, to begin an imaginative account of the nature of the universe he was to call *Eureka*. This "prose-poem" was published in 1848. Poe also attempted to marry Sarah Helen Whitman, but was finally rejected.

By 1849 Poe appeared once more in charge of himself and made plans to launch a new magazine, to be called the "Stylus." He made a trip to Richmond to publicize the new magazine and after a stay of some weeks left for New York. For a few days he disappeared and was found on the streets of Baltimore in deplorable physical condition. He was taken to the Washington College Hospital where he died on Sunday, October 7, 1849.

WORKS: *Tamerlane and Other Poems* (1827). *Al Aaraaf, Tamerlane and Minor Poems* (1829). *Poems. By Edgar A. Poe, Second Edition* (1831). *The Narrative of Arthur Gordon Pym, of Nantucket* (1838). *The Conchologist's First Book* (1839). *Tales of the Grotesque and Arabesque* (1840). *The Prose Romances of Edgar A. Poe: Uniform Serial Edition. No. 1* (1843), contains in pamphlet form the tales "The Murders in the Rue Morgue" and "The Man That Was Used Up." *Tales* (1845). *The Raven and Other Poems* (1845). *Eureka: A Prose Poem* (1848).

ROBERT D. JACOBS
Georgia State University
Atlanta

KATHERINE ANNE PORTER (1890–). Katherine Anne Porter was born Callie Russell Porter, May 15, 1890, in Indian Creek, Tex., the fourth of five children of Mary Alice and Harrison Boone Porter, both Methodists. After the mother's death (1892) the family lived in Kyle, Hays County, Tex., until the grandmother's death (1901). Subsequently they lived in San Antonio where Porter attended the Thomas School, a nonsectarian boarding school. While there, she acted in summer stock. After leaving school she taught classes in music and dramatic reading in Victoria, Tex. In 1906 she married John Henry Koontz, a clerk on the Southern Pacific Railway. In 1908 she adopted her husband's religion, Roman Catholicism.

After eight years of marriage she left for Chicago to become a movie actress (1914). Under mental and physical strain she contracted tuberculosis and during convalescence ran an outdoor school in Dallas for tubercular children (1916). In 1917 she began work on the Fort Worth *Critic* covering theatrical and social events. A year later she began work on the *Rocky Mountain News* in Denver and stayed there for a year, during which she nearly died in the epidemic of influenza.

In 1919 she went to New York and did hack work before leaving for the months in Mexico that provided the basis of her story "Flowering Judas." During 1921–1930 she lived mainly in the eastern United States but made frequent visits to Mexico. She published poetry, book reviews, and stories. Her first story, "Maria Concepcion," appeared in *Century* magazine in 1922. A brief marriage to Ernest Stock, an English World War I pilot, was dissolved in 1926. In 1929 five idyllic months in Bermuda, intended for work on the biography of Cotton Mather, resulted in the germination of the stories which eventually became "The Old Order" and "Old Mortality." When she returned to the United States she finished "Flowering Judas," the story which established her reputation as a writer.

Porter entered her most productive decade in the 1930s, encouraged by a Guggenheim and by the success of her first collection of short stories. She went to Mexico and there met Eugene Pressly, first with the Crane Foundation in Mexico City and after 1931 with the American Embassy in Madrid and then with the American Embassy in Paris. After spending two days on the set of Eisenstein's abortive movie "Que Viva Mexico," which she described in "Hacienda," she left with Pressly for Europe on the journey that provided the basis of *Ship of Fools*. She remained alone in Berlin in the fall of 1931 and later traveled throughout Europe to be near Pressly's embassy postings. They married in 1933 and settled in Paris. After their return from Europe in 1936, she went into seclusion and began "Pale Horse, Pale Rider" and finished "Noon Wine" and "Old Mortality." Separated from Pressly, she went to New Orleans where she met Albert Erskine, business manager of the *Southern Review*. They were married in

1938 and separated two years later. She left for Yaddo, N.Y., where she lived before settling into a home of her own in Saratoga Springs, N.Y. Discouraged by loneliness, financial pressure, and the inability to finish the story which became *Ship of Fools*, she accepted a job as a scriptwriter in Hollywood (1945). When that work proved unpalatable she supported herself by lecture tours and teaching stints at various universities—Stanford, Michigan, Liège, and Washington and Lee. *Ship of Fools*, triumphantly finished in 1962, brought literary acclaim and financial rewards.

The next years saw publication of her collected stories (winning the Pulitzer Prize and the National Book Award) and her collected essays. More honorary degrees were added to those she already held. She settled near the University of Maryland Library which houses, in the Katherine Anne Porter Room, her papers, books, and personal memorabilia.

In 1977 her last book, *The Never-Ending Wrong*, a memoir of the Saco-Vanzetti case, which she protested in 1927, appeared shortly after she had been stricken by a series of strokes.

WORKS: *Flowering Judas and Other Stories* (1930). *Katherine Anne Porter's French Song Book* (1933). *Hacienda* (1934). *Noon Wine* (1937). *Pale Horse, Pale Rider: Three Short Novels* (1939). *The Leaning Tower and Other Stories* (1944). *The Days Before* (1952). *Ship of Fools* (1962). *The Collected Stories of Katherine Anne Porter* (1965). *The Collected Essays and Occasional Writings of Katherine Anne Porter* (1970). *The Never-Ending Wrong* (1977).

JOAN GIVNER
University of Regina
Regina, Saskatchewan

WILLIAM SYDNEY PORTER [O. HENRY] (1862–1910). William Sydney Porter was born near Greensboro, N.C., on September 11, 1862. With youthful enthusiasm for literature and a pharmacist's license, he left Greensboro in 1882, spent two years on a Texas ranch, and began writing sketches of frontier life. From 1884 to 1896 he held various jobs in Texas—as clerk, draftsman, bank teller, and newspaper reporter—but devoted most of his leisure to writing short fiction.

In 1887 Porter married Athol Estes Roach, step-daughter of a prominent Austin merchant. Seven years later, following the birth of Margaret, their second child, he launched a comic weekly, the *Rolling Stone* (1894–1895), apparently subsidized in part by money surreptitiously borrowed from his employers' funds. Indicted for embezzlement in 1896, he fled to Honduras, remaining there until word of his wife's terminal illness drew him back to Austin. Six months after her death Porter was tried (February, 1898), convicted, and sentenced to serve time in the Ohio Federal Penitentiary.

Porter's renown under the pseudonym O. Henry grew out of his prison experience, as stories written there, based on his earlier adventures, captured the attention of New York magazines. In 1902 he moved to New York, and, under the guarded secrecy of his pseudonym, he quickly became the nation's preeminent short-story writer. During his remaining eight years he produced nearly 300 stories, later reissued in fourteen collections. Despite burgeoning fame and income, Porter died a pauper deeply in debt on June 5, 1910; yet subsequent editions of his stories, translated into many foreign languages, have sold millions of copies. Royalties from these and from stage and screen rights enabled his daughter Margaret to repay all his debts before her own death on June 5, 1927. As O. Henry, Porter's fame has become legendary, yet the final chapter in that legend remains to be written.

WORKS: *Cabbages and Kings* (1904). *The Four Million* (1906). *The Trimmed Lamp* (1907). *Heart Of The West* (1907). *The Voice Of The City* (1908). *The Gentle Grafter* (1908). *Roads Of Destiny* (1909). *Options* (1909). *Strictly Business* (1910). *Whirligigs* (1910). *Sixes and Sevens* (1911). *Rolling Stones* (1917). *Waifs and Strays* (1917). *O. Henryana* (1920). *Letters To Lithopolis* (1922). *Postscripts* (1923). *O. Henry Encore*, ed. Mary S. Harrell (1939).

EUGENE CURRENT-GARCIA
Auburn University
Auburn, Ala.

JOHN PORY (1572–1636). Born in Thompson, Norfolk, of a well-to-do farming family, Pory was graduated from Caius College, Cambridge, the university with which relatives had been associated for many years. After teaching Greek at Caius for two years he began private study with Richard Hakluyt, geographer-historian, and assisted in the preparation of Hakluyt's *Voyages* (1600). Pory's own book, *A Geographical Historie of Africa*, appeared later the same year and became the source of most of the impressions of Africa and Africans held by Englishmen, including Shakespeare, well into the eighteenth century. His *Epitome of Ortelius* (1602), a condensation of a larger work, was intended for the growing body of literate Englishmen who could not read Latin.

Pory served in Parliament, 1605–1611, afterwards traveling on the Continent and serving on the embassy staff in Constantinople, 1613–1616. He was a lifelong friend of John Donne; both were incorporated M.A. at Oxford at the same convocation, and Pory delivered letters to Donne in France. He was also a friend of Ben Jonson, and both men participated in a disputation in Paris in 1612, afterwards collaborating in the publication of *The Summe and Substance of a Disputation* (1630).

In 1618 Pory became secretary in the colony of Virginia under Governor Sir George Yeardley, his cousin's husband. In this capacity Pory served as speaker of the first American legislature organizing it along the lines of the House of Commons.

As a writer of newsletters, precursor of the newspaper, Pory is perhaps best known. His letters from 1606 to 1633 touch on innumerable subjects but are of especial interest for their information about Virginia, the Thirty Years' War, affairs of the Court of England, and personal observations of scores of his contemporaries including literary figures, artists, royalty, and the nobility. While in Virginia, Pory explored in the vicinity of the Potomac River and down into what later became North Carolina and in returning to England also visited Plymouth, Mass.

WORKS: *A Geographical Historie of Africa* (1600). *An Epitome of Ortelius* (1602). "The observations of Master John Pory Secretarie of Virginia, in his travels," in John Smith, *The General Historie of Virginia* (1624).

The Summe and Substance of a Disputation, with Ben Jonson (1630). Pory's newsletters and other minor writings are in William S. Powell, *John Pory, 1572–1636: A Man of Many Parts* (1976).

WILLIAM S. POWELL
University of North Carolina
Chapel Hill

MARGARET JUNKIN PRESTON (1820–1897). Margaret Junkin Preston was born in Milton, Pa., on May 19, 1820. She was the daughter of a distinguished minister and educator, Dr. George Junkin. Under his tutelage Margaret learned to read both Latin and Greek by the age of twelve. Indeed, the intense reading associated with her studies seriously impaired her eyesight by the age of 25.

In 1848, after serving as founding president of Lafayette College, Dr. Junkin accepted the presidency of Washington College (now Washington and Lee University) in Lexington, Va. Here Margaret spent nine happy years in her father's house, devoting her free time to writing. In 1856 her first novel, *Silverwood*, was published anonymously. The following year she married Major J. T. L. Preston, a professor of Latin at Virginia Military Institute and a widower with seven children. In 1861 her father, a Unionist, resigned from the presidency of Washington College and left Virginia with Margaret's sister. Margaret, however, was firmly loyal to her adopted state and remained in Lexington.

From 1862 to 1865, while her husband fought in the Civil War and served on the staff of General Stonewall Jackson, Margaret kept a detailed journal which became the source for her long narrative poem, *Beechenbrook, A Rhyme of War* (1865). This story of a family whose father is serving in the Confederate Army was reprinted eight times and spread Mrs. Preston's name throughout the South as the poetic spokeswoman for "proud Virginia."

Through Reconstruction Margaret Preston continued to combine the roles of housewife, mother, and poet. She published four collections of poetry and a travelbook between 1870 and the loss of her eyesight in the late 1880s. In these collections she demonstrated a wide range of technique and subject matter, from European folk legends and American ballads, to sonnets and poetic vignettes drawn from Vasari's lives of the great Italian artists. She died in Baltimore at the home of her son on March 28, 1897.

WORKS: *Silverwood: A Book of Memories* (1856). *Beechenbrook: A Rhyme of War* (1865). *Old Song and New* (1870). *Cartoons* (1875). *Centennial Poem for Washington and Lee University: Lexington, Virginia, 1775–1885* (1885). *A Handful of Monographs, Continental and English* (1886). *For Love's Sake: Poems of Faith and Comfort* (1886). *Colonial Ballads, Sonnets and Other Verse* (1887). *Semi-Centennial Ode for the Virginia Military Institute: Lexington, Virginia, 1839–1889* (1889). *Aunt Dorothy: An Old Virginia Plantation Story* (1890).

RITCHIE D. WATSON, JR.
Randolph-Macon College
Ashland, Va.

REYNOLDS PRICE (1933–). One of the South's most talented writers, Edward Reynolds Price was born on February 1, 1933, in Macon, N.C. Combining native syntax in his dialogue with natural descriptions of rural Carolina, Price has created a people-centered fictional world, recognizably part of the southern literary tradition but unique in many ways. Warren County provides settings for his rural protagonists who search for meaning and identity, often to discover it, when they are fortunate, in gratuitous acts of giving or sharing. The movement of the fiction is from provincial beginnings toward universal implications.

The son of William Solomon and Elizabeth Rodwell Price, Price is a 1955 Phi Beta Kappa graduate of Duke University and a former Rhodes Scholar at Merton College, Oxford. He has been on the Duke University faculty since 1962, the same year his first novel, *A Long and Happy Life*, was published by Atheneum. The book received the Sir Walter Raleigh Award and the William Faulkner Award (for the most notable first novel published by an American in that year). The people he describes have been shaped by Protestant fundamentalism and their Scotch-Irish and English backgrounds. Their world is the Piedmont South, not the aristocratic Tidewater South or the exotic, complex, Deep South.

In 1963 Price published a collection of his stories under the title *The Names and Faces of Heroes*. Some of these had previously appeared in *Shenandoah*, the *Virginia Quarterly Review*, and other journals. Some of his stories have been included in the annual editions of *O. Henry Prize Stories*. Price received a Guggenheim Fellowship in 1964, and the following year he was writer-in-residence at the University of North Carolina. Since then he has continued teaching at Duke and has published four novels, collections of stories, translations, essays, a play, and a volume of poetry, *Late Warnings*. In his most recent novel, *The Surface of the Earth* (1975), he has followed several generations of the fictional Mayfield and Kendal families in a complex narrative. The book includes large segments of letters, monologues, and dreams which reveal the impact of passing time on a clearly defined section of rural America.

WORKS: *A Long and Happy Life* (1962). *The Names and Faces of Heroes* (1963). *A Generous Man* (1966). *Late Warning* (1968). *Love and Work* (1968). *Permanent Errors* (1970). *Things Themselves* (1972). *The Surface of the Earth* (1975). *Early Dark* (1977). *A Palpable God* (1978).

KIMBALL KING
University of North Carolina
Chapel Hill

JAMES RYDER RANDALL (1839–1908). Poet and journalist, James Ryder Randall is best known for his patriotic poem "Maryland, My Maryland." His father was a descendant of English and Irish Randalls who came to Maryland in the seventeenth century and for whom Randallstown was named. His mother was a descendant of Acadian exiles who settled in Baltimore in 1755; René Leblanc, the Notary in Longfellow's "Evangeline," was Randall's great-great grandfather. Randall was born on January 1, 1839.

Taught by Joseph H. Clarke, Poe's schoolmaster in Richmond, Randall afterward entered Georgetown College where he was recognized as an exceptional student of English and as a writer of poetry. Illness prevented him from finishing his final year. Following a trip to the West Indies he worked as a printer in Baltimore and then as a clerk in New Orleans before accepting the position of Professor of English and Classics at Poydras College in Louisiana.

Prompted by an account in the New Orleans *Delta* of fighting in Baltimore between Maryland and Massachusetts troops in April, 1861, and of the death of a college friend, Randall, a fervent secessionist, wrote "Maryland, My Maryland." After it was published in the *Delta* and later set to the music of "Tannenbaum, O Tannenbaum" by the Carey sisters of Baltimore, the poem's wartime success was assured.

Randall's remaining years were spent as a journalist and poet, the popularity of his "Maryland" overshadowing a rather substantial number of other war poems of merit. He died on January 14, 1908, before he was able to collect and publish his poems, though a volume hastily edited appeared in the year of his death, and a better one in 1910. Just prior to his death he was honored as the official guest of the state of Maryland at the Jamestown Exposition, and at Homecoming Week by the city of Baltimore. He was survived by his wife and four of his eight children.

WORKS: *Maryland, My Maryland and Other Poems* (1908). *The Poems of James Ryder Randall*, ed. Matthew Page Andrews (1910).

WILLIAM OSBORNE
Memphis State University
Memphis, Tenn.

JAMES INNES RANDOLPH, JR. (1837–1887). Second of the many children of J. I. Randolph of the "Turkey Island" family and the former Marguerite S. P. Armistead, Randolph was born on October 25, 1837, at Barleywood homestead, Frederick County, Va., attended Hobart College, Geneva, N.Y., and graduated from the State and National Law School, Poughkeepsie, N.Y. In 1859 he married Anna Clare King of Georgetown, D.C.; the couple had four children. Randolph served throughout the Civil War as a topographical engineer, rising to the rank of major. He then settled at Richmond as a newsman for the *Examiner* and entered into his most fecund period as light versifier and fiction writer. None of his tales, which earned him local renown, has been identified, and his poetry was only posthumously collected. Therein the "Vignettes" are remarkable as free verse. The internationally popular jeremiad against the Union beginning, "Oh, I'm a good old Rebel," was first sung by him at meetings of the Mosaic Club, Richmond, during the war, but apparently published only on July 4, 1867, in the Augusta, Ga., *Constitutionalist*.

In 1868 Randolph took his family permanently to Baltimore and commenced practice of law. Journalism shared his energies, and he worked variously for nearly all the city's newspapers, becoming chief editorial writer for the *American* and gaining repute as its music critic. In 1884 the paper sent him to Europe as its political and social correspondent. He distinguished himself as an amateur athlete, painter, sculptor, and musician, performing on virtually every instrument, especially the violoncello. He died on April 28, 1887, of heart disease and is buried in an unmarked grave of the Randolphs in the Green Mount Cemetery, Baltimore.

WORKS: *The Grasshopper: A Tragic Cantata* (1878). *Poems* (1898).

CURTIS CARROLL DAVIS
Baltimore, Md.

JOHN CROWE RANSOM (1888–1974). John Crowe Ransom was born on April 30, 1888, in Pulaski, Tenn., the home of his mother's (Ella Crowe Ransom) parents. After brief periods in California and Cuba, his father, John James Ransom, a learned Methodist minister who had spent ten years as a missionary in Brazil, returned to Tennessee, where he served as a Methodist minister until his retirement in 1922. Between 1891 and 1899, from the time John Crowe Ransom was three until he was eleven, his father served four churches in middle Tennessee: Spring Hill, Franklin, Springfield, and North High Street, Nashville. Because of these frequent moves, which usually occurred in early autumn, John Crowe Ransom did not enter public school until he was eleven, receiving private tutoring from his father and mother and reading in the excellent library his father had collected for the use of the members of the rural churches he served. After only one year in public school, Ransom entered the Bowen School in Nashville. In 1903, a few days after his fifteenth birthday, he took the strenuous examinations required for admission to Vanderbilt University and scored the highest mark in English, history, and mathematics.

At the end of his second year at Vanderbilt, financial necessity forced him to withdraw from the university and seek a teaching position. He taught one year at the Taylorsville, Miss., public school and one year at the Haynes-McLean School in Lewisburg, Tenn. He returned to Vanderbilt in the fall of 1907 and was graduated two years later, Phi Beta Kappa and number one in his class. After one more session at the Haynes-McLean School, he entered Christ Church College of Oxford University as a Rhodes Scholar and in the spring of 1913 received a degree in *Literae Humaniores*. He taught Latin at the Hotchkiss School of Lakeville, Conn., for one year before joining the faculty of Vanderbilt University in the fall of 1914, a position he retained, except for two years in the army in World War I, until the fall of 1937, when he became a professor of English (later Carnegie Professor of Poetry) at Kenyon College in Gambier, Ohio. He died in Gambier on July 30, 1974.

Between April, 1922, and December, 1925, Ransom and a small group of literary associates—including Allen Tate, Robert Penn Warren, and Donald Davidson—published the *Fugitive*, a magazine of verse and brief critical commentary. This little magazine, one of the best known of its kind ever published in America, contains much of Ransom's most mature verse. Although he had published one book of poetry, *Poems About God* (1919), before the first issue of the *Fugitive* appeared and wrote a half dozen or so poems after the magazine ceased publication, his career as active poet coincides almost exactly with the lifespan of the *Fugitive*. Almost all of the poems that Randall Jarrell has called "almost perfect lyrics" were written between 1922 and 1925. In 1939, shortly after he moved from Vanderbilt, Ransom founded and edited for more than 20 years the *Kenyon Review*, a journal which did much to disseminate the New Criticism by publishing some of the most influential critical essays of this century.

After 1925 his work lay in another direction: critical and philosophical prose. Along with eleven other southerners, Ransom contributed to the symposium *I'll Take My Stand* (1930), in which he and his fellow contributors assailed some of the major vices of modern America: an unquestioning confidence in industrial capitalism, the rampant growth of materialism, the need of an inscrutable God, and a belief in the fallibility of the natural and social sciences. All of these concerns, particularly the last, carry over into the three books he published in the 1930s and 1940s: *God Without Thunder* (1930), *The World's Body* (1938), and *The New Criticism* (1941). He argues for a God of thunder, one which man cannot apprehend with his senses nor explain with his reason, and he insists that man can fully realize human experience only through art.

As poet, critic, and editor, John Crowe Ransom was one of the most significant and influential American men of letters of the first half of the twentieth century.

WORKS: *Poems About God* (1919). *Chills and Fever* (1924). *Grace After Meat* (1924). *Two Gentlemen in Bonds* (1927). *God Without Thunder* (1930). *The World's Body* (1938). *The New Criticism* (1941). *Selected Poems* (1945). *Poems and Essays* (1955). *Selected Poems* (1963). *Selected Poems*, rev. and enl. (1969). *Beating the Bushes* (1972).

THOMAS DANIEL YOUNG
Vanderbilt University
Nashville, Tenn.

BEATRICE RAVENEL (1870–1956). Of the group of poets most active in the Poetry Society of South Carolina in the 1920s, Beatrice Witte Ravenel is perhaps least known, in large part because unlike DuBose Heyward, Hervey Allen, and Josephine Pinckney she did not subsequently achieve a reputation as a writer of fiction. During her long lifetime she published only a single book, *Arrow of Lightning* (1925). Yet in her use of language, in her strong sense of place and of history, she produced some few poems that avoid the immediately exotic and picturesque uses of local color writing and are striking in their imaginativeness and in their richness and specificity of imagery.

Born in Charleston on August 24, 1870, she was the third of six daughters of Charles Otto Witte, German-born and a prominent businessman and civic leader, and Charlotte Sophia Reeves Witte. She was educated privately, and in 1889 enrolled in the women's division of Harvard University. There she played a prominent role in a group of literary young men and women, including William Vaughn Moody, Trumbull Stickney, and Norman and Hutchins Hapgood, wrote for the *Harvard Monthly* and the *Advocate*, and published poems in *Scribner's Magazine*, the *Chap-Book Magazine*, and the *Literary Digest*.

In 1900 she married Francis Gualdo Ravenel, whose mother, Harriet Horry Ravenel, was a writer and biographer of some note. For some years the Ravenels and their daughter, Beatrice St. Julien, born in 1904, lived on a plantation south of Charleston, the setting for several of her best poems, which deal with the Yemassee Indian heritage of the Carolina low country. Frank Ravenel was no businessman; by the late 1910s the sizable fortune left Beatrice Ravenel by her father was gone, and she helped support the family by writing fiction for *Ainslie's*, *Harper's*, and the *Saturday Evening Post*, and after 1919 she wrote editorials for the Columbia (S.C.) *State*.

In the late 1910s she began writing poetry again, and in the early 1920s came an abrupt change in her verse. Almost overnight she put aside the sentimental abstractions of the waning genteel tradition and began producing free verse of a notable economy of diction, precision of language and vivid imagery. The formation of the South Carolina Poetry Society brought her into contact with other poets, including visitors such as Amy Lowell, with whom she formed a strong friendship.

In 1926, six years after her first husband's death, she married Samuel Prioleau Ravenel. It was no longer necessary for her to support her daughter and herself through journalism and fiction. The Ravenels traveled extensively. Though she wrote little poetry during her later years, one sequence based on the West Indies, unpublished in her lifetime, is among her most accomplished work. She died on March 15, 1956, at the age of 85. A selection of her work was published in 1969.

WORKS: *Arrow of Lightning* (1925). *The Yemassee Lands* (1969).

Louis D. Rubin, Jr.
University of North Carolina
Chapel Hill

MARJORIE KINNAN RAWLINGS (1896–1953). Marjorie Kinnan was born on August 8, 1896, in Washington, D.C., and educated in the public schools of that city and at the University of Wisconsin. In 1919 she married Charles A. Rawlings and worked as a newspaper reporter and feature writer in Louisville, Ky., and Rochester, N.Y., until 1928 when she left city and job for a 40-acre orange grove in the tiny hamlet of Cross Creek in north-central Florida. Here she found in the wild beauty of the Florida countryside and her "cracker" neighbors a remnant of the American frontier which deeply stirred her writer's imagination. With the publication of her first Florida stories (1931) she became a protégé of Maxwell Perkins, the famous editor at Scribner's, and thus joined a literary elite which included Wolfe, Hemingway, and Fitzgerald.

Her writings give expression to pastoral themes in the tradition of Thoreau, Cooper, and Jefferson. She had a remarkable ear for folk speech and wrote a series of comic stories in dialect in the vein established by Mark Twain. These qualities mark *The Yearling*, her greatest success. She was divorced from Charles Rawlings in 1933 and was remarried in 1941 to Norton S. Baskin. She was working on a biography of Ellen Glasgow when she died at her beach home near St. Augustine on December 14, 1953. She was taken for burial to Island Grove, Fla., in the midst of the Cross Creek country she had loved so well.

WORKS: *South Moon Under* (1933). *Golden Apples* (1935). *The Yearling* (1938). *When the Whipporwill* (1940). *Cross Creek* (1942). *The Sojourner* (1953). *Secret River* (1955).

Gordon Bigelow
University of Florida
Gainesville

OPIE PERCIVAL READ (1852–1939). Opie Percival Read was born on December 22, 1852, in Nashville, Tenn., youngest child of Guilford and Elizabeth Wallace Read. At nineteen he was setting type for the Franklin *Patriot* in Simpson County, Ky., then worked his way through the now defunct Neophegen College in Gallatin, Tenn., and two years later was back in Allen County, Ky., publishing the Scottsville *Argus*. In 1878 he became city editor of the Little Rock *Daily Arkansas Gazette*; in 1881 he went to Cleveland for a brief stint with the *Leader*; and in 1882 he was back in Little Rock, where he founded the weekly *Arkansaw Traveller*. Read's genius as a story teller, his extravagance and exaggeration tempered with homely philosophy, his scorn for traditional concepts of culture and polish in the Old South and the East, and his ineradicable faith in the individualism of the Old Southwest won a circulation of 85,000 for the paper.

In 1887 he moved the editorial offices to Chicago, his permanent home thereafter. In 1891 he resigned the editorship of the *Traveller* and concentrated on lecturing and writing novels and short stories. The bulk of his fiction came in the next decade and a half, after which he produced only three novels, a humorous pamphlet on golf, and the autobiography, *I Remember* (1930). He spent most of his active years on the Chautauqua and other lecture circuits. His novels were popular at the time, and it is said that *The Jucklins* (1896) sold over a million copies.

Read has been quoted as saying that he based his style on the readers of William Holmes McGuffey and his appreciation of literature from the Shakespearian quotations in the readers. His unbridled sentiment and insistent moralizing surely reflect the influence of McGuffey, and his unlikely melodramatic plots and popular stereotypes recall some Elizabethan traditions. Read, six feet, three inches, and 250 pounds, was called the "greatest literary shortstop of his time" (*Time*, November 13, 1939). He was a survivor of the heroic era of Trans-Appalachia. He died November 2, 1939.

WORKS: *Len Gansett* (1888). *Up Terrapin River* (1889). *A Kentucky Colonel* (1890). *Mrs. Annie Green: A Romance* (1890). *Emmett Bonlore*

(1891). *Selected Stories* (1891). *Twenty Good Stories* (1891). *The Colossus: A Story* (1893). *A Tennessee Judge: A Novel* (1893). *The Tear in the Cup and Other Stories* (1894). *The Wives of the Prophet* (1894). *Miss Polly Lopp and Other Stories* (1895). *On the Suwanee River: A Romance* (1895). *An Arkansas Planter* (1896). *The Captain's Romance, or, Tales of the Backwoods* (1896). *The Jucklins* (1896). *My Young Master: A Novel* (1896). *Bolanyo: A Novel* (1897). *Odd Folks* (1897). *Old Ebenezer* (1897). *The Waters of Caney Fork: A Romance of Tennessee* (1898). *A Yankee from the West: A Novel* (1898). *The Carpetbagger: A Novel* (1899). *Judge Elbridge* (1899). *In the Alamo* (1900). *Our Josephine, and Other Tales* (1902). *The Starbucks: A New Novel* (1902). *The Harkriders: A Novel* (1903). *The American Cavalier* (1904). *"Turk": A Novel* (1904). *An American in New York: A Novel of To-day* (1905). *Old Lim Jucklin: The Opinions of an Open-air Philosopher* (1905). *Opie Read in the Ozarks, Including Many of the Rich, Rare, Quaint, Eccentric, Ignorant, and Superstitious Sayings of the Natives of Missouri and Arkansaw* (1905). *The Son of the Swordmaker: A Romance* (1905). *"Turkey Egg" Griffin ("Turk"): A Novel* (1905). *"By the Eternal": A Novel* (1906). *Tom and the Squatter's Son: A Stirring Tale of Adventure in the Pioneer Days for Boys from 7 to 60* (1910). *The New Mr. Howerson* (1914). *Opie Read on Golf* (1925). *"Come on Buck"* (1926). *The Gold Gauze Veil* (1927). *I Remember* (1930). *Mark Twain and I* (1940).

LAWRENCE S. THOMPSON
University of Kentucky
Lexington

JAY SAUNDERS REDDING (1906–). Jay Saunders Redding—scholar, educator, man of letters—was born in Wilmington, Del., on October 13, 1906. He attended Lincoln University in Pennsylvania for one year before entering Brown University where he completed requirements for undergraduate (Ph.B., 1928) and graduate degrees (M.A., 1932). Since 1932 he has been presented with six honorary degrees and many other awards, including Rockefeller and Guggenheim fellowships, the National Urban League Service Award, and the Mayflower Award. He has taught at Morehouse College (1928–1931), Louisville Municipal College (1933–1935), Southern University (1936–1938), Elizabeth City State Teachers College (1938–1943), Hampton Institute (1943–

1966), and at many other major colleges and universities. When he retired in 1975, he was the Ernest I. White Professor of American Studies and Humane Letters at Cornell University. Redding has also lectured in India for the State Department, in Africa for the American Society of African Culture, and throughout America at scholarly assemblies. He has served on the editorial board of the *American Scholar* (1954–1962); he has directed the Division of Research and Publication, National Endowment for the Humanities (1966–1969); and his own articles and reviews have appeared in numerous periodicals, notably the *American Scholar, Atlantic Monthly, Harper's, Nation, Negro Digest, Phylon, Saturday Review*, and *Transition*.

Among Redding's book-length publications, *No Day of Triumph* has often been adjudged his best volume. It won the North Carolina Historical Society's Award of 1942 for the year's best book by a North Carolina resident. Combining autobiography with a report of observations made while traveling through the South, Redding presents a dramatic account of southern Negro life in the 1940s. Besides this excellent book, he has written or edited nine others, including fiction, biography, history, and literary criticism. In each work his writing is effective and revelatory of his impressive knowledge of Negro American history, literature, and culture.

WORKS: *To Make a Poet Black* (1939). *No Day of Triumph* (1942). *Stranger and Alone* (1950). *They Came in Chains* (1950). *On Being Negro in America* (1951). Ed., *Reading for Writing*, with Ivan E. Taylor (1952). *An American in India* (1954). *The Lonesome Road* (1958). *The Negro* (1967). Ed., *Cavalcade: Negro American Writing from 1760 to the Present*, with Arthur P. Davis (1971).

PATSY B. PERRY
North Carolina Central University
Durham

BYRON HERBERT REECE (1917–1958). Byron Herbert Reece was born on September 14, 1917, at the foot of Blood Mountain in north Georgia to Juan and Emma Reece. Reece lived as a young boy in a secluded mountain area, not seeing an automobile until he was eight years old. Before entering the Choestoe Elementary School in 1923, Reece had read *Pilgrim's Progress* and much of the Bible, upon which many of his later ballads were based.

In June, 1935, Reece was graduated from Blairsville High School and entered Young Harris College in September. There he published numerous poems in the small poetry journals and attracted the attention of Ralph McGill, editor of the Atlanta *Constitution*. Reece left Young Harris College without being graduated because he refused to take the required courses in French, which he considered an affectation.

He returned to his parents' farm where he did heavy farm work during the day and at night composed literary mountain ballads. He attracted the attention of Jesse Stuart who had read Reece's work in *Prairie Schooner*. On Stuart's recommendation E. P. Dutton published *Ballad of the Bones* in October, 1945, which immediately received wide and favorable critical acclaim. After Reece published a novel, *Better a Dinner of Herbs* (1950), he was invited to the University of California at Los Angeles as poet-in-residence. In 1953 he was invited to Young Harris College as poet-in-residence but was forced early in 1954 to enter Battey Hospital at Rome, Ga., because of tuberculosis.

By early 1956 Reece had recovered sufficiently to become poet-in-residence at Emory University. He returned the following fall to Young Harris College. The following summer he received a Guggenheim award, but illness and depression forced him to return to his mountain home. After another academic year at Young Harris College, he committed suicide on June 3, 1958.

WORKS: "The Hills Not Home," in *Three Lyric Poets* (1942). *Ballad of the Bones* (1945). *Remembrance of Moab* (1949). *Better a Dinner of Herbs* (1950). *Bow Down in Jericho* (1950). *A Song of Joy* (1952). *The Season of Flesh* (1955). *The Hawk and the Sun* (1955).

RAYMOND A. COOK
Valdosta State College
Valdosta, Ga.

ISHMAEL REED (1938–). Novelist, poet, and critic, Ishmael Reed was born February 22, 1938, in Chattanooga, Tenn., the son of Bennie Stephen and Thelma Coleman Reed. He moved at an early age to Buffalo, N.Y., where he attended school and "served time" at Buffalo Technical High School. From 1956 until 1960 he attended the State University of New York at Buffalo, but left school because of the "wide gap between social classes." Reed then moved "into Buffalo's notorious Talbert Mall Project (a horrible experience)," and says of this period, "A time of political activism was followed by one of cynicism."

He married Priscilla Rose in September, 1960; they have one daughter, Timothy Brett. Reed and his wife separated in 1963 and were subsequently divorced. He is now married to Carla Blank.

In 1962 Reed moved from Buffalo to New York City, where he participated in the Umbra Workshop, writing and studying Afro-American culture. He moved to California, where he taught at the University of California at Berkeley (1968–1969) and at the University of Washington in the winter of 1969. He resides in Berkeley, Calif.

A member of the Authors League of America and of P.E.N., Reed has received numerous awards—among them an award from the National Institute of Arts and Letters (1975), a writing fellowship from the National Endowment for the Arts (1974), and a Guggenheim Fellowship (1975).

From the publication of his first novel, *The Free-Lance Pallbearers* (1967), Reed has received considerable critical attention for his experiments in forms of fiction and poetry, for his satirical examination of black and white American culture, and for his knowledge and use of Afro-American folklore and myth in his work. *Mumbo Jumbo* (1972) firmly established Reed's reputation as an important American novelist. Although Reed has lived most of his life outside the South, his fiction and poetry—especially *Chattanooga: Poems* (1973)—show his indebtedness to his Afro-American and southern heritage.

WORKS: *The Free-Lance Pallbearers* (1967). *Yellow Back Radio Break-Down* (1969). *Catechism of the Neo-American HooDoo Church* (1970). Ed., *19 Necromancers From Now* (1970). *Mumbo Jumbo* (1972). *Conjure: Selected Poems, 1963–1970* (1972). *Chattanooga: Poems* (1973). *The Last*

Days of Louisiana Red (1974). *Secretary of the Spirits* (1976). *Flight to Canada* (1976).

ROBERT BAIN
University of North Carolina
Chapel Hill

LIZETTE WOODWORTH REESE (1856–1935). Poet and teacher, Lizette Woodworth Reese, a twin and one of four daughters, was born on January 9, 1856, to David Reese and Louisa Gabler Reese and reared in Waverly, Md., a suburb of Baltimore. Graduating from Eastern High School, she began teaching and publishing poetry before she was 20. Before her retirement in 1921 she had taught for several decades in various public and private schools in the Baltimore area, including a high school for black children.

Her first published poem, "The Deserted House," appeared in the *Southern Magazine* in 1874, and her first volume of poetry, *A Branch of May*, was published in Baltimore in 1877. This volume, one of fourteen that would be published during her lifetime and posthumously, was well received, and gained her the friendship of the critic Edmund Clarence Stedman.

Although the period from 1897 to 1919 was a relatively barren one, *Scribner's Magazine* published her best-known poem, the sonnet "Tears," in 1899. Her career picked up in 1920, and she published steadily almost until her death at 79, her writings consisting not only of poetry but also of essays, stories, and an unfinished novel, *Worleys*.

Her poetry was intensely personal, direct, and economical, her traditional idiom and subject matter little affected by the "new poetry" and the free verse vogue. In verse and prose she provided a believable portrait of life in her Victorian Maryland village.

The alumni of Western High School, where she had taught for 20 years, honored her in 1923 by giving the school a bronze scroll inscribed with her poem "Tears." Other honors she received were election to Phi Beta Kappa at William and Mary as an honorary member in 1925, and an honorary Doctor of Letters from Goucher College in 1931.

She died on December 17, 1935, was buried in the churchyard of St. John's Church in Waverly, where she had begun her teaching career.

WORKS: *A Branch of May* (1887). *A Handful of Lavender* (1891). *A Quiet Road* (1896). *A Wayside Lute* (1909). *A Victorian Village: Reminiscences of Other Days* (1920). *Wild Cherry* (1923). *The Selected Poems of Lizette Woodworth Reese* (1926). *Little Henrietta* (1927). *White April and Other Poems* (1930). *The York Road* (1931). *Pastures and Other Poems* (1933). *The Old House in the Country* (1936). *Worleys* (1936).

WILLIAM OSBORNE
Memphis State University
Memphis, Tenn.

JAMES REID *(fl.* **1768).** Like so many southern colonial writers, James Reid left few discernible tracks. He was evidently born and schooled in Edinburgh, Scotland, where he was a classmate and contemporary of the blind poet, Thomas Blalock (1721–1791). Reid had migrated to Virginia by the late 1760s, perhaps as a tutor, even an indentured tutor, to a planter. Evidence indicates that Reid served as schoolmaster to the family of Colonel Robert Ruffin, who during the winter of 1768–1769 moved from his Mayfield plantation in Dinwiddie County to Sweet Hall or to the adjoining plantation of Windsor Shades in King William County to be nearer a daughter married to a Claiborne. Reid, whose religious sympathies have been characterized as Old Light Presbyterian, found the move to King William County unsatisfactory. He satirized the King Williamites as arrogant, crude, and ignorant.

Under the pseudonym of "Caledoniensis," Reid published between September 15, 1768, and March 30, 1769, nine or ten poems and four essays in the *Virginia Gazette* of Purdie and Dixon. Three of the essays deal with religious and theological problems, and the fourth with abuses of language. The poems range in subject from mock elegies to love poems to verse satires.

Reid's long prose satire, *The Religion of the Bible and Religion of K[ing] W[illiam] County Compared*, written in 1769 but not published until 1967, depicts the young Virginia gentry not as esquires, but as "Ass-queers." The Ass-queer "drinks, fights, bullies, curses, swears, whores, games." "This," says Reid, "comprehends his whole life, and renders him a Polite Gentleman, or to use the modern elegant phrase—a damn'd honest Fellow." Reid presents a view of the Virginia gentleman current among immigrants and back-country people of the day, and his attitude counterpoints that of many romantic versions of the nineteenth century. Scholars have not discovered further biographical details.

WORKS: *The Religion of the Bible and Religion of K[ing] W[illiam] County Compared*, ed. Richard Beale Davis, *The Colonial Virginia Satirist* (Philadelphia, 1967) in *Transactions of the American Philosophical Society*, New Ser., LVII, Pt. 1, pp. 43–71. Richard Beale Davis, "James Reid: Colonial Virginia Poet and Moral and Religious Essayist," in *Literature and Society in Early Virginia: 1608–1840* (Baton Rouge: Louisiana State University Press, 1973), 168–91.

ROBERT BAIN
University of North Carolina
Chapel Hill

ALICE CALDWELL HEGAN RICE (1870–1942). Alice Caldwell Hegan Rice was born on January 11, 1870, in Shelbyville, Ky., the older of two children of Sallie Caldwell Hegan, of old Kentucky and Virginia stock, and Watson Hegan, an art dealer of Irish extraction. She was educated at home and at Miss Hampton's Girls School in nearby Louisville. In her autobiography, *The Inky Way* (1940), she describes her experiences with a mission Sunday school in a run-down section of Louisville then called the Cabbage Patch, and she expressed her admiration for the way in which the people survived their poverty with fortitude and cheerfulness. After a debut she continued her social work as well as her literary endeavors, begun at an early age when she wrote stories. At the Louisville Authors' Club she was encouraged to write her first and most important work, *Mrs. Wiggs of the Cabbage Patch*, a novel based on her experiences in the slums. S. S. McClure published it in 1901, and over the years it sold over a half million copies and was widely translated.

In 1902 she married Cale Young Rice, and they joined the

McClures for a European tour, the first of many trips in Europe and the Orient which are reflected more in his writings than in hers. In 1903 she wrote another Cabbage Patch story, *Lovey Mary*, her only other work which approached *Mrs. Wiggs* in popularity. Most of her works are gently humorous, full of sympathy for human foibles, and with a particular sensitivity for children (the Rices had no children of their own). Her one serious novel was *Mr. Opp* (1909). Mr. Opp was a failure in business but had a basic gentility which lent meaning to his life. She died on February 10, 1942.

Mrs. Rice's strength lay in her choice of themes from personal experience. She continued her interest in the Cabbage Patch, where she and Louise Marshall established a settlement house that continued to grow in service throughout her life. Her creative work abated somewhat in the 1920s due to ill health, but financial problems which beset the couple in the depression stimulated both to more writing, little of which is significant.

works: *Mrs. Wiggs of the Cabbage Patch* (1901). *Lovey Mary* (1903). *Sandy* (1905). *Captain June* (1907). *Mr. Opp* (1909). *A Romance of Billy-Goat Hill* (1912). *The Honorable Percival* (1914). *Calvary Alley* (1917). *Miss Mink's Soldier and Other Stories* (1918). *Turn About Tales*, with Cale Young Rice (1920). *Quin* (1921). *Winners and Losers*, with Cale Young Rice (1925). *The Buffer: A Novel* (1929). *On Being "Clinnicked" (a Bit of Talk over the Alley Fence)* (1931). *The Lark Legacy* (1935). *Passionate Follies: Alternate Tales by Alice Hegan Rice and Cale Young Rice* (1936). *My Pillow Book* (1937). *Our Ernie* (1939). *The Inky Way* (1940). *Happiness Road* (1942).

Lawrence S. Thompson
University of Kentucky
Lexington

CALE YOUNG RICE (1872–1943). Cale Young Rice was born on December 7, 1872, in Dixon, Webster County, Ky., and resided in Evansville, Ind., between the ages of seven and seventeen. He graduated from Cumberland University, Lebanon, Tenn., and subsequently went to Harvard "to consult the sages" and took two degrees. There he studied under William James, Josiah Royce,

George Santayana, and Hugo Munsterberg. After leaving Harvard in 1896 he taught at Cumberland for a while, but he soon settled in Louisville where he married Alice Caldwell Hegan in 1902 and devoted the remainder of his life to creative writing. The childless but singularly happy marriage lasted until Mrs. Rice's death in 1942 and was punctuated by extensive travel in Europe and the Orient, where he gathered many themes for his poetry and plays. He wrote his autobiography, *Bridging the Years*, in 1939 and appended at the end an essay entitled "Poetry's Genii" on his theory of poetic inspiration. After his wife's death he sold his home and donated a large portion of his private library to the University of Kentucky (often with his signature as owner never annotated). He continued to write for another year, but despondency over the loss of his wife drove him to suicide on January 23, 1943.

Rice was an earnest but prolific and somewhat uncritical writer. His work attracted attention from professional critics on occasion, for example, Gilbert Murray, who stated that "his books open up a most varied world of emotion and romance." On the other hand, he was a rigid traditionalist in form and content; and no single poem, play, story, or essay shows exceptional inspiration. His themes are largely from his reading and travel rather than from personal experience or emotion. Most of his eight plays have tediously complicated plots, implausible motivation, and banal characters. When Clarence Loomis set *Yolanda of Cyprus* to music and it was performed by the American Opera Company in 1930, the score was condemned as a pale imitation of Debussy and Wagner and the libretto passed over as "conventional." Rice's personal popularity in Louisville won him wide local acclaim.

WORKS: *From Dusk to Dusk* (1898). *With Omar* (1900). *Song-Surf* (1901). *Charles di Tocca: A Tragedy* (1903). *David: A Tragedy* (1904). *Plays and Lyrics* (1904). *A Night in Avignon: A Drama* (1907). *Yolanda of Cyprus* (1908). *Nirvana Days* (1909). *Many Gods* (1910). *The Immortal Lure* (1911). *Far Quests* (1912). *Porzia* (1913). *At the World's Heart* (1914). *Collected Plays and Poems*, 2 vols. (1915). *Earth and New Earth* (1916). *Trails Sunward* (1917). *Songs to A.H.R.* (1918). *Wraiths and Realities* (1918). *Shadowy Thresholds* (1919). *Mihrima, and Other Poems* (1922). *Youth's Way* (1923). *A Pilgrim's Scrip: Poems for World Wanderers*

(1924). *Bitter Brew* (1925). *A Sea Lover's Scrip* (1925). *Selected Plays and Poems* (1926). *Stygian Freight* (1927). *Early Reaping* (1929). *Seed of the Moon* (1929). *The Swamp Bird: A Drama* (1931). *High Perils* (1933). *Love and Lord Byron: A Drama* (1936). *Bridging the Years* (1939).

> LAWRENCE S. THOMPSON
> University of Kentucky
> Lexington

AMÉLIE RIVES [PRINCESS TROUBETZKOY] (1863–1945). Born in Richmond, Va., on August 23, 1863, Amélie Louise Rives descended from Virginia antecedents that included a U.S. senator, a minister to France, an explorer, a Confederate officer, and several authors. Both her family background and her formative years, which were spent at Castle Hill, the Rives estate in Albemarle County, Va., proved important in shaping her temperament, talent, and social conscience.

She was educated by governesses and was allowed to read at will from the library of her grandfather, William Cabell Rives. She began to write almost as soon as she learned to read, though until she was 23, she entertained no thoughts of publication. But when a house guest discovered one of her manuscripts, he was given permission to publish it anonymously. This story, "A Brother to Dragons," appeared in the *Atlantic Monthly* in March, 1886. This and several subsequent stories were romantic tales of adventure, often narrated in dialect, and they gained the author a following. However, with the publication of *The Quick or the Dead?* (1888), which sold more than 300,000 copies, a strain of psychological realism was introduced that would be developed throughout the remaining years of her career.

Amélie Rives's personal life was also much publicized. One of the great beauties of her generation, she married in 1888 John Armstrong Chanler, a wealthy descendant of John Jacob Astor. After she separated from Chanler in 1894, Oscar Wilde introduced her to Prince Pierre Troubetzkoy, a noted portrait artist, whom she married in 1896. She enjoyed social and intellectual life in both England and America until World War I. Thereafter, believing that the England she had known as a young woman was permanently changed, she spent most of her time in New York and at Castle Hill. Her final fifteen years were generally unhappy, and she wrote little after 1930. She died in Charlottesville on June 16, 1945.

WORKS: *A Brother to Dragons and Other Old-Time Tales* (1888). *Herod and Marianne* (1888). *The Quick or the Dead?* (1888). *Virginia of Virginia* (1888). *The Witness of the Sun* (1889). *According to St. John* (1891). *Athelwold* (1893). *Barbara Dering* (1893). *Tanis, the Sand-Digger* (1893). *A Damsel Errant* (1898). *Seléné* (1905). *Augustine the Man* (1906). *The Golden Rose* (1908). *Trix and Over-the-Moon* (1909). *Pan's Mountain* (1910). *Hidden House* (1912). *World's-End* (1914). *Shadows of Flames* (1915). *The Ghost Garden* (1918). *As the Wind Blew* (1920). *The Sea-Woman's Cloak and November Eve* (1923). *The Queerness of Celia* (1926). *Love-in-A-Mist* (1927). *Firedamp* (1930).

WELFORD DUNAWAY TAYLOR
University of Richmond
Richmond, Va.

ELIZABETH MADOX ROBERTS (1881–1941). Doubly descended from eighteenth-century Virginians who trekked into Kentucky through Boone's Trace, Elizabeth Madox Roberts was born in Perryville, Ky., on October 30, 1881, to Simpson and Mary Brent Roberts. Her father, a sometime scholar, schoolmaster, surveyor, and farmer, moved the family to Springfield, Ky., in about 1884, and there—except for high school years in Covington, Ky., at her grandmother Brent's (1896–1900), several visits to Colorado between 1910 and 1916 for her health, and her years at the University of Chicago (1917–1921)—was to be her home for the rest of her life as well as the characteristic setting for much of her writing.

Her second inheritance from Simpson Roberts was an early exposure to classical culture and the philosophical idealism of Berkeley which, interacting with her family sense of involvement in Kentucky and American history, was to constitute the intellectual framework which she brought to her art. It is also probable that her father's overprotectiveness served to nurture the development of both the frailty that was to delay her college education and plague her throughout her life as well as the sensitivity and stubborn energy that drove her to be a writer.

In Chicago her mature life began. She became devoted to a group of younger writers (Glenway Wescott, Yvor Winters, Janet Lewis, Monroe Wheeler), was accepted as a poet in the wider world of Harriet Monroe's *Poetry*, and found the self-confidence to launch herself as a novelist. *The Time of Man* and *The Great Meadow* gained her an international reputation as a writer of authentic regional power with a talent for rendering the feminine sensibility in lyrical prose.

In her last years—beset by chronic anemia and the fatal Hodgkin's disease—both critical and commercial success eluded her. She died in Orlando, Fla., on March 13, 1941, and was buried in Springfield, Ky.

WORKS: *In the Great Steep's Garden* (1915). *Under the Tree* (1922). *The Time of Man* (1926). *My Heart and My Flesh* (1927). *Jingling in the Wind* (1928). *The Great Meadow* (1930). *A Buried Treasure* (1931). *The Haunted Mirror* (1932). *He Sent Forth a Raven* (1935). *Black Is My True Love's Hair* (1938). *Song in the Meadow* (1940). *Not by Strange Gods* (1941).

EARL ROVIT
City College of New York
New York City

ADRIEN-EMMANUEL ROUQUETTE (1813–1887). Adrien-Emmanuel Rouquette was born on February 13, 1813, in New Orleans but spent most of his childhood years at his family's home in the woods outside of the city, where he developed his love for solitude, nature, and the Choctaw Indians who lived nearby. After attending schools in New Orleans, Kentucky, and Pennsylvania, he went to France in 1829 and received his baccalaureate from Rennes in 1833. Then he studied law in France and Louisiana, but he abandoned his legal studies in 1839.

His lyric poems, *Les Savanes*, met with critical success when published simultaneously in Paris and New Orleans in 1841. Soon afterwards, Rouquette decided to enter the priesthood and was ordained in 1845. During the next fourteen years he sought permission to live as a hermit and missionary among the Indians. He published his defense of the contemplative, eremitic life, *La Thébaïde*, in 1852, and became a missionary to the Choctaws in 1859. He won acceptance from the Indians who called him Chata-Ima (Choctaw-like), a name Rouquette often used to sign his works. An antisecessionist, he saw the Civil War and postbellum change ruin his efforts to help the Choctaws. Throughout his life he remained close to his brother, François-Dominique Rouquette (1810–1890), the only other important author of French poetry in Louisiana. Rouquette died on July 15, 1887.

His works include an unpublished dictionary of Choctaw; numerous poems, reviews, and essays in periodicals; *Wild Flowers* (1848), his English poems; *L'Antoniade* (1860), religious and patriotic poems; *La Nouvelle Atala* (1879), a romance; and *Aboo and Caboo* (1880), a pamphlet viciously attacking G. W. Cable's portrayal of the Creoles in *The Grandissimes*. Rouquette's writings reveal a deep love for the Indians and for the simple, primitive life close to nature, a religious mysticism, and a patriotic faith in America.

WORKS: *Les Savanes, poésies américaines* (1841). *Wild Flowers, Sacred Poetry* (1848). *La Thébaïde en Amérique ou Apologie de la vie solitaire et contemplative* (1852). *L'Antoniade ou la Solitude Avec Dieu (Trois Ages) Poème Erémitique* (1860). *La Nouvelle Atala ou la Fille de l'Esprit, Légende Indienne* (1879). E. Junius (pseud.), *Critical Dialogue between Aboo and Caboo or a Grandissime Ascension* (1880).

ALFRED BENDIXEN
University of North Carolina
Chapel Hill

ROBERT CHESTER RUARK (1915–1965). Son of Robert Chester, Sr., and Charlotte Atkins Ruark, Robert Ruark was born on December 29, 1915, in Wilmington, N.C., but spent most of his boyhood in nearby Southport, where his paternal grandfather tutored him in hunting and fishing. From New Hanover High School in Wilmington, he went to the University of North Carolina at Chapel Hill, studying journalism and writing for student publications. After graduating in 1935, he was general factotum at the Hamlet (N.C.) *News-Messenger* for three months, worked for the Works Progress Administration as an accountant, and went to sea as an ordinary seaman. Back in journalism, Ruark moved from copyboy at the Washington (D.C.) *Star* to the Washington *Daily News* and soon was on the sports staff. In 1938 he was married to Virginia Webb of Washington. His experiences during three years as a naval officer in World War II resulted in several magazine articles.

After the war, he became a Scripps-Howard columnist and achieved almost immediate success with his brash, breezy condemnations of such of his "pet hates" as southern cooking, progressive schools, Texans, military brass, politicians, and American women. Two spoofs of the then-popular bosoms-and-bourbon historical romances established him as the "nonthinking man's writer." His lucrative newspaper column allowed him to pursue a hard, fast life. From an East Africa safari during the summer of 1951 came the novels *Something of Value* and *Uhuru*. Although they were best sellers, as was *Poor No More*, rags-to-riches story of a southern go-getter, *The Old Man and the Boy* is considered his best book. In 1955 Ruark purchased a villa near Barcelona, Spain; and there he was buried after his death in London on July 1, 1965. His voluminous papers are deposited in the University of North Carolina library at Chapel Hill.

WORKS: *Grenadine Etching* (1947). *I Didn't Know It Was Loaded* (1948). *One for the Road* (1949). *Grenadine's Spawn* (1952). *Horn of the Hunter* (1953). *Something of Value* (1955). *The Old Man and the Boy* (1957). *Poor No More* (1959). *The Old Man's Boy Grows Older* (1961). *Uhuru* (1962). *The Honey Badger* (1965). *Use Enough Gun* (1966). *Women* (1967).

RICHARD WALSER
North Carolina State University
Raleigh

ROWLAND RUGELEY (*ca.* **1735–1776**). Little is known about Rowland Rugeley's life. His exact year of birth is uncertain but is believed to have been 1735. He emigrated from England to South Carolina sometime around 1766, prior to which he published a volume of *Miscellaneous Poems and Translations from La Fontaine and Others* (London, 1763) and made frequent contributions to the British magazines.

Local records indicate that in 1766 Rugeley purchased a large tract of land on the banks of the Ashley River near Charleston. A contemporary diary describes him as a "merchant" and mentions that he had three brothers and three sisters, also of Charleston. Rugeley died of unknown causes in the autumn of 1776, possibly from the same epidemic that killed his wife and youngest child a few weeks later. A death notice in the *South Carolina and American General Gazette* states that he was an honest man and a jovial companion whose poetry was "very generally admired" and entitled him to "some Rank in the Literary World."

Rugeley is perhaps best remembered today as the author of *The Story of Aeneas and Dido Burlesqued: From the Fourth Book of the Aeneid of Virgil* (1774). This lively parody of Virgil written in the tradition of Paul Scarron and Charles Cotton was printed in Charleston by Robert Wells. It reveals that its author was a man of uncommon learning and is the first classical burlesque written in America.

WORKS: *Miscellaneous Poems and Translations from La Fontaine and Others* (1763). *The Story of Aeneas and Dido Burlesqued: From the Fourth Book of the Aeneid of Virgil* (1774).

JAMES A. LEVERNIER
University of Arkansas
Little Rock

IRWIN RUSSELL (**1853–1879**). Irwin Russell was born on June 3, 1853, in Port Gibson, Miss., son of Dr. William McNab and Elizabeth Allen Russell, teacher in the Port Gibson Female College. The family moved to St. Louis in 1853 after Russell survived yellow fever, but returned when war began. After Appomattox the boy, always precocious and frail, entered what is now St. Louis University and was graduated in 1869. Despite restlessness that often sent him roaming from his studies, he read law in Port Gibson under Judge L. N. Baldwin and was admitted to the bar at nineteen. In time he took over an increasingly large portion of Judge Baldwin's practice.

As much interested in literature as in law, he was active in social life and, as a member of the Port Gibson Thespian Society, wrote and directed a play now lost, "Everybody's Business; or, Slightly Mistaken." About 1869 he began improvising dialect verses to his own banjo accompaniment. Signed poems appeared in *Scribner's Monthly* and other national magazines from 1871 until his death, and he is known to have published other unsigned, hence unidentifiable, poems.

During the yellow fever epidemic of 1878 Russell endeared himself to his fellow townsmen by working as Dr. Russell's assistant. Physically and emotionally exhausted, he moved to New York in December but could not write despite the emotional support of Richard Watson Gilder, R. U. Johnson, and H. C. Bunner, who tried to curb his drinking. Dr. Russell's death (May, 1879) plunged him deeper into depression and illness. Penniless and fleeing his friends, he signed as fireman on a steamboat to New Orleans, where he contributed irregularly to the *Times* until his death on December 23, 1879.

Russell called Burns his idol. The influence shows especially in the ironic and loving details of "Christmas Night in the Quarters" (1878). Despite chronic alcoholism and early death, Russell left a permanent literary legacy of value greater than his one volume of verse. As Joel Chandler Harris and Thomas Nelson Page recognized, Russell introduced blacks into American literature—not as symbols or stock characters, servants or victims, but as individuals who happened to be emancipated, independently unreconstructed, and as memorable as Burns's crofters.

WORKS: *Poems by Irwin Russell* (1888; enl., 1917).

HARRIET R. HOLMAN
Clemson University
Clemson, S.C.

ARCHIBALD RUTLEDGE (1883–1973). Archibald Hamilton Rutledge, first poet laureate of South Carolina, was born on October 23, 1883, in McClellanville, S.C., the son of Henry Middleton and Margaret Hamilton Rutledge. His ancestors included a chief justice of the Supreme Court, a signer of the Declaration of Independence, and a governor of South Carolina. He was educated at Porter Military Academy in Charleston and Union College in New York. From 1904 until his retirement in 1937, he taught in and headed the English Department at Mercersburg Academy in Pennsylvania. In 1907 he married Florence Louise Hart; they had three sons, Archibald, Jr., Henry Middleton, and Irvine Hart. Mrs. Rutledge died in 1934, and in 1936 Rutledge married Alice Lucas, a childhood sweetheart.

Beloved by his admirers, Rutledge received many tributes to his literary efforts: seventeen honorary degrees, more than 30 medals, including the John Burroughs Medal for nature writing, election to the American Society of Arts and Letters, and in 1934, appointment as poet laureate of South Carolina.

In most of his writing, Rutledge applauds the beauties and traditions of Hampton Plantation, the Rutledge ancestral home built in 1730. His poetry is reminiscent of the lyricists of the Old South —Simms, Wilde, and Pinkney. His short stories and personal essays recount his hunting, his appreciation of nature, and his experiences with relatives and friends. Most of his more than 1,000 poems and articles contributed to popular magazines and literary journals appeared in book form.

After his retirement, Rutledge returned permanently to South Carolina, continued to write, and restored the old Hampton Plantation, part of which he deeded to the state in 1970. Rutledge died on September 15, 1973, a few miles from Hampton at Summer Place, the log house retreat in which he had been born.

WORKS: *The Heart's Quest* (1904). *Under the Pines, and Other Poems* (1906). *The Banners of the Coast* (1908). *Spirit of Mercersburg* (1909). *New Poems* (1915). *Tom and I on the Old Plantation* (1918). *Songs from a Valley* (1919). *Old Plantation Days* (1921). *Plantation Game Trails* (1921). *South of Richmond* (1923). *Days Off in Dixie* (1924). *Heart of the South* (1924). *Collected Poems* (1925). *A Monarch of the Sky* (1926).

Children of Swamp and Wood (1927). *Life's Extras* (1928). *Bolio and Other Dogs* (1930). *The Flower of Hope* (1930). *Peace in the Heart* (1930). *Veiled Eros* (1933). *When Boys Go Off to School* (1935). *Wild Life in the South* (1935). *Brimming Chalice* (1936). *An American Hunter* (1937). *My Colonel and His Lady* (1937). *It Will be Daybreak Soon* (1938). *The Sonnets of Archibald Rutledge* (1938). *Rain on the Marsh* (1940). *Christ Is God* (1941). *Home by the River* (1941). *Love's Meaning* (1943). *Hunter's Choice* (1946). *The Beauty of the Night* (1947). *God's Children* (1947). *The Angel Standing; or, Faith Alone Gives Poise* (1948). *The Everlasting Light and Other Poems* (1949). *A Wildwood Tale: A Drama of the Open* (1950). *Beauty in the Heart* (1953). *The Heart's Citadel and Other Poems* (1953). *Brimming Tide and Other Poems* (1954). *Those Were the Days* (1955). *Bright Angel and Other Poems* (1956). *Santee Paradise* (1956). *From the Hills to the Sea: Fact and Legend of the Carolinas* (1958). *Deep River: The Complete Poems of Archibald Rutledge* (1960; rev., 1966). *The World Around Hampton* (1960). *The Ballad of the Howling Hound and Other Poems* (1965). *Willie Was a Lady* (1966). *How Wild Was My Village* (1969). *I Hear America Singing* (1970). *Poems in Honor of South Carolina's Tricentennial* (1970). *The Woods and Wild Things I Remember* (1970). *Voices of the Long Ago: Bible Stories Retold* (1973).

HAROLD WOODELL
Clemson University
Clemson, S.C.

ABRAM JOSEPH RYAN (1838–1886). Abram Ryan was born on February 5, 1838, the son of Matthew and Mary Coughlin Ryan, in Hagerstown, Md. He was educated at the Seminary of St. Mary's of the Barrens at Perryville, Mo., the Christian Brothers Cathedral School in St. Louis, and later at Niagara University in New York under the Vincentian Fathers. He entered Vincentian novitiate in 1854, took solemn vows in 1856, and was ordained a priest on September 12, 1860. Accounts of his activities in the years immediately following his ordination are clouded by contradiction, but it appears that he taught briefly at Niagara University, at the diocesan seminary at Cape Girardeau, Mo., and served briefly at St. Mary's Parish, Peoria, Ill. An ardent sympathizer with the Confederate cause, he tried unsuccessfully to become a commissioned military chaplain, but did join the Confederate service as a free-lance chaplain. After learning that no clergyman would accept the assignment to Gratiot Prison in New Orleans, Ryan ministered to the smallpox victims there.

Following his brother's death in action, Ryan wrote "In Memory of My Brother" and "In Memoriam." After the war he published such poems as "The Conquered Banner," "The Sword of Robert E. Lee," "The Lost Cause," "Gather the Sacred Dust," and "March of the Deathless Dead," the popularity of which led to his becoming known as the "Poet-Priest of the Confederacy." Of his poems, now largely forgotten, he said that they were "written at random, —off and on, here, there, anywhere,—just as the mood came, with little of study and less of art, and always in a hurry."

After the war, Ryan resided briefly near Beauvoir, Miss., and then served as curate of St. Patrick's in Augusta, Ga., where he edited the *Pacificator* and later *Banner of the South*. While pastor in New Orleans, he edited a Catholic weekly, the *Star*. He also served churches in Biloxi, Miss.; Nashville, Knoxville, Clarksville, Tenn.; Macon, Ga.; and finally Mobile, Ala., where he remained from 1870 to 1883. He died on April 22, 1886, at the Convent of St. Bonifacius in Louisville and was buried at Mobile.

WORKS: *Father Ryan's Poems* (1879). *Poems, Patriotic, Religious, and Miscellaneous* (1880). *A Crown for Our Queen* (1882).

EUGENE NOLTE
University of Central Arkansas
Conway

EMMA SPEED SAMPSON (1868–1947). The great-granddaughter of George Keats, brother of poet John Keats, Emma Speed Sampson was born on December 1, 1868, at Chatsworth, a farm just outside Louisville, Ky., and spent part of her youth in nearby Shelbyville. She later studied art at the Art Students League in New York and with Charles Lazar in Paris. She taught for a time in Louisville before marrying Henry Aylett Sampson in 1896. After living in various parts of America, the Sampsons moved to Richmond, Va., which became their permanent home.

Shortly after settling in Richmond, the Sampsons were joined by her sister, Nell Speed, who was completing her fourth novel—featuring a college undergraduate named Molly Brown. Nell Speed knew that she was dying, so she convinced her sister to continue the series of books. Thus, at age 45, Emma Speed Sampson wrote her first book. This juvenile novel, *Molly Brown's Post-Graduate Days* (1914), was ultimately followed by three more titles in the same series. During the early years of her career, Sampson, using the name of her sister, which had been willed to her, wrote several volumes in the "Tucker Twins" and "Carter Girls" series.

When a fellow author found that these books were required to run 50,000 words but commanded only $200, she admonished Sampson to change publishers. She wrote to Reilly & Lee, the Chicago firm that had published Frances Boyd Calhoun's *Miss Minerva and William Green Hill* (1909). They suggested that she write a sequel to this best seller, and two months later she complied with *Billy and the Major* (1918). The manuscript was accepted by return mail and was published under Sampson's own name. It was the first of eleven volumes she wrote as continuations of the prototype.

After her husband's death in 1920, Sampson's career became varied. She continued to write—additional "Miss Minerva" titles, an undetermined number of "Campfire Girl" books, several non-series novels, two "Priscilla" novels for girls (written in collaboration with her daughter, Emma Keats), and continued the "Mary Louise" series that had been begun by L. Frank Baum under the name of Mrs. Edith Van Dyne. She also served for several years on the Virginia board of motion picture censors and was a staff writer for the Richmond *Times-Dispatch*. She died on May 7, 1947.

WORKS: *Billy and the Major* (1918). *Mammy's White Folks* (1919). *Miss Minerva's Baby* (1920). *The Shorn Lamb* (1922). *Miss Minerva on the Old Plantation* (1923). *The Comings of Cousin Ann* (1923). *Masquerading Mary* (1924). *Miss Minerva Broadcasts Billy* (1925). *Miss Minerva's Scallywags* (1927). *Miss Minerva's Neighbors* (1929). *The Spite Fence*

(1929). *Miss Minerva's Cook Book* (1931). *Miss Minerva's Goin' Places* (1931). *Miss Minerva's Mystery* (1933). *Miss Minerva's Problem* (1936). *Miss Minerva's Vacation* (1939).

WELFORD DUNAWAY TAYLOR
University of Richmond
Richmond, Va.

SONIA SANCHEZ (1934–). Sonia Sanchez was born on September 9, 1934, in Birmingham, Ala., but later moved to New York where she graduated from Hunter College of the City College of New York in 1955. She has taught black literature and creative writing at the City College of New York and the University of Massachusetts at Amherst. Married and the mother of three (Anita, Morani, and Mungu), Sanchez converted to the Nation of Islam recently and is presently a staff writer with the weekly Muslim news organ, *Bilalian News.*

Sanchez is poet, playwright, short story writer, and essayist. All of her creative efforts address the problems of blacks in the western white world. She provides an analysis of their dilemma and outlines a program for their survival. Her solution is straightforward: eradicate the white man's social, political, and economic stranglehold on things black and replace the structure with a redefined set of social and political institutions firmly rooted in the black experience, generally the black family and more particularly the black community.

Sanchez is unashamedly a black female artist. The adjectival order is crucial. An early and vigorous supporter of the Black Arts Movement, Sanchez has no patience with, art-for-art's-sake. Her art is utilitarian. Sanchez is also conscious of her special role as a black woman. As such, she is concerned with the proper education of her children. Both the *Adventures of Fat Head and Square Head* and *The Afternoon of Small Head, Fat Head, and Square Head* respond to the critical need for creative, healthy, entertaining reading for young blacks.

The poetic canon itself shows a wide range of textures, sensibilities, and techniques. Aware of the pitfalls in the English language for the black poet, Sanchez's best efforts show an impressive, largely accurate ear for the varieties of rhythms and syntax in northern urban black speech. The grammar stress patterns and songlike rhythms produced with her delicate play on vowel sounds are in the main urban black innovations.

Sanchez has written three plays. *Sister Son/ji* was produced by Joseph Papp in 1972. Her dramatic efforts share the themes of her poetry. There is, however, more emphasis on the black woman's role as black mother and black wife. Sanchez lives in Chicago and is currently at work on a novel.

WORKS: *Homecoming* (1969). *We a BaddDDD People* (1970). *Broadside No. 34* (1970). *The Bronx Next* (prod. 1970). *Dirty Hearts '72 in Scripts 1* (1971). *It's a New Day for Young Brothas and Sistahs* (1971). *Sister Son/ji* (prod. 1972). Ed., *Three Hundred Sixty Degrees of Blackness Comin' at You* (1972). *Love Poems* (1973). *A Blues Book for Blue Magical Women* (1973). *The Adventures of Fat Head and Square Head* (1973). Ed., *We Be Ward Sorcerers! 25 Stories by Black Americans* (1973).

WALLACE R. PEPPERS
North Carolina A & T State
University
Greensboro

GEORGE SANDYS (1578–1644). Sandys was an English traveler, poet, colonist, and early foreign service career officer. The seventh and youngest son of Edwin Sandys, archbishop of York, and brother of Edwin Sandys, he was born near York, on March 2, 1578. He studied at St. Mary's Hall, Oxford, and Corpus Christi College and in 1596 was admitted to the Middle Temple. Probably about two years later he married Elizabeth Norton, his father's ward. By 1606 the marriage had ended in permanent separation.

In May, 1610, Sandys set out on the travels described in *A Relation of a Journey begun An: Dom: 1610* (1615), which went through nine editions during the seventeenth century and was used as source material by Sir Francis Bacon, Sir Thomas Browne, Milton, and other writers. Sandys returned home in March, 1612, and was active in the companies established for colonization in America. His brother, Sir Edwin Sandys, had been instrumental in drawing up the Virginia Company's charter (1609), and George had been a member of the company since 1607. In July, 1621, he accompanied his nephew-in-law, the governor, Sir Francis Wyatt, to Virginia as its first resident treasurer and director of industry and agriculture, continuing in these duties when the crown took over government of the colony in 1624. On his return to England (1625), Sandys was made a gentleman of the king's privy chamber. For about fifteen years he was a member of various committees administering the colonies and, finally (1640), agent for the Virginia colony.

On his voyage to, and while in, the New World, Sandys completed a translation of Ovid's *Metamorphoses*, published in 1626. In 1632 he brought out a revised edition that was expanded to include commentaries from numerous other classical authors and many allusions to the Virginia the author had known. On this work, composed in remarkably compressed heroic couplets, Sandys' poetic fame largely rests. His later and less well-known works reflect his interest in theology. Sandys' last years were spent in London, in Oxfordshire with the Falkland circle at Great Tew, and in Kent with Sir Francis Wyatt at Boxley Abbey, where he died in March, 1644, being buried at Boxley Church on March 7.

WORKS: *A Relation of a Journey begun An: Dom: 1610. Four Books containing a description of the Turkish Empire, of Egypt, the Holy Land, of the Remote Parts of Italy, and Islands adjoyning* (1615). Trans., Ovid's *Metamorphoses* (1626, 1632). *A Paraphrase upon the Psalmes of David* (1636). *A paraphrase upon the Divine Poems* (1638). Trans., Grotius' *Christus Patiens*, as *Christ's Passion* (1640). *A Paraphrase upon the Song of Solomon* (1641). *The Poetical Works of George Sandys*, 2 vols.; ed. Richard Hopper (1872).

RICHARD BEALE DAVIS
University of Tennessee
Knoxville

HERBERT RAVENEL SASS (1884–1958). Novelist, journalist, historian, and naturalist, Herbert Ravenel Sass was born in Charleston, S.C., on November 2, 1884. From his family Sass inherited a lifelong interest in literature, nature, and history, especially the history of South Carolina. His father, George Herbert Sass, was the famous Confederate poet known under the pen name of Barton Grey. His mother, Anna Eliza Ravenel Sass, was the daughter of Harriott Horry Rutledge Ravenel, a distinguished South Carolina writer and wife of Dr. St. Julien Ravenel, the noted scientist and inventor.

Sass was educated at the College of Charleston where he received a B.A. in 1905, M.A. in 1906, and an honorary Litt.D. in 1922. After graduating from college Sass worked as assistant director of the Charleston Museum. Upon his father's death in 1908 he joined the staff of the Charleston *News and Courier* where he worked as city editor and later assistant editor until 1924 when he resigned from journalism to pursue a full-time career in free-lance writing. As a free-lance writer Sass contributed numerous articles, essays, and short stories to such magazines as the *Saturday Evening Post*, *Country Gentleman*, *National Geographic*, *Collier's*, *Harper's*, *Cornhill*, the *Atlantic Monthly*, the *Saturday Review*, and *Good Housekeeping*, among many others. Sass also wrote several novels and book-length essays.

In later life Sass's concern for the future of South Carolina led him to write more exclusively about its history and politics. He died at his home in Charleston on February 18, 1958, after a lengthy illness.

WORKS: *The Way of the Wild* (1925). *Adventures in Green Places* (1926, enl., 1935). *Gray Eagle* (1927). *War Drums* (1928). *On the Wings of a Bird* (1929). *Look Back to Glory* (1933). Intro., William Smith, *Old Charleston* (1933). *A Carolina Rice Plantation of the Fifties*, with Alice R. Huger Smith (1936). *Fort Sumter*, with DuBose Heyward (1938). *Hear Me, My Chiefs!* (1940). *Emperor Brims* (1941). *Charleston Grows* (1949). *Outspoken: 150 Years of the News and Courier* (1953). *The Story of the South Carolina Lowcountry* (1956).

JAMES A. LEVERNIER
University of Arkansas
Little Rock

LYLE SAXON (1891–1946). Born in Baton Rouge, La., on September 4, 1891, to Hugh and Katherine Chambers Saxon, Lyle

Saxon became one of the more notable men of letters in Louisiana. After receiving his B.A. from Louisiana State University in 1912, he worked as a reporter in Chicago. In 1918 he came to the New Orleans *Item* and later to the *Times-Picayune* as a feature writer until 1926. Associated with the *Doubledealer*, he contributed stories and articles to magazines and won the O. Henry Award in 1926. One of his stories was collected in *O'Brien's Best Short Stories* in 1927. He was not married and lived in the Vieux Carré, where William Faulkner, Sherwood Anderson, Roark Bradford, and Edmund Wilson were visitors to his home. He later resided at Melrose Plantation at Natchitoches and the St. Charles Hotel in New Orleans.

His only novel, *Children of Strangers* (1937), reflects his experience at Melrose as it explores the mulatto and Negro people in and about a Cane River country plantation. Saxon focuses on Famie, a beautiful mulatto girl who has just turned sixteen. The novel begins at Easter in 1905 and concludes on an ironic note as he punctures some of the illusions that many have held about Negroes.

Most of Saxon's writing is nonfiction. In 1927 *Father Mississippi*, which in part emphasizes a child's growing up on a river plantation, appeared. A year later *Fabulous New Orleans* presented a series of descriptive "impressions" and "stories." In 1929 he finished *Old Louisiana*, a realistic account of plantation life. His biography of the pirate Jean Lafitte was published in 1930. As director of the Federal Writers' Projects in Louisiana, he edited *A Collection of Folk Tales: Gumbo Ya-Ya*, which was published in 1945. When Saxon died on April 9, 1946, he left behind his books and a growing coterie of admirers.

WORKS: *Father Mississippi* (1927). *Fabulous New Orleans* (1928). *Old Louisiana* (1929). *Lafitte the Pirate* (1930). *Children of Strangers* (1937). *A Collection of Louisiana Folk Tales: Gumbo Ya-Ya* (1945). *The Friends of Joe Gilmore* (1948).

THOMAS BONNER, JR.
Xavier University of Louisiana
New Orleans

JANET SCHAW (*ca.* 1739–post-1778). Janet Schaw was probably born at Lauriston, a suburb of Edinburgh, Scotland, about 1739, one of six children of Gideon and Anne Rutherfurd Schaw. Her birth date is uncertain, but she was between 35 and 40 years old when she made her trip to the West Indies, North Carolina, and Portugal in 1774–1776. Nothing is known of her education, but the *Journal* of her trip, Schaw's only known work, indicates that she was well read.

In the company of her brother, Alexander, three children of a kinsman, John Rutherfurd of North Carolina, and others, Janet Schaw sailed from the Firth of Forth on October 25, 1774, aboard the *Jamaica Packet* for the West Indies and North Carolina. The purpose of the journey was apparently to return the Rutherfurd children to their parents and to visit her brother, Robert Schaw, who had migrated to North Carolina by 1751, first as an apprentice, then later a merchant, and at the time of Janet Schaw's visit, a planter in the Cape Fear country. After spending time at Antigua and St. Christopher's, Schaw sailed aboard the *Rebecca* for North Carolina, arriving in February, 1775, and remaining there until November of that year. She returned to Scotland by way of Portugal, but little is known of her thereafter. Schaw's *Journal*, of which there are three manuscript copies, was dedicated to her brother, Alexander, and dated "St. Andrews Square, March 10, 1778." She probably never married.

Schaw's *Journal*, published in 1921, gives a lively picture of the Cape Fear country on the eve of the Revolution, for she was a careful observer of people, places, manners, and customs. A witty woman and an ardent Tory, Schaw abhorred the "most disgusting equality" that she found in North Carolina. In the summer of 1775 she compared the North Carolina militia, then gathered for review at Wilmington, with Falstaff's rag-tag crew from Shakespeare's *Henry IV*. When she read the newspaper accounts of the British losses at the Battle of Bunker Hill, she wrote, "But tho' 'tis all false together, I hope the publishers will be hanged." She kept her *Journal* in the form of letters to friends.

WORKS: *Journal of a Lady of Quality; Being the Narrative of a Journey from Scotland to the West Indies, North Carolina, and Portugal, in the*

Years 1774 to 1776, ed. Evangeline Walker Andrews and Charles M. Andrews (1921).

ROBERT BAIN
University of North Carolina
Chapel Hill

EVELYN SCOTT (1893–1963). Evelyn Scott was born Elsie Dunn in Clarkesville, Tenn., on January 17, 1893. Her mother, Maude Thomas, of Clarksville, and her father, Seeley Dunn, of New Orleans, were members of wealthy families. Privately tutored, but with intermittent attendance at public schools, she spent most of her childhood and early youth in Clarksville where she was raised in an elegant Greek revival mansion as a southern belle. Strikingly beautiful, she was well equipped to play such a role, but she early rebelled against social conventions and began to develop her remarkable intellect. She wrote her first fiction at age nine, published her first story at thirteen, and began her professional career at sixteen. She completed her formal education at Sophie Newcomb College and Newcomb Art School, Tulane University. On December 26, 1913, a few weeks before her 21st birthday, she left New Orleans with Frederick Creighton Wellman, head of the School of Tropical and Preventative Medicine, Tulane University, to establish a common-law marriage. In this deliberate act of commitment to unconventional values, the couple changed their names to Cyril Kay Scott and Evelyn Scott and moved to Brazil.

During five poverty-ridden years pioneering in Brazil, recounted in the uniquely poetic autobiography *Escapade*, Scott began her serious writing isolated from outside stimulation, yet developed many of the techniques of impressionism, stream of consciousness, and symbolic realism. During this period she published, mainly poetry, in *Poetry Journal*, *Dial*, the *Egoist*, *Others*, and *Poetry*. Returning to the United States in 1919, she was almost immediately recognized as an important new writer. Her reputation for innovations in form and technique, for intellectual depth, for the breadth and scope of her materials, grew steadily until 1937, but declined after her attack on Communist mentality which prefaced *Bread and a Sword*.

Evelyn Scott married the English novelist John Metcalfe in 1930, and from the beginning of World War II until 1952 remained in London where she continued to write under extremely difficult circumstances. She returned to the United States in 1952 to try to reestablish her literary career. Although plagued by ill health and near poverty, she completed two long novels, "Before Cock Crow" and "Escape into Living," perhaps her most important works, but never found a publisher. She died in New York City on August 3, 1963.

WORKS: *Precipitations* (1920). *Love: A Drama in Three Acts* (1921). *The Narrow House* (1921). *Narcissus* (1922). *Escapade* (1923). *In the Endless Sands: A Christmas Book for Boys and Girls*, with Cyril Kay Scott (1925). *The Golden Door* (1925). *Ideals: A Book of Farce and Comedy* (1927). *Migrations: An Arabesque in Histories* (1927). *The Wave* (1929). *Witch Perkins: A Story of the Kentucky Hills* (1929). *On William Faulkner's "The Sound and the Fury"* (1929). *Blue Rum* (1930). *The Winter Alone* (1930). *A Calender of Sin, American Melodramas* (1931). *Eva Gay: A Romantic Novel* (1933). *Breathe Upon These Slain* (1934). *Billy the Maverick* (1934). *Bread and a Sword* (1937). *Background in Tennessee* (1937). *The Shadow of the Hawk* (1941). Works unpublished: "Before Cock Crow: A Novel" (1930–62). "Escape Into Living: A Novel" (1952–62). "The Gravestones Wept," poetry (1950–60). "The Youngest Smiles," poetry (1955–60).

ROBERT L. WELKER
University of Alabama
Huntsville

MOLLY ELLIOT SEAWELL (1860–1916). Born on a plantation in Gloucester County, Va., on October 23, 1860, Molly Seawell was the daughter of John Tyler and Frances Jackson Seawell. Both her father, a lawyer and classics scholar, and her uncle, Joseph Seawell, a seaman, contributed much to her future literary endeavors. She was educated chiefly in the informal fashion at home, but also received some formal instruction at Virginia schools. It was her girlhood in the Tidewater region that perhaps provided the greatest influence on her writing career.

While in Norfolk in 1886, Molly Seawell modestly began her literary duties. A sojourn in Europe added to her storehouse of subject matter, and, upon her return to Virginia, she initiated publication of several magazine pieces under various pen names. Moving to Washington, D.C., she submitted numerous political articles to New York papers and, throughout her years, continued her political involvement which culminated in the 1903 publication of *Despotism and Democracy*, a critique of society and politics in Washington, and the 1911 publication of *The Ladies' Battle*, an antisuffragist tract.

By far the most important aspect of her writing was fiction. From her first novel, *Hale-Weston*, in 1889, her fiction was characterized by a lilting, pleasant style with humor and a major emphasis on setting. In variety, the novels have discussed antebellum Virginia, English history, Parisian society, the American navy, and Washington fact and fancy.

Several of her works, such as *The Sprightly Romance of Marsac* (1896), *The History of Lady Betty Stair* (1897), and *The Fortunes of Fifi* (1903), received a certain degree of popular acclaim, although she is little remembered today. Molly Seawell died in Washington, D.C., on November 15, 1916, and was buried in Baltimore.

WORKS: *The Berkeleys and Their Neighbors* (1888). *Hale-Weston* (1889). *Little Jarvis* (1890). *Throckmorton* (1890). *Midshipman Paulding* (1891). *Maid Marian and Other Stories* (1891). *Children of Destiny* (1893). *The Sprightly Romance of Marsac* (1896). *A Strange, Sad Comedy* (1896). *A Virginia Cavalier* (1896). *The History of Lady Betty Stair* (1897). *Twelve Naval Captains* (1897). *The Loves of the Lady Arabella* (1898). *The Lively Adventures of Gavin Hamilton* (1899). *The House of Egremont* (1900). *Papa Bouchard* (1901). *Franceska* (1902). *The Fortunes of Fifi* (1903). *Despotism and Democracy* (1903). *The Chateau of Montplaisir* (1906). *The Victory* (1906). *The Secret of Toni* (1907). *The Last Duchess of Belgarde* (1908). *John Mainwaring, Financier* (1908). *The Imprisoned Midshipman* (1908). *The Whirl: A Romance of Washington Society* (1909). *The Ladies' Battle* (1911). *Betty's Virginia Christmas* (1914). *The Diary of a Beauty* (1915).

ROBERT M. WILLINGHAM, JR.
University of Georgia
Athens

MARY LEE SETTLE (1918–). Born at Charleston, W.Va., on July 29, 1918, to Joseph Edward Settle, a civil engineer, and Rachel Tompkins—both of English and Scottish descent—Mary Lee Settle's youth was spent in Cedar Grove, W.Va., in Greenbriar County, W.Va., and in eastern Kentucky. In 1936 she graduated from Charleston High School after which she attended Sweet Briar College. There Joseph Dexter Bennett, one of her teachers, encouraged her to write. Although she began with verse, her published works have been fiction and nonfiction. In 1942 she joined the Women's Auxiliary Air Force (WAAF), Royal Air Force. She remained in England fourteen years after the war and married Douglas Newton. They are now divorced.

Her first novel, *The Love Eaters*, describes the emotional and professional tensions found in an amateur theatrical group of an Allegheny coal town. Although her first major work was well received in England and the United States, her reputation rests on her Beulah Land trilogy about the settlement of West Virginia from 1754 to present—*O Beulah Land, Know Nothing*, and *Fight Night on a Sweet Saturday*. After *O Beulah Land* appeared, she received a Guggenheim Fellowship. Her sixth and latest novel, *Prisons*—"based on a true incident of the English Civil War"— "evokes the many levels of struggle for personal, political, and spiritual freedoms that stretch from Cromwell's time to the present." Her nonfiction includes *All the Brave Promises*, a nostalgic recall of one small corner of wartime life—the WAAF; and three juvenilia: *Story of Flight, The Clam Shell*, and *The Scopes Trial*. Always active, she enjoys hunting, outdoor life, and trotting. Her works reflect that love of the vigorous life and her dedication to historic research.

WORKS: *The Love Eaters* (1954). *The Kiss of Kin* (1955). *O Beulah Land* (1956). *Know Nothing* (1960). *Fight Night on a Sweet Saturday* (1964). *All the Brave Promises* (1966). *Story of Flight* (1967). *The Clam Shell* (1971). *The Scopes Trial: The State of Tennessee v. John Thomas Scopes* (1972). *Prisons* (1973). *Blood Tie* (1977).

JAMES A. GRIMSHAW, JR.
United States Air Force Academy
Colorado Springs, Colo.

WILLIAM GILMORE SIMMS (1806–1870). A writer of great talent and energy, William Gilmore Simms was a poet, novelist, critic, historian, biographer, essayist, writer of tales, and dramatist. He edited ten periodicals and published over 80 volumes and enough uncollected material to fill another 20. Little of this material has survived, but in his time Simms was preeminently the man of letters of the Old South.

Simms was born in Charleston, S.C., on April 17, 1806, the son of an Irish immigrant tradesman. When he was two, his mother died; his father went to Tennessee and finally to Mississippi; and he was left in the care of his maternal grandmother. His six years of formal schooling were brief and poor, and he was largely self-educated. At twelve he was apprenticed to an apothecary, a trade he deserted. In 1824–1825, while visiting his father in the Southwest, he saw Indian and frontier life in Alabama, Mississippi, and Louisiana—an experience he put to good use in his fiction. He read law and was admitted to the bar in 1827. His marriage to a childhood sweetheart in 1826 ended with her death in 1832.

He published a monody on the death of General C. C. Pinckney (1825) and was one of the editors of a literary journal, the *Album* (1825), and the *Southern Literary Gazette* (1828–1829). In 1830 he purchased a daily newspaper, the Charleston *City Gazette*, in which he supported the Union in the Nullification Controversy, a position which cost him so many readers that he had to sell the newspaper in 1832.

Then he went North to establish his literary fortunes. He had already published four volumes of poetry and had another, *Atalantis*, ready for publication. In New York he became associated with the Knickerbocker writers, most notably his lifelong friend William Cullen Bryant. His first book of fiction, *Martin Faber*, appeared in 1833, and *Guy Rivers* (1834), the first of his "Border Romances," laid in frontier Georgia, won him a wide audience. In 1835 he published *The Yemassee*, a romance of Indian warfare in Carolina in 1715 and his best novel, and *The Partisan*, the first of seven romances of the Revolution.

In 1836 he married Chevilette Roach and moved to her father's plantation, Woodlands, in Barnwell District, 70 miles inland from

Charleston. For the remainder of his life, he made Woodlands his home, spending his winters there and his summers in northern publishing centers. There he wrote most of his works and entered politics, serving from 1844 to 1846 in the South Carolina legislature. During the 1840s he was actively associated with the New York "Young America" group which sponsored nationalism in literature. From 1836 to 1860 he edited several magazines, among them the *Southern and Western Monthly Magazine* (1845) and the *Southern Quarterly Review* (1849–1855). During these years he wrote six other Revolutionary War Romances: *Mellichampe* (1836), *The Scout* (1841, originally entitled *The Kinsman*), *Katharine Walton* (1851), *Woodcraft* (1852, originally entitled *The Sword and the Distaff*), *The Forayers* (1855), and *Eutaw* (1856). He also wrote other border romances, notably *Richard Hurdis* (1838) and *Border Beagles* (1840), romances of Spanish history such as *Pelayo* (1838), *The Damsel of Darien* (1839), and *Count Julian* (1845), and continued to write poetry, criticism, history, and biography, including lives of John Smith, Francis Marion, and Nathanael Greene. His last novel published during his lifetime was *The Cassique of Kiawah* (1859). His collected poems, in two volumes, were published in 1853.

Simms vigorously defended slavery, contributing to *The Pro-Slavery Argument* (1852). A close friend of James Henry Hammond, U.S. senator from South Carolina (1857–1860), he counseled him on disunion.

In 1862 Woodlands was burned and partially rebuilt. The following year his wife died, and in 1865, Woodlands was again burned, this time by Sherman's troops. Simms spent the last years of his life writing desperately for money to sustain his life and that of his children. He died in Charleston, on June 11, 1870, asking that his epitaph be: "Here lies one who, after a reasonably long life, distinguished chiefly by unceasing labors, has left all his better works undone." It was not carved on his tombstone, but it would have been appropriate.

works: *Monody on The Death of Gen. Charles Cotesworth Pinckney* (1825). *Lyrical and Other Poems* (1827). *Early Lays* (1827). *The Vision of Cortes, Cain, and other Poems* (1829). *The Tri-Color, or the Three Days of Blood, in Paris With Some other Pieces* (1830). *Atalantis: A Story of the Sea* (1832). *The Remains of Maynard Davis Richardson, with a Memoir of His Life* (1833). *Martin Faber: The Story of a Criminal* (1833). *The Book of My Lady: A Melange* (1833). *Guy Rivers: A Tale of Georgia* (1834). *The Yemassee: A Romance of Carolina* (1835). *The Partisan: A Tale of the Revolution* (1835). *Mellichampe: A Legend of the Santee* (1836). *Martin Faber: The Story of a Criminal; and other Tales* (1837). *Carl Werner: An Imaginative Story, with Other Tales of Imagination* (1838). *Richard Hurdis: or, The Avenger of Blood* (1838). *Pelayo: A Story of the Goth* (1838). *Southern Passages and Pictures* (1839). *The Damsel of Darien* (1839). *Border Beagles: A Tale of Mississippi* (1840). *The History of South Carolina* (1840). *The Kinsmen: or the Black Riders of Congaree, a Tale*, later renamed *The Scout or The Black Riders of Congaree* (1841). *Confession: or, The Blind Heart, a Domestic Story* (1841). *Beauchampe: or The Kentucky Tragedy, a Tale of Passion* (repr. 1856, Vol. I was retitled *Charlemont: or The Pride of the Village, a Tale of Kentucky*, and Vol. II, *Beauchampe: or The Kentucky Tragedy, a Sequel to Charlemont*) (1842). *Donna Florida: A Tale* (1843). *The Geography of South Carolina* (1843). *The Life of Francis Marion* (1844). *Castle Dismal: or, The Bachelor's Christmas, A Domestic Legend* (1844). *The Prima Donna: A Passage from City Life* (1844). *Helen Halsey: or, The Swamp State of Conelachita, A Tale of the Borders* (1845). *The Wigwam and the Cabin* (1845). *Count Julian: or, The Last Days of the Goth* (1845). *Views and Reviews in American Literature, History and Fiction* (1845). *Grouped Thoughts and Scattered Fancies: A Collection of Sonnets* (1845). *Areytos: or, Songs of the South* (1846). *The Life of Captain John Smith, the Founder of Virginia* (1846). *The Life of the Chevalier Bayard: "The Good Knight"* (1847). *Charleston and Her Satirists: A Scribblement* (1848). *Lays of the Palmetto: A Tribute to The South Carolina Regiment in the War with Mexico* (1848). *The Cassique of Accabee: A Tale, with Other Poems* (1848). Ed., *A Supplement to the Plays of William Shakespeare: Comprising the Seven Dramas, Which Have Been Ascribed to His pen, but which are not included in his writings in modern editions* (1848). *Father Abbot: or, The Home Tourist* (1849). *Sabbath Lyrics: or, Songs from Scripture* (1849). *The Life of Nathanael Greene, Major-General in the Army of the Revolution* (1849). *The Lily and the Totem: or, The Huguenots in Florida* (1850). *The City of the Silent: A Poem . . . Delivered at the Consecration of Magnolia Cemetery* (1850). *Katherine Walton: or, The Rebel of Dorchester* (1851). *Norman Maurice; or, The Man of the People: An American Drama. In Five Acts* (1851). *Michael Bonham: or, the Fall of Bexar: A Tale of Texas in Five Parts* (1852). *The Sword of the Distaff: or, "Fair, Fat and Forty."* A *Story of the South at the close of the Revolution*, later retitled *Woodcraft or Hawks about the Dovecote* (1852). *The Golden Christmas: A Chronicle of St. John's, Berkeley* (1852). *As Good as a Comedy: or, The Tennessean's Story* (1852). *Vasconselos: A Romance of the New World* (1853). *Eqeria: or, voices of Thought and Counsel* (1853). *Marie De Berniere: A Tale of the Crescent City*, also entitled *The Maroon: A Legend of the Caribees* (1853). *Poems Descriptive, Dramatic, Legendary, and Contemplative,* 2 vols. (1853). *South Carolina in the Revolutionary War* (1853). *Southward Ho! A Spell of Sunshine* (1854). *The Forayers: or, The Raid of the Dog-Days* (1855). *Eutaw: A Sequel to The Forayers: or, The Raid of the Dog-Days* (1856). *A Tale of the Revolution* (1856). *The Cassique of Kiawah: A Colonial Romance* (1859). *Simms's Poems: Areytos or Songs and Ballads of the South, with other Poems* (1860). *Sack and Destruction of the City of Columbia, S.C.* (1865). *The Army Correspondence of Colonel John Lawrens . . . with a Memoir* (1867). *Voltmeier or The Mountain Men* (1969). *Joscelyn: A Tale of the Revolution* (1975).

C. HUGH HOLMAN
University of North Carolina
Chapel Hill

CHARLES ALPHONSO SMITH (1864–1924). C. Alphonso Smith, a professor and popularizer of literature, was born in Greensboro, N.C., on May 28, 1864, to Jacob Henry and Mary Kelly Watson Smith. He received his early education in Greensboro and earned an A.B. (1884) and an A.M. (1887) at Davidson College. For four years Smith taught school in small North Carolina towns. In 1889 he matriculated at the Johns Hopkins University where he received his Ph.D. in 1893. In his subsequent academic career, Smith served as a professor of literature at Louisiana State University, 1893–1902; the University of North Carolina, 1902–1909; the University of Virginia, 1909–1917; and the United States Naval Academy, 1917–1924. In 1910–1911 he was Roosevelt Professor of American History and Institutions at the University of Berlin, the first southerner since the war to occupy that chair. Smith died in Annapolis on June 13, 1924.

Although a university professor, Smith always sought to interest a wider audience in literature. To do so, he frequently employed his considerable talent as a public lecturer and in 1913 published a tract on the value of literature. Entitled *What Can Literature Do for Me?*, this book appeared in several editions.

After initial work on grammar and syntax, Smith devoted his scholarly attention to the essay, short story, and oratory, especially of his native region. He edited one volume of *The Library of Southern Literature* and assisted with others. Smith wrote a biography of his boyhood friend William Sydney Porter and a book on Edgar Allan Poe. He also developed an interest in the collection of ballads, lectured widely on the topic, and helped found the Virginia Folk-Lore Society in 1913. After his death his widow published some of his short pieces on individual southerners and trends in southern literature as *Southern Literary Studies*.

WORKS: *Repetition and Parallelism in English Verse: A Study in the Technique of Poetry* (1894). *An Old English Grammar and Exercise Book with Inflections, Syntax, Selections for Readings, and Glossary* (1896). *An English-German Conversation Book*, with Gustav Krüger (1902). *Our Language* (1903). *Studies in English Syntax* (1906). *Die Amerikanische Literatur: Vorlesungen, Gehalten an der Königlichen, Friedrich-Wilhelms-Universität zu Berlin, von Dr. C. Alphonso Smith* (1912). *What Can Literature Do for Me?* (1913). *O. Henry Biography* (1916). *New Words Self-Defined* (1919). *Keynote Studies in Keynote Books of the Bible* (1919). *Edgar Allan Poe: How to Know Him* (1921). *What Reading Can Do for You*, new ed. *What Can Literature Do for Me?* (1925). *Southern Literary Studies: A Collection of Literary, Biographical, and Other Sketches* (1927).

GAINES M. FOSTER
University of North Carolina
Chapel Hill

CHARLES FORSTER SMITH (1852–1931). Charles Forster Smith was born on June 30, 1852, in what is now Greenwood County, S.C., the fifth of eleven children. His parents were the Reverend James Francis and Juliana Forster Smith. He received his earliest education at neighboring schools before he went in 1868 to Wofford College, S.C., where he received an A.B. in 1872. He also attended Harvard University (one semester, 1874), the University of Berlin (1874–1875), and the University of Leipzig (1874–1875, 1879–1881). At the latter he was awarded a Ph.D. in 1881; his dissertation, *A Study of Plutarch's Life of Artaxerxes, with Especial Reference to the Sources*, was published the same year. The University of Arkansas and Wofford College awarded him the honorary LL.D. in 1910.

Smith married Anna L. Du Pre on August 21, 1879, and they were the parents of five children. She died April 26, 1893.

Smith held teaching positions in Greenwood, S.C., until 1874, at Wofford College (classics and German, 1875–1879), at Williams College, Mass. (assistant professor of Latin and Greek, 1881–1882), at Vanderbilt University (professor of modern languages, 1882–1883); Chair of Greek (1883–1894), at the University of Wisconsin (professor and chairman of the Department of Greek and Classical Philology, 1894–1917; emeritus, 1917), and at the American School of Classical Studies in Athens (annual professor, 1920–1921). He was associate editor of *Classical Philology* from its founding in 1906 to 1931 and president of the American Philological Association, 1902–1903.

Smith was the editor of several college texts in the classics and wrote "The South's Contribution to Classical Studies" for Vol. VII of *The South in the Building of the Nation* (1909). At Wofford College, one of Smith's colleagues was William Malone Baskervill. During his last years he was working on an unfinished book on the Old South. He died on August 3, 1931, in Racine, Wisc.

WORKS: *A Study of Plutarch's Life of Artaxerxes, with Especial Reference to the Sources* (1881). Ed., *Thucydides, Bk. 7* (1886), *Bk. 3* (1894). Trans., Hertzberg's *Geschichte* (1900). Ed., Xenophon, *Anabasis* (1905). Ed., *Herodotus, Bk. 7* (1907). *Reminiscences and Sketches* (1908). Ed., *Thu-*

cydides, Bk. 6 (1913). Trans., *Thucydides*, Loeb Classical Library, 4 vols. (1919–1923). *Charles Kendall Adams* (1924).

RANDALL G. PATTERSON
Belhaven College
Jackson, Miss.

CHARLES HENRY SMITH (1826–1903). Charles Henry Smith, creator of "Bill Arp," was born in Lawrenceville, Ga., on June 15, 1826. One of ten children born to Asahel Reid and Caroline Ann Maguire Smith, he attended Gwinnet County Manual Labor Institute. In 1844 he entered Franklin College (later the University of Georgia) but left in 1847 before completing his degree because of family illness. Smith married the sixteen-year-old Mary Octavia Hutchins in 1849 and eventually had thirteen children, ten of whom lived to adulthood. After a brief study of the law, Smith became a lawyer traveling for the Georgia circuit court. In 1851 he and his growing family moved to Rome where he was elected alderman six times and mayor once.

As an active supporter of the southern cause during the Civil War, Smith procured supplies, tried cases of treason, and served as an officer in the Army of Northern Virginia and in the Forrest Artillery Company. After the war he continued to be active in law, politics, and business until 1877, when he moved to a farm some five miles from Cartersville. His main source of income from then until his death came from his Bill Arp letters and public lectures. His death at Cartersville on August 24, 1903, was mourned by thousands of admiring readers throughout the South.

Charles Henry Smith's contribution to southern literature, the Bill Arp letters, is a series of more than 2,000 informal essays written between 1861 and 1903. The persona Bill Arp is a simple, strong, conservative Georgia cracker whose letters to the editor chronicle the successes and failures, hopes and frustrations, of an average southerner during the war and Reconstruction. Over the years the voice of Arp changes from that of a semiliterate given to comic misspellings to that of a gentleman, educated and literary. Most of the letters appeared in Atlanta newspapers, the *Southern*

Confederacy and the *Constitution*, and according to one estimate were also printed in over 700 newspapers during the peak of their popularity.

WORKS: *Bill Arp, So Called* (1866). *Bill Arp's Peace Papers* (1873). *Bill Arp's Scrap Book: Humor and Philosophy* (1884). *The Farm and the Fireside: Sketches of Domestic Life in War and in Peace* (1891). *A School History of Georgia* (1893). *Bill Arp: From the Uncivil War to Date* (1903).

HAROLD WOODELL
Clemson University
Clemson, S.C.

FRANCIS HOPKINSON SMITH (1838–1915). F. Hopkinson Smith, as he signed his works, was born in Baltimore, Md., on October 23, 1888. Because his family could not afford to send him to college, he worked in an iron foundry, then learned mechanical engineering. He married in 1866 and spent some 30 years in constructions that included the foundation for the Statue of Liberty. His hobby was painting and drawing. He was a prize-winning watercolorist and an illustrator of some of his own books.

He became a popular after-dinner speaker and lecturer. His first publications were books that he illustrated and supplied stories for, such as *Old Lines in New Black and White* (poetry by Lowell, Holmes, and Whittier, 1885) and *Well-Worn Roads* (a travel book, 1886). Toward the end of his life he produced other similar works.

In his 50s he became a popular novelist and short story writer, producing best sellers until his death. Several of his books have autobiographical bases. His best-liked book was *Colonel Carter of Cartersville* (1891), featuring a Virginia gentleman who told after-dinner stories. *Tom Grogan* (1896) was a novel about labor strife on the New York waterfront, with a female protagonist. In *The Tides of Barnegat* (1906), perhaps his best-written novel, he dealt with divorce and family problems in a New Jersey fishing community.

Smith was a descendant of Francis Hopkinson, poet, composer, and signer of the Declaration of Independence. In his time Smith was taken so seriously as an author that a 23-volume collection of his *Works* was issued in 1915. He died in New York on April 7, 1915.

WORKS: *Old Lines in New Black and White* (1885). *Well-Worn Roads in Spain, Holland and Italy* (1886). *A White Umbrella in Mexico* (1889). *A Book of the Tile Club* (1890). *Colonel Carter of Cartersville* (1891). *A Day at Laguerre's and Other Days* (1892). *American Illustrators* (1892). *A Gentleman Vagabond and Some Others* (1895). *Tom Grogan* (1896). *Gondola Days* (1897). *Venice of To-Day* (1897). *Caleb West, Master Diver* (1898). *The Other Fellow* (1899). *The Fortunes of Oliver Horn* (1902). *The Under Dog* (1903). *Colonel Carter's Christmas* (1904). *At Close Range* (1905). *The Wood Fire in No. 3* (1905). *The Tides of Barnegat* (1906). *The Veiled Lady* (1907). *The Romance of an Old-fashioned Gentleman* (1907). *Peter* (1908). *Forty Minutes Late* (1909). *Kennedy Square* (1911). *The Arm Chair at the Inn* (1912). *Charcoals of New and Old New York* (1912). *In Thackeray's London* (1913). *In Dickens' London* (1914). *Enoch Crane* (1916).

WILLIAM K. BOTTORFF
University of Toledo
Toledo, Ohio

CAPTAIN JOHN SMITH (1580–1631). John Smith was baptized on January 9, 1580, at the parish church of Willoughby, Lincolnshire, England; presumably he was born earlier in the same month. The eldest son of George Smith, a freeman farmer, and his wife Alice, he attended school in his early teens in nearby Louth, served a brief apprenticeship to a merchant, and on the death of his father (when Smith was sixteen) inherited his farm. He served for several years with English troops in the Netherlands, and upon the declaration of peace there, having found a calling, he headed for Hungary, whose soldiers were fighting against the Turks. He fought in several battles in the Balkans as part of the army of the Holy Roman Empire. He was commissioned captain. After winning recognition as a soldier, he was captured by the Turks and taken to Constantinople. He was next shipped across the Black Sea and up the Don River, where he escaped. After further travels, he returned to England.

In December, 1606, Smith left with the first group of colonists headed for Virginia. At Jamestown, the town they founded, his leadership qualities brought him the position of supply officer and later president of the governing council. During his 30 months in America he carried the colony through severe trials and prepared two reports, one on his experiences and one on the character of the place. In October, 1609, he was badly burned in a powder explosion and forced to return to England. Less than 30 years old, Smith was to find his most memorable days and his most significant achievements now behind him.

Despite ambitions, he was able to visit America only once more, in 1614, when he explored the coast of the area that he named New England. Henceforth he was to serve the cause of colonization through his writings, which are largely autobiographical and promotional, with some hack work. He wrote a pamphlet *Description of New England*; he compiled, from his own writings and from the writing of others, *The Generall Historie of Virginia, New England, and the Summer Isles* [Bermuda]; he described the virtues of New England in *Trials*; and he prepared *Advertisements* for planters of New England "or any where." He recalled his European experiences in what he insisted were *True Travels*. Although his reliability was later to be questioned, he is now judged to have been truthful if egotistical. His exaggerations concerning his own importance can be attributed to the painful frustrations felt by a proved leader. He was denied the opportunity to return to the America on which he had set his heart, though he lived on till June 21, 1631.

Captain John Smith has been called the first American writer, since his letter or report of 1608 from Jamestown was published that year in London, the first publication in English written from America. Although his prose is sometimes obscure and disjointed, it conveys a strong sense of the man and what he saw in America, as well as what he hoped—he was a deep-dyed optimist—for the land he so loved.

WORKS (short titles): *A True Relation* (1608). "A Description of Virginia" in *A Map of Virginia* (1612). *A Description of New England* (1616). *New England Trials* (1620; 2nd ed., 1622). *The Generall Historie of Virginia,*

New England and the Summer Isles (1624). *An Accidence* (1626). *A Sea Grammar* (1627). *The True Travels* (1630). *Advertisements for the Unexperienced Planters of New-England, or Any Where* (1631).

EVERETT EMERSON
University of Massachusetts
Amherst

LILLIAN EUGENIA SMITH (1897–1966). Lillian Smith, who gained both fame and fortune with her first novel, *Strange Fruit* (1944), was born in Jasper, Fla., on December 12, 1897. A strong influence on her early life came from her maternal grandfather, William Henry Simpson, a New Yorker, who had been educated to be a Jesuit priest. Simpson left the Church and migrated to Georgia where he married Caroline Peeples, a member of an aristocratic Tidewater family. A daughter of this marriage, Anne Simpson, married Calvin Warren Smith of Ware County, Ga. The Smiths, who settled in Jasper, had nine children, of whom Lillian Eugenia was the seventh. In 1915 Smith moved his family to Clayton, Ga., where he operated a hotel and a children's camp. During 1915–1916, Lillian attended nearby Piedmont College; in 1916–1917 she worked with her father; and in 1917–1918 she studied piano at Peabody Conservatory, Baltimore. In the summer of 1918, she returned to Clayton to teach school and enroll in a Student Nurse Corps. She studied piano at Peabody Conservatory (1919–1922), and then taught music at Virginia School, Huckow, Chekiang Province, China, for three years.

In 1925 Smith returned to Clayton to direct her father's summer camp; during 1928–1929 she studied at Teachers College, Columbia University; from 1930 to 1935 she resided in Clayton and Macon, Ga., where she drafted two novels and a novella, all later destroyed by fire. From 1936 to 1946, she coedited a little magazine, *South Today*, which reflected her liberal stance on race relations. Among early contributors were W. J. Cash and Gerald W. Johnson.

During 1938–1939 Smith spent the winter in Brazil, working on *Strange Fruit*. In 1939 and again in 1940, she received Julius

Rosenwald fellowships for a travel-study project in the South. In 1944 shock waves crossed the country when *Strange Fruit*, the story of a love affair between a white man and a black woman, was published. Charges of obscenity obscured the quality of the novel. In 1945, with her sister Esther, Smith dramatized *Strange Fruit* for a brief run on Broadway.

From October, 1948, to September, 1949, Smith wrote a weekly column, "A Southerner Talking," for the Chicago *Defender*; and during 1964–1966 she wrote sixteen book reviews for Chicago *Tribune Books Today*. She received honorary degrees from Howard University and Oberlin College in 1950 and from Atlanta University in 1957. Suffering from cancer, beginning in 1953, she died on September 28, 1966, in Atlanta.

WORKS: *Strange Fruit* (1944). *Killers of the Dream* (1949). *The Journey* (1954). *Now Is the Time* (1955). *One Hour* (1959). *Memory of a Large Christmas* (1962). *Our Faces, Our Words* (1964).

LOUISE BLACKWELL
Florida A. & M. University
Tallahassee

WILLIAM JAY SMITH (1918–). William Jay Smith was born in Winnfield, La., on April 22, 1918, and spent his childhood in Louisiana and in Missouri. His father and his grandfather were soldiers, the latter serving in the Confederate Army. Smith studied in France (1938) and received his B.A. (1939) and M.A. (1941) at Washington University, with a major in French. In World War II he served in the U.S. Naval Reserve, achieving the rank of lieutenant. After the war he taught for a year at Columbia, was a Rhodes Scholar at Oxford (1947–1948), and spent the following two years at the University of Florence in Italy.

In 1947 Smith married Barbara Howes, a poet, by whom he had two sons. His first marriage ended in divorce in 1964, and in 1966 Smith married Sonja Haussmann of Paris.

For a two-year term, Smith served in the Vermont house of representatives. He has taught at Williams College and now is at Hollins College. He has been writer-in-residence at Arena Stage in Washington, D.C., and consultant in poetry at the Library of Congress. He has traveled and lectured for the Department of State in the Far East in 1969 and in Russia and Europe in 1970.

Smith began writing early, his first poem being published nationally when he was fourteen. He has also garnered a number of awards, the first for a poem as an undergraduate in *College Verse*. Two volumes of poetry were nominated for the National Book Award (1957, 1966). He received the Henry Bellamann Major Award (1970) and the Russell Loines Award for poetry (1972). The same year he also received a grant from the National Endowment for the Arts.

Smith has translated poetry from France, Italy, and Austria, has written poems for children, has published two volumes of essays and criticism, and has written a comedy with accompanying music.

WORKS: *Poems* (1947). *Celebration at Dark* (1950). *Valéry Larbaud: Poems of a Multimillionaire* (1955). *Selected Writings of Jules Laforgue* (1956). *Poems, 1947–1957* (1957). *The Spectra Hoax* (1961). *The Tin Can and Other Poems* (1966). *Poems from France* (1967). *New and Selected Poems* (1970). *The Streaks of the Tulip: Selected Criticism* (1972). *Poems from Italy* (1972). *Queen of Coins* (1975). *Venice in the Fog* (1976).

JOE ROSS
University of Alabama
Birmingham

EMMA DOROTHY ELIZA NEVITTE SOUTHWORTH (1819–1899). This most prolific of southern lady novelists was known as E.D.E.N. Southworth, author of over 60 books, most of them sentimental or melodramatic novels with a southern setting. She was born in Alexandria, Va., on December 26, 1819, the oldest daughter of Charles LeCompte Nevitte, and spent much of her childhood in St. Mary's County, Md., home of her Catholic ancestors in America. After the death of her father, her mother, Susanna, married Joshua Henshaw, secretary to Daniel Webster, who soon opened a school for girls in Washington. There Emma was first a pupil and later a teacher. In 1840 she married Frederick Southworth, moved to Wisconsin, taught school there briefly, but in 1844 returned to Washington, apparently deserted by her husband.

She resumed teaching, but the pay ($250 per year) was low and the expenses for her two children high; so she supplemented her income by writing sketches, first for the Baltimore *Visitor* and later for Gamaliel Bailey's *National Era*. At the *Era* she received ten dollars a column, and for it, in 1847 and 1848, she wrote stories in two-to-six parts, leading to *Retribution*, her first full novel, in 1849, which appeared in fourteen weekly installments. "From that time I never had a manuscript refused," she claimed, and she always seemed to have a manuscript in hand.

Her success led to her purchase of Prospect Cottage, a fourteen-room dwelling overlooking the Potomac in Georgetown, and for the rest of the century it was a well-known literary meeting place for the District of Columbia. At the *Era* she met Whittier, then a corresponding editor, who introduced her to Harriet Beecher Stowe. Stowe is supposed to have stayed at Prospect Cottage while making arrangements for the publication of her famous novel in the *Era*, and certainly the two writers became lifelong friends. Later, on a trip to England to see to the sale of her books, Emma met and became another American friend of Lady Byron.

In this country, while continuing to write regularly for the *Era*, she made arrangements with the *Saturday Evening Post*, so that through 1856 she sometimes had separate novels running serially in each magazine. But in 1857 she became another of Robert Bonner's stable of writers for the New York *Ledger* and thereafter restricted her writing to its pages. She made few pretensions about the literary merit of her novels, but her early and authentic treatment of Negro speech, her use of local legends, her occasional light touches, and her shrewd grasp of feminine psychology are better than anything of the sort in Sylvanus Cobb, Harriet Lewis, or other writers of the *Ledger* breed. Her own favorite of her novels was *Ishmael* (1863), based on the life of William Wirt, but her best-known and most widely reprinted was the melodramatic *The Hidden Hand* (1859). She believed fully and seriously that novels could provide both escape and instruction, and her hundreds of thousands of readers clearly found the first and were ready to escape again in the next week's installment. Southworth continued to write until 1886, and even thereafter reprints continued well into this century. She died at Prospect Cottage on June 30, 1899.

WORKS: The following list is of book publication when possible, and of the first copyright date, when known. When a Southworth novel has appeared under different titles (some, including pirated editions, have appeared under four titles), the original title only has been used. *Retribution* (1849). *The Three Beauties* (1850). *The Deserted Wife* (1850). *The Mother-in-Law* (1851). *The Curse of Clifton* (1852). *The Discarded Daughter* (1852). *Virginia and Magdalene* (1852). *India* (1853). *Old Neighborhoods and New Settlements* (1853). *The Wife's Victory* (1853). *The Lost Heiress* (1854). *Broken Pledges* (1855). *The Missing Bride* (1855). *Vivia* (1856). *The Lost Bride* (1858). *The Hidden Hand* (1859). *Capitola's Peril* (1859). *The Lady of the Isle* (1859). *Kathleen Vernon* (1860). *The Haunted Homestead* (1860). *The Gipsy's Prophecy* (1860). *Love's Labor Won* (1860). *Hickory Hall* (1861). *Eudora* (1861). *Astrea* (1862). *Captain Rock's Pet* (1862). *The Broken Engagement* (1862). *The Fatal Marriage* (1863). *Ishmael* (1863). *The Widow's Son* (1863). *The Bride of Llewellyn* (1864). *Self-Raised* (1864). *The Bridal Eve* (1864). *Allworth Abbey* (1865). *The Changed Brides* (1867). *The Coral Lady* (1867). *The Bride's Fate* (1867). *Fair Play* (1868). *Elfie's Vision* (1868). *How He Won Her* (1869). *Cruel as the Grave* (1869). *Tried for Her Life* (1869). *The Family Doom* (1869). *The Maiden Widow* (1870). *The Christmas Guest* (1870). *The Artist's Love* (1872). *The Lost Heir of Linlithgow* (1872). *A Noble Lord* (1872). *A Beautiful Friend* (1873). *Victor's Triumph* (1874). *The Spectre Lover* (1875). *The Mystery of Dark Hollow* (1875). *The Fatal Secret* (1877). *Gloria* (1877). *David Lindsay* (1877). *A Love Lost and Won* (1877). *The Phantom Wedding* (1878). *The Bride's Ordeal* (1878). *Her Love or Her Life* (1878). *Erma, the Wanderer* (1878). *A Skeleton in the Closet* (1878). *Brandon Coyle's Wife* (1879). *When Love's Shadows Flee* (1879). *Sybil Brotherton* (1879). *A Leap in the Dark* (1881). *The Mysterious Marriage* (1882). *Her Mother's Secret* (1883). *Love's Bitterest Cup* (1883). *When Shadows Die* (1883). *Why Did He Wed Her?* (1884). *For Woman's Love* (1884). *An Unrequited Love* (1885). *A Deed Without a Name* (1886). *Dorothy Harcourt's Secret* (1887). *To His Fate* (1887). *When Love Gets Justice* (1888). *Nearest and Dearest* (1889). *Little Nea's Engagement* (1889). *Unknown* (1889). *The Mystery of Raven Rocks* (1889). *Between Two Fires* (1889). *The Lost Lady of Love* (1890). *The Struggle of a Soul*

(1890). *The Unloved Wife* (1890). *When the Shadow Darkens* (1890).
Lilith (1890). *Em* (1892). *Em's Courtship* (1892). *Em's Husband* (1892).
Only a Girl's Heart (1893). *Gertrude's Sacrifice* (1893). *The Rejected
Bride* (1894). *A Husband's Devotion* (1894). *Gertrude Haddon* (1894).
Reunited (1894). *The Trail of the Serpent* (1907). *A Tortured Heart*
(1907). *The Test of Love* (1907). *Love's Suspense* (1907). *The Bride's
Dowry* (1910). *For Whose Sake?* (1910). *The Rector's Daughter* (1910).
The Three Sisters (1910).

C. CARROLL HOLLIS
University of North Carolina
Chapel Hill

ALFRED BENNETT SPELLMAN (1935–). Alfred Bennett
Spellman, Jr., was born on August 7, 1935, in Nixonton, N.C.,
a small northeastern coastal town near Elizabeth City. He left
North Carolina in 1952 for Howard University in Washington,
D.C., where he graduated in 1956. He took a degree from the
university's law school in 1959.

Spellman's early penchant for words and music never left him.
He spent much of the early 1960s managing a Greenwich Village
bookstore and writing poetry and record reviews for *Kulchu Jazz*
(now defunct), *Metronome*, and *Downbeat*. His portraits of jazz
artists, *Four Lives in the Bebop Business*, was published in 1966.
In these sketches he explored the lives and contributions of jazz
musicians Cecil Taylor, Ornette Coleman, Herbie Nichols, and
Jackie McLean. Spellman observed the bittersweet extremes of
joy and pain flowing through the history of jazz and the lives of
jazzmen and noted that such extremes characterized living everywhere.

The Beautiful Days, Spellman's only collection of poems, appeared in 1965. Predictably, jazz subjects and rhythms dot the collection. The work is strong, masculine, unpretentious, and it is
sensual with no hint of the lewd. The poems show no trace of
bitterness or hate or didacticism. They just explore raw, authentic
experiences of men and women together and alone.

In the early 1970s Spellman produced and wrote two TV shows,
"Ebony Beat" and "Ebony Beat Junior." Both "Say Brother" and

"Essays in Black Music" produced and written for WGBH-TV in Boston were syndicated throughout New England. Presently Spellman hosts a daily fifteen minute "Jazz Calendar" for a Washington, D.C., Pacifica Network station. Spellman lives in Washington, D.C., is married, and has two children, Malcolm and Toyin.

WORKS: *The Beautiful Days and Others* (1965). *Four Lives in the Bebop Business* (1966).

WALLACE R. PEPPERS
North Carolina A & T State
University
Greensboro

ANNE SPENCER (1882–1975). Born on February 6, 1882, in Henry County, Va., Annie Bethel Scales spent most of her childhood with her mother in Bramwell, W. Va., after her parents separated about 1887. Barely literate when in 1893 her mother enrolled her in Virginia Seminary in Lynchburg, Va., she wrote her first poem, "The Skeptic," at age fourteen, a poem motivated by her disagreement with religious doctrine taught at the seminary. Annie progressed rapidly in her studies and graduated from the secondary division of the seminary in 1889. After two years of teaching primary school in rural West Virginia, she married her classmate, Edward A. Spencer, in 1901 and moved to Lynchburg, Va., where she lived for the remaining 74 years of her life.

Spencer spent most of her adult life reading and writing, cultivating her flower garden, and working actively in community affairs. Her efforts to help organize the Lynchburg chapter of the NAACP in 1917–1918 brought her into contact with James Weldon Johnson, then field secretary for the NAACP, who, while a guest at the Spencers' home, accidentally found some of her poetry and arranged for its publication in *Crisis*, an organ of the NAACP. Always modest about her writings, Spencer did not write with the intent of seeing her works in print. In every case her literary friends arranged for the publication of her poems. During the decade original pieces by Anne Spencer were published in *Crisis*,

Opportunity, and other magazines and were included in several anthologies.

From 1924 to 1946 she was librarian at Dunbar High School, having charge of the first library in Lynchburg to serve black patrons. Beginning in the 1920s, for four decades her home at 1313 Pierce Street in Lynchburg was frequented by such prominent persons as James Weldon Johnson, Countee Cullen, W. E. B. Du Bois, and Langston Hughes. After the early 1950s Anne Spencer lived an increasingly secluded life. Her poems have appeared in French and Spanish translations, have been widely anthologized since the 1920s, but have not been collected into a single volume. When she died in July, 1975, she was working on a free verse poem of seven cantos about the illustrious abolitionist John Brown.

WORKS: "Before the Feast of Shushan" (*Crisis*, February, 1920). "Dunbar" (*Crisis*, November, 1920). "At the Carnival," "Translation," "The Wife-Woman," in *The Book of American Negro Poetry* (1922), ed. James Weldon Johnson. "White Things" (*Crisis*, March, 1923). "Lady, Lady" (*Survey Graphic*, March, 1925). "Lines to a Nasturtium" (*Psalms*, October, 1926). "Creed," "I Have a Friend," "Innocence," "Life-Long, Poor Browning," "Neighbors," "Questing," "Substitution," in *Caroling Dusk*, ed. Countee Cullen (1927). "Sybil Warns Her Sister" (rev., "Letter to My Sister"), *Ebony and Topaz*, ed. Charles S. Johnson (1927). "Rime for the Christmas Baby" (*Opportunity*, December, 1927). "Grapes: Still-Life" (*Crisis*, April, 1929). "Requiem" (*Lyric*, Spring, 1931). "For Jim, Easter Eve," in *The Poetry of the Negro, 1746–1949*, ed. Langston Hughes and Arna Bontemps (1949). J. Lee Greene, *Time's Unfading Garden: Anne Spencer's Life and Poetry* (Baton Rouge: Louisiana State University Press, 1977) collects the poems.

J. LEE GREENE
University of North Carolina
Chapel Hill

ELIZABETH SPENCER (1921–). Elizabeth Spencer was born on July 19, 1921, at Carrollton, Miss., the daughter of Mary McCain and James Luther Spencer, descendants of families who have lived in Carroll County for generations. After a childhood plagued by ill health but enhanced by a vivid delight in myth, biblical stories,

Arthurian romance, and accounts of Mississippi's participation in the Civil War, she was graduated valedictorian of her high school class in 1938. She had already begun to write stories, and as a student at Belhaven College, Jackson, Miss., she edited the Belhaven newspaper, received the Chi Delta Poetry Award, and placed second in the short-story division of the Southern Literary Festival. After graduation from Belhaven in 1942, she enrolled as a graduate student in English at Vanderbilt, where Donald Davidson encouraged her to continue writing. After receiving her M.A. in 1943, she taught at Northwest Junior College in Senatobia, Miss., and at Ward-Belmont College in Nashville, Tenn. After a brief interval as a newspaper reporter for the Nashville *Tennessean*, she resolved to become a full-time writer of fiction.

The success of her first novel, *Fire in the Morning* (1948), encouraged her to continue writing. In 1948 she joined the faculty of the University of Mississippi, teaching English and creative writing. Her second novel, *This Crooked Way* (1952), won for her a grant from the National Institute of Arts and Letters, and the following year a Guggenheim Fellowship enabled her to live and write in Italy.

In Italy, Spencer met John Arthur Blackwood Rusher, a language school director, whom she married in 1956. The last of her novels to be set in Mississippi, *The Voice at the Back Door*, won the Rosenthal Award for 1957. In 1958 she moved with her husband to Canada where she now lives.

WORKS: *Fire in the Morning* (1948). *This Crooked Way* (1952). *The Voice at the Back Door* (1956). *The Light in the Piazza* (1960). *Knights and Dragons* (1965). *No Place for an Angel* (1967). *Ship Island and Other Stories* (1968). *The Snare* (1972).

JOHN PILKINGTON
University of Mississippi
Oxford

LAURENCE TUCKER STALLINGS (1894–1968). Laurence Stallings, whose life and writing were dominated by World War I, was born in Macon, Ga., on November 25, 1894. Physically active as a boy, he was captivated by stories from the southern past, especially those of chivalric heroism from the Civil War. Entering Wake Forest College in 1912, he played football and was an excellent student. In 1917, a year after graduation, he joined the Marines and was wounded at Belleau Wood in June, 1918, a wound that necessitated the amputation of his right leg in 1922. Later that year he joined the New York *World*.

Stallings' literary career began sensationally. His autobiographical novel *Plumes* (1924), which contrasted his chivalric idealism through college with his bitter despair following the war, was widely hailed as an example of postwar disillusionment. His first play, *What Price Glory* (1924), written with Maxwell Anderson, succeeded tremendously using the war to symbolize a world without meaning. With Anderson he quickly wrote two more plays that failed commercially, though one, *First Flight* (1925), is an interesting tall tale about Andrew Jackson in North Carolina. And before leaving the *World* in 1926, he also wrote the highly acclaimed motion picture *The Big Parade*.

Stallings published short stories (uncollected) into the early 1930s, dramatized Hemingway's *A Farewell to Arms* (1930), compiled *The First World War: A Photographic History* (1933), and produced a play *The Streets Are Guarded* (1944; unpublished). But after leaving the *World* his literary career was virtually over. Retiring to North Carolina in 1927, he returned to New York for newspaper work in the early 1930s, then went to Hollywood in 1934. Following duty in World War II, he settled in Whittier, Cal., where he died on February 29, 1968. The major work of his last years was a narrative history of American soldiers in World War I, *The Doughboys* (1963).

WORKS: *Plumes* (1924). *Three American Plays [What Price Glory*, with Maxwell Anderson, *First Flight, The Buccaneer]* (1926). *The First World War: A Photographic History* (1933). *The Doughboys: The Story of the AEF, 1917–1918* (1963).

LAURENCE G. AVERY
University of North Carolina
Chapel Hill

MAX STEELE (1922-). Max Steele, writer and teacher at the University of North Carolina, was born on March 30, 1922, in Greenville, S.C. His early education was in Greenville; his undergraduate studies at Furman University (1939-1941) and the University of North Carolina (1942) were interrupted by service in the Army Air Force. As a meteorology cadet he attended Vanderbilt University (1943-1944) and UCLA (1944). He received a B.A. in 1946 from the University of North Carolina. Steele also did graduate work in painting at the Academie Julien (1951) and in the French Language and Literature at the Sorbonne (1952-1954) while he was an advisory editor to the *Paris Review*.

Steele's novel, *Debby*, received both the Harper Prize and the Mayflower Award in 1950, but he has received awards for both writing and for teaching. In 1955 and 1969 his stories were chosen for the O. Henry Prize Story collections; and in 1967 and 1970 he received fellowships from the National Foundation on the Arts and Humanities. In 1971 he was given both the Standard Oil Award for excellence in undergraduate teaching at the University of North Carolina, and the Distinguished Alumnus award from Furman University. Belmont Abbey College awarded him the honorary Litt.D. in 1970.

Steele served as lecturer in the Department of English at the University of North Carolina, 1956-1958, and as lecturer at the University of California at San Francisco, 1962-1964. He returned to the University of North Carolina as writer-in-residence, 1966-1967. Since 1967 he has headed the creative writing program at Chapel Hill where he now holds the rank of professor.

Essentially a short story writer, Steele's fiction has appeared in many national publications since August, 1944, when his first story was published in *Harper's*. Some 30 stories appeared between 1944 and 1977. Some of these stories have been collected in his book *Where She Brushed Her Hair* and in other anthologies. A book for children, *The Cat and the Coffee Drinkers*, was published by Harper & Row in 1969. In addition Steele writes book reviews, introductions, and interviews.

Steele is married to the former Dianna Whittinghill. They have two sons—Oliver Whittinghill and Kevin Russell. He is presently at work on a novel, "The Gorgon and the Bridegroom," and during the summers teaches at Squaw Valley, Community of Writer's Workshop, sponsored by the University of California at Davis. He has been a director of the workshop since 1970.

WORKS: *Debby* (1950). *Nichts gegen Debby!* (Hamburg, 1950). *The Goblins Must Go Barefoot* (1966, *Debby* retitled). *Where She Brushed Her Hair* (1968). *The Cat and the Coffee Drinkers* (1969). *American Literary Anthology*, #3, ed. with George Plimpton, Joyce Carol Oates *et al.* (1970).

JEANNE R. NOSTRANDT
James Madison College
Harrisonburg, Va.

WILBUR DANIEL STEELE (1886–1970). Wilbur Daniel Steele was born in Greensboro, N.C., on March 17, 1886, during the time his New England father was principal of Bennett Seminary. From theological studies in Germany, where Wilbur attended kindergarten, his father moved in 1892 to the University of Denver faculty. Steele graduated there in 1907, then studied art in Boston, but turned to writing after his first short story was published in 1910. For the next 45 years he produced over 200 stories for popular and literary periodicals, wrote ten novels and numerous plays, his acclaim attested by frequent awards and citations in the annual O'Brien *Best Short Stories*. In Provincetown, Mass., Steele was a roommate of Sinclair Lewis, wrote scripts for the Provincetown Players, and was a friend of Eugene O'Neill. Though his penchant for travel—to Italy, England, France, Switzerland, Tunisia, South America, and the Caribbean—provided a variety of locales for his stories, a majority of his characters were westerners and Cape Cod fishermen.

Beginning in 1927 he spent four years in the Carolinas, first in Charleston and later in Chapel Hill. Among his southern stories are "The Silver Sword," "Conjur," "A Bath in the Sea," "Can't Cross Jordan by Myself," "Pioneers," "A Way with Women," "Light," and two of his best, "Man and Boy" and "How Beautiful with Shoes." After the death of his wife, the artist Margaret Thurston, by whom he had two sons, he married Norma Mitchell. Thereafter his home was in Connecticut, where he died on May 26, 1970. In the 1930s the fashion for Steele's psychologically morbid stories, with their intricate plots and improbable twists, faded, and he turned to "western" novels, but only *That Girl from Memphis* was a commercial success. Martin Bucco's critical biography (1972) analyzes the career of a man once considered America's outstanding writer of short stories.

WORKS: *Storm* (1914). *Land's End* (1918). *The Shame Dance* (1923). *The Giant's Stair* (1924). *Isles of the Blest* (1924). *The Terrible Woman and Other One Act Plays* (1925). *Taboo* (1925). *Urkey Island* (1926). *The Man Who Saw Through Heaven* (1927). *Meat* (1928). *Tower of Sand* (1929). *Undertow* (1930). *Post Road*, with Norma Mitchell (1935). *Sound of Rowlocks* (1938). *That Girl from Memphis* (1945). *The Best Short Stories of Wilbur Daniel Steele* (1945). *Diamond Wedding* (1950). *Full Cargo* (1951). *Their Town* (1952). *The Way to the Gold* (1955).

RICHARD WALSER
North Carolina State University
Raleigh

JAMES STERLING (1701–1763). Born in obscurity in Downrass, King's County, Ireland, James Sterling gained his first notoriety soon after taking his B.A. at Trinity College, Dublin, in 1720. Perhaps the earliest Irish tragic playwright, he saw two of his plays performed on the Irish stage before taking Holy Orders in 1734 and entering the king's service as an army chaplain. Leaving behind a collection of his *Poetical Works*, the Reverend James Sterling emigrated to America in 1736 to undertake a clerical career.

Eventually settling in Kent County on Maryland's eastern shore, Sterling married and prospered in his rural parish from 1740 until his death. His literary and spiritual concerns did not prevent him from securing passage back to England in 1751, where he lobbied successfully for a lucrative appointment as collector of customs at Chester on the Chesapeake Bay. Opposition to Sterling's secular self-promotion was considerable and frustrated his more grandiose economic schemes, but he returned to Maryland in 1752 a man of unshakable means. In publicly disseminated sermons and magazine poetry, he celebrated America as a land of economic opportunity, natural beauty, and colonial loyalty during the last ten years of his life. He died on November 10, 1763.

Sterling's literary reputation rests largely on his competent, if rarely distinguished, neoclassic verse, his early application of sentimentalism to American subjects, and his recurring literary nationalism. These qualities are particularly evident in his major poems, *An Epistle to the Hon. Arthur Dobbs, Esq.* (1752) and "A Pastoral" (1758). The *Epistle* mixes neoclassic genres in high-flown language to praise Dobbs, the American explorer-hero, to describe the American wilderness, and to speculate on the advantages to trade of the discovery of the Northwest Passage. "A Pastoral" attempts to yoke a pastoral elegy mourning Pope's death with a progress piece describing the westward movement of the arts to the New World.

WORKS: *The Rival Generals: A Tragedy* (1722). *The Poetical Works of the Rev. James Sterling* (1734). *The Parricide: A Tragedy* (1736). *An Epistle to the Hon. Arthur Dobbs, Esq.* (1752). *A Sermon preached before his Excellency the Governor of Maryland, and Both Houses of Assembly at Annapolis, December 13, 1754* (1755). "A Pastoral," *American Magazine or Monthly Chronicle*, I (May, 1758), 390–97. "Verses Occasioned by the Success of the British Arms in the Year 1759," *Maryland Gazette* (January 3, 1760), 1.

WILLIAM L. ANDREWS
University of Wisconsin
Madison

JAMES STILL (1906–). Born on July 16, 1906, in Lafayette, Ala., the son of J. Alex (a veterinarian) and Lonnie Lindsey Still, James Still since 1932 has lived in a pre–Civil War log house on a farm nine miles from Hindman (Knott County), Ky., where he has combined writing, teaching, librarianship, farming, and research in Mayan civilization. Pursuing the latter interest, he has spent five winters in Mexico and Central America.

Still received his B.A. from Lincoln Memorial University, Harrogate, Tenn., 1929, his M.A. in literature from Vanderbilt, 1930, and the B.S. in Library Science from the University of Illinois, 1931.

Between 1933–1939 and 1952–1961 Still supported himself primarily as a staff member at Hindman Settlement School, and between 1962 and 1970 as a member of the English department of Morehead State University. He served in the U.S. Army Air Corps (Africa and the Middle East) from March 10, 1942, to September 5, 1945.

Among the honors Still has received are the O. Henry Memorial Prize (1939), two Guggenheim fellowships (1941, 1946), and in 1947 an award from the Academy of Arts and Letters and the National Institute of Arts and Letters in recognition of "his gift of style and mastery of character and scene."

Set in the mining camps and on the small farms of eastern Kentucky, both his poetry and fiction depict the lives of people who follow the rounds of the seasons in an almost timeless cycle of birth, growth, seedtime, and death.

Although Still uses southern Appalachia for his settings, most of his work is distinguished by the traits that *Time* magazine said make *River of Earth* "a small masterpiece": his skillful use of the English language and his clean, spare style elevate the regional to the universal.

WORKS: *Hounds on the Mountain* (1937). *River of Earth* (1940). *On Troublesome Creek* (1941). *Way Down Yonder on Troublesome Creek* (1974). *The Wolfpen Rustics* (1975). *Jack and the Wonder Beans* (1976). *Sporty Creek* (1977). *Pattern of a Man* (1977).

> DEAN CADLE
> University of North Carolina
> Asheville

WILLIAM STITH (1707–1755). Minister and historian of Virginia, William Stith was born in 1707, the son of Captain John Stith of Charles County, Va., and Mary Randolph Stith, daughter of William Randolph. After attending the Grammar School of the College of William and Mary, Stith entered Queens College, Oxford University, on May 21, 1724, and received his B.A. on

February 27, 1728. He was ordained a minister in the Anglican Church on April 12, 1731, and returned to Williamsburg.

Stith was elected master of the Grammar School of William and Mary College on October 25, 1731, and he also acted as chaplain to the Virginia House of Burgesses. In July, 1736, he became minister of Henrico Parish, Henrico County, where he remained for sixteen years. On July 13, 1738, he married his cousin, Judith Randolph, daughter of Thomas Randolph. Late in 1751 Stith was chosen as minister of St. Ann's Parish, but before he took this post, he was appointed the third president of the College of William and Mary on August 14, 1752. During this time, Stith also served as minister of York-Hampton Parish in York County. He was president of William and Mary until his death on September 19, 1755.

Stith published three sermons in the 1740s and 1750s but he is best known for *The History of the First Discovery and Settlement of Virginia*, published at Williamsburg in 1747. Using the accounts of Captain John Smith and of Robert Beverley and the unpublished records in the possession of William Byrd II and his uncle, Sir John Randolph, Stith carried his account of the founding of Virginia through 1624. Although Thomas Jefferson believed Stith's "details often too minute to be tolerable," and though Stith's account is partisan and critical of the policies of James I, his *History* is still a valuable source for information about early Virginia. Discouraged by the Virginians' reception of his *History*, Stith did not continue the work.

WORKS: *A Sermon Preached Before the General Assembly at Williamsburg, March 2, 1745–46* (1746). *The History of the First Discovery and Settlement of Virginia: Being an Essay Towards a General History of the Colony* (1747). *The Sinfulness and Pernicious Nature of Gaming: A Sermon Preached Before the General Assembly of Virginia* (1752). *The Nature and Extent of Christ's Redemption: A Sermon Preached Before the General Assembly* (1753).

ROBERT BAIN
University of North Carolina
Chapel Hill

JAMES HOWELL STREET (1903–1954). James Street was born in Lumberton, Miss., on October 15, 1903, the son of John C. and William [sic] Thomson Street. He was educated at the Massey School, Southwestern Theological Seminary, and Howard College. The son of a liberal Roman Catholic lawyer, Street was reared in Laurel, Miss., where he began a journalism career that eventually led to appointments with the Hattiesburg *American* (1922–1923); Pensacola *Journal* (1926); *Arkansas Gazette* (1927); Associated Press in Memphis (1928), Nashville (1929), Atlanta (1930–1933); New York *American* (1934–1936); and New York *World-Telegram* (1937). After marrying Lucy Nash O'Briant in 1923, Street interrupted his newspaper career to serve Baptist ministries in St. Charles, Mo., Lucedale, Miss., and Boyles, Ala. (he later became an Episcopalian). In 1938 Street moved to Old Lyme, Conn., and became a free-lance writer. Returning to the South in 1945, he resided in Chapel Hill, N.C., until his death on September 28, 1954.

His previous careers gave Street much material. *Look Away— A Dixie Notebook* (1936), his first book, describes the violence and turmoil of the South in sociological transition. In novels like *The High Calling* and *The Gauntlet* one follows the spiritual struggles of a minister. Street also wrote several historical romances such as *The Velvet Doublet*, based on the life of Juan Rodrigo Bermejo, who sailed with Columbus. In *Tomorrow We Reap* and *Mingo Dabney* he presents the various fortunes of the Dabney clan of Lebanon, Miss. Popular histories by Street include *The Civil War* and *The Revolutionary War*. *Captain Little Ax*, completed by novelist Don Tracy, covers the exploits of a seventeen-year-old Confederate captain. *James Street's South* is a collection of articles on southern states, cities, and rivers. Two short stories, "Nothing Sacred" and "The Biscuit Eater," became movies, and the former was eventually a musical comedy, *Hazel Flagg* (1953).

WORKS: *Look Away—A Dixie Notebook* (1936). *Oh, Promised Land* (1940). *In My Father's House* (1941). *The Biscuit Eater* (1941). *Tap Roots* (1942). *By Valour and Arms* (1944). *Short Stories* (1945). *The Gauntlet* (1945). *Tomorrow We Reap* (1949). *Mingo Dabney* (1950). *The High Call-*

ing (1951). *The Velvet Doublet* (1953). *The Civil War* (1953). *Good-bye, My Lady* (1954). *The Revolutionary War* (1954). *James Street's South*, ed. James Street, Jr. (1955). *Captain Little Ax*, with Don Tracy (1956).

JOHN T. HIERS
Valdosta State College
Valdosta, Ga.

MARY DALLAS STREET (1885–1951). Born on May 31, 1885, into a substantially wealthy and socially acceptable family in Richmond, Va., Mary Street was the daughter of Mary Gormley and George Levick Street. The only other surviving child was George, Jr., four years younger than Mary. Her father was president of a company that manufactured parts for railroad cars.

The family lived at 703 East Grace Street while Mary was growing up, but in 1919 moved to 815 West Franklin, a home she inherited after her parents' deaths in the 1920s. There Street remained until 1935, when financial problems and a bitter break with her brother over the family business probably contributed to her moving to New York City, where she lived until shortly before her death on November 10, 1951. She died in Charlottesville and is buried in Richmond's Hollywood Cemetery.

Educated at Miss Jennie Ellett's School and in Chestnut Hill, Pa., Street enjoyed horseback riding, membership in the right clubs, and travel abroad. Large and masculine, she wore tailored clothes and was known to have passionate attachments to other women.

One of the four editors of the *Reviewer*, a literary magazine of the early 1920s, she contributed funds as well as 27 pieces of her writing to the journal: twelve book reviews, six poems, five short stories, three sketches, and one editorial. Then, she seems to have published nothing for over a decade when her first novel appeared in 1936. A second novel followed ten years later.

Her writing is conventional, romantic, and often sentimental. The plots in the novels are full of coincidence, but Street shows a modest gift in describing place. She was a minor writer in the lively Richmond literary community of the 1920s.

WORKS: *At Summer's End* (1936). *Christopher Holt* (1946).

DOROTHY McINNIS SCURA
University of Richmond
Richmond, Va.

T[HOMAS] S[IGISMUND] STRIBLING (1881–1965). Born in the small river village of Clifton, Tenn., on March 4, 1881, Thomas Sigismund Stribling grew up against a background of contrast— his mother's side of the family having fought for the Confederacy and his father's side, the Union. The result was that Tom Stribling became, in his own words, "a doubter and a questioner," particularly of morals, manners, and social settings, a position well documented by his fiction.

Although Stribling prepared for teaching at the Florence, Ala., Normal School and studied law at the University of Alabama, his interest in writing—an interest he had developed as a child—was so great that he was discontented doing anything else. Rejecting teaching school and practicing law, he began his career writing stories for Sunday school magazines, but was soon writing adventure stories. In 1921 *Century Magazine* published his first serious novel, *Birthright*, a book dealing with the problems of a black man educated at Harvard who returns to his hometown in Tennessee hoping to do something uplifting for his race.

Between *Birthright* and his last novel, *These Bars of Flesh* (1937), Stribling turned out a dozen novels and a number of short stories, winning the 1933 Pulitzer Prize for *The Store*, the middle novel of a penetrating trilogy of the South that covers the years from the Civil War to the early 1920s. After 1937 Stribling continued to write stories for the *Saturday Evening Post* and various detective magazines. He died on July 10, 1965, in the Tennessee hill country he loved so much.

Stribling contributed significantly to American letters by presenting a new view of the South, thus clearing the way for later writers working in the same area.

WORKS: *The Cruise of the Dry Dock* (1917). *Birthright* (1922). *East Is East* (1922). *Fombombo* (1923). *Red Sand* (1924). *Teeftallow* (1926).

Bright Metal (1928). *Strange Moon* (1929). *Clues of the Caribbees* (1929). *Backwater* (1930). *The Forge* (1931). *The Store* (1932). *The Unfinished Cathedral* (1934). *The Sound Wagon* (1935). *These Bars of Flesh* (1938).

WILTON ECKLEY
Drake University
Des Moines, Iowa

DAVID HUNTER STROTHER [PORTE CRAYON] (1816–1888). David Strother was born on September 26, 1816, in Martinsburg, now W.Va. He briefly attended Jefferson College in Cannonsburg, Pa., before moving to New York City during the 1830s to study art under Samuel F. B. Morse and John Gadsby Chapman. Between 1840 and 1843 he continued his studies in Italy, but after his return to the United States he failed to make a living as portrait painter. In 1853 he submitted to *Harper's* a humorous account, illustrated with pen-and-ink sketches, of a camping expedition into the Blackwater Falls wilderness of western Virginia; the publication of "The Virginian Canaan" under the pen-name "Porte Crayon" launched Strother as a travel writer. During the 1850s he wrote four serials for *Harper's*: *Virginia Illustrated* (published in book form, 1857 and 1871), *North Carolina Illustrated*, *A Winter in the South*, and *A Summer in New England*. During this period he resided in Berkeley Springs, Va., and assisted his father in the management of a resort hotel. For *Harper's Weekly* he prepared eyewitness accounts of the John Brown trial and execution.

No abolitionist, Strother was nevertheless unwavering in his support of the Union. At the outbreak of the Civil War he attached himself to the topographical corps of the Union army and subsequently served as officer on the staffs of Banks, Pope, McClellan, Sigel, and Hunter. His active service included the battles of Second Manassas, Antietam, the Tesche, and the Valley campaigns of 1864. As brevet brigadier general he summarized his military observations in an eleven-part serial in *Harper's* titled *Personal Recollections of the War by a Virginian* (1866–1868), a valuable source for historians of the Civil War. Ostracized by many relatives and friends for his support of the Union, Strother continued to manage his Berkeley Springs hotel until the late 1870s when hard times wiped out his investment. President Hayes saved Strother and his family from poverty by appointing him consul general to Mexico in 1879. During his six years in Mexico, Strother acquired financial solvency but never completed his projected serial *Mexican Notes*. In 1885 he returned to Berkeley Springs and four years later died of pneumonia in Charles Town, his wife's home, on April 3, 1889.

WORKS: *Virginia Illustrated* (1857; 1871). *The Old South Illustrated*, ed. Cecil D. Eby (1959). *A Virginia Yankee in the Civil War*, ed. Cecil D. Eby (1961).

CECIL D. EBY
University of Michigan
Ann Arbor

DABNEY STUART (1937–). Dabney Stuart was born on November 4, 1937, in Richmond, Va., the son of Walker Dabney, Jr., and Martha von Schilling Stuart. As he has written, his roots go deep in Virginia. He began writing poetry when he was fourteen at summer camp, echoing Edgar Allan Poe; many of his poems are about places in the state where he has lived, or fished and hunted. After finishing high school in Richmond, he entered Davidson College, where he began publishing poetry in the campus literary magazine and other poetry journals. Elected to Phi Beta Kappa, he was awarded his A.B. in English in 1960 and attended Harvard University on a Woodrow Wilson Fellowship, receiving his A.M. in 1962. His marriage to Martha Varney ended in divorce; he has since remarried and is the father of three children.

Since leaving Harvard, Stuart has combined writing and editing with teaching. From 1961 until 1965 he was on the staff of the College of William and Mary. Since then he has taught at Washington and Lee University, where he is currently professor of English and poetry editor of *Shenandoah*.

Although primarily known for his poetry, Stuart has also published fiction and critical studies of such modern authors as Kafka and Nabokov. His first collection of poetry, *The Diving Bell*, composed mostly of traditional lyrics, was published in 1966. He has subsequently published poems in nearly 100 magazines, and nearly a dozen anthologies. Since his first book he has moved away from fixed forms, experimenting with new modes and surrealistic images. Once labeled a confessional poet because of his poems about his ancestors and family relationships, he is no longer easy to categorize. He has clearly been influenced by Eliot and Yeats, and he stresses the necessity for changing styles. Dabney Stuart has won the Dylan Thomas Award of the Poetry Society of America, the Howard Willett Prize and has been the recipient of a Literary Fellowship from the National Endowment on the Arts.

WORKS: *The Diving Bell* (1966). *A Particular Place* (1969). *The Other Hand* (1974). *Friends of Yours, Friends of Mine* (1974). *Round and Round: A Triptych* (1977). *Nabokov: The Dimensions of Parody* (1978).

GUY OWEN
North Carolina State University
Raleigh

JESSE STUART (1907–). Jesse Stuart was born on August 8, 1907, in W-Hollow, Greenup County, Ky., the first of seven children born to Mitchell and Martha Hilton Stuart. Graduated in 1926 from Greenup High School, he entered Lincoln Memorial University and took a B.A. in 1924. He became principal of Warnock High (1929), then of Greenup High in 1930 when he also published his first book, *Harvest of Youth*. He studied at Vanderbilt University, 1931–1932, but left without taking his master's when his dormitory burned with all of his belongings, including an almost completed thesis.

Stuart returned to positions in Greenup schools and began to publish poetry and short fiction. He published his most important book of poetry *Man with a bull-tongue Plow* in 1934. In 1937 he spent a year abroad on a Guggenheim Fellowship.

Stuart returned to the United States in 1938 for a continuous career of teaching, lecturing, and writing (poetry, novels, short stories, and articles). He married Naomi Deane Norris on October 14, 1939, and moved to his boyhood home in W-Hollow which, greatly changed and refurbished, remains his home today (1977).

Stuart's writing, domesticated almost completely in the hilly terrain of W-Hollow, is very prolific and has won him many honors, including the $2,500 Thomas Jefferson Southern Award for the best southern book of the year (1943) and the $5,000 Fellowship of the Academy of American Poets (1961). His works have been published on five continents and in many languages. He has traveled widely (70-odd countries and all of the 50 states).

His basic theme is the Antaean theme that man derives his ultimate strength from the earth; if divorced from the earth we ultimately wither and die. Stuart is very likely the best-known and most widely read of living Appalachian writers.

WORKS: *Harvest of Youth* (1930). *Man with a bull-tongue Plow* (1934). *Head O' W-Hollow* (1936). *Beyond Dark Hills* (1938). *Trees of Heaven* (1940). *Men of the Mountains* (1941). *Taps for Private Tussie* (1943). *Mongrel Mettle* (1944). *Album of Destiny* (1944). *Foretaste of Glory* (1946). *Tales From the Plum Grove Hills* (1946). *The Thread That Runs So True* (1949). *Hie to the Hunters* (1950). *Clearing in the Sky and Other Stories* (1950). *Kentucky is My Land* (1952). *The Good Spirit of Laurel Ridge* (1953). *The Year of My Rebirth* (1956). *Plowshare in Heaven* (1958). *Huey, the Engineer* (1960). *God's Oddling* (1960). *Hold April* (1962). *A Jesse Stuart Reader* (1963). *Save Every Lamb* (1964). *Daughter of The Legend* (1965). *My Land Has a Voice* (1966). *Mr. Gallion's School* (1967).

RUEL E. FOSTER
West Virginia University
Morgantown

RUTH MCENERY STUART (1852–1917). Ruth McEnery Stuart was a writer of local color stories set in Louisiana and Arkansas. Born on February 19, 1852, in Marksville, Avoyelles Paris, La., she grew up in New Orleans. Her father, a cotton merchant, was from Ireland; her mother was of Scotch ancestry. Married in 1879 to an Arkansas cotton planter, Alfred Oden Stuart, she was a widow four years later. She returned to New Orleans, where she began to write fiction. Her first story was published in 1888, and, benefiting from the ready national market for picturesque southern literature, she published prolifically for fifteen years thereafter. After 1903 she published less new fiction but more verse. Shortly after her first acceptances she moved to New York and remained a southern lady in a northern city, a charming and fashionable hostess for literary gatherings. She died on May 6, 1917.

Stuart wrote in three forms—the lyric often based on southern songs, the local-color sketch of whites or blacks, and the extended story not quite a novel. With few exceptions her work follows a sentimental, optimistic formula. The tales are often set at Christmastime and revolve around marriages or middle-aged romances. In almost all her stories she tries to capture dialect, also the key to her popular public readings from her own work. Most of her writing about whites is set in either the Italian section of New Orleans or her fictional town, Simpkinsville, Ark. Her many tales of blacks, usually domestic and picturesque, include none about interracial conflict and none with the vicious blacks of Thomas Dixon. In 1916 Hyder Rollins claimed her Negroes were more realistic than those of Page, Harris, or even Dunbar, but described her successes as "the illiterate, happy-go-lucky, good-natured Negro who is typical of the new South."

WORKS: *Carlotta's Intended* (1891). *A Golden Wedding and Other Tales* (1893). *Carlotta's Intended and Other Tales* (1894). *The Story of Babette, a Little Creole Girl* (1894). *Gobolinks or Shadow-Pictures for Young and Old*, with Albert Bigelow Paine (1896). *Sonny . . .* (1896); future eds. published as *Sonny, a Christmas Guest. Solomon Crow's Christmas Pockets and Other Tales* (1896). *The Snow-Cap Sisters: A Farce* (1897). *In Simpkinsville: Character Tales* (1897). *Moriah's Mourning, and Other Half-Hour Sketches* (1898). *Holly and Pizen and Other Stories* (1899). *The Woman's Exchange of Simpkinsville*, separate ed. of story included in *A Golden Wedding* (1899). *Napoleon Jackson: The Gentleman of the Plush Rocker* (1902). *George Washington Jones: A Christmas Gift That Went A-Begging* (1903). *The River's Children: An Idyl of the Mississippi* (1904). *The Second Wooing of Salina Sue and Other Stories* (1905). *Aunt Amity's Silver Wedding and Other Stories* (1909). *The Unlived Life of Little Mary Ellen*, separate ed. of story included in *In Simpkinsville* (1910). *Sonny's Father* (1910). *The Haunted Photograph* [and other stories] (1911). *Daddy Do-Funny's Wisdom Jingles* (1913). *The Cocoon: A Rest-Cure Comedy* (1915). *Plantation Songs and Other Verse* (1916).

JOHN BASSETT
Wayne State University
Detroit, Mich.

WILLIAM STYRON (1925–). Born in Newport News, Va., on June 11, 1925, William Styron was the only child of William Clark, a shipyard engineer, and Pauline Margaret Abraham Styron. After the death of his mother, Styron entered, in 1938, Christchurch, an Episcopal boarding school, in Middlesex County, Va. In 1942 he entered Davidson College, but soon entered the Marine Corps V-12 program at Duke University. By 1945 he was commissioned a lieutenant, reaching Okinawa just as the war ended.

Upon discharge Styron returned to Duke, graduating in 1947. While there he studied creative writing under William Blackburn; one of his stories was published in an anthology of student writing. From Duke Styron went to New York City, where he became an associate editor for Whittlesey House, the trade book division of McGraw-Hill. After six months he was fired.

Living as best he could, Styron began to write a novel, with the encouragement of Hiram Haydn, under whom he took a writing course at the New School for Social Research. That novel, about a deteriorating Virginia family, was published as *Lie Down in Darkness* in 1951, while Styron was on active reserve duty in the Marine Corps. The tour of duty was brief, for Styron was discharged because of an eye defect. Soon he went to Paris, where, in six weeks of the summer of 1952, he wrote a novella based on his just concluded military experience. While in Paris he joined the efforts of George Plimpton and others in founding the *Paris Review*.

The same year the American Academy of Arts and Sciences awarded *Lie Down in Darkness* its *Prix de Rome*; the cash award of that prize enabled Styron to travel in Italy for a few months. Soon after his return to the United States he married, on May 4,

1953, Rose Burgunder, daughter of a Baltimore merchant. The Styrons settled in Roxbury, Conn., where they are rearing four children.

While on vacation at Martha's Vineyard in 1962, Styron read Camus' *The Stranger* for the first time and decided that he had found the technique suitable for the book which had been on his mind all of his adult life, a study of Nat Turner, the slave who led the famous uprising in Virginia in 1831. At the same time Styron felt that the insights he gained from James Baldwin, who was his houseguest for five months while finishing *In Another Country*, enabled him to create a valid psychology for his black protagonist.

The Confessions of Nat Turner (1967) has provoked wide and continued controversy, not all of which centers on the novel as a success or failure in literary accomplishment. Since that time Styron has written a play, *In the Clap Shack* (1973), about a young World War II Marine's experiences in the venereal ward of a navy hospital. At the present time he is said to be finishing two novels, "The Way of a Warrior," about a Marine who returns from World War II service in the South Pacific, and "Sophie's Choice," about a young editor, who, after being fired for indecorous behavior, goes home to write a novel.

WORKS: *Lie Down in Darkness* (1951). *The Long March* (1953). *Set This House on Fire* (1960). *The Confessions of Nat Turner* (1967). *In the Clap Shack* (1973).

> LEWIS A. LAWSON
> University of Maryland
> College Park

HOLLIS SUMMERS (1916–). Born in Eminence, Ky., on June 21, 1916, Hollis Summers has pursued an academic as well as literary career since his graduation from Georgetown College, Georgetown, Ky. in 1937. He worked on his higher degrees and taught simultaneously, taking his M.A. from Middlebury College in 1943 and his Ph.D. from the University of Iowa in 1949. Meanwhile he taught in high school in Covington, Ky., and at Georgetown College. From 1949 to 1959 he taught creative writing at the University of Kentucky. Since then he has held the position of Distinguished Professor of English at Ohio University. He married the former Laura Vimont Clarke in 1943 and has two children.

Summers' writing career to date has fallen roughly into three periods. In the decade beginning in 1948 he published four novels, dealing primarily with the Kentucky small-town environment of his childhood and concentrating on the tensions between community expectations and actual living patterns of a fundamentalist minister's family. However, *Teach You a Lesson*, written pseudonymously with James Rourke, is a mystery novel.

Poetry was his concentration in the next decade; *The Walks Near Athens*, published in 1959, was followed by three more collections of verse in the 1960s. His poetry is highly patterned and deliberately unsentimental. Such ordinary experiences as living in a college town, traveling, or observing natural phenomena are frequent subjects.

Since 1968 he has published two novels, three volumes of poetry, and a collection of short stories. *How They Chose the Dead* brings together for the first time the short stories he has published serially since 1954. The stories are marked by his wide variety of central characters and the sharply drawn locale, usually Kentucky. His interest in the short story is further demonstrated by two of the three anthologies he has edited.

WORKS: *City Limit* (1948). *Brighten the Corner* (1952). Ed., *Kentucky Story: A Collection of Short Stories* (1954). Jim Hollis (pseud)., *Teach You a Lesson*, with James Rourke (1956). *The Weather of February* (1956). *The Walks Near Athens* (1959). Ed., *Literature: An Introduction*, with Edgar Whan (1960). *Someone Else: Sixteen Poems About Other Children* (1962). Ed., *Discussions of the Short Story* (1963). *Seven Occasions* (1965). *The Peddler and Other Domestic Matters* (1967). *The Day After Sunday* (1968). *Sit Opposite Each Other* (1970). *Start from Home* (1972). *The Garden* (1972). *How They Chose the Dead* (1973). *Occupant Please Forward* (1976).

NANCY C. JOYNER
Western Carolina University
Cullowhee, N.C.

JOHN BANISTER TABB (1845–1909). John Banister Tabb was born near Richmond, Va., on March 22, 1845, the son of John Yelverton, an Amelia County planter, and Marianna Bertrand Archer Tabb. He received his education almost entirely at home from his mother and from tutors.

Bad eyesight prevented Tabb's early enlistment in the Confederate service, but in 1862 he went to England with an expedition dispatched to bring supplies to the Confederacy, and upon his return to Charleston, he was assigned to the blockade-running steamer *Robert E. Lee*. In the spring of 1864 he carried dispatches on the *Siren* until the ship's capture on June 4, near Beaufort, N.C., after which he was imprisoned at Point Lookout, Md., prison camp where he formed a lasting friendship with Sidney Lanier. Upon his release from prison in February, 1865, he went to Baltimore with the intention of becoming a concert pianist, but in Baltimore he met Alfred Curtis, an Episcopal minister—later a Catholic bishop—who turned his thoughts toward religion. He taught briefly at St. Paul's School, Baltimore, and in 1870 he taught English for a few months at Racine College in Wisconsin. Later, in November, 1872, following his conversion on September 8, he entered St. Charles College, Ellicott City, Md., whence he graduated in 1875. From 1875 to 1877 he taught at St. Peter's Boys' School in Richmond, and from 1877 to 1881 he taught at St. Charles College. In 1881 he entered St. Mary's Seminary in Baltimore and was ordained on December 20, 1884, after which he returned to St. Charles where he taught until blindness forced his retirement in 1907. He died in Ellicott City on November 19, 1909.

Tabb had commenced writing poetry while in the Confederate service, but his first volume, privately printed, was not published until 1882. Between that time and the early 1890s, his poetry did not find ready acceptance by magazine editors, apparently because of its imagistic quality. However, after the publication of *Poems* (1894), his work was eagerly sought by the periodical press, and he published regularly thereafter.

WORKS: *Poems* (1882). *An Octave to Mary* (1893). *Poems* (1894). *Lyrics* (1897). *Child Verse* (1899). *Two Lyrics* (1900). *Later Lyrics* (1902). *The*

Rosary in Rhyme (1904). *Quips and Quiddities* (1907). *Later Poems* (1910). *A Selection from the Verses of John B. Tabb*, comp. Alice B. Meynell (1907). *The Poetry of Father Tabb*, ed. F. A. Litz (1928).

EUGENE NOLTE
University of Central Arkansas
Conway

PATRICK TAILFER (*fl.* 1741). Very little is known about the life of Patrick Tailfer, the satirist who wrote *A True and Historical Narrative of the Colony of Georgia*. Reputedly he was a physician from Edinburgh, Scotland. As a matter of record he did arrive in the colony of Georgia on August 1, 1734, settling at the Colerain Plantation on a 500-acre grant near his wife Mary's brothers John and Robert Williams. He soon became disenchanted with such life-style and removed to Savannah to practice surgery.

In Savannah, Tailfer began to antagonize the Georgia authorities. He joined with several other disgruntled Georgians to form a club that met regularly at Edward Jenkins' tavern. For the most part Scotsmen of independent means, they began to formulate an intricate plan in opposition to the Georgia trustees. They increased their numbers by using such inducements as horse races followed by drinking sessions at the tavern where Tailfer and his friends would address the gathering. Soon they had acquired the appelation "clamorous malcontents" as they protested Georgia's refusal to import slaves, the misleading descriptions of Georgia's landscape, the difficulties with the system of land distribution, and the prohibition of rum.

The grievances of Tailfer reached print only in 1741 after he and his associates had fled to South Carolina. *A True and Historical Narrative of the Colony of Georgia* by Patrick Tailfer, M.D., Hugh Anderson, M.A., David Douglas, and Others, Landholders of Georgia, proved to be an urbane, witty, yet biting view of the difficulties in the new colony. Its dedication to General Oglethorpe gave an immediate air of mockery and sarcasm. The work set forth in detail the problems of the colony as defined by Tailfer. Although vitriolic, much of the criticism was well founded. An obscure

Savannah physician had succeeded in becoming one of early America's most influential satirists.

WORKS: *A True and Historical Narrative of the Colony of Georgia* (1741).

ROBERT M. WILLINGHAM, JR.
University of Georgia
Athens

ALLEN TATE (1899–1979). Allen John Orley Tate was born in the Kentucky Blue Grass region of Winchester, Clark County, on November 19, 1899. He was the son of John Orley and Eleanor Varnell Tate, descended on both sides from English, Scotch, and Irish families of Virginia and Maryland, both Protestant and Catholic. He studied at home in his early years, then attended private and public schools in Louisville, Nashville, and Washington, D.C. He studied briefly at Georgetown University and at the University of Virginia, but because his elder brothers had gone to Vanderbilt University, he followed them to Nashville and entered Vanderbilt in 1918. At Vanderbilt, Tate took freshman writing from John Crowe Ransom, and, according to Ransom's own testimony, quickly revealed his awareness of "a body of literature unknown to his fellow students, and to my faculty associates and myself." Tate was soon invited to join Ransom and Donald Davidson and the other writers who, in 1922, launched the *Fugitive* magazine and started the Southern Literary Renaissance. When he graduated from Vanderbilt magna cum laude in 1922, he was already a professional poet, editor, critic, and founder of a literary magazine that had gained international recognition.

Tate continued as contributor to the *Fugitive* until it ceased publication in 1925, though in 1924 he had married a young novelist, Caroline Gordon (the first of three marriages for Tate), and had moved to New York City, where he worked as a free-lance reviewer and critic until 1928. During the winter of 1925, the Tates shared their rented country house near Patterson, N.Y., with Hart Crane, and in a period of mutual inspiration, Crane began his epic, *The Bridge*, while Tate started his major poem, "Ode to the Confederate Dead." In 1928 Tate published his first book, *Mr.*

Pope and Other Poems, and was awarded a Guggenheim Fellowship, which led him to spend the next two years in France, making friends with American expatriate writers, including Stein, Hemingway, Fitzgerald, and John Peale Bishop. He returned to the United States in 1930, and settled in a house near Clarksville, Tenn. There the Agrarian group was formed from the nucleus of the earlier Fugitive group: Ransom, Davidson, Tate, and Robert Penn Warren. With other southern writers, they published a symposium in 1930, *I'll Take My Stand: The South and the Agrarian Tradition*, which aroused a storm of controversy. The twelve essayists argued variously in favor of the agricultural economy of the South and against the industrial economy of the North, but the arguments were primarily cultural rather than political.

Tate had written biographies of two Confederate heroes, Stonewall Jackson and Jefferson Davis, and he continued to write provocative essays from a southern viewpoint in his first collection of criticism, *Reactionary Essays on Poetry and Ideas*, and in his joint authorship, with Herbert Agar, of *Who Owns America? A New Declaration of Independence*. His only novel, *The Fathers*, was an evocation of the Civil War South in a manner like that of Henry James. During the 1930s, while writing these books and continuing to write poems, Tate taught at Southwestern College in Memphis, at the University of North Carolina at Greensboro, and at Princeton University.

Tate held the Chair of Poetry at the Library of Congress in 1943–1944, when his friend Archibald MacLeish was librarian, and from 1944–1946 edited the *Sewanee Review*. He taught at New York University in the late 1940s, and in 1951, finally received his first tenured university position, a professorship in English at the University of Minnesota, a position he retained until his retirement, as Regents' Professor, in 1968. He served in many visiting positions, including a year as Fulbright Professor at Oxford University in 1958–1959, and several years as Fellow of the Kenyon School of Letters and of the Indiana School of Letters, and he lectured widely and often traveled abroad, including a trip to Florence in 1962 to receive the Gold Medal of the Dante Society. He was awarded the Bollingen Prize for Poetry in 1956, the most important of his many poetic honors, accepted a number of honorary degrees, and served a term as president of the National Institute of Arts and Letters. When he retired from the University of Minnesota, it was to a home near the University of the South at Sewanee, Tenn., where he continued to write and to lecture, and to receive frequent visitors. He died on February 9, 1979.

WORKS: *The Golden Mean and Other Poems*, with Ridley Wills (1923). *Mr. Pope and Other Poems* (1928). *Stonewall Jackson, the Good Soldier: A Narrative* (1928). *Jefferson Davis, His Rise and Fall: A Biographical Narrative* (1928). *I'll Take My Stand: The South and the Agrarian Tradition*, contributor (1930). *Poems: 1928–31* (1932). *Reactionary Essays on Poetry and Ideas* (1936). *The Mediterranean and Other Poems* (1936). *Who Owns America? A New Declaration of Independence*, with Herbert Agar (1936). *Selected Poems* (1937). *The Fathers* (1938). *Reason in Madness: Critical Essays* (1941). *Sonnets at Christmas* (1941). Trans., *The Vigil of Venus: Pervigilium Veneris* (1943). *The Winter Sea: A Book of Poems* (1944). *Sixty American Poets, 1896–1944*, checklist (1945). *Poems, 1920–1945: A Selection* (1947). *Poems: 1922–1947* (1948). *On the Limits of Poetry: Selected Essays, 1928–1948* (1948). *The Hovering Fly and Other Essays* (1948). Ed., *The House of Fiction: An Anthology of the Short Story*, with Caroline Gordon (1951). *The Forlorn Demon: Didactic and Critical Essays* (1953). *The Man of Letters in the Modern World: Selected Essays, 1928–1955* (1955). *Collected Essays* (1959). *Poems* (1960). Ed., *T. S. Eliot, the Man and His Work: A Critical Evaluation* (1966). *Essays of Four Decades* (1968). *The Swimmers and Other Selected Poems* (1970). *Memoirs and Opinions, 1926–1974* (1975). *Collected Poems, 1919–1976* (1978).

WILLIAM PRATT
Miami University
Oxford, Ohio

JOHN TAYLOR OF CAROLINE (1753–1824). John Taylor was born on December 19, 1753, the son of James and Ann Pollard Taylor of Caroline County, Va. Edmund Pendleton, Taylor's uncle, supervised the boy's education following the death of James (*ca.* 1756). Taylor received a classical education from private tutors, attended the College of William and Mary (1770–1771), read law with Pendleton, and was admitted to practice in 1774. He served three tours of duty during the Revolutionary War—first in Virginia (1775–1776), then in the northern campaigns (1776–1779), and again in Virginia (1781). He left the army with the rank of lieutenant colonel.

After the war Taylor devoted his time to farming, to politics, and to political pamphleteering. In 1783 he enhanced his fortune by marrying Lucy Penn, daughter of John Penn, a wealthy lawyer and planter. Six sons and two daughters were born to this union. Taylor acquired three plantations in the 1780s and settled with his family at Hazelwood in Caroline County, his home until his death on August 21, 1824.

Taylor was a member of the Virginia legislature in 1779–1781, 1783–1785, and 1796–1800, and of the U.S. Senate in 1792–1794, 1803–1804, and 1822–1824. A staunch Jeffersonian in 1804, Taylor had by 1809 become associated with the "Tertium Quids," a group opposing both Jefferson and the Federalists—especially Jefferson's support of Madison as his successor. Jefferson and Taylor remained friendly, but their political thinking differed after 1809.

Although he was no prose stylist, Taylor is important as a transitional theorist and thinker between such southern spokesmen as Jefferson and John C. Calhoun. Taylor's early work was largely political pamphleteering attacking Alexander Hamilton's financial policies and the centralization of power in the federal government. Between 1813 and his death, Taylor published five books, two of which remain important for students of southern culture. One is *Arator: Being a Series of Agricultural Essays, Practical and Political* (1813), 61 essays first published in the *Spirit of 'Seventy-Six,'* a Georgetown newspaper, beginning on December 25, 1810. Taylor revised and enlarged *Arator*, essays proposing agricultural reform and attacking northern capitalists, for editions published in 1814, 1817, and 1818. Edmund Ruffin felt these essays important enough to reprint in his *Farmers' Register* in 1840.

Taylor spent 20 years writing *An Inquiry into the Principles and Policy of the Government of the United States* (1814), a 656-page critique of the Federalists' political theories and especially of John Adams' *A Defense of the Constitutions of the Government of the United States* (1787). Though Adams "gravely composed" his "risible muscles" as he read Taylor's treatise, economic historian Charles Beard described *An Inquiry* as being "among the two or three really historic contributions to political science" in the U.S.

As a spokesman for the agrarian South, Taylor anticipated many of the problems that would lead to civil war. Among these were the conflict between the capitalistic North and the agrarian, slave-based economy of the South; the tariff question later addressed by Calhoun; and the growing authority of the federal government. His work warns against encroachments upon the South.

WORKS: "Remonstrance of Virginia" (March, 1781), *Tyler's Quarterly Historical and Genealogical Magazine*, XII (July, 1930), 40–41. *An Examination of the Late Proceedings in Congress, Respecting the Official Conduct of the Secretary of the Treasury* (1793). *Definition of Parties* (1794). *An Enquiry into the Principles and Tendency of Certain Public Measures* (1794). *An Argument Respecting the Constitutionality of the Carriage Tax* (1795). Curtius (pseud.), *A Defense of the Measures of the Administration of Thomas Jefferson* (1804). *A Pamphlet, Containing a Series of Letters* (1809). *Arator: Being a Series of Agricultural Essays, Practical and Political* (1813, 1814, 1817, 1818). *An Inquiry into the Principles and Policy of the Government of the United States* (1814). *Construction Construed, and Constitutions Vindicated* (1820). *Tyranny Unmasked* (1822). *New Views of the Constitution of the United States* (1823).

ROBERT BAIN
University of North Carolina
Chapel Hill

PETER HILLSMAN TAYLOR (1917–). As in his justly praised fiction, the external events of Peter Taylor's life are low key. Taylor's father was a lawyer, state attorney general, and a successful insurance company president. Peter Taylor was born to Matthew Hillsman and Katherine Baird Taylor Taylor on January 8, 1917, in Trenton, Tenn.

Taylor writes about the times and places in which he was reared and educated: pastoral Trenton, Tenn. (1917–1924), Nashville (1924–1926), St. Louis (1926–1932), and Memphis (1932–1937). Taylor's choice of colleges—and perhaps his literary career—was determined by the opportunity to study under several distinguished southern writers. At Southwestern at Memphis in 1936 he studied with Allen Tate. At Vanderbilt in 1937 his mentor was John Crowe Ransom, whom he followed to Kenyon College in 1938. After receiving an A.B. from Kenyon in 1940, Taylor studied briefly at Louisiana State University under Robert Penn Warren and Cleanth Brooks. He served in the U.S. Army, eventually as a sergeant, 1941–1945 in Georgia and in England. In 1943 he married poet Eleanor Lilly Ross (b. 1920) of Norwood, N.C. They have two children, Katherine Baird (b. 1948) and Peter Ross (b. 1955).

Since World War II Taylor's careers as a writer and teacher of creative writing have been intermingled. He taught at the University of North Carolina, Greensboro, intermittently from 1946 to 1966; at Indiana (1948–1949); Chicago (1952); Kenyon (1952–1957); Ohio State (1957–1963); and Harvard (1964). Since 1967 he has been a professor of English at the University of Virginia, Charlottesville.

In the enthusiastic introduction which launched both Taylor's first collection of short stories, *The Long Fourth*, and his career, Robert Penn Warren's views became the prototype for the dimensions and tone of much subsequent criticism. In 1950 Taylor published a delicate, engaging short novel, *A Woman of Means*. Four more volumes of short stories appeared (1954, 1959, 1963, 1969), many of which were first published in the *New Yorker* or various southern literary magazines. These received unanimous critical praise, inclusion in Martha Foley's *Best American Short Story* annuals, and in the O. Henry Prize Stories. Taylor has also been awarded several major fellowships: a Guggenheim (1950); Fulbright (1955); Ford Foundation (1961); Rockefeller Foundation (1964); and membership in the National Institute of Arts and Letters (1969).

Taylor's plays, like his stories, explore the fragile nuances of relationships past and present. They focus on upper or upper middle-class families flourishing, but more often fading, in elegant houses with closets full of sometimes surprising skeletons. The seven short plays in *Presences* deal with ghosts that are more often psychological projections rather than supernatural spirits. Critics agree that Taylor's intricate and subtle explorations of his themes and characters are more effective and natural in his understated stories than in the more explicit plays.

Taylor has remained a consistent, meticulous craftsman, an unsensational but unerring interpreter of modern urban southern domestic life and mores.

WORKS: *A Long Fourth and Other Stories* (1948). *A Woman of Means* (1950). *The Widows of Thornton* (1954). *Tennessee Day in St. Louis: A Comedy* (1957). *Happy Families Are All Alike: A Collection of Stories* (1959). *Miss Leonora When Last Seen and Fifteen Other Stories* (1963). *A Stand in the Mountains* (1965). Ed., *Randall Jarrell, 1914–1965*, with Robert Lowell and Robert Penn Warren (1967). *The Collected Stories of Peter Taylor* (1969). *Presences* (1973). *As Darker Grows the Night* (1976). *In the Miro District and Other Stories* (1977).

LYNN Z. BLOOM
The College of William and Mary
Williamsburg, Va.

MADISON TENSAS. See Henry Clay Lewis.

JOHN REUBEN THOMPSON (1823–1873). Born on October 23, 1823, in Richmond, Va., John Reuben Thompson grew up there, attended the University of Virginia, receiving his Bachelor of Laws in 1845, and began practicing law, but changed soon to working with magazines.

In 1847 he became editor of the *Southern Literary Messenger* and drew around him the best literary talent of the South. He worked closely with Poe and wrote "The Genius and Character of Edgar Allan Poe," which he gave many times as a lecture. He spent six months of 1854 in England and Europe, sending travel articles back to the *Messenger*, and visiting with Thomas Carlyle, Alfred, Lord Tennyson, William Makepeace Thackeray, Charles Dickens, Thomas Macaulay, and Robert and Elizabeth Barrett

Browning. Returning to Richmond, he worked closely with William Gilmore Simms, Henry Timrod, Paul Hamilton Hayne, and Philip Pendleton Cooke, and gave many lectures and contributed to northern magazines, working particularly with Whittier and Bryant. A little later, Whittier wrote to Hayne, "To thee, and John R. Thompson . . . the South must look, for its literary leaders."

In 1860 Thompson left the editorship of the *Southern Literary Messenger* to become for one year editor of the *Southern Field and Fireside* and then devoted himself to helping the Confederacy during the war. Many of his best-known poems are war lyrics: "Lee to the Rear," "The Battle Rainbow," "Music in Camp," and "General J. E. B. Stuart." From 1864 to 1866 he was back in England, to serve on the staff of the *Index* (official organ of the Confederate States in London), and visited again with his literary friends, spending much time in the homes of Tennyson and Carlyle.

Upon his return home he wrote for many journals, and Bryant soon offered him the literary editorship of the New York *Evening Post*, a position which he held until his death on April 30, 1873, in New York City.

While in New York, he worked with Bryant, Parke Godwin, Richard Stoddard, Edmund Stedman, and many other northern writers. Probably few American writers have worked as closely with as many literary figures in England and America as did Thompson. These friendships fitted in well with his work as literary editor, and some advised him about his own poetry.

WORKS: *Poems of John R. Thompson*, ed. John S. Patton (1920). *The Genius and Character of Edgar Allan Poe*, ed. James H. Whitty and James H. Rindfleische (1929).

JOHN O. EIDSON
University System of Georgia
Atlanta

MAURICE THOMPSON (1844–1901). Born on September 9, 1844, in Fairfield, Ind., reared in the north Georgia hills, Maurice Thompson was the son of Grigg Matthew Thompson, a Baptist minister, and Diantha Jaegger Thompson, of New York Dutch ancestry. His mother directed his education, with the help of an occasional tutor. After serving from December, 1862, to May, 1865, in the Confederate Army, Thompson settled in 1868 in Crawfordsville, Ind., working first as a civil engineer in railroad construction, and later as a lawyer. He was elected to one term (1879) in the Indiana House of Representatives. From 1866 onward he published poetry, fiction, nature sketches, and criticism, mostly in minor journals, but after 1873 in such magazines as *Atlantic*, *Independent*, *Harper's*, *Lippincott's*, and *Scribner's Monthly*. By 1880 most of his energies were going into literature, and in 1889 he became literary editor and principal book reviewer for the *Independent*, perhaps the most influential nonsectarian religious weekly of the period.

The Ethics of Literary Art best represents Thompson's criticism: eclectic, moralistic, viewing art as a potent agent in shaping character. The values to be served are nonsectarian Christianity, Manifest Destiny, and small-town Victorian gentility. *The Witchery of Archery* displays Thompson's generally Theocritan approach to nature, offering a pastoral ideal as a refuge from urban-industrial blight. Thompson's first collection of poetry was *Songs of Fair Weather*, enlarged later as *Poems*. The dominant themes are the pastoralism of nature, domestic love, and patriotism. His form is eclectic: the free ode, the four-stress or five-stress couplet, the "fourteener." In fiction, Thompson wrote local-color stories in dialect (*Hoosier Mosaics* and *Stories of the Cherokee Hills*), sentimental romance (*A Tallahassee Girl*), Howellsian realism (*A Banker of Bankersville*), and historical romance (*Alice of Old Vincennes*).

Although the *Independent* was a New York journal, Thompson lived and worked in Crawfordsville. Throughout his career he vigorously expressed the view that the culture of the midwestern small town, though not unflawed, represented the highest development of human life. He died on February 15, 1901, in Crawfordsville.

WORKS: *Hoosier Mosaics* (1875). *The Witchery of Archery* (1878). *How to Train in Archery* (1879). *A Tallahassee Girl* (1882). *His Second Cam-*

paign (1883). *Songs of Fair Weather* (1883). *At Love's Extremes* (1885). *By-Ways and Bird Notes* (1885). *The Boys' Book of Sports* (1886). *A Banker of Bankersville* (1886). *Sylvan Secrets* (1887). *A Fortnight of Folly* (1888). *The Story of Louisiana* (1889). *Poems* (1892). *The King of Honey Island* (1893). *The Ethics of Literary Art* (1893). *Lincoln's Grave* (1894). *The Ocala Boy* (1895). *Stories of Indiana* (1898). *Stories of the Cherokee Hills* (1898). *My Winter Garden* (1900). *Alice of Old Vincennes* (1900). *Sweetheart Manette* (1901). *Rosalynde's Lovers* (1901).

OTIS WHEELER
Louisiana State University
Baton Rouge

WILLIAM TAPPAN THOMPSON (1812–1882). William Tappan Thompson was born on August 31, 1812, in Ravenna, Ohio, the son of David and Catherine Kerney Thompson. His formal education ended when, being orphaned at the age of fourteen, he went to Philadelphia to work in the office of the *Daily Chronicle*. By 1830 he had moved to Tallahassee in the employ of James D. Westcott, then secretary of the territory of Florida. In 1835 he was employed by A. B. Longstreet on the *States' Rights Sentinel* in Augusta, Ga., where he married in 1837, and in March, 1838, founded the *Mirror*. He also served briefly in 1836 in the Seminole campaign in Florida. Early in 1842, he merged the *Mirror* with the Macon *Family Companion* to form the *Family Companion and Ladies' Mirror*.

The popularity during the 1830s of Seba Smith's Major Jack Downing, Longstreet's *Georgia Scenes*, and the Crockett stories provided Thompson with models for humorous sketches of rustic life. The first Pineville story appeared in the *Family Companion and Ladies' Mirror* in March, 1842; the first Major Jones letter in the same journal in June, 1842. Shortly thereafter the journal failed, and Thompson became editor of the *Southern Miscellany* in Madison, Ga., where some 30 letters appeared between August 20, 1842, and February 9, 1844. In 1843 the first sixteen letters were collected in a pamphlet as a subscription premium for the *Miscellany*, constituting the first edition of *Major Jones's Courtship*. An enlarged second edition of 26 letters appeared in 1844;

an eighth edition in 1847 added two more letters. By 1900 the work
had been reprinted nearly 30 times.

In the character of Major Joseph Jones, Thompson expressed
in native dialect, and from a realistic and humorous perspective,
the tastes and morals of a middle-class southern, farmer-townsman.
Kindly, domestically committed, yet shrewdly enjoying human
frailty, Major Jones gave a large reading public hearty amusement
without the distressing overtones of cruelty and animalism that
emerge from the stories of Sut Lovingood or Simon Suggs.
Suggs.

Despite the popularity of his creation, Thompson profited little
from the Major Jones books, but enjoyed increasing success as an
editor and publisher. In 1850 he founded the Savannah *Morning
News* which he actively edited until his death on March 24, 1882.

WORKS: *Major Jones's Courtship* (1843, 1844, 1847). *Major Jones's
Chronicles of Pineville* (1845). *John's Alive: or The Bride of a Ghost*
(1846). *Major Jones's Sketches of Travel* (1848). *Polly Peablossom's Wedding* (1851). *Rancy Cottem's Courtship* (1879).

OTIS WHEELER
Louisiana State University
Baton Rouge

THOMAS BANGS THORPE (1815–1878). Descended from
seventeenth-century New England settlers, Thorpe was born on
March 1, 1815, in Westfield, Mass., to Thomas and Rebecca Farn-
ham Thorpe. His father, a Methodist minister, died when Thomas
was four, and his mother took the family to live first with her
parents in Albany, and later to New York City. In 1830 Thorpe
studied art with John Quidor. From 1834 until 1836 he attended
Wesleyan University, where he was friendly with the sons of
southern planters being educated there.

In 1836, for his health, he moved to Louisiana, where he lived
in St. Francisville, Baton Rouge, and New Orleans, painting portraits for the planters. Dissatisfied with the economic and social
position of the artist in the South, he began, in 1843, to publish
a series of Louisiana newspapers, holding minor political offices,

and supporting Whig candidates and causes. In 1852 he ran for state superintendent of education, lost with his party, and shortly moved back to New York City. During the Civil War he served as colonel with the Union forces in New Orleans. After the war he returned to New York to continue painting and writing until his death, on September 20, 1878.

As early as 1839 he had begun contributing sketches of Louisiana and Arkansas frontier life to national journals, such as the New York *Spirit of the Times*, the *Knickerbocker Magazine*, *Graham's*, *Harper's*, and others. His one antislavery novel, and his essays on art and artists retain a minor significance. "The Big Bear of Arkansas" (*Spirit*, 1841), admired by William Faulkner, can be called, because of Thorpe's skillful use of myth, symbol, and comic meaning, the best single story in the tradition of Southwestern Humor.

WORKS: *The Mysteries of the Backwoods* (1846). *Our Army on the Rio Grande* (1846). *Our Army at Monterey* (1847). *The Taylor Anecdote Book* (1848). *The Hive of "The Bee-Hunter"* (1854). *The Master's House* (1854).

MILTON RICKELS
University of Southwestern
Louisiana
Lafayette

HENRY TIMROD (1828–1867). Had it not been for the Civil War, Henry Timrod, although considered the best southern poet of his time except for Poe, would be almost unknown today. In view of his reputation as chief of the southern poets of the war—he is characterized in such rebarbative phrases as "Laureate of the Confederacy" and "Harp of the South"—his life and thought are rich in ironies.

He was born on December 8, 1828, in Charleston, S.C., the only son among the four children of William Henry and Thyrza Prince Timrod. The father, who died when Henry was ten years old, was an unprosperous bookbinder and the author of *Poems on Various Subjects* (1814). William's father was Heinrich Dimroth, an emigrant from Kusel, Rheinpfalz, Germany, in 1765. Dimroth established himself as a merchant tailor, acquired land, signed himself *gentleman*, and anglicized his name. Timrod's mother was the great granddaughter of one Hannah Caesar, a small shop-keeper, whose testimony during a court trial in 1786 was objected to on the grounds that she was a mulatto. The evidence for Negro ancestry remains dubious.

For most of his life Timrod lived meagerly and in a state of dependency. He attended a private school, then with the assistance of a Charleston merchant went for less than two years to the University of Georgia. Tutoring with plantation families was his chief occupation until the outbreak of the war. Although never an ardent secessionist, soon disenchanted with the war, and tubercular, he made abortive efforts to engage in war service. He did go briefly to the western front as a correspondent, arriving in time to be caught up in the disastrous retreat from Shiloh. In 1864 a bene-factor made it possible for him to buy part interest in and become an editor of the Columbia *South Carolinian*. Feeling momentarily secure, he married a young English girl, Kate Goodwin. Sherman's troops sacked and burned Columbia in February, 1865, however, and from that time until his death on October 7, 1867, the conditions of Timrod's life were unmitigatedly painful.

Antebellum southern writers were often at odds with their culture. Until the war stifled adverse criticism, a strain of bitter candor ran through Timrod's excellent prose. Although Charleston was the publishing center of the South, Timrod's essays describe the region as a literary backwater, archaic in taste, unformed in judgment, materialistic, prosaic, uninterested in intellectual and poetic knowledge. Except when conforming to the pressures of the war, he opposed southernism in literature and emphasized that poetry must belong to the world. To some of the older generation of Charleston literary men, Timrod seemed extravagantly avant-garde: his principal heroes and models were Wordsworth and Tennyson.

Timrod's life fits the romantic conception of the sensitive, doomed poet, but his theory and his better poems are tempered by classicist ideas and habits. He insisted that after inspiration must come artistry; that excessive subjectivity spoils verse; and that poetry must be true and ethical. His apprentice verses show him zealously experimenting in forms and meters, and variant versions of mature poems indicate that he was an assiduous reviser. Sidney Lanier wrongly held that Timrod possessed a dainty artless art but never had time to learn the craft of the poet. His lyricism is most successful when most considered: his verse lacks spontaneity, intensity, and figurative imagination; his ideas and metrics are unoriginal. He was in a sense an occasional poet whose work is remarkably free of the sentimental verbosity and formlessness characteristic of his southern contemporaries.

Amative and nature poetry make up the bulk of Timrod's verse, but the critical consensus is correct in judging his war poetry to be his best. Only a few of his war poems are militant; the majority stress the losses and sorrows of the conflict.

Nearly all of Timrod's verses were first published in southern newspapers and magazines, usually for no pay. The *Southern Literary Messenger*, of Richmond, and *Russell's Magazine*, of Charleston, were the most important of the miscellanies to which he made regular contributions. Friends guaranteed the costs of the one slim volume of his verse that appeared during his lifetime. Posthumous collections more than double the number of poems contained in that first volume.

WORKS: *Poems* (1859). *The Poems of Henry Timrod* (1873). *Poems by Henry Timrod* (1899). *The Last Years of Henry Timrod* (1941). *The Uncollected Poems of Henry Timrod* (1942). *The Essays of Henry Timrod* (1942). *The Collected Poems of Henry Timrod* (1965).

GUY A. CARDWELL
Cambridge, Mass.

MELVIN BEAUNORUS TOLSON (1900–1966). Melvin Tolson was born on February 6, 1900, in Moberly, Mo., not far west of Mark Twain's birthplace. Tolson's mother was a Cherokee Indian (and an unpublished poet); his father, a Methodist minister, was a good provider for his wife and their four children.

During Tolson's boyhood his family lived in several towns in Iowa and Missouri. The last of these towns was Kansas City, where Tolson, captain of the football team and valedictorian of his class, finished high school. He worked for a year in a meat-packing plant, spent his freshman year of college at Fisk in Nashville, then went on to Lincoln University in Pennsylvania, from which he took a bachelor's degree after marrying, in his junior year, a wife who would remain a treasure to him unto his death.

Wide acclaim as a poet came to Tolson only in his later years. But at Wiley College in Texas, where he taught English for over 20 years, and at Langston University in Oklahoma, to which he removed from Wiley, he acquired, within the relatively compact Negro college world of his day, a legendary reputation for excellence in the classroom and influence on his students. He was appointed the first Avalon Professor of the Humanities at Tuskegee in 1965. He still held that post when he died of cancer in Dallas on August 29, 1966.

Humanity gleamed in Tolson. He made debate a major sport at Wiley. Simultaneously he spent his nights, despite the gravest personal danger, unionizing Negro sharecroppers in the country around his campus. He was the mayor of Langston for four terms. For his poetry he was named poet laureate of Liberia. And through it all he was an affectionate father whose two sons both achieved Ph.D.s and whose late daughter was a librarian at Howard University.

Study on his master's degree, which he received at Columbia, drew Tolson to Harlem as the Harlem Renaissance was ending in 1930. He was writing poetry then. His subject matter remained constant, the Negro life which he knew intimately at all levels. His sophisticated mastery of form derived principally from long years of assimilating Browning, Masters' *Spoon River Anthology*, the symbolists and imagists, Eliot, Pound, Pasternak, and the New Critics, among others. He spoke, he felt, with a voice heedful of Africa and all of western culture as well as of America and the experience of American blacks. Allusive, erudite, elliptical, often remorselessly succinct, his verse eventually demanded of its reader the most arduous attention. Through it he affirmed, without apology, his race. But through it, also, he sought a universal audience. He carried his intended masterpiece, *Harlem Gallery*, through only one of its projected five books. Even so, there are those who reckon him a leading poet of his time.

WORKS: "Caviar and Cabbages," Washington *Tribune*, November 26, 1938–February 9, 1939 (newspaper column). *Rendezvous with America* (1944). *Libretto for Liberia* (1953). *Harlem Gallery: Book I, The Curator* (1965).

> BLYDEN JACKSON
> University of North Carolina
> Chapel Hill

JEAN TOOMER (1894–1967). Nathan Eugene Toomer, son of Nathan and Nina Pinchback Toomer, was born on December 26, 1894, in Washington, D.C. Deserted in infancy by his father, orphaned in adolescence, Toomer was reared in Washington in the household of his maternal grandfather, P. B. S. Pinchback, the Georgia-born Afro-American who was lieutenant governor of Louisiana during Reconstruction. Known as Eugene Pinchback in his youth, Toomer's identity was further confused by his light complexion, his uncertainty regarding his vocation, and his unsettled beliefs. Between 1914 and 1919 he pursued five academic majors in as many colleges, held four different jobs, converted from Christianity to atheism to a nonorthodox theism, and embraced capitalism, socialism, then capitalism again. During this period, Toomer began his lifelong pattern of indecisiveness and evasiveness about his race.

In 1920, supported by a $600 legacy, Toomer read widely and met such literary figures as Edward Arlington Robinson, Waldo Frank, Lola Ridge, and—later—Malcolm Cowley, Van Wyck Brooks, Hart Crane, Kenneth Burke, and Robert Littell. He also defined himself a writer and named himself Jean Toomer.

None of Toomer's earliest work was published, and only a play and the fragments of an autobiographical novel survive. Both of these treat the repressed American Negro. Then in 1921, the 27-year-old Jean Toomer spent three months in Sparta, Ga., where he discovered that his roots were in the Deep South and that his true subject matter was the southern land and its rural blacks. He also discovered his lyrical voice. In 1922 he wrote *Cane*, a novel-like collection of thematically related prose, verse, and dramatic vignettes lyrically depicting black life in rural Georgia and urban Washington. Part I presents a young black's impressionistic response to lives and scenes set in a romantically vibrant South. Part II describes spiritually paralyzed blacks living in Washington. The last section, "Kabnis," depicts an urban black in Georgia, aware of but unable to share in the black peasants' vitality.

For a brief moment, Toomer wrote and lived effectually as southerner, Negro, and artist. This equilibrium was soon lost. In the summer of 1923 he urged his publisher not to advertise *Cane* as the work of a Negro (this despite Waldo Frank's Introduction proclaiming Toomer's ancestry). That same year Toomer came under the influence of Georges Ivanovitch Gurdjieff and began using his talent to express his new psychological and philosophical vision. In 1931 he married a Caucasian who died bearing their daughter. In 1934 he married another Caucasian who supported him as he wrote, lectured, and worked with the Philadelphia Quakers.

No longer writing lyrical sketches of blacks, Toomer could find no publisher. Only one play (*Balo*, 1927), a privately published collection of aphorism (*Essentials*, 1931), and a handful of essays, stories, and poems were published after *Cane*. At his death in 1967, Toomer left three unpublished novels, four unpublished plays, eight unpublished philosophical pieces, two unpublished volumes of poetry, six unpublished stories, and four unpublished autobiographies, all now in the Fisk University Toomer Collection.

WORKS: *Cane* (1923). *Essentials* (1931).

LADELL PAYNE
Claremont Men's College
Claremont, Calif.

WILLIAM PETERFIELD TRENT (1862–1939). William Peterfield Trent was born November 10, 1862, in Richmond, Va., to Peterfield and Lucy Carter Burwell Trent. Both of his parents had distinguished Virginia ancestors; after serving the Confederacy and sacrificing much of his means to the southern cause, his father, a physician, died in 1875. After attending private schools in Richmond, Trent enrolled at the University of Virginia where he edited the literary magazine and received a B. Litt. in 1883 and the A.M. in 1884. From 1884 to 1887 he read law and taught in private schools in Richmond. In 1887 he went to Johns Hopkins University for a year of postgraduate study in history and political science.

In 1888 he joined the faculty of the University of the South at Sewanee, Tenn., as professor of English and acting professor of political economy and history. While Trent was at Sewanee, his main interests shifted from history to literature. In 1892 he was a leader in founding the *Sewanee Review* and was its editor for seven years. Always a prolific worker, while he was at Sewanee Trent edited eleven texts, wrote 65 articles for periodicals, and published eight books. A biography of William Gilmore Simms for the American Men of Letters series was controversial in the South, for it contended that slavery had been a great evil in part because it had diverted the talents of a man like Simms from a potentially great achievement in belles lettres to a defense of the peculiar institution.

On December 8, 1896, Trent married Alice Lyman, and they were the parents of a daughter and a son. In 1900 he accepted a professorship of English literature at Barnard College of Columbia University. There Trent continued to be a pioneer in teaching the appreciation of literature for its own sake.

One of the major projects of Trent's career was *The Cambridge History of American Literature*, in four volumes, which he edited with Carl Van Doren, John Erskine, and Stuart P. Sherman (1917–1921). Another was the Columbia edition of *The Works of John Milton*, in eighteen volumes (1931–1938), which Trent first suggested in 1908; he served as editor in chief until ill health forced him to resign in 1925. A paralytic stroke in Paris in the summer of 1927 ended his teaching duties. He died of a heart attack at Hopewell Junction, N.Y., on December 6, 1939.

WORKS: *English Culture in Virginia: A Study of the Gilmer Letters and an Account of the English Professors Obtained by Jefferson for the*

University of Virginia (1889). *William Gilmore Simms* (1892). *The Makers of the Union—Benjamin Franklin* (1897). *Southern Statesmen of the Old Regime: Washington, Jefferson, Randolph, Calhoun, Stephens, Toombs, and Jefferson Davis* (1897). Ed., Edgar Allan Poe, *The Raven, The Fall of the House of Usher, and Other Poems and Tales* (1897). Ed., Edgar Allan Poe, *The Gold Bug, The Purloined Letter, and Other Tales* (1898). *The Authority of Criticism and Other Essays* (1899). *John Milton: A Short History of His Life and Works* (1899). *Robert E. Lee* (1899). *Verses* (1899). Ed., Robert Louis Stevenson, *The Poems of Robert Louis Stevenson* (1900). Ed., Honoré de Balzac, *The Works of Honoré de Balzac*, 32 vols. (1900). Intro., *Historic Towns of the Southern States* (1900). *War and Civilization* (1901). Ed., Herman Melville, *Typee: Life in the South Seas* (1902). *A History of American Literature, 1607–1865* (1903). *Progress of the United States of America in the Century* (1903). *A History of the United States*, with Charles Kendall Adams (1903). Ed., *Colonial Prose and Poetry*, with Benjamin W. Wells, 3 vols. (1903). *A Brief History of American Literature* (1904). Intro., Frederick Law Olmstead, *A Journey in the Seaboard Slave States in the Years 1853–1854, with Remarks on Their Economy*, 2 vols. (1904). *Greatness in Literature, and Other Papers* (1905). Ed., *Southern Writers; Selections in Prose and Verse* (1905). Ed., *The Best American Tales*, with John Bell Henneman (1907). Intro., *The History of the Literary and Intellectual Life of the South*, vol. VII of *The South in the Building of the Nation* (1909). *Longfellow and Other Essays* (1910). *Littérature Américaine* (1911). *An Introduction to the English Classics*, with Charles L. Hanson and William T. Brewster (1911). *Great American Writers*, with John Erskine (1912). *Daniel Defoe: How to Know Him* (1916). Ed., *The Cambridge History of American Literature*, with John Erskine, Stuart P. Sherman, and Carl Van Doren, 4 vols. (1917–21). Ed., Washington Irving, *The Journals of Washington Irving*, with George S. Hellman (1919). *Verse-Jottings* (1924). Ed., John Milton, *The Works of John Milton*, with Frank A. Patterson *et al.*, 18 vols. (1931–38).

RANDALL G. PATTERSON
Belhaven College
Jackson, Miss.

GEORGE TUCKER (1775–1861). The son of Daniel and Elizabeth Tucker, George Tucker was born on August 20, 1775, in Bermuda, where he received private instruction and began reading the law. In 1795 he moved to Virginia and studied law at William and Mary in Williamsburg, where he met and married (in 1797) Mary Byrd Farley, a Virginia heiress. When she died in 1799, he became involved in complicated litigation concerning the estate and was forced to open a practice in Richmond, where, in 1802, he married Maria Bell Carter. During his six years there, he gained a reputation as a man of letters and went deeply into debt. For several years the Tuckers lived with her family in the Shenandoah Valley before moving to Pittsylvania County. There Tucker succeeded as a lawyer and politician. He was elected to the state legislature in 1816, continued to publish essays, and improved his financial position. In 1819 he was elected to Congress from Lynchburg. During his three terms in Congress, Tucker supported the standard Virginian positions and made no significant contribution to legislation, perhaps because he had begun again to gamble and to spend more money than he made. His second wife died in 1823 during pregnancy.

Tucker hoped to become a professional novelist. In 1824 he published *The Valley of Shenandoah, or, Memoirs of the Graysons*, which depicts a society in the process of inevitable economic and social evolution and effectively builds upon the tension resulting from the conflict between Tucker's belief in the justice of economic laws and his nostalgia for old-time values and traditions. Although it is his chief contribution to American literature, the novel failed financially, thus helping Tucker decide to accept the chair of moral philosophy at the University of Virginia in 1825. He had been offered the position on the recommendation of Madison and Jefferson, both of whom had read and admired his *Essays on Various Subjects of Taste, Morals, and National Policy* (1822).

Tucker's professorship at the University of Virginia lasted for 20 years, during which he taught moral philosophy and metaphysics, political economy, and belles lettres and rhetoric, closely following the tenets of Scottish Common Sense philosophy and literary criticism. Along with his colleague, Dr. Robley Dunglison, he founded and edited the *Virginia Literary Museum* (1829–1830), in which he published many essays and short stories. *A Voyage to the Moon* (1827) was a satire intended to ridicule "the errors of the day in science and philosophy," but most of Tucker's energies were directed toward political and economic issues. In 1837 he published *The Laws of Wages, Profits and Rent Investigated* and a two-volume *Life of Thomas Jefferson*. Before his death on April 10, 1861, Tucker completed four other books on economics and a four-volume *History of the United States*. A prophet of the "New South," Tucker was an apologist for slavery who aimed to protect property, enhance the economic welfare of the South, and retain for the well-to-do the political control of Virginia.

WORKS: *Letters from Virginia, Translated from the French* (1816). *Essays on Various Subjects of Taste, Morals, and National Policy* (1822). *The Valley of Shenandoah; or Memoirs of the Graysons* (1824). *A Voyage to the Moon: With Some Account of the Manners and Customs, Science and Philosophy, of the People of Morosofia and Other Lunarians* (1827). *The Laws of Wages, Profits and Rent Investigated* (1837). *The Life of Thomas Jefferson, Third President of the United States, with Parts of His Correspondence Never Before Published, and Notices of His Opinions on Questions of Civil Government, National Policy, and Constitutional Law* (1837). *Theory of Money and Banks Investigated* (1839). *Progress of the United States in Population and Wealth in Fifty Years, as Exhibited by the Decennial Census* (1843). *Progress of the United States in Population and Wealth in Fifty Years, as Exhibited by the Decennial Census, with an Appendix, Containing an Abstract of the Census of 1850* (1855). *A History of the United States from Their Colonization to the End of the Twenty-Sixth Congress, in 1841* (1856–58). *Political Economy for the People* (1859). *Essays, Moral and Metaphysical* (1860).

ROBERT C. McLEAN
Washington State University
Pullman

NATHANIEL BEVERLEY TUCKER (1784–1851). The son of St. George and Frances Randolph Tucker and the half-brother of John Randolph of Roanoke, Beverley Tucker was born in Chesterfield County, Va., on September 6, 1784. He graduated from William and Mary in 1801 and practiced law for a time with small success. He served in the War of 1812, and in 1815 moved to Missouri, where he rose to a judgeship. After the deaths of his first two wives, he married again in 1830. He returned to Virginia in 1833 and a year later was appointed professor of law at his alma mater, a post that afforded him a platform for his intransigent defense of state sovereignty. Tucker early espoused a peaceful secession from what he saw as a despotic Union, and he championed a slave-based economy until the day of his death on August 26, 1851.

Tucker's many letters and writings on politics and economics remain valuable to the student of southern nationalism, but his literary reputation must stand upon three novels: *George Balcombe* (1836), *The Partisan Leader* (1836), and *Gertrude*, serialized in 1844–1845 in the *Southern Literary Messenger*. *Gertrude* is a sentimental trifle, but *George Balcombe*, set in Virginia and Missouri, won the admiration of William Gilmore Simms and Edgar Allan Poe. The title page of *The Partisan Leader* carried the fictitious date of 1856, suggesting that this forecast of war between the North and South was no mere fancy. Tucker might have been gratified that his prophecy was reprinted in the North in 1861 as *A Key to the Disunion Conspiracy* and in Richmond in 1862 as "A Novel, and an Apocalypse of the Origin and Struggles of the Southern Confederacy." Tucker's literary production was not substantial, but its intense sectionalism and its idealized portraits of plantation society contributed importantly to the later fictional treatment of the Lost Cause.

WORKS: *George Balcombe* (1836). *The Partisan Leader* (1836). *A Discourse on the Importance of the Study of Political Science* (1840). *The Principles of Pleading* (1846). *A Series of Lectures on the Science of Government* (1845).

J. V. RIDGELY
Columbia University
New York, N.Y.

ST. GEORGE TUCKER (1752–1827).

Born on June 29, 1752, in Bermuda, St. George Tucker came to Virginia to become a student at the College of William and Mary, graduating in 1772. Two years later he was admitted to the bar and practiced in Williamsburg. In 1775 he returned to Bermuda, but soon after the outbreak of the Revolution came back to Virginia, joined the Virginia militia, serving as a lieutenant colonel during the Yorktown campaign, during which he was wounded. He married Frances Randolph, the widowed mother of John Randolph, on September 23, 1778. Nathaniel Beverley Tucker and Henry St. George Tucker were their sons.

In 1786 he was a delegate to the Annapolis Convention, in 1788 was elected a judge of the General Court of Virginia, from 1790 to 1803 was professor of law at the College of William and Mary, from 1804 to 1811 was a judge in the Virginia Superior Court of Appeals, and from 1813 to 1825 a judge of the Federal District Court of eastern Virginia. Three years after the death of his first wife, he married in 1791 Lelia Shipworth Carter. He died on November 10, 1827, in Nelson County, Va., where he had retired after his distinguished career in public life.

Tucker's annotated *Blackstone's Commentaries* became one of the most important law books of his time. He also contributed occasional poems to periodicals, but much of his writings—plays, essays, and poems—remain unpublished. When collected, they may prove him to have been among the more talented literary men of his time.

WORKS: *The Knight and the Friars: An Historical Tale* (1786). *Liberty: A Poem on the Independence of America* (1788). *A Dissertation on Slavery: With a Proposal for the Gradual Abolition of It, in the State of Virginia* (1796). *Probationary Odes of Jonathan Pindar, Esq.* (1796). Redaction of *Blackstone's Commentaries*, 5 vols. (1803). *The Poems of St. George Tucker of Williamsburg, Va., 1752–1827*, ed. William S. Prince (1977).

LEWIS LEARY
University of North Carolina
Chapel Hill

JOSEPH ADDISON TURNER (1826–1868). Joseph Addison Turner was born in Putnam County, Ga., on September 23, 1826, the son of William and Lucy Butler Meriwether Turner. He suffered a childhood illness that left him permanently lame. As a result of this illness he received his early education at home from his father. Later he attended a local academy from 1838 to 1842 and briefly the first part of 1845, and Emory College from August to November, 1845, but he was mainly self-educated. On November 28, 1850, he married Louisa Dennis, the daughter of a wealthy Eatonton, Ga., merchant and planter, and four children were born to this union. The following year he bought and settled on a Putnam County plantation, which he later named Turnwold.

Like many other southern writers of the antebellum period, Turner was highly versatile. He was a teacher, planter, lawyer, politician, writer, and editor, but his main desire was to excel as a writer. To this end he projected numerous literary works and published two collections of poems, two long poetic satires, and many short selections in prose and verse. He also edited several short-lived periodicals, to which he contributed his writings. His most ambitious periodical was the *Plantation: A Southern Quarterly Journal*, printed in New York by Pudney and Russell in 1860. But his most successful periodical was the *Countryman*, printed weekly at Turnwold from March 4, 1862, to May 8, 1866, the only break occurring between June 27, 1865, and January 30, 1866. During the first part of its history the paper was modeled on the famous eighteenth-century periodical essays, but from the beginning of 1864 on, it resembled *Niles' National Register*, although it retained a literary department.

As a writer Turner failed to achieve the success he desired, but as an editor he exerted a significant influence. Moreover, he taught a sound theory of literature which bore fruit in his disciple, Joel Chandler Harris.

WORKS: *Kemble's Poems* (1847). *Turner's Monthly* (3 nos., 1848). *Red Lion* (a review, 1 no., 1849). *Hasty Plate of Soup* (a little journal, 2 nos., 1852). *The Times* (poem, 1853). *Tomahawk* (magazine, 1 no., 1853). *Independent Press* (newspaper, 1854–55). *A Letter to Hon. N. G. Foster, Candidate for Congress in the 7th Congressional District of Ga. . . .* (1855). *The Cotton Planter's Manual* (1857). *The Discovery of Sir John*

Franklin, and Other Poems (1858). *Plantation: A Southern Quarterly Journal* (1860). *Countryman* (1862–66). *The Nigger: A Satire* (n.d.).

LAWRENCE HUFF
Georgia Southern College
Statesboro

MARK TWAIN. See Samuel Langhorne Clemens.

JOHN DONALD WADE (1892–1963). All his life John Donald Wade maintained close ties with Marshallville, Ga., where he was born on September 28, 1892, the son of John Daniel and Ida Frederick Wade, and where he was buried in the Methodist churchyard following his death on October 9, 1963. The way of life which was practiced and the humanistic values which were cherished by the first settlers of this middle Georgia community and their descendants profoundly influenced him.

Educated at the University of Georgia (A.B., 1914), Harvard University (A.M., 1915), and Columbia University (Ph.D., 1924), Wade achieved recognition as a scholar and writer with the publication of his doctoral dissertation entitled *Augustus Baldwin Longstreet: A Study of the Development of Culture in the South* (1924). As an early scholarly biography of a southern literary figure and as a pioneer work on southern humor, this book established Wade's reputation as a leading authority on southern life and thought.

Wade served on the English faculties of the University of Georgia (1919–1926 and 1934–1950) and Vanderbilt University (1928–1934). Before going to Vanderbilt he spent a year in England working on a biography of John Wesley and another year in Washington as an editor of *The Dictionary of American Biography*. While at Vanderbilt he contributed his best-known shorter narrative, "The Life and Death of Cousin Lucius," to the essays published by the Nashville Agrarians as *I'll Take My Stand* (1930).

By the time he returned to the University of Georgia in 1934, Wade had perfected both his distinguished prose style and his use of the biographical essay about southerners to reflect his views about the South and the world. In 1947 he founded the *Georgia Review*.

Wade and his first wife, Julia Floyd Stovall, had one daughter. Following the death of his first wife he married Florence Lester of Marshallville.

WORKS: *Augustus Baldwin Longstreet: A Study of the Development of Culture in the South* (1924). *John Wesley* (1930). *I'll Take My Stand: The South and the Agrarian Tradition*, contributor (1930). *Selected Essays and Other Writings* (1966).

CLAUD B. GREEN
Clemson University
Clemson, S.C.

MARGARET WALKER (1915–). Margaret Walker, the daughter of a minister of the African Methodist Episcopal Church, was born July 7, 1915, in Birmingham, Ala. During her childhood and youth in New Orleans, she attended the schools of that city, including Gilbert Academy. She continued her education at Northwestern University, from which she received a B.A. The University of Iowa conferred an M.A., accepting a collection of her poems as fulfillment of the thesis requirement. This collection, published in 1942 as *For My People*, won the Yale University Younger Poets competition for that year. In 1965 Walker received her Ph.D., also from Iowa. Her novel *Jubilee* satisfied the doctoral dissertation requirement.

In addition to her literary productions, her career has included other experiences. She was awarded a Rosenwald Fellowship and has made extensive lecture tours. Walker has been a professor of English at Livingstone College in Salisbury, N.C., and West Virginia State College in Institute, W.Va. She is presently a professor of English at Jackson State College in Jackson, Miss.

Margaret Walker is married to F. James Alexander and is the mother of four children.

WORKS: *For My People* (1942). *Jubilee* (1967). *Prophets for a New Day* (1970). *How I Wrote Jubilee* (1972). *October Journey* (1973). *A Poetic Equation*, with Nikki Giovanni (1974).

ELAINE MITCHELL NEWSOME
Fayetteville State University
Fayetteville, N.C.

ROBERT PENN WARREN (1905–). When the National Book Committee in 1970 honored Robert Penn Warren with the National Medal for literature, it was neither the first nor the last time he was recognized for his artistic achievement. The only writer to have won the Pulitzer Prize for both fiction (in 1947, for *All the King's Men*) and poetry (in 1958, for *Promises*), he was also awarded in 1975 the Emerson-Thoreau Medal of the American Academy of Arts and Sciences, which cited his achievement in diverse forms. No other figure in modern American literature, including Edmund Wilson and Warren's friend Allen Tate, has been able, with the same authority as Warren, to lay claim to the title of man of letters. Equally adept as a poet and novelist, Warren is also a brilliant practical critic whose influential *Understanding Poetry* and similar textbooks, written with Cleanth Brooks, virtually revolutionized the teaching of literature in the United States. Although in his long career he has contributed books and essays on cultural history, journalism, sociology, and biography, Warren began as a poet, and it is as poet that Warren the man of letters would prefer to be remembered—"my central and obsessive concern," as he puts it in *Democracy and Poetry*.

Born in Guthrie, Ky., on April 24, 1905, Warren was educated in the public schools in Guthrie and Clarksville, Tenn. Although he went to Vanderbilt intending to study chemistry, he soon fell under the sway of Donald Davidson and John Crowe Ransom, English professors and poets. Warren joined the Fugitives, to which his roommate Tate already belonged, read and discussed the members' work, and began writing his own poetry under the aegis of the most rigorous communal criticism of the 1920s. After his first volume of poems in 1935, he was to publish verse regularly for the rest of his career. After graduating in 1925, Warren earned his M.A. at the University of California (1925–1927) and attended Yale briefly (1927–1928) before going as a Rhodes Scholar to New College, Oxford (B. Litt., 1930). Many of the themes, images, and character types which recur, sometimes obsessively, in later works —the ambiguity of truth, the corruption of the idealist, the difficulty of self-knowledge—are anticipated in Warren's first book, an unorthodox biography of John Brown, and in his first published fiction, "Prime Leaf," a novella which was reworked as his first novel, *Night Rider*.

During the 1930s, Warren taught exclusively at southern institutions: Southwestern University in Memphis (1930–1931), Vanderbilt (1931–1934), and Louisiana State University (1934–1942), where he helped to establish the *Southern Review*. In 1942 he moved to the University of Minnesota as professor of English and in 1950, as professor of playwriting in the school of drama, to Yale. *All the King's Men* was originally a play ("Proud Flesh"), and the novel, in turn, was recast as a play, which was produced several times in various versions, most notably in 1948 at the New School for Social Research. Warren's interest in drama can also be seen in a work which eludes generic classification, *Brother to Dragons*.

Despite a dramatic and lyric facility, Warren's great power—in poetry, fiction, and nonfiction prose—has always been a feel for narrative, especially those stories, legends, ballads, and historical episodes in which he sees distilled the moral significance of southern culture. Through the juxtaposition of generational angles of vision (*All the King's Men*, *World Enough and Time*, *Brother to Dragons*) and the impingement of modern dilemmas on nineteenth-century situations (*Band of Angels*, *Wilderness*, *Audubon*, and some of the poems in *Promises*), Warren articulates a belief in the meaning and influence of continuities—disabling flaws as well as manifest strengths. Although *The Legacy of the Civil War*, a "meditation" on "the great single event of our history," is perhaps the most cogent demonstration of that concern, his series of studies of American authors—Mark Twain, John Greenleaf Whittier, Herman Melville, Nathaniel Hawthorne, Theodore Dreiser—speaks to his commitment to art, which keeps alive "the sense of self and the correlated sense of a community."

In 1950 Warren and his first wife Emma Brescia were divorced after 20 years of marriage. He and his second wife, the writer Eleanor Clark, whom he married in 1952, have two children, Rosanna Phelps and Gabriel Penn. In 1975 Warren retired from Yale, with which he had been associated for a quarter of a century.

WORKS: *John Brown: The Making of a Martyr* (1929). *Thirty-Six Poems* (1935). *An Approach to Literature*, with Cleanth Brooks and John Thibaut Purser (1936, 1939, 1952, 1964). Ed., *A Southern Harvest: Short Stories by Southern Writers* (1937). *Understanding Poetry: An Anthology for College Students*, with Cleanth Brooks (1938, 1950, 1956, 1960). *Night Rider* (1939). *Eleven Poems on the Same Theme* (1942). *At Heaven's Gate* (1943). *Understanding Fiction*, with Cleanth Brooks (1943, 1959). *Selected Poems, 1923–1943* (1944). *All the King's Men* (1946). *The Circus in the Attic and Other Stories* (1947). *Modern Rhetoric*, with Cleanth Brooks (1949, 1958, 1961). *Fundamentals of Good Writing: A Handbook of Modern Rhetoric*, with Cleanth Brooks (1950). *World Enough and Time: A Romantic Novel* (1950). Ed., *An Anthology of Stories from the "Southern Review,"* with Cleanth Brooks (1953). *Brother to Dragons: A Tale in Verse and Voices* (1953). Ed., *Short Story Masterpieces*, with Albert Erskine (1954). *Band of Angels* (1955). Ed., *Six Centuries of Great Poetry*, with Albert Erskine (1955). *Segregation: The Inner Conflict in the South* (1956). Ed., *A New Southern Harvest: An Anthology*, with Albert Erskine (1957). *Promises: Poems 1954–1956* (1957). *Remember the Alamo!* (1958). *Selected Essays* (1958). *The Cave* (1959). *The Gods of Mount Olympus* (1959). *How Texas Won Her Freedom: The Story of Sam Houston and the Battle of San Jacinto* (1959). *All the King's Men: A Play* (1960). *The Scope of Fiction*, with Cleanth Brooks (1960). *You, Emperors, and Others: Poems, 1957–1960* (1960). *The Legacy of the Civil War: Meditations on the Centennial* (1961). *Wilderness: A Tale of the Civil War* (1961). *Flood: A Romance of Our Time* (1964). *Who Speaks for the Negro?* (1965). Ed., *Faulkner: A Collection of Critical Essays* (1966). *Selected Poems, New and Old, 1923–1966* (1966). Ed., *Randall Jarrell, 1914–1965*, with Robert Lowell and Peter Taylor (1967). *Incarnations: Poems, 1966–1968* (1968). *Audubon: A Vision* (1969). *Homage to Theodore Dreiser, August 27, 1871–December 28, 1945, on the Centennial of His Birth* (1971). Ed., *Selected Poems of Herman Melville* (1971). Ed., *John Greenleaf Whittier's Poetry: An Appraisal and a Selection* (1971). *Meet Me in the Green Glen* (1971). *Or Else—Poem/Poems 1968–1974* (1974). Ed., *American Literature: The Makers and the Making*, with Cleanth Brooks and R. W. B. Lewis (1974). *Democracy and Poetry* (1975). *Selected Poems: 1923–1975* (1976). *A Place to Come To* (1977).

JAMES H. JUSTUS
Indiana University
Bloomington

BOOKER TALIAFERRO WASHINGTON (1856–1915). The slave son of a slave mother and an anonymous white father, Booker T. Washington was born near Roanoke, Va., on April 5, 1856. The Civil War was barely over when he was resettled in Malden, five miles from Charleston, W.Va. Brutal work in the salt mines of Malden did not prevent him from going to school. In 1871 he secured a job working at the home of Mrs. Viola Ruffner, whose husband owned the salt mines. Mrs. Ruffner was from New England. She instilled in young Washington the virtues of her native region. In 1872 Washington, almost penniless, enrolled in Hampton Institute.

At Hampton, Washington came under the strong influence of General Samuel Armstrong, Hampton's head and founder. Washington finished Hampton in 1875. His mother, whom he loved devotedly, had died in 1874. From 1875 until 1878 Washington taught at Malden. He spent an academic year studying at Wayland Seminary in Washington and some months helping to campaign for the selection of Charleston to replace Wheeling as the capital of West Virginia. He thus acquired valuable training in public speaking. In 1879, invited by General Armstrong, he returned to Hampton to teach.

In 1881 he went to Tuskegee. When he arrived, Tuskegee Institute existed only as a $2000 appropriation of the Alabama state legislature. Students, buildings, teachers, grounds, as well as support and a reputation soon worldwide: all of these must be attributed to him. His three wives served Tuskegee as wholeheartedly as he. For Tuskegee was to him undoubtedly a religion. The gospel of industrial education which it enshrined, we may suspect now, resolved itself too much into artisanships, the heyday of which was passing even as Tuskegee espoused them. But he combined his championship of trades and agriculture with an emphasis on character which hardly seems anachronistic in any age.

It has been said that no other Negro has ever been as powerful in America as Washington. As early as 1884 he addressed, in Madison, Wis., the National Education Association. His famous speech at the Cotton States Exposition in Atlanta in 1895 made him the unquestioned leader of his people in the eyes of most Americans.

But to many—as, preeminently, to W. E. B. Du Bois—he represented a hateful Uncle Tomism. Still, four presidents, Theodore Roosevelt especially, turned to him for advice. Princes of industry and finance treated him as an equal. He started the National Negro Business League, serving as its president until November 14, 1915. His sometimes surreptitious control of most of the Negro press was a fact. For years hardly an appointment of consequence of any Negro was made without his assent. Writing for him was an avocation. Even so, his *Up From Slavery* was a phenomenal success, and a classic of American autobiography.

WORKS: *The Future of the American Negro* (1899). *The Story of My Life and Work* (1900). *Up From Slavery* (1901). *Working with the hands* (1904). *Tuskegee and Its People* (1905). *My Larger Education* (1911). *The Negro Problem*, with others (1903). *The Negro in the South*, with others (1907). *Frederick Douglass*, with S. Laing Williams (1907). *The Story of the Negro*, with Robert Park (1909). *The Man Farthest Down*, with Robert Park (1912).

BLYDEN JACKSON
University of North Carolina
Chapel Hill

HENRY WATTERSON (1840–1921). Henry Watterson was born in Washington, D.C., on February 16, 1840, the son of a Democratic congressman from Tennessee. As a young man, he had literary ambitions, and, turning to journalism until they could be realized, he was briefly a music critic for the New York *Times* before going to the nation's capital in 1858, where he worked as a reporter on the Washington *States*. Although he thought secession wrong, he joined the Confederate army and edited a wandering army newspaper named the *Rebel*. Watterson was editor of the Louisville *Courier-Journal* from 1868 to 1919, and achieved national recognition for pungent, vivid editorials that reflected his flamboyant personality. He fought for the restoration of southern home rule, promoted Samuel J. Tilden's candidacy for the presidency, and served as a Tilden floor leader in the House of Representatives during the disputed 1876 electoral contest. He was awarded a Pulitzer Prize in 1917 for two editorials supporting America's entry into World War I. When Watterson died on December 22, 1921, the American press eulogized him as the last great personal editor.

Watterson edited *Oddities in Southern Life and Character* (1883), a collection of genre stories by southern humorists. A ghostwritten *History of the Spanish-American War* (1898), to which he lent his name, was a dismal failure. He collected his major speeches as *The Compromises of Life and Other Lectures and Addresses* (1903). While revealing Watterson's abiding interest in sectional and national unity, they lacked in print the warmth of his personality which had made them popular when delivered from a platform. *History of the Manhattan Club* (1915) was a short account of that famous Democratic organization. His rambling, anecdotal memoirs, appearing as a serial in the *Saturday Evening Post*, proved so popular that they were published in 1919 in two volumes under the title of *"Marse Henry." The Editorials of Henry Watterson*, compiled by Arthur Krock, appeared posthumously in 1923.

WORKS: *Oddities in Southern Life and Character* (1883). *History of the Spanish-American War* (1898). *The Compromises of Life and Other Lectures and Addresses* (1903). *History of the Manhattan Club* (1915). *"Marse Henry": An Autobiography*, 2 vols. (1919). *The Editorials of Henry Watterson*, ed. Arthur Krock (1923).

NORMAN D. BROWN
University of Texas
Austin

RICHARD M. WEAVER (1910–1963). In the role of classical rhetor, Richard M. Weaver has applied his discipline to a wide range of concerns—literary criticism, social and intellectual history, and the state of contemporary culture. This wide application has made his views on the nature and practice of rhetoric among the most controversial, stimulating, and significant of contemporary theorists of rhetoric.

Born in Weaverville, N.C., on March 3, 1910, the son of Richard Malcolm and Carrie Embry Weaver, he spent his early youth in Lexington, Ky., and graduated from the University of Kentucky in 1932. He then went to Vanderbilt University for his M.A. and was in attendance when Donald Davidson and John Crowe Ransom were still members of the faculty and the Fugitive-southern Agrarian concepts were strong. (Ransom directed Weaver's M.A. thesis, "The Revolt Against Humanism," 1934.)

Weaver remained at Vanderbilt as a teaching fellow until 1936 when he left to become an instructor at Alabama Polytechnic Institute (Auburn University) for one year and an assistant professor at Texas A. & M. College from 1937 to 1940. He studied during summers at Harvard, the Sorbonne, and the University of Virginia and regularly attended Louisiana State University where he received his Ph.D. in 1943. His doctoral dissertation, "The Confederate South, 1865–1910: A Study in the Survival of a Mind and Culture," was revised and published in 1968 as *The Southern Tradition at Bay*. After a one-year period as a special instructor in the Army Specialized Training Corps at North Carolina State College, he went to the College of the University of Chicago where he was to become a professor of English and remain until his death on April 3, 1963.

Having gone through stages of socialism and party-line liberalism, being long associated with the University of Chicago, and being profoundly influenced by the perspectives and tenets of his earlier mentors and associates—Davidson, Ransom, Robert Penn Warren, Cleanth Brooks, Arlin Turner—Weaver achieved a passionately involved objectivity that combined with his discipline in rhetoric to permit him to explore the moral, ethical, cultural, and intellectual uses and misuses of rhetoric.

WORKS: *Ideas Have Consequences* (1948). *The Ethics of Rhetoric* (1953). *Composition: A Course in Reading and Writing* (1957). *Relativism and the Crisis of Our Time* (1961). *Academic Freedom: The Principle and the Problems* (1963). *Visions of Order* (1964). *Life Without Prejudice and Other Essays* (1965). *The Southern Tradition at Bay: A History of Postbellum Thought*, ed. George Core and M. E. Bradford (1968). *Language*

Is Sermonic: Richard M. Weaver on the Nature of Rhetoric, ed. Richard L. Johannesen, Rennard Strickland, and Ralph T. Eubanks (1970).

ROBERT L. WELKER
University of Alabama
Huntsville

EUDORA WELTY (1909–). Probably the greatest living writer of southern fiction with an achieved body of work, Eudora Welty has made her literal and fictional home primarily in Mississippi. She was born in Jackson on April 13, 1909, the only daughter, with two younger brothers, of Christian Webb and Mary Chestina Andrews Welty. Her father, president of the Lamar Life Insurance Company, had come from Ohio soon after his marriage to her mother, a schoolteacher from West Virginia whose family had come from Virginia. Eudora attended Jackson Central High School, and then spent two years at Mississippi State College for Women. In 1927 she transferred to the University of Wisconsin, where she received her B.A. in 1929. As a child and young woman she had been bright, imaginative, an inveterate reader of fairy tales, legends, Mississippi history, much loved and encouraged by her tender and protective father and adventurous mother. In college she developed an interest in such modern writers as Chekhov, Yeats, Faulkner, and Forster. In 1929–1930 she attended the Columbia University Graduate School of Business, where she studied advertising.

The year 1931 was a time of beginnings and endings. Her formal education completed, she emerged on the depression job market, and returned to Jackson. Her father died, a deep personal loss. However, she was able to find part-time work with radio and newspapers, and put her father's typewriter to use by writing stories. Then she found the job which was to be as formative to her literary career as the tactics of advertising had proved largely useless to it. From 1933 to 1936 she worked as a publicity agent for the Works Project Administration. Traveling all over the state, talking and listening to people, doing feature stories on various projects, taking photographs, and above all, observing, she gathered many

of the basic materials of her art and developed one of its central
focal points: the importance of place in fiction. The countryside
and towns of Mississippi, especially those along the Natchez Trace,
were to provide the settings for much of her best fiction.

For a while her stories met with rejection slips. She seemed
more successful in showing her informal photographs of Mississippi black people, which were displayed in a small New York
camera shop. (Several of these photographs were to be published
in *One Time, One Place* in 1971.) But in 1936 "Death of a Traveling Salesman" appeared in a small magazine, *Manuscript.* Soon
her talent was discovered by Robert Penn Warren and Cleanth
Brooks, who began to publish her stories in the *Southern Review*,
which they were then editing. Ford Madox Ford was also helpful,
as well as Katherine Anne Porter, who wrote an introduction to
Welty's first collection of stories. By 1941, the date *A Curtain
of Green* appeared, her stories had been accepted by such nationally circulated magazines as the *Atlantic Monthly*, and a series
of awards commenced with O. Henry Memorial Contest prizes
for "A Worn Path" and "The Wide Net." As other publications
followed—collections of stories, a first novel (*Delta Wedding*) and
a short-story cycle (*The Golden Apples*)—so did recognition of her
literary gifts: a poetic, metaphorical style; a command of widely
varied literary types, including comedy, tragedy, satire, fantasy;
a complex vision of human identity and relationships; an impressive grasp of the rhythms of southern speech. With that recognition came honors and awards: among them, Guggenheim fellowships in 1942 and 1949, election to the National Institute of Arts
and Letters in 1952, the William Dean Howells Medal of the
American Academy for *The Ponder Heart* in 1955. However, she
seemed still a writer mostly for connoisseurs, largely devoted but
some disaffected by what they regarded as an increasing obscurity
and precocity of style or lack of social consciousness. The impressionistic stories collected in *The Bride of Innisfallen* (1955) intensified this response, though a dramatic adaptation of *The Ponder
Heart*, which had a successful run on Broadway in 1956, brought
some popular recognition. "Why Can't Jackson Be More Aware
of Its Most Celebrated Citizen?" the Jackson *Daily News* scolded

in 1958, despite the fact that the citizen had always been "underfoot locally."

The next several years found Eudora Welty lecturing on fiction; reading and teaching at a number of colleges and universities all over the United States and at Cambridge University, England; receiving medals, grants, awards, and honorary degrees at the rate of almost one a year; being interviewed, becoming more widely known, and having to deal, therefore, with some of the side effects of fame—particularly, in the 1960s, the expectation of liberals that she become, in and out of her fiction, an active crusader in the civil rights struggle. (She dealt with the latter problem in an October, 1965, *Atlantic* article in which she argued that the novelist's objectives, in depicting the timeless and universal truths of the human heart, must necessarily be broader than those of the crusader, who risks oversimplifying life and becoming quickly outdated.) Meanwhile, she was working on a novel which was to be her longest and perhaps most ambitious work, *Losing Battles*. Published in 1970, it was generally a critical and popular success. A long private ordeal, ending in her mother's death, led to the most autobiographical of her novels, *The Optimist's Daughter*, a Pulitzer Prize winner. With this award, which followed upon her being elected to the American Academy of Arts and Letters in 1971, and receiving the Gold Medal for Fiction of the National Institute in 1972, her national honors were complete. Her fellow Mississippians had long since begun to honor her for her achievement: May 2, 1973, was, in fact, proclaimed Eudora Welty Day by Governor William L. Waller.

WORKS: *A Curtain of Green* (1941). *The Robber Bridegroom* (1942). *The Wide Net and Other Stories* (1943). *Delta Wedding* (1946). *The Golden Apples* (1949). *Short Stories* (1950). *The Ponder Heart* (1954). *The Bride of Innisfallen and Other Stories* (1955). *Place in Fiction* (1957). *Three Papers on Fiction* (1962). *The Shoe Bird* (1964). *Losing Battles* (1970). *One Time, One Place: Mississippi in the Depression, A Snapshot Album* (1971). *The Optimist's Daughter* (1972). *The Eye of the Story* (1978).

RUTH M. VANDE KIEFT
Queens College
Flushing, N.Y.

ALEXANDER WHITAKER (1585–1617). An Anglican clergyman, Alexander Whitaker was born at Cambridge, England, in
1585, the son of William and Susan Culverwell Whitaker. His
father was a noted Puritan divine who remained inside the Established Church, who was appointed Regius Professor of Philosophy
at Cambridge in 1580, and who became master of St. John's College in 1587. By 1595 Whitaker's parents were dead, and a kinsman, Alexander Nowell, apparently helped with his education.

Whitaker spent four years at Eton (1598–1602), and in the fall of
1602 he entered Trinity College, Cambridge, taking a B.A. (1605)
and M.A. (1608). Following his ordination in the Church of England in 1609, Whitaker spent two years as a minister in the north
of England (probably Yorkshire) before volunteering to go to Virginia as minister and missionary. Late in March, 1611, he sailed
from London with Sir Thomas Dale and 300 colonists, reaching
Virginia May 19, 1611.

Soon after, Whitaker joined a group founding a new settlement
named Henrico (sometimes called Henricopolis) on the north bank
of the James River 50 miles up-river from Jamestown. Whitaker
built a parsonage, Rock Hall, on the south bank opposite Henrico,
and in addition to his duties at Henrico, he ministered to another
settlement, Bermuda Hundred, about five miles from Rock Hall.

As early as August 9, 1611, Whitaker wrote to friends in England
of his pleasure with the Virginia adventure. His *Good News from
Virginia*, completed by July 28, 1612, was not intended for publication, but as a report to the Virginia Company. The company's
council, pleased with Whitaker's report, decided to print it so that
"the naked and plaine truth may give a just affront to the cunning
and coloured falsehoods devised by the enemies of this Plantation." Published in the form of a sermon, Whitaker's *Good News
from Virginia* appeared in London in 1613. The 45-page
pamphlet describes the plenty of the country, urges conversion
of the Indians, and argues for continued support of the Virginia
colony.

Whitaker's pastoral duties evidently included instructing Pocahontas in Christianity and baptizing her before her marriage to

John Rolfe. He drowned crossing the James River in the spring of 1617. He never married.

WORKS: *Good News from Virginia* (1613).

ROBERT BAIN
University of North Carolina
Chapel Hill

DANIEL KIMBALL WHITAKER (1801–1881). Daniel K. Whitaker was born on April 13, 1801, in Sharon, Mass., to Mary Kimball and Jonathan Whitaker, a Congregationalist minister. After receiving the A.B., 1820, and the A.M., 1823, at Harvard, he studied theology and was licensed to preach. In 1822–1823 he edited the *Christian Philanthropist* in New Bedford.

In poor health, Whitaker moved south in 1823. He lectured and preached widely and organized a congregation in Augusta, Ga., before abandoning the ministry and settling in South Carolina. In 1828 he married Mary H. Firth, a widow with two large tracts and 62 slaves in St. Paul's Parish. As a rice and cotton planter, Whitaker was active in agricultural and literary affairs and actively supported nullification in the early 1830s.

Prepared for the bar under James L. Pettigru's direction, he opened a law office in Charleston. There in 1835 he began the *Southern Literary Journal and Monthly Magazine*, which he edited until 1837. He edited the *Southern Quarterly Review* from its beginning in 1842 through 1847. In 1849 he married a widow, Mary Scrimzeour Furman Miller, a writer of poetry and fiction. With her he edited *Whitaker's Magazine: The Rights of the South* in Charleston and Columbia, 1850–1853. After it was absorbed by the *Southern Eclectic*, Whitaker edited the latter (1853–1854) in Augusta, first with J. H. Fitten and later alone.

Having held a minor position in Washington under Buchanan's administration, he served in Richmond in the C.S.A. Post Office Department and Quartermaster General's Department. After moving to New Orleans in January, 1866, he edited the *New Orleans Monthly Review*, 1874–1876, attempting to revive it as the

New Orleans Quarterly Review in 1878 and as the *Southern Quarterly Review*, 1879–1880. In 1878 he joined the Roman Catholic Church. He died while visiting in Houston on March 23, 1881.

WORKS: *Sidney's Letters to William E. Channing, D.D., Occasioned by His Letter to Hon. Henry Clay, on the Annexation of Texas to the United States* (1837).

> WILLIAM M. MOSS
> Wake Forest University
> Winston-Salem, N.C.

ANDREW WHITE, S. J. (1579–1656). Although biographical details of Father Andrew White's early life are sketchy, he was apparently born in London in 1579. Like other English Catholics, he was educated on the Continent, matriculating at Douai College in April, 1593, then entering St. Alban's College, Valladolid. In 1605 he took his vows as a priest at Douai. Following this, a mission to England ended in banishment, White having the misfortune to be there at the time of the Gunpowder Plot. In 1607 he was admitted as a Jesuit novitiate at St. John's College, Louvain. As a Jesuit, White, ignoring a death sentence, held several missionary posts in England where, sometime between 1619 and 1622, he evidently met George Calvert through whom he became interested in Lord Baltimore's plans to colonize what was to become Maryland.

Before sailing to America with Lord Baltimore on November 22, 1633, Father White, often called the Apostle of Maryland, wrote the first Maryland colonization tract: *A Declaration of the Lord Baltimore's Plantation in Mary-land*, an eight-page pamphlet, revised by Calvert, describing in glowing terms the new colony and the advantages of settling there. After arriving in the New World, he wrote a second promotional tract, *A Relation of the Successful Beginnings of the Lord Baltimore's Plantation in Mary-land* (1634), which enthusiastically described the beauty and bounty of the colony through specific details and incidents set in a narrative frame. White's account of the Indians in particular looks forward to his work in converting them to Christianity and, in the process, to his making of a grammar and dictionary of their language. This tract was followed in 1635 by a third colonization tract, composed largely by Father White, *A Relation of Maryland*.

Father White's work in Maryland, although often interrupted by illness, continued until 1644 or 1645 when he was captured by Virginia Puritans and sent to England for trial on the spurious charge of "being a Priest in England." After several years in Newgate, he was released. He was never able to return to Maryland, living instead on the Continent and then in England where he is recorded as having died on December 27, 1656.

WORKS: *A Declaration of the Lord Baltimore's Plantation in Mary-land* (1633). *A Relation of the Successful Beginnings of the Lord Baltimore's Plantation in Mary-land* (1634). *A Relation of Maryland* (1635).

PETER L. ABERNETHY
Texas Tech University
Lubbock

JOHN BLAKE WHITE (1781–1859). Born in Berkeley County, S.C., on September 2, 1781, John Blake White soon moved to Charleston, where his father, a former Revolutionary soldier, was a builder. From 1801 to 1803, White studied painting in England with Benjamin West and met Washington Allston, whose relative, Elizabeth Allston, he later married. White tried painting in Charleston and Boston but found no encouragement for historical subjects. In Charleston he practiced law and became active in cultural affairs. He was elected to the state legislature as a Democratic-Republican in 1818 and during nullification was a Unionist. White persevered as a historical artist, and four of his works now hang in the Capitol, among which is his best known, *The Camp of Marion*. He was later employed at the Customs House in Charleston, where he died on August 24, 1859.

White was the first dramatist in the South to write a substantial number of plays, five in all. Three were performed in Charleston. He is significant for turning from foreign to native subjects and as a writer of reform plays. His *Foscari* (1806), a romantic tragedy set in Venice, was the first tragedy written in the state. *The Mys-*

teries of the Castle (1807) provoked an argument over the plausibility of melodramatic villains in the Charleston press. *Modern Honor* (1812) is the first antidueling play in America. White also dramatized the Battle of New Orleans in *The Triumph of Liberty* (published 1819, but not performed). The purpose of this play was to support Jackson's actions in the Seminole War of 1818. *The Forgers*, an early temperance drama, was composed in 1829, but not performed. It was published in the *Southern Literary Journal* (1837). White's interest in social reform included abolition of capital punishment, about which he wrote an essay for *The Charleston Book* (1845).

WORKS: *Foscari* (1806). *The Mysteries of the Castle* (1807). *Modern Honor* (1812). *The Triumph of Liberty, or Louisiana Preserved* (1819). *The Forgers* (1837).

CHARLES S. WATSON
University of Alabama
Tuscaloosa

WALTER FRANCIS WHITE (1893–1955). Walter White, born in Atlanta, on July 1, 1893, was 1/64th Negro. He had blond hair, blue eyes, and a very light skin; he could have "passed." But the terrible Atlanta race riots, which he witnessed with his father on September 23, 1906, seemed to fix in his mind forever that he was black.

After graduating from Atlanta University in 1916, White worked for an Atlanta insurance company, but in 1918 James Weldon Johnston convinced him to come to New York City to become assistant secretary of the NAACP. In 1922 he married Leah Gladys Powell, and in that same year he met H. L. Mencken, who urged him to write a novel about Negro life "from the inside." *The Fire in the Flint* (1924) focuses upon a Negro doctor, Harvard-trained, who returns to his home town in Georgia to practice medicine. White's objectives were to show "what an intelligent, educated Negro feels" and to illustrate Mencken's thesis in "The Sahara of the Bozart" that the South had become an intellectual and moral waste land after the Civil War. White's second novel, *Flight* (1926), was influenced by Sinclair Lewis, who became a close friend. In it, he satirized the stuffy, provincial bourgeoisie of both races. During the 1920s, he recommended young black writers to Carl Van Vechten and Alfred Knopf, who were both interested in promoting the Negro Renaissance.

A major turning point in White's life occurred in 1927 when he went to southern France on a Guggenheim Fellowship, ostensibly to write a novel about three generations of a black family. What he wrote instead was *Rope and Faggot: A Biography of Judge Lynch* (1929). It was not fiction but rather a sociopsychological study of the illegal execution of Negroes. White subsequently gave up his literary career to become more active in politics. In 1931 he replaced Johnson as executive secretary of the NAACP; in 1937 he was awarded the Spingarn Medal for activity against lynching; and in 1942 and 1943 he helped settle the race riots in Detroit and Harlem. He also investigated the alleged mistreatment of black troops in Europe during World War II, and his findings took form in a book, *A Rising Wind* (1945). He and his first wife divorced in 1948. He married Poppy Cannon in 1949, and this marriage to a white woman did some damage to his reputation within the NAACP. Her biography of his last years is titled *A Gentle Knight* (1956). He died on March 21, 1955.

WORKS: *The Fire in the Flint* (1924). *Flight* (1926). *Rope and Faggot: A Biography of Judge Lynch* (1929). *A Rising Wind* (1945). *A Man Called White* (1948).

CHARLES SCRUGGS
University of Arizona
Phoenix

JAMES WHITEHEAD (1936–). Born in T. S. Eliot's birthplace— St., Louis, Mo.,— on the Ides of March, 1936, James Whithead spent most of his growing-up days in Mississippi where he graduated from Jackson Central High School. He then attended Vanderbilt (B.A., Philosophy; M.A., English) and the University of Iowa (M.F.A.). While in college, he studied under R. V. Cassill, Donald Davidson, and Donald Justice. After graduation he taught at Millsaps College in Jackson (1960–1963) and is currently associate professor of English, University of Arkansas, Fayetteville, and co-director of the creative writing program.

He received the Robert Frost Fellowship in Poetry of the Breadloaf Writers' Conference for his first book of poems, *Domains*. His second major publication is *Joiner*, a novel about the self-discovery of one man, Eugene "Sonny" Joiner—NFL tackle, killer, teacher, husband. The successes of his first two books mark him as a writer with promise. Whitehead is married to Gen Graeber; they have seven children.

WORKS: *Domains: Poems* (1966). *Joiner: A Novel* (1971).

JAMES A. GRIMSHAW, JR.
United States Air Force Academy
Colorado Springs, Colo.

ALBERY ALLSON WHITMAN (1851–1901). Albery Allson Whitman was born on May 30, 1851, in Hart County, Ky. Both his parents were slaves, as was he. Both were dead in 1863, the year when President Lincoln's proclamation emancipated Whitman.

A freed lad, Whitman worked in Kentucky and Ohio, received some months of formal schooling, taught at Carysville, Ohio, as well as near his Kentucky birthplace and, in 1870, enrolled at Wilberforce University, where he became a student and protégé of Daniel Alexander Payne, Wilberforce's founder and first president and a bishop of the African Methodist Episcopal Church. Although Whitman apparently never finished at Wilberforce, he worked for it as its general financial agent. His poem of over 5,000 lines, *Not a Man and Yet a Man*—long mistakenly assumed to be the longest poem of Negro authorship—was intended to raise money for Wilberforce. As an A.M.E. minister, noted for his pulpit histrionics, Whitman pastored, and, in some cases, founded churches in Ohio, Kansas, Texas, and Georgia. His last charges were in Savannah and Atlanta. After contracting pneumonia in Anniston, Ala., he died within a week at his Atlanta home, on June 29, 1901. His death was hastened by his addiction to alcohol.

Whitman was a mulatto; his wife, Caddie, a strikingly beautiful octoroon. She recited his poetry with great effect. Her four daughters, two of whom may have been only Whitman's stepdaughters, eventually formed the Whitman Sisters, who were active in vaudeville as entertainers and booking agents until the 1930s.

It now seems to some critics that Whitman, and not Frances Ellen Watkins Harper, may have been the best Negro poet of his age. He began with Longfellow as his idol. A facile versifier, he was the first Negro poet to use the Spenserian stanza. He narrated well, but tended also toward melodramatic romance. His pride in his race was unmistakable. In his poetry, however, it did not prevent his expression of other concerns.

WORKS: *Essays on the Ten Plagues and Miscellaneous Poems*(1871?). *Leelah Misled* (1873). *Not a Man and Yet a Man* (1877). *The Rape of Florida* (1884). *Twasinta's Seminoles*, a reissue of *The Rape of Florida* (1885, 1890). *Drifted Leaves* (1890). *World's Fair Poem* (1893). *An Idyl of the South* (1901).

BLYDEN JACKSON
University of North Carolina
Chapel Hill

RICHARD HENRY WILDE (1789–1847). A lawyer, Congressman, poet, and translator, Wilde was born in Dublin, Ireland, on September 24, 1789. His parents, Richard and Mary Newett Wilde, moved to Baltimore, Md., in 1797, and in 1803 his widowed mother went to Augusta, Ga., to open a ladies' dress shop. In this Georgia town Wilde grew to manhood.

He studied law on his own, and, after passing the necessary examination, started a law practice. In 1811 he became attorney general of Georgia. He was elected as a representative from Georgia to the Fourteenth, Twenty-First, Twenty-Second, and Twenty-Third Congresses of the United States and filled two additional vacancies. In 1819 he married a widow, Caroline Buckle. In 1835, as a result of political defeat, the then widowed Wilde went to Europe and settled in Florence, Italy, enjoying the study of Italian literature. His sister and two sons joined him. In 1841 he returned to America for financial reasons. After trying unsuccessfully to practice law in Augusta, he moved in 1844 to New

Orleans. He was a fairly successful lawyer there and was to have been one of the first professors in the new Tulane law school, but he died on September 10, 1847, during a yellow fever epidemic.

Wilde wrote many original poems, including the one entitled "The Lament of the Captive" beginning "My life is like the summer rose," which was involved in a plagiarism controversy. While in Italy he started a life of Dante; he also wrote short biographies of other Italian poets and translated a number of their poems.

WORKS: *Hesperia* (1867). *The Italian Lyric Poets* (1966). *Poems, Fugitive and Occasional* (1966).

EDWARD L. TUCKER
Virginia Polytechnic Institute
and State University
Blacksburg

ELIZA WILKINSON (1757–?). A chronicler of events during and immediately following the Revolutionary War in South Carolina, Eliza Wilkinson was born on February 7, 1757, the daughter of Sarah Clifford and Francis Yonge, Sr., of Yonge's Island, St. Paul's Parish, near the South Carolina coast. Her first husband, Joseph Wilkinson, apparently died before the Revolution and after only twelve months of marriage. It was as his widow that Wilkinson wrote her letters describing the events of the Revolutionary War in and around Charleston. She married her second husband, Peter Porcher, Sr., of St. Peter's Parish, on January 9, 1786. Apparently they had only one child, Francis Younge Porcher. Wilkinson's date of death is not known.

In 1781 and 1782 she wrote a series of letters to a friend, Mary Porcher, in which she recalled the invasion of South Carolina and the taking of Charleston by the British in 1779. These letters, written in an entertaining, consciously literary style somewhat in the manner of the epistolary novel tradition, were edited and arranged by Caroline Gilman (whose daughter, Abby Louisa, had married Wilkinson's grandson, Francis J. Porcher) and published in her magazine the *Southern Rose Bud*, irregularly from 1832 to

1835. In 1839 Gilman collected them in book form as *Letters of Eliza Wilkinson*.

In addition to the published letters, there are fifteen other letters and one poem which have remained unpublished. These letters are generally less literary and more personal in nature, but they are nevertheless of interest for the discerning picture they present of Charleston and plantation society. There is nothing remarkable about the poem. All of these writings were copied in manuscript by Wilkinson into a quarto letterbook which served as Gilman's text for her edition. This manuscript book was in the possession of the Porcher family at the turn of the century; transcriptions of the letters may be found in the South Caroliniana Library at the University of South Carolina.

WORKS: *Letters of Eliza Wilkinson*, ed. Caroline Gilman (1839).

EDWIN T. ARNOLD
University of South Carolina
Columbia

SYLVIA WILKINSON (1940–). Sylvia Wilkinson was born on April 3, 1940, in Durham, N.C., the daughter of Thomas Noell and Peggy George Wilkinson. At the University of North Carolina in Greensboro, she studied with poet-critic Randall Jarrell and received her B.A. in painting and writing in 1961. She continued her study at Hollins College in English and creative writing, earning her M.A. in 1963. She won in 1965–1966 the Wallace Stegner Creative Writing Fellowship at Stanford University, where she completed her second novel.

Wilkinson has taught or been writer-in-residence at several colleges and universities, among them Asheville-Biltmore College, the College of William and Mary, Sweet Briar College, and the University of North Carolina at Chapel Hill. Her honors include a Hollins College Creative Writing Fellowship (1963), the Eugene Saxton Memorial Trust Fund (1964) for *Moss on the North Side*, and a Creative Writing Fellowship from the National Endowment for the Arts (1973–1974).

In addition to her full-length works, Wilkinson has published numerous short stories, poems, critical essays, and articles on sports car racing—one of her hobbies. She has also produced a sizable collection of paintings and other art works that are frequently modeled on characters, animals, and objects in her fiction. As a result of her work with the Learning Institute of North Carolina, she published *Change: A Handbook for the Teaching of English and Social Studies in the Secondary Schools* (1971). A biography of John Brock, the national race car champion, appeared in 1973 with the title *The Stainless Steel Carrot: An Auto Racing Odyssey*.

Wilkinson's first three novels are set in rural eastern North Carolina. In 1977 she published *Shadow of the Mountain*, a novel dealing with the murder of a young woman in the North Carolina mountains and the tracing of her life up to her death.

WORKS: *Moss on the North Side* (1966). *A Killing Frost* (1967). *Cale* (1970). *Change; A Handbook for the Teaching of English and Social Studies in the Secondary Schools* (1971). *The Stainless Steel Carrot: An Auto Racing Odyssey* (1973). *Shadow of the Mountain* (1977).

LOTTIE H. SWINK
Hickory, N.C.

BEN AMES WILLIAMS (1889–1953). Ben Ames Williams, who has been described as a historical novelist who cared for history, was born at Macon, Miss., on March 7, 1889. He was the son of Daniel Webster and Sarah Marshall Ames Williams. When Williams was a boy his father became editor of the Jackson (Ohio) *Standard Journal*, a position he held for 30 years. Ben Ames attended Allen School in West Newton, Mass., and then went for one year to Cardiff, Wales, where his father served as United States consul.

After receiving a B.A. from Dartmouth in 1910, Williams became a newspaper reporter for the Boston *American*; in 1912 he married Florence Trafton Talpey of York, Me. After selling a few short stories, he resigned his job as reporter in 1916 to devote full time to writing. During the next 20 years he sold more than 400 short stories; he then turned to longer works, writing 35 novels and editing two books over the years. His keen interest in studying Americans in wartime prompted him to write *Come Spring* (1940), set during the Revolutionary period; *Thread of Scarlet* (1939), set during the War of 1812; and *House Divided* (1947), a saga of the Civil War period, in which he utilized some historical figures, including his great-uncle, Confederate general James Longstreet. *The Unconquered*, published posthumously, is a sequel to *House Divided*. Two novels, *The Strange Woman* (1941) and *Leave Her to Heaven* (1944), were best sellers and became successful motion pictures. At the time of his marriage, Williams settled in Maine, later moving to Chestnut Hill, Mass., and maintaining a summer home at Searsmont, Me.

He took an active interest in hunting, fishing, riding, and curling, participating in several international curling matches. He collected books in the field of Americana and early Colt revolvers. On February 4, 1953, while engaged in a curling contest at the Brookline Country Club, he collapsed and died of a heart attack.

WORKS: *All the Brothers Were Valiant* (1919). *The Sea Bride* (1919). *The Great Accident* (1920). *Evered* (1921). *Black Pawl* (1922). *Thrifty Stock* (1923). *Sangsue* (1923). *Audacity* (1924). *The Rational Hind* (1925). *Silver Forest* (1926). *Immortal Longings* (1927). *Splendor* (1927). *The Dreadful Night* (1928). *Death on Scurvy Street* (1929). *Touchstone* (1930). *Great Oaks* (1930). *Pirates Purchase* (1931). *An End to Mirth* (1931). *Money Musk* (1932). *Honeyflow* (1932). *Pascal's Mill* (1933). *Mischief* (1933). *Hostile Valley* (1934). *Small Town Girl* (1935). *Crucible* (1937). *The Strumpet Sea* (1938). *Thread of Scarlet* (1939). *The Happy End* (1939). *Come Spring* (1940). *The Strange Woman* (1941). *Time of Peace* (1942). Ed., *Amateurs at War* (1943). *Leave Her to Heaven* (1944). *It's a Free Country* (1945). *House Divided* (1947). Ed., *Mary B. Chesnut: Diary from Dixie* (1949). *Fraternity Village* (1949). *Owen Glen* (1950). *The Unconquered* (1953).

LOUISE BLACKWELL
Florida A. & M. University
Tallahassee

JOAN WILLIAMS (1928–). Joan Williams was born on September 26, 1928, the daughter of Priestly H. and Maude Williams of

Memphis, Tenn. During her junior year at Bard College (1949) she won *Mademoiselle's* short-story contest for "Rain Later." After graduation she lived briefly in New Orleans and New York, where she worked for *Look*. On March 6, 1954, she married Ezra Bowen and divorced him May, 1970. They have two sons, Ezra and Matthew. She presently resides in Westport, Conn.

In 1949 Williams arranged to meet William Faulkner through John Reed Holley of Oxford, Miss. Faulkner soon asked her to collaborate on *Requiem for a Nun*. Finally abandoning this collaboration, they were more successful with Williams' "The Morning and the Evening" (*Atlantic*, 1953) and with her first novel, *The Morning and the Evening* (1961; Faulkner's suggested title). A television script, "The Graduation Dress," was sold in September, 1960, under their names. Faulkner claimed the story was essentially hers; Williams remembers only some discussion of characters' names. By August, 1952, she had become Faulkner's lover; but by November she informed him that their age difference was too great. However, she remained his friend.

Winner of the John P. Marquand First Novel Award (1962), *The Morning and the Evening* presents a small Mississippi community's unjust treatment of an idiot (recalling Faulkner's Benjy and Ike Snopes) and later guilt over his death. *Old Powder Man* (1966) traces the legendary life of Dynamite Wynn (Williams' father, a dynamite salesman, is his prototype). Centering on the Mississippi levee construction after the great flood of 1927, this novel dramatizes southern frontier humor and character which disappear with urbanization. Her latest novel, *The Wintering* (1971), follows the emotional maturation of a neophyte writer through her increasingly intimate relationship with an older, acclaimed novelist. Williams also has written several short stories.

WORKS: *The Morning and the Evening* (1961). *Old Powder Man* (1966). *The Wintering* (1971).

JOHN T. HIERS
Valdosta State College
Valdosta, Ga.

JOHN A[LFRED] WILLIAMS (1925–). John Alfred Williams was born on his grandfather's farm near Jackson, Miss., on December 5, 1925. His parents had come South for John's birth and shortly thereafter returned to Syracuse, N.Y., where he grew up. Before completing high school, Williams entered the United States Navy in 1943, serving part of his duty in the Pacific. He began writing free verse poetry while in the navy. After his discharge from the navy in 1946, Williams graduated from Syracuse's Central High School. He enrolled briefly at Morris Brown College in Atlanta before entering Syracuse University, from which he received an A.B. in 1950. The following year he enrolled in a graduate program at Syracuse. During his college years he married Carolyn Clopton, a marriage which, after two sons, ended in divorce in 1953.

During the 1950s and 1960s Williams held a variety of jobs in communications. Shortly after leaving the navy, he worked for a black newspaper in Syracuse, and from 1952 to 1953 as a public relations officer for Doug Johnson and Associates. Moving to California in 1953, Williams was employed from 1954 to 1955 by the Columbia Broadcasting System in Hollywood as a staff member for radio and television special events. He returned to New York in 1955, and since the early 1950s has worked for more than fifteen newspapers and magazines; he was European correspondent for *Ebony* and *Jet* magazines from 1958 to 1959 and a correspondent in Africa for *Newsweek* from 1964 to 1965.

The 1960 publication of *The Angry Ones* launched Williams's career as a novelist. Two years later *Night Song* won him a literary fellowship to the Rome Academy from the American Academy of Arts and Letters. However, the National Institute of Arts and Letters, parent body of AAAL, rescinded the award because the Rome Academy rejected Williams as the recipient. The NIAL later awarded him a grant for his contributions to American literature.

Williams met Lorrain Isaac while both were working for the same publishing house. They married in 1965. *Holiday* magazine commissioned him in 1963 to take an automobile trip across the United States and gauge the racial attitudes of the country. He published his findings as *This Is My Country Too* (1965). With

The Man Who Cried I Am (1967), it was evident that the guarded optimism expressed in his earlier works had taken a more pessimistic stance.

WORKS: *The Angry Ones* (1960). *Night Song* (1961). *Africa: Her History, Lands and People* (1962). *The Angry Black* (1962). *Sissie* (1963). *The Protectors*, with H. J. Anslinger (1964). *This Is My Country Too* (1965). *Beyond the Angry Black* (1966). *The Man Who Cried I Am* (1967). *Sons of Darkness, Sons of Light: A Novel of Some Probability* (1969). *The Most Native of Sons* (1970). *The King God Didn't Save: Reflections on the Life and Death of Martin Luther King, Jr.* (1970). *Captain Blackman* (1972). *Flashbacks: A Twenty-Year Diary of Article Writing* (1973). *Mothersill and the Foxes* (1975). *The Junior Bachelor Society* (1976).

J. LEE GREENE
University of North Carolina
Chapel Hill

JONATHAN WILLIAMS (1929–). Jonathan Williams, most of whose poems are one-page artifacts carefully made of short lines, favors condensation along with carbonation, even in autobiographical notices: "The basic facts are: born in Asheville, North Carolina, in 1929 [March 8]. Educated at St. Albans School; un-educated at Princeton University. Studies in painting with Karl Knaths; in graphic arts with Stanley William Hayter. At Black Mountain College (1951–56), the counsel of such men as Charles Olson, Aaron Siskind, Robert Duncan, and Lou Harrison. Having read in public more than 800 times and having published 27 books of my own, and directed the publication of some 80 titles in my *Jargon Society* series of new writers, there has been constant travel for 20 years, and I have known more artists than anyone deserves—or could stomach. The antidote has been to take to my feet, along the rivers and mountains of the USA & UK, to listen to people with *ground* sense, good ears and eyes, and a knowledge of the names of things. . . . I live about eight months a year in a farm cottage in Dentdale in the Pennines; and go back to North Carolina for the winter season to encourage students, see old friends, and pay my respects to the Great Smokies, the Galax leaves, and the Pileated Woodpecker." This "Note on JW by JW" is dated August 28, 1974.

For all of his adult life, Jonathan Williams has, with impressive energy and intelligence, worked as an avant-garde all-around man of letters: poet, essayist, lecturer, scold, photographer, book-designer, and publisher. In the same league as New Directions, his Jargon Press has been consistently and uniquely bold in the publication of the work of some of the best writers to emerge since 1950, including Charles Olson, Robert Creeley, Louis Zukovsky, and Denise Levertov. Unlike most of the publications of small presses, Jargon books are integrally designed and proficiently manufactured.

WORKS: *Garbage Litters the Iron Face of the Sun's Child* (1951). *Red/Gray* (1951). *Four Stoppages* (1953). *The Empire Finals at Verona* (1959). *Amen/Huzza/Selah* (1960). *Elegies and Celebrations* (1962). *In England's Green &* (1962). *Lines about Hills above Lakes* (1964). *Polycotyledonous Poems* (1967). *Descant on Rawthey's Madrigal* (1968). *Mahler* (1969). *An Ear in Bartram's Tree: Selected Poems 1957–67* (1969).

WILLIAM HARMON
University of North Carolina
Chapel Hill

MILLER WILLIAMS (1930–). Miller Williams was born on April 8, 1930, in Hoxie, Ark. His father, Ernest B. Williams, was a Methodist minister; and his mother, who now resides in Baton Rouge, La., is Ann Jeannette Miller Williams. In 1951 Williams married Lucile Day, with whom he had three children: Lucinda (1953), Robert (1955), and Karyn (1957). That marriage ended in divorce after fifteen years.

Planning to pursue a career in research biology, Miller Williams earned a bachelor's degree in biology from Arkansas State College at Jonesboro (now Arkansas State University) and a master's in zoology and anthropology from the University of Arkansas at Fayetteville. After ten years of teaching in premedical and science programs, he acknowledged his insatiable hunger for language properly used and redirected his efforts towards literature. A Bread Loaf Fellowship in Poetry for 1961 marked the formal beginning of his new career.

His first volume of poetry, *A Circle of Stone* (1964), appeared while Williams was teaching at Louisiana State University. That book heralded the beginning of the publishing career of a major voice in southern American literature. During the years between this first volume of verse and the latest, *Why God Permits Evil* (1977), Williams has written and traveled and taught widely. With the Amy Lowell Award, he spent 1963–1964 as Visiting Professor of American Literature at the University of Chile and there began translating Latin American poetry. A Fulbright scholarship enabled him to spend 1970 in Mexico where he further pursued his work in translation. Since his return from Mexico in 1970, Williams has resided with his second wife, Rebecca Jordon Hall Williams, in Fayetteville, Ark., where he teaches in the graduate program in creative writing at the University of Arkansas. Winner of the 1976 Prix de Rome in Literature, Williams spent 1976–1977 based in Rome. From there he traveled throughout Europe and the Middle East, reading his work in such major cities as Rome, Madrid, Vienna, Delhi, Calcutta, Athens, and Amsterdam.

Aside from original poetry, translation, and critical writing, Williams has edited, alone or in collaboration, seven books—the most notable being the 1975 revised edition of *How Does a Poem Mean?*, with John Ciardi.

WORKS: *A Circle of Stone* (1964). Ed., *19 Poetas de Hoy in los EEUU* (1966). Ed., *Southern Writing in the Sixties: Fiction*, with John William Corrington (1966). Ed., *Southern Writing in the Sixties: Poetry*, with John William Corrington (1967). Trans., *Poems and Antipoems of Nicanor Parra* (1967). *So Long at the Fair* (1968). Ed., *Chile: An Anthology of New Writing* (1968). *The Achievement of John Ciardi* (1969). *The Only World There Is* (1971). Ed., *Contemporary Poetry in America* (1972). *The Poetry of John Crowe Ransom* (1972). *Halfway from Hoxie* (1973). Ed., *How Does a Poem Mean*, 2nd ed., with John Ciardi (1975). Ed., *Railroad: Trains and Train People in American Culture*, with James Alan McPherson (1976). *Why God Permits Evil* (1977).

BEVERLY JARRETT
Louisiana State University
Baton Rouge

TENNESSEE [THOMAS LANIER] WILLIAMS (1911–). Tennessee Williams was born in Columbus, Miss., on March 26, 1911, the first son and second child of Cornelius Coffin and Edwina Dakin Williams. His mother, of genteel upbringing, was the daughter of a minister. She and the two older children lived in the home of the grandparents, whom Williams adored, during their early years. Williams' father, of a Tennessee family whose ancestry included Tennessee's first governor and first senator as well as Sidney Lanier, was of the aggressive man's-man type who enjoyed life as an itinerant shoe salesman. In about 1919 he was promoted to the shoe company's headquarters in St. Louis. The move represented a traumatic change in life style for both Williams and his sister, Rose, though the degree to which *The Glass Menagerie* represents the facts is not altogether clear. In some respects it clearly does not, since Williams' father never deserted his family, since the second son (Dakin, born about the time of the move) is not in the play, and since the family was never so poverty-stricken or badly housed as the play suggests.

Williams went first to the University of Missouri, then (after three years of unhappy work at the shoe company) to Washington University, finally graduating from the University of Iowa. There ensued, and intervened, periods of widespread wandering, which in a sense have never ceased. Williams is a roamer, alighting most frequently in Key West, New Orleans, New York, and Italy. His life has been deeply affected not only by the move to St. Louis and ill feeling between himself and his father, but also by serious illnesses in his childhood and youth which left him hypochrondriac, and which have sporadically continued; by the mental illness and eventual prefrontal lobotomy of Rose, to whom he was, and remains, very close, and for whose excellent care he has for many years been responsible; and by his discovery and acceptance, as revealed in his *Memoirs*, of his homosexuality.

Williams began writing early; but success came first with the production of *The Glass Menagerie* in 1944 in Chicago and in 1945 in New York, where it won the Drama Critics' Circle Award. Earlier, Williams had won a prize from the Group Theater in New

York for a collection of one-act plays; had as a result become a client of the successful literary agent Audrey Wood; had won a Rockefeller grant for playwriting; had worked briefly as a script-writer for MGM; and in 1940 had a full-length play, *Battle of Angels*, produced in an unsuccessful tryout in Boston.

After *Menagerie*, and after an unsuccessful collaboration with Donald Windham, *You Touched Me* (1945), Williams' next produc-tion was one which became and remains his standard play, a per-manent part of dramatic repertory and of American literature: *A Streetcar Named Desire* (1947). *Streetcar's* two central charac-ters, Blanche Dubois and Stanley Kowalski, fallen southern aristo-crat and flamboyant son of the slums, are among the most vivid and memorable creations in modern drama. The play won the Critics' Award and also a Pulitzer Prize.

From that time until the early 1960s, Williams was a successful playwright, his more important plays being *Summer and Smoke* (1948; more popular in later revival), *The Rose Tattoo* (1951), *Camino Real* (1953), *Cat on a Hot Tin Roof* (1955; won Critics' Award and Pulitzer Prize), *Suddenly Last Summer* (1958), and *The Night of the Iguana* (1961; won Critics' Award). Since *Night of the Iguana*, his plays have been largely unsuccessful, with both critics and public. His most important recent work is his *Memoirs* (1975). He has also written novels, poetry, and an original movie script (*Baby Doll*, 1956).

All of Williams' full-length plays through 1962 are laid in the South, except *The Glass Menagerie*, *Camino Real* (a mythical Latin America), and *The Night of the Iguana* (Mexico). His plays, vary-ing from darkly gloomy to seriously affirmative to comic, represent a broad and frequently searching study of life in the South, though at their best, as in *Streetcar*, they rise above regionalism to uni-versality. His plays frequently grow out of earlier short stories and one-acters, and he is given to frequent revision, before, during, and after production, as well as to providing different titles for more or less the same play, thus creating serious problems for scholar and editor.

While his critical reputation varied widely for years, it is now clear that Williams is one of the two or three most important American playwrights, the most important to come out of the South.

WORKS: *Five Young American Poets*, third series (1944). *Battle of Angels* (1945). *The Glass Menagerie* (1945). *You Touched Me*, with Donald Windham (1946). *27 Wagons Full of Cotton* (1946). *A Streetcar Named Desire* (1947). *Summer and Smoke* (1948). *One Arm and Other Stories* (1948). *American Blues* (1948). *The Roman Spring of Mrs. Stone* (1950). Intro., Carson McCullers, *Reflections in a Golden Eye* (1950). *The Rose Tattoo* (1951). *I Rise in Flame, Cried the Phoenix* (1951). *Camino Real* (1953). *Hard Candy: A Book of Stories* (1954). *Cat on a Hot Tin Roof* (1955). *Lord Byron's Love Letters* (1955). *In the Winter of Cities* (1956). *Baby Doll* (1956). *Orpheus Descending* (with *Battle of Angels*; 1958). *Suddenly Last Summer* (1958). Intro., William Inge, *The Dark at the Top of the Stairs* (1958). *Sweet Bird of Youth* (1959). *Period of Adjustment* (1960). *Three Players of a Summer Game* (1960). *The Night of the Iguana* (1962). *Garden District* [*Something Unspoken* and *Suddenly Last Summer*] (1962). *The Milk Train Doesn't Stop Here Anymore* (1964). *The Eccentricities of a Nightingale* (with *Summer and Smoke*; 1964). *Knightly Quest and Other Stories* (1967). *Kingdom of Earth: The Seven Descents of Myrtle* (1968). *Small Craft Warnings* (1972). *Out Cry* [*Two Character Play*] (1973). *Eight Mortal Ladies Possessed* (1974). *Moise and the World of Reason* (1975). *Memoirs* (1975). *Tennessee Williams' Letters to Donald Windham, 1940–65*, ed. Donald Windham (1977).

JACOB H. ADLER
Purdue University
Lafayette, Ind.

CALDER BAYNARD WILLINGHAM, JR. (1922–). Calder Willingham was born on December 23, 1922, in Atlanta, Ga. The son of Eleanor Churchill Willcox and Calder Baynard Willingham, he was educated at the Darlington Preparatory School (1936–1940), the Citadel (1940–1941), and the University of Virginia (1941–1943). In 1945 he married Helene Rothenberg, and they had one son before the marriage was dissolved in 1950. Jane Marie Bennett became his wife on September 15, 1953, and has since borne him three sons and two daughters.

Willingham's first novel, *End as a Man* (1947), a satire on life in a military academy in the South, created a stir and later served him as a basis for a Broadway play of the same title in 1953 and a movie under the title of *The Strange One* in 1957. By 1975 he had published *The Gates of Hell* (1951), a collection of short stories and sketches, and eight other novels. He has also been active as a writer of screenplays and has among his credits *Paths of Glory* (1957; nominated for a Writers Guild Award); *One-Eyed Jacks* (1961); *The Graduate* (1967; nominated for an Academy Award and received a Writers Guild Award); and *Little Big Man* (1970). Aside from *The Graduate*, however, he is known best as a novelist, as one indeed whose fiction more often than not deals with southern settings or character.

WORKS: *End as a Man* (1947). *Geraldine Bradshaw* (1950). *Reach to the Stars* (1951). *The Gates of Hell* (1951). *Natural Child* (1952). *To Eat a Peach* (1955). *Eternal Fire* (1963). *Providence Island* (1969). *Rambling Rose* (1972). *The Big Nickel* (1975).

RAYBURN S. MOORE
University of Georgia
Athens

AUGUSTA JANE EVANS WILSON (1835–1909). Augusta Evans Wilson, one of the most popular of the domestic sentimentalists of the latter half of the nineteenth century, was born on May 8, 1835, in Augusta, Ga. Following a brief residence in Texas, in 1849 the family moved to Mobile, Ala., where Wilson lived until her death. In 1868 she married Lorenzo Madison Wilson, a Mobile businessman, and enjoyed with him a happy and tranquil life at Ashland, Wilson's estate. She died there on May 9, 1909.

Wilson was uncompromising in her support for the Confederacy, rejecting in 1860 the marriage proposal of James Spaulding, an admirer of her novel *Beulah*, because of his opposition to secession and his support of Lincoln. The avowed purpose of her novel *Macaria, or Altars of Sacrifice* was to champion the Confederacy, "the bodyguard for the liberty of the Republic." *Macaria* was so effective as propaganda that General G. H. Thomas, commander of the Yankee troops in Tennessee, banned the novel among his troops and burned all copies that could be found.

St. Elmo, the novel by which she is best known, employs nearly all of the standard devices of the sentimental novel. The style is marked by erudition; quotations and abstruse references abound. The pathos is excessive. Edna Earl, the idealized heroine, over-comes adversity and leads St. Elmo, the idealized hero, from sin to salvation. The moral, heavily laid on, reflects Wilson's view that art must teach the highest principles of Christianity. Soon after *St. Elmo* appeared, Charles H. Webb published *St. Twel'mo*, or the *Cuneiform Cyclopedist of Chattanooga*, a parody in which he attributes Edna Earl's turgid erudition to the fact that as a child she swallowed an unabridged dictionary. In 1965 the Springer Opera House in Columbus, Ga., presented an original musical version of *St. Elmo*.

WORKS: *Inez: A Tale of the Alamo* (1855). *Beulah* (1859). *Macaria or Altars of Sacrifice* (1864). *St. Elmo* (1866). *Vashti* (1869). *Infelice* (1875). *At the Mercy of Tiberius* (1887). *A Speckled Bird* (1902). *Devota* (1907).

MARION C. MICHAEL
Texas Tech University
Lubbock

WILLIAM WIRT (1772–1834). William Wirt was born on No-vember 8, 1772, in Bladensburg, Md., the youngest of six chil-dren of Jacob and Henrietta Wirt. His father, a Swiss immigrant and tavern keeper, died when the boy was two years old. His German mother died when he was eight. Wirt was brought up by his Uncle Jasper with the help of Peter Carnes, a lawyer, who later married his sister. He attended a variety of schools, became a tutor at age fifteen, studied law, was admitted to practice in Cul-pepper County in northern Virginia (1792), and eventually became one of the most powerful orators in America.

As a young lawyer Wirt inhabited a very select social set includ-ing Jefferson's nephew Dabney Carr (with whom he developed a lifelong friendship), Jefferson himself, Madison, Monroe, Francis Walker Gilmer, and Dr. George Gilmer, whose daughter Mildred he married on May 28, 1795. She died on September 17, 1799, and he moved to Richmond, where he served as clerk in the House of Delegates during three sessions of the Assembly. His second marriage—(September 7, 1802) to the aristocratic Elizabeth Gamble, the second daughter of Colonel Robert Gamble, a wealthy Richmond merchant—marked a turning point in his life. In 1803 he moved to Williamsburg, where he became friends with St. George Tucker. In 1804 Littleton W. Tazewell persuaded him to move to Norfolk as his law partner. In 1806 he was back in Richmond again, to escape the occasional yellow fever in Norfolk but also to further his legal career.

As a literary figure Wirt is important for his work with the familiar essay. The first and most successful of these was *The Letters of the British Spy* (1803), ten anonymous essays in the tradition of *The Spectator* published in the Richmond *Argus*. From the viewpoint of an English traveler he presented recognizable portraits of such figures as James Monroe, John Marshall, Edmund Randolph, and John Wickham, entertaining criticism of Virginia society, and discussions of such topics as education, government, classical and modern oratory, and injustice to Indians. Less successful were *The Rainbow* (1804), a series of ten didactic essays, and *The Sylph* (1810) published in the Richmond *Enquirer*. But *The Old Bachelor* essays (1810–1811) were better received. In these Wirt had the help of several friends—Dabney Carr, St. George and George Tucker, *et al*.

But it was *Sketches of the Life and Character of Patrick Henry* (1817) that constituted Wirt's greatest popular success (15 editions by 1859). Apparently influenced by Jefferson's view, Wirt played up Henry's oratorical powers while minimizing his shortcomings as governor and soldier. Posterity will always owe Wirt a debt for piecing together (from various sources) the famous "Give me liberty, or give me death" speech.

In politics Wirt used his pen to support Madison's campaign for president, served one term in the Virginia legislature (1808–1809), but declined Jefferson's invitation to run for Congress. Madison appointed him attorney general, a post he held from 1817 to 1829, when he retired to Baltimore. In the 1832 campaign for the presidency Wirt opposed Jackson. Although he had been a Mason, he ran on an anti-Mason ticket, hoping thereby to unite the Whigs. Other highlights of his political career were his defense of James Callender—during an Alien and Sedition Acts libel trial (1800) before Judge Salmon P. Chase (Wirt's former law student)—and his part in the prosecution of Aaron Burr (1807). He died on February 18, 1834.

WORKS: *An Oration Delivered in Richmond on the Fourth Day of July 1800; the Anniversary of American Independence* (1800). *The Letters of the British Spy* (1803). *The Rainbow* (1804). *The Sylph* (1810). *The Old Bachelor* (1810–11). *Sketches of the Life and Character of Patrick Henry* (1817).

RICHARD E. AMACHER
Auburn University
Auburn, Ala.

THOMAS WOLFE (1900–1938). Thomas Wolfe was born on October 3, 1900, in Asheville, N.C. He was the youngest child in the large family of Julia Elizabeth Westall and William Oliver Wolfe, a prosperous mason and stonecutter. His first novel, *Look Homeward, Angel*, reflects both the gusto and the troubles of the Wolfe family life and especially the neglect young Tom suffered when his mother established the Old Kentucky Home boarding-house. At the North State Fitting School, however, he found a mother-substitute in his teacher, Margaret Roberts, who developed and guided his taste for literature. In 1916 he enrolled at the University of North Carolina where he concentrated in classics and in English literature and where, as a member of the Carolina Play-makers, he began his writing career.

He continued his playwriting at Harvard, 1920–1923, in Professor George Pierce Baker's drama workshop. Besides earning a master's degree in English, he wrote *The Mountains*, a play about a family feud, and *Welcome to Our City*, an expressionistic drama about a race riot in a southern town, and he resolved to become a professional writer.

In 1924 he became an instructor in English at New York University where he taught intermittently until 1930. Not able to find a producer for *Welcome to Our City*, or for *Mannerhouse*, his Civil War drama, he began work on a novel about a boy named Eugene Gant growing up in the South, searching for an understanding of the world around him. In this project he was encouraged by the love and financial help of Aline Bernstein, a wealthy stage designer, who was nineteen years his senior. She appears in his later fiction as Esther Jack. Because of its passionate intensity and its lyric style, *Look Homeward, Angel* (1929) found an enthusiastic audience when it appeared.

Wolfe next set to work on a novel of epic scale, which would characterize the restlessness of the modern American and would render a sense of the vastness and variety of the American continent. As he labored, his ideas multiplied to the extent that he developed a plan for a series of novels spanning the history of the nation. After three years, he became overwhelmed by the bulk and complexity of his scheme and turned for aid to Maxwell Perkins, his editor at Scribner's, who helped him to order a portion of his material and to piece together *Of Time and the River* (1935). Under those conditions, the book emerged an uneven piece of work, anthologylike in its variety. Parts were magnificent, conveying the quality of the American character and nation and presenting sensitive impressions of the twentieth-century scene as the narrative carried Eugene Gant to Harvard, to New York, and to Europe. But other parts were overwritten, wearisome in their expansiveness.

After his next publication, *From Death to Morning* (1935), a collection of stories, Wolfe decided to set aside the six-volume series while he wrote a different kind of work, a story about an innocent, gullible man discovering life's harsh truths through trial and disillusionment. As he worked, he gradually drew upon the material he had already written for the Eugene Gant cycle, and he began to fashion a long chronicle about a new autobiographical character, George Webber. At the same time he broke with Scribner's and Perkins in order to demonstrate his independence as an artist. Although Wolfe did not live to see his new work completed, he published several sections which show his continued strength of passionate statement, together with new powers of satire and social criticism.

On September 15, 1938, Wolfe died after a sudden siege of pneumonia led to complications and unsuccessful surgery, and he left behind a fragmentary narrative of over a million words. Out of this huge manuscript Edward Aswell of Harper's drew three books: *The Web and the Rock* (1939), the story of George Webber's growing up and of his tumultuous love affair with Esther Jack; *You Can't Go Home Again* (1940), Webber's further adventures as a young novelist who finds that one cannot escape change and its responsibilities; and *The Hills Beyond* (1941), an incomplete cycle of tales about Webber's mountain kinsmen.

Although Wolfe always stuck to autobiographical material for his fiction, he raised his autobiographical hero above the level of realism to become an archetypal figure engaged in the quest for self-discovery and trying to understand his place in the national scene and his relationship to the universe. Despite the unevenness of his work, his lyric intensity and his narrative power combined to make his series of novels the nearest approximation to an American epic that can be found in the twentieth century.

WORKS: *Look Homeward, Angel* (1929). "A Portrait of Bascom Hawke," *Scribner's*, XCI (April, 1932). *Of Time and the River* (1935). *From Death to Morning* (1935). *The Story of a Novel* (1936). "The Return of Buck Gavin" and "The Third Night," *Carolina Folk Plays*, 1st, 2nd, 3rd Ser. (1938). *The Web and the Rock* (1939). *You Can't Go Home Again* (1940). *The Hills Beyond* (1941). *Mannerhouse* (1948). *The Letters of Thomas Wolfe* (1956). *Welcome to Our City* (play), *Esquire*, XLVIII (October, 1957). *Thomas Wolfe's Purdue Speech*, "Writing and Living" (1964). *The Letters of Thomas Wolfe to His Mother* (new ed., 1968). *The Notebooks of Thomas Wolfe* (1970). *The Mountains* (1970).

RICHARD KENNEDY
Temple University
Philadelphia, Pa.

TOM WOLFE [THOMAS KENNERLY WOLFE, JR.] (1931–).

Tom Wolfe was born on March 2, 1931, in Richmond, Va. Reared in upper-class Richmond society, he graduated in 1947 from St. Christopher's, a private Episcopal boys' school in the city. In 1951 Wolfe took his bachelor's degree from Washington and Lee University and then pitched two seasons of semiprofessional baseball. Wolfe took his Ph.D. in American Studies from Yale in 1957, but did not seek an academic position. Instead, he entered newspaper journalism, working initially for the Springfield (Mass.) *Union* and in 1959 moving to the Washington *Post*, where he later became a Latin American correspondent. In 1962 he became a reporter for the New York *Herald Tribune*.

In the spring of 1963, Wolfe contracted to do a free-lance article for *Esquire* on the hot rod and custom car scene in Los Angeles. He could not pull the article together; and so he agreed to prepare notes and turn them over to an *Esquire* staff writer. In the course of typing the notes, Wolfe hit upon a style that he has since dubbed "the wowie!"—a collection of "vignettes, odds and ends of scholarship, bits of memoir, short bursts of sociology, apostrophes, epithets, moans, cackles, anything that came into my head, much of it thrown together in a rough and awkward way." *Esquire* published his 49-page memorandum.

Since 1963 Wolfe has written numerous articles about contemporary American lifestyles and has published four collections of his articles in book form. He is best known for his interpretations of middle-class California culture and of high-class New York society, and for his study of Ken Kesey, author and drug guru.

Wolfe has become a spokesman for the New Journalists. He argues that modern novelists have abandoned "the richest terrain of the novel: namely, society, the social tableau, manners and morals, the whole business of 'the way we live now,' in Trollope's phrase." Wolfe and the other New Journalists have therefore moved into the novelist's domain and have even begun to use traditional novelistic techniques to portray scenes in contemporary society.

WORKS: *The Kandy-Kolored Tangerine-Flake Streamline Baby* (1965). *The Pump House Gang* (1968). *The Electric Kool-Aid Acid Test* (1968). *Radical Chic & Mau-Mauing the Flak Catchers* (1970). Ed., with E. W.

Johnson *The New Journalism* (1973). *The Painted Word* (1975). *Mauve Gloves & Madmen, Clutter & Vine* (1976).

JAMES L. W. WEST III
Virginia Polytechnic Institute
and State University
Blacksburg

CHARLES WOODMASON (*ca.* **1720–1776**). Little is known of Woodmason's early life other than that he was probably born in Gosport, Hampshire, England, was an Anglican of the gentry class, at some time knew London, married, and had a son. In 1752 he sailed without his family to South Carolina where he acquired large tracts of land in various parts of Prince Frederick Winyaw Parish. He lived in this region for a decade as a planter, merchant, storekeeper, and holder of virtually every local office. During the 1750s he published several writings, verse and prose, in the *Gentleman's Magazine* in England.

After a brief return to England in 1762, Woodmason lived in Charleston where he was generally popular as justice of the peace and member of two Assembly commissions. In 1765 he applied to become a stamp distributor, and late in the same year he petitioned for the position of itinerant Anglican minister in the upper part of St. Mark's Parish. After an ordination in England, he returned to take up his frontier post with Camden as headquarters. Here, as a highly literate writer and one who knew both Charleston and the backcountry, he became penman for the poor frontier settlers who, terrorized by gangs of lawless men and ignored by the government in Charleston, organized the so-called Regulator movement. On their behalf Woodmason wrote a number of angry, passionate, sometimes moving appeals, including the great Remonstrance of 1767. His pages were filled with vivid rhetoric, irony, sarcasm, and satire.

Aging, ill, his congregations weakened by the deluge of New Light Baptists, Woodmason left South Carolina in 1772. He preached at various places in Virginia and Maryland and in 1774 sailed for England where for two years he preached in the vicinity of Bristol. After November, 1776, all records of him cease.

WORKS: "C. W. in Carolina to E. J. at Gosport," *The Gentleman's Maga-*
zine, XXIII (July, 1753), 337–38. "To Benjamin Franklin Esq; of Philadelphia, on his Experiments and Discoveries &c.," *ibid.*, XXIV (February, 1754), 224–26. "The Art of Manufacturing Indigo in Carolina,"
ibid., XXV (June, 1755), 201–203, 256–59. "A Political Problem," *South
Carolina Gazette and Country-Journal*, March 28, 1769. The "Remonstrance" and other political writings are in *The Carolina Backcountry
on the Eve of the Revolution*, ed. Richard J. Hooker (Chapel Hill, 1953).

RICHARD J. HOOKER
Englewood, Fla.

RICHARD WRIGHT (1908–1960). Richard Wright, whose novel
Native Son (1940) probably did more than any other single literary
event to pave the way for the emergence of black literature after
World War II, was born on September 4, 1908, on a cotton plantation 25 miles from Natchez, Miss. His father, Nathan, was a mill
worker; and his mother, Ellen, was a country schoolteacher. His
childhood was a series of struggles against impossible obstacles;
but it provided as well the subject matter and tone for his greatest
writing. Nathan Wright deserted the family when Richard was
five. Not long after, Ellen Wright suffered a series of paralytic
strokes. As a result, Richard was shuttled back and forth between
other members of the family. Finally, at age fifteen, he left home
to work as a porter-messenger in Memphis. It was in Memphis
that he first decided he wanted to write; and he began reading all
the books mentioned in Mencken's *Book of Prefaces*.

After a year in Memphis, Wright migrated further north to Chicago, a city which remained his home for ten years. He held jobs
there as a dishwasher, a postal clerk, a porter, a life insurance
salesman, and at other times subsisted on relief. During this time
he continued his reading and began to write; and he became involved in politics, serving as an assistant precinct captain for the
Republican party. In 1933 Wright joined the Communist party, attracted more by the fact that it included many intellectuals and by
its support for oppressed people of all colors than by its specific
political views. With the encouragement of fellow members, he

began writing poetry and short stories and reading the avant-garde writers of the period. His work, heavily imbued with the radical passions of the Party, began to appear in journals like *New Masses*, *Left Front*, *Partisan Review*, and *International Literature*, and he began work for the Federal Writers' Project. Feeling that his writing career was suffering because of the demands made on his time by the Party in Chicago, in 1937 he moved on to New York, where again he would remain for ten years. This decade was to be the most productive of his life and at its conclusion, he would have an international literary reputation.

In December, 1937, after months of frustration during which he had his novels continually turned down by New York publishers, Wright won the $500 first prize in a contest sponsored by *Story* magazine for FWP members. This in turn led to Harper's acceptance for book publication *Uncle Tom's Children* (1938), a collection of four long short stories dealing with racism in the South and the terror that it instilled in blacks. On March 1, 1940, Harper's published *Native Son*; and Wright's celebrity was assured. The novel was chosen as a selection by the Book-of-the-Month Club; a stage version by Wright and Paul Green was produced by Orson Welles; and the book sold 200,000 copies in less than three weeks. A novella, "The Man Who Lived Underground" (1942), showed the influence of his reading in Dostoevsky. Wright's fictionalized autobiography, *Black Boy* (1945), dealt only with the years before the move to Chicago but did so in such moving and vivid detail that it achieved almost as much popular success as had *Native Son*.

In March, 1941, after a brief first marriage to Dhimah Rose Meadman, Wright married Ellen Poplar. In 1946 the Wrights and their daughter, Julia, visited Paris, returning the next year to live there until the end of his life. Wright's later work never achieved either the popularity or the quality of *Native Son* and *Black Boy*. A novel, *The Outsider* (1953), is interesting chiefly for the influence upon it of Sartrean existentialism. *The Long Dream* (1958) is a novel about a Negro boy in Mississippi. While in France, he openly renounced his affiliation with the Communist party. During the last period of his life, he wrote a series of travel books: *Black*

Power (1954), on Africa's Gold Coast; *The Color Curtain* (1956), on the Bandung Conference of Asian and African nations; and *Pagan Spain* (1957), a bitter view of Franco's Spain. He died in Paris of a heart attack on November 28, 1960, hailed at his death as "a great American writer." Two of his works appeared posthumously, *Eight Men* (1961), a collection of short stories, and *Lawd Today* (1963), one of the novels he had unsuccessfully tried to publish during his early days in New York.

WORKS: *Uncle Tom's Children* (1938). *Native Son* (1940). *Twelve Million Black Voices* (1941). *Black Boy* (1945). *The Outsider* (1953). *Savage Holiday* (1954). *Black Power* (1954). *The Color Curtain* (1956). *Pagan Spain* (1957). *White Man, Listen!* (1957). *The Long Dream* (1958). *Eight Men* (1961). *Lawd Today* (1963).

JACKSON R. BRYER
University of Maryland
College Park

FRANK [GARVIN] YERBY (1916–). Frank Yerby was born on September 5, 1916, in Augusta, Ga. His father was Rufus Garvin Yerby, a postal clerk. His mother was Wilhelmina Smythe Yerby. Yerby married Flora Williams on March 1, 1941. They were divorced, and he married Blanca Calle-Perez on July 27, 1956. Yerby has four children, three by the first marriage. He received an A.B. in 1937 from Paine College, an M.A. from Fisk University in 1938, and did further graduate study at the University of Chicago in 1939. He began a teaching career at Florida A & M in 1939 with stints at Southern University through 1941. During World War II he worked as a laboratory technician at Ford and was a chief inspector for Fairchild Aircraft, 1944–1945. After 1945 he became a full-time writer. He has been a resident of Madrid, Spain, since 1959.

Yerby's writing career actually began with the publication of "Health Card" in *Harper's* (May, 1944); it was later chosen as an O. Henry Memorial Prize Award story. It is a bitter story of America's rejection of blacks as humans objectively narrated by an observer of injustices visited upon a black couple by military police. He published several other stories in 1945–1946, notably "White

Magnolias." Collectively, they concern racial matters in Georgia and the South. His first and most popular novel, *The Foxes of Harrow*, was published in February, 1946. In contrast to his earlier works, *The Foxes of Harrow* virtually abandoned racial material for stock historical romance. Yerby admits that it was written for the popular market, but many critics have praised the book's authenticity and the stirring action that includes duels, sex, societal clashes, and memorable characterizations. Since *The Foxes of Harrow*, Yerby has published, with regularity, historical novels that, in his words, attempt to correct the reader's historical perspective on themes of slavery, the Civil War, and Reconstruction. He has published 27 novels, the latest in May, 1976. Five are modern, including *The Old Gods Laugh; Speak Now*, his most serious work; *The Voyage Unplanned; Tobias and The Angel*; and *A Rose for Ana Maria*, all recent. Of the historical novels, Yerby rates *An Odor of Sanctity; Judas, My Brother; Goat Song*; and *The Garfield Honor* as serious novels.

WORKS: *The Foxes of Harrow* (1947). *The Vixens* (1948). *The Golden Hawk* (1948). *Pride's Castle* (1950). *Floodtide* (1950). *A Woman Called Fancy* (1951). *The Saracen Blade* (1952). *The Devil's Laughter* (1953). *Benton's Row* (1954). *Bride of Liberty* (1954). *The Treasure of Pleasant Valley* (1955). *Captain Rebel* (1956). *Fairoaks* (1957). *The Serpent and the Staff* (1958). *Jarrett's Jade* (1959). *Gillian* (1960). *The Garfield Honor* (1961). *Griffin's Way* (1962). *The Old Gods Laugh: A Modern Romance* (1964). *An Odor of Sanctity* (1965). *Goat Song: A Novel of Ancient Greece* (1968). *Judas, My Brother* (1968). *Speak Now* (1969). *The Dahomean* (1971). *The Girl from Storyville* (1972). *The Voyage Unplanned* (1972). *Tobias and The Angel* (1975). *A Rose for Ana Maria* (1976).

BRIAN J. BENSON
North Carolina A & T University
Greensboro

STARK YOUNG (1881–1963). Stark Young was born on October 11, 1881, the son of Mary Clark Starks and Alfred Alexander Young, in Como, Miss. Through his grandmother, Caroline Charlotte McGehee, Young was related to the large and distinguished

McGehee family who appear as characters in his fiction. His father served in the Confederate Army and after the war became a physician. At the death of his mother in 1890, Young went to live with his granduncle, Hugh McGehee. In 1895, when his father married again, Young moved to Oxford and entered the University of Mississippi. Upon graduation in 1901, he became a graduate student at Columbia University, receiving an M.A. in 1902. In 1904 he joined the faculty of the University of Mississippi. From 1907 to 1915 he taught English at the University of Texas and directed plays for the Curtain Club, which he founded, but left to lecture at Amherst College. Shortly afterward he began to publish articles of literary and social interest in many periodicals.

In 1921 Young resigned from Amherst to become a free-lance writer in New York. In 1922 Edith Isaacs named him a member of the editorial board of *Theatre Arts Magazine*, and Herbert Croly appointed him theater critic and contributing editor of the *New Republic*. During the next few years, Young established himself as a leading theater critic on Broadway. Meanwhile, he directed Henri Lenormand's *The Failures* and Eugene O'Neill's *Welded*. Although Young's own plays, *The Saint*, produced in 1924 at the Greenwich Village Theatre, and *The Colonnade*, produced in 1925 by the London Stage Society, were praised by critics, theater-goers were only mildly enthusiastic. From August, 1924, to August, 1925, Young was drama critic for the New York *Times*, but resigned to return to the *New Republic*.

Although Young continued to write theater criticism for the *New Republic* and *Theatre Arts Magazine*, for the next eight years (1926–1934) he devoted considerable time to writing four southern novels and an essay for *I'll Take My Stand*, the Agrarian manifesto of 1930. After the death of Herbert Croly in 1930, Young found the atmosphere at the *New Republic* becoming less and less congenial.

In 1938 Alfred Lunt and Lynn Fontanne scored a notable success in Stark Young's translation of Anton Chekhov's *The Sea Gull*. During the 1940s, Young observed a decline in the quality of plays offered on Broadway; and when his space in the *New Republic* was sharply curtailed, he resigned his position on July 12, 1947.

In his career as critic and writer for the *New Republic*, he wrote more than 500 essays, sketches, reviews, and articles.

Although officially "retired," Young continued to engage in literary activities. In 1948 he collected his best theater essays in *Immortal Shadows*, and, in 1951, Scribner's brought out his autobiography, *The Pavilion*. In 1953 Young helped Donald Davidson prepare a new edition of *So Red the Rose*, first published in 1934 and his best-known novel. Meanwhile, he continued to translate Chekhov's plays for productions at the Fourth Street Theatre; in 1956 Random House published Young's translations as the *Best Plays of Chekhov*.

Young suffered a stroke in May, 1959, and never returned to active work. After spending several months in a nursing home, he died on January 6, 1963, in New York. He is buried in Friendship Cemetery, near Como, Miss.

WORKS: *Guenevere* (1906). *The Blind Man at the Window and Other Poems* (1906). Ed., *The English Humorists of the Eighteenth Century by W. M. Thackeray* (1911). *Addio, Madretta and Other Plays* (1912). *Three One-Act Plays: Madretta, At the Shrine, [and] Addio* (1921). *The Queen of Sheba* (1922). *The Flower in Drama* (1923). *The Colonnade* (1924). *The Three Fountains* (1924). *Glamour: Essays on the Art of the Theatre* (1925). *The Saint* (1925). *Sweet Times and The Blue Policeman* (1925). *The Twilight Saint* (1925). *Encaustics* (1926). *Heaven Trees* (1926). *Theatre Practice* (1926). *The Theater* (1927). Trans., *Mandragola by Machiavelli* (1927). *The Torches Flare* (1928). *River House* (1929). *The Street of the Islands* (1930). *I'll Take My Stand: The South and the Agrarian Tradition*, contributor (1930). *So Red the Rose* (1934). *Feliciana* (1935). Ed., *Southern Treasury of Life and Literature* (1937). Trans., *The Sea Gull by Anton Chekhov* (1939). *Artemise* (1942). Ed., *Selected Poems of Sidney Lanier* (1947). *Immortal Shadows: A Book of Dramatic Criticism* (1948). *The Pavilion: Of People and Times Remembered, of Stories and Places* (1951). *The Flower in Drama & Glamour* (1955). Trans., *Best Plays of Chekhov: The Sea Gull; Uncle Vanya; The Three Sisters; The Cherry Orchard* (1957). *The Theatre* (1958). *Stark Young, A Life in the Arts: Letters, 1900–1962*, ed. John Pilkington.

JOHN PILKINGTON
University of Mississippi
Oxford

JOHN JOACHIM ZUBLY (1724–1781). John Joachim Zubly was born on August 27, 1724, in St. Gallen, Switzerland. He attended a local gymnasium, but was ordained in a German-speaking church in London on August 19, 1744. In the same year he moved to Perrysburg, S.C. In 1746 he married Ann Tobler. They had two daughters. In 1760 he was called to the Independent Presbyterian Church of Savannah, Ga. In 1770 the College of New Jersey (now Princeton) awarded him an honorary A.M.; in 1774, an honorary D.D.

At different South Carolina churches Zubly preached sometimes in German, sometimes in English, and he would also occasionally preach in German to Lutheran churches during his pastorate at his Presbyterian church in Savannah. He opposed what he called the "Episcopal oppression"; his published series of letters to the Reverend Samuel Frink, rector of Christ Church in Georgia, concerning payment of the same sexton both ministers had used for tolling the bell shows at least one cause of his differences with this church. But in his sermon *The Nature of that Faith without which it is impossible to please God*, he also attacked one of the Calvinist leaders of the Great Awakening, Joseph Bellamy of Bethlehem, Conn. Zubly's published sermons show his wide reading in five different languages—Latin, French, Dutch, German, and English—and in the works of Coke and Blackstone, Rapin, and Montesquieu. At least one of his works, *The Real Christians Hope in Death*—an extensive anthology of deathbed scenes—reveals his almost morbid mysticism.

In the period preceding the American Revolution, Zubly was one of the ablest pamphleteers against British tax policies, for which he largely blamed the earl of Dartmouth. He was elected delegate to the provincial congress in Georgia in July, 1775, and representative from Georgia to the Continental Congress in Philadelphia. A man of considerable property in a largely Tory area, Zubly opposed a complete break with England. When Samuel Chase accused him of disloyalty to the American cause, Zubly, "greatly indisposed," returned to Georgia, where he was arrested, had half his estate confiscated, and was banished. For two years he lived in South Carolina. When royal government was restored in Georgia in 1779, he returned there to take up his pastoral work. He died in Savannah on July 23, 1781.

WORKS: *Leichenpredigt* (1746). *Eine Leicht-Predigt* (1747). *Eine Predigt* (1749). *Evangelisches Zeugnuss. Vom Elend und Erlösung der Menschen in zwei Predigten abgelegt Und auf Hoffnung Mehrer Erbauung dem Druck Überlassen* (1751). *The Real Christians* [sic] *Hope in Death* (1756). *The Stamp-Act Repealed; A Sermon Preached in the Meeting at Savannah in Georgia, June 25th, 1766* (1766). *An Humble Enquiry into the Nature of the Dependency of the American Colonies upon the Parliament of Great-Britain and the Right of Parliament to lay Taxes on the said Colonies. By a Freeholder of South-Carolina* (1769). *Funeral Sermon on the Death of the Rev. George Whitefield* (1770). *A Letter to the Rev. Samuel Frink, A.M., Rector of Christ-Church Parish in Georgia, Relating to Some Fees demanded of some of his Dissenting Parishioners* [1770?]. *The Wise Shining on the Brightness of the Firmament and they that turn many unto Righteousness as Stars for ever. A Funeral Sermon Preached at Savannah, in Georgia, Nov. 11, 1770, on the Much Lamented Death of Rev. George Whitefield, A.M.* (1770). *The Nature of that Faith without which it is impossible to please God, considered in a Sermon* (1772). *The Faithful Minister's Course Finished: A Funeral Sermon, Preached Aug. 4, 1773, in the Meeting at Midway in Georgia, at the Interment of the Rev. John Osgood, A.M.* (1773). *The Law of Liberty: A Sermon on American Affairs preached at the Opening of the Provincial Congress of Georgia Addressed to the Right Honourable the Earl of Dartmouth. With an Appendix Giving a Concise Account of the Struggles of Swisserland* [sic] *to Recover Their Liberty* (1775). *Pious Advice* (1775). *Letter to Mr. Frink* (1775). *To the Grand Jury of the County of Chatham, State of Georgia* (1777).

RICHARD E. AMACHER
Auburn University
Auburn, Ala.